The Collected Essays of Leslie Fiedler

BY LESLIE A. FIEDLER

Nonfiction

An End to Innocence
No! in Thunder
Love and Death in the American Novel
Waiting for the End
The Return of the Vanishing American
Being Busted

Fiction

The Second Stone
Back to China
The Last Jew in America
Nude Croquet

The Collected Essays of Leslie Fiedler

VOLUME I

STEIN AND DAY/*Publishers*/New York

First published in 1971
Copyright © 1971 by Leslie A. Fiedler
Library of Congress Catalog Card No. 76-122420
All rights reserved
Published simultaneously in Canada by Saunders of Toronto Ltd
Printed in the United States of America
Stein and Day/*Publishers*/7 East 48 Street, New York, N.Y. 10017
SBN 8128-1333-2

Contents

No! in Thunder

ESSAYS ON MYTH AND LITERATURE

PART ONE: THE ARTIST

PART TWO: THE GENERATIONS

Acknowledgments

THE AUTHOR wishes to thank the editors and publishers of the following firms and periodicals under whose imprints parts of this book originally appeared:

BEACON PRESS for Preface, *An End to Innocence*, 1955; Foreword and Introduction, *No! in Thunder*, 1960.

COLUMBIA UNIVERSITY PRESS for "Shakespeare and the Paradox of Illusion," first published as "The Defense of the Illusion and the Creation of the Myth," *English Institute Essays 1948*, 1949.

COMMENTARY for "Peretz: The Secularization of the Absurd," first published as "Mediator Between Past and Future," December 1948; "William Faulkner, Highbrows' Lowbrow," first published as "William Faulkner, An American Dickens," October 1950; "Hiss, Chambers, and the Age of Innocence," December 1950; "Dead-End Werther," September 1951; "Roman Holiday," April 1954; "The Search for the Thirties," September 1955.

DELL PUBLISHING COMPANY, INC., for "Whitman: Portrait of the Artist as a Middle-Aged Hero," first published as Introduction to *Whitman, The Laurel Poetry Series*, Leslie A. Fiedler, ed., © copyright 1959 by Richard Wilbur.

ENCOUNTER for "Afterthoughts on the Rosenbergs," October 1953; "The 'Good American,'" March 1954; "McCarthy and the Intellectuals," August 1954; "Images of Walt Whitman," January 1955 (also appeared in *Whitman After 100 Years*, published in 1955 by the Stanford University Press); 'The Un-Angry Young Men," January 1958.

ESQUIRE for "Class War in British Literature," April 1958.

FOLIO for first part of "Malamud: The Commonplace as Absurd," first published as "In the Interest of Surprise and Delight," Summer 1955.

HOLT, RINEHART AND WINSTON, INC., for "R.L.S. Revisited," first published as Introduction to *The Master of Ballantrae* by Robert Louis Stevenson, Rinehart, 1954.

THE KENYON REVIEW for "Italian Pilgrimage," Summer 1952; "Introducing Cesare Pavese," Autumn 1954; 'Dante: Green Thoughts in a Green Shade," Spring 1956.

MIDSTREAM for "Negro and Jew: Encounter in America," Summer 1956.

THE NEW LEADER for "Kafka and the Myth of the Jew," March 6, 1948; "Toward Time's Cold Womb," July 22, 1950; "Some Notes on F. Scott Fitzgerald," April 9, April 16, 1951; "Invention of the Child," March 31, 1958; "Good Good Girl and Good Bad Boy," April 14, 1958; "Boys Will Be Boys," April 28, 1958; "From Redemption to Initiation," May 26, 1958; "The Profanation of the Child," June 23, 1958; "Leopold and Loeb: A Perspective in Time," first published as "Final Thoughts on the Leopold Case," November 17, 1958. Material from all except the first and last essays has also been incorporated in *Love and Death in the American Novel,* Criterion, 1960, revised edition Stein and Day, 1966.

THE NEW REPUBLIC for "Fiction as Opera," first published as "Romance in the Operatic Manner," September 22, 1955.

PARTISAN REVIEW for "Come Back to the Raft Ag'in, Huck Honey!" June 1948; "Montana," December 1949; "Seneca in the Meathouse," April 1952; "Looking Backward," May-June 1952; "The Ant on the Grasshopper," first published also as "Image of the Twenties," Summer 1955.

THE RECONSTRUCTIONIST for second part of "Malamud: The Commonplace as Absurd," first published as "The Commonplace as Absurd," February 21, 1958.

THE SEWANEE REVIEW for "Archetype and Signature," Spring 1952; "In the Beginning Was the Word," Summer 1958.

Introduction to the Collected Essays

THE FOLLOWING essays were written over a period of slightly more than two decades extending from my thirtieth year to just beyond my fiftieth. They record impressions and responses, therefore, to a period bounded by two Cold Wars: the first between the two great powers on either pole of Europe, who came inevitably into conflict once their initial revolutionary impetus had turned into imperialist expansionism; the second between the old and the young, parents and children in the whole region between those two poles. Some of these essays deal directly with the politics created by the first of the two Cold Wars, and some with the cultural changes created by the second. Others are concerned primarily with literature, but these, too, are necessarily influenced by the series of cultural revolutions and political counterrevolutions through which we have all been living over the past twenty years.

Almost all of these essays were occasional to begin with, which is to say, were prompted by public events or the appearance of certain books, as well as by the demands of editors or the organizers of forums and symposia. They seem to me, however, to have survived their occasions, which is why I have chosen them out of the several hundred similar articles which I wrote and published between 1948 and 1970. Even when I have changed my mind radically about matters treated in one or another essay, I have not revised or altered anything. The reader patient enough or moved enough to read through to the end of these two volumes will discover not only where I am now in my feelings and ideas, but also where I have been all along the way. It is tempting to falsify one's past in the light of the present, but really impossible for a writer like me who has always insisted in rushing into print before he has had time enough for second thoughts.

This collection is intended to record not only one man's sentimental and political education, but an experience shared by the overlapping generations who have come of age within the two decades it spans, generations which now find it mutually useful to pretend that a cultural "gap" separates them. What separates them in fact, however, is precisely what they have in common: the living memory recorded here of a loss of innocence which has kept the twice-born fathers of my own generation disconcertingly young, so that their sons have had, in order to seem even younger, to retreat from adolescence to childhood—from the show of sophistication to the profession of naïveté. If I were as close to twenty-five or thirty-five at the moment as I am to fifty-five (and if in addition I were blessedly Black), I would be writing just such an anatomy of the New Innocence as I once wrote of the Old; but trapped in time, I must content myself with the republication of old criticisms, hoping for new readers capable of perceiving in these volumes analogies to their own situation which it would be mischievous or irrelevant or downright boring for me to make clear.

Introduction to Volume I

APPEARING together for the first time in this volume are the two collections of essays I have already published, one in 1955 and the other in 1960. The most recent essay included, therefore, represents a Me as well as a world now over ten years distant, and I can, therefore, regard them with a certain kind of detachment, even with real objectivity.

Almost all of my books have suffered the fate of being badly read, but none has been as passionately and systematically misinterpreted as *An End to Innocence*. Three essays, especially, have stirred continuing hostile responses, not so much to what they said as to what it was imagined they said, what certain readers had to believe they said to make any sense of them at all. These are "Come Back to the Raft Ag'in, Huck Honey!" "Montana; or the End of Jean-Jacques Rousseau," and "Afterthoughts on the Rosenbergs." The first has especially confused and annoyed literary critics, the second a handful of loyal Montanans, and the third all sentimental or ritualistic left-wingers in the past as well as the present. All three express a complicated kind of allegiance to what they insist on exposing in ways the more tender-minded may find shocking: the basic erotic myths of American literature; the hypocrisies and concealed despair of professional Westerners; the self-deceiving apologetics of "radicals," whose total program had become a defense of the Soviet Union—in short, that outworn pretense to innocence which characterized all of American culture, Right, Left and Center, as the first half of the twentieth century came to a close.

To understand the stance of the Me who wrote *An End to Innocence* and to hear the voice in which that book speaks, a reader should really first come to terms with the general position presented in the title essay of *No! in Thunder,* though this did not appear until five years after the first book. That I am the offspring and heir of all those movements I have most passionately criticized has never been a secret from me, and I hope remains a secret to no one else. My mind was made by the same politics that turned the Rosenbergs into palpable liars, by the same West that has been commercialized in rodeos and roadside stands selling buffalo burgers, by the same unachievable dream of a love that can transcend interracial hatred which joins Huck and Jim on the raft. To know the weaknesses and failures of all these things and speak them out is the only way of repaying the debt one feels.

It is not just filial gratitude which leads to biting the hand that feeds one, but a sense that such a course of action is at least better than its only real possible alternative; namely, biting the ass one kisses. It is in short, a way of ending the innocence with which one begins in order to be able to move to the next innocence which at first one can scarcely imagine. I like to think, at any rate, that my rejection of the traditional ways of responding to older American literature, as well as of traditional ways of behaving on the old Left and in the old West, have made it possible for the generations which have come of age since to create for themselves a new American literature, a new Left, a new West, plus a new innocence which I confess I did not foresee, but which I cannot manage to despise.

An End to Innocence

ESSAYS ON CULTURE AND POLITICS

FOR MY FATHER

Introduction to the
Second Edition of
An End to Innocence

THOUGH some of the essays included in this volume are now more than twenty years old and none less than fifteen, certain subjects with which they deal have recently come back into the center of everyone's concern, especially that of the young, while others have continuously vexed and titillated all of us during the intervening decade or two.

I myself, for instance, have expanded the central insights first developed in the few pages of "Come Back to the Raft Ag'in, Huck Honey!" into the thousand-page trilogy which begins with *Love and Death in the American Novel*, goes on to *Waiting for the End*, and concludes with *The Return of the Vanishing American*. And these books have become for a new generation of teachers in universities, colleges and high schools, the basis for a new understanding of our classic books and of our culture in general, as well as the model for critical studies which do not even bother to acknowledge their source—as if everyone had always known what was really at issue between Huck and Jim on the raft.

Even more importantly, that erotic archetype which I began to explore in 1948 has come closer and closer to the surface of the nonacademic American mind, appearing quite explicitly as a controlling theme in currently popular novels like Ken Kesey's,

One Flew Over the Cuckoo's Nest, in recent movies like *The Defiant Ones* and *The Fortune Cookie,* and even in presumably unsophisticated television series like *I Spy.* And, finally, during the past year Mark Twain's masterpiece has been rewritten by John Seelye as *The True Huckleberry Finn,* a version in which the line, "Come back to the raft again, Huck Honey," actually composed by me for my own purposes, appears twice over in the dialogue.

Less clearly, but just as inevitably, many of the contradictory impulses memorialized in *Montana; or the End of Jean-Jacques Rousseau*—impulses which led me first to abandon the East, then to criticize the place to which I had come—presently possess the minds of the those young men and women, the children of fathers who unlike me stayed in the Urban East, who are just now abandoning the city and moving into what survives of the West. Such young wanderers constitute a third westward migration which promises to become as significant in the making of American culture as was the mid-nineteenth-century first wave. I can now see my own move as part of a small second wave, whose goals were more ironically and less sentimentally defined than either of the other two since we sought not mining camps (like the first) or communes (like the third) but only universities and colleges, fortresses of culture in a dying wilderness. But we managed all the same to keep alive in a time of paralysis and timidity the notion of heading westward, the dream of getting out.

Most crucial to the moment, however, are my essays on Alger Hiss and the Rosenbergs, since the latter especially are being refurbished as political heroes, noble victims appropriate to an age when leftwing politics has become fashionable once more. There is something touchingly absurd in the attempt to make such devious spokesmen of a movement whose chief aim was to remain invisible into symbols of a proud and courageous resistance to an oppressive system. They sought only to seem like good servants of that system, faithful bureaucrats or loyal technicians —as averse to treason as anyone; and their posthumous recasting as rebels is a function of that ignorance of history which is the special blessing as well as the fatal handicap of the young. What irked me, however, when I first wrote about the Rosenbergs (in what few remember was intended to be a protest against their pointless execution) and Hiss was their refusal of candor and heroism, their failure to stand up in court and define just what it was they had done and just what beliefs had prompted their actions. I like to think that, however current sentimentality may falsify the actual situation of the Rosenbergs, it was precisely such exposures of their cowardice and confusion which make it possible now in a new age of political oppression for defendants like the Chicago Seven to stand up in court and to shout loud and clear just what they are guilty of, rather than to whimper about their innocence and superior patriotic devotion. I hope, in any event, that in the decades to come, even if some of those more candid revolutionaries have to die, none of them will try to seem to die for nothing, to die by mistake, as did the Rosenbergs.

I reread and rethink these essays at a moment when I myself am living through a political trial, and I find it a little uncanny to discover how my imagination has always haunted the courtroom, which has from the first seemed to me not merely a forum but a theater where those uninhibited and courageous enough can perform a kind of drama absurd enough to seem true in a time of total absurdity. I would have preferred not to have been an actor on such a stage, though obviously I have long dreamed myself there in others' boots—as Alger Hiss, as Julius Rosenberg, as the now nearly anonymous victims of Joe McCarthy—dreamed myself, that is to say, failing the chance to say in the spotlight and to a packed house who I really am and for what I am truly prepared to suffer. But circumstances have taken the choice out of my hands so that reprinting the record of such dreams now constitutes a way of making amends in advance for my own inevitable failure to be quite brave or quite true enough.

Preface

Reading over my essays for the purpose of making this collection has been an instructive, though somewhat sobering, experience. Certain phrases that must have struck me once as apt or beautiful I have found not even comprehensible; while certain emphases seem now excessive, and certain declarations of conviction over-rhetorical. I have not hesitated to prune and amend and rewrite where it seemed profitable, though in no case have I made a major change; and several of these pieces I have not retouched at all. I have, as a matter of fact, been pleased to discover how often I have managed to tell what still seems to me the truth about my world and myself as a liberal, intellectual, writer, American, and Jew. I do not mind, as some people apparently do, thinking of myself in such categorical terms; being representative of a class, a generation, a certain temper seems to me not at all a threat to my individuality. As one who dearly loves a generalization (this the reader will soon discover), I relish all that is typical, even me; and I like to think of myself as registering through my particular sensibility the plight of a whole group.

I must hasten to add, however, that the groups for which I think I speak often regard me not as their appointed mouthpiece but as a rather presumptuous apostle to the gentiles; and this (I confess) I do not find *altogether* distasteful. By instinct and training I am polemical — and preaching to the converted has no appeal for me at all. Of course, I do not enjoy being misunderstood, and have suffered in the past when something written in pure rage and love (my Rosenberg article) has been called "gloating." But I will always remember with real joy the cry from the soul of a young man I met for a moment and by chance. Discovering that I had written "Come Back to the Raft," he looked at me reproachfully through a long minute of silence, and then in an impassioned whisper asked: "Why did you *do* it?" This, I suspect, is success.

My essays are not only polemical; they are occasional. I have really a certain uneasiness about committing myself to print, and I certainly do not have the kind of temperament that permits me to make a list of "important subjects" and write on them one by one. It is only when infuriated by some stupid or malicious argument or harried by an importunate editor (usually both) that I can begin to write; and I must express here my thanks to the editors who have harried me out of indolence and silence, especially Irving Kristol, formerly with *Commentary* and now co-editor of *Encounter,* who has persuaded me, protesting and stalling, to get down much that I should regret having left unsaid. The origin of these articles is therefore various; some began life as book reviews or speeches, one as a lecture in Italian to an advanced class in English in a high school in Reggio Calabria. And yet they have common metaphors, common themes, a common center. There is even from essay to essay an occasional repetition of phrase, the reiteration of a key fact, which I have preferred to leave rather than recast the pattern of the individual pieces.

The title of this book is intended not, I trust, to impose but to make explicit the real unity which has been present in my writing over the last several years, and of which I was not until now quite aware. This thematic unity runs, I think, not only through the kind of article to which this selection is limited, but through my stories and poems, as well as my "purely" literary essays. In the three sections of this book, however, the reader will find primarily pieces dealing with political events, the American scene, and literature as a cultural fact, evidence of attitudes and archetypes that shape our relations to each other and the rest of the world. The articles on Fitzgerald and the American novel go beyond this, but in the context I suspect that their sociological aspects will be emphasized out of proportion.

Indeed, I feel just a little misrepresented by a first book so largely political. I think of myself as *primarily* a literary person, though one whose interest in works of art is dictated by a moral passion rather than a cooler technical concern; and I do not hesitate to admit that I write of politics reluctantly, in a world where to ignore them would mean to be less than human. I have no expert knowledge in political matters and am an indifferent researcher; but I have lived (deeply, though somewhat grudgingly, involved) through a crisis in liberalism which seems to me a major event in the development of the human spirit. This crisis I feel peculiarly qualified to describe, precisely *because* I am a literary man, immune to certain journalistic platitudes and accustomed to regard men and words with a sensibility trained by the newer critical methods. It is a "close reading" of recent events that I should like to think I have achieved, a reading that does not scant ambiguity or paradox, but tries to give to the testimony of a witness before a Senate committee or the letters of the Rosenbergs the same careful scrutiny we have learned to practice on the shorter poems of John Donne.

L. A. F.

PART ONE

AN AGE OF INNOCENCE

CHAPTER ONE

Hiss, Chambers, and the Age of Innocence

You will either aid in moulding history, or history will mould you, and in the case of the latter, you can rest assured that you will be indescribably crushed and maimed in the process. . . . History is not a blind goddess, and does not pardon the blindness of others.

— WHITTAKER CHAMBERS (1931)

Alger Hiss went to prison on March 29, 1951. The last legal judgments have been passed. The decision of the courts stands: guilty as charged — guilty in fact of treason, though technically accused only of perjury. It is time, many of us feel, to forget the whole business: the prison doors have closed; let us consider the question also closed. But history is not so easily satisfied. Like some monumental bore, it grabs us by the lapels, keeps screaming into our faces the same story over and over again. The case of Judith Coplon, the case of Julius and Ethel Rosenberg, the inevitable case of tomorrow's Mr. X — the names change but the meanings are the same, and we protest that we have long since got the point. But have we? Of what was Alger Hiss guilty anyhow?

The statute of limitations protected Hiss against the charge of having passed secret material from State Department files to his accuser Whittaker Chambers, of having placed in the hands of agents of the Soviet Union documents which, whatever their intrinsic value, enabled our present enemies to break some of our most important codes. The transaction had taken place in 1936 and 1937 — a war away, in years we ourselves

3

find it difficult to remember, in years some of us don't want to remember. It is a painful thing to be asked to live again through events ten years gone, to admit one's identity with the person who bore one's name in a by now incredible past. It is hardest of all to confess that one is responsible for the acts of that past, especially when such acts are now placed in a new and unforeseen context that changes their meaning entirely. "Not guilty!" one wants to cry; "that is not what I meant at all!"

And yet the qualifying act of moral adulthood is precisely this admission of responsibility for the past and its conse-quences, however undesired or unforeseen. Such a recognition Hiss was called upon to make. Had he been willing to say, "Yes, I did these things — things it is now possible to call 'treason' — not for money or prestige, but out of a higher allegiance than patriotism"; had he only confessed in the name of any of the loftier platitudes for which men are prepared publicly to admit the breaking of lesser laws — then he need not even have gone to prison. Why did he lie?

Had Hiss told the truth, the whole meaning of the case might have been different, might have attained that dignity of tragedy for which Alistair Cooke* looks through its dossiers in vain. The defenders of Hiss, and of the generation they take him to represent, would have been delivered from the intolerable plight that prompted them, during the trials, to declare at one

---

*Alistair Cooke, *A Generation on Trial.* In addition to Mr. Cooke's book, a thorough and scrupulous work, though one with many of whose interpre-tations I disagree, I have used for this article De Toledano and Lasky's *Seeds of Treason,* which is marred by a journalistic and melodramatic style, but contains much valuable background material and sets the Hiss case in an illuminating context of Communist espionage on two continents. I have also consulted the newspaper accounts of the case, particularly those of the New York *Times,* and the printed hearings of the House Un-American Activities Committee; for the further background, I have turned to the *New Masses* for 1931, and various other official Communist publications. I do not know personally either of the principals in the case, nor have I made any attempt to communicate with them. I have no private or special sources of information. What I have attempted in this piece is an analysis based on publicly available documents, considered in the light of my own experience and knowledge of that world of values and beliefs out of which the incidents of the case arose. It is the lack of such experience and knowledge which makes even Mr. Cooke's careful and subtle book miss what seems to me the essential point.

and the same time that (a) Hiss was innocent of the charges, the victim of a malevolent psychopath, and (b) even if he was technically guilty, he had the moral right, in those years of betrayal leading to Munich, to give his primary loyalty to the Soviet Union. Why did he lie and, lying, lose the whole point of the case in a maze of irrelevant data: the signature on the transfer of ownership of a car, the date a typewriter was repaired . . . ?

The lie, it is necessary to see, was no mere accident, but was of the essence of the case, a clue to the deepest significance of what was done and to the moral atmosphere that made the deed possible. We can see Hiss's lie now in a larger context, beside the fantastic affirmations of innocence by Julius and Ethel Rosenberg. These were not, after all, common criminals, who plead innocent mechanically on the advice of counsel; these were believers in a new society, for whose sake they had already deceived their closest friends and endangered the security of their country. In the past (and even yet in the present — the Puerto Rican nationalists, for instance), such political idealists welcomed their trials as forums, opportunities to declare to the world the high principles behind their actions, the loyalty to the march of history and the eventual triumph of socialism that had brought them to the bar. They might have been, in some eyes at least, spectacular martyrs; they chose to behave instead, before the eyes of all, like blustering petty thieves.

Not that the avowals of innocence, especially in the case of Hiss, were not affecting. Despite the absurdity of his maunderings about "forgery by typewriter," there was something moving — for a generation brought up on stories of Dreyfus and Tom Mooney, and growing to social awareness through the Sacco-Vanzetti trial and the campaigns to free the Scottsboro boys — in Hiss's final courtroom pose as The Victim. Even now, it is hard to realize how little claim he has to the title. For here was no confessed revolutionary, marked by his avowed principles, his foreign accent, his skin color, as fair game for the frame-up; here was a super-eminently respectable civil servant from the better schools, accused by the obvious outsider, the self-declared rebel and renegade, Whittaker Chambers. Hiss seemed to desire both the pathos of the persecuted and the aura of unblemished respectability. His is, as we shall see, the Popular Front mind at bay, incapable of honesty even when there is no hope in anything else.

After the hung jury, the second trial, the reams of evidence that frittered away the drama in boredom, one thing is quite clear. Twenty of twenty-four jurors, presumably twenty of twenty-four of us, believed that Alger Hiss was guilty of the perjury with which he was charged, of the treason with which he could not be charged.

For many, that verdict may be sufficient; for some, it is not enough. These cannot help feeling that the total issue of the guilt or innocence of Alger Hiss remains still to be solved. The verdict of the courts applies only to the "facts" as defined by precedent and law, a few fragments torn from their rich human contexts and presented to a group of men deliberately chosen for their relative ignorance of those contexts, and for the likelihood of their not being sympathetically involved with the passions and motives which underlay them.

Is there any sense in which Hiss is *symbolically* innocent — in which he may, indeed, have made the mistake of having passed certain papers via Chambers to the Russian agent, Colonel Bykov, but out of such naive devotion to the Good that it is a travesty of justice to find him on merely technical grounds "guilty"? It sometimes seems possible that when a Rosenberg or a Hiss speaks publicly of his "innocence," he is merely using a convenient shorthand for an account of motives and actions too complex to set before an ordinary juryman without completely re-educating him. One of the distinctive features of the recent series of "spy" trials has been that the accused and the chief accusers have been intellectuals, whereas the jury, the lawyers on both sides, even the judges, were not. And since in this country the intellectuals have been notoriously set apart from the general public, living, especially since the Russian Revolution, by different values and speaking a different language, communication is difficult. How can people who do not read the same books, and whose only relationship is one of distrust, arrive at a common definition of innocence and guilt?

One might argue on these grounds that what a jury could have meant by voting "guilty" is ridiculously far from the truth; that Hiss is not what the average mind, brought up on E. Phillips Oppenheim and pulp fiction, means by a "traitor"; that he can surely feel himself neither venal nor skulking, for he has always been faithful in intent to his true fatherland, Humanity; that if in fact he has ended up by helping the interests of just another imperialist power, the Soviet Union, it is not his crime but that of the Soviet Union, which he took in good faith to be the deputy of mankind's best interests.

This was Henry Julian Wadleigh's defense: a minor source of information for Chambers in the pre-war years, and a witness at the Hiss trials, he attempted to declare his innocence and guilt at the same time. With no sign of contrition, he admitted passing secret documents to Chambers but insisted that his course had been justified by history; it had not even occurred to him, he explained condescendingly, as a matter of conscience — though merely joining the Communist party had, and he had finally *not* signed up.

The comic aspects of Wadleigh strike one first — the cartoonist's pink-tea radical, with his thick glasses, disordered hair, and acquired Oxford accent. The articles which he wrote for the New York *Post* are classics of unconscious humor, monuments to smugness and self-pity, and trailers for the novel which (of course!) he was busy writing about his Experience. When Hiss's lawyers found they could not pin on Wadleigh the stealing of the papers Chambers had disconcertingly produced, they were content to make him the butt of their jokes. At several points during his questioning, the judge had to cover his mouth with his hand to preserve the dignity of the court. Wadleigh is the comic version of Alger Hiss.

The clowning of Wadleigh reveals what is not so easily read in Hiss: a moral obtuseness which underlies the whole case. Mr. Cooke tries to make of Wadleigh his tragic figure, but the true protagonist of tragedy suffers and learns. Wadleigh has learned nothing. He cannot conceive of having done anything *really* wrong. He finds in his own earlier activities only a certain excessive zeal, overbalanced by good will, and all excused by — Munich. Was he not a better man for having

tried to counter, however ineptly, the shameful appeasement
of Hitler? That the irony of events had made him, just in so far
as he was more idealistic and committed, more helplessly the
tool of evil, he cannot conceive. In the end, his "confession"
is almost as crass a lie as the denial of Hiss — a disguise for
self-congratulation, a device for clinging to the dream of innocence. He cannot, even in the dock, believe that a man of
liberal persuasion is capable of wrong.

It was this belief that was the implicit dogma of American
liberalism during the past decades, piling up a terrible burden
of self-righteousness and self-deceit to be paid for on the day
when it would become impossible any longer to believe that
the man of good will is identical with the righteous man, and
that the liberal is *per se* the hero. That day came at different
times to different people: for some it was the Moscow Trials,
for others the Soviet-Nazi pact, and for a good many — including a large number who had, during the war, regained lost
illusions — it came on August 17, 1948, when Hiss and
Chambers were brought face to face before the House Committee on Un-American Activities.

The facts were clear from the moment of confrontation, but
for many the facts did not matter. Chambers stated flatly that
Hiss had been a Communist, his associate in the "underground"; Hiss as flatly denied it. Simply to ask *cui bono* would
have been enough: which one of the men stood to gain by
lying? But somehow such a common-sense approach seemed
excluded. The most fantastic psychological explanations were
dredged up. One heard via the intellectual underground the
unlikeliest proto-Dostoevskian stories to suggest reasons for
Chambers' self-vilifying testimony. *Psychopathia Sexualis* was
hauled out and Freud quoted glibly by the same skeptics who
had laughed at the psychologizing explanations of the Moscow
Trials.

But there remained still the detailed circumstantiality of
Chambers' memories, the documents stolen from the office in
which Hiss had worked, the microfilms taken from the dusty
dumbwaiter in Brooklyn and hidden in the famous pumpkin
on Chambers' Maryland farm. For all the theatrical instincts
of Chambers, who seemed to possess a flair for adding one

artistic touch too many to any situation (out of God knows what compulsion), the documents were there — the undeniable goods.

An unbiased look at the proceedings of the House Committee reveals that from the start Hiss quite apparently lied, or, more precisely, half lied and equivocated with the canniness of the trained lawyer. During the trials his version of the events was delivered with great aplomb, but before the Committee one can see him uncertainly feeling his way into the situation, cautiously finding out at each point how much he will have to admit to escape entrapment.

At first, he said simply that to the best of his knowledge (the qualifying phrase hardly seemed significant, a lawyer's habit), he had never met the man Chambers who had named him as one of a Washington cell of infiltrators. There was no mention of espionage, it must be remembered, until Hiss had forced Chambers' hand. Then, advised perhaps of the convincing nature of Chambers' testimony, he began slowly to shift ground, first, however, taking the initiative and charging with increasing surliness that the Committee had been leaking back to Chambers everything he said. At this point the Committee, which had handled him until then with more than normal sympathy, began to press him hard. He could not say for sure, Hiss now testified, but he thought that certainly he had known no one who called himself "Chambers," or anyone who looked very like the photographs he had been shown. They were, however, not very good pictures; so he could not be positive. Indeed, the face on the photograph before him might be that of the chairman of the Committee. It was his last joke.

Finally, he admitted that he had, after all, known the man in question, under a name he had written down on a pad in front of him. It was "George Crosley" (Chambers was later to say that, although he had used many names, he was quite sure he had never used that one), a dead-beat writer whom he had known casually, and with whom he had occasionally talked over possible story material, though he had really found the man despicable. As a matter of fact, he had even once, for certain obscure reasons, let the dead-beat move into his apartment for a couple of days, or was it weeks; and when Crosley had welshed on the rent, Hiss, for reasons even more obscure, had given him a car — just a little old car, it must be understood, with a "sassy" rumble seat, though one, Hiss admitted, to which he had been sentimentally attached. It is a fantastic story, enough to send anyone less well placed to jail without further ado. Later, there was to be a good deal of trouble over the dates of this strange transaction — and records were to turn up proving that the car had never been presented to Crosley-Chambers at all, but apparently to the Communist party!

All the while this amazing farrago was being served up by Hiss, Chambers was patiently building up the story of their actual relationship, born in intrigue and common devotion to an ideal, and destined to end in bitterness and mutual accusation. They had been comrades and close friends, Chambers said, he and the promising young lawyer, whom he was still able to describe as "of a great gentleness and sweetness of character." At first, their dealings were concerned only with dues and reports, but they quickly grew closer together, in the sort of relationship hard to parallel outside the party, the two of them utterly dependent on each other's loyalty, and both betting their self-esteem on the truth of the Marxist-Leninist dream.

They are men who could never have met outside the Communist movement, and even as Communists they were utterly different: Chambers the romantic recruit of the 1920's, hating a world that had rebuffed him at every encounter, and choosing the movement as an alternative to suicide; Hiss, universally respected, and by nature an opportunist, but with a streak of social conscience (personified in his earnest wife, who could not even let a casual visitor call the day "fine" without reminding her of the plight of the sharecroppers), choosing the party to protect himself from a merely selfish kind of success. Different as they were, Chambers had found Hiss a "real Bolshevik," perhaps sensing in him a kind of hardness to which he himself could only aspire, and had defended him against the sneers of their Russian boss, Bykov, who always referred to Hiss condescendingly as "our dear lawyer."

The quality of the feeling that must have existed between the two men is revealed by Chambers' last-minute attempt to draw Hiss with him out of the party, after he himself had become convinced that the Soviet Union was serving not justice but her own selfish national interests. Feeling that he might well be killed by party agents after his desertion (such political murders have occurred even in America), Chambers nevertheless risked exposing himself by a final visit to Hiss's home. But Hiss had stood firm, scarcely listening to the arguments of Chambers, though he had finally wept a little (the scene stays in the imagination, the completely unexpected, uncharacteristic tears), and had given to Chambers a trivial Christmas present for his daughter — "a little rolling pin."

Perhaps, even before the break, Hiss was already tired of Chambers as a person, a little ashamed of his admiration for the shabby writer who wrote nothing, and who had a tendency to remake his experience as he told about it, retouching and bringing up the highlights here and there. Mrs. Hiss had distrusted him from the first, finding him, with a strange inconsistency for a genteel internationalist, "too foreign." They had pretended finally, Alger and "Crosley," that "Crosley" was a Russian, which made him all right, of course; and Chambers had played up to it with all his love of subterfuge.

Whatever the status of their personal relations, when Chambers had come to Hiss with his talk about the Moscow Trials and the betrayal of the revolution, Hiss already could not afford to listen to him. He had by then too much to lose; for, without ceasing to be a Bolshevik, he had become a "success," a respectable citizen. To acknowledge that Russia could be fundamentally wrong would have changed the whole meaning of his own life, turned what had perhaps seemed to him his most unselfish and devoted acts, the stealing of State Department documents, into shameful crimes — into "treason"! Only the conviction that there was no final contradiction between his activities, public and private, could have made Hiss's life tolerable. He must have felt that what he had done as a New Deal lawyer, helping to expose the "munitions makers" in the Nye committee, or working for the AAA in the Department of Agriculture, did not contradict what he tried to do as a member of a left-wing faction in the State Department, urging certain attitudes toward Chiang Kai-shek;

and that what he had sought in both these capacities was merely completed by his "secret" work as a purveyor of information to warn the Soviet Union — his Soviet Union, mankind's Soviet Union — of the forces that worked for and against her in the inner world of diplomacy.

He was not a "traitor"! What the Un-American Activities Committee could not understand, what the two juries were certainly not able to comprehend, is that, to Hiss, his service to the party and the Soviet Union is an expression of "loyalty," not "treason." Before consenting to marry him, Remington's former wife had made him solemnly pledge "not to succeed"; to so many of the generation of Remington and Hiss, the bourgeois success of the American Dream was the final treachery, and each step forward in their personal careers had to be justified in terms of opportunities provided for infiltration. Hiss offered his "espionage" as an earnest to the inner few whose opinion mattered to him (in those days chiefly Chambers, and always himself) that he had not "sold out" to the bourgeois world in which he was making a splendid career.

No wonder Hiss was inaccessible to Chambers' arguments against the party! No wonder he seemed scarcely willing to admit Chambers' existence, refusing him his very name! It was as if Hiss had wanted to shrug off his accuser, not like a real being in the outside world, but like a nightmare. Indeed, the persistent voice of the man he had once admired must have seemed to him to possess the quality of a nightmare, speaking in its characteristic half-whisper the doubts, thrust down in himself, that could destroy his self-esteem.

And so Hiss had spoken out over the condemning voice, protesting his innocence with a vigor that contrasted oddly with Chambers' quiet tone. All the accounts speak of the voice of the accuser as one that, symbolically enough, could scarcely be heard. There is, even in the printed testimony, a sense of a counter-desire not to be heard along with the resolve to speak out. Far from seeming the vindictive persecutor of some accounts, Chambers strikes us as oddly reluctant, willing for a long time to risk perjury rather than reveal the full guilt of his former comrade. What Chambers really seems to be after is a confession of the truth from Hiss; he does not feel he can hide forever what Hiss has done, but he would prefer him to speak out himself.

Hiss, on the other hand, baits Chambers furiously, daring him to become the complete "rat," as if knowing Chambers will suffer in speaking out, as if wanting to shame and punish him. He seems to have felt sure that Chambers could not really harm him. A man does not unflaggingly succeed from high-school days to early middle age without losing something of humility, and forgetting that a single failure of the most superb luck is enough for destruction. When the end comes, when the threat of a suit for defamation against Chambers leads to the disclosure of the damning papers, to the trials of Hiss for perjury, and to the final conviction, one has the sense that both of the men are surprised.

Some of the commentators on the case have spoken of the anti-Red "hysteria" that prevailed at the time of the case, as if in such an atmosphere the cards were hopelessly stacked against Alger Hiss. But precisely the opposite is the case. He is just the type that does not normally get caught in the indiscriminate "witch hunt," which tends to pick out those who look like "witches," the visible outsiders. A woman like Assistant Secretary of Defense Anna M. Rosenberg, for instance, foreign-born and a Jew, is much more likely to be haled up without any evidence against her, while a man like Hiss can slip past the ordinary Congressman, to whom "Red" really means loud-mouth or foreigner or Jew. (Rankin, who was on the Committee when it examined Hiss, apparently spent his spare time thumbing through *Who's Who in American Jewry,* and turned all his fire on — Chambers!)

The Committee did not want to believe Chambers. They were convinced by his, and his wife's, astonishingly specific memories: though some members of the Committee had been eager to "get the goods" on the New Deal, to catch out the State Department at last, they had apparently found it difficult to put much faith in Chambers. It was impossible to like him, as one instinctively liked Hiss for the boyish charm we think of as peculiarly American. Chambers seems to have worn his unprepossessing air (he is the sort of person of whom one believes immediately quite unfounded stories of insanity and

depravity) deliberately, as if he had acquired in his revolutionary days the habit of rebuffing all admiration based on anything but his role in the party.

Every word he spoke declared him an ex-traitor, a present
turncoat and squealer; and Hiss, sensing his inestimable advantage in a society whose values are largely set in boyhood when
snitching is the ultimate sin, had traded on his role as the
honest man confronted by the "rat." Really, Hiss kept insisting, they'd have to call the Harvard Club, say he'd be a few
minutes late to dinner — after taking care of this unpleasant-
ness. For a while it came off quite successfully, coming from
one who visibly belonged, whose clothes beautifully fitted,
whose manners were adequate to all occasions.

We learned later, of course, how much the genteel aspect
of Hiss was itself a mask, imposed on a background of disorder and uncertainty not unlike Chambers': the suicide of
his father and sister, the undefined psychological difficulties of
his stepson, into whose allowance from his actual father, we
remember, the Hisses sometimes dipped for contributions to the
party. It was as if Alger Hiss had dedicated himself to fulfill-
ing, along with his dream of a New Humanity, the other dream
his father had passed on to him with his first name — from
rags to riches. How strangely the Marxist ideal and the dream
of Horatio Alger blended into the motives of his treason. . . .

Any good bourgeois bristles when confronted with Whittaker Chambers His years as an editor on *Time* (he is "brilliant," of course, but the adjective is itself ambivalent), his
later role as a small farmer, cannot conceal his real identity
as the outsider: the "butterball who could not even learn to
play marbles," the writer of poetry for little magazines, the
obnoxious young radical expelled from college, the uncomfortable spirit that either blasphemes or is too religious for respectability. At one point, Chambers is asked by a Committee
member how he spent his time during a week-long period
when he had borrowed Hiss's apartment; and when he says,
"Reading . . . ," one feels the troubled silence. How could
anyone read so long? It is the suspicious vagary of the kind
of man who once believed in Stalin and now believes in the
Devil.

After his years in the "underground," he still seems ill at
ease in our daylight world; and beneath the guise of the magazine executive (assumed only, we remember, to establish an
"identity" for himself as a protection against being murdered
by the GPU), the old Chambers persists. Everyone who had
known him in his revolutionary days — except Hiss, of course
— had no difficulty in recognizing Chambers at the time of
the trial.

The jowls and the new teeth do not fundamentally change
the face we can still see on the inside back cover of the Communist literary magazine, the *New Masses,* for July 1931.
After twenty years, the young Chambers looks up at us still
with the sullen certainty of one who has discovered in the revolution an answer to the insecurity and doubt which had
brought his brother to suicide, himself to months of despair
and near paralysis. In the movement he had found a way out
of immobility, a way to join with the other insulted and injured of the earth to change the world which excluded them.
To appear in the *New Masses* in those days was not merely to
be a writer, but to subscribe to a new myth of the writer,
summed up in the blurb under the photograph: "Youth as a
periodically vagrant laborer in Deep South, Plains, Northwest.
Brief Columbia College experience ending with atheist publication. . . . Joined revolutionary movement 1925. . . ."

Hiss, who really knew Chambers, of course, better than
anyone else except Chambers' wife, put his finger on the
sources of this myth when he told the Committee that Chambers thought of himself as a kind of Jim Tully or Jack London.
To understand Chambers, one must understand the concept
of the literary bum as hero that came out of Tully and London, a special Marxist class-angling of the old bohemian ideal.
Chambers' once living in the same quarters with an old whore,
and his stealing of library books of which Hiss's lawyers and
psychiatrists were to make so much during the trials, his name-
changing and wandering, were all standard procedure for the
rebel-intellectual in those days.

The life style he adopted was perfected in the Communist
"Third Period," in the years before 1935, and it is the Third
Period we must first of all understand. The term is Lenin's,

invented to describe that last stage of imperialism, the age of cataclysmic wars and revolutions; but it comes also to describe the way of life of those who believed themselves the sole carriers of the future in those final days. To the young comrades in their blue work shirts or flat-heeled shoes, there was no need to come to terms with the dying bourgeois world; Marx had told them that the point was to change it. They lived in a fine apocalyptic fury, issuing leaflets to ROTC units in Midwestern agricultural colleges, urging the "peasants and soldiers" to turn their guns the other way; they cried for an autonomous Negro republic to be carved out of the Deep South; and in the few cities where they had sufficient numbers, they were forever rushing "into the streets" to shout their resolve to "Defend the Soviet Union" against their own bourgeoisie in case of war. The only reality in their paranoid world was the Workers' Fatherland, still encircled and unrecognized by our own government. Here is a typical passage from an editorial that appeared in the *New Masses* in 1931, and so might have been written by Chambers:

> It is only a question of time until all the imperialist powers mobilize their manpower and hurl its bleeding masses in a rain of steel across the frontiers, to destroy the first Socialist Republic. In this situation what are the intellectuals to do? . . . They realize, however imperfectly, that the Union of Soviet Socialist Republics represents the advance guard, the hope of human progress and civilization. . . . And they desire, the most advanced of them, to employ their minds as weapons in the fight to save the Soviet Union from its reactionary enemies.

Reread in the pages of the old magazine, in the heavy black format that seems to shriek at us across the years, and surrounded by the pen-and-ink drawings with their incredibly depraved bosses and their unbelievably noble workers, the banal paragraph seems merely unconscionably funny, like a bad silent film. But when we remember the universal loss of faith in those years of mass unemployment and of seemingly endless depression, we can appreciate the attractiveness of the Marxist answer, guaranteed by the miraculous existence of the Soviet Union, the last best hope of human culture. We sense, too, the appeal of violence in a world of words — an instant of bloodshed and the whole golden future unfolds!

No Third Perioder could have become, like a later type of Communist, really a "traitor" as distinguished from a mere "spy." How could they betray a world they publicly disavowed? Romantic and ridiculous, they were still revolutionaries, their allegiance single and unconcealed. When such Communists went underground they hid, but they never pretended to be good bourgeois. When the call came in 1932 from Max Bedacht, asking Chambers to disappear as the individual he had been in order to take on "special" work, Chambers seems to have welcomed the chance. He had already sacrificed his will to party discipline, his fate to history. He had little more to offer up beyond his name and the small fame that had become attached to it in the movement: the praise he had received in the Russian press for his stories of Communist life, the popularity of the play *Can You Hear Their Voices?*, based on one of his works, already presented at Vassar and about to be produced in Russia.

Something in his temperament seems to have greeted the prospect of self-immolation; even before he entered what the Communists mean by the "underground," he had been, in the Dostoevskian sense, an underground man, his own enemy. It had apparently pleased him to take the final step, to become one whose death it would be forbidden to notice. What did Mundt or Rankin or Nixon know of Dostoevsky, or those twenty-four jurors of the kind of alienated life that conditioned Chambers? What trick of history brought them and him into the same room, pushed them toward an uneasy alliance?

It was Hiss — the embodiment of the subsequent Popular Front era, as Chambers was the embodiment of the Third Period — who provided the common link: Hiss who had as desperately to look respectable as Chambers had not to. The New Deal had moved American politics left, and had opened the doors of the trade unions and the Washington bureaus to the university intelligentsia at the very moment when that intelligentsia had been penetrated by the Communists, and Communism had undergone two decisive changes: first, the national Communist parties had lost all initiative and internal democracy, coming under the absolute control of the Russian bureaucracy; and, second, world Stalinism had adopted the

Popular Front line of collaboration with the bourgeoisie.

No longer was the ideal Bolshevik the open rebel, the poet-bum chanting songs of protest, but the principled government worker with the pressed suit and the clean-cut look. It was the day of "fronts" and "mass organizations," of infiltrating and "capturing" and "boring from within." As the headlines in the *Daily Worker* declared peace-with-capitalism, a new kind of underground Communist moved into Washington, unnoticed among the purer, pragmatic New Dealers.

Hiss is the prototype of the new-model Bolshevik (Lee Pressman and Henry Collins and John Abt, Noel Field and George Silverman were others) who was the more valuable as he seemed less radical. Far from being urged to sell the party press, he was even discouraged from reading it. These new secret workers had never been open members of the party; they did not merely hide, but pretended to be what they were not. For the first time, a corps of Communists existed for whom "treason," in the sense of real deceit, was possible. These were not revolutionaries but Machiavellians, men with a double allegiance, making the best of two worlds and often, like Hiss, profiting immensely within the society they worked so hard to destroy.

Doubtless some of these new Bolsheviks were able to deceive themselves into believing that there was no actual contradiction between their real allegiance and their pretended one. What helped the self-deception was the rise of Nazi Germany as the chief threat on the world scene, and the changing role of the Soviet Union in international affairs. The blanket phrase "anti-Fascism" covered over conflicts as deep as life itself. On the one hand, the New Deal had finally recognized the new Russian regime; and, on the other hand, Communist Russia had joined the fellowship of nations. In the League of Nations (which Lenin had long before called "a den of thieves"), Litvinov was calling for the unity of the anti-Fascist world. The watchword was no longer "Defend the Soviet Union!" but "Establish Collective Security!" The Communists insisted that the interests of Russia and the United States were forever identical, and the majority of liberals collaborated in the hoax — which was to crash with the signing of the Soviet-Nazi pact, be ridiculously revived during the war when we were "allies," and collapse once more at the foot of the Iron Curtain. Here are the words of Earl Browder, written in the first flush of the Popular Front honeymoon:

In this world movement, there stand out before the peace-loving peoples of the world two centers of resistance to the fascist flood, two points from which leadership and inspiration can be given to the majority of mankind struggling for democracy and peace, two rallying grounds for the hard-pressed forces of progress and culture — the Soviet Union and the United States. . . . . The Soviet Union and the United States have common problems, common interests and common enemies. That is a central fact in the new world situation.

The platitudes, read in their context of rallies-for-Spain sponsored by the "big names" from Hollywood and Broadway, seem only a little less old-fashioned and absurd than those of 1931, but we must read them with attention, remembering that they made treason easy. The bureaucrat, busy making himself a niche in the government service while transmitting secret material to the Russians, didn't even have to pose to himself a moral "either-or"; in both his roles, he could consider himself serving what Browder liked to call "the spirit of Jefferson, Jackson, and Lincoln."

Before the Popular Front Communist the ordinary Congressman is helpless, unless there is a "renegade" willing to make revelations. The average legislator pursues ordinarily one of two policies in regard to Communists, springing from his profound inability or unwillingness to tell a Stalinist from a liberal. Either he lumps together as "Reds" everybody left-of-center (and even an occasional right-winger by mistake), or he refuses to recognize as a Communist anyone who denies it. The one kind of Communist likely to be missed by both approaches is the genteel Bolshevik who keeps his nose clean and never even reads the *New Republic*.

That is why the Committee was at first so completely buffaloed by Hiss. When he thundered righteously, "I am sorry but I cannot but feel to such an extent that it is difficult for me to control myself that you can sit there, Mr. Hébert, and say to me casually that you have heard that man [Chambers] and you have heard me, and that you just have no basis for judging which one is telling the truth," Hébert could only stutter lamely something about the degrading necessity of using low "stool pigeons" like Chambers and Miss Bentley.

It is easy enough to understand the shouts of "red herring!" raised in the earlier days of the case by certain old-line Democrats led by President Truman. They did not dissent on principle, but merely on party lines. If a venture sparked by Republicans is admitted to have succeeded, the Democrats stand to lose votes; and one denies anything that might lose votes. But the real liberals, in and out of the Democratic party, from whose ranks most of the actual believers in the innocence of Hiss are drawn, are a different matter. They had not even listened to the earlier testimony, out of a feeling that paying any heed to the House Committee on Un-American Activities was playing into the hands of the enemy, and that, in any event, the personnel and procedures of that Committee made it impossible for it to arrive at the truth. During the trials they paid attention for the first time.

Chambers' documentary evidence was still there, of course, and his circumstantial story was told again; but by this time Hiss was able to make a better showing than he had, taken unawares, before the Committee. He was imperturbable and glib in his testimony; and his lawyers were able to make Chambers seem more than ever a "moral leper," turning his very virtues (the lies and half-revelations by which he had attempted to protect Hiss) against him, and mocking his new-found religion. All the world distrusts a convert, but no part of it does so more heartily than the liberals. Finally, there were the psychiatrists, prepared on the basis of courtroom observation to call Chambers seriously unbalanced.

But, most important of all, there arose to stand beside Hiss, one by one, a series of respectable character witnesses, an elite corps, as it were, of the New Deal, distinguished civil servants and honored judges, until it seemed as if the whole movement that from 1932 on had swept the country out of fear and toward prosperity was staking its very reputation on the innocence of this single man. We know the character witnesses did not deliberately lie. But if they were not liars — as they certainly were *not* — they were, in some sense, fools.

It is not an easy admission, certainly not for them, but not even for those (among whom I include myself) who have admired in them a vision of national life that still appears worth striving for.

Even the wisdom of Franklin Roosevelt, the final culture hero of our liberal era, is brought into question. For he seems personally to have pooh-poohed the suspicions, relayed to him in 1940 by Ambassador Bullitt, about the reliability of Hiss. How could he have done otherwise? Was not Hiss one of those young men, mocked by the reactionary press as "brain-trusters," it had been his special pride to bring into political life? The big-city bosses, the unprincipled "experts," and the party hacks he had been forced to carry with him for expediency's sake; but these young idealists he had supported for the sake of principle. Superficially, the history of Hiss is the prototypical history of the New Dealer at his best: the distinguished years at Harvard Law School, the secretaryship to the almost mythical Justice Holmes, the brilliant career that began in the Nye committee and culminated at Teheran.

Certainly, a generation was on trial with Hiss — on trial not, it must be noticed, for having struggled toward a better world, but for having substituted sentimentality for intelligence in that struggle, for having failed to understand the moral conditions that must determine its outcome. What is involved is not any question of all or most of the younger New Dealers having been, like Hiss, secret agents of the GPU, but the question of their having been so busy denying that there was a GPU, or that it mattered, that they could not identify an enemy of all the values in which they most profoundly believed.

They cannot even flatter themselves on having been fooled by master tricksters. Hiss was, perhaps, an extraordinarily accomplished dissembler; but what of the Pressmans and the Wadleighs, more obvious in their intended deviousness? Lest the New Dealers seem "Red-baiters," they preferred to be fools. Even in the case of Hiss, disquieting reports were transmitted to his superiors from time to time, and it was noticed, on at least one occasion, that information which passed through his hands had an odd way of leaking out.

At one point A. A. Berle, after a conversation with Chambers, had gone to Dean Acheson, then Hiss's immediate superior, to report the rumor that "the Hiss boys" were members of a secret Communist group; and Acheson called in Donald Hiss to ask him if he and his brother were really Reds.

The naïveté of the thing is monumental! He asked Donald Hiss, and when Hiss said *no*, Acheson was "satisfied." After all, he had known "the Hiss boys" since they were children; they had gone to the same schools, belonged to the same clubs, could speak man to man. Dean Acheson simply could not bring himself to believe that if the Hisses, who were gentlemen, were also Communists, they would as a matter of course lie. One thinks of Mrs. Roosevelt, under somewhat similar circumstances, calling the leaders of the American Student Union into her drawing room, asking them please to tell her the real truth: were they Communists?

In part, the lack of realism shared by Acheson and Mrs. Roosevelt came from belonging to a world in which liberals and conservatives (and even radicals) are assumed to share the same moral values, the values of the old Judeo-Christian ethical system, however secularized; but, in another sense, it arises from long conditioning of the public mind by the "front organizations" of the late 1930's, through which the bulk of the liberals learned to maintain the paradox that (a) there were really no Communists, just the hallucinations of "witch hunters," and (b) if there were Communists, they were, despite their shrillness and bad manners, fundamentally on the side of justice. After all, the Communists are "left," and everyone knows that only the "right" is bad. This absurd metaphor of "leftness" managed to conceal from men of good will and some intelligence the essential fact that the Communists had ceased to subscribe to a political morality universally shared, whatever its abuses, until 1917. How many victims of this confusion were able to spend years moving in and out of Communist fronts and say blandly in the end, "To the best of my knowledge, I have never known an actual Communist"!

Seen in this larger context, the half-deliberate blindness of so many decent people, which is a vital part of the total Hiss

case, explains itself. The erstwhile defenders of Hiss's innocence show a growing tendency to remain silent; but their
silence does not mean, alas, that they are finally convinced.
Looking through Carey McWilliams' book *Witch Hunt,* for
instance, one is startled to discover, in a study of the rising
tide of accusations of Communism, no mention of the name
of Alger Hiss — nor, indeed, of Klaus Fuchs. So significant
an oversight must mean, if not active skepticism about Hiss's
guilt, a feeling that his case is somehow less relevant than
those in which charges of Communism have not been sub-
stantiated.

We must clearly understand that the failure of Hiss to confess, far from casting doubt on his guilt, merely helps to define
its nature. If Hiss's guilt is of the sort I have tried to indicate,
it is clear that, without some change of heart or values, he
could not possibly have confessed. One has only to think of
the recent trial of the twelve members of the national committee of the Communist party. Even these avowed and open
leaders of the movement, whom one had perhaps expected to
cry out their faith proudly before the tribunal, could only
plead — so ingrained had the Popular Front lie become — in
the teeth of the evidence of their own early writings, that (a)
they had never advocated revolution and (b) by God, it was
their inalienable right as American citizens to do so. What
could one expect from Hiss?

If there is a note of tragedy in the case, it is provided by
Chambers, the informer driven to mortify himself and to harm
those he still loved. The Third Perioder, still pursuing the
absolute, makes a tragic final appearance as the scorned
squealer; the Popular Fronter can only exit in the role of
the hopeless liar. It is difficult to say what factor is most decisive in cutting Hiss off finally from the great privilege of
confession; opportunism or perverted idealism, moral obtuseness or the habit of Machiavellianism — they are all inextricably intermingled.

In the end he failed all liberals, all who had, in some sense
and at some time, shared his illusions (and who that calls
himself a liberal is exempt?), all who demanded of him that
he speak aloud a common recognition of complicity. And yet,

perhaps they did not really want him to utter a confession; it would have been enough had he admitted a mistake rather than confessed a positive evil. Maybe, at the bottom of their hearts, they did not finally want him to admit anything, but preferred the chance he gave them to say: He is, we are, innocent.

American liberalism has been reluctant to leave the garden of its illusion; but it can dally no longer: the age of innocence is dead. The Hiss case marks the death of an era, but it also promises a rebirth if we are willing to learn its lessons. We who would still like to think of ourselves as liberals must be willing to declare that mere liberal principle is not in itself a guarantee against evil; that the wrongdoer is not always the other — "they" and not "us"; that there is no magic in the words "left" or "progressive" or "socialist" that can prevent deceit and the abuse of power.

It is not necessary that we liberals be self-flagellants. We have desired good, and we have done some; but we have also done great evil. The confession in itself is nothing, but without the confession there can be no understanding, and without the understanding of what the Hiss case tries desperately to declare, we will not be able to move forward from a liberalism of innocence to a liberalism of responsibility.

CHAPTER TWO

Afterthoughts on the Rosenbergs

Since the execution of the Rosenbergs, it has become possible to see clearly what was for a long time obscured: that there were *two* Rosenberg cases, quite distinct though referred to by a single name; and that this ambiguity made it difficult for the pro- and anti-Rosenberg forces ever to engage in a real dialogue. How often we were talking about quite different things under the same label!

The first Rosenberg case, which reached its climax with their trial in March 1951, involved certain questions of fact about the transmission of secrets to the Soviet Union, culminating in the handing over of sketches for the detonating device of the atom bomb. Implicated in this first case were: the brother of Ethel Rosenberg, David Greenglass, who made a full confession; Morton Sobell; Anatoli Yacovlev, the Russian vice-consul who had got safely out of the United States in December of 1946; and the notorious Communist "drop," Harry Gold. Through Gold, the Rosenberg case was linked with those of the confessed espionage agents, Klaus Fuchs and Allan Nunn May, woven inextricably into a context against which their guilt appeared clear beyond doubt. The denials of the Rosenbergs seemed merely the mendacious pleas of two people fighting for their lives in the face of overwhelming evidence.

In this initial open-and-shut case, scarcely anyone was very interested. In the United States, it did not stir up nearly as much discussion as the Hiss-Chambers affair, or even the trivial business of Judith Coplon. In Europe, it was ignored or meagerly reported, so that the European defenders of the

Rosenbergs tended to be happily ignorant of the first or factual case in its real interconnections; and this ignorance in many cases they fought desperately to preserve. The Communists themselves maintained a strange official silence about the Rosenbergs for more than a year after their arraignment, wary, presumably, about identifying themselves with a pair at once so central to their whole espionage effort and so flagrantly guilty; and baffled, no doubt, at how to defend two comrades who had been underground for six years and who refused to admit their party membership in court.

The second, or legendary, Rosenberg case was invented, along with the Committee to Secure Justice in the Rosenberg Case, at the end of October 1951 in Knickerbocker Village, a housing settlement in New York City. The place of the double birth seems almost too apt; the Rosenbergs themselves had once inhabited that melancholy block of identical dwelling units that seem the visible manifestation of the Stalinized petty-bourgeois mind: rigid, conventional, hopelessly self-righteous — the mind which dreamed the odd parody of the martyr which was the role of the Rosenbergs in their second case.*

The Rosenbergs stood alone in the new version of their plight — alone except for certain honorable ghosts. Gone were the real accomplices: Yacovlev and Sobell, Harry Gold, Klaus Fuchs and Allan Nunn May, though "Davy" Greenglass, recruited to the Movement at the age of twelve by his nineteen-year-old sister, remained to play the shadowy villain — replaced by the evoked figures of Sacco and Vanzetti, Tom Mooney, the Scottsboro Boys, and, especially, Dreyfus. The cue had been given by the "progressive" *National Guardian*, which had opened the defense campaign with a story headlined: "Is the Rosenberg Case the Dreyfus Case of America's Cold War?" The revised Rosenbergs were no longer spies, but "political prisoners" in the European sense, victims of the class struggle and the Cold War, defenders of the peace, a perse-

---

*The Rosenbergs of the second case possess a certain kind of immortality; that is, they will continue to live in the official history and art of the Communist Movement, until, for one reason or another, their particular segment of history is forgotten or refalsified. But not yet! In 1954, the hit of the season on the Warsaw stage was a play called *Ethel and Julius*.

cuted minority — these very people, it must be remembered, who would not confess their political allegiance in court, and who for six years had been under instructions not even to appear "progressive."

The long-drawn-out process of appeal in the American courts had made it possible to set up the symbolic Rosenbergs in place of the real ones; between the first exposure of two spies and the appeal of the "framed up victims before the bar of world opinion" came the year (soon two, and three) of separation and imprisonment and real suffering. The Communists banked on this stretch of time to screen their sleight-of·hand; and it worked. Even those who had followed the first trial carefully found it difficult to keep it in mind; and the maintenance of the anti-Rosenberg position soon fell largely into the hands of those who countered liberaloid sentimentality and rancor not with facts but with their own even more wretched "Down with the Communist Rats — God Bless America" sentimentality and rancor. The second, the legendary, Rosenberg case possessed the imagination of the world.

It is that second case which I wish to discuss. There is no point in rehearsing the first; as far as I am concerned, the legal guilt of the Rosenbergs was clearly established at their trial, and it is from an assumption of that guilt that I begin. What I want to examine (and this, after all, is the enduring point of the matter) is why the Rosenbergs, for all their palpable guilt, won their second case before the world; why there arose such a universal condemnation of their sentence; and why so many, in the teeth of the evidence, even believed in their innocence.

One can say in a general way that in the second case the Rosenbergs were not tried at all, but that by a bit of prestidigitation they, too, disappeared along with Gold, Yacovlev, and the rest; and that we were called upon to judge in their places Sacco and Vanzetti or Dreyfus. And how did they get in? Through the evocation of these almost traditional victims, a kind of moral blackmail was practiced on us; the flags of the gallant old causes were unfurled, and we were expected to respond by revivifying the battered belief that the political dissident (but in what sense is the present-day flag-waving Communist a dissident?), the proud rebel (but in what sense were the Rosenbergs, peering slyly out from behind the Fifth Amendment, rebellious or proud?), the Jew (but in what sense were the Rosenbergs Jews?) is always framed, that the guilt is always on the other side.

What a relief to be able to reassert that simple-minded article of faith after Fuchs and Nunn May and Hiss, and after the thousand betrayals of the Soviet Union. The fact that the Rosenbergs were remarkable chiefly for their difference from the older martyrs, that the whole point of their affair lay in that difference, was hardly remarked; scarcely anyone wanted to see them as they were, but merely to *use* them for self-exculpation — for joining together once more the ranks that had marched unbroken for Vanzetti, but had since fallen hopelessly apart.

And yet the question remains. Why this occasion rather than another; why this improbable pair; and why (outside of the United States itself) so nearly unanimous a response to their plight? To disentangle the motives that found a focus in the pro-Rosenberg movement is to write a thumbnail moral history of our time.

One must begin, I suppose, by separating out the absolute cynics, the Communist bureaucrats who used the case coldly when it was convenient to use it, as they had ignored it calmly when it was convenient to ignore it; and who knew that they could not lose in any event. For if the freeing of the Rosenbergs would have been for them a minor victory, their death was a major one in the struggle against the United States. After a certain point, the energies of such functionaries were patently directed at insuring that clemency would not be granted. I do not want to seem to make master-minds out of shabby Communist bureaucrats, but surely a certain elementary cunning rather than mere stupidity led them to do everything that would infuriate official American opinion, make any revision of the death sentence seem an admission of a judicial error.

It is no accident, I think, that the only plea which came near saving the Rosenbergs was prompted by an outsider who had been expelled from both the Communist party and the Communist-controlled defense committee. The suffering and death of the Rosenbergs were *willed* by the makers of Communist opinion and relished by them, as every new lynching in America, every bit of violence against the Jews, is willed and relished as further evidence that they are right! These are the professional accomplices of calamity; and if they cried "innocent," it was because they thought that the greatest possibility of disaster lay in such an assertion.

These conscious exploiters of the case were a tiny minority, yet one which had ready to hand a mass of naïve communicants already trained to believe, sincerely and even fervently, what that minority decided they should believe. In this sense, one can think of the bacterial-warfare campaign and the various "peace" petitions as preparations for the Rosenberg case, as the Rosenberg case in turn is no end in itself but a rehearsal for the next real or manufactured issue on the Communist agenda. This prefabricated public is made up not only of the naïver party members, activists to whom ideas are unknown and the mute attenders of meetings, but also of fellow-travelers and the "innocents" who read nothing but the Communist press, or even only the Communist posters (knowing, of course, that all other sources of information are "bought"). For such believers an event does not even *exist*, much less have a significance, until it is recognized by their journals; and so for them there had simply been *no* Rosenberg case until the party had given the go-ahead signal after months of discreet silence. For them, only the legendary case was real.

The Communists have long controlled in Europe large numbers of "advanced" workers, peasants, and petty bourgeois by manipulating a mythology inherited from a hundred years of political struggle: the belief that the state and its courts are always wrong; that the bourgeoisie is always wrong; and especially that the United States, the bastion of capitalism, is always wrong* — with the corollaries that no Negro, Jew, or "progressive" (i.e., Communist or sympathizer) can ever be anything but innocent. This group was joined by an even larger periphery, stalinized to the extent of not believing its own

---

*Only the notion that priests are always wrong could not be exploited in the Rosenberg case; otherwise it was a perfect ritual expression of the sub-Marxist catechism.

press and of accepting in critical instances the opinions screamed in the piazzas by those whom they consider more "devoted" and "unselfish" than themselves, because they are louder and more assured. Together these formed a sizable public which appears really to have believed that the Rosenbergs were innocent in the basic sense of the word, guiltless of the crime with which they were charged. This they knew, not from scrutinizing the record, but from consulting the opinions of those who had always defined for them the truth. They would have believed it quite as firmly if there had been no such people as the Rosenbergs — as, in a sense, there were not.

Such a rank and file, stalinized at second and third remove, did not exist in the United States, which possesses in their place a mass of people politically innocent and merely indifferent to such affairs in a way no European can understand. To this oppositely corresponding American group, the *second* Rosenberg case had no existence; so that between them and their European opposite numbers there was not even ground enough for real disagreement.

In both Europe and America, however, a substantial minority of intellectuals shared a third position which asserted the innocence of the Rosenbergs, or at least maintained the final irrelevance of their guilt. This position combined in varying proportions two complementary attitudes: the *wish* that the Rosenbergs might actually be innocent; and the conviction that they were *symbolically* guiltless whatever action they may have committed. The first feeling led to an incantatory declaration of the Rosenbergs' guiltlessness, based on the belief that what these intellectuals repeated with truly unselfish fervor could not help but prove true; and, in any event, the Rosenbergs *couldn't* have done it, couldn't have committed treason — or these intellectuals, too, might have been guilty of as sordid a crime when in their own heedless youth they also had been Communists or had at least defended in perfect self-righteousness their Communist friends against the "Redbaiters."

But, even if the Rosenbergs *had* performed the act, this line of argument continues, treason was not what they had meant; they had been acting for a better world, for all Humanity (i.e., for the Soviet Union, whose interests all the more enlightened had once known were identical with those of mankind); and, anyhow, Russia had been our ally when the Rosenbergs gave them a helping hand, standing with us side by side against the Nazis; and, after all, Russia had not yet used the Bomb, will never use it, never, never, *never* (to stop believing this would mean having to rethink their whole lives), so that sharing the atomic secret in this somewhat unorthodox fashion was really a blow for world peace: just look at the present *détente*, etc., etc. In light of all which, isn't it better simply to declare that the Rosenbergs are "innocent," as a kind of shorthand for an analysis too complicated to explain to the uninitiated without re-educating them completely.

How near the conscious surface such reasoning was carried on must have varied from case to case; but in almost every instance it led to the by-now-customary double bookkeeping of the Communists' friends, the exploitation of a vocabulary which makes it possible to say, at one and the same time, "They didn't do it at all; it's a frame-up!" and, "After all, they had a right; their hearts were pure!" This is a fantastic enough position in any event, but when held by the accused themselves (and it *was* held by the Rosenbergs, as I shall show), it becomes utterly fantastic, the obverse of those equally absurd "symbolic" declarations of guilt in the rigged Russian trials.

Finally,* one is left with those who cried only for mercy, for the conversion of the death sentence, "even if they were guilty as charged." It is difficult to disentangle the position itself from those who maintained it; to redeem it from the scandalous way it was used by the Communists, who sought to confuse hopelessly the two kinds of protest, to make every cry for grace seem an assertion of innocence, and more: a condemnation of the United States, the Atlantic Pact, the European Army, and God knows what else. One is so ap-

---

*I am relegating to this footnote the "diplomatic" advocates of mercy — those who urged a revision of the sentence in order to "placate world opinion" or in order "not to give the Communists a martyr." This was not an important group, and the point of the whole case is precisely that the Rosenbergs were *incapable* of becoming martyrs.

palled at the cynicism of many of the exploiters of "mercy," with their own record of political executions without appeal, without trials — and after the most ignominious of self-degradations — that he is tempted to discount the whole movement.

Even where the Communists played only a secondary role, there was evident in the shrillness of the cries of horror (rising from countries where only a little while before the lynching of political enemies was considered an act of virtue) a desire to celebrate the fall of America from innocence, to indulge in an orgy of self-righteousness at our expense. There is no political act (and the simplest cry for clemency was inevitably a political act) that is not marred these days by the obsessive envy and anguish of the Europeans in our regard. If the Europeans could only have believed as firmly as they pretended that we had utterly yielded to hysteria and persecution, the balance of guilt that tilts so annoyingly in their direction would have been righted; and they might have loved us more, not less. But they could only *want* to believe this, not really credit it — any more than they have been able to really accept the stories of germ warfare in Korea. In a Europe that tends to admire where it is horrified, and to be overwhelmed by the fascination of ruthlessness, even our approximate innocence, or the mere inefficiency at terror that is its equivalent, is a reproach.

Yet, allowing for all that was stage-managed or disingenuous in the pleas for clemency; discounting the rather professional nature of some of the ecclesiastical protests; allowing for the sob sisters who are ready to howl bitterly at the sentencing of the most sadistic wretch; setting aside the pleading based on a general condemnation of the death penalty, which does not bear precisely on this case; and discounting the almost mechanical reflex of those to whom since Hitler any threat to any Jew seems a recrudescence of the old horror, one comes to a residual protest that cannot be explained away, and in the face of which we must as Americans admit a real, a perhaps tragic, failure of the moral imagination.

The final protest that existed behind all the others based on stupidity or malice or official dogma was the humane one. Under their legendary role, there were, after all, *real* Rosenbergs, unattractive and vindictive but human; fond of each other and of their two children; concerned with operations for tonsillitis and family wrangles; isolated from each other during three years of not-quite-hope and deferred despair; at the end, prepared scientifically for the electrocution: Julius' mustache shaved off and the patch of hair from Ethel's dowdy head (and all this painfully documented by the morning papers in an America that can keep no secrets); finally capable of dying. This we had forgotten, thinking of the Rosenbergs as merely typical, seeing them in the context of a thousand other petty-bourgeois Stalinists we had known, each repeating the same shabby standard phrases. That they were individuals and would die they themselves had denied in every gesture — and we foolishly believed them. In the face of their own death, the Rosenbergs became, despite themselves and their official defenders, symbols of the conflict between the human and the political, the individual and the state, justice and mercy; and this symbolic conflict only those who knew they were guilty could fully appreciate.

It is, in the end, no mere matter of protesting an excessive sentence, but of realizing that they *count,* these people moved always like puppets from above, that they count as *human,* though they committed treason in disregard of all real human considerations in the name of an intolerably abstract "Humanity." It is wonderful in a way that two individuals did still count to so many people in a world as accustomed as ours to mass slaughter and injustice become mere routine.

There is no sense in becoming enraged at the fact that these two, our *only* two victims, should have stirred up the response that could not be brought to focus for the millions of victims of Soviet firing squads; that most of the world should have been crying out for the lives of two American spies, convicted by due process, at the very moment when Willy Goettling and a score of nameless others were being summarily shot in Soviet Berlin. We should rather be flattered that as a nation we continue to act on a plane where moral judgment is still possible; elsewhere assertions of human value seem merely pointless, and the only possible protest is silence, the resolve at least not to hail institutionalized murder as social justice.

Some Americans have, indeed, felt flattered at being among the last peoples to whom real protest is still conceivable, not merely permitted by law, but possible to the uncorrupted moral sense; and they have been willing to stop there, arguing that this very fact sanctions the execution of the Rosenbergs, by proving it the sort of exceptional act we can still morally afford when political considerations demand it. But the point is surely that clemency to the Rosenbergs was what we could *not* afford to deny. The world had turned to us (that part at least still not hopelessly stalinized) for a symbolic demonstration that somewhere a government existed willing to risk the loss of political face for the sake of establishing an unequivocal moral position. A minority at least understood that the Communists were doing everything in their power to make any concession on our part seem a cowardly retreat; but they hoped we would have the courage to seem in that sense cowardly. I cannot help feeling that even among the rank-and-file Stalinists there existed on some deeply buried level the shadowy desire for someone somewhere to assert that the political man was not all of man, that our humanity is neither fictional nor irrelevant.

This opportunity we let slip away from us, in part because of our political innocence, in part through a lack of moral imagination, but also through a certain incapacity to really believe in Communists as people. In the official declarations of Eisenhower, one senses behind the cold reasoning from cause to effect, and the shaky conclusion that the secrets transmitted by the Rosenbergs unleashed the Korean War, the failure of the military mind to see beyond a justice defined in codes. In the justifications of Judge Kaufman, on the other hand, one feels a personal hysteria — a fear of Communism magnified by the sense that in the United States, where so many Stalinists have been Jews, the acts of the Rosenbergs were an attainder of the whole Jewish population. But the Rosenbergs were not, after all, excessively punished merely because their fates happened to rest in the hands of a military man and a Jew, but because mass opinion in America, in so far as it took notice of them at all, *wanted* their deaths, as an example and token.

When counter-pickets to the Rosenberg defenders carried

placards demanding "Death to the Communist Rats!" there was involved, beyond an old American metaphor for spies, a wish to believe that the enemy is subhuman, an animal to exterminate rather than a man to confront. Needless to say, the Communists themselves need no lessons in this sort of maneuver; we have only to remember the words of the Rosenbergs' lawyer before the White House on the eve of their death: "I don't know what animals I am dealing with, but I know that I am dealing with animals." Yet we have no right to let ourselves be provoked into answering the Communists with equivalent strategies; differently from them, we still have much to lose; and in trying to dehumanize our opponents we may end by dehumanizing ourselves.

When the news of the Rosenbergs' long-delayed execution was announced before the White House, the counter-pickets cheered. A critical episode in the moral and political coming of age of America had reached its climax; the hopes for a world of equity and peace that had moved the more sensitive and intelligent in the 1920's and 1930's, had been used as camouflage by a brutally imperialistic power and had ended by leading two undistinguished people into a trap of lies and espionage and death; and the counter-pickets *cheered!* One is tempted to echo the words of Irwin Edelman* just before he was chased out of Pershing Square by an irate crowd: "If you are happy about the execution of the Rosenbergs, you are rotten to the core!" But, if this reaction seems the final indignity, there is much worse to come.

Our failure placed in the hands of the Communists the

---

*Edelman is one of the most extraordinary figures in the whole affair. Thrown out of the Communist party in Los Angeles in 1947 for advocating more inner party democracy, and expelled from the official Rosenberg defense committee as a heretic, he nonetheless provided the nearest thing to a legal out for the Rosenbergs. His pamphlet, *Freedom's Electrocution,* inspired two rather eccentric lawyers to make the plea which brought into special session the Supreme Court, which had recently reviewed a case against Edelman himself on a charge of vagrancy. He enters and exits from the affair in a style that provides a real contrast to the Rosenbergs' sly, maddeningly mendacious conduct. He seems a survival of the old-fashioned American radical, refreshingly honest beside the new "underground" models. One would bid those who think the Rosenbergs were killed for being radicals to notice that in a presumably hysterical America it was the real radical who was free to come to their aid.

advantage of being able to exploit the very human considerations that they were least capable of feeling. And there was an additional advantage in their cynicism itself, which left them able to *use* the Rosenberg children, the coincidence of the electrocution date with the fourteenth wedding anniversary of Ethel and Julius, their frustrated love, and the shocking physical details of their death with a complete lack of squeamishness. On the hoardings of the whole world, the embraces of the Rosenbergs and their approach to the Chair were turned into clichés, occasions for public orgies of sentiment. The Judaism of the condemned pair was played on tearfully by the same activists who had screamed for the death of the Russian Jewish doctors until the line was changed; and the believers that religion is the opium of the people cried out against executing the Rosenbergs on the Sabbath.

But all this, it must never be forgot, was not until the leaders of the party had decided it was *safe* to be sorry — safe for the party, of course, and not for the Rosenbergs. The disregard of the Stalinists for the individuals whose causes they support, their willingness to compromise their very lives for the sake of making propitious propaganda, has been known to everyone since the days of the Scottsboro boys. But unlike those boys, or Tom Mooney, or the other classic cases, the Rosenbergs were actual comrades. This did not mean, however, that there was any more real desire to save them; indeed, as enlightened and disciplined members they would be expected to approve the tactics that assured their deaths in order to blacken the United States in the eyes of the world. Their actual affiliation was, in fact, an embarrassment, something not to be played upon but concealed. The Manchester *Guardian* and other liberal journals might talk of "making martyrs for the Communists," but the Communists, victims of the frantic game of hide-and-seek they had been playing with themselves ever since the dawning of the Popular Front, expended a good deal of energy to hide the fact that these martyrs were "theirs."

"Death for the Rosenbergs Is a Victory for McCarthy!" the posters read, and who, in Europe, at least, remembered that McCarthy had never had anything to do with the affair? Surely the chief evil of McCarthyism consists in branding honest men as Communists out of malice and stupidity. But how does this concern calling a Communist a Communist, or with deciding by legal process that a spy is a spy? These creatures of Soviet foreign policy were labeled the defenders of all "freedom-loving peoples," sacrificed to nothing less than their love for "American Democracy."

There were no limits to the absurd masquerade. A hundred marching Communists in London put flowers at the foot of a statue of Franklin Roosevelt, with an attached card reading: "That Roosevelt's Ideas May Live the Rosenbergs Must Not Die!" Not Marx or Lenin's ideas, please note, but Roosevelt's. It is all of a piece. Julius draped after his death not with a red flag but with the ritual prayer shawl of the Jews; not "The Internationale" sung but "Go Down, Moses" and the Psalms; the American flags flying brazenly over the cortege and the rabbi to intone unbelieved-in prayers at the grave. But the hoax would not quite hold to the end, for the crowd at the funeral parlor booed when a rabbi invited for the sake of camouflage, reminded them that the Jewish religion teaches forgiveness of enemies. In an instant, the fake piety and humanity had disappeared from the carefully prepared faces, and those who had cried for mercy a little while before hooted down the mention of its name.

But there was worse yet. I was in Rome when the news of the Rosenbergs' death came through, and I can speak only of what I actually witnessed; but there, at least on the faces of the Communist crowds surging and screaming before the American Embassy, I saw evidence of *joy*. They were glad, these young activists, that the Rosenbergs were safely dead; for a little while they had been afraid that some last-minute reprieve might cheat them out of their victory celebration, that they would be unable to go through the streets in their Sunday best chalking up "Death to the Killers of the Rosenbergs!" and to sit afterwards over a bottle of wine content with a good day's work. But even this is not the utterest obscenity.

That the American public should deny the humanity of their enemies is terrible enough; that the Communists should deny the humanity of their comrades much worse; but that two people should deny their *own* humanity in the face of death is the ultimate horror, the final revelation of a universal moral calamity. For even at the end the Rosenbergs were not able to think of themselves as real people, only as "cases," very like the others for which they had helped fight, Scottsboro and Harry Bridges and the Trenton Ten, replaceable puppets in a manifestation that never ends. There is something touching in their own accounts of reading each issue of the *National Guardian* (not the frank *Daily Worker,* but the crypto-Communist sheet) to share in the ritualistic exploitation of themselves. But even before the "progressive" journal had begun to spread their story, they themselves had written to each other the foreseeable platitudes of the propaganda on their behalf. From the start, they had not been able to find any selves realer than those official clichés. If there is a tragedy of the Rosenbergs, this is it.

The persistently evoked image of Sacco and Vanzetti had led many to expect in the correspondence of the Rosenbergs some evidence of an underlying honesty, some frank and simple declaration of faith; but they could not hit upon any note that rang true. Reading the "death-house letters" of the Rosenbergs, one has the sense that not only the Marxist dream of social justice but the very possibilities of any heroism and martyrdom are being blasphemed. It is a parody of martyrdom they give us, too absurd to be truly tragic, too grim to be the joke it is always threatening to become.

Ethel's last appeal to President Eisenhower was the first of their letters I read; and it is surely among the most embarrassing, combining with Ethel's customary attempts at a "literary" style, and the constitutional inability to be frank which she shared with her husband, a deliberate and transparent craftiness. She, who had already been writing about Eisenhower in private as "our gnaedige Gauleiter," refers in a painfully adulatory beginning to that embarrassment "which the ordinary person feels in the presence of the great and famous" and which has kept her from writing to the President before. Only the example of Mrs. Oatis,* who "bared her

---

*The evocation of the Oatis case raises problems which demand another article: the prefabricated stalinoid public's celebration of Oatis' re-

heart to the head of a foreign state," has led Ethel, she explains, to look for "as much consideration from the head of her own." She has been unable to avoid the note of reproach in this comparison of mercy on either side of the Iron Curtain, but to take off the curse she hastens to protest her ignorance, in the typical gesture of the Communist who has felt obliged to praise, however mildly, something publicly identified with his real allegiance. "Of Czechoslovakia I know very little, of her President even less than that. . . ." This unconvincing avowal, however, does not satisfy even her, so she tries the alternative gambit of gratuitous flag-waving, announcing quite inconsequently that for America she "would be homesick anywhere in the world."

She then reminds Eisenhower that before he became President he was a "Liberator," but it is not really a congenial memory to her who has still ringing in her ear her own cry of "gauleiter" and the conventional Communist characterization of the American general staff as "heirs of the Nazis." The transition to this note is easy: her execution will be, she charges, "an act of vengeance," and not the first, she reminds Eisenhower, identifying herself and her husband with the 6,000,000 hounded Jews of Europe, and the President with the masters of Buchenwald — those "ghastly mass butchers, the obscene fascists," who are presently "graciously receiving the benefits of mercy," while "the great democratic United States is proposing the savage destruction of a small unoffending Jewish family. . . ."

At last she is at home. The hatred, the obvious irony, the ready-made epithets of the Communist press are released like a dog's saliva at the *ting* of a bell. How happily she forgets that she has been defending the concept of mercy, and using the word "democratic" of her own country without sarcasm. But "a small unoffending Jewish family" — it seems incredible that anyone could speak so about herself, her own children.

---

lease as an unparalleled act of generosity; his own attitude toward himself and his sentence; etc. Here I would like to note merely how neatly this reference joins together two problems that are really one. Why do the guiltless confess on the other side of the Curtain, while the guilty protest their innocence here? In both cases, "symbolic" truth-telling, a shorthand for the uninitiate, is at stake.

At last she is ready for the final series of elegantly unctuous appeals: in the name of "fealty to religious and democratic ideals," as "an offering to God," in the name of the President's wife who will "plead my cause with grace and felicity," or of "the province of the affectionate grandfather, the sensitive artist, the devoutly religious man." And the rhetoric reaches its high point with the reminder that "truly the stories of Christ, Moses and Gandhi hold more sheer wonderment and spiritual treasure than all the conquests of Napoleon." Against the shadow of these names the alternating venom and flattery seem especially evident; and we are left astonished at the self-righteousness that dared evoke them.

The letters which the Rosenbergs wrote to each other from their cells in Sing Sing seem at first glance superior at least to this. Ethel, to be sure, is still hopelessly the victim not only of her politics but of the painfully pretentious style that is its literary equivalent; but Julius, more the scientist in his view of himself, manages from time to time to seem sincere and touching. One is moved by his feeling for his wife, which is more than love — an almost frantic dependence and adulation; and by the tears that stand in his eyes after the visits of his children. But even these scenes, we remember, were, if not staged, at least edited for publication; published in a context of the most banal thumbnail editorials ("I was horrified to read . . . that our government is planning an accord with Spain . . . to ally ourselves with the most reactionary, feudal, and Fascist elements in order to defend democracy . . . something is very rotten in Denmark . . ."*) at the wish of the Rosenbergs themselves.

In part, their self-exposure was aimed, as they declared, at raising money for their children; but, in part, it must have been intended to make political capital out of their own misery and frustrated passion. Finally, the letters are incomprehensible either as genuine expressions of feeling or as partisan

---

*The reader checking these quotations against the English text of the letters will find certain discrepancies, for I am translating them back from the French text of the *Figaro Littéraire,* the only one available to me. There is however, a certain justice in this procedure; for the documents of the legendary Rosenberg case were intended primarily for Europe, and should be seen backward through Europe to be truly appreciated.

manifestoes, since they consist almost equally of intimacies which should never have been published, and lay sermons which should never have been written to each other by a husband and wife confronting their deaths. The line between the person and the case, between private and public, had been broken down for them long before and could not be redrawn even in the extremest of situations. A single logic connects the Communist hating on order the person he has never seen; the activist ignoring on the street yesterday's best friend who has become a deviationist; the wife leaving her husband the day after he is expelled from the party; the son informing on the father; the accused in Russia slavishly vilifying themselves in court — and the Rosenbergs exploiting their final intimacies to strike a blow in the Cold War.

It is in light of this failure to distinguish the person from the cause, the fact from its "dialectical" significance, that we must understand the lies (what are for us, at least, lies) of the letters. The most flagrant, of course, is the maintenance by the Rosenbergs of the pose of innocence to the very end and *to each other!* We have grown used to Communist spies lying in court with all the conviction and fervor of true victims; there was the recent example of Alger Hiss, to name only one; but we had always hoped that to their wives at least, in darkness and whispers, they spoke the truth. Yet the Rosenbergs played out their comedy to the end; and this we should have foreknown.

Some, I recall, advocated a conversion of their sentences on the tactical grounds that they might in the long run confess; and some have even been shaken by their consequent persistence in the cry, "We are innocent!" An occasional less-convinced Stalinist, bullied into complicity like David Greenglass, can be bullied out again into a frank admission; but the true believer believes above all in his own unimpeachable innocence. Precisely because the Rosenbergs could have committed espionage as they did, they could not ever confess it. A confession would, in a certain sense, have shed doubt on their complicity.

They were able to commit their kind of treason because they were incapable of telling treason from devotion, deceit from honesty. It was not even, though this would be easier to accept, that they chose deliberately between rival allegiances: the Soviet Union versus the United States. They did not know that such a choice existed; but believed in their own way what they continued to assert, that they had always loved and served "American Democracy." It is misleading to think of them as liars, though their relationship to everything, including themselves, was false. When Julius, who had stuck up in his cell a copy of the Declaration of Independence clipped out of the New York *Times,* refers to it as if in passing so that all the world will know he is really a misunderstood patriot, one is tempted to call him a poseur and a hypocrite; but he is something much more devious.

When he and his wife carefully observe the coming of each Jewish holiday and sentimentalize over their double heritage as Americans and Jews, they are not deliberately falsifying, though they neither know nor care what Judaism actually is about; they will use as much of it as they need, defining it as they go. "In two days," Julius writes, "it will be Passover, which recalls the search of our people for liberty. This cultural heritage has for us a special significance, because we are imprisoned . . . by the Pharaohs of today. . . ." And in another place he remarks that "the culture of my people, its fight to liberate itself from slavery in Egypt" is astonishingly like "the great traditions in the history of America" — and, one understands though it is left unsaid, like those of the Communist party.

Ethel, typically, insists on defining her enlightened position more clearly. Thrilled by the sound of the shofar, she thinks of the Jews everywhere hastening to the synagogues to pray for a Happy New Year, but hastens to remind them via her husband that "we must not use prayer to the Almighty as an excuse for avoiding our responsibilities to our neighbors . . . the daily struggle for social justice." And she concludes, astonishingly, with the appeal: "Jews and non-Jews, Black and White, we must all stand together, firm, solid, and strong." It is like the curtain line of an *agit-prop* choral production at the combined celebration of *Rosh Hashanah* and the anniversary of the Russian Revolution.

Judaism happens to lie closest to hand because of the accident of the Rosenbergs' birth, but any other tradition would have done as well — and does. Not only the Christ, Gandhi and Moses of Ethel's letter to the President, but Roosevelt and "Butch" LaGuardia in their letters to each other — the list might be extended indefinitely. For they have been told, and are prepared to believe a priori, that they are the heirs of all the ages: Lincoln, Washington, Jefferson, Isaiah, Confucius, Leonardo da Vinci, Ivan the Terrible, Charlie Chaplin, and Christopher Columbus have all contributed to their patrimony.

They even like to think of themselves as sharing in the peculiarly American mana of the Brooklyn Dodgers. "The victory of the Dodgers," Ethel writes, "over the Phillies quickly restored me to my customary good spirits," and one takes it for a relatively harmless example of the pursuit of the popular and folksy that led Ethel to sing folk songs in the death house. But she cannot leave it at that; the editorial follows the next day, between declarations of love: "It is the Dodgers' unconquerable spirit which makes people love them. But where they have especially covered themselves with glory is in making an important contribution to the rooting out of racial prejudice." We have moved from melodrama to comedy, but the point is always the same. What is involved is the system of moral double bookkeeping invented to fool the Examiners, but so successful that it has ended by bamboozling the bookkeeper himself.

Nothing is what it seems: the Communist parties advocate revolution, and they do not; the Communist International has been dissolved, but it exists; one commits crimes, but he is innocent. Anyone can call war peace, or lies the truth; but to believe such assertions so that one will face death for them requires a trained will and imagination. For such belief, the Rosenbergs had been in training ever since they had combined wooing with the study of Communist literature; and they had finally reached a degree of perfection which enabled them to attain the final stage of subterfuge, to go "underground."

To me, even more extraordinary (for it seems on the face of it *pointless*) than the assertion of their innocence is the Rosenbergs' stubborn silence about their political affiliations.

In court, they had refused to speak on constitutional grounds; in their letters to each other, these "martyrs of the Communist cause" never mention the word "Communism," unless in quotation marks as an example of the slander of their enemies; while the name of the Soviet Union is, needless to say, avoided like a dirty word.

The expurgation goes sometimes to fantastic lengths, of which the most amusing example occurs in a letter of Ethel's written on June 21, 1951. "My beloved husband," she begins, "I feel so discouraged by this unjustifiable attack on a legally constituted American party! The specter of Fascism looms up, enormous and menacing . . ." But she does not identify the party beyond labeling it "American"; and the explanatory note attached by the defense committee in the published volume is equally coy. "Seventeen men and women had been arrested and convicted in New York under the recently passed Smith Act." If one already knows that those otherwise unqualified "men and women" were the leaders of the Communist party, all well and good. If not, it is apparently better to persist in one's ignorance.

The upshot of the whole business is that the Rosenbergs were quite incapable of saying in their last letters just what it was for which they thought they were dying. Not only had they excluded themselves from the traditional procedure of the old-style radical, who rises up in court to declare that he has acted in the teeth of accepted morality and law for the sake of certain higher principles; they could not even tell the world for what beliefs they were being framed. Beyond the cry of frame-up, they could only speak in hints and evasions; so that they finished by seeming martyrs only to their own double talk, to a handful of banalities: "democracy and human dignity," "liberty and peace," "the greatest good of our own children, our family, and all families," and finally "the interests of American Democracy, of justice and fraternity, of peace and bread and roses and the laughter of children."

To believe that two innocents had been falsely condemned for favoring "roses and the laughter of children," one would have to believe the judges and public officials of the United States to be not merely the Fascists the Rosenbergs called them, but monsters, insensate beasts; and perhaps this was partly their point. But one must look deeper, realize that a code is involved, a substitution of equivalents whose true meaning can be read off immediately by the insider. "Peace, democracy, and liberty," like "roses and the laughter of children," are only conventional ciphers for the barely whispered word "Communism," and Communism itself only a secondary encoding of the completely unmentioned "Defense of the Soviet Union." The Defense of the Soviet Union — here is the sole principle and criterion of all value — and to this principle the Rosenbergs felt that they had been true; in this sense, they genuinely believed themselves innocent, more innocent than if they had never committed espionage.

The final pity was that they could not say even so much aloud — except in certain symbolic outcries of frame-up and persecution, and only through the most palpable lies. It is for this reason that they failed in the end to become martyrs or heroes, or even men. What was there left to die?

Yet despite all this, *because* of it, we should have granted them grace. The betrayal of their essential humanity by their comrades and themselves left the burden of its defense with us. This obligation we failed, and our failure must be faced up to. Before the eyes of the world we lost an opportunity concretely to assert what all our abstract declarations can never prove: that for us at least the suffering person is realer than the political moment that produces him or the political philosophy for which he stands. Surely it is not even a paradox to assert that it is our special duty to treat as persons, as real human beings, those who most blasphemously deny their own humanity.

CHAPTER THREE

McCarthy and the Intellectuals

Tell the truth or trump, but take the trick.
— PUDD'NHEAD WILSON'S CALENDAR

Recently a major wire service carried the story of a man released from prison after more than fifty years, who confessed to never having heard of Joe McCarthy. The implication of the article was clear: the *only* man in the United States, the last man in the world still unaware of the Junior Senator from Wisconsin . . . It is a hyperbole, of course, but a modest one, almost the literal truth. McCarthy, McCarthyism — the two names have become familiar in most of the tongues of the earth. Choose a passer-by at random in any of the great cities of the world and ask him to identify the "X" in the following quotation: "Beware, Commies, spies, traitors, and foreign agents! X, with all loyal, free men behind him, is looking for you, ready to fight until the last one of you is exposed for the yellow scum you are."

"McCarthy," he will tell you, "Joe McCarthy, of course," though he might be incapable of saying whether the actual lines were a publicity release from McCarthy's supporters or a parody of such a release by his worst enemies. Actually, the name for which I have substituted an "X" is "Captain America," and the warning is taken from a comic book for small boys. But the implied commentary is apt: in our world, what seems to one group a howling travesty strikes another as a clarion call to action; and a legend has become confused with a man.

Here is the clue to the many paradoxes that surround Mc-

Carthy: the discrepancy between his reputation and his accomplishments; between the special aura of fear which surrounds him and the banality of his personality; between the real terror which has spread and the equally real freedom with which the terrified speak of being gagged; between his disavowal by the whole respectable press and his continuing popular support; between the piety and assurance of his attackers among themselves and their hedging before his committee; and finally, between the millions of words written about McCarthy and the sense that he has not yet been explained.

Even to himself McCarthy is apparently a double man; his way of referring to his official self in the third person is well known; and there appears to be a real difference between "McCarthy," the public presence, humorless and vindictive, and "Joe," the private person who jokes and sets up the drinks and has managed to make lifelong friends even of some whom the political "McCarthy" betrayed. Being his own legend has become a full-time job, so that the real Joe comes to have, not only less and less relevance, but less and less time to exist. Somewhere along the line, he found time to marry Jean Kerr, who had been his assistant, but he has never managed to unpack his wedding presents; and one sees him camped among the unopened boxes, his palsied head trembling, his throat closing with what may be a cancer of the larynx, as if his body and his voice rebelled against the role into which they are forced. One can almost feel pity for the man who has become as vividly unreal as a political slogan, or as the newspaper headlines that reinvent him daily.

To make matters more confusing, there are not one but two legendary McCarthys, the first of which he has defined himself: the figure scarcely distinguishable from "Captain America," the embodiment of an "Americanism that is ready to stand up and fight Communism." The other has been created by the Communists in their pose of abused "progressives," and has been adopted by many liberals and some conservatives: McCarthy as the spirit of "warmongering hysteria and the witch hunt." There have been other aspirants for this two-faced legendary status: William Randolph Hearst and Martin Dies, Father Coughlin and Captain Patterson and a score of others; but only Hearst has ever stirred the archetypal hatred which McCarthy compels, and even he did not flourish at so apt a moment. It is a time for nightmares and the need to project them: the traditional enemies of the hyper-patriot in confusion at the final revelation of the perfidy of the Soviet Union; America learning to face up for the first time to endemic frustration and to loneliness, as the whole world threatens to desert us out of hostility or cowardice or indecision. The Red Scare which for years remained a journalistic luxury, a Hallowe'en false face for bored chauvinists, comes to resemble more and more the bad dream from which we cannot awaken, the bad dream of history.

Those who believe, on the one hand, that there are *no* Communists or spies (I suppose this is the final implication of crying "witch hunt" in an age of enlightenment) or, on the other, that everyone who challenges middle-class orthodoxy is a lackey of Russia have been long trying to make their stereotypes flesh. They have evoked McCarthy; the rest of us merely suffer him. But for all of us he comes into existence at the same moment, some time just after 8 P.M. on the evening of February 9, 1950. From the moment he rose before the Women's Republican Club of Wheeling, West Virginia, McCarthy's history has been in the public domain. What most people know of his earlier career in the Senate — his opposition to sugar rationing and public housing; his leading though unofficial role in saving from the death sentence German storm troopers convicted of shooting down 250 American and Belgian prisoners at Malmédy in 1944 — all this has been reinterpreted in light of the unbroken series of charges and counter-charges that have followed the Wheeling Lincoln Day address.

McCarthy on the one side; the State Department, the Democratic party and international Communism on the other; a threatened America between — this is our modern *East Lynn,* a melodrama (but about who is the hero, who the villain, we cannot agree) played over and over with an almost mindless persistence and lack of variation, in the newspapers, on the radio, on television. The names and dates change, but the meaning of the play is always the same: the conspiracy exposed, the "liberal" revealed as camouflaged Communist or understrapper of the Communists; or, alternately, as the traduced innocent, rounding on his tormentors in all the radiance of his virtue. Sitting in the same playhouse, the two audiences see two quite different plays acted simultaneously by the same cast: John Carter Vincent and Owen Lattimore and Philip Jessup and Edward G. Posniak or Theodore Kaghan or . . . In the end, one can no longer remember who is in the title role.

From the very first the plot, the tone were set, half-comic, half-terrifying: the attack without warning, wild, self-contradictory, almost random; and never better documented or better prepared really, merely better prepared *for* with the press conference that announces another press conference at which the hyperbolic accusation is launched in the conspiratorial setting, as McCarthy raps a pencil against the mouthpiece of his telephone, turns on the water in the sink. He is surrounded by dictaphones, one is given to understand, spied on and harried. No matter how often the performance is repeated, the air of improvisation is never lost, the sense of one who rides the tiger, driven endlessly to defend and justify the indefensible first statement by an indefensible second, the indefensible second by a shameless diversion: "a list of 205 known to the Secretary of State as being members of the Communist Party . . . still working and shaping policy . . ." "I do not believe I mentioned the figure 205. I believe I said 'over 200' . . ." "I told him three times. I read the speech to him. I told him I said there were 57 Communists in the State Department . . ."

We hesitate between laughter and exasperation, until we realize that some are neither annoyed nor amused, that our buffoon and villain is someone else's hero, certainly his own hero. Against those who harass him, he strikes out with a holy rage possible only to one convinced he is justified. Indeed, he is at his most ferocious against the relatively innocent who merely challenge his exposés of his first targets: General Marshall, because of a demurrer in favor of Jessup, became the victim of a 60,000-word attack on the floor of the Senate, later transformed into a book; while Senator Tydings, whose committee investigation of the Wheeling charges ended in an indictment of McCarthy, was stalked and slandered and defeated at the polls; and Secretary of the Army Stevens has recently had to fight a series of engagements after a rather modest protest over McCarthy's publicity on presumable Communist infiltration in the Army Signal Corps. Finally, President Eisenhower himself, for siding with Stevens, has become a target of abuse. The process begun at a venture becomes institutionalized and self-perpetuating, like the Russian treason trials, and can end only with universal capitulation or universal accusation.

Against opponents whom even he would not call Communists, McCarthy displays his notorious willingness to edit stubbornly unrevealing facts to make clear hidden truths: a composite portrait of Tydings and Earl Browder, or a picture of Secretary Stevens and McCarthy's former assistant, G. David Schine, emended by the discreet use of scissors — these appear to McCarthy legitimate enough weapons to use against an enemy who he is convinced is ultimately backed by the Soviet secret police.

But it is vain to attempt to gather the historical *facts* about McCarthy; in simple truth, there are no such facts, only issues. McCarthy does not deal in documents, he deals in polemics; and it is impossible to get behind them. Regret it as we may, we have to admit finally that there *is* no behind; McCarthy and McCarthyism exist only on the surface — that is to say, in the newspapers. It is not the recorded proceedings of the Permanent Subcommittee on Investigations or the remarks on the floor of Congress that we read and remember, but what the daily paper chooses to tell us, what the radio considers it good editorial policy to excerpt.

Many people have deplored what they consider to be the excessive attention paid to McCarthy by our press, and some have even suggested trying to ignore him out of existence; but bad economic reasons have helped to preserve us from such a censorship of good intentions, since McCarthy apparently does more to sell newspapers than newspapers do to sell McCarthy. In an annual poll taken among the political reporters in Washington, McCarthy has more than once been voted the worst of the ninety-six Senators by those who do most to spread his name and fame, and only thus can make amends to themselves. Between McCarthy and the press in general there is a state of chronic feud, which erupts from time to time into particular squabbles with editors like William Evjue and James Wechsler, columnists like Drew Pearson, and radio commentators like Edward R. Murrow; and yet he has the best press in the country. It is a minor paradox among the major ones that define his meaning, and is simply enough explained.

The very reporters who as men despise him, as reporters recognize in him the newsman's blessing, the story that writes itself. His statements do not have to be touched up or toned down to make good journalistic fare; McCarthy may have babbled in headlines as precociously as certain poets are said to have lisped in numbers. His releases have that swollen, emotion-ridden air, that immunity to documentation, of the journalistic statement at its lowest level; and his legend has been dreamed by the kind of mind to which the press habitually condescends. It is not a matter of politics at all; the rhetoric which makes McCarthy kin to the rightist Chicago *Tribune* also relates him to the late communoid *PM*.

But McCarthy is not his only press agent; he has also the Communist party, which by a simple act of inversion turns his own hyper-patriotic image into one of *their* stereotypes; and this in turn is adapted by the vague anti-capitalists all over the world who borrow from official Soviet propaganda whatever depreciates America. It is easier, however, to forgive the foreign manipulators of the meaning of McCarthy than the American ones; for it requires at this juncture, when we are an embodiment of the least palatable necessities of history, superhuman virtue to love us from abroad. But the motives that make most Americans recast the doubleness of McCarthyism into some easy singleness are less creditable. Whether we be hyper-Americans or doctrinaire liberals, to assess McCarthyism justly means to admit that good and evil are divided, though not evenly, between ourselves and our enemies; that there is not an entirely innocent "we" opposed to an absolutely guilty "they." It is easier to slip into the one-sided platitudes that preserve our self-righteousness and identify us like a campaign badge: "whitewash" and "willful coddling" on the one side; "witch hunt" and "putrid slander" on the other.

The Tydings investigation is a case in point. Any approximately objective study of the relevant documents reveals that *two* things are true at once. First, the investigation itself was partisan and inefficient, a mere token glance at the questions raised, and its official report misrepresents what the committee did, or rather failed to do. From its title page on, the Tydings report is dubious, for it claims to be a report of a whole committee to which it was never submitted — as, indeed, it was not even submitted before release to the minority (Republican) members of the subcommittee actually involved. Moreover, the findings of the Tydings committee have been falsified in discussion ever since, as they are for instance in the Mc-Carthy issue of the *Progressive,* where Senator Lodge is quoted as having said that the investigations found no Communists in the State Department, but where his qualification that most of the case material was insufficiently followed up to *prove anything either way* is misleadingly omitted, as is his specific comment that "sufficient evidence was not developed with regard to Mr. Lattimore to enable me to clear him or not to clear him."

On the other side, a mere glance at the documents makes clear how shifty and unreliable a witness McCarthy was, uneasily dodging from number to number, completely contemptuous of dates, and unwilling, despite boasts to the contrary, to strip himself of senatorial immunity and take the legal consequences of his statements. It must be said finally that, on the one hand, McCarthy has never attempted to claim the $25,000 Tydings offered in 1950 if McCarthy could convict anyone in the State Department of being a Communist; but that, on the other, at least 11 persons named by McCarthy on his final list of 81 were subsequently removed from their positions or resigned under fire. Interestingly enough, one of the cases in McCarthy's original list was that of William Remington, who was, of course, in the Department of Commerce rather than the State Department (departments mean even less to McCarthy than numbers) but who certainly is not above suspicion.

In the same way, it is easy enough to talk horrifiedly of "book burning" in condemning McCarthy's campaign against the libraries of the United States Information Service, or to snicker at his advocating the removal of detective stories by Communists as sources of infection; but it must be observed that on the shelves of our own propaganda libraries at a moment when we were presumably engaged with Russia in a struggle for the minds of Europe there were political tracts by Earl Browder and William Z. Foster — and even a book by Ilya Ehrenburg. To find in such choices evidence of treason is, of course, absurd; if traitors do not keep themselves better occupied than that, they are not worth their hire. What the selection of these books indicates is an uncertainty about what Communism is and about its relationship to the American tradition — a feeling, perhaps only half confessed, that there is no *real* contradiction between the particular goals of the Communists and the general aspirations of the democratic world.

The case of Owen Lattimore, in its interconnections with *Amerasia*, the Institute of Pacific Relations, and State Department policy, must do as a final example chosen from an embarrassing overplus. McCarthy has almost succeeded in completely obscuring the facts of the Lattimore case in his attempt to remake a self-righteous party-line professor into a "top espionage agent." Most people do not even realize that at the present moment Lattimore stands indicted on three counts of perjury (there were originally seven) for his testimony before the McCarran committee, because his appearance before the grand jury fell between the premature rejoicing of almost the whole liberal world after his clearance by the Tydings committee, and a comic coda in which McCarthy "discovered" a completely invented plot to get Lattimore out of the country. Those who sprang so quickly to Lattimore's defense on the simple grounds that, if he was accused by McCarthy, he *must* be innocent, should be required to read through Lattimore's testimony, and writhe with him as he tries to explain how, when he uses the word "radical," he means it in its pure etymological sense, or why, after he had informed our ambassador that Outer Mongolia was a state completely independent of Russia, he applied for a travel visa to that unfortunate country at the Russian Foreign Office. We must recognize finally that

Lattimore is not a hired spy in a melodrama, but simply a defender of the Moscow trials as a higher form of justice; not an official "high in the State Department" but yet a person of considerable influence on the policymakers in that Department.

To write off the whole desire to learn the role of Communist influence in shaping our late mistaken China policy as a bugaboo scared up by the "China Lobby" is as facile and wrong as to interpret that policy to be the fabrication of disloyal or suborned officials. The notion of the Chinese Communists as "agrarian reformers" or "the representatives of a nationalist revolution" or "at least preferable to the corrupt Chiang Kai-shek" is merely a particular development of a widespread liberal willingness to see a better side to expanding Communism even where it did not exist. To label that impulse harmless and blameless is to the advantage only of the Communists; to indict it as utterly stupid or perverse is only to McCarthy's; but to see it in all its ambiguity is to the advantage of all whose first allegiance is to the truth.

We must, I am convinced, see this ambiguity or become its victims; and it is difficult to be sufficiently on guard. I do not mean, of course, that we must moderate our fight against McCarthyism in an excess of scrupulosity; merely that we must understand what it is that we are fighting, so that we do not waste our energy in stalking the enemy where he is not. It is better, I am sure, to fight windmills than not to fight; but where there are real monsters it is a pity to waste one's blows on windmills. Even the rallying cry which seems superficially most sound — the contention that McCarthyism, on whatever half-truths it may be based, has by its methods created an atmosphere of suspicion, a stifling pressure of conformity — is only one piece of a double truth.

It can be asserted with almost equal justice that there is nothing easier in America at the present moment than to speak ill of McCarthy. In academic circles, for instance, particularly in the East, it is generally the pro-McCarthy position which occasions resentment and even ostracism; while in the country's major newspapers and on the chief radio networks the majority opinion, quite openly expressed, is unfavorable to the Senator from Wisconsin. For intellectual respectability (and one can understand "intellectual" in its broadest possible scope), it is required that one consider McCarthyism a major threat to liberty. I doubt that there has ever been gathered together a broader or more articulate united front than the one which opposes the tactics of the former chairman of the Permanent Subcommittee on Investigations. Aside from the Communists and their more intimate friends (actually well aware that it is to their best interests that McCarthy continue to spread confusion), this front includes socialists and libertarians, Old Guard and New Deal Democrats, leading spokesmen for Jewish, Protestant, and liberal Catholic groups, and a strong representation of Republicans, including apparently the President and Vice-President of the United States.

It need hardly be said that such a group has little trouble in making itself heard; the daily press and the radio are open to their statements; their books are prominently and favorably reviewed, whereas the partisans of McCarthy find a certain resistance not easy to overcome. McCarthy is notoriously well covered by day-to-day reporting, to be sure, but I do not find in the *Book Review Digest,* for instance, a single notice of his book *The Fight Against Communism;* and the recent favorable study of McCarthy by Buckley and Bozell has received comment almost universally hostile. It is instructive, in this regard, to look through the additional material included in the Appendix to the *Congressional Record,* in which the opponents of McCarthy are able to quote from the leading newspapers of his own state and from journals ranging from the social-democratic *New Leader* through the Jesuit *America* to the Republican *Time,* while he and his friends can eke out the Hearst and McCormick press only with excerpts from the scarcely literate editorials of back-country weeklies.

And yet the statement made in article after article by the attackers of McCarthy, a statement repeated by the commentators and re-echoed by commentators on the commentators, is that McCarthyism threatens if it does not actually bludgeon into silence the hostile press. From one end of the country to another rings the cry, "I am cowed! I am afraid to speak out!" and the even louder response, "Look, he is cowed! He is afraid to speak out!" In my own town, where it proved almost impossible to turn up a pro-McCarthy speaker for a recent forum, and where no library contains a copy of McCarthy's major book, though Lattimore's version of his encounter with the McCarran committee is available, I have been told over and over that there is "something" now in the air which makes one swallow unsaid what he might once have spoken without a second thought.

One is tempted to laugh at first, to find only comedy in this constant frightened twittering back and forth among people who are in almost universal agreement, and who rise, with all the air of Christians entering the arena, to address those who listen with the set jaw of Galileo muttering, *"Eppur si muove!"* And yet — and yet, it was only with difficulty that I refrained from adding a parenthesis to the last sentence of the preceding paragraph, to read: ". . . needless to say, our librarians are far from being Communists." The "needless to say" would have been only a sop; obviously there was some need to say, some nagging fear that a careless reference *under the circumstances* might get the unimpeachable guardians of our books into trouble. I am convinced that the intellectual community has been an accomplice to this situation of fear, compounding it out of pride and guilt; but it has been an accomplice after the fact. There have been reprisals against the holders of ideas unpopular with McCarthy: some nervous regents have dropped instructors in universities and colleges; in the public-school system, there has been an occasional firing; sponsors on the radio, cowed by an advertising-agency legend of public opinion, have been particularly jittery; and in certain government agencies there has been a real terror, as McCarthyism has combined with the standard vagaries of bureaucratic administration and the usual rumormongering of bureaucratic underlings.

Even if we attribute to McCarthyism a whole atmosphere of suspicion of which it is a symptom rather than a cause, it can be said that its effects (I do not mean the firing of proven Communists, in which many anti-McCarthyites would concur, but the intimidation of all unorthodoxy and especially of the outspoken critics of intimidation) have been small in proportion to the anxiety they have created. I should suppose that the excessive fear of the "intellectuals," in so far as it is more than a tic of anxiety, is based on the suspicion that McCarthy represents not merely himself, his own ambition and chicanery, but a substantial popular hostility, immune to argument and logical proof, to their own *raison d'être*. Certainly, it was disconcerting to discover not many months back that the majority of the American people were favorably disposed toward McCarthy, despite the fact that the larger part of their semi-official spokesmen were bitterly opposed to him. In a certain sense, McCarthyism not only flourishes in but *is* this hostility between the community and its intelligence. An occasional intellectual apologist, whether an embittered "premature anti-Communist" like James Burnham or a black young radical like Buckley, makes little difference. The price of supporting McCarthy is self-abnegation, and there is no reward.

The forces that McCarthy really represents (I mean his mass support, not the Texas millionaires of whom so much is made; anyone who persists in politics in America, whether he be right or left or center, McCarthy or the Communists or F.D.R., can get himself a millionaire or two) find their expression in the resolutely anti-intellectual small-town weeklies and in the professionally reactionary press, which continue to say in his name precisely what they have been saying now for thirty-five years. To realize this is to understand that McCarthyism is, generally speaking, an extension of the ambiguous American impulse toward "direct democracy" with its distrust of authority, institutions, and expert knowledge; and, more precisely, it is the form that populist conviction takes when forced to define itself against a competing "European" radicalism. McCarthy is a new voice for these forces though scarcely a different one, with his automobile salesman's pitch, his proffering of inaccuracy and the inability to stay on a point as evidence that he talks the customer's language. The astonishing thing about McCarthy is his closeness to a standard kind of Midwestern political figure, usually harmless and often comical. What defies analysis is the aura of fear which surrounds him.

Certainly, the facts of McCarthy's early life add scarcely anything to a comprehension of the phenomenon for which he stands. There is so little in his career sinister or even calculated, and so much clearly banal and accidental, that one who dislikes him finds himself tempted to overinterpret unfavorable data in a way embarrassingly reminiscent of McCarthy himself. There is a quality in the man that makes McCarthys of us all, unless we are content to accept a paradox for our conclusion. He is not (though it would be comfortingly simple to believe so) any of the things we ordinarily mean by the word "Fascist"; and comparisons with Huey Long are beside the point. McCarthy is not, to begin with, a spellbinder in the Hitlerian sense, but almost anti-rhetorical in his effect, confidential and bumbling, an expert harrier of witnesses but a mover of masses only in a queer, negative way. Certain crowds seem to find his very lack of glibness an assurance that he is their voice — and quite inexplicably they roar; but an even mildly sophisticated audience finds it easy to laugh him down. He is not a racist, and, indeed, in the early days of his career was opposed by the old-school, anti-Semitic native Fascists. Though more recently he has been hailed and even supported by known anti-Semites,* he has himself never been recorded as playing on the racist fantasies common enough among his own constituency; and his association with certain clearly identifiable Jews like Cohn and Schine works in quite another direction. Indeed, when the latter two were on their famous quick European investigation tour, one sensed in certain of the adverse comments on them (the comparisons to Gallagher and Shean, for instance) the faintest and most polite undercurrent of anti-Semitism working in the anti-McCarthy direction. Moreover, one of the bitterest McCarthy onslaughts against the Voice of America was for cutting down its Hebrew broadcasts at a point when it might

---

*The case of which the most has been made by those who would find McCarthy an anti-Semite is that of Mrs. Anna Rosenberg, whose appointment as Assistant Secretary of Defense he challenged. There is no doubt that leading racists closed in like vultures during the affair, among them Gerald L. K. Smith; but the original charges, though unjustified, seem to have been made in good faith (on the basis of a confusion of identities) by one who far from being an anti-Semite was actually a Jew.

have been possible to make capital of the anti-Semitic tone of the Slansky trial in Czechoslovakia. Because it baffles a convenient stereotype if McCarthy is not a racist, the charge continues to be made, and American Jews as a group were in the middle of 1953 the only section of the population to oppose McCarthy by a large majority; but the verdict is at least: unproven.

Certainly, he has left behind the backwoods doctrine which identifies the Elders of Zion with the International Bankers, and the Bankers with the Bolsheviks; for McCarthy, Communism is no diabolic expression of an outcast race, but quite simply the foreign policy of the Soviet Union. It would be ridiculous to claim for McCarthy (as he occasionally does for himself when visiting easy scorn on some innocent Army intelligence officer who cannot distinguish between Marxism and Marxism-Leninism) any real theoretical understanding of Communism; he keeps a stock of experts on hand for such matters, satisfactorily repentant ex-Communists and an occasional amateur like G. David Schine, who once prepared a brochure on the subject for circulation in his father's hotels. McCarthy seems, however, to have been twice victimized by Communist *agents provocateurs,* once in the almost prehistoric days of the Congressional debate on the Malmédy massacre, when he was completely duped by a German Communist called Rudolf Aschenauer, who apparently supplied McCarthy with manufactured evidence that American interrogators extorted confessions from German storm troopers by torture; and once when he was taken in by a young American Negro, Charles Davis, who offered faked evidence to prove that John Carter Vincent was in contact with Soviet agents. When McCarthy refused to recognize Davis, after the latter had been deported from Switzerland, Davis filed a suit for libel, confessing in the course of the proceedings that he had been a member of the Communist party. The combination of naïveté with an eagerness to accept any evidence against an enemy as true has made McCarthy the victim of almost as many frauds as he has himself perpetrated.

But it needs no sophistication to understand Communism in 1954; history has defined for anyone with a sense of political fact what Marxism-Leninism has become — namely, the rationalization and defense of that which Russia or its agents do for the sake of expansion or self-defense. In the light of this, it is a little disingenuous to complain, as some critics have done, that McCarthy never defines in his books and speeches his key term, "Communism." In the formal and academic sense, he certainly does not; but it is hard to deny that the term has been defined for him, as for all of us, with distressing clarity.

The story of McCarthy's life is at first glance disconcertingly the rags-to-riches idyl of campaign literature: the son of a poor Wisconsin farmer, he worked hard from childhood on, taking from his father a small section of land that, single-handed at the age of sixteen, he made into a paying poultry farm. Indeed, he seemed on the very verge of prosperity when he broke down from overwork; and, when he recovered, his ambitions had changed. He began the slow movement toward the big city which he has followed ever since, transferring first to the little town of Manawa, Wisconsin, where he became not merely the successful manager of a grocery store but the town's darling. Deciding that he needed an education to fulfill the hopes he had aroused in his fellow-townsmen, Joe finished an entire high-school course in the single year before he reached twenty-one, alternating extraordinary feats of memorization with equally fervent bouts of physical activity; and went on to Marquette University, where he soon switched from engineering to law, though he was a shy and awkward speaker in public.

In college, McCarthy became a boxer of considerable ability, learned painfully to debate, was elected president of his class, and was graduated without particular academic distinction. After two years of law practice, he entered a political campaign for the first time, being defeated for Shawano County attorney on the Democratic ticket, and decided, though he had glowed earlier with a hatred for Hoover in particular and the Republicans in general, that his future lay in their party. In 1939, at the age of thirty, he was elected judge of Wisconsin District 10, winning an utterly unforeseen victory. All his early political activity was characterized by an incredible willingness to take pains, a complete contempt for expert predictions, and a fantastically unflagging energy.

As a judge, he proceeded immediately to wipe out in a matter of months an apparently permanent backlog of 250 cases and never dropped behind in his calendar again, though keeping up meant holding court in session past midnight on many occasions. When the war came, he took a leave of absence from his judicial post to enlist in the Marine Corps, where he served as an air intelligence officer behind the front lines, volunteering from time to time to accompany bombing flights as an unofficial tailgunner. Before the war was over, he left the Marine Corps to enter national politics, making a first vain bid to get the Wisconsin senatorial nomination away from Alexander Wiley in 1944. He was finally elected to the Senate in 1946, after taking, in a victory that characteristically astonished everyone but himself, the Republican nomination from an overconfident Bob LaFollette, who had scarcely troubled to campaign.

Superficially the record is a cliché, embodying only too patly the Pluck and Luck of the legend; but one must accept as real the unquestioning will to victory (across his tent in Guadalcanal McCarthy hung a banner reading: "McCarthy for U. S. Senate," though he was willing to pass it off as a joke) and the compulsive drive toward hard work, which led McCarthy after his election to slip off anonymously and work in the wheat fields. He is an American instance, and must be understood in terms of our myths and compulsions rather than in adapted European terms.

It has often been alleged that McCarthy lacks principles; and certainly he is immune to most of the traditionally noble ones, desiring to succeed chiefly for success' sake and loving the feel of overextended strength as an end in itself. To punish and be punished, to yield voluptuously to the fury of struggle — these *are* his principles, the fundamental values to which he is devoted. "I don't claim to be any smarter than the next fellow," he told a reporter after his election to the Senate, "but I do claim to work harder." One has the sense that he is reciting a part rather than making a statement. Though, as his name indicates, McCarthy's background is Irish and

Catholic, he has none of the amiable fecklessness one associates with his stock; he is the puritan we all tend to become, with the puritan's conviction that the desire to win is the guarantee of being chosen, the gift of energy a sign of salvation. He has apparently never doubted this, though he was for a while uncertain of what end he had been chosen for, aside from the important one of being Joe McCarthy. But his discovery of the Communist issue settled his doubts quickly, giving to his undefined conviction of a mission a sanction at once religious and political. His notorious shopping around for a cause up until 1950 must, in the light of this, be considered something far more complicated than simple opportunism.

A closer look at the record reveals the shoddy underpinnings of the American legend — but this also is typical. From the start, McCarthy's career has been marked by broken promises and betrayals of confidence (his very first office was obtained behind the back and at the expense of his law partner, who had similar ambitions); and by a series of "deals," petty or large (beginning with the trivial episode of the high-school teacher wooed into making possible his record secondary-school career). His appearance of simple virtue goes to pieces under the most superficial scrutiny; though he has been able all along to establish legal innocence of various charges against him, he has emerged always morally indicted. In his early campaign for the judgeship, he apparently overspent the statutory allowance and in campaign literature consistently mis-represented his opponent's age; and even in his famous clearing up of the docket he turns out to have shown more haste than discretion. He connived in a series of astonishingly quick divorces for friends, personal and political, though it meant by-passing the divorce-counsel system of which Wisconsin likes to boast; and he attained special notoriety for not only acquitting the Quaker Dairy of unfair price practices on the odd grounds that the law involved would go out of date in six months, but also destroying a vital part of the court record. He seems also to have contravened the clear intent of a Wisconsin law forbidding judges to run for public office while maintaining tenure on the bench; he could not be convicted because he was running for federal rather than state office.

McCarthy's whole subsequent career has followed the same pattern: from the production of a pamphlet on housing for which he was paid $10,000 by Lustron, a private manufacturer of prefabricated housing, much interested in the legislation before McCarthy's housing committee; through his tangled relations with sugar consumers that earned him the nickname of the "Pepsi-Cola Kid"; to his long history of alleged misrepresentation and barely legal accommodation in preparing his income-tax reports.

It would be foolish to portray McCarthy as extraordinarily corrupt in these respects. He is a hopelessly ordinary politician in all things: his manipulation of his finances, his willingness to "arrange" matters behind the scenes, his barely legal maneuverings to escape uncomfortable restrictions. This is the standard procedure of the standard elective official, and is standardly revealed from time to time in standard investigations; but between such orgies of exposure and righteousness the ordinary American voter not merely condones but applauds evidence of such minor duplicity in his representatives as a sign of political acumen.

McCarthy has been shown up, too, in another favorite practice of the politician: the refurbishing of his own record and the blackening of his opponent's by the discreet manipulation of truth. McCarthy's election as judge at the age of thirty is not considered striking enough: it must be made twenty-eight; his enlistment as a first lieutenant in the Marine Corps must be revised for public consumption into enlistment as a private who then worked his way up through the ranks. A job as an intelligence officer must become an assignment as tailgunner; a leg smashed up during horseplay aboard ship must be turned into a combat wound, recognized with the Purple Heart — and finally metamorphosed into "ten pounds of shrapnel" carried with an exaggerated limp. It is possible that McCarthy does not even consider such conventional accommodation of facts to be lying; he seems especially proud of his own truthfulness, and whenever he and some opponent come into absolute conflict over a question of fact, he typically cries out for a lie-detector test with all the air of a much-abused citizen turning to science to redeem him.

He practices in addition the college debater's device (I can dimly remember my own debate coach recommending it to me with a wink) of waving about irrelevant papers as he makes some especially undocumented statement. This is a clue, I think, to his whole attitude, the "plain man's" conviction that figures are useful only for bolstering after the fact an intuitive judgment or insight. Despite his extensive research staff, and his recent willingness to do a little homework on his charges, McCarthy seems still incapable of believing that it *really* matters whether there are 200, 205, 81, or 57 Communists in a certain branch of the government. He appears clearly convinced that those of his opponents who concern themselves with such discrepancies are stupidly or insidiously trying to divert attention from what truly matters: are there *any* Communists in the department concerned?

It is tempting to identify McCarthy's lying with the Big Lie of Hitler; but it seems more closely related to the multiple little lies of our daily political forum, to a fact of our national life too often ignored by those looking for analogies instead of roots. McCarthyism is, in part, the price we pay for conniving at or ignoring the alderman's deal with the contractor, the mayor's boast that he was always labor's friend. Yet McCarthy's distortion of the truth is not merely a particular development of the cheap politician's hyperbole; it is also the courtroom lawyer's unchallenged device for "making a case" rather than establishing a fact. The politically naïve citizen called for jury duty in any town in the United States begins by being horrified at what seems to him at first a contempt for the truth, but is revealed later as the lawyer's assumption that *there is no truth:* that guilt and innocence are matters, not of moral judgment or even of established fact, but of a decision arrived at inside a devious technical code of procedure. But the naive are never horrified enough.

I do not place McCarthy in this context to justify him, but rather to condemn the system of which he is a pathological symptom. Anyone unwilling to believe how *like* most other lawyers McCarthy is should volunteer to serve on a jury; or, short of that, should read the reports of other Congressional investigations, preferably of those with whose ends one is in general sympathy — of war profiteers, say, or of organizers of anti-labor violence. It would suffice, perhaps, to read through the report of the Tydings subcommittee which condemned McCarthy to see how clearly such investigations distinguish between looking into facts and proving a case. To change the rules of *all* Congressional investigating committees so that at least the safeguards of the courtroom will be provided for what has become a judicial procedure, to insist on the right of confrontation, representation by counsel, etc. — all this will help; but it will not solve the underlying problem I have tried to define. In certain ways, it would seem more desirable to make the proceedings of Congressional investigation *less formal,* less like trial procedure, leaving to the courts the business of establishing technical innocence or guilt, and reserving for the legislative branch, as our national conscience, the task of seeking the truth of morality and feeling. One can imagine no person less equipped for such a task than the run-of-the-mill lawyer trained in the cynical school of the community courtroom.

But there remains in McCarthy's handling of the truth a more sophisticated and "modern" use of the lie than the politician's or the lawyer's. It is a concept of "symbolic" truth-telling, which has, of course, always existed, but which has entered into public life with especial vigor in recent years. It is tempting to call it a "totalitarian" concept, for it has been much exploited by Communists and Fascists; but it is, alas, a favorite device of hard-pressed liberals and conservatives; once the process is begun on either side, the other seems forced to respond in kind. A McCarthyite will say, for instance, "There are hundreds, thousands of Communist espionage agents in the State Department," meaning merely that the influence of Communist ideas, at one remove or another, has helped determine State Department policy for the worse. To this the liberal will answer, "There is not a single Communist in the State Department and there has never been one," meaning simply that, in so far as men and notions influenced by Communists have played a role in the State Department, they have been "idealist" in inspiration, and therefore have done more good than harm.

Or, on a more specific level, a McCarthyite will howl, "Lattimore is the top espionage agent in the United States," which translated means that Lattimore's ideas coincide remarkably with those of the Communists; to which the liberal answers, "He is entirely innocent, a good man," or decoded, "Well, whatever his ideas, they were ones that some quite close friends of mine agreed with once, etc." The Communists themselves have a "scientific" way of saying all this, making the charge, for instance, that the Jewish Social Democrats were "objectively" on the side of Hitler.

McCarthy, of course, is not capable of distinctions between objective and subjective allegiance, any more than he can distinguish between ends and means; but his intellectual and proto-intellectual supporters are quite willing to sustain him on these grounds both publicly and to themselves. There is no doubt in my own mind that Robert Taft, for instance, supported McCarthy (despite waverings and reservations) because he himself had long been convinced that "objectively" socialists were no different from Communists, and leftish New Dealers no different from either; so that calling any supporter of the "welfare state" a Communist might be rude and impolitic but was not actually wrong. Still, Taft was always a little *uncomfortable* about it all, as the handful of more intellectual fellow-travelers of McCarthyism continue to be uncomfortable.

The simple-minded McCarthyite, however, has no trouble at all; he is not disturbed about the problem of whether a lie can be objectively true, because a political lie does not seem to him to be morally reprehensible. McCarthy's position depends not at all upon fair play or respect for conscience, whereas the moral *raison d'être* of his opponents is their scrupulousness; and it is for this reason that these opponents, once betrayed into playing his game of symbolic truth-telling, are at a disadvantage. They find themselves in a terrible dilemma in this regard; granted the discrepancy between their values and that of the vast public, even the non-McCarthyites, they can hardly ever be quite candid without seeming to confess a guilt they do not feel; and, granted their own morality, they cannot trifle with the truth without feeling a guilt they do not confess.

How have the intellectuals fallen into such a plight? Even ten or fifteen years ago, they would have stood up proudly to hoot down McCarthy's equivalent; and that equivalent, bold enough among his own buddies or on the floor of Congress, would have been on the defensive, shouting a little, enraged before the superior tittering of an audience that sympathized with his heckler. The defeat of J. Parnell Thomas, one-time head of the House Un-American Activities Committee, made a laughingstock and finally convicted of petty crime, symbolizes the older state of affairs; the apparent invulnerability of McCarthy the new. As the nation's current Grand Inquisitor, McCarthy is perhaps a good deal smarter than Thomas, but he is not otherwise notably different. What has happened? Chiefly, the main body of liberals has recognized that the Soviet Union, once considered a rallying point for the opposition to Fascism, has replaced Fascism as a symbol of social evil; and that, therefore, "Red-baiting" when directed against real Reds is far from a certain sign of indecency.

The typical confrontation by McCarthy of his witnesses (when those witnesses have not been Communists, open or concealed) has been the legendary confrontation by the Hundred-Percent American of the Enlightened Internationalist at the moment of discomfiture for the Internationalist. There has always been a greater or lesser split in the United States between the Ordinary Voter and the Man Seriously Interested in Politics; but this difference was exaggerated and specially defined in the years between the triumph of the Russian Revolution and the Great Depression. Unlike Western Europe, where a gradually Marxianized people and intelligentsia have found a way of neutralizing old tensions in their attitude toward the Soviet Union, in America the influence of Marxism, however remote, has served only to separate the intellectuals decisively from the mass of people.

The intellectuals, including brighter college students, newspaper reporters, lawyers, and professional people, as well as artists and political theorists, have had as a typical initiation into the intellectual community (the case of Oppenheimer, recently much bruited, is a classic though untypically belated instance) a brief bout of membership in the Communist party, fellow-traveling, or at least the experience of collaboration and friendly intercourse with Communists and fellow-travelers. Communists and liberals seemed in those days to be bound together not only by a passionate revulsion from war and the inequities of capitalism, but more positively, too, by certain tastes in books and in the arts, by shared manners and vocabulary — and especially by the sense of moral engagement that used to be called "social consciousness." From this fellow feeling, the great United Front organizations of the late 1930's were forged, in the teeth, as it were, of the ordinary voter, who, immune to all this, identified not only the Communists but their most distant friends with free love, looting, and general bloodshed; and who were condescended to majestically by the enlightened, thus storing up a special resentment for the hour of disillusion.

To the stereotyped cry of "Red!" the intellectual, who was above stereotypes, shouted back "Fascist!"; and on both sides the notion of two irreconcilable camps grew. From the time of the Sacco-Vanzetti case — that is to say, from 1927 — until 1946 (when those unshaken by Spain and the Moscow trials and the Soviet-Nazi pact were jarred loose by the Cold War), it seemed that America had chosen sides in a bloodless civil war. To the liberal-intellectual,* "we" consisted of the supporters of trade unionism, social security, and the rights of Negroes, Jews, and other minorities, including socialists and even Communists ("rude but on our side"); while "they" consisted of "Red-baiters," readers of Hearst, supporters of Franco, Pinkertons, and *ad libitum* members of the Catholic hierarchy, William Green and the A.F.L., Southern Senators and football players, American Legionnaires, etc. The questioning of Reed Harris, deputy administrator of the Interna-

---

*I cannot in all honesty resist defining this term, though I should have preferred to leave its meanings implicit. To describe the allegiances of the group is to define it sufficiently; but it is perhaps wise to forestall objections by stating explicitly that I use the word "liberal" (and "intellectual" is, for better or worse, historically synonymous with it in America) to mean all those who believe or believed Sacco was innocent, who considered the recognition of the Soviet union not merely wise strategically but a "progressive" step, and who identified themselves with the Loyalist side during the Spanish Civil War. It is perhaps unnecessary to say that I consider myself one of this group.

tional Information Administration, illustrates the difficulties such a conventional categorizing can occasion years later. Despite his subsequent record of loyal service in government, Harris was quizzed at length over a book he had written when just out of college called *King Football;* and the McCarthy committee thought it worthwhile to quote, as a presumable example of disloyalty, Harris' identification of someone as "a sadistic butcher who is now probably the commander of some American Legion post." The complicated innocence of such a remark made in the 1930's is almost impossible to explain to someone whose proudest boast has always been his membership in the Legion.

It is perhaps worth adding that anti-Stalinist leftists of all kinds, especially Trotskyites, were most usually included in the liberals' "they," and that in a strange way a distaste for energetic anti-Communists often survives any sympathy for Communism and the Soviet Union. Often enough, the reconverted liberal, though prepared to grant the decency of A.F.L. organizers, American Legion post commanders, and members of the Kiwanis club (at least in public), feels no qualms about expressing contempt for such "traitors" as Whittaker Chambers or Louis Budenz or Benjamin Stolberg, even though what they have "betrayed" is what he now believes to be evil. There is a sizable minority of non-Communist liberals to whom the "hysterical anti-Communist" (which is to say, *all* anti-Communists) and the "professional informer" (which is to say, anyone who exposes even the most flagrant traitor in the Communist party) are objects of almost irrational horror. This is the last negative persistence of the belief in the Soviet Union as a touchstone of human decency — not a conviction really but a tic, which leads to a compulsive closing of the eyes before the evidence that would make, say, a Chambers right and a Hiss wrong.

I do not want to exaggerate even polemically the Communist influence on American life; in a political sense, the movement was a failure in the United States, for it never appealed to any large number of the workers and poorer farmers to whom it presumably spoke most directly. Indeed, it never won the total allegiance, much less the actual adherence, of the intellectuals; but it *did* manage to establish itself in the intellectual community as an acceptable variant of the liberal-humanistic tradition — and, even more, made its acceptance as such a variant the test of political decency. This established confusion not only enabled such party members as Hiss to regard their activities as the expression of a higher loyalty to "humanity," but even made it possible for others like Wadleigh, too "liberal" to join the party, to commit espionage on behalf of the Soviet Union. And it has bequeathed to us the bewildering concept of an undefinable "left" which obscures for us the actualities of the political situation.

The liberal-internationalists found presumable justification for their self-righteousness in the knowledge of their own superiority to the practicing politician in personal morality. Bribery and logrolling, patronage and "fixing," were as exceptional among the liberals as they were common among those who hated them. Besides, the liberals knew that they were immune to platitudes and conventional rhetoric; that they were more intelligent, read better books, liked superior music and pictures; could use the vocabularies of advanced thought. Certainly intelligence in itself is an advantage, and surely the majority of the intelligent were on the liberal side; but intelligence is not synonymous with virtue nor is it a specific against either political error or malice. The intelligent do not make the same mistakes as the others, or at least they do not make them for the same reasons; but even when they are buttressed with good will they do make mistakes. And they were wrong, drastically wrong, about the most important political fact of our time. The unpalatable truth we have been discovering is that the buffoons and bullies, those who *knew* really nothing about the Soviet Union at all, were right — stupidly right, if you will, accidentally right, right for the wrong reasons, but damnably right.

This most continuing liberals, as well as ex-Communists and former fellow-travelers, are prepared to grant in the face of slave labor and oppression and police terror in the Soviet Union; but yet they, who have erred out of generosity and open-mindedness, cannot feel even yet on the same side as Velde or McCarthy or Nixon or Mundt. How desperately they wish in each case that the Hiss, the Lattimore who speaks their language might be telling the truth; that the hyper-patriot who combines the most shameless stock phrases of nationalism with behind-the-scenes deals, who distrusts litera-ture and art and intelligence itself, might be lying.

How happy the liberals are when McCarthy out of malice or ignorance miscues, traducing the innocent or bullying the merely timid. How gratefully they welcome his contempt for legal safeguards and elementary fairness; but, despite all, they cannot convince themselves that these are the *whole* issue. They know that McCarthy is sometimes right or half-right, and even then (perhaps then even more) they resent his charges for reasons they are no longer prepared to defend, feeling, against all reason, their side, themselves, somehow indicted. It is hard to say this precisely without seeming to accuse honest people of conscious duplicity; but no one who shared once the liberal concept of an innocent "we" and a guilty "they" can appear before an investigating committee without a double sense of guilt: over having once lived his past and over being now obliged to betray it.

Some try to evade the problem by simplification: either choosing silence on the grounds of the Fifth Amendment and thus avoiding the second guilt completely; or identifying them-selves with the investigators and atoning publicly for the first. But the non-cooperators find themselves in the company of the Communists who, like McCarthy, want to perpetuate the confusion of liberals and "left" totalitarians; and, in so far as they know that the human spirit is offended and maimed wherever Communist governments exist, they bear the burden of having chosen to shelter as a "lesser evil" the enemies of all they most love. They tell themselves in vain that the *particular* Communists they knew and once worked with may have long since changed their political convictions; and that they were, at any rate, "idealists" who would never have committed espionage or condoned terror. But they know that Klaus Fuchs or the Rosenbergs seemed to some intelligent people of good will equally "idealistic" and harmless.

Meanwhile a very few ex-liberals or repentant radicals find not peace but further exacerbation in acknowledging publicly

the rightness of those they long despised. They become either
superior apologists for McCarthy in journals that most Mc-
Carthyites never read, or else employees of investigating committees, to which they supply the minimal information about
Marxism that their employers are capable of understanding.
Aside from one another, they find few sympathizers with their
course; those they work for cannot really communicate with
them, while the majority of their intellectual compeers regard
them as unclean. Actually, the intellectual informers range
i⸱ reliability and basic decency through the normal spectrum;
but some find themselves trapped in the need to continue informing, and end by substituting fantasy for memory in the
effort to justify themselves from day to day. In any case, their
shrillness betrays a nagging sense of guilt which no public
accolade can allay.

Between the evasion of the non-cooperaters and the over-
cooperation of the confessers lies a troubled and difficult
course: what seems to me the truly liberal one. Such a course
has been variously followed before one committee or another
by Robert Gorham Davis and Stewart Alsop and James
Wechsler. Naturally, it seems to do no *immediate* good, to
satisfy neither side. When such a witness speaks out bluntly
in opposition to something which McCarthy believes, he is
charged by the hyper-patriots with being a stooge or even a
secret member of the Communist party; and when he identifies
for the investigators the utterest scoundrel in the pro-Soviet
camp, he finds himself scorned and ostracized by the kind of
"sincere" liberal who gasps horrifiedly: "He named names!"
— as if to "rat" were the worst of crimes. It is not, however,
really the boys' code of not squealing which is at stake, but the
whole dream of an absolute innocence.

The honest witness's worst enemy will be finally neither the
hyper-patriot nor the sentimental liberal but himself. The
opportunities for self-deception will be many, and even his
most legitimate strategy may turn out to be a trap. He may
be tempted to begin by making clear his present opposition
to the Soviet Union, to bid against McCarthy in terms of the
fervor if not the priority of his convictions: to produce, perhaps, out of McCarthy's own past naïvely favorable statements

about Stalin or refusals to reject Communist votes. But especially he will feel compelled to boast: "I also am opposed to . . ."; "I have always fought against totalitarianism . . ." Such statements can be made in bland good faith by those who have simply forgotten that once, of course, "totalitarianism" did not for them include the Soviet Union. One would be wrong to call this falsification; it is the scarcely conscious adjustment of fact made by the happily married man asked fifteen years later about a disreputable love affair.

Too much of what the witness wants to say is forbidden to him: not only cut off by the ridiculous yes-and-no questioning, the setting up of leading questions for quotable answers, though this is a source of exasperation and dismay; but barred to him by the impossibility of communicating in his own language. He wants to say, perhaps, that having been inoculated with philo-Communism once, he is now immune; that his former allegiance is a special guarantee of his present integrity. He may even have the mischievous impulse to declare: "Just as we glory in what made us wrong in 1936, though we deplore our wrongness, so you should be thoroughly ashamed of what made you right then. You were opposed to Communism then, and are still, for reasons which make us enemies and not allies!" But these things remain unspoken, because speaking them would be unpolitic before a committee to whom they would seem a confession of treason; and because the witness is not quite sure how far or in what sense he really believes them himself. Even James Wechsler, by far the most effective witness ever to face McCarthy, got himself into trouble in this way. I quote this passage in the hearing not to detract from the honor due Wechsler, but to illustrate the difficulty of candor and communication under the best circumstances.

Though Wechsler began his testimony with the air of one determined to expose with the weapons of frankness and forthrightness a procedure that had thriven on the fear and deviousness of previous witnesses, he himself fell into equivocation on three main issues: Had he ever written favorably of any ex-Communist? Had he ever approved of *any* chairman of an investigating committee? Had he voluntarily submitted to the FBI a list of former associates after his presumed break with Communism? Confronted with these three shibboleths, the turncoat, the "Red-baiter," and the cop — unchallenged heroes to all his inquisitors and villains in the legendary melodrama he had believed in as a youth — Wechsler hedged and squirmed. He seemed especially unsure on the issue of the FBI, and his questioners, scenting weakness, closed in on him, McCarthy and Roy Cohn hammering away by turns, six, seven, eight, nine times.

Now, did you go to the FBI, after you broke with the movement in 1937?
No, I did not go to the FBI, but over a period of years . . . I was visited at times by FBI men. I was visited . . .

Have you ever in your editorial columns, over the last two years, praised the FBI?
Well, sir, I would have to go back and read our editorials for the last two years. I did not understand that I was being called down here for . . .

Did you at any time . . . go to the FBI and offer to give them what information you might have to aid them in their fight against Communism. . . ?
I did not go to the FBI . . . I was visited on several occasions by FBI men . . . I answered freely and to the best of my knowledge. . . .

Mr. Rushmore since he broke with the movement has been of great assistance to the FBI. . . . This is the first time Mr. Wechsler has given a list of names.
That statement, sir, is not consistent with the facts!
Did you give a list of names before?
I was not asked for it.

The unspoken point is clear, though Wechsler does not feel it politic to make it. In his generation and in the world in which he moved, one simply did not "give a list of names" in any case, and certainly not to the FBI, who seemed an especially insidious form of the Enemy. It is hard to re-create that world in a time when coeds inform on suspicious boy friends to the proper government agency; but one raised in it can never recover completely from its assumptions. Wechsler has, indeed, come a long way, being prepared now to admit that the FBI "does not deserve to be denounced as it has been denounced in some quarters as a Fascist-Gestapo agency"; but this concession is less than meaningless to those who have never had any doubts about the virtue and wisdom of J. Edgar Hoover.

What Wechsler did not succeed in declaring openly — that the FBI is in some of its aspects comic; that its men are often incapable of telling who is a Communist; that its immunity to criticism is a menace to freedom — these convictions are quoted from his published writings as evidence of perfidy. And yet how could he have declared what he truly felt to a group which shared not at all the central experience of his life; and which, at its friendliest, felt the need to assert in the words of the Democratic member, Senator Symington: "First, I want to say that nobody believes in the FBI more than I do, and I am sorry if Mr. Wechsler has criticized the FBI."

No wonder that baffled witnesses (and most are considerably more baffled than the alert and articulate Wechsler) seek to right the balance outside of the committee room, crying out "corruption" and "reckless charges" and retailing in print circumstantial descriptions of the bullying, intimidation, and misrepresentation they have endured. The epithet "Fascist!" is shouted and the image of Huey Long evoked; the sincerity of McCarthy's anti-Communism is impugned, and it is suggested variously that he is self-seeking, an unwitting tool of the Communists, and/or a creature of the Texas oil men and the Catholic hierarchy (though at the same time it is pointed out how many influential Catholics oppose him). The whole arsenal of liberal mythology is drawn upon, until what began as a genuine bill of particulars ends as paranoid speculation, paranoia answering paranoia: McCarthyism of the left and center, McCarthyism of the right.

Just as McCarthy is incapable not only of believing that those who disagree with him may be right, but even of granting that they may be wrong through misjudgment or normal stupidity; and as he is convinced that behind the opposition to him there is a conspiracy or plot; so his opponents fall into a similar belief. The plot discovered is the finding of evil where we have always known it to be: in the *other*. But the final joke and horror of the situation is that there *are* in our days conspiracies which baffle common sense. Even the most fantastic accusations of McCarthy are lent a certain plausibility by the revelations of the Hiss case, in which it scarcely matters whether you opt for the Communist-espionage-ring theory of Hiss's guilt, or the equally fantastic forgery-by-typewriter theory of his innocence. What an absurd world we live in where only half the audience, or less, laughs aloud when McCarthy charges that James Wechsler himself wrote the Communist editorials attacking him.

But the Red-baiter and the liberal do not really charge each other with equal conviction. The liberal is uncertain even when, closing his eyes in desperation (but all the time, he *knows*), he repeats ritually: "Lattimore is pure; Hiss was framed; the Rosenbergs are a mirage; there never was a Klaus Fuchs; Harry Dexter White was maligned . . ." And as a final charm: *"No harm has been done, no harm has been done, no harm has been done!"* The McCarthyites, however, answer with more certainty (their eyes have always been closed and they do not even suspect it) and equal ritual insistence: "Yalta and China, Hiss and Marzani and Harry Dexter White; treason and the coddling of treason: *guilty, guilty, guilty!*"

It is no use protesting that McCarthy himself has revealed no dangerous hidden Communists; that the Marzanis, the Hisses, and the Rosenbergs of whom he boasts were turned up by other agencies, before the opening of McCarthy's much-advertised campaign. In so far as Joe McCarthy is an individual, he has proved little beyond the foolishness and uncertainty of many who have appeared before him; even his single prize, Lattimore, is no "espionage agent." But in so far as McCarthy is the personification of a long-inarticulate movement, of the sullen self-consciousness of a sizable minority, he *begins* with a victory that he cannot fritter away, no matter how many errors he makes or how many downright lies he tells.

The emergence of McCarthy out of the wreckage of the La Follette Progressive movement in Wisconsin is a clue to what he represents. He inherits the bitterest and most provincial aspects of a populism to which smooth talking has always meant the Big City, and the Big City has meant the Enemy. Traditionally that enemy has been identified with "Wall Street," but from the mid-1920's there has been a tendency to give an equal status to the non-native rebels who claim also to oppose the bankers. Indeed, Robert La Follette, Jr., had gone so far in the latter direction that in 1946 the Communists, through the Wisconsin CIO council, supported McCarthy against him. It was not until 1950, however, that McCarthy discovered a symbolic butt in the State Department "Red," the "Park Avenue Pinko," capable of welding together the fractured Populist image of the Enemy. In light of this, it is just as important that McCarthy's initial attack was directed against the State Department under Acheson (and against Harvard behind him) as that it was directed against the Communists. Acheson is the projection of all the hostilities of the Midwestern mind at bay: his waxed mustache, his mincing accent, his personal loyalty to a traitor who also belonged to the Harvard Club; one is never quite sure that he was not invented by a pro-McCarthy cartoonist.

With something like genius, McCarthy touched up the villain he had half-found, half-composed, adding the connotations of wealth and effete culture to treachery, and topping all off with the suggestion of homosexuality. McCarthy's constant sneering references to "State Department perverts" are not explained by his official contention that such unfortunates are subject to blackmail, but represent his sure sense of the only other unforgivable sin besides being a Communist. The definition of the Enemy is complete — opposite in all respects to the American Ideal, simple, straightforward, ungrammatical, loyal, and one-hundred-percent male. Such an Enemy need not be *proven* guilty; he is guilty by definition.

It is interesting by way of comparison to see how much less sure McCarthy is before even a scoundrel who shares his own "American" prejudices. Certainly, no traduced liberal has ever faced him down as he was faced down by Isador Ginsberg, a war profiteer and former leader of a veterans' organization, who appeared before McCarthy when he was on the housing committee. "I want to say, sir," the grey-marketeer cried out in the midst of the questioning, "Ginsberg is as proud as McCarthy. I don't believe you can possibly pass legislation to prevent me, and honest men like me, from making a fair profit. Only in Russia can that be done!" And McCarthy, an "honest man" like Ginsberg, after all, and no friend of Russia, had to confess he was right: that only the enemies of profit and the defenders of Communism were outside the pale.

But the Enemy for McCarthy is not only a dandy, a queer, an intellectual, and a Communist; he is (or was, at least, in the beginning) a Democrat or a Democrat's friend. The struggle between the liberal intellectual and the old-line Red-baiter has been absurdly confused with the contest for votes between the Democratic and Republican parties. This seems, in part, clearly accidental. McCarthy himself was, for a while at least, a Democrat (his chief counsel Roy Cohn still proudly declares himself one); and at the start his charges were taken up largely as ammunition to be used against the ins, who happened to be Democrats, by the outs, who happened to be Republicans. It was possible at first to believe that there was no anti-Communist conviction at all behind McCarthy's campaign against the State Department, but merely a desire to slander his opponents and advance the fortunes of his own party; but one senses in him the happy coincidence of conviction and strategy. Blessed is the man who can at the same time gather in votes and vent the fear and hostility that the encroachments of Soviet imperialism have stirred in most American hearts!

Does the Republican party have any right to claim the mantle of Communist-hunting as its own? Certainly, there have been leading "Red-baiters" in both parties; and dupes of the Communists in both, too. Everyone remembers, I suppose, that among the friends of Alger Hiss was not only Acheson but also John Foster Dulles. Yet it is true that the Democratic party had become, in the early days of the New Deal, not liberal perhaps, but certainly liberal-colored; finding a place in its ranks somewhere between the big-city bosses and the Southern reactionaries for communoid and liberaloid professors, left-wing CIO trade unionists, and especially for a new kind of practical politician who had learned in Depression times to adapt the vocabulary and attitudes of the true liberal to his own constant opportunism.

Roosevelt himself was a representative of this group, and his own approach to the Soviet Union (the recognition of which became a leading slogan of the party), to England, and to China, for example, were deeply conditioned by the stereotypes and conventional allegiances of the liberal, at a point when the liberals were most victimized by illusions about the Soviet Union. The influence of such attitudes on our military activity in Europe and Asia and on our diplomatic activity as at Yalta and Potsdam, as well as the actual presence of Communists or sympathizers in key spots at key moments, have been documented and are outside the scope of this essay; but perhaps a word should be said about F.D.R.'s Vice-President, who symbolized the various stages of the liberalization of the Democratic party.

There is a shift of revolutionary scope between Garner, who represented an assurance to the right wing of the party that Roosevelt did not intend to go overboard in a radical direction, and Henry Wallace, who stood for an exactly opposite assurance to the left. Wallace is the blindly "idealist," hands-across-the-sea approach to the Soviet Union made flesh; and his symbolic role reaches a climax in his famous junket to Soviet Asia, under the partial tutelage of Owen Lattimore, during which Wallace failed to see anything blameworthy though he passed through one of the larger slave-labor camps. Later, he was to plead that he had been taken in by the wily camouflage of the Soviets, and (most interestingly) that he had been instructed not to look too hard for negative evidence, but to concentrate on what might bind us to our ally in amity. The ditching of Wallace for Truman meant on the surface a counter-gesture of reassurance to the right; but it actually represented the final penetration of the new ideology into the party, with the emergence of the liberalized party man, who makes unnecessary the window-dressing principledness of Wallace. Truman is basically the old-style politician, brought up inside the Machine, where fixes and deals are the order of the day, and where party or personal loyalty is ranked above the "reformer's" morality; but he has learned, on the one hand, to dedicate his political craft to liberal ends; and, on the other, to sanction his means by the pious evocation of those ends. It is no accident that it was Truman who cried loudest at the charges of Communist infiltration into his party's ranks: "Red herring!"

It remains to be added that the Roosevelt administration pushed the safeguards for labor and provisions for social security to the verge of what Republican conservatives like to call the "welfare state"; and, though the latter cannot, of course, undo such progressive measures, they can deplore them or condemn the "philosophy" behind them; which is to say, they can call liberal-colored improvisation a philosophy, and name it "creeping socialism." The spokesmen for this ideological opposition to the New Deal were tempted to use the exposure of real or alleged Communists in the Roosevelt bureaucracy as objective proof of a kinship of ideas between left-wing Democrats and Bolsheviks.

Whatever the justification before the fact for the Republican identification of the Democratic party with the liberal intellectuals and the Communists, they found in the jittery and uninformed reactions of men like Truman more fuel than they had hoped for. Fearful that granting any truth to the Republican charges might lose them votes, the Democrats arrayed themselves in strict party lines over every issue from the Tydings subcommittee report (when the anti-New Deal Tydings found himself backed by those who had tried to defeat him in the previous primaries) to the Army-Schine squabble. Once the Democrats had put themselves in the absurd position of denying Chambers' allegations about Hiss, and of screaming, every time Harry Dexter White's name was mentioned, that he was *dead* so loudly that they never heard the evidence against him, the way was open to make the whole New Deal seem nothing but a cover-up for Communist infiltration and espionage.

In the polemics which have followed, it has become impossible to speak of the sense in which the New Deal *did* put into positions of trust a few men with a double allegiance, and *did* encourage many colleagues of such men to look on that double allegiance as no more than an annoying foible, without seeming to ascribe to the "realistic" New Dealers more stupidity or Machiavellianism than they deserve. It would be foolish to accuse the Democrats, who under Truman launched a creditable program of opposing Communism abroad, with any real desire to protect Communists at home; but they did often choose to deny what they knew to be true in the interests of vote-getting; and after a while they came to speak of hysteria and "witch hunts" as if the danger of Communist espionage were not merely exaggerated but non-existent.

It was a strange and embarrassing opportunity for the Republicans, who found themselves on the popular side of an issue for the first time since 1932. In America anti-Communism has never been an exclusively bourgeois attitude; indeed, the only sizable group ever to challenge it was completely bourgeois. It has always been strongest among farmers, unorganized workers, and the lowest level of the middle class; and, once McCarthy had brought into the open a problem which opposed to the People the Intellectuals rather than "the Economic Royalists," a new kind of Republican was needed to assume leadership, the kind of Republican represented on varying levels of respectability by Nixon and McCarthy. This Senator Taft, for instance, appears to have sensed; perhaps he knew all along that though he was called "Mr. Republican" he could not make the populist appeal. Certainly, in this light his otherwise inexplicable support of McCarthy, his willingness to tout him in speeches dedicated to "political morality," makes a kind of sense.

The votes which clinched McCarthy's first senatorial victory came not only from the wealthier Catholic farmers of Wisconsin but from the working-class districts of Kenosha and Racine and Milwaukee ordinarily considered safe for the Democrats. If there is a blackness in McCarthy, it is not the reactionary blackness of the oil interests or of the Catholic Church, but of something in the American people which grows impatient with law and order, with understanding and polite talk, when it feels it has been betrayed. The ordinary American who has for years thundered in his Legion post against Reds cannot understand why, at a time when we are being baffled by Reds on three continents and are actually committing troops to battle against them, there should be a single Communist or defender of the Communists in a position of trust. He is only enraged when one speaks to him of safeguards and due process; of the difficulties of adjusting from a period in which the Communists were not only a legal party but our allies; of the actual equivocal status of Communists under the law. The Army, caught up in the toils of its own involved legality, finds itself forced to promote a Communist dentist before it can discharge him; and those who always have equally distrusted red tape and Reds scream in anguish through McCarthy, who is their mouthpiece.

The spirit that speaks is fundamentally a lynch spirit, the cry of those convinced that recognized evil cannot be touched by the law: "Let's get them before it's too late. Let's do it now!" But the lynchings have been only verbal so far, moral lynchings, which compared even to the reprisals against radicals that followed the First World War appear relatively calm and sane. The fight against McCarthyism must be carried on, but those who wage it must be aware that they are fighting a whole section of our people unable to understand a situation in which moral condemnation of a group has far outstripped the community's legal procedures for dealing with them. It is therefore hard to undercut McCarthy, especially because most of those who attack him have always been considered by his supporters to be their natural enemies; and because, more and more, the picture is established in the minds of his adherents of Joe the Giant-Killer — a limited but dedicated man, fallen among fast-talkers and slickers.

In light of this, the constant hope of the already enlightened that McCarthy's following can be split away if only some forcefully written exposé could be got into the right hands, or if only someone would stand up to him boldly enough at the hearings, is revealed as fantasy. Equally chimeric is the dream that "given enough rope he will hang himself," that some lie revealed, some exceptionally absurd accusation hastily dropped, will damn McCarthy in the eyes of his fondest followers. It is this sort of eternally deferred hope that leads to final despair: the Dorothy Kenyon case, the Wechsler case, the Benton charges, the Army scandal — each hoped-for blunder, each eagerly awaited revelation, finds McCarthy unshaken and assured, his pathos more firmly established for his supporters.

I am not trying to suggest that McCarthy cannot be dislodged from his place of power. I am sure that, if the Republican National Committee cuts him off unequivocally, those of his adherents who are allured only by the aura of success will depart, even some of those to whom he represents the triumph of principle. A glance at the decline of McCarthy's vote from 1946 to 1952 indicates how much damage can be done even by the defection of a few influential people inside his own party; and certainly the opposition to McCarthy continues to grow in Republican ranks: even those who seem at first glance closest to him begin to edge away. Vice-President Nixon is the representative figure; himself an inquisitor (he must get the chief credit for Hiss's exposure before the House Un-American Activities Committee) and an exploiter of anti-Communism as a campaign issue, he has nonetheless a yearning for intellectual respectability. "This is just a note," he wrote to James Wechsler in January of 1950, "to tell you that I thought your editorial on the Hiss case . . . was one of the most able and fair appraisals of a very difficult problem I have ever seen. Since you probably have me categorized as one of the 'reactionaries' . . . I thought you might be particularly interested in my reaction." This letter to one whom McCarthy finds it politic to call a concealed Communist reveals clearly the difference in Nixon's approach that must force him to a final break with the traducers of the anti-Communist position as he understands it.

Most recently, McCarthy has created a new kind of resentment with his defense of the "young officer" who transmitted to him for use against the Department of Defense a classified FBI report on Communists in the Army, and his assertion that all government employees "are duty bound to give me information even though some bureaucrat may have stamped it secret." Under a Democratic administration, his Republican colleagues might have found it possible to ignore the positing of a "higher" allegiance, embarrassingly reminiscent of Communist theory; but with their own man in the White House they have felt forced to take a stand. Attorney General Brownell set the tone by blasting publicly "an individual [coyly unnamed] who may seek to set himself above the laws of the land"; and even some of McCarthy's staunchest supporters hastened to dissociate themselves from his position. But most leading Republicans were apparently not yet sure that McCarthy could be disavowed without losing votes, and on second thought they shifted from attacking him to accusing the Democrats of plotting to split the Republican party on the McCarthy issue.

The melancholy conclusion is that, whatever personal resentments or principled differences may exist within the Republican party, McCarthy will not be cast off until it is politically expedient. Perhaps what will sink him in the end is a rather personal quirk, the almost compulsive hatred of the Army and its brass which has led to his most unpopular moves: the investigation of the Malmédy massacre, the (since-repented) attack on MacArthur, the book-length onslaught on General Marshall (with unfavorable side-glances at Eisenhower); and the tongue-lashing of General Zwicker which helped precipitate the Army-McCarthy hearings. This is an age of generals, and McCarthy's distaste for them may eventually compromise him, though liberals will be able to find small comfort in such a dog-eat-dog defeat.

But none of this will touch the hard core for whom McCarthy establishes in history the nightmare they have dreamed in private; and that group which preceded Joe McCarthy will survive him, as McCarthyism itself, whatever new name it bear, will outlive the death of its present form. The fight against McCarthyism is more than the fight against McCarthy; it is a struggle against the outlived illusions of the left as well as the distortions of the right, against the superciliousness of the intellectuals as well as the resentment of those to whom they condescend. It is the fight against our own comfortable lies as well as the disquieting ones of our enemies, against self-righteousness as well as slander. It is a war for the truth we cannot help betraying even as we defend it; and in this war each victory is only a new way to begin.

A Postscript

Though the Army-McCarthy hearings did not, of course, produce a clear-cut condemnation of the Senator from Wisconsin; though they did not, indeed, even raise the issues everyone felt to lurk behind the superficial question of who was lying, McCarthy or the Army (or, more precisely, who had lied first and more egregiously), they have in an indirect and unexpected way led to the partial collapse of McCarthy's prestige. His double defense of, on the one hand, portraying himself as the champion of the legislative branch against the executive, and, on the other, revealing with what unclean hands his presumably high-minded opponents came against him, was only too successful. As far as his mass support is concerned, any exposure of the incidental lack of virtue on his part remains, as I have tried to show above, beside the point. The convinced McCarthyites, his scarcely articulate admirers, who applaud him almost more for bucking his glib upper-class opponents than for blasting Communists — these have not been touched.

And yet, at the end of the late televised hearings, everyone but those *lumpen* advocates was left with a sense of shame, a feeling that he had been personally besmirched by the whole ignoble affair. It was not only that nobody directly involved in the circus managed to perform with distinction or tact, but that even those not directly implicated, the nation itself, sat transfixed for weeks before their television receivers in a voyeuristic orgy — unable to turn away from the often vacuous bluster of Jenkins, the somewhat oleaginous piety of Welch, the surly and unprincipled "cleverness" of Roy Cohn, the aggrieved smugness of McCarthy himself. Supporters of one side or the other tried hard to find moments for enthusiasm; but as the affair wore on, as Secretary Stevens weakly stumbled (with a last-minute, useless kind of courage) from point to point, as any semblance of order and coherence disappeared and the "actors" preened for the cameras, the reigning feeling in most hearts was self-contempt for being unable simply to turn off the sets and go away to useful work or decent play.

Never before had television revealed itself quite so clearly as the electronic keyhole from which it is impossible to remove one's eye no matter what disgustingness is being played out behind it. Never before had the underlying triviality, the small dirtiness behind the large statements of McCarthyism, been so patent. In the morning after the orgy of the hearings, it became clear to many that no one could join McCarthy's ranks or even combat him on issues of his own choosing without being degraded. The dignity of the nation and the government seemed at stake.

It is in light of this morning-after revulsion that the recent report of the Watkins committee must be read. The function of that committee was not so much to investigate certain particular charges against McCarthy for behavior unworthy of the Senate, as to redeem the total dignity of that body. It is for this reason that the procedure of the committee has been as important as its findings: its decision to forego the more grotesque excesses of publicity, its refusal to lose all coherence in a welter of irrelevant "points of order." But it is also for this reason that the accusations against McCarthy sustained by the Watkins committee are so uncentral to the problem of McCarthyism. He has been found guilty not of failing to fight effectively the enemy against whom he blusters, Communism; not of attacking civil liberties; not even of setting loyalty to himself above government regulations and the standard procedures for handling confidential material. The latter conflict he managed to put in the light of a struggle between legislature and the executive, and the committee chose to evade it.

No, the charges sustained against him are the use of vile language to fellow-Senators and his refusal to testify before an earlier legislative committee on the score of financial matters. What McCarthy says in self-defense is, of course, deplorably true: that on these points (the use of vituperation and the discreet manipulation of income-tax reports) he is scarcely more guilty than many other legislators. It is a little like the case of the gangster whose kidnapings, assaults, and murders cannot for one reason or another be proved against him, and who is finally jailed for income-tax evasion.

The Democrats on the committee really found, *as* Democrats, McCarthy guilty for stealing the Communist issue and hence votes from their party; the Republicans, *as* Republicans, for disrupting the unity of their party and sniping excessively at their administration; all of them as Senators for his public besmirching of the upper house by behavior common enough in milder form but unforgivable in this flagrant version. In McCarthy, what is for other Senators incidental vice becomes published as public virtue; and this, in a country still in a residual sense puritan, is unpardonable. McCarthy will not pay vice's customary tribute of hypocrisy to virtue; and in the end it is for his sullen honesty in dishonesty that he has been condemned.

Besides which, time has run out on the Senator. So many of his colleagues in both parties have for so long been joined with him in rooting out Communist influence, both real and fancied, in all branches of government, that there no longer appear to be any spectacular unexplored areas. The great diversionist finds himself at the moment of his supreme discomfit without any diversion at hand; the man who has based his whole claim to regard on the constant harrying of Reds is fresh out of Reds. It is not merely a matter of being distracted from his hunt, as McCarthy keeps declaring; much of the game has been flushed and bagged. No wonder he has recently retreated to the hospital, overwhelmed by the respiratory ailment that nags him like a reproach; and that the face he raises on current television shows is that of a man badly hurt if not beaten. No wonder he begins to boast of his own impending defeats as voluptuously as he once forecast his victories. McCarthyism, the psychological disorder compounded of the sour dregs of populism, the fear of excellence, difference, and culture, remains still a chronic disease of our polity; but its acute form, our most recent attack, seems to have passed the crisis.

PART TWO

INNOCENCE ABROAD

CHAPTER FOUR

Italian Pilgrimage: the Discovery of America

For shipboard reading en route to Italy, I took along with me *The Marble Faun*. It was a toss-up between that and *Innocents Abroad*. There seemed no use in trying to kid myself — no American just goes to Italy; he makes willy-nilly a literary journey, and his only choice is between melodrama and comedy. Hawthorne or Mark Twain? You pays your money and you takes your choice — if it is a choice; for after all each writer confesses, according to his own conventions, the same meanings of the voyage: a Pilgrimage to the shrines of an idea of man (or more accurately, I suppose, to the visible forms of a culture in which that idea is entombed) and a Descent into Hell. Moreover, both books agree in telling us, what we might have guessed anyhow, that the Descent into Hell is for us the real pleasure of the venture, while the Pilgrimage threatens always to become a bore.

Even the distinction between comedy and melodrama is not final. With Hawthorne's romance of terror clutched firmly in hand, two generations of Innocents Abroad dutifully followed in the steps of the writer who had in turn dutifully followed in the steps of his wife. And I, once arrived, dutifully followed at third hand the now fashionable itinerary of those foolish and innocent ghosts, standing before the "Faun" on the Capitoline, and in the dim innards of the Church of the Capuchins looking at the insufferable St. Michael of Guido Reni. It is a lesson in humility to contemplate such works of

91

art, once extravagantly admired; though no one ever quite believes that his own enlightened preference for Caravaggio and the figures on Etruscan tombs will seem one day as inconceivably and nostalgically ridiculous.

The comedy of the journey is no more final than the melodrama. One forgets too easily that *Innocents Abroad* is one of our saddest books. At first glance, shipboard life had seemed to promise passages of pure comic Twain, and things threatened to reach a hilarious climax when we disembarked briefly at Barcelona to make our first penetration of Europe. We had only a few hours ashore and everyone piled into the sightseeing buses at the dock. I found myself just behind a large, enthusiastic lady, almost purple with the strain of being an American. She had thrust eagerly down the gangplank but, getting her first whiff of the Old World, had begun holding her nose in ostentatious and growing disgust, until finally, in the shadow of her first cathedral, she had turned to all of us, imploring us to join in "God Bless America!" It was impossible to laugh; she was so obviously afraid.

The setting of comedy is conservative, and one can still play Mark Twain straight, but the décor and personnel of melodrama have changed drastically, and hell itself has been refurnished and completely recast to suit our shifting taste. To Hawthorne, Italy had seemed a Gothic inferno, an underworld familiar and traditional for all its terror, with the Wandering Jew making a not-unexpected appearance in the catacombs, and the legend of the Cenci once more evoked. For us, however, Italy has become a politicalized, a "neo-realistic" hell; it is the comic-tragic shade of Mussolini that haunts our underground (half the Jack Oakie of Chaplin's *Great Dictator,* and half the bloody, head-down corpse of the obscene newsreel shots that fade indistinguishably into the montage of a handful of recent Italian movies). Beatrice Cenci walks no more; and instead of the print of that tragically theatrical face we are likely to take home with us the image of the latest twelve-year-old rape victim from some seedy suburb; not the figure of classic incest and terror, but of mechanical lust and meaningless violence. The malaria is gone, and we who know all about mosquitoes and germs can believe no longer in a curse, a miasma arising from the almost timelessly compounded evils of Empire and Papacy. But there is still overcrowding and poverty and hunger raised to the power of the exotic; and, to delight the liberal Protestant imagination, the vision of a land harried by evil landlords and by a clergy which can no longer kidnap and torture but which, by opposing birth control, continues its dastardly work.

No, Italy is hell enough for us still; what is disconcerting, however, is the realization that for many Italians we do not seem the gingerly visitors from an upper world that we appear to ourselves, but refugees from our own authentic and ultimate inferno. America has become the hell of its own favorite hell! This is the most disturbing and diverting thing I have learned thus far in Italy. I have had the unexpected sense of Italy as a mirror, a distorting mirror to be sure, one of those diabolical things from a Coney Island Fun House, that gives you for the laughs a brutal caricature, at once a nightmare and a joke, a travesty and a disturbing criticism of yourself.

I am never able to doubt that the portrait of America I find reflected here is a portrait of my own America. Unfair, I may find it, even occasionally dishonest, but it never seems to me the limning of someone else. I have, indeed, felt here as I have never felt before that there is only *one* America. To be sure, an occasional homegrown speaker, visiting under the auspices of the United States Information Service, and reviving the familiar banalities about the infinite variety of our land and the misrepresentations of writers like Faulkner, will arouse in me a suspicion that the monolithic America the Italians dream is a hoax. But, at this distance and inside another view, I see clearly my own ironies and dissents as a necessary part of an overall pattern; and this does not upset me. I have come across occasional detached Americans who seem eager to attest, by loudly certifying the Italian picture of their country, their own dissociation from that picture. "Yes," they declare, "it is true of those others, but we, on the other hand . . .": and they devote themselves to exposing unfortunate American influences in current Italian movies and novels. These are our last true Innocents Abroad, the last claimants to what seemed once our unquestioned birthright. For whoever admits his complicity in the existent America, down to the crassest Philistine, avows a sense of guilt.

The Italian attitude toward our country is, however, not really available to the innocent expatriate, still linked to us, strain as he will, by a bond of ennui, the last vestige of familiar love. There is no tedium in the Italian's view; he may tremble in hatred before his own image of our civilization, but his connection is essentially passionate and desperate — as if we were, indeed, a *femme fatale*. We have become quite absurdly the blonde Dark Lady, the Beatrice Rappacini of the Italian world. It is ridiculous, one keeps wanting to cry out: the roles are reversed, the drama miscast!

And yet, if the mythic America has seemed for the Italians an inferno, it has also seemed to them a symbol of salvation. But this is, of course, no real contradiction; for why else does one descend into hell, except to find his way home or to heaven or to the promised fatherland, which is to say, into his own yet unravished margins of consciousness. Within the last twenty years, America has come to stand to the Italians for a new idea of man, a humanism beyond their official Humanism, lost in a compulsive rhetoric and captured by the makers of Fascist propaganda. Italian intellectuals had remained strangely immune to the earlier idyllic Americas of the French; though Cooper in translation made a popular success, there never was an Italian Chateaubriand, much less an Italian Crèvecoeur. Not out of the expurgated forests of *Atala* or *The Last of the Mohicans,* but out of the ravaged landscapes of *Sanctuary* and *Winesburg, Ohio,* the Italians have contrived a utopia. Imagine the wit and desperation necessary to such a conceit!

But this is the final America of Italy, the America of its present poets; and one must come to it last of all, through the other Americas which greet the initial glance of the uninitiated traveler, who sees first the apartment houses of the fashionable quarters and the newsstands everywhere: the imaginary America of the upper bourgeoisie, complete with steam radiators and nylons and electric refrigerators, enshrined in the resolutely un-Roman, the really inhuman, "functional" architecture of the Parioli district; and the popular America of comic books, illustrated periodicals, detective stories, and movie magazines. Perhaps there is no other really popular culture except our own. Certainly, no one in Italy seemed capable of filling the vacuum of expectation left after the civil war. The traditional guardians of Italian culture had compromised themselves by coming too easily to terms with Fascism; and the bright young men, who at first flocked almost unanimously to Stalinism, could only *talk* of a new people's culture, at once generally available and uncompromisingly complex. While they chattered and debated, a debased popular literature, made in the image of our own, simply grew.

On every street-corner kiosk, one now sees displayed side by side a half-dozen Italian imitations of *Life* and *Look* and *Pic,* reducing all events through the camera lens to the same values and consequence — the monotone of the spectacle. And, in contrast to their slick black and white, the colored comic books (colored only on every fourth page, one discovers, for Italy after all is not as rich as some countries) translating the adventures of Pecos Bill and "Jane Calamity," of Donald Duck and Mickey Mouse. Mickey especially, re-baptized Topolino in Italian, is everywhere: lending his name to a caramel penny candy, a new Canasta set, a movie house for children — and providing an affectionate nickname for the midget cars that tear through the Roman streets with all the abandon and pace of a Disney cartoon. Only the Superman type of comics have not taken, whether because the sock in the jaw means little in Italian symbology, or in simple reluctance to adopt an urban mythology, I can't say. Certainly, the Romans seem to prefer to linger in the legendary Far West with "Jane Calamity," and they even insist on Mickey Mouse being sent week after week to their own tormentingly lost "Far West," the jungles of Africa.

The translation of American *gialli,* murder mysteries, is a major industry; and, along with the equivalent films, such works provide on the popular level the vision of America as the utopia of violence ("At least your country is young, exciting!") which the intellectuals derive from Erskine Caldwell or William Faulkner. Indians, outlaws, and gangsters flow together with Communist-inspired versions of the American G.I. (on every wall during the recent NATO conference, a

death's-head or a thug's face under a swastika-marked helmet
— and *Via Americani! Americani Get Out!*) into a single
image of the Tough Guy, infinitely repulsive and infinitely
alluring — an ambivalent image of potency.

But the movies provide other Americas, too, Americas of
luxury: the oversize purring automobile, the long-legged girl,
the penthouse towering above the swarming streets; and it is
the movies in their endless repetition that are decisive in the
end. Whatever political paper a man may read, his myths
are made in the dark before the screen; and the Italians are
still moviegoers with an intensity and enthusiasm that has
been gone from America for fifteen years. The provincial
opera house, which once sustained a local art, now shows *Tea
for Two* and *All About Eve,* and the outraged cries of the
nostalgic grow weaker and weaker. Two-thirds of the pictures
one sees advertised on the hoardings are American films, despite the excellence of the Italian product and the substantial
fine which an operator must pay if he does not show a certain
proportion of Italian movies. For most Italians the voyage to
America is a cinematic one — a ritual more honored than
the Mass.

What is hard to see at home, where we are oppressed by the
real vulgarity and triviality of our ordinary films, is the exu-
berant confidence they manage to convey to a society as
anxious and unstable as Italy's. The Italian moviegoer can
only conceive of our life in terms of strength; and it is in this
sense that he finds it easy to reconcile his double view of us
as a Land of the Heart's Desire (the old-fashioned notion of
Golden America has survived the reality of our Depression
and thirty years of Fascist and Communist "revelations") and
as a threat to peace and prosperity. The average moviegoer
would vote Communist, of course; but his willingness to vote
for Togliatti does not mean that he would not be delighted to
emigrate to the United States — to join himself to our mana,
our potency.

The "American" in a quite wonderful current Italian comedy, *Guardie e ladri* ("Cops and Robbers"), is the incarnation
of present Italian stereotype: a bureaucrat, bluff, hearty, a
little overfed, but offensively strong in his checked overcoat

— he is fair game for the Italian con-man, despite the fact (perhaps, after all, because) he has come over to distribute food packages to poor children. Though he is temporarily hoaxed, he is never defeated; though he is blustering and ridiculous, his unassailable confidence and health still overwhelm both the Italian policeman and the crook, who serve or undermine a state in which they cannot believe and inhabit bodies on whose livers they cannot depend. Liver trouble and sexual failure — these are the calamities that fill the columns of Roman newspapers with advertised cures. *Povera Italia!* In America, similar space is occupied by minor anxieties about B.O. and dull teeth. After a while, one cannot help seeing in the eternal newspaper offers to cure impotency a symbolic expression of a general fear of failing virility, from which the rhetoric of Mussolini was able to deliver the Italians for a little while.

Our political "friends" do not challenge the picture of us our enemies cherish; they merely assess it a little differently. A Roman daily newspaper that has supported the Atlantic Pact, describing our crop-headed, ignorant young soldiers with condescending enthusiasm, assures its readers that Stalin would hesitate to attack if he could only see our strength (these strange giants who are capable of washing down a huge meal with ice water!), and ends by assimilating us to a myth of Imperial Rome — a civilization of luxury hedged about by its Praetorian Guards, who fortunately (though quite by accident) became also the guardians of Western European civilization.

We have moved now to the middling level of Italian culture — to the essay on the third page of the daily newspaper with which the serious writer and the professor still manage in Italy to meet the mass mind. The nearest thing to "third page" style, at its not infrequent worst, is to be found in American life in the kitschy program note, which, you may be sure, also flourishes over here. Elmer Rice's *Dream Girl* was playing in Rome when I first arrived, in an Italian version called *Sogno ad occhi aperti* ("Dream with Open Eyes") — and the program note attempted to make clear to its audiences exactly how Rice's trivially amusing, philistine piece was a political lesson of great importance (Americans should continue to dream with eyes wide open and with "the Declaration of Rights in their fist"), and a revelation to America of its own true self. Both the style and the attitude are typical enough to bear quotation. In Rice's work, we are told, we are to find "an expression . . . made in U.S.A. . . . athletic and muscular, well adapted to drawing rooms and martinis . . . a revolt against the labels on canned foods, the black journalism of Hearst, and the fame of Coca Cola." And in Georgina Allerton, the heroine of the play, we are to see not the mad romantic she might seem at first, "riding her European despair like a Lady Godiva," but a true-blue American girl capable of throwing over Freud for the Sane Living of Doctor Hauser. (If the last reference baffles you, you can look up Doctor Hauser in your nearest bookstore, or order the Italian version, if the American edition is exhausted.) The general philistinism of Rice is taken as a special plea to Americans to give up the false pursuit of culture (all the Italians' own weariness with European culture is being projected continually and savagely upon us) and to reveal themselves as what they truly are: lovable noble savages, who "dance the boogie, secretly read the comic strips, are in love with Clark Gable, and walk along Fifth Avenue in all the glory of their long-limbed bodies."

It is the long-limbed blondness of a Georgina Allerton which defines the erotic image of the modern Italian; it is hard for us, for whom the sexually potent primitive tends to be thought of as dark, to understand the Latins' blonde dream — testified to by the outrageously unconvincing peroxided heads one is forever passing in Rome. The American woman is no longer, if indeed she ever was, a "Snow Queen" for the Italians, but a sexual mana-object like her male counterpart, to whom is also attributed a mythical sexual allure. In a recent scandalous murder case, the mother of the child victim turned out to be a whore, "honest," however, the papers all assured us, until she was corrupted during the war by "anglo-saxon" troops; and the unhappy woman who only last week slashed her wrists in a seedy hotel room had been, of course, abandoned by "an American diplomat." There is a popular movie actress called Tamara Lee, with pale-gold hair and legs of extraordinary length, who appears in film after film as the Anglo-Saxon *femme fatale,* scarcely speaking, merely moving across the screen to register her archetypal self. And it is one of those symbolic and inevitable "accidents" that the foremost Italian "Americanist," a poet and translator, committed suicide a year ago, apparently as the result of an unhappy affair with "an American moving picture actress." A posthumous volume of his poems had just appeared, some written in English and dedicated to the beloved "C." — yet another record of the pursuit of the elusive image which is America and death.

It is only on a more serious literary level, however, that the relationship of contemporary Italy to America has come to full consciousness. The confrontation of Italy and America is of recent origin — though it is not as recent as our awareness of it in the United States. We are likely to think of the encounter as a post-World-War-II phenomenon, a result perhaps of the actual penetration of Italy by our troops — a function of an enthusiasm for us as "liberators." Nothing could be further from the truth. The relationship of the Italian intellectuals to our culture begins in horror and disgust, at a point when Italy is in the midst of Fascism and we are at the beginning of our greatest Depression.

It is not the image of a triumphant and flower-crowned army that presides over the start of Italian interest in us, but a vision of soup kitchens and bowery bums, bloody corpses of gangsters and lynched Negroes. *America amara* ("Bitter America") — that is the title of the almost legendary travel book by Emilio Cecchi, "its assonance," as he says, "most exact in every sense," the book which transformed America from a geographical and social entity to a fact of the Italian imagination. The Cecchi volume did not appear until 1938, and it had been preceded in 1935 by Mario Soldati's *America primo amore* ("America, First Love"), the story of an emigration that failed. But Cecchi had already been registering his impressions in the earliest 1930's; and Soldati's book, the work of a very young man, unequal and marred by self-pity, has tended to fuse its meanings into those of the more expert and coolly bitter exposé of Cecchi. In both, after all, there is the same vision of a land ravaged by senseless violence, ruled by women, and presided over intellectually by professors who despise ideas and love bridge; and in both there is the view of a desperate materialism brought to the edge of despair, though the New Deal, by Cecchi's time, is trying to resuscitate the American dream of happiness, that "joy of the child about to collapse into tears."

In Cecchi and Soldati the journey to America becomes literature; and in Cecchi, at least, there is a clue to the next step, in which literature is to become a journey to America. In the midst of the desert of American life, Cecchi finds the unexpected fact of American literature, despising and despised by America. Watching American women in a cafeteria, eating with their curious coldness "a few peas and an ice," Cecchi thinks that on just such a diet Ligeia must have subsisted; reading the account of a particularly repulsive crime in the South, he reflects that America does not have to read Faulkner to imitate him; and, entering New York, he remembers the frantic night journey of Pierre and Isabella into the city. Poe, Faulkner, and Melville — in the phrase of D. H. Lawrence, the minority of ardent and sorrowing spirits lost in a vast republic of fugitive slaves — they are welcomed by the Italian essayist as witnesses against their own civilization, whose barbarity he feels as a threat to his own.

It is important to keep sight of the fact that the contemporary Italian interest in American literature begins with a search for documents to justify a revulsion, to explain an enemy; that it ends in finding a utopia and a cue for emulation is a splendid irony, and betrays perhaps an ambivalence in Cecchi himself, a secret hunger for the madness and primitive rage he chose to read into America. At any rate, whatever his intentions, his essays on American literature (collected in *Scrittori inglese e americani* in 1935) helped release an interest in American writing which burgeoned beyond all foreseeing; and which eventually led to a belated revolution in Italian prose style (the so-called "neo-realism" of Pavese, Vittorini, etc.), with which Cecchi has found it hard to sympathize; and which even contributed to the anti-Fascist movement a motivating myth, though Cecchi himself is a self-declared sympathizer with "cops on horses."

Since about 1930, there has taken place in Italy one of the most extraordinary feats of translation and assimilation in the history of culture; hundreds of American books have been turned into Italian, provided with prefaces, critically discussed, and, most important of all, read with a fantastic eagerness. The figures of Poe, Melville, and Whitman, Hawthorne, Hemingway, O. Henry, and Faulkner have become real presences to the Italian imagination — living and important figures available even to the commonest reader, who will find from time to time in his daily newspaper stories by the older writers, even pieces by Saroyan or Eudora Welty. A new language has been invented — an Italian remade by American prose rhythms (a hybrid like the Mayakovsky-English of the Communist poets in the 1930's), a sometimes deplored idiom, common to the translations and the latest "neo-realistic" novels. If America welcomes warmly the flood of new Italian fiction (and the closely related pseudo-documentary films), it is welcoming itself, a deliberate reflection of its own moods and stylistic devices. What Italy itself had been to England in the Renaissance, what Germany to Europe when Romanticism was beginning — America is (or has been until only yesterday) to contemporary Italy.

In the ten years from 1930 to 1940, the literary discovery of America was made twice over. History has moved so fast, and events have so tended to blur, that for a while the double discovery seemed one. Ten more years, however, have sufficed to show clearly the differences between the two experiences, essentially contradictory, even inimical: the discovery of a barbaric culture and its literature, a new Ossian, by a generation of cultivated and tolerant humanists, who managed to live at peace with Fascism and whose own style was never touched by the American example; and the rediscovery of a land that was at once its particular self and a myth of deliverance. Emilio Cecchi is, as we have seen, the leading figure of the first group; Vittorini and Cesare Pavese and Giaime Pintor, typical figures in the second.

It is both odd and just that the Italian double vision of the journey to America corresponds part for part to the American double vision of the journey to Italy: a Descent into Hell,

and a Pilgrimage to the shrines of an idea of man. For the
generation of Cecchi, the American experience is the pure
Descent into Hell. In his introduction to *Americana,* a thousand-page analogy of American prose, edited by Elio Vittorini,* Cecchi remembers a phrase of D. H. Lawrence which
he has already quoted in *America Amara;* of certain documents
of American life, Lawrence said: "They seem more terrible
than the Oedipus or the Medea; and beside them, Hamlet,
Macbeth and King Lear are eyewash." Lawrence is for the
Italians the Virgil of their infernal descent. It is impossible
here in Italy to pick up a book or listen to a lecture on American literature that does not draw on *Studies in Classic American Literature,* that shrill, self-indulgent, insightful book so
little honored still in American universities. After all, it is "un-
scholarly," as Cecchi was told in 1930, when he read from it
in an attempt to persuade his students at the University of
California to rediscover Melville! To an Italian, of course, the
rhetoric of Lawrence's book (so committed and uncorseted
and disturbing to the professor with a pipe) is an earnest that
he is *simpatico,* on their side; and so their classic American
literature, their Melville and Hawthorne and Cooper, are to
this very day essentially Lawrence's.

But Cecchi is not, after all, quite prepared to grant to
American writing the tragic status which Lawrence's remark
seems to imply. For all their fragmentary brilliance, American
prose and poetry are from the beginning "demented and shaken
by a St. Vitus dance," and, indeed, it tends to become more
and more frantic as a civilization, never dedicated to anything
higher than "well-being and material felicity," collapses in its
hour of crisis into "hopeless disillusion." To be heard among
the exhortations of "the medicine men and Jewish grey emi-
nences of the New Deal" and the baleful cries of American
women harrying their men to bed to celebrate orgies of a
"frozen and frenetic paganism," the American writer must
scream louder all the time. The dialog between him and his
public comes to be more and more like that between Hamlet

---

*Apparently, Vittorini had written a too-friendly introduction — and the
intervention of the Facist censors prompted the last-minute substitution of
the Cecchi essay, a rehash of his earlier pieces.

and Laertes in the grave of Ophelia, a contest of imprecation; and he ends in a kind of sadist *concettismo*, a baroque of the horrible.

As if he were a little afraid of his own yearning toward the madness of American literature, Cecchi keeps reminding himself that, after all, the Hemingways and Faulkners may well turn out to be the Macphersons and Radcliffes of our time, "primordial romantics," forerunners of little intrinsic merit — interesting finally only as documents, as "social and historic testimony" of a culture already sick to death in its youth.

This point of view is met head-on by Cesare Pavese, the brilliant novelist and translator of *Moby Dick*. His collected essays have just appeared posthumously, not only the studies of American literature, but a fascinating series developing a new theory of the relation of myth and literature. In his earliest pieces, written between 1930 and 1934, he boldly spurns the comforting official theory of the American artist as the enemy of his own culture, the foe of that upstart "puritan" system of values, which the Fascist press was always discovering in the act of "threatening our 2000-year-old culture." (Like two boys fighting, Pavese says, one of whom boasts, "I'm the son of a general!") In his studies of Whitman and Dreiser, Sinclair Lewis and Edgar Lee Masters, Pavese sets himself the task of showing how certain works which, read as satire or polemics, create an anti-America, read as poetry, reveal an essential, positive America, America's consciousness of itself; a complex and ironic affirmation, which must also be taken into account along with the strikes, the lynchings, the "materialism," and the "emancipated women" that are its occasions.

To a writer like Pavese, the facts of life in the United States as perceived by Cecchi matter only in their whole context, in which they come to seem minor components of an astonishing attempt to come to terms with the modern world in all its immediacy; to find words for dealing with motives and passions whose very existence a tradition-ridden Italian official culture denied. This search for an anti-rhetorical rhetoric and the honesty which prompted it were essential to America, and not the "babel of clamorous efficiency," "the cruel, neon-lighted optimism," which, after all, were precisely what the Fascists

would have liked for Italy — "granted always a civilized veneer
of Roman hypocrisy." In the mirror of America, the young
Italian intellectuals recognized themselves, their deepest long-
ings, which the official culture wanted to persuade them were
spiritual vices. "America was not another country . . . but
only the giant theater where with greater candor was played
out the drama of us all."

Though the leaders of the Italian state were never willing
openly to oppose the interest in American culture, the young
soon came to feel each act of criticism or translation, the
simple reading of an American text, as symbolic revolutionary
acts, secret heresies. Years later Pavese wrote of this period:
"It can be said frankly that the new mania for American writing helped not a little to perpetuate and nourish the political
opposition. . . . For many people the encounter with Steinbeck, Caldwell, Saroyan, or even with the old Lewis . . .
aroused the first suspicion that not all the culture of the world
ended with the fasces."

There is in a great deal of the critical writing about American literature under Fascism a sense of an intended ambiguity,
a deliberate double-entendre; the young Italian writers (for
the Americanists were also the leading novelists and poets)
talked about "style" and "expression" — as if, in Pavese's
words, they were studying "the past, Elizabethan drama or
the poetry of the *stil nuovo*" — but one understands that they
are really interested in the living drama, the myth, the problem
of America. And the literary attacks on the "hermeticists" and
"aesthetes" must be understood, in part at least, as a veiled
political foray against the social system with which the older
generation of "aesthetes" had made their peace. A revolution
of the word that aimed at changing the world! Whatever they
may have intended, however, the young intellectuals accomplished a vital renewal of language which is still bearing fruit
— whereas the political revolution of which the literary one
was to be the type appears to have been stillborn. There is
little vital democracy in Italy today, but there is "neo-realism."
If this is a wry kind of joke, it is also a real achievement.

It is worth noting, by the way, that the very literature from
which our best young writers have been seeking to be de-

livered, the post-Dreiserian tradition, particularly in the forms
it took in the 1930's, has been for the Italian fictionist precisely a means of delivery. Cecchi, to be sure, deplores the
mean catalogs of Dreiser, the ephemeral slang of Hemingway;
but for the contemporaries of Pavese a kind of practice which
impresses us with its exhaustion provided exemplars of a passionate fidelity to the brute given world, of a language that tries
impatiently to be things, and of a tradition that exists only in
being sought.

In the light of the uses they have made of our literature, it
is possible to understand certain Italian estimates of our
authors, so different from our own. Masters and Dreiser, Anderson and Sinclair Lewis, and, oddest of all, O. Henry, have
seemed to them central; while the "bourgeois and Europeanizing" James has appeared irrelevant for all his undeniable merit
— and Eliot, though he has been well translated and much
admired, has seemed a product of their own familiar culture
rather than of the mythic America with its "miraculous immediacy of expression."

On the other hand, even those Italian intellectuals who have
since become Communists have never, like some of our home-
grown "liberals," judged our writers on the basis of their
"progressivism," but always on the score of their attitudes
toward experience and language. So that Faulkner, for instance, political reactionary though he may be, is for them,
as for us, the best of our living writers; and Melville the greatest of our classics. There is something heartening in this core
of agreement, which rises solidly amid the swirl of our peripheral differences. It is obvious how sympathetic, under the
circumstances, the Italians must have found the critical work
of Matthiessen, who perhaps alone in America tried to combine
in quite their own way a regard for the claims of poetry and a
program of political action. If Lawrence is the Virgil of the
Italian Descent into Hell, Matthiessen is the Cato of their
ascent toward the imagined Earthly Paradise of a new view of
man as the master of a society "in which there is an organic
unity between culture and the world of work."

It was not until 1946, however, that Pavese discovered
Matthiessen, in a post-war era of new possibilities and disap-

pointments. Right up through the war years, the anti-Fascist Americanists had continued to publish side by side with the pro-Fascists under the aegis of Lawrence. The culmination of this ill-assorted united front was the anthology *Americana,* in which Cecchi and Vittorini collaborated, their contradictions concealed amid the quotations from *Studies in Classic American Literature,* and the pictures of American whores, gangsters, and mountains.

In 1943, to be sure, the 24-year-old critic Giaime Pintor had written a review of that anthology, in which he had separated out the confused tendencies* in a brilliant piece of exposition that had to wait until 1945 to be published (it can be read now in a corrected version in the collection of Pintor's essays called *Il sangue d'Europa*). Pintor himself died at the end of 1943, blown up by a German mine while attempting to pass into occupied Italy to join the partisans; but his essay remains the classic discussion of the two discoveries of America. "Cecchi has scrupulously collected a museum of horrors, where he has isolated diseases and decadence, and recognized a world in which it is impossible to trust; while we have heard a voice profoundly sympathetic to us, that of true friends and our first contemporaries. . . . Bureaucratic corruption, gangsters, and economic crisis, all has become nature in a growing body. And that is the whole story of America: a people that grows, that covers with its unbroken enthusiasm the errors it has already committed, and with great good will risks future errors." The true religion of this America is the "exaltation of man," and its so-called materialism, even its love of money, is a front for this abstract fury, "the impulse toward man which animates American youth. And all the weary aesthetes who think of themselves as contemporaries of Pericles . . . the journalists who have taken upon themselves the 'defense of the West' . . . impose on American civilization the stupidity of a phrase: materialistic civilization." It is this despised

---

*The confusing of the two views again has resulted from more recent Communist attempts to sponsor a higher anti-Americanism. At a meeting of the "Charlie Chaplin Cinematographic Society" in 1952, I was handed a leaflet in which a quotation from Pavese (one of his unfriendliest) was combined with a lengthy comment by Ilya Ehrenburg, the whole headed with the famous title of the pro-Fascist Cecchi, *America amara.*

and vital America, which "has no cemeteries to defend," that has invented a new kind of fiction and perfected a new medium, the movies, thus "instituting the first colloquy between the great masses of the world and a unified culture."

Needless to say, Pintor is aware of the possibility that his "anti-Romantic" America, center of resistance to a Romantic Germany which "celebrated the revolt of the myth against man," may itself be a myth, a local name and habitation for a state of mind. "In our words dedicated to America," he concludes his essay, "much may be ingenuous and inexact, much may refer to arguments perhaps extraneous to the historical phenomenon of the U.S.A. in its present form. But it matters little: because, even if the continent did not exist, our words would not lose their significance. This America has no need of a Columbus; it is discovered within ourselves; it is the land which is approached with the same faith and the same hope by the first immigrants and by whoever has decided to defend at the price of pains and error the dignity of the human lot."

Hier oder nirgends ist Amerika— once more! As soon as the self-conscious words are said, a myth is dying; and if it is possible to write about the Italian discovery of America, it is because a dream has become history. The older books on our country continue to be reprinted; the scattered essays of an earlier period are gathered together; the shop windows are full of American novels, and the translations continue. Everybody translates American books (even my doctor is working on a popular handbook about babies), but translation is no longer a passion, merely a habit or even an industry; and no longer is the latest book from the United States picked up with a sense of furious haste, as if somehow everything depended on it.

As early as 1947, Pavese was able to head a new essay, "The days are gone in which we discovered America!"; and the intellectuals, who just after the war were generally Communists and are now more and more merely disillusioned, have been explaining to themselves and everyone else for nearly five years now that they really translated American literature in order to find out what they themselves were not; that American books are no longer as good as they were in the 1930's;

that America, having lost Fascism as an ideal opponent, has lost its vitality; that the American G.I. has been Europeanized to the point of dissipating his "exotic and tragic straightforwardness"; etc., etc. Meanwhile, the more conservative writers who once "defended the West" against America have now discovered us as allies in a new "defense of the West." The very youngest generation is discovering new utopias, a few in Moscow, even more in the vanished Social Republic of Mussolini — but without real conviction or enthusiasm. It is, alas, a time for common sense: "Many countries in Europe and in the world are today laboratories where one creates form and style . . . and even one living in a monastery may say a new word."

One can foresee the discussion five thousand years from now, when the scraps of some of these documents are being dug out of Italian soil, as to whether there ever really was an America, or only a metaphor like Atlantis, a fable for poets . . .

CHAPTER FIVE

The "Good American"

I have been haunted, ever since my return to the United States from Italy, by the image of a typical discussion at the end of which, as inevitably as in a recurring dream, I find myself heated, shouting a little, defending America with a passionate self-righteousness I should like to disown. But it is a true recollection and I cannot disavow it. What *was* I doing, playing the earnest advocate, the patriot at bay — I who, by temperament and on principle, have always been a critic and dissenter, and who had hoped in Europe to open a dialogue based on fairness and moderation? I cannot say I was not forewarned. Before my departure, several friends had told me of their own experiences, of how they, too, had found themselves for the first time forced into the role of apologists and ambassadors extraordinary. But I did not take what they said quite seriously, understanding it as a figure of speech, a hyperbole to express their exasperation with European intellectuals.*

I was prepared to meet with frankness the Europeans who trotted out the conventional criticisms of our culture; to grant that some of us, many of us, indeed, are smug, boorish, conformist, contemptuous of what we do not understand, virtually cultureless. I was resolved not even to assert in protest what I have long known — that the average European has as little living connection with his country's traditional culture as any

---

*I use "European intellectuals" in an extended sense on the basis of limited experience. My first-hand acquaintance with intellectuals abroad was largely confined to Italy, but I believe it applies, in one degree or another, to most of the other countries of Western Europe — though not, I should suppose, to Great Britain.

Midwestern farmer; for I knew that in Europe at least no one is proud of such ignorance, that the European is likely to be in regard to culture a pretentious hypocrite rather than a surly Pharisee. And this difference I was ready to admit was a European advantage.

I suppose I had not quite realized that the European intellectual would not, as we ourselves do, hate our failings in us, but rather hate us for those failings, taking our faults for our essence. And surely I assumed that no European would forget that he had, indeed, learned of our faults from us; that his current picture of our world had been transmitted to him by those American novelists, of the last century and this, for whom we share an admiration; so that the European observer notoriously sees, even when he visits us, only a fictional America, the world he has learned to expect from Melville and Hawthorne, from Dreiser or Sherwood Anderson or William Faulkner. I had hoped that the European intellectual, in this sense the heir of an American tradition of dissent, would think of us as a society almost pitifully eager to confess its faults, to measure and assess them in the world's eye.

I should have realized (and in a way did) that Europeans have an odd habit of reading our most poetic books as anthropological documents. I had seen in New York, for instance, several years ago, Sartre's melodrama, *The Respectful Prostitute,* and knew what happened when one took Faulkner's parochial symbols of universal human guilt and endurance as a factual account of life in the specific American South. But such disingenuous misunderstandings seemed to me then peripheral and comic.

At any rate, I did not quite understand how anyone could overlook the fact that the myth of a "Bitter America" (Emilio Cecchi, the inventor of the phrase, was a leading critic of our literature) was made in the United States by writers who are as real a part of us as the Snopses or Babbitts whom they have created, and who, by these very creations, bear witness to a vigor and freedom of the imagination which is also America.

I had even hoped that my own small heterodoxies might serve as evidence that not all Americans think alike out of ignorance or choice or abject surrender. But I soon realized that any unorthodox comment I might make would be taken solely as testimony against my country, though I might personally be credited with a courage to which I had no claim. Whatever willingness I disclosed in conversation with my European acquaintances to admit vice or inadequacy in American society was most often regarded not as a sign that America still fostered in some of us the critical intelligence but as an indication of almost superhuman virtue on my part. Such evidence of virtue would be greeted with overt praise, and not a little concealed contempt; for I would have become not only a hero but also an accomplice — my off-the-cuff comments carefully distorted and filed away among the anti-American stereotypes of my auditors. It is only too easy to become the "Good American" of the anti-American Europeans; all one has to do is to talk before them precisely as one has always talked among friends at home, critically, skeptically, bitterly.

But the "Good" in "Good American" has exactly the tone and weight of the same adjective applied to the "Good Jew" of the anti-Semite. One is good in so far as he is different — i.e., not really a Jew or an American, not really the unmodifiable legendary figure of contempt. The anti-Americanism of many European intellectuals has reached the stage where it is almost immune to facts. An automatic selector has been built into the stereotype, which thus becomes self-sustaining and everlasting. The lowest common denominator of tourist making his expected gaffes, the American soldier abroad hailing all foreigners with a "Hey, boy!" — these count because they fit. But the American intellectual, the writer abroad who rejects the label of expatriate, the very novelists who have won universal acclaim — these somehow do not matter, except as they are willing to testify to the depravity of their country.

Some Americans (especially the young, whose own America is as mythic as that of their European friends) submit to the role imposed upon them, flattered by the social success it brings, and by the sense of belongingness that costs only a willingness to bear witness on demand. But most American intellectuals will not abide so ignoble an exploitation; and they fall into the counter-strategy of patriotic defense. It takes only a little while to bring to the surface of one's mind the virtues of his society, which he has, behind all criticism, always taken for granted: its hostility to hypocrisy, its eternal discontent.

He finds quickly that most Europeans are not only ignorant of these virtues but choose to remain so. A sufficiently platitudinous comment on our simplicity and animal vigor, or on the nastiness of McCarthy, is perfectly acceptable. But a favorable remark on the structure of our courts, or an unfavorable one on such legendary victims of them as Alger Hiss or the Rosenbergs, brings forth the supercilious smile, the unspoken but unmistakable rejoinder, "Propaganda!" Even literary remarks may stir suspicion; a derogatory word about the style of Theodore Dreiser or the criticism of F. O. Matthiessen, an unfavorable comment on a Negro poet — and one is labeled an apologist or the dupe of apologists. It is at this point that the shouting properly begins.

One soon learns that it is unwise to be polite about the most hackneyed and apparently harmless observation. Grant without qualification that American soldiers are ignorant, unacquainted with *The Scarlet Letter* and *Moby Dick,* and your interlocutor will follow up by observing in a conspiratorial tone, "It's easy for us [*us!*] to understand how such barbarians can be persuaded to use germ warfare against Korean peasants!" Or admit the abuses of Congressional investigating committees, and you will be expected to grant that the United States has resigned from Western civilization. One must refuse the gambit, protest loudly from the start.

To be sure, shouting is undignified and it solves no ultimate problems; but it leads to some interesting disclosures, perhaps clears the atmosphere that stifles real discussion. When you have cried out at last in exasperation, "What's the matter with you people? Why has the blind criticism of America become for you an obligatory assertion of your independence, while criticism of Russia is considered evidence of cowardice and venality? Surely when you compare the two countries . . ." — your European opposite number does not even let you finish.

"Naturally, there is no comparison," he tells you. "The Soviet Union has nothing in common with us. But America, now! When we criticize America, we are criticizing ourselves. Culturally you represent the most advanced stage of what we are all fast becoming."

Now one knows that this is, in a sense, true. American serious literature among the intellectuals, American mass culture among the people, moves inexorably into Europe. The Americanization of cultural life on all levels is a complement to, perhaps a cause of, anti-Americanism.

"Why do you make your forecast so sadly?" you ask your European friends. "Under our system you will survive. You will be harassed by movies, television, the comic books; but you will be permitted to fight back and you may win in the end. Under the Soviet system of mass culture, you would have to choose among conformism, silence, or death!"

"Would the death of an intellectual be so terrible an event?" Your interlocutor gives you his most cynical and pityingly European smile.

Here is the giveaway, the clue to why anti-Americanism has become a psychological necessity to many Europeans. The self-distrust of the intellectuals, their loss of faith in their function and in the value of their survival, blends with the Marxist dogma that one's own bourgeoisie (if you are a bourgeois, yourself!) is the worst enemy. Conditioned by this principled self-hatred, the European intellectual finds it hard to forgive America for being willing and able to let him live; and even harder to forgive himself for knowing that he could be, in our "McCarthy-ridden" land, if not happy at least unhappy in his customary way. Both these resentments he takes out on a mythicized image of all he hates, which he calls America.

It should be clear that even as self-hatred such a feeling is impure. For the European intellectual ends up via his anti-Americanism hating in himself and his world only what can be called "America," which is to say, "the Other." In the end, anti-Americanism of this type permits the European to indulge simultaneously in self-hatred and self-righteousness. So handy a psychological device is not readily surrendered.

Yet unless it be surrendered, unless the European intellectual learns to see the menace as well as the promise of his future not in a legendary America but in his actual self, self-pity will answer self-righteousness on both sides of the Atlantic — and we will delay yet longer in taking up that dialogue between the European and American intellectual upon which the solution of our problems, cultural and political, in part depends. Perhaps for now a real basis for disagreement is all we can hope to find; but certainly it is better for us to shout at each other in the same world rather than to smile condescendingly from our several nightmares.

CHAPTER SIX

Roman Holiday

It is difficult really to believe in Passover in Rome. By the time I had set out with my two older sons in search of matzos and a community Seder, Holy Week was at hand, and the streets were full of tourists: the Germans (back in force this year) carefully avoiding every eye and speaking only to each other; the seedy herds of Austrians following their guides from crowded bus to crowded bus; the Americans resting between churches at chic sidewalk cafés. It was no use to remind my boys that, after all, the Last Supper was a Seder, too; nothing could redeem the sense of moving in loneliness against the current that flowed toward the great basilicas, the celebration of the Tenebrae, the washing of the feet, and the final orgy of Easter Sunday when half a million foreigners and Romans would stand flank against flank, the visible body of Christendom awaiting the papal benediction.

It does not matter that scarcely any Roman will confess to a belief in religious dogma — that Rome is also a city of anti-clericalism, with a statue of Giordano Bruno presiding over its busiest market; what is *not* believed is always and everywhere the same. And into each house before Easter is past, the priest will come with holy water and a blessing (only the most ferocious Communist will bar his way) to wash believer and non-believer clean for the new year. The rhythms of the year, the rhythms of life itself, are the rhythms of the Church; and to be outside those rhythms as an American and a Jew is to be excluded as no one can ever be in America, where one's loneliness is what he shares with all his neighbors.

Yet the history and legend of Rome belong also to the Jews.

My sons and I travel down the Corso where the *ebrei* were once forced to race against asses; we skirt the Forum whose furthest limit is the Arch of Titus, with its image of the defeated Jordan borne on a stretcher; and my oldest boy asks me if it is true that no Jew is permitted to walk under that memorial to the fall of Jerusalem. I tell him that this was once a commonly held belief, and that, for all I know, the Orthodox may still hold it; and I go on to recount the legend of how the Golden Candlestick of the Temple fell from the hands of a triumphal Roman procession into the Tiber. My sons argue about whether it was an accident or an act of God, and they make up a story about finding it again, gold in the black mud.

But by this time the modern Roman Synagogue stands behind us, dignified and ugly, "built," as the guidebooks say, "in an imitation Assyro-Babylonian style" — and my mind has wandered off to the melancholy gossip I have heard lately about the former Chief Rabbi who has become a Catholic. I saw him once in the halls of the University where he now lectures, distrait and melancholy — or perhaps it is only that I expected, *wanted,* him to seem so.

An East European type, certain unofficial informants tell me, despised by the "old Roman" members of his congregation, he was left to bear the brunt when the Nazis came, to face the problem of raising the ransom they demanded. Almost all of the rich Jews were in hiding, my informants go on to explain, so that in the end it was the Pope who put up the money. Then, the war over, the aristocratic members of the congregation returned and began to conspire against their somewhat shabby leader, who therefore. . . . God knows whether any of it is true; but that the story itself should exist is enough to confirm my melancholy.

But today there are wreaths in front of the Synagogue, eight or ten of them draped with the Italian tricolor, their green leaves already dusty and turning brown, for they have been standing out since March 24, anniversary of the mass reprisals in the Ardeatine Caves, when sixty or seventy Jews, along with nearly three hundred other Romans, were killed by the Nazis. The monument to the dead, surmounted by the cross and the Jewish star, is brutally impressive (the Romans have never lost their flair for celebrating death); but more moving are the occasional small plaques on nondescript apartment houses — memorializing some individual victim who once lived there. His fellow-tenants, though they may have stolen his furniture once he was dead, will never forget him.

It is better to concentrate only on the dead. We stand beside the wreath and try to ignore the jaunty youngster who approaches us with a "Shalom" and offers to show us what is left of the "old synagogue" on a lower level. He speaks the sort of American a hep kid would have picked up from our soldiers, and his approach is precisely that of a street peddler offering to sell you something or change your money.

I try to tell my children something about the Ardeatine Caves, but I do not know the details they ask (What does the overhanging slab weigh? How old was the youngest victim?); and, anyhow, it is time to meet R. at the Portico of Octavia. More history. One part of the ancient portico has become the atrium of the church of Sant'Angelo, where for hundreds of years the Jews were forced on each Sabbath to hear a sermon urging conversion. Across the front of the church, in Hebrew and Latin, an inscription still thunders against the outcast and stiff-necked people. Beyond lies the old Ghetto; and, since R. has not yet arrived, we walk through the narrow, sodden streets, where my boys are impressed by the smell of filth and oppression. I do not tell them that all the poorer quarters of Rome share equally that ghetto smell.

In a little square that opens with typical suddenness around a fountain, a woman smiles at us hopefully and says, "Shalom." When we answer, "Shalom," we are surrounded by six or eight young men who appear out of nowhere. Each of them is the twin of the boy before the Synagogue; each has a genuine Swiss watch or Parker 51 pen to sell. My children haggle with them enthusiastically, and they ask us about America; until, even more suddenly than they materialized, they have all disappeared. We see only the soles of feet flashing down a twisting alley. Then we understand, for a cop is riding past, winking at us good-naturedly.

Meanwhile R. has come, and we discuss getting tickets for the community Seder. He knows, he says, a certain kosher

butcher shop where one can buy tickets from a man named
Polacco; he has this on excellent authority. So we go on to
the butcher shop, where no one will confess to having heard of
our Polacco. "Naturally," the butcher tells us, wiping more
blood off his hands onto an already sufficiently bloody apron,
"there are many Polaccos. Which one, is the question, and
what do we want him for anyway? Tickets for the community
Seder? Naturally, there are several Seders. Which one, is the
question? Right or left, or — "

Right or left? In our bewilderment, R. and I consult each
other in English; and someone taps me on the shoulder, draws
me aside: a middle-aged man with a loud, impatient voice,
who unexpectedly speaks excellent English. He is sure we
would only be interested in the most Orthodox celebration.
"Naturally, where you don't have to worry about the food!"
He turns aside to consult an elderly man with a beard who has
been pretending all along not to be with him; I think they are
speaking Yiddish, but they whisper and I can't be sure. "The
price will be only — " The tickets are already in his hand,
and he presses them enthusiastically into mine.

"But isn't there another?" I ask.

His face loses a little of its not quite plausible friendliness.
"Another Seder? Yes, there is one, not so kosher, for the
younger men, *very* young — " He looks me up and down
carefully, estimating my age. "Twenty-, twenty-five-year-olds.
If anyone wants such company!"

"But isn't there one," I insist, "officially sponsored by the
Synagogue?"

He regards me now with open contempt. "Officially sponsored? Children! A Seder sung by school children — " He
walks off, followed by his accomplice with the beard, who
looks back at us scornfully.

"Aha!" the butcher puts in at this point, "you want the
children. It's the Polacco *School* you want, not Polacco!"

But R. isn't satisfied. He turns suspiciously on the butcher.
"The *other* butcher, isn't he Polacco?" By this time, we do
not know how many real or imaginary Seders there are, or
what lies we may not be told in the interests of one faction
or another.

"Him? He's my brother. We're Terracini."

It had to be Terracini! Not that it isn't a common enough name among Italian Jews: Terracina, Terracini — there must be at least twenty-five in the Rome telephone book, including the dealer in Catholic church supplies; but R. and I are momentarily taken aback. Terracini is also the name of the Communist Senator who was one of the leaders of the recent rioting in the Parliament. That very day a session has ended with the Communists hurling inkbottles at the president of the Senate; and, the day before, R. watched Terracini himself banging his desk with a stick in concert with his colleagues, so that the roll call would not be heard. . . . And it was Terracini, too, who a couple of months before explained away at a meeting of Roman Jewish intellectuals the anti-Semitic trials in Prague, denouncing as a Nazi and hireling our friend Professor T., who rose to challenge his lies.

But at last we have found the Polacco School, a *yeshiva* across the Tiber from the Synagogue, and Terracini is forgotten. The tickets and the matzos are being sold next door to each other; and the children are so delighted at reaching the end of our quest that we are not even disturbed at the curtness with which the young women in charge treat us. Never have they been so busy, so important! "Speak up! Speak up!" They have no time to waste over our indecision.

While we try to figure out the difference between Swiss matzos and regular matzos, we are good-naturedly but efficiently mauled by the large crowd, which struggles for first place with elbow and knee in the approved Roman style. They even look just like Romans, my children insist sadly; they don't look like Jews at all. And the matzos are called *azzime,* and they, too, are different in texture and shape from what we are used to. Even the Pesach wine (we buy everything in sight, flour, meal, wine; there will be complaints when we get home, but who cares!) turns out to be the customary *vino bianco* from Frascati, not the syrupy red stuff to which the children have been looking forward. But later we are all relieved and happy, balancing the awkward packages in our arms; we smile with a new and perilous sense of having found a community as we pass others carrying similar packages.

Next door, the lady in charge is delighted to see us; there will be another American at the Seder, she tells us, a woman with a small child. We will be like manna to them, for neither of them can speak anything but English. The Seder will be wonderful, *wonderful!* If we listen we can hear the children practicing now. It is true; we can just make out their voices, faint and sweet. We are pleased to be so wanted; and as we depart enthusiastically, the friendly *signora* assures us that the rabbi himself will be there. It is to be the next night, and the children can hardly wait.

Perhaps the rabbi *was* there, after all: we could never find out. It is true that there was at the head table a fine-looking, white-bearded old man, very genteel; but he could equally well have been an Italian Senator (even Terracini!), and he seemed throughout the celebration as bored as everyone else. The "American" woman turned out to be a South African who did not have a child at all, and she regarded the R.'s and us with dim hostility from the start. We arrived too early, of course, though we had allowed a half-hour past the announced time; and so we began under the terrible burden of shame borne by the first guest. The children from the school were already at their prayers, dressed in the Italian student uniform; but the white-draped tables which formed a square around their long crowded one were empty; and the teacher who led them glanced up from his book to us with what seemed to me a look of annoyance.

It was hot, and I walked up and down outside with R., watching the arrival of the other paying guests. They turned out to be mostly very old ladies, who drove up in expensive cars and were helped trembling up the steps by their chauffeurs. If they participated at all in the Seder, beyond nibbling a little from each of the plates set before them, I certainly could not tell. They were quite obviously only performing an act of charity.

Three young men came in at the last minute, dark and reticent, but obviously more at home than we, though they confessed later to being Americans. They seemed quite familiar to me, the kind of good Jewish boys who refuse invitations to dinner because they have promised their mothers to keep kosher. After the Seder, they told us in horror about the heterodoxies of the Roman Synagogue, about which I can remember only the fact that it celebrates Bat Mitzvah, the equivalent of Bar Mitzvah but for girls. Imagine it!

The Seder service itself was badly cut and extremely dull, despite the real charm of the children (there was one girl with the black, ugly-beautiful face of a Bedouin) and the freshness of their voices. The only emotion I could sense was the anxiety of the teacher that they get through it all without too horrible a blunder. The sacrifice was just a bone on a plate, the egg only something to eat; and the earnestness of the performing children (even the littlest ones did not squirm noticeably until the end) was canceled out by the apathy of the paying guests. It was a relief when the voice of the young Bedouin broke and they all giggled; or when the pregnant young wife of the teacher, who sat at the head of the table, reached over to slap her own child, distinguished from the others by not wearing a smock.

Three buxom waitresses in pink uniforms trimmed with the shield of David dashed frantically about with bowls of water for washing, herbs for dipping, etc., but they never managed to get anything to us on time, chiefly because the old ladies took so long waving them away; and we were often passed by completely, to the distress of my boys.

The meal itself was served somewhat more efficiently, though, naturally, not until everything was satisfactorily cold. It was a completely Roman, non-Paschal meal: broth with *pasta,* slices of roast veal, and finally artichokes *alla giudea,* which is to say, Jewish style; for the Jews have long been famous as restaurateurs in Rome, and this is their most notable contribution to the local cuisine. It was somehow the last disconsolate touch. Whether the school children had the same fare or not was difficult to discern, for they did not eat off china, like the guests, but from a single metal bowl, like the setting in a prison or a Dickensian workhouse.

There was more singing after the meal, of course; and for this the parents of the children were let in, ruddy-faced working people, ruddier with washing and the excitement of seeing their offspring perform for the rich. They sat across from us on wooden benches against a farther wall, looking at the pale old ladies and parchment-yellowish rabbi-senator, not in hostility, but like representatives of a different species. Over their heads, a sign read in Hebrew: *With a strong hand!* And it would have taken a Strong Hand, indeed, to have brought us all out of Egypt together.

From this point on, the ceremony was speeded up until I could no longer follow it in the *Haggadah* I had brought along; the children had long since lost interest. Finally, the weary little students were permitted to sing one song in Italian and out of tune: the *"Chad gadya,"* into which they flung themselves with obvious relief, while their parents beamed in approval and the old ladies tried hard to smile. Only then the teacher, who had conducted and prompted in suppressed anguish all evening, rose to explain the symbolism of the egg, the herb, the bitters; but conversation was general on all sides, and the chairs of the children creaked. Only his wife listened to him, earnestly, one hand resting lightly on her swollen belly — poised for the quick slap if her own child grew restive.

Afterward, the old ladies and the bearded gentleman shook the hand of the teacher, who bowed gratefully like a superior servant, while the children trotted off, chattering, on the arms of their parents. I was ashamed to look at my wife or the R.'s, and I wanted even to apologize to my sons; but they were content, after all, for they had been able to wear their new skullcaps with the initials that their great-grandmother had sent them, and they had drunk two glasses of wine apiece. *Next year in Jerusalem!*

There was not a bus or streetcar in sight. The Communist trade unions had called a strike for that day in protest against the new election law passed by the Demo-Christians despite inkwell-throwing and desk-banging. When we had come down to the Seder, there had still been some transportation available; but now everyone had decided to enjoy the stoppage with that frightening good humor with which a Roman crowd greets any disorder. They stood in groups on the street corners joshing each other about getting home, or sat at the tables of sidewalk cafés cursing the government of the priests. All the old ladies had long since been whisked back to the fashionable quarters by their chauffeurs, and no one was left who knew it was Pesach.

We could not even find a taxi, and the R.'s decided to walk. *"Gut yontif,"* we called to each other as we parted, but we did not believe in it. After three-quarters of an hour, during which the children grew wearier and crankier, a bus came lumbering along which would carry us within a mile of our house. On the long ride home, my wife and I argued bitterly, chiefly because I, for some reason I can no longer recall, refused to admit how miserable the whole evening had been. Finally, I was yelling so loud that the two other passengers were watching me, delighted to be so entertained. Despite it all, the children had fallen asleep, and had to be awakened for the hike home; but they were surprisingly cheerful.

We had almost arrived, when someone hailed us. It was an American girl we knew and her Italian husband, both Jewish, both very young, and determinedly liberal.

"A big day," I said, thinking wearily of the holiday.

"The strike, you mean," he answered. "We really tied them up tight! This should be a lesson for De Gasperi and the Vatican, too." He seemed as enthusiastic about it as if he had arranged it all himself.

What was the use of arguing? "We're just coming from a Seder," I said to change the subject.

"A Seder! I'll bet." He laughed, hoping it was a joke.

"No — no — I'm serious. And tomorrow we're having another — a *real* one at home, so the kids will really understand it."

At that his wife could no longer bear it. "How can you do it?" she cried in horror, turning from me to my wife in search of an ally. "Do you mean to say that in this day and age you tell your children — " she could hardly manage to say it — "you teach them that we're the *Chosen People?*"

CHAPTER SEVEN

Looking Backward:
America from Europe

The end of the American artist's pilgrimage to Europe is the discovery of America. That this discovery is unintended hardly matters; ever since Columbus it has been normal to discover America by mistake. Even in the days when it was still fashionable to talk about "expatriation," the American writer was rediscovering the Michigan woods in the Pyrenees, or coming upon St. Paul in Antibes. How much more so now, when the departing intellectual does not take flight under cover of a barrage of manifestoes, but is sent abroad on a Fulbright grant or is sustained by the G.I. Bill. The new American abroad finds a Europe racked by self-pity and nostalgia (except where sustained by the manufactured enthusiasms of Stalinism), and as alienated from its own traditions as Sauk City; he finds a Europe reading in its ruins *Moby Dick,* a Europe haunted by the idea of America.

The American writer soon learns that for the European intellectual, as for him, there are two Americas. The first is the America of ECA and NATO, a political lesser evil, hated with a kind of helpless fury by those who cannot afford to reject its aid. The second is the America invented by European Romanticism — the last humanistic religion of the West, a faith become strangely confused with a political fact. To the European, the literature of America is inevitably purer, *realer* than America itself. Finding it impossible to reject the reality of death, and difficult to believe in anything else, the European is perpetually astonished at the actual existence of a land where only death is denied and everything else considered possible. Overwhelmed by a conviction of human impotence, he regards with horrified admiration a people who, because they are too naïve to understand theory, achieve what he can demonstrate to be theoretically impossible.

From Europe it is easy to understand the religious nature of the American belief in innocence and achievement; to see how even the most vulgar products of "mass culture," movies, comic books, sub-literary novels are the scriptures of this post-Christian faith — a faith that has already built up in Western Europe a sizable underground sect which worships in the catacombs of the movie theaters and bows before the images of its saints on the newsstands. A hundred years after the *Manifesto*, the specter that is haunting Europe is — Gary Cooper! Vulgar, gross, sentimental, impoverished in style — our popular sub-art presents a dream of human possibilities to starved imaginations everywhere. It is a wry joke that what for us are the most embarrassing by-products of a democratic culture, are in some countries almost the only democracy there is.

It seems to me that it has become absurd to ask whether a democratic society is worthwhile if it entails a vulgarization and leveling of taste. Such a leveling the whole world is bound to endure, with or without political guarantees of freedom; and the serious writer must envision his own work in such a context, realize that his own final meanings will arise out of a dialectical interplay between what he makes and a given world of "mass culture." Even the Stalinists, though they thunder against American jazz and cowboy suits for children, can in the end only kidnap our vulgar mythology for their own purposes. The sense of an immortality here and now, so important to American culture and parodied in Forest Lawn Cemetery, finds its Soviet counterpart in the mummification of Lenin or the touting of Bogomolets; while our faith in progress and achievement finds an *ersatz* in the Five Year Plans and the statistics doctored to assist belief. In its Russian form, what is possible in America has become compulsory, an unofficial rite has been made an orthodoxy. And even in our own country there have been occasional attempts to impose optimism (and eventually, one can only suppose, youth and naïveté) by law.

Yet, for us, hope has never become *just* official, a mere camouflage for actual exploitation, though indeed two generations of writers just before us believed so; and it was their sense of having alone penetrated our hoax of prosperity and happiness that nourished their feelings of alienation. The error of such writers was double (such errors, naturally, do not preclude good writing; being *right* is, thank God, optional for the writer). Not only was the American *mythos* real and effective, the very opposite of the hypocritical and barren materialism it seemed; but also everywhere, down to the last layer of babbittry, there existed beside this belief its complement: an unspoken realization of the guilt and terror involved in the American experience. In his sense of lonely horror, the writer was most one with everyone else.

Precisely the uncompromising optimism of Americans makes every inevitable failure to accomplish what can only be dreamed an unredeemable torment. Among us, nothing is winked at or shrugged away; we are being eternally horrified at dope-addiction or bribery or war, at things accepted in older civilizations as the facts of life, scarcely worth a tired joke. Even tax evasion dismays us! We are forever feeling our own pulses, collecting statistics to demonstrate the plight of the Negro, the prevalence of divorce, the failure of the female organ, the decline of family Bible reading, because we feel, we *know*, that a little while ago it was in our power, new men in a new world (and even yet there is hope), to make all perfect. How absurd of our writers to have believed that only they were pained at the failure of love and justice in the United States! What did they think our pulp literature of violence and drunkenness and flight was trying symbolically to declare? Why did they suppose that the most widely read fiction in America asks endlessly, "Whodunit? Where is the guilt?"

I think we are in the position now to understand that the concept of the "alienated artist" itself was as much a creation of the popular mind as of the artist. It is no accident that Edgar Allan Poe is both the prototype of the American Poet as Despised Dandy, and the inventor of the most popular genres of "mass culture." The image of the drunken, dope-ridden, sexually impotent, poverty-oppressed Poe is as native to the American mind as the image of the worker driving his new Ford into the garage beside the Cape Cod cottage; together they are the American's image of himself. Poe, Crane, Fitzgerald — each generation provides itself with its own lost artist — and their biographies are inevitable best-sellers.

I do not mean to imply that the role of scapegoat is not actually painful for the artist; his exclusion and scourging is the psychodrama of us all, but it is played out in earnest. Poe was in a certain sense a poseur, but he died of his pose; and the end of Fitzgerald was real terror. I want only to insist that the melancholy and rebellious artist has always been a collaborator in American culture — that it is only when he accepts the political or sentimental half-truths of democracy, when he says *yes* too soon, that he betrays his role and his countrymen — and that the popular mind at its deepest level is well aware of this.

Of all peoples of the world, we hunger most deeply for tragedy; and perhaps in America alone the emergence of a tragic literature is still possible. The masterpieces of our nine-teenth-century literature have captured the imagination of readers everywhere, precisely because their tragic sense of life renews vicariously the exhausted spirit. In Western Europe, the tragic tension no longer exists; it is too easy to despair and to fall in love with one's despair. Melodrama, *comèdie larmoyante,* learned irony, and serious parody — these are the forms proper to the contemporary European mind. In the orbit of Communism, on the other hand, despair has been legislated away; justice triumphs and the wicked suffer — there is no evil except in the other. Some lies are the very stuff of literature, but this is not among them; it breeds police forces rather than poetry.

Only where there is a real and advancing prosperity, a con-stant effort to push beyond all accidental, curable ills, all easy cynicism and premature despair toward the irreducible re-siduum of human weakness, sloth, self-love, and fear; only where the sense of the inevitability of man's failure does not cancel out the realization of the splendor of his vision, nor the splendor of his vision conceal the reality and beauty of his failure, can tragedy be touched. It is toward this tragic margin that the American artist is impelled by the neglect and love of his public. If he can resist the vulgar temptation to turn a quick profit by making yet one more best-selling parody of hope, and the snobbish temptation to burnish chic versions of elegant despair, the American writer will find that he has, after all, a real function.

Indeed, he is needed in a naked and terrible way, perhaps unprecedented in the history of Western culture — not as an entertainer, or the sustainer of a "tradition," or a recruit to a distinguished guild, but as the recorder of the encounter of the dream of innocence and the fact of guilt, in the only part of the world where the reality of that conflict can still be recognized. If it is a use he is after and not a reward, there is no better place for the artist than America.

PART THREE

THE END OF INNOCENCE

CHAPTER EIGHT

Montana; or The End of Jean-Jacques Rousseau

Hier oder nirgends ist Amerika.
GOETHE

There is a sense, disturbing to good Montanans, in which Montana is a by-product of European letters, an invention of the Romantic movement in literature. In 1743 a white man penetrated Montana for the first time, but there was then simply nothing to *do* with it: nothing yet to do economically in the first place, but also no way of assimilating the land to the imagination. Before the secure establishment of the categories of the *interessant* and the "picturesque," how could one have come to terms with the inhumanly virginal landscape: the atrocious magnificence of the mountains, the illimitable brute fact of the prairies? A new setting for hell, perhaps, but no background for any human feeling discovered up to that point; even *Sturm und Drang* was yet to come.

And what of the Indians? The redskin had been part of daily life in America and a display piece in Europe for a couple of hundred years, but he had not yet made the leap from a fact of existence to one of culture. *The Spirit of Christianity* of Chateaubriand and the expedition of Lewis and Clark that decisively opened Montana to the East were almost exactly contemporary, and both had to await the turn of the nineteenth century. Sacajawea, the Indian girl guide of Captain Clark (the legendary Sacajawea, of course, shorn of such dissonant realistic details as a husband, etc.), is as much a product of a new sensibility as Atala — and neither would have been possible without Rousseau and the beautiful lie of the Noble Savage. By the time the trapper had followed the explorer, and had been in turn followed by the priest and the prospector, George Catlin in paint and James Fenimore Cooper in the novel had fixed for the American imagination the fictive Indian and the legend of the ennobling wilderness: the primitive as Utopia. Montana was psychologically possible.

One knows generally that, behind the thin neo-Classical façade of Virginia and Philadelphia and Boston, the mythical meanings of America have traditionally been sustained by the Romantic sensibility (the hero of the first American novel died a suicide, a copy of *Werther* lying on the table beside him); that America had been unremittingly dreamed from East to West as a testament to the original goodness of man: from England and the Continent to the Atlantic seaboard; from the Atlantic seaboard to the Midwest; from the Midwest to the Rocky Mountains and the Pacific. And the margin where the Dream has encountered the resistance of fact, where the Noble Savage has confronted Original Sin (the edge of hysteria: of the twitching revivals, ritual drunkenness, "shooting up the town," of the rape of nature and the almost compulsive slaughter of beasts) we call simply: the Frontier.

Guilt and the Frontier are coupled from the first; but the inhabitants of a Primary Frontier, struggling for existence under marginal conditions, have neither the time nor energy to feel *consciously* the contradiction between their actuality and their dream. Survival is for them a sufficient victory. The contradiction remains largely unrealized, geographically sundered; for those who continue to dream the Dream are in their safe East (Cooper in Westchester or New York City), and those who live the fact have become total Westerners, deliberately cut off from history and myth, immune even to the implications of their own landscape. On into the second stage of the Frontier, it is dangerous for anyone who wants to *live* in a Western community to admire the scenery openly (it evokes the Dream); such sentiments are legitimate only for "dudes," that is to say, visitors and barnstorming politicians.

But the schoolmarm, pushing out before her the whore,

symbol of the denial of romance, moves in from the East to marry the rancher or the mining engineer (a critical cultural event intuitively preserved as a convention of the Western movie); and the Dream and the fact confront each other openly. The schoolteacher brings with her the sentimentalized Frontier novel, and on all levels a demand begins to grow for some kind of art to nurture the myth, to turn a way of life into a culture. The legend is ready-made and waiting, and speedily finds forms in the pulps, the movies, the Western story, the fake cowboy song — manufactured at first by absentee dudes, but later ground out on the spot by cultural "compradors." The Secondary Frontier moves from naïveté to an elementary consciousness of history and discrepancy; on the one hand, it falsifies history, idealizing even the recent past into the image of the myth, while, on the other hand, it is driven to lay bare the failures of its founders to live up to the Rousseauistic ideal. The West is reinvented!

At the present moment, Montana is in some respects such a Secondary Frontier, torn between an idolatrous regard for its refurbished past (the naïve culture it holds up defiantly against the sophistication of the East, not realizing that the East *requires* of it precisely such a contemporary role), and a vague feeling of guilt at the confrontation of the legend of its past with the real history that keeps breaking through. But in other respects, Montana has gone on to the next stage: the Tertiary or pseudo-Frontier, a past artificially contrived for commercial purposes, the Frontier as bread and butter.

In the last few years, Montana has seen an efflorescence of "Sheriff's Posses"; dude ranches; chamber of commerce rodeos, hiring professional riders; and large-scale "Pioneer Days," during which the bank clerk and the auto salesman grow beards and "go Western" to keep the tourist-crammed coaches of the Northern Pacific and the Great Northern rolling. The East has come to see its ancient dream in action — and they demand it on the line, available for the two-week vacationer. What the Easterner expects, the Montanan is prepared to give him, a sham mounted half in cynicism, half with the sense that this is, after all, what the West really means, merely made visible, vivid. There is, too, a good deal of "play" involved, a not wholly unsympathetic boyish pleasure in dressing up and pulling the leg of the outlander, which overlays and to some degree mitigates the cruder motives of "going Western." But in Montana's larger cities and towns a new kind of entrepreneur has appeared: the Rodeo and Pioneer Days Manager, to whom the West is strictly business. There is scarcely a Montanan who does not at one remove or another share in the hoax and in the take; who has not, like the nightclub Negro or the stage Irishman, become the pimp of his particularity, of the landscape and legend of his state.

Astonishingly ignorant of all this, I came from the East in 1941 to live in Montana, possessing only what might be called the standard Eastern equipment: the name of the state capital (mispronounced); dim memories of a rather absurd poem that had appeared, I believe, in *The Nation,* and that began: "Hot afternoons have been in Montana"; some information about Burton K. Wheeler; and the impression that Montana (or was it Idaho?) served Ernest Hemingway as a sort of alternative Green Hills of Africa. I had, in short, inherited a shabby remnant of the Romantic myth; and, trembling on an even more remote periphery of remembering, I was aware of visions of the Indian (out of Cooper and "The Vanishing American") and the Cowboy, looking very much like Tom Mix. I was prepared not to call cattle "cows," and resolutely to face down any student who came to argue about his grades armed with a six-shooter.

I was met unexpectedly by the Montana Face.* What I had been expecting I do not clearly know; zest, I suppose, naïveté,

---

*Natives of Montana, it is only fair to say, don't believe in, don't *see* the Montana Face, though of course they can describe the Eastern Face, black, harried, neurotic. It takes a long time before newcomers dare confide in each other what they all see, discover that they have not been enduring a lonely hallucination; but the unwary outlander who sets down for public consumption an account of what he has noticed before he forgets it or comes to find it irrelevant must endure scorn and even hatred. Since the first publication of this essay, I have been reviled for putting in print my (I had supposed) quite unmalicious remarks on the "Montana Face" by men who have never read the *Partisan Review* — indeed by some who, I suspect, do not read at all. Yet some of those most exercised have been quite willing to admit the inarticulateness, the starvation of sensibility and inhibition of expression, of which "the Face" is an outward symbol. To criticize the soul is one thing, to insult the body quite another!

a ruddy and straightforward kind of vigor — perhaps even honest brutality. What I found seemed, at first glance, reticent, sullen, weary — full of self-sufficient stupidity; a little later it appeared simply inarticulate, with all the dumb pathos of what cannot declare itself: a face developed not for sociability or feeling, but for facing into the weather. It said friendly things to be sure, and meant them; but it had no adequate physical expressions even for friendliness, and the muscles around the mouth and eyes were obviously unprepared to cope with the demands of any more complicated emotion. I felt a kind of innocence behind it, but an innocence difficult to distinguish from simple ignorance. In a way, there was something heartening in dealing with people who had never seen, for instance, a Negro or a Jew or a Servant, and were immune to all their bitter meanings; but the same people, I knew, had never seen an art museum or a ballet or even a movie in any language but their own, and the poverty of experience had left the possibilities of the human face in them incompletely realized.

"Healthy!" I was tempted to think contemptuously, missing the conventional stigmata of neurosis I had grown up thinking the inevitable concomitants of intelligence. It was true, certainly, that neither the uses nor the abuses of conversation, the intellectual play to which I was accustomed, flourished here; in that sense the faces didn't lie. They were conditioned by a mean, a parsimonious culture; but they were by no means mentally incurious — certainly not "healthy," rather pricked invisibly by insecurity and guilt. To believe anything else was to submit to a kind of parody of the Noble Savage, the Healthy Savage — stupidity as mental health. Indeed there was, in their very inadequacy at expressing their inwardness, the possibility of pathos at least — perhaps even tragedy. Such a face to stand at the focus of reality and myth, and in the midst of all the grandiloquence of the mountains! One reads behind it a challenge that demands a great, liberating art, a ritual of expression — and there is, of course, the movies.

The seediest moving-picture theater in town, I soon discovered, showed every Saturday the same kind of Western picture at which I had yelled and squirmed as a kid, clutching my box of jujubes; but in this context it was different. The children still eagerly attended, to be sure — but also the cowhands. In their run-over-at-the-heels boots and dirty jeans, they were apparently willing to invest a good part of their day off watching Gene and Roy, in carefully tailored togs, get the rustlers, save the ranch, and secure the Right; meanwhile making their own jobs, their everyday work into a symbol of the Natural Gentleman at home.

They *believed it all* — not only that the Good triumphs in the end, but that the authentic hero is the man who herds cattle. Unlike, for instance, the soldier at the war picture, they never snickered, but cheered at all the right places; and yet, going out ·from contemplating their idealized selves to get drunk or laid, they must somehow have felt the discrepancy, as failure or irony or God knows what. Certainly for the bystander watching the cowboy, a comic book under his arm, lounging beneath the bright poster of the latest Roy Rogers film, there is the sense of a joke on someone — and no one to laugh. It is nothing less than the total myth of the goodness of man in a state of nature that is at stake every Saturday after the show at the Rialto; and, though there is scarcely anyone who sees the issue clearly or as a whole, most Montanans are driven instinctively to try to close the gap.

The real cowpuncher begins to emulate his Hollywood version; and the run-of-the-mill professional rodeo rider, who has turned a community work-festival into paying entertainment, is an intermediary between life and the screen, the poor man's Gene Autry. A strange set of circumstances has preserved in the cowboy of the horse opera the Child of Nature, Natty Bumppo become Roy Rogers (the simple soul ennobled by intimacy with beasts and a virginal landscape), and has transformed his saga into the national myth. The boyhood of most living Americans does not go back beyond the first movie cowpuncher, and these days the kid without a cowboy outfit is a second-class citizen anywhere in America. Uncle Sam still survives as our public symbol; but actually America has come to picture itself in chaps rather than striped pants.*

*The myth of the Cowboy has recently begun to decline in popular favor, crowded out of the pulps by the Private Eye and the Space Pilot; and is being "secularized," like all archetypes that are dying, in a host of more or less highbrow reworkings of the archetypal theme: *Shane, High Noon*, etc.

Since we are comparatively historyless and culturally dependent, our claim to moral supremacy rests upon a belief that a
high civilization is at a maximum distance from goodness; the
cowboy is more noble than the earl.

But, on the last frontiers of Montana, the noble lie of Rousseau is simply a lie; the face on the screen is debunked by the
watcher. The tourist, of course, can always go to the better
theaters, drink at the more elegant bars beside the local property owner, dressed up for Pioneer Days. The cowhands go to
the shabby movie house off the main drag and do their drinking
in their own dismal places. And when the resident Easterner
or the visitor attempts to pursue the cowpuncher to his authentic dive, the owner gets rich, chases out the older whores, puts
in neon lights and linoleum — which, I suppose, serves everybody right.

But the better-educated Montanan does not go to the West-
erns. He discounts in advance the vulgar myth of the Cowboy,
where the audience gives the fable the lie, and moves the
Dream, the locus of innocence, back into a remoter past; the
surviving Cowboy is surrendered for the irrecoverable Pioneer.
It is the Frontiersman, the Guide who are proposed as symbols
of original nobility: Jim Bridger or John Colter, who outran
half a tribe of Indians, barefoot over brambles. But this means
giving up to begin with the possibilities that the discovery of
a New World had seemed to promise: a present past, a primitive *now*, America as a contemporary Golden Age.

When the point of irreconcilable conflict between fact and
fiction had been reached earlier, the Dream had been projected
westward toward a new Frontier — but Montana is a *last
Frontier;* there is no more ultimate West. Here the myth of
the Noble Woodsman can no longer be maintained in space
(the dream of Rousseau reaches a cul-de-sac at the Lions Club
luncheon in Two Dot, Montana); it retreats from geography
into time, from a discoverable West into the realm of an irrecoverable past. But even the past is not really safe.

Under the compulsion to examine his past (and there have
been recently several investigations, culminating in the Rockefeller Foundation-sponsored Montana Study), the contemporary Montanan, pledged to history though nostalgic for myth,

becomes willy-nilly an iconoclast. Beside a John Colter he discovers a Henry Plummer, the sheriff who was for years secretly a bandit; and the lynch "justice" to which Plummer was brought seems to the modern point of view as ambiguous as his career. The figure of the Pioneer becomes ever more narrow, crude, brutal; his law is revealed as arbitrary force, his motive power as — greed. The Montanan poring over his past comes to seem like those dance-hall girls, of whom a local story tells, panning the ashes of a road agent who had been lynched and burned, for the gold it had been rumored he was carrying. Perhaps there had never been any gold in the first place. . . .

+ It is in his relations with the Indian that the Pioneer shows to worst advantage. The record of those relations is one of aggression and deceit and, more remotely, the smug assumption that anything goes with "Savages." There are honorable exceptions among the early missionaries, but it is hard for a Protestant culture to make a Jesuit its hero. For many years the famous painting of Custer's Last Stand hung in the state university, where the students of history were being taught facts that kept them from taking Custer for the innocent Victim, the symbolic figure of the white man betrayed by crafty redskins that he is elsewhere. In Montana it is difficult to see the slaughter at Little Big Horn as anything but the result of a tactical error in a long warfare with whose motives one can no longer sympathize.

Driving across Montana, the conscientious sightseer who slows up for the signs saying "Historic Point 1000 Feet" can read the roadside marker beside US 2 at Chinook, which memorializes "The usual fork-tongued methods of the white which had deprived these Indians of their hereditary lands," "One of the blackest records of our dealings with the Indians . . ." Or at Poplar he can learn how the Assiniboines "are now waiting passively for the fulfillment of treaties made with 'The Great White Father.' "*

---

*I have since been told that these signs were composed by a self-conscious "rebel," who later accommodated to the ruling powers and grew rich; but such an account is itself an American Legend — and anyway the words of the "rebel" have never seemed inappropriate to legislator, road commissioner, or traveler on the highways.

It is at first thoroughly disconcerting to discover such confessions of shame blessed by the state legislature and blazoned on the main roads where travelers are enjoined to stop and notice. What motives can underlie such declarations: The feeling that simple confession is enough for absolution? A compulsion to blurt out one's utmost indignity? A shallow show of regret that protects a basic indifference? It is not only the road markers that keep alive the memory of the repeated betrayals and acts of immoral appropriation that brought Montana into existence; there are books to document the story, and community pageants to present it in dramatic form. The recollection of a common guilt comes to be almost a patriotic duty.

What is primarily involved is, I think, an attempt to *identify* with the Indian. Notice in the sentences quoted from highway signs the use of Indian terminology, "fork-tongued," "Great White Father" — the attempt to get *inside* the Indian's predicament. If the Pioneer seems an ignoble figure beside the Indian, it is perhaps because he was, as a Noble Savage, not quite savage enough; as close as he was to nature, the White Pioneer, already corrupted by Europe and civilization, could not achieve the saving closeness. "Civilization," a road sign between Hysham and Forsyth ironically comments, "is a wonderful thing, according to some people." The corpse of Rousseau is still twitching.

At the beginnings of American literature, Cooper had suggested two avatars of primeval goodness: Pioneer and Indian, the alternative nobility of Natty Bumppo and Chingachgook; and the Montanan, struggling to hang on to the Romantic denial of Original Sin, turns to the latter, makes the injured Chief Joseph or Sitting Bull the Natural Gentleman in place of the deposed Frontiersman.

But the sentimentalized Indian will not stand up under scrutiny either. "The only good Indian is a dead Indian," the old folk saying asserts; and indeed the Montanan who is busy keeping the living Indian in the ghetto of the reservation cannot afford to believe too sincerely in his nobility. The cruelest aspect of social life in Montana is the exclusion of the Indian; deprived of his best land, forbidden access to the upper levels

of white society, kept out of any job involving prestige, even
in some churches confined to the back rows, but of course
protected from whisky and comforted with hot lunches and
free hospitals — the actual Indian is a constant reproach to
the Montanan, who feels himself Nature's own democrat, and
scorns the South for its treatment of the Negro, the East for
its attitude toward the Jews. To justify the continuing exclusion of the Indian, the local white has evolved the theory that
the redskin is *naturally* dirty, lazy, dishonest, incapable of
assuming responsibility — a troublesome child; and this theory
confronts dumbly any attempt at reasserting the myth of the
Noble Savage.

The trick is, of course, to *keep* the Indian what he is, so
that he may be pointed out, his present state held up as a
justification for what has been done to him. And the trick
works; the Indian acts as he is expected to; confirmed in indolence and filth, sustained by an occasional smuggled bout
of drunkenness, he does not seem even to have clung to his
original resentment, lapsing rather into apathy and a certain
self-contempt. The only thing white civilization had brought
to the Indian that might be judged a good was a new religion;
but one hears tales now of the rise of dope-cults, of "Indian
Christianity," in which Jesus and Mary and the drug *peyote*
are equally adored. Once I traveled for two days with an
Indian boy on his way to be inducted into the Army; and,
when he opened the one paper satchel he carried, it contained:
a single extra suit of long underwear and forty comic books —
all the goods, material and spiritual, with which our culture
had endowed him.

On the side of the whites, there is, I think, a constantly
nagging though unconfessed sense of guilt, perhaps the chief
terror that struggles to be registered on the baffled Montana
Face. It is a struggle much more difficult for the Montana
"liberal" to deal with than those other conflicts between the
desired and the actual to which he turns almost with relief: the
fight with the Power Company or the Anaconda Copper Mining Company for the instruments of communication and the
possibilities of freedom. The latter struggles tend to pre-empt
the liberal's imagination, because on them he can take an

unequivocal stand; but in respect to the Indian he is torn with inner feelings of guilt, the knowledge of his own complicity in perpetuating the stereotypes of prejudice and discrimination. In that relationship he cannot wholly dissociate himself from the oppressors; by his color, he is born into the camp of the Enemy.

There is, of course, no easy solution to the Indian problem; but so long as the Montanan fails to come to terms with the Indian, despised and outcast in his open-air ghettos, just so long will he be incapable of coming to terms with his own real past, of making the adjustment between myth and reality upon which a successful culture depends. When he admits that the Noble Savage is a lie; when he has learned that his state is where the myth comes to die (it is here, one is reminded, that the original of Huck Finn ended his days, a respected citizen), the Montanan may find the possibilities of tragedy and poetry for which so far he has searched his life in vain.

CHAPTER NINE

Come Back to the Raft Ag'in, Huck Honey!

It is perhaps to be expected that the Negro and the homosexual should become stock literary themes in a period when the exploration of responsibility and failure has become again a primary concern of our literature. It is the discrepancy they represent that haunts us, that moral discrepancy before which we are helpless, having no resources (no tradition of courtesy, no honored mode of cynicism) for dealing with a conflict of principle and practice. It used once to be fashionable to think of puritanism as a force in our lives encouraging hypocrisy; quite the contrary, its emphasis upon the singleness of belief and action, its turning of the most prosaic areas of life into arenas where one's state of grace is tested, confuse the outer and the inner and make hypocrisy among us, perhaps more strikingly than ever elsewhere, *visible*, visibly detestable, the cardinal sin. It is not without significance that the shrug of the shoulders (the acceptance of circumstance as a sufficient excuse, the sign of self-pardon before the inevitable lapse) seems in America an unfamiliar, an alien gesture.

And yet before the continued existence of physical homosexual love (our crudest epithets notoriously evoke the mechanics of such affairs), before the blatant ghettos in which the Negro conspicuously creates the gaudiness and stench that offend him, the white American must make a choice between coming to terms with institutionalized discrepancy or formulating radically new ideologies. There are, to be sure, stopgap devices, evasions of that final choice; not the least interesting is the special night club: the "queer" café, the black-and-tan joint, in which fairy or Negro exhibit their fairy-ness, their Negro-ness as if they were mere divertissements, gags thought up for the laughs and having no reality once the lights go out and the chairs are piled on the tables by the cleaning women. In the earlier minstrel show, a Negro performer was required to put on with grease paint and burnt cork the formalized mask of blackness; while the queer must exaggerate flounce and flutter into the convention of his condition.

The situations of the Negro and the homosexual in our society pose quite opposite problems, or at least problems suggesting quite opposite solutions. Our laws on homosexuality and the context of prejudice they objectify must apparently be changed to accord with a stubborn social fact; whereas it is the social fact, our overt behavior toward the Negro, that must be modified to accord with our laws and the, at least official, morality they objectify. It is not, of course, quite so simple. There is another sense in which the fact of homosexual passion contradicts a national myth of masculine love, just as our real relationship with the Negro contradicts a myth of that relationship; and those two myths with their betrayals are, as we shall see, one.

The existence of overt homosexuality threatens to compromise an essential aspect of American sentimental life: the camaraderie of the locker room and ball park, the good fellowship of the poker game and fishing trip, a kind of passionless passion, at once gross and delicate, homoerotic in the boy's sense, possessing an innocence above suspicion. To doubt for a moment this innocence, which can survive only as *assumed,* would destroy our stubborn belief in a relationship simple, utterly satisfying, yet immune to lust; physical as the handshake is physical, this side of copulation. The nineteenth-century myth of the Immaculate Young Girl has failed to survive in any *felt* way into our time. Rather, in the dirty jokes shared among men in the smoking car, the barracks, or the dormitory, there is a common male revenge against women for having flagrantly betrayed that myth; and under the revenge, the rather smug assumption of the chastity of the revenging group, in so far as it is a purely male society. From what other source could arise that unexpected air of good clean fun which overhangs such sessions? It is this self-congratulatory buddy-buddiness, its astonishing naïveté that breed at once endless opportunities for inversion and the terrible reluctance to admit its existence, to surrender the last believed-in stronghold of love without passion.

It is, after all, what we know from a hundred other sources that is here verified: the regressiveness, in a technical sense, of American life, its implacable nostalgia for the infantile, at once wrong-headed and somehow admirable. The mythic America is boyhood — and who would dare be startled to realize that the two most popular, most *absorbed,* I am sure, of the handful of great books in our native heritage are customarily to be found, illustrated, on the shelves of the children's library. I am referring, of course, to *Moby Dick* and *Huckleberry Finn,* so different in technique and language, but alike children's books or, more precisely, *boys'* books.

There are the Leatherstocking Tales of Cooper, too, as well as Dana's *Two Years Before the Mast* and a good deal of Stephen Crane, books whose continuing favor depends more and more on the taste of boys; and one begins to foresee a similar improbable fate for Ernest Hemingway. Among the most distinguished novelists of the American past, only Henry James completely escapes classification as a writer of juvenile classics; even Hawthorne, who did write sometimes for children, must in his most adult novels endure, though not as Mark Twain and Melville submit to, the child's perusal. A child's version of *The Scarlet Letter* would seem a rather farfetched joke if it were not a part of our common experience. Finding in the children's department of the local library what Hawthorne liked to call his "hell-fired book," and remembering that *Moby Dick* itself has as its secret motto *"Ego te baptizo in nomine diaboli,"* one can only bow in awed silence before the mysteries of public morality, the American idea of "innocence." Everything goes except the frank description of adult heterosexual love. After all, boys will be boys!

What, then, do all these books have in common? As boys' books we should expect them shyly, guiltlessly as it were, to proffer a chaste male love as the ultimate emotional experience

— and this is spectacularly the case. In Dana, it is the narrator's melancholy love for the *kanaka*, Hope; in Cooper, the lifelong affection of Natty Bumppo and Chingachgook; in Melville, Ishmael's love for Queequeg; in Twain, Huck's feeling for Nigger Jim. At the focus of emotion, where we are accustomed to find in the world's great novels some heterosexual passion, be it "platonic" love or adultery, seduction, rape, or long-drawn-out flirtation, we come instead on the fugitive slave and the no-account boy lying side by side on a raft borne by the endless river toward an impossible escape, or the pariah sailor waking in the tattooed arms of the brown harpooner on the verge of their impossible quest. *"Aloha, aikane, aloha nui,"* Hope cries to the lover who prefers him to all his fellow-whites; and Ishmael in utter frankness tells us: "I found Queequeg's arm thrown over me in the most loving and affectionate manner. You had almost thought I had been his wife . . . he still hugged me tightly, as though naught but death should part us twain . . . Thus, then, in our heart's honeymoon, lay I and Queequeg — a cosy, loving pair . . . he pressed his forehead against mine, clasped me around the waist, and said that henceforth we were married."

In Melville, the ambiguous relationship is most explicitly rendered; almost, indeed, openly explained. Not by a chance phrase or camouflaged symbol (the dressing of Jim in a woman's gown in *Huck Finn*, for instance, which can mean anything or nothing at all), but in a step-by-step exposition, the Pure Marriage of Ishmael and Queequeg is set before us: the initial going to bed together and the first shyness overcome, that great hot tomahawk-pipe accepted in a familiarity that dispels fear; next, the wedding ceremony itself (for in this marriage like so many others the ceremonial follows the deflowering), with the ritual touching of foreheads; then, the queasiness and guilt the morning after the *official* First Night, the suspicion that one has joined himself irrevocably to his own worst nightmare; finally, a symbolic portrayal of the continuing state of marriage through the image of the "monkey rope" which binds the lovers fast waist to waist (for the sake of this symbolism, Melville changes a *fact* of whaling practice — the only time in the book), a permanent alliance that provides mutual protection but also threatens mutual death.

Physical it all is, certainly, yet somehow ultimately innocent. There lies between the lovers no naked sword but a
childlike ignorance, as if the possibility of a fall to the carnal
had not yet been discovered. Even in the *Vita Nuova* of Dante,
there is no vision of love less offensively, more unremittingly
chaste; that it is not adult seems beside the point. Ishmael's
sensations as he wakes under the pressure of Queequeg's arm,
the tenderness of Huck's repeated loss and refinding of Jim,
the role of almost Edenic helpmate played for Bumppo by
the Indian — these shape us from childhood: we have no
sense of first discovering them or of having been once without them.

Of the infantile, the homoerotic aspects of these stories we
are, though vaguely, aware; but it is only with an effort that
we can wake to a consciousness of how, among us who at the
level of adulthood find a difference in color sufficient provocation for distrust and hatred, they celebrate, all of them, the
mutual love of *a white man and a colored*. So buried at a
level of acceptance which does not touch reason, so desperately repressed from overt recognition, so contrary to what
is usually thought of as our ultimate level of taboo — the
sense of that love can survive only in the obliquity of a symbol,
persistent, obsessive, in short, an archetype: the boy's homoerotic crush, the love of the black fused at this level into a
single thing.

I hope I have been using here a hopelessly abused word
with some precision; by "archetype" I mean a coherent pattern
of beliefs and feelings so widely shared at a level beneath consciousness that there exists no abstract vocabulary for representing it, and so "sacred" that unexamined, irrational restraints inhibit any explicit analysis. Such a complex finds a
formula or pattern story, which serves both to embody it, and,
at first at least, to conceal its full implications. Later, the
secret may be revealed, the archetype "analyzed" or "allegorically" interpreted according to the language of the day.

I find the complex we have been examining genuinely
mythic; certainly it has the invisible character of the true archetype, eluding the wary pounce of Howells or Mrs. Twain, who

excised from *Huckleberry Finn* the cussing as unfit for children, but who left, unperceived, a conventionally abhorrent doctrine of ideal love. Even the writers in whom we find it attained it, in a sense, dreaming. The felt difference between *Huckleberry Finn* and Twain's other books must lie in part in the release from conscious restraint inherent in the author's assumption of the character of Huck; the passage in and out of darkness and river mist, the constant confusion of identities (Huck's ten or twelve names; the question of who is the real uncle, who the true Tom), the sudden intrusions into alien violences without past or future, give the whole work, for all its carefully observed detail, the texture of a dream. For *Moby Dick* such a point need scarcely be made. Even Cooper, despite his insufferable gentlemanliness, his tedium, cannot conceal from the kids who continue to read him the secret behind his overconscious prose: the childish, impossible dream. D. H. Lawrence saw in him clearly the boy's Utopia: the absolute wilderness in which the stuffiness of home yields to the wigwam, and "My Wife" to Chingachgook.

I do not recall ever having seen in the commentaries of the social anthropologist or psychologist an awareness of the role of this profound child's dream of love in our relation to the Negro. (I say Negro, though the beloved in the books I have mentioned is variously Indian and Polynesian, because the Negro has become more and more exclusively for us *the* colored man, the colored man *par excellence.*) Trapped in what have by now become shackling clichés — the concept of the white man's sexual envy of the Negro male, the ambivalent horror of miscegenation — they do not sufficiently note the complementary factor of physical attraction, the archetypal love of white male and black. But either the horror or the attraction is meaningless alone; only together do they make sense. Just as the pure love of man and man is in general set off against the ignoble passion of man for woman, so more specifically (and more vividly) the dark desire which leads to miscegenation is contrasted with the ennobling love of a white man and a colored one. James Fenimore Cooper is our first poet of this ambivalence; indeed, miscegenation is the secret theme of the Leatherstocking novels, especially of

The Last of the Mohicans. Natty Bumppo, the man who boasts always of having "no cross" in *his* blood, flees by nature from the defilement of all women, but never with so absolute a revulsion as he displays toward the *squaw* with whom at one point he seems at the point of being forced to cohabit; and the threat of the dark-skinned rapist sends pale woman after pale woman skittering through Cooper's imagined wilderness. Even poor Cora, who already has a fatal drop of alien blood that cuts her off from any marriage with a white man, in so far as she is white cannot be mated with Uncas, the noblest of redmen. Only in death can they be joined in an embrace as chaste as that of males. There's no good woman but a dead woman! Yet Chingachgook and the Deerslayer are permitted to sit night after night over their campfire in the purest domestic bliss. So long as there is no mingling of blood, soul may couple with soul in God's undefiled forest.

Nature undefiled — this is the inevitable setting of the Sacred Marriage of males. Ishmael and Queequeg, arm in arm, about to ship out, Huck and Jim swimming beside the raft in the peaceful flux of the Mississippi — here it is the motion of water which completes the syndrome, the American dream of isolation afloat. The notion of the Negro as the unblemished bride blends with the myth of running away to sea, of running the great river down to the sea. The immensity of water defines a loneliness that demands love; its strangeness symbolizes the disavowal of the conventional that makes possible all versions of love. In *Two Years Before the Mast,* in *Moby Dick,* in *Huckleberry Finn* the water is there, is the very texture of the novel; the Leatherstocking Tales propose another symbol for the same meaning: the virgin forest. Notice the adjectives — the virgin forest and the forever inviolable sea. It is well to remember, too, what surely must be more than a coincidence, that Cooper, who could dream this myth, also invented for us the novel of the sea, wrote for the first time in history the sea story proper.

The rude pederasty of the forecastle and the captain's cabin, celebrated in a thousand jokes, is the profanation of a dream; yet Melville, who must have known such blasphemies, refers to them only once and indirectly, for it was *his* dream that they threatened. And still the dream survives; in a recent book by Gore Vidal, an incipient homosexual, not yet aware of the implications of his feelings, indulges in the reverie of running off to sea with his dearest friend. The buggery of sailors is taken for granted everywhere, yet is thought of usually as an inversion forced on men by their isolation from women; though the opposite case may well be true: the isolation sought more or less consciously as an occasion for male encounters. At any rate, there is a context in which the legend of the sea as escape and solace, the fixated sexuality of boys, the myth of the dark beloved, are one. In Melville and Twain at the center of our tradition, in the lesser writers at the periphery, the archetype is at once formalized and perpetuated. Nigger Jim and Queequeg make concrete for us what was without them a vague pressure on the threshold of our consciousness; the proper existence of the archetype is in the realized character, who waits, as it were, only to be asked his secret. Think of Oedipus biding in silence from Sophocles to Freud!

Unwittingly, we are possessed in childhood by these characters and their undiscriminated meaning, and it is difficult for us to dissociate them without a sense of disbelief. What — these household figures clues to our subtlest passions! The foreigner finds it easier to perceive the significances too deep within us to be brought into focus. D. H. Lawrence discovered in our classics a linked mythos of escape and immaculate male love; Lorca in *The Poet in New York* grasped instinctively (he could not even read English) the kinship of Harlem and Walt Whitman, the fairy as bard. But of course we do not have to be conscious of what possesses us; in every generation of our own writers the archetype reappears, refracted, half-understood, but *there*. In the gothic reverie of Capote's *Other Voices, Other Rooms,* both elements of the syndrome are presented, though disjunctively: the boy moving between the love of a Negro maidservant and his inverted cousin. In Carson McCullers' *Member of the Wedding,* another variant is invented: a *female* homosexual romance between the boy-girl Frankie and a Negro cook. This time the Father-Slave-Beloved is converted into the figure of a Mother-Sweetheart-Servant, but remains still, of course, satisfactorily black.

It is not strange, after all, to find this archetypal complex in latter-day writers of a frankly homosexual sensibility; but it recurs, too, in such resolutely masculine writers as Faulkner, who evokes the myth in the persons of the Negro and the boy of *Intruder in the Dust*.

In the myth, one notes finally, it is typically in the role of outcast, ragged woodsman, or despised sailor ("Call me Ishmael!"), or unregenerate boy (Huck before the prospect of being "sivilized" cries out, "I been there before!") that we turn to the love of a colored man. But how, we cannot help asking, does the vision of the white American as a pariah correspond with our long-held public status: the world's beloved, the success? It is perhaps only the artist's portrayal of *himself*, the notoriously alienated writer in America, at home with such images, child of the town drunk, the hapless survivor. But no, Ishmael is in all of us, our unconfessed universal fear objectified in the writer's status as in the outcast sailor's: that compelling anxiety, which every foreigner notes, that we may not be loved, that we are loved for our possessions and not our selves, that we are really — *alone*. It is that underlying terror which explains our incredulity in the face of adulation or favor, what is called (once more the happy adjective) our "boyish modesty."

Our dark-skinned beloved will take us in, we assure ourselves, when we have been cut off, or have cut ourselves off, from all others, without rancor or the insult of forgiveness. He will fold us in his arms saying, "Honey" or "Aikane"; he will comfort us, as if our offense against him were long ago remitted, were never truly *real*. And yet we cannot ever really forget our guilt; the stories that embody the myth dramatize as if compulsively the role of the colored man as the victim. Dana's Hope is shown dying of the white man's syphilis; Queequeg is portrayed as racked by fever, a pointless episode except in the light of this necessity; Crane's Negro is disfigured to the point of monstrosity; Cooper's Indian smolders to a hopeless old age conscious of the imminent disappearance of his race; Jim is shown loaded down with chains, weakened by the hundred torments dreamed up by Tom in the name of bulliness. The immense gulf of guilt must not be mitigated any more than the disparity of color (Queequeg is not merely brown but monstrously tattooed; Chingachgook is horrid with paint; Jim is portrayed as the sick A-rab died blue), so that the final reconciliation may seem more unbelievable and tender. The archetype makes no attempt to deny our outrage as fact; it portrays it as meaningless in the face of love.

There would be something insufferable, I think, in that final vision of remission if it were not for the presence of a motivating anxiety, the sense always of a last chance. Behind the white American's nightmare that someday, no longer tourist, inheritor, or liberator, he will be rejected, refused, he dreams of his acceptance at the breast he has most utterly offended. It is a dream so sentimental, so outrageous, so desperate, that it redeems our concept of boyhood from nostalgia to tragedy.

In each generation we *play out* the impossible mythos, and we live to see our children play it: the white boy and the black we can discover wrestling affectionately on any American sidewalk, along which they will walk in adulthood, eyes averted from each other, unwilling to touch even by accident. The dream recedes; the immaculate passion and the astonishing reconciliation become a memory, and less, a regret, at last the unrecognized motifs of a child's book. "It's too good to be true, Honey," Jim says to Huck. "It's too good to be true."

CHAPTER TEN

Images of Walt Whitman

It is difficult to remember that *Leaves of Grass* is, in its conception at least, an anonymous poem. Even its author seems more than once in the course of thirty years of revision to have forgotten that fact; and certainly he became convinced before the end of his life that it was a guilty secret, to be hidden with all the resources of a furtiveness of which he liked to boast. The signed proem, the endless insistence upon the first person, the deliberate confusion of the Mask and the self — all these come to conceal the truth which the authorless title page of the first edition confesses: that the "Walt Whitman" of *Leaves of Grass* is a persona really created by the poems it fictionally creates. An "eidolon" Whitman preferred to call it in his own highfalutin vocabulary, an "avatara," or more simply, "My Fancy." At the end of his life, he confesses under this name the doubleness of image and self:

> Good-bye my Fancy!
> Farewell dear mate, dear love!
> I'm going away, I know not where,
> Or to what fortune, or whether I may ever see you again,
> So Good-bye my Fancy.

It is his farewell to his truest love, cherished with a passion beyond "amativeness" or "adhesiveness," and he will not admit finally that even dying can sever them.

> Yet let me not be too hasty,
> Long indeed have we lived, slept, filter'd, become really blended into one;
> Then if we die we die together, (yes, we'll remain one,) . . .
> May-be it is yourself now really ushering me to the true songs, (who knows?)
> May-be it is you the mortal knob really undoing, turning . . .

There is the real romantic madness in this (and the metaphysics which lies beyond it), the irrational conviction that made Balzac cry out on his deathbed for a doctor of his own inventing, and which leads Whitman to dream that he and his fictive "Walt" will share all eternity.

But we must not let the final metaphysics blind us to the initial assumption upon which the wit and pathos of the poems really depend. Emerson, who felt so deeply into *Leaves of Grass* in his first reading, knew its namelessness, realized that the poem's "Walt Whitman" could not really exist. "I did not know until I last night saw the book advertised in a newspaper that I could trust the name as real and available for a post-office," he wrote to Whitman; but he let the newspaper fact convince him, and opened a correspondence that could only end in comedy and equivocation. It was not, of course, "Walt" who answered but "Walt's" promoter, rubbing his hands together and bowing like a salesman over his shoddy goods. "Master, I am a man who has perfect faith. Master, we have not come through centuries, tastes, heroisms, fables to halt in this land today. . . ."

It sounds like an impersonation, even a parody, and in a sense it is. Later, Whitman was to learn to play his own eidolon with more conviction in reviews, introductions, and conversation; but never, except in his most intense poetic moments, could he help somehow travestying the beloved Fancy that possessed him only when it would. I do not share an admiration for Whitman's prose, which has for me generally the sense of pushing, thrusting — being by brute force Walt Whitman. The comparison suggests itself to the medium who feels obliged to fake at blank moments the real experience that fails him.

It is Whitman's own fault (and that of the disciples whom he suffered only too willingly) that metaphors of table tapping and the Beyond come so readily to our minds. One does not become a child of nature in the nineteenth century by attempting to eschew culture; one becomes, in so far as he fails, a *literary* version of the child of nature; and, in so far as he succeeds, a creature of subculture: of the world of "cosmic consciousness" and phrenology that lurks beneath the surface of ideas proper. In the latter sense, Whitman is the Mary Baker Eddy of American poetry; in the former, he is its Ossian; and it is upon the literary analogy that I want to insist in order to redeem him from animal magnetism to art.

Ossian and Chatterton, the examples of the faked antique, the artificial "natural," of the higher hoax as Romantic poetry, suggest themselves; and Ossian, at least, Whitman has confessed to feeling as a temptation to be resisted. Whitman has actually much in common with such poets, especially the sense (one suspects) that the seeming fraud is the real truth, that the writer is truly possessed by the spirit he seems to invent, but also the anonymity prompted by the desire both to take in the reader and to establish the higher truth of the impersonation. In the Ossianic poet only the fictive singer is real; it is McPherson who does not exist — and if there is no forger there can be no forgery. Whitman has the advantage, to be sure, of playing a contemporary role, so that he is free to drop the cumbersome device of the "translated" or "discovered" manuscript — and has only to become in public life the person he invents, that is to say, to counterfeit himself rather than the text.

It is tempting to the stern moralist to see Whitman as the tragic victim of his own imposture. As the years and editions went by, the name "Walt Whitman" crept from its place in the poem to the spine of the book; and the anonymous author almost irrevocably disappeared, lying, distorting, destroying all evidence of any life outside the legend. Even his face changed, along with his stance and costume, as he willed himself from photograph to photograph into the image of the Rowdy, the Christ, the Workman's Friend, the Beard and the Butterfly, the Good Gray Poet. The one portrait of the anonymous author, an indolent dandy with a pert beardlet, shocks us. We tend to believe only what the poem tells us, that Walt never dressed in black, that he is

> Of pure American breed, of reckless health, his body perfect, free from taint from top to toe, free forever from headache and dyspepsia, clean-breathed
> Ample-limbed, a good feeder ... bearded, calm, unrefined ...

The unexpected revelations of the autopsy ("the left suprarenal capsule tubercular . . . a cyst the size of a pigeon's egg") or the glimpses in the accounts of early acquaintances of the shy misfit who drank only water and was never "bothered up" by a woman — these affect us like slander: nature slandering art, the actual the mythical.

But Whitman was finally the master of the actual, achieving by sheer will the Mask he dreamed. It is revealing to see him through the letters of *The Wound-Dresser*, walking the wards of the Washington hospitals during the Civil War: oppressed by headaches, worried about his weight, fussing like an old grandmother with his jars of jam, secretly titillated by all those beautiful young men so touchingly maimed; and yet somehow *really* exuding the strength and health he did not possess, convincing and helping others by his mythic powers; and paying for it all finally, paying for the legend of absolute participation, the boast: "I was there!"

By the time he had invented the Good Gray Poet, he had burned away all of himself that was not the image. "The secret" at which he eternally hinted was now untellable; perhaps he had actually forgotten it. With the death of his mother, the anonymous poet (who had been, above all, that mother's boy) was dead; and Whitman's subsequent paralysis was a declaration, as it were, that his body was now quite simply the book — to be slipped into the blouses of young men, to lie next to their flesh in innocence.

> Or if you will, thrusting me beneath your clothing,
> Where I may feel the throbs of your heart or rest upon your
> hip . . .

The poem had become a man, but the man in turn had become the poem. If this is a "pose" or "fraud," it is not one which we can despise.

No, if we are uncomfortable these days with Walt Whitman, it is not because he pretended to be what he was not; our judgments are not so simple. "Above all to thine own self be true" was good enough advice in the mind of one surer than we are what *is* the self. It is because the motives of his masquerade were so literary and conventional, and the image of the poet he proposed himself such a ragbag of *Versunkene*

Kulturgüte, Rousseau, Goethe, George Sand, Carlyle, Emerson, and God knows what else, eked out with phrenology and Fourth of July rhetoric, that we hesitate to accept him. If Whitman were really the monster of health and sympathy he paints himself, really the solemn discoverer of a New Sex or even of a hypostasized America as his early followers came to believe, we should not abide him for a moment. It is the poet who feared literature, the sly old maid finally trapped by his own cunning, who is *our* Whitman; and the point of *our Leaves of Grass* lies precisely in the distance between the poet and his eidolon. If that distance did not exist, Whitman would have been laughed out of existence by the first sophomore who snickered at "There is all that lot of me, and so luscious . . ."

I remember not many years ago a black-bordered notice in *Furioso,* advising certain rejected contributors that Walt Whitman was dead! And it is true that *a* Walt Whitman, a series of Walt Whitmans, has been destroyed, leaving only the poet we were not sure for a while was there at all: the poet who peers slyly from behind his most portentous statements to tip us the wink:

> To begin with take warning, I am surely different from what you suppose;
> Do you suppose you will find in me your ideal? . . .
> Do you think I am trusty and faithful?
> Do you see no further than this façade, this smooth and tolerant manner of me?
> Do you suppose yourself advancing on real ground toward a real heroic man?

or who, in double irony, speaks as the persona doubting the reality of the Whitman who creates it: "that shadow my likeness" who goes "chattering, chaffering" about the business of earning a living. "How often," remarks the poetic image coolly, "I question and doubt whether that is really me." The continual trifling with the illusion in *Leaves,* the ambiguity of the "I's" and the shifting irony of their confrontations ("O take my hand Walt Whitman! What do you hear Walt Whitman?"): this is far from the rant of a naïvely egoistic poet; it is a mannerist device, subtle and witty. To remember that

Leaves of Grass is an anonymous poem is to notice that it is a humorous one.

This is a sense of Whitman long lost behind the constructions of those searching the poem for "a real heroic man," or hopefully taking its size for a guaranty of its epic qualities. But the lyrical impulse swollen to epic proportions (this is a discovery of our age) produces either conscious irony or unwitting absurdity. In Whitman there is much of both; the latter has been pointed out sufficiently by all but the most fervent apologists; the former has been noticed sympathetically in the past only by Constance Rourke. "At the same time he remained within a sphere which . . . had been defined in popular comedy, that of the acutely self-aware." Whitman was not unconscious of this, and his confession of his awareness should not be held against him as Esther Shephard has tried to do. "I pride myself on being a real humorist underneath everything else," he once remarked. And to someone who warned, "After all, you may end up as a comedian," he responded, "I might easily end up worse." And he did, poor Walt Whitman, he *did!* But this he foresaw, too.

> Nor will my poems do good only, they will do just as much evil, perhaps more,
> For all is useless without that which you may guess at many times and not hit, that which I hinted at . . .

Out of his image of himself, not only the living, wittily qualified eidolon of his best lines, but out of the ersatz of that eidolon provided by the poetry at its worst, out of ghostwritten adulatory reviews and memoirs there emerged a quadruple figure with a fictional life — the Prophet of the New Era, the Faith Healer, the Sexual Emancipator, the Democrat at Home. The "hot, little" subprophets of the first generation, Burroughs and O'Connor and Bucke, soon detached the image of the Prophet, confronting lines from *Leaves* with lines from the Upanishads, suggesting a comparison with that other notable carpenter's son, Jesus; defining the state in which the Mask of Walt possessed the poet with Dr. Bucke's "Cosmic Consciousness"; in short, turning Whitman's poem into the scriptures of yet another homemade American religion. "Has our age produced a Christ — a Buddha? Has it given us a New Bible? I believe that in Walt Whitman we have the Prophet of a New Era, and that in his Leaves of Grass we have a book that will one day become a Bible to many seekers after light . . ." Within a generation the converts to the New Belief, the Whitmaniacs at large, had become a standard literary type. What had the poet done to deserve it?

Certainly, there is in him a vagueness, a failure to distinguish the poetic experience from the velleities that surround it, which blurs out into religiosity. It cannot be denied that Whitman wrote at times the sort of indeterminately ambitious verse that has been defined as "spilt religion" — and those to whom "spilt religion" is the only acceptable kind can hardly be blamed for finding in him evidences of their kind of sainthood. It must be said, further, that Whitman exemplifies a modern mystery, a kind of "conversion" (or, perhaps, "possession": one scarcely knows what to call it), elsewhere found in Rousseau, in which a third-rate mind, sentimental, obtuse, and indolent, is illuminated with inexplicable suddenness by reading a phrenologist's report or the announcement of an essay contest in a local newspaper. But it is not the cosmos that inspires Rousseau or Whitman, not any Otherness — but precisely the dazzling vision of themselves. In their moments of ecstasy what is made flesh is not God but Jean-Jacques or Walt.

Whitman as Christ has fared ill in our age that moves toward the poles of orthodoxy or unbelief, and from either pole regards the religioid with contempt. The image of the Source of Radiant Health has not done much better. The more intellectual turn to the analyst's couch or the orgone box for renewal, and the vulgar have their own non-literary prophets. What Mary Baker Eddy does not sufficiently cover ("I am he bringing help for the sick as they pant on their beds"), Dale Carnegie has claimed as his birthright ("Do you not see how it would serve to have such a body and soul that . . . everyone is impressed with your personality?").

In his role of Sexual Emancipator, however, Whitman has had a more successful career. About exactly what *kind* of emancipation Whitman promises, there has been considerable disagreement, some finding in him the celebrator of paganism, a free heterosexual life; others (André Gide, for example) discovering comfort and reassurance for the homosexual, the normalizing of the abnormal; still others presenting him as the celebrator, if not the inventor, of what the Germans call the *Zwischenstufe,* what Edward Carpenter has translated as "the Intermediate Sex." As a deliverer of *verse* from sexual taboos, a forerunner of D. H. Lawrence, willing to be abused and abandoned to redeem the phallus and the orgasm to the imagination, Whitman deserves the credit he has been given. It is not, however, to the poems but to an image of Whitman that the legend of the Sexual Emancipator refers, to an image he himself sponsored of himself as the Defender of the Body against the overweening claims of the soul; as the Deliverer from Christianity with its antithesis of flesh and spirit and its distrust of passion; as the savior not of poetry but of *us.*

Those who would preserve this legend of Whitman as the spokesman for total physical love find themselves in the uncomfortable position of having to underestimate the role of homosexuality in his verse. Havelock Ellis is typical in this regard, brushing aside the homosexual sensibility as "negligible," and crying aloud that "Whitman represents for the first time since Christianity swept over the world, the reintegration, in a sane and whole hearted form, of the instincts of the entire man." In his own neo-Freudian terms, Ellis recapitulates the new-religious interpretation of Whitman as a beneficent anti-Christ. "Here is no thing of creeds and dogmas. Here is no stupefying list of 'Thou shalts' and 'Thou shalt nots' . . . To Whitman the Devil is dead, and the forces of good are slowly but surely working for the salvation of all." Reading for the "devil" God in any of the conventional senses of the word (He who says, "Thou shalt" and "Thou shalt not") one sees the master-clue to the Whitman imago as the God of the Godless, the Father of the Fatherless, the Son of the Mother. The anti-Christian meaning of Whitman explains the odd united front that gathered about him: the "religious" Dr. Bucke and the "irreligious" Colonel Robert Ingersoll joined with the Nietzschean André Gide in his worship. Only D. H. Lawrence has ever challenged Whitman's claim to this honor, finding in him a final failure of nerve: "Then Whitman's mistake. The

mistake of his interpretation of his watchword: Sympathy.
. . . He still confounded it with Jesus' LOVE, and with Paul's
CHARITY. Whitman, like all the rest of us, was at the end of
the great emotional highway of Love. . . . The highway of
Love ends at the foot of the Cross. There is no beyond. . . .
He needed to supersede the Christian Charity, the Christian
Love . . . in order to give his Soul her last Freedom. . . .
And he failed in so far as he failed to get out of the old rut of
Salvation." But one can hardly expect Lawrence to be fair,
since he coveted for himself the title of the anti-Christian
Christ.

To all other enemies of the superego as Church or State or
paterfamilias, culture or Europe or "literature," Whitman has
seemed a sufficient idol, the bearded but motherly papa. In
this sense, even his homosexuality is necessary, not publicly
proclaimed but "unconsciously" *there* for his disciples as for
himself. It is as the Patriarch who is not a father, and who has
no Father on earth or in heaven, that Whitman appeals to the
Socialist, the advocate of the New Poetry, the professional
American, the undefined Democrat. Not realizing the necessity to his myth of his impotence, his femininity, Whitman fell
into the error of inventing for himself six bastards when he
was accused of physically loving men; but it was a half-hearted
addition to the legend, imagined late and discounted even as
it was told by the most ardent of his disciples.

The true "sons" of Whitman are necessarily "spiritual,"
those legendary readers who have never, of course, really read
him, but who correspond to the legendary poet: the mechanic,
the bus driver, the wounded soldier, bound to him by a love
as pure as Dante's for Beatrice. How careful he is in separating
sex from sentiment (*Children of Adam*), and sentiment from
sex (the *Calamus* poems) — and how American! Too American, perhaps, for any of us to see; certainly, it is only García
Lorca, a stranger in New York, who invokes this image precisely:

> Beautiful, Old Walt Whitman your beard full of butterflies . . .
> your thighs of a virginal Apollo . . . you moaned like a bird
> with its sex pierced with a needle . . .
> You dreaming of being a river and sleeping like a river
> with that comrade who would place in your breast
> a tiny pain of an ignorant leopard.

It is the heartbreaking innocence of this aspect of Whitman which Lorca seizes, the unfallen tenderness of America behind the machine-ridden cities; and he contrasts him sharply with the corrupted of the cities, whose meanings are quite different:

> queers of the cities, with your tumified flesh and your sullied
> thought . . .
> harpies, assassins of doves
> slaves of women . . .

"Sleep, Walt," the Spanish poet concludes, finding in his virginal poet an odd promise of salvation, "and let a black boy announce to the golden whites the arrival of the reign of an ear of corn."

Not many worshipers of Walt, however, have been willing to accept him as the prophet of so ritual and mystic a revolution (surely the allusion to the Eleusinian mysteries that makes Walt the Ceres to the "black boy's" Kore is deliberate). From the beginning, he has been claimed as the forerunner of a more real, a more political "freedom," and as history has defined that ambiguous term more and more diversely, each faction, asserting its right to some meaning of the term, has held aloft its own image of Whitman. There has always been, to be sure, a suspicion that Whitman's "democracy" might be merely a rationalization of "adhesive" love; and in Germany, for instance, what began as a struggle between the "Uranians" and the Social Democrats over whether Whitman prophesied the coming of socialism or the emergence of the third sex ended in a rather vicious debunking of the "Yankee Saint" by the Uranian party.

But Socialists have always clung to Walt, raising his eidolon beside that of Karl Marx, while to others he has seemed linked to Mazzini and republicanism in general, as he is imagined in that most improbable of tributes by Swinburne (who later qualified his admiration drastically):

> Send but a song overseas for us,
>   Heart of their hearts who are free,
> Heart of their singer, to be for us
>   More than our singing can be;
> Ours, in the tempest at error
> With no light but the twilight of terror;
>   Send us a song oversea!

For the English poet, at first only uncertain as to whether he admired Whitman more as the apostle of freedom or of "the great god Man, which is God," Whitman stood for a specifically American experience. But in other European minds, both those that approved and those that were horrified, he was associated with an image of revolt that knew no national boundaries; and he was especially confused with those other serenely bearded rebels, Tolstoy and Hugo, in a way that reveals in the case of all three how different is their common mask from their stubbornly divergent selves. To the Continental who saw him as "the American" and America as somehow unitary, his image was blended with such improbable fellow-countrymen as Theodore Roosevelt, the "professor of energy" (by Rubén Darío), or President Wilson (in post-World-War-I Germany, where it is said he was considered the real author of the Fourteen Points).

But strangest of Whitman's posthumous avatars was that of a Marxist saint. While the French had been discovering in the author of *Leaves of Grass* a Nietzsche-like patron of intellectual anti-Christianity and an ancestor of *symbolisme,* the Germans had been finding behind the poem a figure that Johannes Becher was to name, finally, *Bruder Whitman,* Brother Whitman, Comrade Whitman; and they turned him willy-nilly into a dangerous poet, a revolutionary, whom the Central European police, convinced by the myth, felt obliged to ban just after the First World War. The *facts* matter not at all: that Whitman was a supporter of capitalism despite certain cagey reservations; that he despised trade unions; that after his one long interview with a Socialist proselytizer he murmured only, "What a beautiful young man!" — all this counted for certain sober critics and commentators, but not for the rank-and-file Marxists who knew only that Whitman represented the "Future" and so did they! In a sense, they were right, of course; for the legendary person he had created and released had taken on a life of its own and could make strange conversions long after the poet's death.

In Russia, too, an imaginary Whitman was drafted into the ranks of the revolutionaries, and by 1917 had become in the popular mind an unquestioned ancestral figure, so that *Leaves of Grass* was one of the first American books officially sponsored in translation by the Bolshevik government. But, even before that, a poem by Whitman had been placed in the hands of the Soviet troops fighting the American Expeditionary Forces, as if to assure them that they, not the soldiers of the United States, were "America" as Whitman had defined it.

> Then courage European revolter, revoltress!
> For till all ceases neither must you cease.

"To a Foil'd European Revolutionaire" is, as poetry, Whitman at his worst — and the poetry inspired by "Comrade Whitman" does not rise above this example. Oddly enough, the redefined Communist Whitman was reimported into the United States, where along with translated Mayakovski, it became the official standard for "Proletarian Poetry" as practiced with fervor and imprecision in the darker 'thirties. The figure of Whitman that informed this kind of verse is classically invoked in a poem by Ben Maddow called "Red Decision," a brief citation from which must stand for all the rest:

> Broad-hearted Whitman of the healthy beard
> stiffen my infirm palate for this bread,
> whose gritty leaven shall embowel me
> to hold and nourish, with reasoning pity and force,
> past fear and comfort or tranquillity,
> in solemn hands, my tough majestic pen.

It is tempting and easy to mock efforts of this sort, which are, after all, no worse than Swinburne or most of the other poets destroyed by the image they chose to sponsor them. Whitman is an almost impossible muse, but it has taken us a long time to discover it. In recent years the Marxists have found themselves in almost uncontested possession of the figure of Whitman (challenged only by an occasional homespun versifier from the hills) as the practice and piety of our younger poets have shifted toward tradition and elegance; but for a while they stood in apparent solidarity with all that was "new" in American literature, with a whole horde of enthusiasts for whom Whitman was not only the whole future of poetry, but America itself.

The image of Whitman as the Bard, the popular voice, the

very definition of the United States arises from a profound
ambiguity in the poet himself; for one of the names he called
his Fancy, his Mask was "America." "I hear America singing
. . . I celebrate myself and sing myself . . ." The image of
Walt swells and is extended until it merges indistinguishably
with the body of an imaginary continent, and the continent
with the vision of comradeship, with "Democracy *ma femme.*"
In the end, there are two wives of Whitman and the two are
one: himself and his country: Walt Whitman *ma femme* and
America *ma femme.* The French is not merely accidental and
comical; it gives away the whole game.

Walt Whitman's America was made in France, the Romantic notion out of Rousseau and Chateaubriand of an absolute
anti-Europe, an utter anti-culture made flesh, the Noble Savage
as a Continent. And from the same sources Whitman derived
the ideal of a national poetry, the belief that a country did not
really exist until a poet discovered it for the imagination. The
irony of such literary ideas is that they must pretend to be
unliterary, anti-literary, the expression of a purely native and
ingenuous humanism.

> Come, Muse, migrate from Greece and Ionia,
> Cross out please those immensely overpaid accounts . . .

But no European is long fooled by the pose of barbarity that
Europe invented; Thomas Mann, for instance, who loved Whitman, identified his meaning with the *humanitas* of Novalis —
and with the thought of Goethe himself.

We have come to understand that the only American writers
who can transcend the European tradition are those who begin
frankly from it; that the "pure" Americans endure becoming
unconsciously stereotypes devised by Europeans weary of the
burden of their culture. The unreality of Whitman's America
— that is, of the European dream of America — is revealed in
its need to be forever moved toward a vanishing horizon, to be
defined as the Absolute West. It is never the known and experienced world, but always the dreamed one over the next
ridge, beyond the next river: the world of a legendary innocence, of Experience as Innocence, where one can undergo
all and remain virgin. It is for this reason that Whitman the

New Yorker was redreamed (in part by himself) as the poet of a "West" which he had not even visited when *Leaves of Grass* took shape. It is utterly misleading to remember Whitman as a populist, plein-air poet; for at his best he is a singer of urban life, like Baudelaire, dedicated to redeeming for the imagination the world of industry, the life of cities. It is not to field or farmland that he invites the Muse, but to the urban kitchen with its window opening on the view of factories:

> By thud of machinery and shrill steam-whistle undismay'd,
> Bluff'd not a bit by drain-pipe, gasometers, artificial fertilizers;
> Smiling and pleased with palpable intent to stay,
> She's here, install'd amid the kitchen-ware.

But this is a witty Whitman and a precise observer who jibes ill with the figure of the diffuse and humorless Tribal Bard that the all-American Whitmanites have tried to create. *Their* Whitman has been classically defined by Edgar Lee Masters. "It is not because Whitman is a better poet than Emerson that he may be called the father of American poetry. . . . It is because Whitman wrote for the American tribe and the American idea. . . . Whitman was the tribal prophet and poet. . . . Whitman had the right idea, namely, that poetry, the real written word, must come out of the earth. . . . It is no wonder that a man as sincere as Whitman, whose sincerity chose prosody without rhyme, meter or ornament, had to endure the sneers and chatter of New York critics . . . who often miss the important, the real and truly American art."

But, one wants to protest, all these ideas come precisely out of "books and erudition" — and it is no use pleading in self-defense that they are bad books and spotty erudition: the fear of New Yorkers (critics or Wall Street bankers, it scarcely matters), provinciality as true virtue, "sincerity" as the sole aesthetic criterion, the notion that rhyme and meter are somehow meretricious, the adulation of the "tribe." What good to point out that these are the dreams of the effete at their most exhausted, the last nostalgia of the hyper-aesthete for a mythic "natural." Such ideas die hard because they appeal to those haters of literature unprepared to appear under their true colors: "emancipated" puritans and social reformers, superpatriots and Communists who fear and distrust art but like to boast that some of their best friends are poets. When challenged to name one, they can always evoke Walt Whitman. Poor Walt! It is the final indignity: to have become the image of the anti-artist, of the poet as despiser of poetry, of America as an anti-culture.

It gets harder and harder to remember that once (only two wars ago!) his name was the rallying cry of the literary avant-garde; New Sex, New Society, and New Poetry: they seemed three persons of a single god, and Whitman was its prophet. *Poetry*, the magazine founded by Harriet Monroe, still carries a tag from Whitman; and in its pioneer days it evoked as a syndrome, anti-conventional and anti-bourgeois, T. S. Eliot, Pound, Whitman, Amy Lowell, imagism, free verse, Sandburg, Frost, and E. A. Robinson. Then and for a long time afterward, other little magazines were sponsoring with equal fervor new directions in social organization and in experimental verse. To this blur of enthusiasm the prophetic blur at the heart of the Whitman image corresponded exactly; he is the presiding genius of an alliance based on the single slogan: "Make It New!"

It was an alliance that could not survive its first victories; quite soon the Socialist new poet was regarding the converted Catholic novelist with hostility; the rediscoverer of metaphysical wit and classical form was watching warily the exponent of uncorseted dithyrambs; the advocate of escape from emotion was wondering how he had ever enlisted beside the enthusiasts of phallic consciousness. In an introduction to the *Selected Poems* of Ezra Pound, Eliot has put his own protest on record: "I did not read Whitman until much later in life, and had to conquer an aversion to his form, as well as much of his matter, in order to do so. I am equally certain — it is indeed obvious — that Pound owes nothing to Whitman. This is an elementary observation." Amy Lowell had already detached herself with a haughty statement: "Often and often I read in the daily, weekly and monthly press, that modern vers libre writers derive their form from Walt Whitman. As a matter of fact, most of them got it from French Symbolist poets." It was toward Walt's Communist kidnapers that she was glancing, for she added: "The last ignominy to him would be the usage of his words to tear down the governmental structure that he loved." And she concluded with the coolest of snubs: "It is perhaps sadly significant that the three modern poets who most loudly acknowledge his leadership are all of recent foreign extraction. . . ."

This is the beginning of an attack that does not end until Whitman is transformed from a figure symbolizing the way poetry must go to a half-comic image personifying the wrong turning, the temptation to formlessness and disorder, the blind alley of the pseudo-poet. Pound's offer of a negotiated peace finds no supporters even among his own followers:

> I make a pact with you, Walt Whitman —
> I have detested you long enough.
> I come to you as a grown child
> Who has had a pig-headed father;
> I am old enough to make friends.

This is an entirely new resistance to *Leaves of Grass,* not the protest of the anti-Jacobin and the genteel, the demurrer of a James Russell Lowell or a Holmes, feeling the hungry generations treading him down; not the horrified "scientific" rejection of a Nordau or Lombroso, classifying Whitman as insane — but the refusal of a poet by the very future on which he had staked all. It is the liveliest minds that begin to turn away from him, not only the reactionary wits like Wyndham Lewis: "Walt Whitman was, I feel sure, the father of the American Baby. . . . Walt showed all those enthusiastic habits we associate with the Baby. He rolled about naked in the Atlantic surf, uttering 'barbaric yawps' . . . he was prone to 'cosmic raptures.' . . . He was a great big heavy old youngster of the perfect Freudian type, with the worst kind of enthusiasm in the Greek sense of the word." To begin with, it is against the Mask of Whitman that they revolt, for they do not want the Son of the Mother for *their* Father; they are after new ancestors, a tradition not of the traditionless but of the traditional. But they find it hard to believe that there is a genuine poet behind the distasteful persona. Only in Europe does Whitman continue to belong to the young, to the creating writers; in the United States he becomes the possession of those new philistines who love the renewal of the day before yesterday — and of the more liberal-minded scholars.

It is these scholars who have been in recent years creating a legend of Whitman's fame, a rags-to-riches story of a slow, but unbroken triumph over the reservations of the short-sighted genteel; and in the interests of this legend they have failed to record (perhaps they have not even noticed) the decline of their poet's reputation among our best practicing poets. Yet the *essential* fact about Whitman as a force in American poetry is precisely what Gay Wilson Allen, for instance, does not even hint at in his *Handbook:* that for the last twenty-five years Whitman has been a chief whipping boy of many of our best poets and critics.

The defeat of Whitman as the informing image of the Poet, as our bearded Muse of the New, is ironically sealed by an attempted celebration in Hart Crane's *The Bridge* of his figure as the Meistersinger of America.

> *Panis Angelicus!* Eyes tranquil with the blaze
> Of love's own diametric gaze, of love's amaze . . .
> Our Meistersinger, thou set breath in steel;
> And it was thou who on the boldest heel
> Stood up and flung the span on even wing
> Of that great Bridge, our Myth, whereof I sing!
>
> .   .   .   .
>
> My hand
>   in yours,
>   Walt Whitman —
>
>   so —

This is hardly Crane at his best. Even the characteristic incoherence is a faked, a second-rate incoherence — not a blending at incandescent temperature but an ersatz fusion; and the attack on the failures of Crane's poem which followed its publication centered on this passage and on the image behind it. The *locus classicus* is the review by Yvor Winters that appeared in *Poetry* for June 1930, asserting that *The Bridge* at its best "carries the epic quality of the Whitmanian vision (the vision of humanity *en masse* or undifferentiated) to the greatest dignity and power of which it is, probably, capable," thus proving under the most favorable conditions "the impossibility of getting anywhere with the Whitmanian inspiration. No writer of comparable ability has struggled with it before, and, with Mr. Crane's wreckage in view, it seems highly unlikely that any writer of comparable genius will struggle with it again."

Doubtless, one of the troubles with the "Cape Hatteras" section of Crane's poem is the falsification by Crane (probably even to himself) of his relation to the image of Whitman. The homosexual sensibility which they shared is ignored in favor of Whitman's legendary representativeness as an "American"; besides, Crane, attracted with one part of his mind to Eliot, is already ridden with doubts about Whitman's true worth. A letter to Allen Tate reveals his ambivalence. "It's true that my rhapsodic address to him [Whitman] in the Bridge exceeds any exact valuation of the man. . . . There isn't much use in my tabulating the qualified, yet persistent, reasons I have for my admiration of him. . . . You've heard me roar at too many of his lines to doubt that I can spot his worst, I'm sure." The myth and the poet had begun to come apart for Crane; and I suspect they cannot be put together by an act of will. Certainly, one has the impression that "Cape Hatteras" is not believed in but *worked up.*

Whatever the truth about these matters, the failure of *The Bridge* was interpreted not as Crane's failure, but as Whitman's. Tate, Blackmur, and others seconded Winters, and this judgment of the Whitmanian imago via *The Bridge* soon became a standard conviction of the "New Critics" — indeed, one of the few beliefs which actually are shared by that ill-assorted congeries. In Blackmur a typical contrast is added to complete the position: "Baudelaire aimed at control, Whitman at release. It is for these reasons that the influence of Whitman was an impediment to the *practice* (to be distinguished from the reading) of poetry, and that the influence of Baudelaire is re-animation itself."

What began as an "advanced" minority opinion has tended to become at least an important orthodoxy, if not *the* orthodoxy of the young, changing emphasis along the way so that Whitman is regarded not only as a bad "influence" but even as a bad poet, the founder of an inferior tradition. William

Van O'Connor sums up the position in his recent study, *Sense and Sensibility in Modern Poetry*. "But Whitman and his followers — like Robinson Jeffers, Vachel Lindsay, Edgar Lee Masters, Carl Sandburg, Stephen Vincent Benét and William Rose Benét, and later Paul Engle, August Derleth, Muriel Rukeyser, Ben Maddow, and Alfred Hayes . . . are not in the line of American writers who have deepened our knowledge of human motivation or action. They are, in so far as they are followers of Whitman, away from the tradition which runs from Hawthorne and Melville through James and Eliot."

Though such amalgams as this seem to me to exploit shamelessly the device of "guilt by association," I sympathize with Mr. O'Connor's effort to isolate the exploiters of what he calls "the historico-mythic equivalent of America." I, too, am repelled by those who do not make poems but manipulate a prefabricated theme and feel that by naming an undefined essence "America" they can turn it into a universal touchstone. I do not even object to setting the "Whitmanians" against whatever equivalent of the metaphysical-symbolist tradition can be found in our literature, except as such a contrast implies that one tradition guarantees, or another makes impossible, poetry. Whitman, at least, succeeds, whatever his assumptions, in being a poet more often than it is ever possible to remember; he is not *merely* his myth, either as he himself expresses it or as it persists in this line of spiritual descent.

I know why Mr. O'Connor and many others find it hard to admit Whitman's excellence; one does not easily come to love a poet who is used as a weapon against oneself and one's favorite writers. And Whitman has become precisely such a weapon in the hands of those who (Van Wyck Brooks is an example) condemn Eliot or Pound on the grounds that they have rejected all that Whitman affirms. It is vain to retort with the commonplace that "poetry affirmeth nought," for Whitman has taught us otherwise. Besides, it is turn and turn about; once the sides were chosen up — Baudelaire against Whitman; Poe, Melville, or Hawthorne against Whitman; Eliot against Whitman — warfare was inevitable. You cannot beat Whitman over the head with Eliot and be surprised when the process is reversed. Such conflicts have a certain strategic value so long as we remember that the causes for which they are fought are not really the poets who bear the same names, but merely their images, tricked out to horrify or allure. Whitman is no more devil than messiah. He is a poet whom we must begin now to rescue from parody as well as apotheosis.

We shall not return to the same Whitman from which we started; twenty-five years of dissent cannot be undone. It is to our *own* Whitman that we come back, and we come by our own roads, via authors whom Whitman would perhaps have despised. It is not from his friends that we ask letters of recommendation but from those who had no reason to love him, from Henry James, for instance, or from Gerard Manley Hopkins. Even Randall Jarrell has felt obliged to remind us (albeit ironically), in a recent admirable essay, that James was moved almost to tears in reading Whitman to Edith Wharton, and that Hopkins wrote to Bridges: "I always knew in my heart Walt Whitman's mind to be more like my own than any other man's living." One laughs a little remembering Yeats's account of how he scarcely listened to Hopkins, whom he met in his father's studio, because he was carrying in his own pocket *Leaves of Grass;* but one laughs wryly, for it is the joke of history which is always on *us!*

It is not to the life-affirmer we are returning, but to the elegiac Whitman, the poet of death. "Merging! And Death!" D. H. Lawrence wrote accusingly of Whitman. "The great merge into the womb. Woman. And after that, the merging of comrades: man-for-man love. . . . Woman is inadequate for the last merging. So the next step is the merging of man-for-man love. And this is on the brink of death. It slides over into death." But the case for the prosecution has become the case for the defense: another joke of history. Dismayed by an optimism in which we no longer believe, a self-assurance that seems to us obscene, we find with relief in *Leaves of Grass* that "blackness ten times black" which Melville once thrilled to discover in Hawthorne. We are pleased to find surviving the hearty eidolon, the melancholy poet who began writing stories about the poor boy flogged to death by a wicked teacher, to honor "the dusky demon and brother" whom Walt did not forget. It is his attackers who have defined for us the Whitman we can love; even such negative and furious onslaughts as those of Esther Shephard and Harvey O'Higgins have succeeded in destroying not the poet but the legend which obscured him.

How different the meaning of what such critics have found is for us than it was for them! Discovering among Whitman's papers the cardboard butterfly with which he faked the famous portrait; learning that the untainted American family of which he liked to boast was ridden with madness and disease; finding a host of proofs that the New Orleans love affair, the vaunted bastards were deliberate hoaxes — his debunkers were ready to write off Walt as "insincere." To them this seemed to destroy his validity as a poet-prophet, to reveal him as "only" a self-advertiser, a poseur, not original or a Democrat or even a lusty breeder. But those of us who know that poetry (God forbid that we should attempt to judge the *man!*) is precisely a matter of cardboard butterflies on real fingers, that the wit and tension of a poem depend on the distance between the given and the imagined, are grateful to Miss Shephard and Mr. O'Connor for having rescued Walt Whitman from "life" (i.e., the clichés of politics and pseudo-mysticism) and having restored him to art.

Our Walt Whitman is the slyest of artificers, the artificer of "sincerity"; and, if this sounds like a joke, there is no reason why even the greatest poetry cannot be a joke on someone, not excluding its author. It does not seem to me enough to say, as G. W. Stonier has in one of the more perceptive comments on Whitman, "His duplicity staggers. He was a fine poet and a charlatan," because this implies that his fine poetry is based on something other than his charlatanism. Whitman's trickery is essential, not accidental, to his poems. Like the mannerists, like Shakespeare, who is the greatest among them, he is a player with illusion; his center is a pun on the self; his poetry is a continual shimmering on the surfaces of concealment and revelation that is at once pathetic and comical.

His duplicity is, I feel, a peculiarly American duplicity, that doubleness of our self-consciousness which our enemies too easily call hypocrisy, but which arises from our belief that what we dream rather than what we are is our essential truth.

The Booster and the Pharisee are the standard caricatures of
the American double man, and Whitman was both Booster and
Pharisee. Condemned to play the Lusty Innocent, the Noble
Savage, by a literary tradition that had invented his country
before he inhabited it, Whitman had no defenses. The whole
Western world demanded of him the lie in which we have been
catching him out, the image of America in which we no longer
believe; the whole world cried to him: "Be the Bard we can
only dream! Chant the freedom we have imagined as if it
were real!"

But he was not "America"; he was only a man, ridden by
impotence and anxiety, by desire and guilt, furtive and stubborn and half-educated. That he became the world's looked-
for, ridiculous darling is astonishing enough; that he remained
a poet through it all is scarcely credible. He has survived his
images; and at last the outlived posturing, the absurd ideas,
the rhetoric borrowed and misunderstood fall away, until only
the poetry remains, and the poet — anonymous in the end as
they were in the beginning.

I and this mystery here we stand.

CHAPTER ELEVEN

Some Notes on
F. Scott Fitzgerald

I. *Nothing succeeds like failure*

The case of F. Scott Fitzgerald belongs first of all to the history of taste in our time. It is immensely difficult at the present moment to distinguish our responses to Fitzgerald's achievement from our self-congratulatory feelings about certain recent changes in our own literary standards. We are likely to overestimate his books in excessive repentance of the critical errors of the 'thirties — for having preferred Steinbeck or James T. Farrell for reasons we would no longer defend. Fitzgerald has come to seem more and more poignantly the girl we left behind — dead, to boot, before we returned to the old homestead, and therefore particularly amenable to sentimental idealization.

And so a fictionist with a "second-rate sensitive mind" (the term is Tennyson's description of himself, and evokes the tradition of late Romanticism in which Fitzgerald worked) and a weak gift for construction is pushed into the very first rank of American novelists, where it becomes hard to tell his failures from his successes. Who cares as long as the confetti flies and the bands keep playing! It is all to the good, of course, that hundreds of thousands of us require the reprinting of his books, actually read him again along with the recent Mizener biography. He had threatened for too long to remain a "case" about whom everyone merely *talks*. If we were only content with reclaiming an imperfect good writer, who achieved just once a complete artistic success, but who in every book at some point breaks through his own intolerable resolve to be charming above all and touches the truth!

But, Lord have mercy on us, we want a "great" writer. It is at once the comedy and tragedy of twentieth-century American letters that we simply cannot keep a full stock of contemporary "great novelists." In the novel, unlike recent poetry in which certain reputations have grown slowly and steadily, we have had an erratic market: reputations fantastically overpriced are in an instant deflated, and new booms are launched. From moment to moment we have the feeling that certain claims, at least, are secure, but even as we name them they shudder and fall. Who now mentions James Branch Cabell? And who can think of Dos Passos and Steinbeck without a twinge of shame for dead enthusiasms? Dreiser and Farrell find a few surly defenders — but even their granted merits seem irrelevant to our current situation. Whom have we left? Faulkner and Hemingway, and even now the stock of the latter has begun to fall; a thousand imitators reveal the weaknesses we had not seen, and the younger critics begin, to the shrill screams of Hemingway's contemporaries, the drastic revision. Into our depopulated pantheon, therefore, we impress Fitzgerald.

Who else? There are several reasons that impel the choice: we have reached the point from which the 'twenties, Fitzgerald's 'twenties, can be regarded with the maximum nostalgia; we readopt the hairdos, the songs — and the authors. We see him now as one who refused to whore after strange Marxist gods, our lonely St. Anthony, faithful to literature in the sociological desert. The versions of Fitzgerald that these estimates imply are perhaps not quite true, but they are believed in and will do. And yet the *essential* appeal of Fitzgerald is elsewhere — astonishingly enough, in his *failure*.

Mr. Schulberg in his recent novel has remarked that in America nothing fails like success; but of course the obverse is also true: among us, nothing succeeds like failure. We are, behind a show of the grossest success-worship, a nation that dreams of failure as a fulfillment. The Christian paradox of the defeated as victor haunts our post-Christian world. None of us seems *really* to believe in the succeeding of success, though we do not know how to escape from its trap; and it has become one of the functions of our writers to supply us with vicarious failures for our second-hand redemption.

Edgar Allan Poe provides the prototype, of course: dope, whisky, the shadow of madness, poverty and early death — and Fitzgerald is the perfect modern avatar. It is the Fall not of a King, but of an Artist, the disaffected son of the middle class, of us all, that we demand to stir our pity and terror. For the great quasi-literate public, Fitzgerald is providing right now the *tragic experience:* creating, in the great amphitheater without walls of articles in *Life,* abridgments in the *Atlantic Monthly,* paragraphs in the papers, and 25-cent reprints, a debased equivalent of what the Athenian found in the *Oedipus Rex.* When any American writer refuses to live into the conventional public myth, the people remake him, as even Poe was retouched by Griswold, who invented in malice the American Writer, and as Stephen Crane was lied and vilified into the image necessary to us all.

But Fitzgerald *willed* his role as a failure, for all his paeans to success. Long before his own actual crack-up, he dreamed it, prophesied it in his stories and novels; and if one cannot read his true desire in the fictional projections, Mr. Mizener's account of the life more than confirms the intimations. Mr. Mizener's greatest merit as a biographer is that he does not cut the fabric of Fitzgerald's life to his own views, but by balancing a half-dozen partial readings of his career permits still others (including this one) that do not suggest themselves explicitly to him. Instinctively, Fitzgerald hoarded his defeats like his truest treasures: his rejection as a young man by Ginevra King, his expulsion from Princeton, the imagined attacks of tuberculosis and the real ones (a disease in which the will is all), the cutting to pieces of his prized movie script by Joe Mankiewicz — and above all, the drinking.

II. *Booze done it!*

From the beginnings of Western literature, there has been a tradition of the flaw as essential to the writer, but at various times there have been various notions of the ideal charismatic weakness: blindness in the most ancient days, incest in the Byronic period, homosexuality in the *fin de siècle*. But in America the flaw has been pre-eminently drunkenness, from Griswold's Poe dead in the gutters of Baltimore to Schulberg's Halliday-Fitzgerald dying among the undergraduates at Dartmouth. It was quite another sort of culture hero, the battered John L. Sullivan, who said mournfully, "Booze done it!"; but the words make an appropriate epitaph for our typical writer.

Every writer in Fitzgerald makes his first staggering entrance loaded: McKiscoe in *Tender Is the Night*, "Four-eyes" in *Gatsby*, Wylie in *The Last Tycoon;* the profession is inseparable from the vice. It is, I suppose, because the 'twenties were the time when drinking became quite simply the American Character, or at least its public face, that Fitzgerald was so much at home in that world, unalienated from the general binge. Mr. Mizener's book makes quite clear the pathetic hollowness of Fitzgerald's claim to be a spokesman for the 'twenties in the formal sense, a kind of higher John Held, Jr.; and a quick, embarrassed rereading of *This Side of Paradise,* with its queasy panegyrics of "kissing" and "petting," reveals a writer far too naïve and principled to speak for a time without principle. And yet Fitzgerald and his audience were, until the 'twenties died, at home with each other; the American citizen as lush and the American artist as lush cried into the same beer. It was not that only Americans, or American writers, drank (there was always James Joyce, as Hemingway reminded Fitzgerald between drinks), but that for Americans it so much *mattered;* and that in the United States, before drinking could become an overwhelming habit, it had first to be forbidden. It is surely no accident that the protagonist of Fitzgerald's best book has, like his author, grown wealthy on Prohibition, the sensitive bootlegger as the last Romantic — the "great" Gatsby, for whom only the drunken writer turns out to mourn after his inevitable defeat.

The greatest drunken writer whom Fitzgerald created, however, appeared in none of his books — being, of course, Fitzgerald himself. A part of the apparent waste of Fitzgerald's life stems from his having invested most of his energy in composing himself; and his Collected Works have not been finished until ten years after his death. One cannot claim to have read him without having read *The Far Side of Paradise* or the letters and reminiscences collected in *The Crack-up*. It is the glory and the curse of the Romantic writer that his achievement cannot survive his legend without real loss. When the lives of Scott and Zelda are forgotten, or when they have become merely chronologies without the legendary distortions and pathos, his books will be less rewarding. Think of Byron, to whom his sins are as necessary as drunkenness and the madness of his wife are to Fitzgerald!

III. *Portrait of the artist as a young girl*

The obverse of the Romantic habit of living one's life as if it were a work of art is that of writing one's books as if they were autobiographies. Fitzgerald is wary in this respect, but his dodges are superficial and ineffective. In his later books, he resolutely refuses to use the writer or artist as protagonist or point-of-view character. Even in *The Last Tycoon,* where the writer Wylie is obviously the character through whom the story of Stahr *must* be told, Fitzgerald's resolve to keep the writer as character peripheral quite ruins any possibility of a coherent organization; and in the end Fitzgerald smuggles himself into the skin of Stahr and of the young girl through whom the events are seen. Nothing is gained, and a good deal is lost — organization, certainly, and consistency of characterization.

It is not by pretending that one's central character is a gangster or psychiatrist or producer that one avoids turning art into confession; it is a question of method and irony and detachment, the devices that made *Stephen Hero* into *Portrait of the Artist as a Young Man,* the devices that Fitzgerald never mastered.

Any one of Fitzgerald's novels will illustrate the point; but perhaps *Tender Is the Night* will serve best of all. Almost all the main characters (Nicole Diver, the female lead, is of course based on Zelda), whatever their outsides, turn out to be F. Scott Fitzgerald. Dick Diver, the protagonist, who seems from a distance the assured aristocrat, the obverse of the author, reveals on the first close-up the Irish lilt, the drunkenness, the tortured sensibility that are Fitzgerald's. The pretentious novelist (enter drunk, to be sure!), Albert McKiscoe, is Scott in caricature, his social insecurity, his pretenses, even the early success he feared and hated. Abe North, faintly disguised as a musician, is Ring Lardner; but Ring Lardner was Fitzgerald's favorite *alter ego,* in whom he liked to see the image of his own doom (exit drunk, of course!). One could do a marvelous movie with all these parts played by the same actor — a different stance, different costuming, and as the camera moves close: the same face.

Even the young moving-picture actress, Rosemary Hoyt, turns out to be a version of the author. She is Irish (always a clue), full of embarrassment and guilty pride at a too-sudden success, and quite indeterminate in her sex. Indeed, the book is shot through with a thematic playing with the ambiguity of sex: Dick Diver makes his first entrance in a pair of black lace panties, and homosexuals, male and female, haunt the climaxes of the novel. "Economically," Rosemary's mother tells her at one point, "you're a boy, not a girl." Economically! One recalls the portrait of Fitzgerald as the most beautiful showgirl in the Triangle Show.

I had felt all this before reading in Mr. Mizener's biography that in *The World's Fair,* an abandoned book from whose fragments the first part of *Tender Is the Night* is made, Rosemary was indeed a boy, who was to kill his mother according to the original plot. It has been observed by Malcolm Cowley that Fitzgerald has always a double vision of himself, as outsider and insider at once, the man of the world and the bumpkin gawking at him; but it has not been remarked that at the end of his writing career the outsider had become defined as the Young Girl, a kind of anima figure, desiring hopelessly the older man who is *also* Fitzgerald, himself double: in the eyes of the girl all power and glamor, in his own view aging and corrupt or at the point of death.

In his last two novels, the same relationship appears, and the same sort of character as narrator, a portrait of the artist as a breathless young girl, still virgin though not without

experience. Each time the affair ends in a deflowering without love and an eventual desertion, Diver-Fitzgerald abandoning Rosemary-Fitzgerald for Nicole-Zelda, and Stahr-Fitzgerald
leaving Cecilia-Fitzgerald for Kathleen; the protagonists choosing both times that Other Woman by whom Fitzgerald symbolizes the lure of death and destruction which is stronger
even than self-love.

This constant impulse to confuse himself with his characters
destroys first of all the consistency of the people in his books;
but, even worse, it leads Fitzgerald into an indulgence in
self-pity, which is the grossest manifestation of his prevailing
sentimentality. He is sentimental about everything — Princeton, the First World War, sex (egregiously!), Skull and Bones,
Gold Star Mothers — but especially about his own plight.
Everywhere in his work there is a failure of irony and detachment that amounts finally to a failure of intelligence, an indulgence of the "second-rate sensitive mind."

Like most American writers, Fitzgerald had to work without
an accepted tradition to sustain him or received standards
against which to measure himself. All his life, he moved uncertainly between the demands of his own erratic sensibility
and a desire to please a great, undefined audience — to be
loved by everybody. Like one of his own epicene coquettes,
he postured and flirted with all comers, trying to cling meanwhile to a virginity which became more and more a techni-
cality. To be wanted and admired, he was willing to seem to
say less than he meant, to appear merely chic; so that it is
still possible to read even his best books with no understanding
and much pleasure. How could he ever find time to learn how
to put a novel together with skill! All his life, point-of-view
baffled him, and he was forced to make his transitions with
such awkward links as: "To resume Rosemary's point of view,
it should be said . . ." or "This is Cecilia taking up the
story . . ."

IV. *What terrible and golden mystery . . .*

And yet . . . there is always the style of the details, the
glow and motion of the close of *Gatsby* or the opening of

Tender Is the Night, those wonderful approaches and fade-outs. There is always the naïve honesty of reminiscence, the embarrassing rightness of his adolescents. And there is the supreme negative virtue: Fitzgerald's refusal to swap his own lived sentimentalities for the mass sentimentalities of social protest that swamp the later Hemingway. Even the compulsive theme of the *femme fatale,* the All-American banality of woman as destroyer, is capable of subtleties forever beyond the "proletarian novel." When Fitzgerald treats social themes he is absurd; surely there appears in the overrated fragment, *The Last Tycoon,* the least convincing Communist in American fiction. But he resisted the temptation to end *Tender Is the Night* with Dick Diver sending his kids off to the Soviet Union, a close that might well have won him the plaudits he so needed in 1934.

But, beyond all this, one feels in his work a great theme, however elusive and imperfectly realized. It is not love, though love is superficially everywhere in his writing; nor is it Europe, though he lived there and set one book and many stories in the expatriate background. Though he was educated in Catholic schools, it is not religion. His books have no religious insights, only religious décor — the obsessive metaphor of the "ruined priest," a theatrical making of the cross to close a book, a belated Aubrey-Beardsley-ish priest. The sensibility of the Catholic in America becomes, like everything else, puritan: the devil, self-consciously introduced in *This Side of Paradise,* shrinks to an evil aura around a tart's head. There is in Fitzgerald no profound sense of evil or sin, only of guilt; and no gods except the Rich.

The Rich — there is the proper subject matter of Fitzgerald, as everyone has perceived: their difference from the rest of us, and the meanings of that difference. That "other woman" who is death is also wealth; the girl, like Daisy, with gold in her voice. Of course, the wealthy in Fitzgerald are not *real,* but that is precisely the point. Whether in declared fantasy like "A Diamond as Big as the Ritz" or in nominally realistic novels, they resemble veritable millionaires as little as Natty Bumppo resembles an actual frontiersman. But they are, at least — like that Cooper character and unlike the nasty rich in proletarian novels — myths rather than platitudes, viable to the imagination.

It is not just snobbishness that drew Fitzgerald to the rich, the boy from St. Paul dreaming his life long of an imagined Princeton. In all his writing, one senses Fitzgerald in search of an American equivalent to *les grands,* the aristocracy to whom the French writers were able to turn in their reversion from the grubby bourgeois world. Was there anywhere, in America or among Americans abroad, a native aristocracy to whom "style" was a goal and a dream? It is not money getters, but spenders, to whom Fitzgerald turned in his search for allies, out of a sense that the squandering of unearned money was an art, like writing, that squandering of an unearned talent; and that among the very rich there might be a perpetual area of freedom, like that in which the artist momentarily feels himself in the instant of creative outpouring.

The world where a penny saved is a penny earned is the world of anti-art. The lower middle class in particular, Fitzgerald felt, were the enemies of style. He wanted a class that knows how to *use* writers, or at least desires a kind of life in which the imagination would have a chance to live. It was a hopeless dream, and in the end Fitzgerald learned two things: first, that the rich, whatever the quality of their living, regard the artist not as an ally but as a somewhat amusing *arriviste;* and, second, that to live the life of high style is to remain a moral child, who destroys whatever does not suit his whim. To be "rich," in the sense he dreamed, is to refuse responsibility, to deny fate, to try (as in the terrible scene toward the close of "The Diamond as Big as the Ritz") to bribe God. There is implicit in such a life a doom as absolute as its splendor, and in this sense alone the career of the very rich is like that of the artist.

It is a vision atrocious and beautiful enough to be true, and it survives in Fitzgerald's work, despite the incoherence and sentimentality, with the force of truth. It is fitting that our chronicler of the rich be our prophet of failure. To those who plead that Fitzgerald could not face up to life and success, it can be said that at least he kept faith with death and defeat.

CHAPTER TWELVE

Dead-End Werther: The Bum as American Culture Hero

There are certain books in a tradition which, after a while, everyone stops reading but no one can stop writing. The less aware a novelist is of these books, the more he is likely to submit to their pattern; and this is one of the best reasons for insisting that writers be educated. *The Sorrows of the Young Werther* is such an archetypal book — the first anti-bourgeois bourgeois novel, the celebration of suicide as the only possible consummation for the young man afraid that sex may harden into marriage, a work of art become the occasion for mere success, and the very act of living turn imperceptibly into accommodation to the world of convention. The only airtight Bohemia is death.

Werther is also, in the guise of a story about "true love," an attack on the role of woman in the middle-class world: cake-eater and haver *par excellence,* able to use a bourgeois husband for security and a rebellious lover for spiritual satisfaction, to flirt with death and accede to life. It is an embarrassing book, particularly when one recalls that its author went on living at the expense of his character and of all his sad young readers not able to discriminate so nicely between art and life.

James Jones's *From Here to Eternity* (best-seller and improbable choice of at least one critic as our greatest recent novel) is the latest version of *Werther,* and this it is important to notice as no one seems to have done, bored or titillated by its use of obscene language, or led off too quickly into observations on "naturalism." I take it that when a critic says that

From Here to Eternity is in the tradition of "naturalism," he
means nothing more spectacular than that it is badly written in
a special and quite deliberate way. In a certain sense, this is
merely belaboring the obvious: even Hollywood in an all-star
production found no difficulty in producing a movie that was
stylistically superior to the book; indeed, the movie-makers are
too much the prisoners of their own technical excellence to do
anything else. Only bankruptcy could betray them into the
sloppiness that Jones has striven for with all the means at his
command, striven for *on principle*. This principle one might
just as well call "naturalism," though the incautious use of
the term has, I am aware, led to a ridiculous sort of civil war
among the critics. On the darkling plain which is literary
discussion, one army advances under a banner reading, "Art
Is Morality! Without Form Only Confusion! (*signed*) HENRY
JAMES"; while the other side rallies under the device, "Not
Art But Life! X (*Theodore Dreiser his mark*)."

I shall, therefore, try to make quite clear what I mean when
I say that James Jones's book is a "naturalistic" version of
Werther, in which the *poète maudit* appears a bugler, and the
aristocracy and middle classes are blended into the officers,
a scarcely human group that make the Noble Savages, i.e., enlisted men, bear off the sanitary napkins of their women while
they themselves infect their wives with venereal diseases they
have picked up wenching. In all the writings in the line of
Werther, there is a hopeless confusion between the class
struggle and the inability of a sensitive (artistic or quasi-
artistic) young man to adjust to *any* given world. This
is reflected in an attempt to find a style in intent a protest
against current conventions, in fact a challenge to the whole
concept of literature, to language itself. The Storm-and-Stress
style of Goethe, however paradoxical at its heart (an anti-
conventional convention), was at least a new style, a radical
one — the beginning of something; but the protestant, unbuttoned prose of James Jones belongs to an already weary
mode that only ignorance can take for revolt, a mode compromised and, in a way it can never confess, slick. This is no
beginning but an end.

The name of that end is "naturalism," which is to say, any

combination of methods the defects of whose qualities are grossness, clumsiness, and the sentimentalizing of the given and those who live on most intimate terms with it. Opposed to it is what might just as well be called "formalism," which lapses at its worst into gentility, overelaboration, and the sentimentalizing of detached insight and of those most capable of exploiting it. To the formalist to write badly is a sin; to the naturalist it is a virtue.

Like arguments about manners and whether or not costume or ritual are important, this conflict over taste is felt to be essentially a *class* struggle, a clash between Ivy Leaguers and the descendants of slaveowners on the one side, and the sons of immigrants, proletarians, and poor farmers on the other; so that defections from one camp to the other are thought of as renegadism. It is a myth of the "proletarian" side (variously sustained by Lawrence and Hemingway and now Jones) that the difference is also a sexual one: those with *cojones* and a real joy in their natural functions versus the impotent, sterile, or genteelly homosexual, who won't even admit that they sweat.

Like many novels of its class, *From Here to Eternity* exists on one level as a work of criticism, stating a theory of what the work of art should be and providing an instance of that theory in practice. It is at its worst the victim of its own doctrine, "successful" according to its own lights — which is not to say "natural" or "free," since *any* theory (even an antitheoretical one) is a trap, and the fear of complexity can be as crippling as the horror of simplicity. One does not write in a state of nature merely for having disavowed the high traditions of his culture; he becomes rather the victim of the lower ones: in *From Here to Eternity*, the note of elegiac self-pity out of *Portrait of the Artist as a Young Man* via *Look Homeward, Angel;* the compulsive detail and the merciless reproduction of overhead speech usually associated with Dreiser; Hemingwayoid hard-corny descriptions of the orgasm; and, above all, a kind of Jack London hallelujah-I'm-a-bum stance — "This ain't *art,* Jack, it's the real McCoy."

The material rendered in this conglomerate style ranges from the documentary "real" (descriptions of barracks life, the stockade, etc.), through masturbatory fantasies (all whores are beautiful, all officers' wives seducible, yet somehow pure), to sophomoric bull sessions reported dead-pan as "ideas." It is the authority of the documentation that is forever saving the book from its own ambitions. Its value as literature, slight, intermittent, but undeniable, lies in its redeeming for the imagination aspects of regular Army life never before exploited, and in making certain of those aspects (the stockade, for instance, our home-grown "concentration camp") symbols of the human situation everywhere.

The essential subject of the *Werther* novel is always innocence and decadence — what is innocence and how can it be preserved in a corrupt world? This is, of course, a subject peculiarly American; indeed, our country makes its formal début almost at the moment of the publication of Goethe's book, and the hero of the first novel written in the United States dies with that tearful story open on the table beside him. In *From Here to Eternity*, the long sigh is sighed again; one has the sense that the good world, the world of innocents, has just passed away. The book is an inglorious wake in honor of the good old days: before the Wobblies were defeated, before Eagle Scout Roy Rogers replaced the bum Buck Jones as the kids' idol, before the movies were commercialized (i.e., when you could still see pictures like *The Grapes of Wrath*), before the draftees descended on "Wahoo" and a man could get laid in peace. One phrase recurs like a theme: "They are a vanishing race." No more good old First Sergeants! No more real Thirty Year Men!

Yet, even though the Golden Age is gone, the world irrevocably lost to the middle classes (who supported Hitler in Germany and appear in their latest disguise as the commissars in Russia), there exists a saving remnant, Noble Savages untouched by the general degeneracy. These are the men who can be "killed but not eaten," beaten to death or driven into exile, but never forced into apologizing for their revolt or becoming accomplices of the system that crushes them. These are the men whose lives prove the essential innocence of us all, if only "they" would leave us alone — the innocence of self-love and brute courage. The only sin in Jones's world is the belief in sin; and his ultimate villain is the Priest.

Dillinger is the archetype of the saved, but a whole company surrounds him: the misfit, the individual non-conformist, the bum. "In France we called it the Underground, which was a heroic term. Here we called it the under*world* but it was the same world and the same kind of people with the same purpose" — mutual defense against the bourgeoisie. Among the underground men, there is a hierarchy: those simply on the bum and in the county jails, those in the federal prisons, those in the Army as enlisted men, those in the Army stockades, and finally the winnowed few who make (via solitary confinement) Ward Two, the quintessential Good Place of Jones's vision. In this ultimate womb, from which a rebirth to freedom is possible, the absolute bolshevik is at home, the "super-arch revolutionary . . . a sort of perfect criminal type, very dangerous, a mad dog that loves underdogs." It is here that Prew, Jones's protagonist, feels himself one at last with Dillinger and Joe Hill and Big Bill Haywood and Buck Jones, one with "the old American tradition of woodsmen and ground-clearing farmers" — a remnant of toughness in a world gone soft, the only force that can save America.

It is in Ward Two that the prophet of Jones's book, Jack Malloy, speaks the novel's final wisdom: the denial of sin, the belief in reincarnation (that strange sentimental religion so attractive to those who believe there is always one more chance), the use of passive resistance; the turning of the defeated into a rock against which their conquerors will dash themselves to death. What Malloy has finally to offer turns out to be the way of Werther: suicide. "Every man has the right to kill himself. . . . It's the only absolutely inviolable right a man does have . . . the old Anglo-Saxon idea of 'freedom' came from that." The final innocence, the ultimate America, the true freedom is — death!

It is in terms of this desolate vision of freedom that the artist has to choose his role and style; and *From Here to Eternity* deals centrally with the education of an artist for this choice. But one must be careful of the word "artist"; Prew, who is careful to make a grammatical error in every sentence (in this, as in so much else, his author's man), is the poor man's creator, a bugler and one of the collaborators in the "Re-enlistment Blues," a "folk song" printed at the end of the book, and intended apparently to be a poetic distillation of the pathos of the whole fable. Jones should have left the words to our imaginations, for they turn out to be in fact bad in a way he could not have foreseen, palpably faked. What Prew as a *Lumpen*-intellectual learns is that he must not accommodate his talents to the world's accepted evil: not bugle where favoritism overrides merit; not box (another of his popular arts) for the reputation of the regiment or his own promotion; not become a flunky in jail, or an officer in the company, or a married man in life. He learns in short to become the poor man's bohemian, to know promotion and marriage and success as the lures that turn a man from the purity of death — but especially to distrust marriage. To marry is to accept complicity, to recognize one's participation in universal guilt, for women do not know enough to die. They are driven hopelessly to conform, that is, to live and make life possible by endless lying, to bear children and to bring them up, to lure strong men into the trap of status and responsibility.

The really "good" feelings of the book are of the innocent-homosexual variety: the camaraderie of the joint trip to the whorehouse (bursting into your buddy's room with a bottle of booze to see how he's doing), and the games in the tough ward of the stockade — allowing yourself to be butted and slugged by your comrades to test how long you can take it. The ruling passion of the novel (despite all the pursuit of "tail" and all the talk about it) turns out to be a desire to spit out teeth, to be beaten and scarred, to be hurt past endurance and to endure (all, of course, just among the boys) — to anticipate the promise of death that is to be the book's climax, when Prew turns deliberately into a rain of machine-gun bullets. It takes a great war in all its initial fury, the bombs and strafing of the attack on Pearl Harbor, to provide a fitting orgasm for the love that is death.

When the writer has learned to rebel and suffer, he is securely joined to those "who could not fight back and win, so they were very strict in their great pride of losing"; and he must then learn *how* to speak for them. The slogan of *"non serviam"* is not enough in itself, for the artist can misguidedly stumble from non-cooperation into a formalist religion of art which scorns and baffles the ordinary Joe. There are, it is indicated, three kinds of art: the commercialized art of frank conformity to the bourgeoisie, the art of the real rebels, and that of the false rebels, the "aesthetes." In the end, the aesthetes only *think* they are rebels; for their rebellion is worthless, either prompted by self-hatred or else made into an end in itself. Oftener than not the decadent rebel is a fairy, dedicated to softness and "conscious aimless beauty." He has no toughness to protect him from the threat of reprisal and the desire for luxury, so that often he passes from unwittingly subserving the middle classes to outright capitulation — even writing slick fiction under a pseudonym in order to keep himself in champagne and to support the plushy apartment where he can seduce young soldiers. The special rancor Jones feels toward the homosexual must be understood in terms of his own stake in the "platonic" love of buddies as the only passion which leads to no commitment to life or society.

But decadents are not only ambiguous sexually; they are also "intellectuals," which is to say, they talk too damn much. To be articulate is to be lost. "Clerks, kings, and thinkers" merely *talk,* but "truckdrivers, pyramid builders, and straight duty men" build and rebuild the world out of their tonguelessness. The clerks ("tall, thin boys with fragile faces": the Army equivalent of intellectuals) talking of Van Gogh and Gauguin lose sight of the true folk sources of art, the clues to a "basic simplicity." It is only the *real* artist, who can mingle unnoticed with the hard guys, the character who has read all the good books (making reading lists out of everything mentioned by Tom Wolfe or Jack London) but would rather die than admit it, who can produce "the song of men who have no place."

As Werther turned to Homer and Ossian and the Ballads in order to touch again the great innocent heart of Nature, so Prew-Jim Jones turns to certain "pure" movies made between '32 and '37, *Grapes of Wrath* and *Dust Be My Destiny,* the on-the-bum pictures with James Cagney, George Raft, and John Garfield (these slick productions he thinks of as not yet commercialized); plus the authentic blues, hillbilly songs, and jazz — perhaps Django Reinhardt also, the three-fingered gypsy guitarist, and Jack London, the American prototype of the artist as bum. Here he hopes to find that "basic artless simplicity" which will be able to crash through the lies of bourgeois art, reach everyone at that core of loneliness which is our only real togetherness.

Finally, in order to prove the innocence of his characters' motives (and his own), their absolute non-complicity, Jones has to prove also their inarticulateness, the tonguelessness of their art and his. For this reason he is driven to contrive (or, perhaps better, to endure) a style which at once speaks and assures us that its message is unsayable. The "basic simplicity" he seeks is so deep beyond words that only a stutter can convey any sense of it. For better or worse then, Jones stutters — and stammers and slobbers and mumbles, all with the utmost conviction, since the lack of slickness is his credentials, his passport into the Utopia of the Natural.

Needless to say, this notion is in the end self-defeating. The absence of positive style makes it possible for the kind of reader Jones most despises to use *From Here to Eternity* for cheap thrills and illegitimate satisfactions. Not the nameless and the defeated, but the very bourgeois who want their pornography in the guise of literature, read his tract as a "dirty book." Any book they can "understand," whose language is no more precise or whose feeling no subtler than their own, this public will use for their own ends; and what *From Here to Eternity* has become in their minds the moving-picture version reveals — at once mawkish and "hot," an orgy of vicarious passion and self-pity. This kind of fate only a high art can escape; and such an art must pass beyond simplicity and nature, beyond the range of perception of those for whom essentially it speaks. It is a baffling dilemma, perhaps a fatal one, but it cannot be sentimentalized out of existence.

CHAPTER THIRTEEN

Adolescence and Maturity in the American Novel

The years since 1940 have been for writers and critics in America a time of disenchantment, marking, one hopes, the passage from the easy enthusiasms and approximate ambitions of adolescence to the juster self-appraisal of maturity. We have been obliged to recognize not only that we have had most recently a narrowing down, if not an actual exhaustion, of the vein of invention and experiment in the novel; but also that much of the work of the earlier twentieth century which seemed a little while ago so exciting and important actually had only a temporary appeal and a parochial interest. It is not that we have not had in the last thirty years at least two novelists of major stature, but that our sense of a full-scale renaissance, of a continually dazzling level of accomplishment, has turned out to be an illusion. Ironically enough, we have come to a realization of our own limitations during the same period in which many Europeans have embraced the illusion we are leaving behind; so that we find ourselves often in the embarrassing position of having to insist upon the inadequacies of American work which critics abroad find it politic to overpraise.

One of the chief disenchantments of American criticism has been the disconcerting way in which the "great" novels of ten or fifteen years back have tended to disappear. Year by year we have greeted new works with enthusiasm, we have remembered them fondly; but looking back for them over our shoulders we have found them inexplicably turned to dust. The novels of Sherwood Anderson, for example, appear to us now incoherent and unconvincing; his diminished reputation rests on a handful of short stories which survive their sentimentality by fixing it precisely, and which can still move us though they seem alien to what we are at present doing. Sinclair Lewis we find it harder and harder to believe we could ever have taken for a serious writer. The figure of Babbitt remains in our mind, a caricature of attitudes to which we no longer respond; but Lewis himself we remember as a cartoonist, a journalist with neither poetic nor psychological depth, the author of a curiously provincial parody of *Madame Bovary*. John Steinbeck we continue to find appealing only where he is least ambitious: his stories about animals touch us, and his sentimental entertainment *Tortilla Flat* we recall with affection; but his attempts to deal with adult human beings in all their complexity, to judge society (in such a book as *Grapes of Wrath*), seem to us marred by maudlin social piety and turgid symbolism.

John Dos Passos has recently been writing books that no one reads; and even turning back to *1919* or *The 42nd Parallel* we feel that all the famous technical devices are no more than mechanical substitutes for poetry, subterfuges to conceal from us the fact that he cannot create a convincing character. James T. Farrell strikes us as a writer who attains occasional passages of genuinely passionate insight almost by mistake, swathing them in such endless stretches of doughy, earnest documentation that we find it hard to remember them. Thomas Wolfe appears to us now as appallingly overblown, a writer still to be responded to enthusiastically, but only at the one moment of adolescence to which his frantic rhetoric is appropriate; certainly he is not a writer for the mature. We tend now to see him backwards through *Raintree County*, that illuminating failure arising from what Wolfe had made of Joyce and Kinsey had made of sex. The early deaths of Lockridge and Wolfe, self-inflicted or merely endured, blur into a single symbol of the plight of the American writer who does not know how to grow old.

Another such symbolic death is that of F. Scott Fitzgerald, leaving unfinished what might have been his only completely adult book. Even our best writers appear unable to mature; after one or two inexpert attempts, they find a style, a subject and tone, usually anchored in their adolescent experience — and these they repeat compulsively, like a songbird his single tune. Ring Lardner is an especially pathetic example, trying to make of his ballplayers occasions adequate to his bitter vision.

In general, our writers have no history, no development; their themes belong to a pre-adult world, and the experience of growing old tends to remain for them intractable. It is merely one aspect of that compulsive veneration of youth, that fear of all which is not simply strong and beautiful, so important in our total culture. When our novelists do not manage to die young or to stop writing completely (plunging into alcoholism as into a dream of the Garden), they are likely simply to get worse, ending often in intolerable parodies of their own best work. Ernest Hemingway is the classic instance of such a development. One of the best writers of the twentieth century, a novelist of immense technical means, and indeed the inventor of a style that has changed the writing of fiction in the whole Western world, Hemingway has still been unable to progress. When he has attempted to move from evocations of lost youth, from studies of impotence and the failure of love, to be "positive" or socially aware, he has seemed merely unconvincing and forced. It is almost as impossible to imagine a Hemingway character having a child (dying in childbed is another matter) as it is to conceive of one of them going to a ballot box. His characters seem never really old enough to vote, merely to blow up bridges; as they seem never old enough to reproduce, merely sufficiently mature to make the motions of the act of love. In every sense except the genital one, they remain children; so that the controlling values of his books are a boy's notion of bravery and honor and devotion, tricked out in the child's images of bullfighting and big-game hunting and playing war. In the earliest and best work, *The Sun Also Rises, A Farewell to Arms,* and some of the short stories, these notions and these images are turned into a nostalgic, desolate poetry, bare and mannered at the same time. But all the novels since *To Have and Have Not* (which enjoys the singular distinction of having had *two* bad movies made from it — and richly deserves the honor) have been failures, more and more disheartening up to the complete fiasco of *Across the River and Into the Trees.*

The Old Man and the Sea returns to a level of technical accomplishment almost equal to the earlier work by stripping away all social implications and any attempt to deal with mature emotions. Hemingway is always less embarrassing when he is not attempting to deal with women; and he returns with relief (with what we as readers at least feel as relief) to that "safe" American Romance of the boy and the old man. The single flaw in *The Old Man and the Sea* is the constant sense that Hemingway is no longer creating, but merely imitating the marvelous spare style that was once a revelation; that what was once an anti-rhetoric has become now merely another rhetoric, perhaps our most familiar one, and that even its inventor cannot revive it for us.

For the youngest American readers, writers barely beginning, the brighter college students, Hemingway has come to seem irrelevant, a little boring; though his immense, diffused influence continues to manifest itself in all American prose writing — and indeed in our speech itself. An occasional direct imitation (Chandler Brossard's *Who Walk in Darkness*, for example) only makes the point more firmly with its inescapably old-fashioned impact. The youngsters of today are disgusted not only by the dated and ridiculous role which Hemingway, more and more frantically, plays in his own life, but also by his failure to project an adult love, an adult commitment, an adult courage — from which they might at least revolt with dignity. His breathless pursuit of wars, swordfish, and lions leaves cold a generation born older than he will ever get.

Generally speaking, our writers no longer go to Africa or the left bank to escape from the dullness of America to a world of pure Experience; they are tourists or art historians or government officials or the holders of grants and fellowships, but they are not Exiles. They may get drunk in Paris or find mistresses in Rome, but they no longer consider their drunkenness a utopia or their sexual adventures a blow for freedom. In the same way, Bohemia has died for them; I do not mean that there are no bohemias, but that they are now escapes *from* writing, not escapes to it from the pressures of bourgeois life. It is for this reason that F. Scott Fitzgerald, who represents the world of bohemia and expatriation as something done with, who presents the world of the 'twenties with the pathos of something already outgrown, with a sense of how naïvely, how *innocently* lost that generation must appear to our post-Dachau vision, is more sympathetic to us than the much more talented Hemingway, to whom the Cult of Experience remains not a lost frenzy of the years after the First World War, but his only faith.

I suppose it is the death of the adolescent faith in Life as Experience which has led to a complementary loss of the ingenuous faith in Literature as Experience. It was once enough for us to know, or believe (it turns out that we were dealing with a legend), that Sherwood Anderson one day suddenly walked out of the office in which he worked, throwing aside bourgeois security for Art and Life. This seemed then a sufficient guarantee of his "integrity" (it was once our favorite word) and of his excellence as an artist. And, alas, this Anderson believed along with the rest of us, so that much of his work remains abortive, because, trusting to Experience to do the whole job, he stopped precisely where he should have begun in real earnest. There was in those days a hopeless confusion between what made a man "good" (i.e., everything his bourgeois parents would have believed bad) and what made a work of art good; "social consciousness," "sincerity," "progressivism" were taken for aesthetic terms. To such a muddled understanding of the relationship between the truth of art, the truth of conscience, and the truth of facts, writers like Upton Sinclair, Sinclair Lewis, and Farrell owe their former successes and their present waning popularity. Hemingway himself, though primarily a stylist and interested only at a second remove in "life," was victimized by similar assumptions, which have led to his continuing pose as a *naïf*, a latterday Mark Twain; and he has felt obliged to invent with great pains a style which seems to take no pains; as some American politicians invest a great deal of art in seeming to speak like the artless common man.

Even so important and courageous a literary pioneer as Theodore Dreiser appears to us now of drastically limited value, despite his ability to create a milieu with all the thick substance of reality itself. It is not merely a matter of his sentimental subjects, those eternally seduced women, or of the gross style interlarded with ladies'-magazine elegancies, nor even of his profound and utterly unsuspected stupidity (intelligence and style alike are optional for the writer — and any subject can be redeemed); but of his failure to develop, his entrapment by the belief that a work of art is equal to its raw materials, and that its moral value is equal to the code its author professes rather than what is *realized* in the text.

It is tempting to say that the central fact of our period is the death of "naturalism" and the decline in reputation of the novelists associated with its seeming triumph. But what has died is only a small part of what is commonly associated with the term: a certain moral obtuseness, political sentimentality and naïve faith in documentation. Much has survived: the breaking of certain taboos about subject matter; the demonstration that no experience is too humble or trivial for the novel; the elevation of a solidly specified environment to equal importance with plot or character; the revolution in the conventions of writing dialogue — all these will never be lost. Yet the contemporary American author no longer believes that a work of art can be judged primarily by its accuracy in reproducing ordinary speech or rendering literally the horrors of Chicago slums; for us, the reality, the value, of a work of art lies in its symbolic depth and resonance, not in the exhaustiveness of its data.

It is for this reason that a vital influence on the contemporary novel is Henry James, who not long since was disowned as too aristocratic, too elaborately trivial to be either a good writer or a true American. In his own day, of course, James was felt, indeed felt himself, in the forefront of the movement toward "realism," while we relish in him what is least like such fellow-realists as William Dean Howells. Our James is the impressionist, the conscious artist, who dared assert that a concern with form is not immoral; and in whom we have come to recognize great poetry, profound images of good and evil, under the slowly elaborated accounts of people who apparently never sweat or blow their noses, and who manage to make love over teacups rather than in bed. From James, our younger novelists (even the ones most impatient with him, most insistent on all he ignores) have learned that a novel is not what its author *says* happened in it, but what is really *rendered*. It is possible to feel now that the Jamesian example has been assimilated, even institutionalized, and that we must be moving on; but there is no way to go except through Henry James, and no writer among us can ever doubt again that a book is made of words rather than facts.

For technique, the newer writers have been able to find a master no further back than the beginnings of realism; but, for an exemplar of the poetic subject, they have had to search behind the Civil War, to the Melville of *Moby Dick,* in whom they have found a blend of secularized puritanism, factual solidity, and symbolic resonance, an erudition and naïveté that point beyond realism. There is a Melville whom one scarcely knows whether to call the discovery or invention of our time, our truest contemporary, who has revealed to us the traditional theme of the deepest American mind, the ambiguity of innocence, "the mystery of iniquity," which we had traded for the progressive melodrama of a good outcast (artist, rebel, whore, proletarian) against an evil bourgeoisie. In James, too, a similar theme is suggested and then almost lost in the embroidery of sensibility; but, having seen once our theme, we do not willingly surrender it or the attitudes proper to it: "the blackness ten times black," the obligation to say *no,* the practice of irony and the acceptance that does not cancel it out. In these, there is the possibility of development and fulfillment, a way out of adolescence.

Guilt and innocence, the mystery of iniquity — most of our present-day writers are not in any orthodox sense religious (though a few are, and many enjoy playing poetically with the counters of orthodoxy: Original Sin and Salvation and the Dark Night of the Soul), but almost all of them feel that there are deeper perceptions of man's plight than the brash optimism of a Rousseau. We remember only too well the generations who tried to convince us that all metaphors of human evil were mystifications, the inventions of priests and aesthetes afraid of "real life." Indeed, during the 'thirties, when American "realism" was captured by the Marxists, such concerns were banned by the exponents of the "proletarian," who preached that the only criterion of good and evil, as well as the true subject of fiction, was the Class Struggle. The record of the so-called "proletarian novel" in the United States is one of the most absurd episodes of our literary history. The names of the "revolutionary" writers who seemed to us in 1935 about to make a new culture are hard to remember: Robert Cantwell, Grace Lumpkin, Jack Conroy, William Rollins — one sees them occasionally in a list of witnesses before a Congressional investigating committee, or on the masthead of a Luce publication. Merely to recite the half-forgotten names and to invoke our old enthusiasm is to learn the lesson which makes us smile a little when we see in Europe today attempts at social realism, at what the French call *"littérature engagée."*

Yet once, even established writers rushed to give assurances that they had graduated from post-war cynicism, Hemingway writing *To Have and Have Not,* and Fitzgerald himself toying with the idea of having Dick Diver become a Communist; and those who would not conform were disowned. It is symptomatic of our new turning that the favorite writer of most of our young novelists now is precisely the author most despised, during the "proletarian" period, as reactionary, ghoulish, and cheaply spectacular — namely, William Faulkner. We do not, to be sure, read his grotesque poems of comedy and horror as realistic reports on the South; for us the truth of Faulkner's world is a symbolic truth; and across his gothic landscape is fought not the historical war between North and South, but the eternal war between the dream of nobility and order and the fact of disorder and failure and sorrow. Naturally, his images are American images and even regional ones: the Negro, the Indian, the ravaged and forgotten wilderness, the miserable mountain farm, the riderless horse disappearing into the night — but their meanings are the meanings of such objects in dreams and not in history, meanings immediately translatable for anyone anywhere. Beyond this, there is Faulkner's concern with rhetoric and form which intrigues us; his stubborn insistence on finding for each book (*The Sound and the Fury* is perhaps the best example) a language and structure so nearly impossible that he is always risking absurdity.

Faulkner and Melville and James: these are the American novelists who function as living influences today. There are others whom we honor, Hawthorne and Mark Twain and Hemingway, for instance; but they do not so directly determine the ambitions of the beginning writer, except as they also contribute to the psychological, symbolic, gothic tradition these define. The strengths of contemporary writing correspond to the strengths of this tradition, boldness of imagery, subtlety of insight, and especially the willingness to plunge deep below the lintel of consciousness; and the weaknesses to its weaknesses, a tendency to involution and hysteria, to a rhetoric that becomes pseudo-poetry at its weakest; and a weakness in dealing with women. The tradition which stems from Melville, James, and Faulkner combines an overall moral maturity with a failure to achieve mature attitudes toward sex; there is a vacuum at the heart of American fiction that James's nervous indirection, Melville's underground homosexuality, and Faulkner's comic anti-feminism cannot fill. But at least there is a tradition at last, compounded ironically by three traditionless and lonely writers; and, beyond them, our newer novelists look to European sources: to the Russian novel of the nineteenth century, especially to Dostoevsky; to Marcel Proust, whose influence blends with that of James; to James Joyce and Thomas Mann; and more recently to Franz Kafka, who seems almost an American writer in his symbolic gothicism and who projected, before we knew we needed it, a style able to reproduce the logical insanity of a German concentration camp or a Russian political trial.

It is a point worth noting that most of our younger writers do not insist upon their *difference* as Americans, feeling themselves sharers in the general development of Western culture; indeed, one of the things that makes us feel alienated from an Anderson, a Dreiser, a Sinclair Lewis is their almost willful cultural naïveté, their fear of the traditional. For we have come to believe that an ignorance of the past and of Europe is the poorest way to ensure our own particularity. In home-made, degenerate form all the clichés of post-Enlightenment thought appear in the work of those writers most set on repro-ducing "pure" American experience; while in James and Mel-ville the fruit of reading and study is an approach at once new and enriched by older sources.

Not all recent American writers, of course, fall into the post-naturalist camp I have been describing. The writers of books describing the Second World War have apparently felt them-selves immune to the shifts I have tried to indicate, and with creditable diligence and woeful lack of invention they have rewritten the typical novels of the war of 1917, changing only dates and place names; while, a few years back, another atavis-tic novel, James Jones's *From Here to Eternity,* won consider-able critical acclaim by reviving and exemplifying the pseudo-realist theory that to write honestly one must write badly, that Art and Truth are mutually exclusive. There survives and flourishes, in addition, the slick sentimental-realist school, represented by John Hersey's *The Wall* and the novels of Irwin Shaw, which manage to combine a banal liberal op-timism with a commercially successful style based on watered-down Hemingway.

But among those writers who, in the phrase of Henry James, have "no ambitions except the highest" the majority are more concerned with symbol than with statement, more drawn to-ward poetry than toward journalism. Their work tends to be the opposite of naïve — in fact, rather difficult; and they are read, therefore, by a relatively small audience as compared not only with the readers of historical romances, but even with those who admire the tough or sentimental pseudo-realists. It is one of the ironies of the present situation in writing that our better novelists are at the same time un-popular and un-experi-mental. Nobody nowadays is doing anything startling or new; the techniques that are being exploited are those that were revolutionary in the 'twenties; but the mass audience has stub-bornly refused to catch up. This is hardly cheering to our younger authors, who tend to be a melancholy lot, having neither the comfort of commercial success nor the thrill of feeling themselves a gallant vanguard. They have tended, in self-defense, to find themselves special audiences for whom they specifically write and by whose acclaim they live; and while this strategy serves a purpose in sustaining them, financially and spiritually, it has tended to create a situation in which we have a series of competing "academies" rather than a conflict of the academic and the anti-academic.

Since it would be impossible to mention more than a few writers of the younger generation without simply compiling a catalogue, I shall limit myself to discussing particularly only two of the competing "academies," the two which seem to me in certain ways most important: one associated with *Harper's Bazaar,* the other with *Partisan Review.* I pick *Harper's Bazaar* to stand for a whole group which includes *Mademoiselle* and *Vogue* and the ill-fated *Flair,* which attempted to be deliberately and whole-heartedly what the others had become partially and almost by accident, and which ended as a parody of itself and of the others. *Harper's Bazaar* is, of course, not primarily a literary magazine at all, but an elegant fashion magazine for women, read not only by those who can afford the goods it advertises but by many who cannot and who participate vicariously in its world of values, picking it up on the table of a beauty-parlor waiting room. Finding a story by, say, Truman Capote tucked away between the picture of a determinedly unbeautiful model and an ad for a brassiere, most of the readers of *Harper's Bazaar,* one assumes, must simply skip the meaningless pages; and, knowing this, the editors (writers, themselves, or friends of writers) know that they can print anything they please.

But the conjunction of Capote and high style is not as accidental as it seems at first glance. We have been evolving in recent years a new sort of sensibility, defined by a taste for *haute couture,* classical ballet, baroque opera, the rites and vestments of Catholicism — and above all for a kind of literature at once elegantly delicate and bitterly grotesque. This new kind of sensibility, although (or perhaps because) it is quite frankly a homosexual one, appeals profoundly to certain rich American women with cultural aspirations, and is therefore sponsored in their salons and published decoratively in magazines that cater to their tastes. The development of new markets for the young writer with this sort of sensibility has gone hand in hand with the development of a kind of high bohemia, which moves freely from New York to Venice to Capri to establish a world that is international and anti-bourgeois without being political or sordid or sullen, like the older bohemias.

The most important writer of this group is Carson McCullers, the most typical Truman Capote (or his latest version, called Speed Lamkin or whatever, since in this world of evanescent youth the hungry generations tread each other down with astonishing rapidity). One can take the latter as almost a caricature of the type: the "queen" as American author, possessing a kind of beauty, both in person and as an artist, which belongs to childhood and early adolescence, and which withers before it can ripen; Southern in origin and allegiance; and gothic (a very refined gothic) in style, blending Edgar Allan Poe and Ronald Firbank in an improbable grafting.

Such writers also descend in a strange way from Faulkner, who provides them with a ready-made *paysage moralisée*, the landscape of the South as a natural symbol for decay and brooding evil. To the distrust and fear of woman in Faulkner, they respond according to their own lights; and what there is in the older writer of the agonizedly male has already been transmuted for them by two transitional writers, both women and both immensely talented, Katherine Anne Porter and Eudora Welty — who began the process of taming and feminizing Faulkner (he has had only one truly male follower, Robert Penn Warren, who falls outside the scope of my present essay), making possible the ingrafting of Henry James which produces the true Magnolia Blossom or Southern Homosexual style: pseudo-magical, pseudo-religious, counterfeiting the symbolism of Faulkner in a rhetoric and rhythm derived from James.

I have used the word "counterfeiting" because I find this kind of fiction often merely chic behind its pretense of being subtle and advanced. Even Capote, who possesses considerable talent, has come more and more to *play* at being an author, to act out for the benefit of his own kind of society the role of the elegant, sad, futile androgyne — half reigning beauty and half freak. His novel *Other Voices, Other Rooms* already represents a falling away from the slight authentic music of such an early story as "Children on Their Birthdays," and some of his most recent work seems more and more just décor — like the quasi-surrealist window dressings of certain Fifth Avenue shops.

There has been a tendency for this school at its periphery, where it touches, let us say, Princeton, to combine in a perhaps foreseeable way with the formal emphasis of the "New Criticism," and to find expression in the more studied Jamesian effects of a writer like Frederick Buechner; but its realest triumphs are achieved in the fiction of Carson McCullers. Her first novel, *The Heart Is a Lonely Hunter,* published when she was only twenty-two, is heartbreakingly wonderful; the melancholy Southern town, the deaf-and-dumb protagonists all make their meanings precisely, scene and symbol fused into a single poetry without strain. The subject of Miss McCullers' work is the subject of her whole group: the impossibility of reciprocal love, the sadness of a world in which growing up means only learning that isolation is the fate of every one of us. Her central characters, those ambiguous boyish girls (Frankie and Mick: the names make the point) who stand outside of everything, even their own sex, lost in a world of freaks — these are strange new heroes of our time.

The *Partisan Review,* around which the second "academy" tends to polarize, is quite another matter, though, indeed, its typical contributors sometimes appear (though not usually with their best or most characteristic work) in *Harper's Bazaar;* while a sensibility, shriller or icier, but not fundamentally different from that which informs the fiction of the ladies' magazines, manifests itself in such *Partisan Review* contributors as Tennessee Williams and Paul Bowles. But the impact, the very appearance of *Partisan* indicate a fundamental difference. It is not an advertising journal that has stumbled into printing advanced fiction, but a review which began as a "little magazine" and has managed (thanks in part to angels, but chiefly to the stubborn devotion of its editors) to become an institution without ever having achieved a large circulation. One of the strangest things about *Partisan Review* is that, though its readers have never numbered more than about 10,000, its name is confidently used in journals with 100,000 and 2,000,000 readers as a symbol for certain values which do not have to be further defined. Certainly, it is resented, hated, and sullenly respected by a much larger number of people than have ever read it.

In its beginnings, it attempted to combine an allegiance to *avant-garde* aesthetic ideals and radical politics; at first, it was quite frankly a Communist publication, though its editors quite soon broke from orthodox Stalinism as the enemy of free culture. Its contributors are characteristically unhappy with each other and with the magazine itself; and they would resent to a man being spoken of as a group, as I am doing now. But they *do* have a good deal in common, not the least of which is their uneasy feeling of independence from each other, the sense that it is only their past which binds them unwillingly together. In politics, for instance, they have grown far apart, becoming variously Anarchists, Trotskyites, Social Democrats, New Dealers, and even Republicans — but they have all of them the complicated political awareness of those who once lived inside of or close to the Communist movement.

They are "political" in the European sense of the word, a sense that does not even exist for most Americans. Not only do they have Marx, accepted or denied, in their blood, but also Freud in much the same way, as well as contemporary sociology, anthropology, and philosophy in general — so that they are likely to take sides passionately in arguments about, say, existentialism or other recent European ideologies. They share the fondness of the Southern group for James and Faulkner, but in some ways Kafka is closer to their hearts (Isaac Rosenfeld, for instance, made a major, not quite successful effort, to create a body of American work in his image), and they feel a real kinship with Dostoevsky and Tolstoy. Precisely because their cultural background is so complex, and also because they have almost all been forced somewhere between 1935 and 1940 to make a radical shift in their political allegiances and aesthetic ambitions, it has taken these writers a long time to grow up. Some critics have even found it comical or disheartening to learn that many *Partisan* writers spoken of as "young" are thirty or thirty-five or forty. But they are in truth, for the reasons I have tried to suggest, still young as writers when middle-aged as men, still *beginning* — not dazzling successes at twenty like Truman Capote. They have matured slowly, but they have matured; and this is exceptional in the American scene.

The best of the group is Saul Bellow, a novelist of exceptional talent and in many ways a typical figure. Like most of the writers I am describing, he is a second-generation Jew (this is important, for the Jews are just now taking a place of peculiar significance in American cultural life; and, as a history-ridden people in a history-less land, they stand in a different relationship to the past and to Europe than any other American group), an urban type, whose world is not the archetypal small town that from Twain to Sherwood Anderson and on to Faulkner has been the world *par excellence* of our fiction. Nor is his city the Big Town seen by the provincial, the bewildering un-home that has haunted the American literary mind from the moment of Pierre's wild trip to New York. Saul Bellow's Chicago (like the New York of Delmore Schwartz) is the only home of the essentially homeless, remembered not idyllically as the Garden but as the desert to which one woke at the moment of the Great Depression.

Bellow's controlling images and myths tend to be social ones; ideas, political and philosophical, are not something intrusive in his work, but the atmosphere, the very condition of life. He feels most deeply where his thought is most deeply involved, and his characters come alive where they are touched by ideas. It is for this reason that the most moving passages in his books are discussions, the interchange of opinions and theories as vividly presented as a love scene or a fight. But his books are never "problem" novels in the sense of the socially conscious 'twenties. Even *The Victim* (which remains in many respects my favorite), though it takes off from the problem of anti-Semitism, does not aim at establishing the smug sense of our own innocence and the other's guilt, but suggests in its muted fable the difficulty of being human, much less innocent, in a world of injustice.

With *The Adventures of Augie March*, Bellow has won for the first time the general recognition he has long deserved, though his two earlier books had won at least equal critical acclaim. Writers of this school have, I think, a special problem in reaching a mass audience to whom the commonplaces of their experience have an inevitable tinge of the remote and abstruse; and *Augie* is a deliberate attempt to break through to such a group out of the parochial world in which Bellow began. *Augie* itself is an uneven book, redundant and untidy, full of a strange tough-abstract poetry that becomes sometimes merely mannered; but it is held together finally by a versatile irony that moves from barely quizzical tenderness to wild burlesque. Ideally, the book should be read after the grey, tight, orderly *Victim* in order to understand the self-imposed limitations against which it is in revolt. In everything but self-understanding and control, it is a better book, richer, more ambitious, funnier, the saga of an improbable Huckleberry Finn: Huck as a metropolitan Jew, a wanderer through cities, fallen among Trotskyites and comedians of ideas as well as grafters and minor machiavellians — but Huck still, the apostle of non-commitment, moving uncertainly but inevitably toward the "happy ending" of un-success. It is an explosive book, a novel powered by the atomization of its own world; and the world fragmented in its humor and violence is the world of the *Partisan Review*, which Augie may never have had time to read.

There are other lesser, but still interesting, writers in this constellation: Lionel Trilling, whose single novel was not quite successful, but who in two short stories perfected a new kind of moral-critical fiction; Delmore Schwartz, a poet and fictionist who evokes the Jewish-American milieu with a studied limpness, half-irritating, half-intriguing; Mary McCarthy, the most wickedly witty of the group, who satirizes the ideas of the *Partisan Review* itself at the point where they tend to die into banalities.

It is because the fictionists of this group are capable of

seeing themselves with a characteristic irony, sad or brittle, because their world is complex and troubled enough to protect them from nostalgia and self-pity, that I see in them evidence of a movement toward a literature of maturity. Yet certain flaws endemic to the whole American scene reappear disconcertingly in the *Partisan* group and mar *Augie* itself. One feels sometimes that only the weaknesses of American literature survive from generation to generation; that the heritage of our writers is a series of vacuums, which by evasion or strategy they must bridge or by-pass.

One waits still, for instance, for the American writer who can render as successfully as, say, any second-rank French novelist of the nineteenth century the complexities and ambiguities of sexual passion, of — (how absurdly hard it is for the American writer to say simply "love") of *love*. The sentimental-love religion has died out of our serious fiction, leaving only a blank, a blank that the nympholeptic stereotypes which play the women's roles in Saul Bellow's book surely do not fill. Among certain *Partisan* writers, there has recently been an attempt to make out of Laurentian reminiscences and Reichian doctrines a new religion — not of love, of course, but of "full genitality"; yet this seems anything but mature.

Moreover, there appears to be a growing impatience inside the *Partisan* academy, superficially directed at the excesses of the newer criticism but actually aimed at the whole Jamesian cult of sensibility, and this threatens to end in a general scalping of all Paleface writers. Yet the urge toward this polar split between "honest crudity" and "elegant introspection" represents as deep a wound in the American aesthetic sense as the analogous distinction of Dark Lady and Fair Lady stands for in terms of our sexual consciousness. There is a kind of tough-minded provincialism implicit in the whole position: an impulse toward "moral realism," a fear of "mystification" (i.e., of religion and metaphysics), which may at any moment explode in a reversion to the simplest Redskin celebration of pure experience.

Against this temptation, Dostoevsky and Tolstoy and Kafka might well be expected to serve as antidotes; but it is hard to say how seriously these writers are finally taken and how far they are merely "culture" in the vulgarest sense of the word, the souvenirs of literary tourism. The "tradition" which sustains the *Partisan Review* remains, in a characteristically American way, partial and *willed*. Its canon develops not organically out of a given cultural past, but by forced breeding out of what a few strong-minded men *happen to know*. It is hard to see how such a situation can be avoided in a society distinguished by the indifference of the many to the making of its taste, and by an unbridgeable gap between its productive present and its only viable literary past.

The America which has survived westward expansion and the mass immigration of the last century can no longer live, except nostalgically, on the puritan-colored metaphysical tradition that was still able to nurture Hawthorne and Melville and Henry James. It is not only that America is comparatively young, but that it no longer possesses even the meager past it has lived; that it has, indeed, deliberately and joyously cast off that burden, so that each new generation must improvise not only its fate but its history. This is, on the one hand, an opportunity but, on the other, a curse; and, opportunity or curse, it cuts us off from the European alternatives of Tradition and Revolt. To be sure, we use these terms frequently but somewhat comically to describe our pious allegiance to or disavowal of values some ten or fifteen years old; and our failure to confess this leads to the constant counterfeiting of new pasts and the restless revaluations that succeed each other among us with bewildering speed.

There has been in recent times a notorious attempt to invent a full-scale synthetic myth of an America of the Open Road to replace the defunct New England version of our country; but this was born as unreal as its predecessor has become, and, as it has grown less and less sympathetic to a second-generation, urbanized world, its sponsors have grown shriller and shriller. The sentimentality of the wholesale American Legend and its corresponding dream of an unlimited mass audience have not directly influenced most serious American writers; but, in their self-satisfaction at having resisted so second-rate a temptation, they are likely to fall prey to the subtler allures embodied in the exclusive little audience with its conviction of the superiority of its special taste. To write deliberately for the few, we have been learning, is as dangerous as writing for the many in a mass society. To shift from the latter aim to the former is to move from the child's desire to buy universal love with perfect obedience to the adolescent's resolve to compel universal recognition with perfect non-cooperation, a resolve that ends typically in complete submission to the mores of one's gang.

The mature writer must write, as he has always written, for neither mass nor sect but for that pure fiction, the ideal understander, for whom we no longer have a name but who was once called the "gentle reader." In traditional cultures, that non-existent perfect reader was postulated in a set of values represented imperfectly but hopefully by a self-perpetuating body of critics. In America, he has never been institutionalized, surviving only in the unwitting parody of the "genteel reader," which at the end of the nineteenth century we rejected with scorn in favor of a more democratic but less useful concept, the "average reader."

The plight of the American writer is at best difficult; aware that the greatest books of our literature remain somehow boys' books, he seeks a way toward maturity. But between him and a mature relationship with his past lies our contempt for what is left behind, the discontinuity of our history; between him and a mature relationship with his public lies the impossibility of institutionalizing values in a democracy which regards taste as a vestige of aristocratic privilege; between him and a mature relationship with experience lies the fact that the only universally *felt* American morality arises from the ersatz religion of sentimentalism.

It is no wonder that our novelists have shuttled between the utopias of form and formlessness, pretending alternately that a technical point-of-view is a sufficient substitute for a moral viewpoint and that reported fact is the equivalent of judged experience. The images of childhood and adolescence haunt our greatest works as an unintended symbolic confession of the inadequacy we sense but cannot remedy. Perhaps it is impossible to attain a mature literature without a continuing tradition in the European sense; for it may be that no individual author alone and in a single lifetime can achieve an adult relationship to his culture and his vision of it. But we can, of course, never have such a tradition, only the disabling nostalgia for one; and quite rapidly the whole world is coming to resemble us in this regard. The essential fact of literature in our age is its inevitable "Americanization," as mass culture advances and the old systems of evaluation go down with the political structures into which they were ingrafted.

In this sense, the Continental vogue of American fiction, which seems otherwise a merely fashionable exoticism or even sometimes a gesture of self-contempt and anti-intellectualism, represents the search of Western literature for its future. Even now, the writers of many other countries begin to stand to their own past in a relation as uneasy as our own; and in our novel they find raised nakedly at last the question that underlay the experimentation of the 'twenties, the "social consciousness" of the 'thirties, the search for formal security of the 'forties: "Can the lonely individual, unsustained by tradition in an atomized society, achieve a poetry adult and complicated enough to be the consciousness of its age?" To have posed that question for the world is the achievement of the American novel at the present moment.

No! in Thunder

ESSAYS ON MYTH AND LITERATURE

To my mother

Introduction to the
Second Edition of
No! in Thunder

ALL MY adult life I have been pulled back and forth between a commitment to literature and a concern with politics, hauled and hunched mercilessly first by my seniors, then by my juniors, always by my more earnest contemporaries surer than I about which was the proper way to go. I suspect that by temperament I am profoundly apolitical, even antipolitical; but growing up in the thirties I was exposed, from the age of twelve or thirteen on, to pressure from friends on the Left who spoke with greater assurance than they perhaps felt in order to convince me that too much time spent thinking about poetry meant betraying the hope of the Revolution. And for some ten years I remained convinced, so deeply convinced in fact that even after I had lost my sense of commitment to the radical politics of that dewy decade, which is to say, my first innocence, I continued to feel that it was my duty to wrestle still with political problems, by exposing all political illusions including and especially my own.

It is for that reason, I suppose, that my first book dealt largely with politics, a politics in dissolution to be sure but politics all the same, whether embraced or disavowed; and the essays dealing with such matters quite untypically, I felt even then, overshadowed the other more literary ones printed beside them. By the time I was ready to put together a second volume

213

of essays, however, I had resolved not to misrepresent myself once more (not only politics, I had learned, but even anti-politics was the opium of the liberals) by listening to the *zeitgeist* rather than to my own inner voice, which spoke in myth and metaphor rather than slogans and statistics.

One excess leads to another, however; and it seems to me now looking back on *No! in Thunder* that it is finally *too* literary in all the conventional sense of the word, too ridden by self-consciousness and the effort to appear solemn or serious, even mantic, at all costs. The shadow of Matthew Arnold had fallen on me as that of Karl Marx had withdrawn, and in the penumbra of either humor withers and dies. How I wish now that there were more jokes in my second collection, even—perhaps especially—bad ones. Not all of the essays in that collection seem to me equally juiceless and joyless, however; the two essays on literary theory which conclude the volume are the most offensive in that respect, though I felt them—I am moved to protest in self-defense—as demihoaxes from the start. The title essay, on the other hand, remains for me still alive and close to the center of my vision of myself as a writer and general critic of society.

It is, I suppose, toward such general criticism that I began moving ten years ago, a little waveringly and uncertainly, in turning from the examination of texts (the reigning mode in the universities at the point when my book appeared) to an exploration of the contexts, social and psychological, in which literature was written and read. Only thus, it seemed to me, could I abandon politics without surrendering moral commitment or betraying my own rage at the inequities and miseries of the society which sustained me.

It is worth noting, I think, that I was still worrying the subject of guilt and innocence as revealed in the courtroom in my essay on Leopold and Loeb, a final pair of antiheroes who seemed to me then strange analogues (immune to political sentimentality) to the Rosenbergs and Alger Hiss; and I reflected on some of the ironies implicit in saying what I believed would be my last word on Symbolic Trials not about great public figures like Dimitrov or Kamenev and Zinoviev or Sacco and Vanzetti, or even such inflated subheroes as Alger Hiss, but two Jewish boys from Chicago, two poor creeps convinced they were supermen.

What most moves me in my second collection on the verge of its rebirth, however, is what is least polemical in it: the series of critical essays in which I was moving from the young man's (necessary) desire to put down all which seems to him alien and shoddy in art toward the (optional) longing of middle age to praise what is best loved—whether established classics like Dante and Shakespeare and Whitman, or more equivocal minor figures like Robert Louis Stevenson and Kafka, Robert Penn Warren and Bernard Malamud. It has taken me a long time to realize that the obligation to praise does not contradict but compliments the necessity to say no. This collection records my first gestures at putting that small wisdom into practice.

Foreword

My second collection of essays has been gathered together in the same hope that inspired the first: the hope of offending all those with "cemeteries to defend," whether the tombstones in those cemeteries memorialize the avant-garde revolt of the twenties, the Marxism of the thirties, the enlightened middle-browism of the forties or the hip pieties of the fifties. I continue to dream of stirring in those entombed in clichés of commitment or disaffection a twinge of shame at not being (while they still have the choice) alive. *Be ashamed that you are dead,* I keep shouting like a fool; *be ashamed that you would rather be dead than uncomfortably aware.* And the answers come back: "You're a position-taker!" or "You're a lackey of the Committee for Cultural Freedom!"—"You're a Freudian!" or "You're not a Freudian!" —"You hate literature!" or simply "You use too many exclamation marks!"

I have not, that is to say, been universally understood or approved of; and I am not sanguine about the prospects for the future, though certain howls of pain and rage, disguised as critical responses to my first book, indicated that some at least had been by its good offices temporarily raised from the dead. Why were they not grateful? To speak frankly, their gratitude would have given me pause; for I am perverse enough to rejoice more in certain enemies made by *An End to Innocence* (literary onanists, academic subscribers to *The Nation,* backwoods patriots and socialists, unreconstructed defenders of Alger Hiss) than by some of its friends. I treasure, however, among the latter those to whom it brought not peace but a sword, not sniggering satisfaction but profound unease. I should hate to think that I write for those who are *glad* that the Rosenbergs, or even Leopold and Loeb, were guilty as charged.

I have heard from time to time reports of friend separated

217

from friend or lover from lover by arguments over one or another of my essays. Such reports, when not mere flattery, are, I fear, part of a legend from which I hope I shall always be able to disentangle my real self. And yet, if I have told in my essays even a part of the truth I have tried to see, they should indeed have had such effects. At the very least, I tell myself, they have brought certain dull parties to bitter and long-overdue ends, leaving perhaps a survivor or two with the conviction that something exists outside the closed circle of standard allegiances and the ennui of self-congratulation.

Nevertheless, I call my new book *No! in Thunder* not as a boast but as a declaration of intent. I know well enough that when a writer believes himself to be thundering, his readers may think he is singing "On the Road to Mandalay." I am not, let it be clear, for all my occasional hamminess, an entertainer; and when I find a reviewer describing a piece of mine as "brilliant," I wince. It is an ambiguous and dangerous epithet, implying sometimes simple condescension, sometimes downright hostility. My aim is to create not the shallow joy felt in the presence of virtuosity but the difficult pleasure possible only to one recognizing a truth which involves a personal humiliation or the surrender of values long held. There is also an illegitimate pleasure derived from seeing someone else's illusions destroyed, or the pretenses of a writer to whom one feels no commitment exposed; but this pleasure, which I cannot help affording certain readers, I want those readers to know I begrudge them.

As for myself, I have in the essays which follow said No! to nothing which it has cost me nothing to reject. I have undercut nothing on which I do not stand or do not remember having been tempted to stand. My book is, therefore, even where it seems least so, an autobiography, a confession: the continuing record of my sentimental education, as well as an account of the world in which I am being educated. It is for this reason that I try to speak always in my own person, never objectively as if I were the voice of an institution or an era. If sometimes I use the "we," this represents not a desire to hide behind the editorial plural, but merely my awareness that in speaking for myself I may also speak for one group or another joined to me by age or skin color or religion or common indignation. I never forget, however, that behind the "we" there remains my singular and quite fallible "I"— an "I" which can go as wrong as anyone's; but this has not seemed to me sufficient reason for qualifying what at any moment I passionately believe.

I hope (probably in vain) that those whom I have felt obliged to dissect, because their work seemed to me representative of what is shallow, self-deceiving or specious in our culture, will somehow realize that I do not think of them as being identical with their work and standing or falling with it. I know that their essential being, quite like my own, is outside of what they write and that only the most despicable of our contemporaries confuse the value of a man's collected works with that of his life. Yet a friend cries, "You write about living men as coldly as if they were *dead*. That's why people cry out against you so hysterically!" And I answer that some presumably living men *are* dead, though I know this seems a metaphor only and therefore something of a quibble. Beyond this, I can add only that I try to keep before me always the awareness that someday not only my subjects but I myself will be literally dead; and that I must say now (regardless of gossip, interest and the possibilities of offense) the words that I would wish to be on record then—the No! that I hope will be heard like distant thunder in a world I shall not see, but that I suspect will only rankle in the heart of some poor writer, his family and friends.

Unlike my first collection, this one consists chiefly of literary theory, comments on literary works and reflections on the role of myth in art and society. I am glad this time to have moved politics to the periphery, not from mere snobbishness (though I do feel something hopelessly trivial in hunting one's subject in yesterday's headlines), but chiefly because I am by temperament and training committed to the world of the imagination rather than that of mere fact. I pledged myself in my first book to give to certain political documents "the same careful scrutiny we have learned to practise on the shorter poems of John Donne"; I pledge myself this time to approach the shorter poems of Donne (or Dante or Shakespeare or Whitman) with the sense that they matter quite as much to the self and the world as the execution of Caryl Chessman or even the suspension of atomic testing.

I have included here no essay which says what I no longer believe, but the language of some of them, after ten or twelve years, I scarcely recognize as my own. Nevertheless, I have resisted the temptation to do more than fill in obvious gaps, update references no longer current, emend outright error, and remedy a slovenliness begotten by haste. Such retrospective comment or qualification as I could not forbear making I have entrusted to footnotes or to the headnotes that introduce the four Parts, thus presenting them as the afterthoughts they really are. The Introduction, written especially for this volume, is intended to cast over the rest of its contents what I should like to think of as the light in which I now live.

Leslie A. Fiedler

MISSOULA, MONTANA
20 MAY 1960

Introduction: No! in Thunder

That the practice of any art at any time is essentially a moral activity I have always believed; indeed, I do not know how to begin to make a book or talk about one without moral commitment. Yet for a long time I tried to keep this secret from myself as well as from others, since in the critical world in which I grew up, a "moralistic approach" to literature was considered not only indecent but faintly comic. Most of my best literary friends, at any rate, considered it strategically advisable to speak of novels and poems *purely* (the adverb is theirs) in terms of diction, structure and point of view, remaining safely inside the realm of the formal. But an author's choice of—or a critic's preference for—one point of view, or type of diction, or kind of structure, or even his emphasis on one of these elements at the expense of the others, involves a judgment of the experience he is rendering; and such a judgement is, implicitly at least, a moral one.

One of the special strengths of modern fiction has been its awareness of the moral dimension of form; and the seminal greatness of Flaubert lies in his willingness to entrust judgment primarily to style: to transform style, in effect, from a social grace to a tool of ethical analysis. The author of *Madame Bovary* seldom comments directly on the social concerns which most deeply vex him; he has, indeed, an almost fanatic resolve *not* to admonish or preach, but his style is his surrogate in this regard. And his style judges—judges Emma and Homais, the clichés of Romanticism and Revolution, the formlessness and falsity of bourgeois life. By the same token, that style judges and condemns, as all serious style continues to judge and condemn, the literature of the market place and those misguided books dedicated to anti-style.

There are, of course, certain counterfeits of style, quite

221

unlike Flaubert's, which are symptoms of the decay of their world rather than judgments of it; for there can be no neutrality in the area of technique. The form of a book represents either a moral critique of man and society, or a moral surrender. The pseudo-styles—which are called, a little misleadingly, "naturalist" and which have been practiced from the time of Émile Zola to that of James Jones—have represented such capitulations before the collapse of discrimination and sensitivity in the world around them; even as earlier Scott's manly carelessness and Dickens' hasty improvisations represented a retreat from moral engagement, and the ecstatic schoolgirl anti-style of Jack Kerouac projects a more recent sort of cowardice. Such writers as Zola, Jones and Kerouac are guilty not only of moral weakness but of hypocrisy as well, for they proffer their sloppiness and their submission to the decay of language as tokens of their sincerity and belongingness. To seem "one of the boys" is especially an American temptation, eternally offered and eternally accepted. But it is not only the principled anti-stylists, populist or Beat, who stand condemned in the court of high art for flagrant immorality, an immorality of form which all their avowed (and guilt-compelled) dedication to quite moral ideas and causes cannot mitigate. Those responsible for books like *Exodus,* or *Advise and Consent,* or whatever improbable contender is currently fighting its way up the best-seller lists, must also be adjudged guilty; since ignorance is no excuse, and good will merely aggravates the crime.

In the realm of fiction, to be inept, whether unwittingly or on purpose, is the single unforgivable sin. To be inept is to lie; and for this, time and the critics grant no pardon. Yet the contemporary audience forgives the liar in art, even adulates him. It knows he is lying, but it needs his lies. In our Do-It-Yourself Age, when no one can really do anything for himself unless provided a kit and instructions, men are plagued by the failure of self-deceit itself, afflicted with a fatal incapacity to believe themselves happy. If happiness is, as Swift insisted, the faculty of being well-deceived, most men can no longer achieve it on their own. They must be lied to every day, and they are willing to pay well for the service.

Our culture is organized around the satisfaction of this demand, and the moral artist, who is the truthteller, is subject (not invariably, but with distressing frequency) to one of two indignities, the first of which is called success, the second failure. Either he is admired, like Faulkner, for the wrong reasons: bought and unread because he is a living "classic" (in the United States, everything is speeded up to a bewildering tempo), his works posthumous before he is laid in the grave; or he is even more enthusiastically bought and *mis*read—like Pasternak, whose *Doctor Zhivago* became the very symbol of being one up on the Russians, or like Nabokov and D. H. Lawrence, the happy authors of once-banned books! Or the moral artist may be condemned out of hand, like Pasternak in Russia or Lawrence in the United States (until only the other day).

The customary charge leveled at the serious writer, until he is ripe for the even more deadly one of being a classic, is that of having written a dirty book. The Russians apparently believe this of all successful American writers who do not sympathize with Soviet objectives; but ironically, the charge is also believed in America of many of the same authors. It is, indeed, part of what has almost assumed the status of a ritual—the standard initiation of the truthteller into the culture of his country, inflicted at the moment when his truth still hurts. One is not startled, perhaps, to discover that Walt Whitman was once called "the dirtiest beast of the age," but it is a little disconcerting to learn that Hawthorne's *The Scarlet Letter* was accused of representing "the beginning of the era of French immorality" in American letters.

Yet it will not do to ignore the difference in the level of hysteria with which such charges were leveled at serious art one hundred years ago and that with which they were made of the first great books in the "modern" tradition at the point when the first of the Great Wars was about to begin. Whatever offense great art has always given and given with particular effect in America seems to have been compounded when, in what is still called, after nearly fifty years, "modern art," that offense was confessed in nonconventional form. Apparently the common man can more easily forgive an attack on home and mother than a flagrant disregard for harmony, or punctuation, or representation. Perhaps it is simply because technical offenses are less easy to overlook or to cancel out by misreading.

I have a clear memory of myself at fourteen or fifteen, struggling for an education in the public libraries of Newark, New Jersey, and having to fight to get Joyce's *A Portrait of the Artist as a Young Man* out of a locked room where it was kept with other dangerous material. Proust's *Remembrance of Things Past* was on the open shelves, but it was no easy matter to get it past the vigilance of a certain librarian who, in her spare time, went through the photography magazines stamping all female nudes three times with the official library stamp (to keep, I suppose, the minds of adolescents pure) and who regarded me as a special challenge. This experience has always seemed to me an archetypal one, my personal myth of The Intellectual Life as Moral Combat; for certainly (to a temperament for which, and in a time when, struggle seemed as necessary as eating) the library became for me an arena in which my morality was pitted against theirs in a war to end all wars! It was not dirty books I was after, I wanted to protest; it was. . . . But I did not know how to explain what it was I sought.

Only a long time afterward did I realize that I had been completely misled by the rationalizations of the guardians of the library, that it was not really the "dirtiness," the frank sexuality, of certain novels that irked the censors, but something quite different. Best sellers—in our country at least—have always been books which exploit sex as far as (and a little farther than) contemporary taboos will permit. From *The Monks of Monk Hall* to *Peyton Place* or the latest paperback by Richard S. Prather, the really popular book has talked of sex on the level of broad suggestion; it has spoken the last common language bearing on the last link (as Moravia has argued) between us and the world of nature. It seems to me now that what must be insisted upon is that even a good book can be a popular success if it can be thought of as dirty, like Nabokov's *Lolita* and Faulkner's *Sanctuary*.

No, the problem of the nonacceptance of serious fiction lies elsewhere: in the fact that *to fulfill its essential moral obligation, such fiction must be negative.* There is a dim sense of this in the popular mind, reflected in the over-the-bridge-table charge that certain great books, whatever their merits, are too "morbid" and responded to by the publishers' defensive assurances on the book jackets: "But beneath the shattering events of that book . . . lies a passionate affirmation" or "This is a book of great themes, of life, death and regeneration, of the dignity and triumph of man." Like the more particular religious reassurances of another age, these vaguely pious assertions are rooted in a profound distrust of art itself; and before them I am moved to resentment and anger. I can never read one without remembering a favorite anecdote of my old teacher, William Ellery Leonard, about how, one night in an inn, he had to share a bed with a man whom he had never met before. He felt no qualms until his bedmate kneeled down beside the bed to pray. "At that point," he liked to say, "I grabbed my wallet and ran!" So I before the book whose jacket assures me that the author is committed to affirmation, or love, or a belief in the dignity of man.

Insofar as a work of art is, as art, successful, it performs a negative critical function; for the irony of art in the human situation lies in this: that man—or better, some men—are capable of achieving in works of art a coherence, a unity, a balance, a satisfaction of conflicting impulses which they cannot (but which they desperately long to) achieve in love, family relations, politics. Yet works of art are *about* love, family relations, politics, etc.; and to the degree that these radically imperfect human activities are represented in a perfectly articulated form, they are revealed in all their intolerable inadequacy. The image of man in art, however magnificently portrayed—indeed, precisely when it is most magnificently portrayed—is the image of a failure. There is no way out.

The self-conscious writer, realizing this irony, feels a demand to make explicit the essentially negative view of man implicit in his work insofar as it is art at all. He is driven to make his avowed attitudes and allegiances congruous with the meaning that his techniques cannot help declaring. Especially in recent times, when the obligations of self-consciousness are imposed on us with a rigor unheard of in the past, the writer becomes aware that his Muse is more like the *Daimon* of Socrates (who appeared only to say *No!*) or the God of Job than like any of those white-draped Ladies of the genteel mythologists. The spirit which speaks to him conveys no reassurances or positive revelations; only the terrible message that what his best friends —in newspaper offices, or the pulpit, or Congress—have been, like Job's, telling him is "the thing which is not right." And that spirit addresses him from the whirlwind, directing his attention from himself to those absurd beasts, the Behemoth and the Leviathan.

Demonic, terrible and negative: this is the Modern Muse— "Bluff'd not a bit by drain-pipe, gasometers, artificial fertilizers," as Walt Whitman had the wit to see; but in his euphoric, comic vision the sense of terror is dissipated. It is to such a writer as James Joyce (who chose for his slogan the device of Satan himself: *Non serviam*, "I will not obey!") or to Henrik Ibsen (whose final words were "On the contrary . . .") or to Whitman's contemporary, Herman Melville, that we must turn for the decisive clue. The secret motto of *Moby Dick* was, Melville once confided: "I baptize you not in the name of the Father, the Son and the Holy Ghost, but in the name of the Devil." Even better, perhaps, because less theatrically gothic, is the phrase Melville attributes to Bartleby the Scrivener, his portrait of the writer in the modern world—a phrase in which there is already implicit Bartleby's insanity and death: "I would prefer not to." Most explicit of all is the comment in a letter to Hawthorne, in which Melville pretends to describe the essence of his beloved contemporary's art, while in fact revealing the deepest sources of his own:

> There is the grand truth about Nathaniel Hawthorne. He says No! in thunder; but the Devil himself cannot make him say *yes*. For all men who say *yes*, lie; and all men who say *no*,—why, they are in the happy condition of judicious, unincumbered travellers in Europe; they cross the frontiers into Eternity with nothing but a carpetbag,—that is to say, the Ego.

It pays to be clear about the nature of the "No! in thunder," which is quite different from certain lesser *no*'s in which a thriving trade is always done: the *no* in newsprint, for instance, and the *no* on manifestoes and petitions. A play written in the 1950s about the Salem witch trials, or a novel of the same period celebrating the revolt of the Maccabees, despite their allegorical intentions, are cheats, exploitations of the pseudo-*no*. Even the attack on slavery in Twain's post-Civil War *Huckleberry Finn*—or, for that matter, in Mrs. Stowe's pre-Civil War *Uncle Tom's Cabin*—like an anti-McCarthyite fiction in the recent past or an excoriation of segregation right now, carry with them a certain air of presumptive self-satisfaction, an assurance of being justified by the future. They are Easy No's, merely disguised *yes*'s, in varying degrees sentimental and righteous; they are *yes*'s by anticipation, tomorrow's *yes*'s. The "No! in thunder" remains a *no* forever; like the *no* implicit in the whole work of the Marquis de Sade, or the deeper *no* of *Huckleberry Finn*—Huck's *no* to womankind, the family and organized society, which remains to this very day a *no*.

The "No! in thunder" is never partisan; it infuriates Our Side as well as Theirs, reveals that all Sides are one, insofar as they are all yea-sayers and hence all liars. There is some evidence that the Hard No is being spoken when the writer seems a traitor to those whom he loves and who have conditioned his very way of responding to the world. When the writer says of precisely the cause that is dearest to him what is always and everywhere the truth about all causes—that it has been imperfectly conceived and inadequately represented, and that it is bound to be betrayed, consciously or unconsciously, by its leading spokesmen—we know that he is approaching an art of real seriousness if not of actual greatness. The thrill we all sense but hesitate to define for ourselves—the thrill of confronting a commitment to truth which transcends all partial allegiances—comes when Dante turns on Florence, Molière on the moderate man, de Sade on reason, Shaw on the socialists, Tolstoy on the reformers, Joyce on Ireland, Faulkner on the South, Graham Greene on the Catholics, Pasternak on the Russians and Abraham Cahan or Nathanael West on the Jews. What people, what party, what church needs an enemy when it has a great writer in its ranks?

Unless he bites the hand that feeds him, the writer cannot live; and this those who would prefer him dead (so they can erect statues of him) can never understand. I remember Faulkner's coming once, rather improbably, to Missoula, Montana, and getting engaged in conversation with a lady Montanan, who cried out at one point, "Why can't So-and-so write a novel that would do for this part of the world what you've done for Mississippi? He *loves* Montana so!" To which Faulkner, of course, answered (maybe I only dreamed it; it all seems so pat), "To write well about some place, you've got to *hate* it." A pause, and then, "The way a man hates his own wife." But this is scandalous in a way with which the righteous cannot seem to come to terms. Not only the Great Audience but also, and even especially, the Little Elite Audiences demand of the writer its disavowal in the name of a kind of loyalty which is for him death. The first attack on me as a critic ever to appear was launched because I had made some rather drastic qualifying remarks about, I think, Thomas Mann—a small god, at any rate, of the avant-garde church to which I was presumably applying for admission. "Aid and comfort to the enemy" was the implicit charge; but this charge the sayer of the Hard No must be willing to face; for he knows that the writer who rejects the negative obligation perishes even as he pleases, perishes though he please only a handful of the very best people—those, for instance, whom he has begun by admiring and whom he never ceases to admire.

It has not always been necessary for the writer to be aware of his denial; his work will do it for him anyhow, if it is honest work. Indeed, at certain periods in the past, it seemed almost better that the writer deceive himself as well as his contemporary audience about his intent: that Dickens, for example, believe himself to be glorifying the purity of woman and the simple heart of the child, while giving us in fact his mad, black-and-white nightmares, in which things live the life of men, and men perform with the lifeless rigidity of things. In the same way, Dostoevsky could think himself the apostle of a revived orthodoxy, and

Samuel Richardson considered his essential task the defense of bourgeois virtue. But these days the writer cannot afford to lose for an instant his sense of himself in opposition to the world; let him pretend, however briefly, that his *no* is a *yes,* and he will end up writing *A Fable* or *The Town,* travesties of his own best work.

Naturally, not all writers in our time accept the negative obligation; and, indeed, its rejection separates the purveyor of commodity-fiction from the serious artist in the novel. There are certain pseudo-novels which are, in fact, transitional stages on the way to becoming movies or substitutes for going to the movies; and these books are obliged to be cheerful, positive, affirmative: to sustain the belief in endurance, piety, hard work and a deliberately maintained, blessed stupidity. Here is the giveaway! Nothing can, after all, be wholly positive; and even the most affirmative of subnovels (say, *Marjorie Morningstar*) must end by denying something: dirt, disorder, eccentricity, nonconformism, skepticism, intelligence—in short, the negative obligation itself! Conversely, the nay-saying writer is not wholly negative; he is in favor of one thing by definition: telling the truth (*Madame Bovary* will do as the counterexample) and accepting the tragic implications of that truth, the vision of an eternal gap between imagined order and actual chaos.

But it is not enough, in our time, for the serious writer to confess *in general* the inevitable discrepancy between dream and fact, between the best man can imagine and the best he can achieve. The artist must be willing specifically to comment on the defeat of a particular dream. The anti-artist, on the other hand, incurs only the most general obligation; despite the particulars in which he apparently deals, he is in fact composing parables, pseudo-myths, to express not wonder and terror but sentimental reassurance. What life refuses, the anti-artist grants: the dying catcher hits a three bagger, and everyone loves him; the coward, at the last moment, finds the courage to fight the segregationist and his hired thugs; the girl in the office takes off her glasses and wins the heart of the boss's playboy son. That these are prefabricated, masturbatory dreams almost everyone (including, I suspect, the authors) would be prepared to admit, yet they do not stir in most of us the moral indignation we feel at the distribution of other habit-forming drugs. They seem more benign than marijuana, which is banned, or tranquilizers, which may soon be sharply regulated; because we accept the fantasies they promote as finally truer than those born of "pot" or happiness pills. Assuring us that man is OK, that men are OK, that we are all—despite our mistakes and the machinations of others—OK, they feed into (at least they do not contradict) the last widely held *Weltanschauung* of the West: the progressive and optimistic, rational and kindly dogma of liberal humanism.

Yet, as some of us are rather disturbedly aware, many if not most of the eminent writers of the twentieth century have found themselves in conflict with this dogma, not always *despite* its nobility, but often because of it. The fact that such otherwise ill-assorted writers as Shaw, Joyce, Faulkner, Yeats, Pound, Eliot, Wyndham Lewis and Samuel Beckett are arrayed against the liberal tradition indicates that it represents for our age the belief against which the serious artist must define himself, the official "Yea!" to which he must say his private "Nay!" As earlier poets had to say "Nay!" to the fifth-century Greeks' belief that their world was really explicable in terms of the Homeric gods, or the Christians' assumption that their society was Christian, or the Enlightenment's conviction that its passion and politics were finally rational, so the artist today must deny the liberal view of the possibilities of man. But liberalism is essentially different from earlier official faiths, religious or secular, in that its ideal is "openness" rather than orthodoxy; and the writer striving toward the Hard No is likely to discover that his most ardent denial is met with a disconcerting "Yes, yes, though all the same . . ." or "I don't finally agree with you, of course, but still . . ."

Nietzsche's assertion that God is dead once shook half the world, and Ibsen's attack on marriage left northern Europe trembling, but they find us merely confused or indifferent—or, as we say when confusion and indifference reach their highest pitch, "tolerant." Only an assault on tolerance itself is able to stir us as Goethe's assault on the ban against suicide once stirred his readers. The very advocacy of adultery, which from the time of the troubadours to that of D. H. Lawrence possessed an almost magic potency to provoke, has now become fashionable and meaningless. The recent redemption of *Lady Chatterley's Lover* in the courts represents not a triumph of literary taste over taboo but a failure of the moral imagination; and Lillian Smith can suggest in her novel *One Hour,* an essentially middlebrow book, that an Episcopalian priest's moment of vision and truth comes when he is in bed with his friend's wife. Who can *épater la bourgeoisie* when the bourgeoisie regards even the grossest scandal as a test of its capacity for understanding and forgiveness?

Yet there is finally a liberal view of man, to deny which is to risk blasphemy: an image of the human situation which persists very like a dogma beneath the undogmatic "openness" of which contemporary society is so proud. This view sees man as the product of a perhaps unplanned but rationally ordered and rationally explicable universe, a product which science can explain, even as it can explain the world which conditions him. The first fictionists who accepted this view of man thought of themselves as protoscientists and of their books as scientific reports on how vice and virtue are produced in the great laboratory of society. Such books, with their blend of rationalism, determinism and quasi-scientific objectivity, were variously hailed when they appeared as examples of Realism, Naturalism, Verism, etc.; and whatever the inadequacy of their styles, they performed in the beginning the essential function of art, the negative one of provocation and scandal. Novelists like Zola and de Maupassant —in America, even so belated a representative of the school as Dreiser—horrified the genteel by exposing the self-delusions of sentimental Christianity. They soon fell victim to the fallacy of imitative form (realism-naturalism did not *have* to eschew style, as the example of Flaubert should have made clear) and proffered anti-style as evidence of their honesty. But even their very bad writing served temporarily a good cause, exposing the pretensions of academic rhetoric.

Purveyors of the old realistic article still circulate among us (James T. Farrell, for instance, and Nelson Algren), but they tell no truths that are not clichés, and they give no valuable offense. Indeed, they have become indistinguishable from the producers of chic Italian movies and from TV entertainers like Paddy Chayefsky—second-rate artists, purveyors of the scandal of the day before yesterday. The day is gone when the tradition of realism-naturalism was so deeply accepted as *the* mode of serious literature that a mannered and artificial stylist like Hemingway, or an exploiter of backwoods rhetoric and gothic nightmare like Faulkner, had to pretend to be a "naturalist" in order to seem respectable. In the first place, realism-naturalism has become an academy itself, sustaining a triumphant orthodoxy instead of challenging one; and meanwhile, certain contraband, smuggled into the presumably objective laboratory report from the beginning, has come to seem more and more essential: political propaganda, heavy-handed symbolism, righteous pornography and sentimentality.

The latter two especially have assumed a disheartening importance in the standard subforms of post-realism, first clearly defined in the United States in the 1930s: the Popular Front Novel, on the one hand, and Regionalist or Protest Pornography on the other. John Steinbeck is the father of the first, having established in *The Grapes of Wrath* the prototype of the pious tract disguised as a sociological report, in which the cruel exploiters of labor are contrasted with simple and kindly men who give candy to children, and women of the people who offer their swollen breasts to the starving unemployed. Erskine Caldwell is the founder of the other, having created in *Tobacco Road* a genre capable of providing all the forbidden thrills of a peep show together with the conscientious satisfactions of deploring the state of the (more exotic) poor. It is hard to remember that Caldwell was considered a serious "proletarian" writer before he became a paperback best seller; one reads with surprise the accounts of his current reception in places like Turkey, where he is still regarded as a pattern for "village literature." In this country, his example has occasioned lately only such bootleg high-school literature as Grace Metalious' *Peyton Place*.

Steinbeck's prototype, however, continues to provide inspiration for the prevailing upper middlebrow form of our time: the serious pseudo-novel as practiced by certain not-quite-first-

rate authors, committed equally to social conscience and success, and sure that these are not mutually exclusive goals. There
is scarcely a moment these days when such authors of the Sentimental Liberal Protest Novel as Irwin Shaw, John Hersey, Budd
Schulberg and James Michener are not fighting for slots on the
list of best sellers; since in our time left-of-center politics has
become, by virtue of converting all its political content to sentiment, the reigning belief of the educated middle classes. In
our genteel age, the class struggle has been translated from a
confrontation of workers and bosses on the barricades to a contest between certain invisible or remote exploiters and all the
rest of us—a contest in which more tears are shed than blood.
The writer dedicated to portraying that struggle is no longer the
man in the work shirt rolled to the elbow and open at the neck,
but the man ashamed of his gray flannel suit—the searcher out
and defender of Victims. For the image of man which possesses
the genteel conscience is the image of the Victim: the snubbed
Jew, the oppressed Negro, the starving Chinese, the atom-scarred
Japanese, the betrayed Hungarian, the misunderstood para-
plegic. For each Victim there is an appropriate book, a last
indignity: *Gentlemen's Agreement, The Wall, The Bridge at
Andau, The Last Pebble, One Hour.* Even the War Novel is
recast in the prevailing form, captured, like *The Young Lions,*
for piety, protest and self-pity. In the end, we are left with the
sense that wars are fought and armies organized (in representative platoons, with all minorities duly represented) so that the
persecuted Jew or tormented Italian can shame his fellows by
proving his unforeseen valor in the end.

Having only a single theme, of a rather simple-minded sort,
the Sentimental Protestors are driven to eke it out, to conceal
its stereotypical bareness with up-to-date details and topical
references. Their eyes are constantly on the headlines; and before
the ink is dry, Michener and Hersey are already embarked for
the scene of the latest indignity—or at least racing for their type-
writers! It is a somewhat comic contest, with the whole reading
world breathlessly waiting to discover who will get Little Rock
first, who the Puerto Ricans. But what is the ersatz morality
which sustains the protest fictionists, from Hersey-Shaw to Jones-

Algren, from the soft-sell defenders of the dark-skinned peoples to the tough apologists for maximum security prisoners and minor hoods? It is the theory that the "Little Man" must be defended against the great and powerful, merely because he is little and "wants only to be let alone." Little! Surely no more degrading label has ever been invented for the exploited, none which has so combined pathos and condescension: the little Jew, the little shopkeeper, the little mixed-up kid, the bewildered little pusher of dope, the little pimp trying to establish himself against the competition of the big operators. . . . Against so abject a surrender to sentiment, one wants to cry out in the terrible words of the Old Testament, "Thou shalt not honor the poor man in his cause." But who could be heard over the voices of those storming their book counters for copies of *Exodus* and *Hawaii?*

What, then, of serious literature in our time? What counter-image of man does it proffer? Not, as so often in the past, an image of man struggling (and failing) to fulfill some revealed or inherited view of himself and his destiny; but of man learning that it is the struggle itself which is his definition. In a time when answers are the business of professional answer men (cheats and delusions carefully rehearsed before the show is put on the air), we have been forced to learn that our humanity is dependent not on the answers we hope for but on the questions we are able to ask. Like Job, we are granted no response except from the apparition which tells us it is time to be still, time to know that man is he who asks what man is. And like Melville's "unincumbered travellers," we must be prepared to leave our Encyclopedia Britannicas and Oxford English Dictionaries behind us, to cross the frontiers of Eternity with no baggage except the Ego. This the most serious writers of our day have taught us, insisting that we endure uncertainty, not as a stage on the way to knowledge, but as our essential condition. Now we see as through a glass darkly. There is no "then."

This view of man opens into a world not of melodrama but of ambiguity, not of the polemical but of the problematical. Saul Bellow's *The Victim*, for instance, will survive *Focus*, *Gentlemen's Agreement*, *The Professor's Umbrella* and all the other earnest and humane tracts on anti-Semitism because, despite its title, it is not a protest novel at all. In Bellow's view, both Jew and gentile are simultaneously Victim and Victimizer; he renders their mutual torment in terms of their common desire to discover what it means to be human, their common need to *be* what is human. Our Jewishness or gentileness, Bellow leaves us feeling, is *given;* our humanity is what we must achieve. There is no more room for sentimentality in such a travesty of the liberal Jewish novel than there is in Robert Penn Warren's similar recasting of the political novel, or Malamud's of the novel about baseball, or James Baldwin's of the standard Negro novel, or Mary McCarthy's of fictional protests against the restriction of academic freedom. Reading, say, *All the King's Men,* one need only think of *The Last Hurrah* or *Advise and Consent*—or picking up *The Natural,* one need only recall Mark Harris' *Bang the Drum Slowly*—to realize how we ordinarily lust to be lied to, and how seldom we are granted the privilege of hearing the truth.

Ambiguity is the first resource of the serious novelist, tempted like all the rest of us to clichés of simplicity; but to say that the good novel is ambiguous is not to say that it is difficult and confused (this is optional), merely to insist that it is *about* moral ambiguity and that it cannot betray its theme. I distrust the writer who claims to know black from white, left from right, Hip from Square, Them from Us—no matter which of the sides he chooses. And I distrust especially the characters in whom he embodies his presumable insights. The protagonists of the best recent books are not self-righteous, long-suffering, diminished prigs, who want only to live in peace and are sure they know what peace is. From the most sympathetic to the least, they are troublemakers like their authors, who will not let the world rest until it acknowledges that they exist. We have by now quite a gallery of such types, including Joyce's insufferable Stephen, too stiff-necked to grant his mother's deathbed wish; Kafka's K., guilty as charged though no one knows quite what the charge is; Nathanael West's Miss Lonelyhearts, trying in vain to be the Christ in whom he does not believe; Ralph Ellison's

Invisible Man, vainly striving to escape the myth of his color; and Faulkner's Popeye, counterfeiting manhood with a bloody corncob.

The contemporary novel through which such characters stalk—bringing harm to those around them, even as they court destruction for themselves—is terror-ridden, dreadful; but it is not humorless. In the midst of Faulkner's grimmest book, *Sanctuary*, a couple of rustics play out a humorous scene in a whorehouse. West's bleakest novel is his funniest, *A Cool Million*, whose title comes from the "Old Saying": "John D. Rockefeller would give a cool million to have a stomach like yours." Kafka, we are told, used to laugh until the tears ran down his cheeks, reading aloud from *Amerika*. Joyce, one sometimes feels, would do anything for a laugh, and Beckett has thought of some things to do which even his master could not imagine; Bellow can be a clown; Mary McCarthy insists on compelling our titters in the midst of our deepest shame; and the British "Angries" have us guffawing like a pack of fools. In this sense, Mark Twain is the true ancestor of the modern writer, and his *Pudd'nhead Wilson* a storehouse of the sort of humor which is not dated by changes of fashion. "*October 12, the Discovery*. It was wonderful to find America, but it would have been more wonderful to miss it." This is our kind of joke, proper to a world in which we may all die laughing—as we like to say.

Such humor is not incompatible with negation, or even terror, for it is not party or factional humor, with which the *in's* satirize the *out's*, and the "normal" put the eccentric in their places. It is total humor, through which men laugh not at their foibles but at their essential selves. The vision of man shared by our greatest writers involves an appreciation of his absurdity, and the protagonists of our greatest books are finally neither comic nor tragic but absurd. To the modern writer, the distinction between comedy and tragedy seems as forced and irrelevant as that between hallucination and reality; his world partakes of both, and he would be hard put to it to say where one ends and the other begins. The conventional definitions of the comic and the tragic strike him as simplifications, falsifications of human life, appropriate to a less complex time. To insist that we regard man, even for the space of three acts or five, as *either* horrible or funny; to require us, through four or five hundred pages, *either* to laugh or to cry we find offensive in an age when we can scarcely conceive of wanting to do one without the other. For us, the great works of the past are those which occupy an intermediate position between comedy and tragedy: the *Bacchae* of Euripides, the *Misanthrope* of Molière, Shakespeare's *Measure for Measure,* Ibsen's *An Enemy of the People,* Twain's *Pudd'nhead Wilson* and Melville's *The Confidence Man.* And the writers of our own time whom we most admire—West, Faulkner and Beckett, among others—pursue a third genre, which suggests that the ludicrous is the source of pity and terror, and that pity and terror themselves are the heart of the ludicrous.

The vision of the truly contemporary writer is that of a world not only absurd but also chaotic and fragmentary. He tries in his work to find techniques for representing a universe in which our perceptions overlap but do not coincide, in which we share chiefly a sense of loneliness: our alienation from whatever things finally are, as well as from other men's awareness of those things and of us. Rapid shifts in point of view; dislocations of syntax and logic; a vividness more like hallucination than photography; the use of parody and slapstick at moments of great seriousness; the exploitation of puns and of the vaudeville of dreams—these experiments characterize much of the best work of recent decades, from Joyce's *Ulysses* through Djuna Barnes' *Nightwood* to Wright Morris' *Field of Vision,* whose winning of the National Book Award so incensed the guardians of middlebrow standards. At the present moment, Morris is almost alone in the United States in his continuing devotion to the themes and techniques of the negative novel. (There is, to be sure, the young novelist John Barth, strangely ignored.) For we have been suffering a general loss of nerve, or a waning of talent, which has persuaded writers of such different origins and generations as Hemingway, Faulkner, Saul Bellow and Mary McCarthy to pursue affirmation in the place of art—disconcerted, perhaps, as they pass from being ignored to relative degrees of fame and victimized by a perverse sort of *noblesse oblige.*

The unearned euphoria of *Henderson, the Rain King;* the

shapeless piety of *A Fable;* the sentimental self-indulgence of
Across the River and into the Trees; the maudlin falsity of *The
Town;* the heavy-handed symbolism and religiosity of *The Old
Man and the Sea,* destined from its inception for the pages of
Life—such failures make over and over the point that the contemporary American writer can abjure negativism only if he is
willing to sacrifice truth and art. For major novelists and minor,
the pursuit of the positive means stylistic suicide. Language
itself decays, and dialogue becomes travesty; character, stereotype; insight, sentiment. The Nobel Prize speech destined for
high-school anthologies requires quite another talent from that
demanded by the novel; and the abstract praise of love requires
another voice from that which cries *No!* to the most noble
temptations, the most defensible lies.

Yet one must not forget, in the face of their recent decline,
the successes of Bellow and Hemingway and Faulkner: the terrible impact of *The Victim, The Sun Also Rises* and *The Sound
and the Fury.* The last, in particular, remains the exemplary
American novel, perhaps the greatest work of fiction produced
in the United States in the twentieth century. And it is no
accident that its title comes from the bleakest passage in Shakespeare, or that its action begins inside the mind of an idiot. The
point is insisted upon bluntly, almost too obviously: life is a tale
told by an idiot, full of sound and fury, signifying nothing. Here
is the ultimate negation, the Hard No pressed as far as it will
go. Yet "nothing" is not quite Faulkner's last word, only the
next to the last. In the end, the negativist is no nihilist, for he
affirms the void. Having endured a vision of the meaninglessness
of existence, he retreats neither into self-pity and aggrieved
silence nor into a realm of beautiful lies. He chooses, rather,
to render the absurdity which he perceives, to know it and
make it known. To know and to render, however, mean to give
form; and to give form is to provide the possibility of delight—a
delight which does not deny horror but lives at its intolerable
heart.

Part One: The Artist

The essays in this group all deal with the artist and his work largely, though not exclusively, in terms of myth; this has been a central concern of mine for a long time. The first four essays, however, as well as the final one, are more formal, less occasional than the kind of thing I usually prefer to do. The one on Shakespeare was, as a matter of fact, originally intended to be part of an ambitious book, and I am a little dismayed at its solemnity; even its jokes are couched in a protective, academic jargon. Yet I believe most of it still, and can regard with nostalgia its style, worked out when I was still young enough to think that the chief danger which threatened a writer was being understood too easily.

The essay on Dante's sestina is often praised by those who regard most of my work as not solid or "scholarly" enough, and who are unmoved by my protest that it was begun as an attempt to explain a quite unacademic poem. The essays on Whitman and Stevenson were both introductions to new editions of works by those authors, and both were aimed to redeeming their subjects (in the classroom itself!) from history to passion, from reverence to use. The piece on Pavese is a gesture of gratitude and affection, an attempt at simulating a conversation with a writer who seems to me more alive than many not cut off from me by distant birth and premature death.

The articles on Peretz, Kafka and Malamud were reviews, done on request, but they strike me now as parts of a continuing quest on my part for the image of the Jew in literature. To have been one of the first to recognize a talent like Malamud's is for a critic the most real of satisfactions; but to have had a sense of the tradition out of which he comes and the way in which he fulfills meanings suggested long before him is to me an even greater joy.

Dante: Green Thoughts
in a Green Shade

Reflections on the Stony Sestina of Dante Alighieri

I have dreamed for many years now of rescuing from silence and misunderstanding the sestina of Dante which begins *Al poco giorno e al gran cerchio d'ombra*. But each time I set to work, I am depressed by the impossibility of rendering even that deceptively simple first line with accuracy or grace; and I end by telling myself that it is all a boy's dream anyhow. What reason is there to think that I am the St. George picked out for the rescue? And even if I achieve it, what then? No one insists on a reward for redeeming Princesses from the powers of darkness, but one looks forward at least to a small crowd of cheering relatives and friends. It is unendurable to contemplate bringing the Maiden back to—nothing. From silence to silence. Yet what else can one reasonably expect?

The professional *dantista*, trained in the language and learned in bibliography, has already what he needs or deserves, an established text and studies ranging from the comically pointless to the poetically illuminating, the fruit of German-trained scholarship and Crocean insight. And the crumbs of this feast are available even to the beginning student. Who else is there? I am aware that we seem to be in the midst of a revival of amateur interest in Dante, a wave of translation and assimilation, which has now reached the grocery-store bookstands with paperback editions of the *Comedy*; but it is with the *Comedy* that the nonprofessional interest begins and ends.

In a way, this is fair enough. To pretend that much beyond the *Comedy* can deeply move one not intimate with the poet's language is to add a further self-deception to a relationship already compromised with fraud and snobbishness. There are enough architectonics, rhetoric and melodrama in the *Commedia* to survive any translation, no matter how breezily colloquial or piously high church. And even the *Vita Nuova* can be read by those who cannot define a *canzone;* for it is blessed with a plot of sorts, a continuous symbolism and an imposed order, which make it possible to ignore the meaning of the poem as the record of a revolution in technique: the perfecting of a new way of making love poetry.

The uncollected lyrics of Dante, however, the so-called *Rime,* are completely at the mercy of the translator; for their appeal is all in their texture and technique. What "story" they possess is at best some vaguely defined and half-ironic myth; and their attitudes the fashionable beliefs of a long-dead "school"; a group of poets who drew from common sources and shared a common metaphysics; who evolved cooperatively a style at once technically "serious" and yet a kind of elegant play; who exchanged compliments and insults and rhyme schemes and lived out their love affairs very largely in those exchanges. The fact that Dante's minor poems are in this sense "love songs" serves only to confuse us. It is hard for us to remember that they are not poems of love, but poems about love; speculations on what it is and demonstrations of how best to express it. Consequently, they are really directed not to the beloved, but to other poet-philosopher-lovers as entries in an endless contest, in which the competitors and judges are the same, and the prize is not love but fame, "*la gloria della lingua.*" Referring to this tradition as it has developed from Guido Guinicelli to Guido Cavalcanti to himself, Dante makes the point quite explicitly behind the barely veiled boast:

> *Così ha tolto l'uno all'altro Guido*
> *la gloria della lingua e forse è nato*
> *chi l'uno e l'altro caccerà di nido . . .*

There have been some recent attempts to find in Dante's love theory a still valid wisdom; but for most of us his Aristotelian (in a technical sense) and Platonic (in the vulgar one) version of the codes of Provence is not merely difficult but tedious and a little silly. It is, in fact, precisely the sort of farrago one would expect from a group of university intellectuals, ridden by homosexuality, possessed by the psychology of scholasticism and haunted by the anti-sexual bias of the Church; but determined to make a poetry based on Provençal models, which thought of love as the noblest subject for verse, and conceived of that love as heterosexual and adulterous.

It is not the *bontà* of Dante's lyric verse, its doctrinal excellence, but its *bellezza*, its adornment and sweet sound, upon which its survival depends. This *bellezza* he apparently conceived as self-sufficient, independent of the *ragione*, the prose meaning of the poem. "If you do not grasp my import fully," the envoy of one *canzone* runs, "at least reflect oɳ how beautiful I am!" (*"Ponete mente almen com' io son bella."*) This essay is intended to be such a reflection on the *bellezza* of the sestina, for me the loveliest of all the minor poems. Unfortunately a mere translation will not suffice, for it does not translate enough; and so I have set my own version beside an earlier one and have accompanied both with a running commentary on the text.*

It is necessary first of all, I suppose, to say what a sestina is. From the point of view of a single stanza, it is a poem which rejects rhyme; and this in a rime-haunted language like Provençal or Italian seems not a relaxation but an effort of the will. From the point of view of the poem as a whole, however, the sestina makes use of monorhyme—that is, of the repetition of identical words in places where one would expect only partial echoes. This means finally that the resemblance-difference we have learned to expect from ordinary rhyming is separated out: the difference insisted upon locally from line to line; the resemblance, become identity, suggested only from stanza to stanza. Such

---

* In my explication, I have drawn on such general knowledge of the tradition as I have derived from De Sanctis, Grandgent, Croce, Vossler, etc.; and I am more specifically indebted to Gianfranco Contini, whose edition of the *Rime* I have used. The rendering I am setting beside my own is Dante Gabriel Rossetti's out of his volume *Dante and His Circle;* this version seems to me as characteristic of Rossetti's age and its uses of Dante as I have tried to make mine of our own. I also refer from time to time to Grandgent's English in his *Ladies of Dante's Lyrics.*

disjunction reinforces that sense of holding apart by sheer will what belongs together by nature which is essential to the sestina.

In addition, the sestina is presided over by a kind of cold mathematics that functions like fate. In each of six stanzas, the same six monorhymes must be repeated, the last one of the first stanza becoming the first of the next, the first becoming the second, the fifth the third, etc., until all the mathematical possibilities are exhausted. Then there is added a *commiato* or *congedo*, in which the six key words must be crowded into only three lines. There is scant room left for invention; what free will is permitted must survive between closely repeated limits, until, at the conclusion, there is scarcely space for it to function at all.

In the *commiato* of Dante, four syllables of each eleven-syllable line are committed in advance; and the poet is confined almost entirely to contriving a syntax to bind together his six obsessive terms. The sestina seems, in this sense, a dialogue of freedom and necessity, like, say, Bach's *Art of Fugue*; but it is one loaded heavily on the side of necessity—a predestinarian dialogue.

The great sestinas of literature—this one of Dante, for example, and its protype in Arnaut Daniel, which begins *Lo ferm voler qu'al cor m'intra*—remain faithful to the metaphysical implications of the form itself. It is only too easy to make the sestina an embodiment of ingenuity rather than necessity, to give the impression that the word at each line ending is sought and prepared for, a prize rather than a trap. On the contrary, the successful sestina must make it seem that each monorhyme is seven times fled and seven times submitted to; that the poet is ridden by a passion which forces him back on the six obsessive words, turn and twist as he may. The periphrasis which is natural to the form (Arnaut, for instance, calls his mother "the sister of my uncle") must never seem a mere device to save the word whose turn has been mathematically determined, but such a giveaway of the poet's hidden madness, such a betraying slip of the tongue as Freud delighted in. *Ubi morbus, ibi digitus.*

Finally, in the *commiato,* there must be the sense (and this only Dante eminently attained) that the key words have managed at last not merely to utter themselves once more, but to achieve their fated relationship, which the poet has desperately evaded through six stanzas. This means that the fulfillment of the *commiato* is likely to be a reversal, to stand in the same relationship to the rest of the poem as the concluding couplet of a Shakespearian sonnet to the first twelve lines.

To keep so complicated a piece of machinery from seeming *merely* a machine is in the power of only the most accomplished poets. Yet mere accomplishment is not enough. The sestina can be handled only by a master poet in a tradition which believes passionately in technique as a good in itself, at the point where the technique is mythicized and becomes the actual subject of the poem. This kind of poet Dante was (though he was more, too), as was Arnaut Daniel, who invented the form. To Arnaut, Dante makes acknowledgment in the *De Vulgari Eloquentia;* and it is, of course, Arnaut who is hailed in Canto XXVI of the *Purgatory* by Guido Guinicelli himself as *"il miglior fabbro,"* the greatest craftsman of language.

This compliment has been adapted by T. S. Eliot to pay his respects to Pound; and these two between them have made the figure of Arnaut a part of the mythology of twentieth-century poetry. The references in Eliot, however, lead only to the Provençal verse which Dante composed for the mouth of his beloved master. And even Pound has not translated (if that is the proper word for his efforts) Arnaut's sestina; so that this amazing poem remains as unknown to most contemporary readers as in the not very distant past, when Grandgent could still call Arnaut "one of the most laborious and tiresome of the Provençal versifiers."

From Arnaut, Dante learned not only the superficial devices of the form, but also the appropriate obsessed tone, the note of barely repressed hysteria, which alone can keep it from seeming a piece of highfalutin' tomfoolery. Love is the required subject, of course, but not the easy adoration or smooth sensuality of other Provençal poets—rather a difficult love come on hard times, an unworthy or hopeless but irrepressible infatuation. The season of Arnaut's suffering is typically winter, and his poems are likely to open in ice or snow among mute and frozen birds, rather than in the musical springtime of the *trobar leu.* The *trobar clus* of which Arnaut is the great representative is a mode which rejects lightness and openness not only in diction, but also in imagery and feeling. Its mythical world endures a perpetual December—and it is to this world that the opening of Dante's sestina belongs, though, characteristically, he specifies his season with a vast astronomical image rather than in terms of Arnaut's more circumscribed background of stripped bushes and trees.

It is not, of course, from Arnaut's sestina alone that Dante has learned to make a poetry at once bleak and complicated, shrill and adorned; and it is not in his own sestina alone that he applies the lesson. *Al poco giorno* belongs to a group of Dante's poems which the Italian commentators call the *"rime pietrose,"* the stony verses. The name is an extension of a pun central to the poems themselves and needs a little explanation. There have survived at least four poems of Dante, similar in tone, diction and technical ambition, all addressed to a certain Donna Pietra (Dante uses the older form "Petra"), and all playing obsessively on the second meaning of her name, which is, of course, "rock" or "stone."

Much vain though amusing speculation has been devoted to the identity of this lady by two opposing wings of Dante scholars, the biographically and the allegorically inclined. One group would have her either a certain Pietra degli Scrovegni or else Pietra di Donato di Bruncaccio, who was Dante's sister-in-law (which "would account for the note of wickedness" in the poems, Grandgent remarks, though he finally dismisses the hypothesis). The others would make her variously the Virgin Mary, whom St. Bernard had called *"pietra,"* or Divine Wisdom or the Church itself, since her name is the feminine form of the nickname of his disciple Simon, on which Jesus punned so disastrously.

The latter misinterpretations Dante has brought upon himself, using with great deliberateness for his monorhymes words of the broadest possible symbolic resonance; but the former interpretations are diseases of an age of biographical criticism—accidental rather than necessary. If one insists upon a historical identification, the dry observation of Boccaccio (a pretty girl from the hills with a goiter) seems far more convincing than the romantic fantasies of some courtly affair or quasi-incestuous entanglement. After all, Boccaccio's no more documented identification of the equally suspicious name of Beatrice (with its equally convenient pun) has had much better luck. The real point is, of course (and here contemporary Italian critical opinion as opposed to "scholarly" speculation has reached an agreement), that the "Donna Pietra" is a myth, a personification of a "moment of Dante's art."

After his shift from an earlier artificial and obscure style to the comparative lucidity of the *stil nuovo,* which is the prevailing mode of the *Vita Nuova,* Dante seems to have turned again, briefly at least, to a second period of *trobar clus.* This second hermetic phase is based directly on the example of Arnaut Daniel, and does not so much woo obscurity out of a contempt for the popular as endure it out of a sense that the pursuit of richness and difficulty and involution may lead to certain reaches of meaning unavailable to perspicuity. It is a useful and (I hope) forgivable anachronism to call this Dante's "symbolist phase."

At any rate, one must imagine his searching for a subject to justify a new style, rather than vice versa (if there is a "true love" behind the *rime pietrose,* it is the love of Arnaut Daniel); and finally projecting into the image of a kind of woman and a kind of love his passionate search for a farfetched and anti-rhetorical rhetoric—"of all things not impossible the most difficult." The Donna Pietra is, then, a symbol of a poetics, an obscure and stony *bellezza;* and if that *bellezza* itself stands for some remoter and larger beauty, this meaning is not stated but hinted. The biographical fact, real or supposed, does not finally matter, and even the symbolic extension of meaning is secondary. What counts is the natural history of the myth constructed in the poems themselves.

The poet finds himself in a frozen world and among limestone hills, confronting a girl, immune to passion, unmoved as stone. He can hope for no easing of his winter with the turning of the seasons, for it is the projection of an inner hopelessness and of advancing age. The youngness of the girl is insisted upon; she is *"nova," "giovane,"* a *"pargoletta";* and though the poet does not directly refer to the years between them, one feels that distance as a final complication, the capstone of the absurdity of the whole affair. The scholars have, as they will, calculated the date of the poems by the (not quite certain) astrological data at the beginning of one of them; and have decided that they were written around 1296. This would make Dante just past thirty, a little young to be the counterpart of his poetic "I," though old enough to feel such a fiction as not utterly alien to him.

At any rate, the poems turn on the paradox of a wintry lover moved like the earth in spring, and a beloved frozen like winter though in the springtime of her life. There seems no chance for any consummation of such a love except a bloody one; for it is by definition absurd, and has been so long baffled that desire has changed to a hope for revenge (*"che bell'onor s'acquisita in far vendetta"*). To tear the Donna Pietra as a bear tears his prey, to grab her by the hair and stare her down, and only at the moment of her greatest terror make peace with the rapist's kiss—these are the lover's sadistic fancies, turned into a language as tortured and feverish as those fancies themselves.

Occasionally, he yields to a more idyllic dream, a vision of his beloved alone in a grassy field, imprisoned among lofty hills and hot with desire for him. But such comparatively gentle images give way to the harsh cry. "Ah, let her yap for me, as I for her, in hell's hot soup!" And finally over all, the cries of desire and the recriminations, and the images of the lover hoar but ardent, the woman green but icy, there hovers a final coldness, the end of both hope and suffering. Each of the poems closes with a prescience of death, half-fear and half-wish, the knowledge that the only stone on which the poet will ever sleep (it is the last and bitterest pun) is the *"poca petra"* of his tomb.

Around this fable, Dante has woven his stony rhymes, though the resulting verses must not be thought of as narrative poems. They are too sluggish on the one hand, too ejaculatory on the other to "tell a story." Their movement is the movement of an obsession, circular within their trap of despair—in their tiny compass, not unlike the motion of Faulkner's *Absalom! Absalom!* This is why the sestina seems so apt an embodiment for the *sentimento* behind the fable of the Donna Pietra. Among the four least-doubtful poems, there is, beside our sestina, a so-called double sestina, which tops the thirty-nine lines on six monorhymes of the former by achieving sixty-six lines with only five repeated words. Dante's double sestina is not without merit; but its coldly proportional inflation of difficulty (excluding the *commiato*, the single sestina is based on a ratio of $36:6 = 6:1$, the *sestina doppia* on one of $60:5 = 12:1$; with the *commiato*, the sum of all the lines of the sestina is thirty-nine, whose integers added give first twelve, then the magical three; the *sestina doppia* gives sixty-six, another twelve which becomes three, etc., etc.) exudes an iciness which is beyond the poet's power to transmute from mathematics to poetry.

Besides, the longer poem, though it clings as it must to the inevitable monorhymes *donna* and *pietra*, substitutes for the *ombra, verde, erba* and *colli* of the shorter one, *freddo, luce* and *tempo:* a movement toward abstraction and away from the objectivity of key words, for which Dante had found a cue in Arnaut, and which he, indeed, carried much further than his master. In *Al poco giorno*, the thematic terms are all substantives (only "green" ambiguously teeters between noun and adjective), all "things" real in terms of the senses; and yet they avoid both the exaggerated "thinginess" and the eccentricity of *oncle* and *ongla* ("uncle" and "fingernail") in Arnaut's most famous sestina. To find another example of a diction as absurd as the latter, as seemingly frivolous yet poetically fruitful, one has to descend to *Le monocle de mon oncle* of Wallace Stevens. Dante is not completely averse to unusual words and fantastic conjunctions, played off in a double dissonance of meaning and sound; indeed, there are sufficient examples in the stony poem which begins with the declaration:

> *Così nel mio parlar voglio esser aspro*
> *com' è ne li atti questa bella petra*

"I would be as harsh in my speech as is this lovely stone in her behavior."

But something in Dante's temperament keeps him from the boast of the Provençal poet: "I am Arnaut . . . who yoke the ox and hare, and swim against the stream." Even in paradox, Dante prefers a certain blandness; and he is content to let his main conceit carry the chief burden of absurdity, substituting for

Arnaut's yoked dissimilars a series of three rather obvious and not discordant contrasts: *donna-petra, erba-colli, verde-ombra.* In each case there is the same playing off of the warm and living against the cold and dead. It is worth noting, however, that at least one of the antinomies is not as obvious as it seems at first glance. The simplest opposite of "green" would be "white," the color of winter versus the color of spring; and inside the lines, this opposition is exploited, as is the other easy contrast of "light" and "shade."

Dante wants, however, to insist upon an opposition less lexical, more deeply symbolic. The typology of Medieval Christianity had linked the color green with the second of the Christian Virtues, hope; while the figure of "the valley of shadow" had made *ombra* a familiar, even homely metaphor for death. It is upon these extended meanings that the not-quite-obvious polarity *verde-ombra,* hope-death, forces our attention. And this, in turn, makes us aware that Dante has deliberately chosen all his monorhymes from words with the widest connotations, so that they may provide a contrast *in depth*—less spectacular but less easily exhausted than Arnaut's. *Petra* is, for instance, the name of a thing, substantial and solid, or rather of a series of things: a girl, a rock, a jewel; yet it also evokes overtones of the Church and of salvation ("on this rock I found my church") which join with the whole penumbra of significance in Donna (mistress—possessor—lady—Our Lady, etc.) to reinforce the sense of how sacred a thing is profaned in the rejection of love.

There are, moreover, three assonances on "o" and three on "e" to underline the threeness of the pattern; indeed, the importance of triplets in the architecture of the sestina has led some commentators on Dante to find in this form the germ of *terza rima* itself. But the sound resemblances are not precisely coincident with the symbolic categories. With *colli* and *ombra,* which belong to the side of cold, is linked *donna* (which assonates both vowels with *ombra*), though the latter stands for all that is most living and desirable; while with the fertile and hopeful *erba* and *verde,* the cruel *petra* is joined by its sound (again in double-assonance with *erba*). But, of course, the ambiguity of "stone" (which is also the name of the beloved) and "lady" is precisely

the point of the poem; and this ambiguity the apparently dis-
placed assonances underline.

I have found it impossible to maintain these subtle and important assonances in my translation, though "grass" and "green"
yield easily enough an alliteration to replace the vowel coincidence of *erba* and *verde*. I have preferred this rendering to the
"leaves" and "green" of Grandgent's translation, out of a sense
that in English a marked consonantal music must bear part of the
burden carried almost exclusively in Italian by vowel play. It is
for this reason that I have not avoided, and indeed have sometimes shamelessly pursued, alliteration. In "green" and "queen,"
I have heretically introduced one full rime among the more fleet-
ing resemblances. Their conjunction is so shifting and so much
at the mercy of the sestina pattern that one is by turns surprised
by their chiming and disappointed by its apparent failure; so that
the feeling of frustration-satisfaction peculiar to the sestina is
rather augmented than diminished by this unorthodoxy.

Besides, "queen" has finally seemed to me the only possible
way to translate *"donna"* in this context of imagery and sound.
"Lady" or "mistress" suggest themselves first; indeed, "mistress"
is quite attractive, rendering very well not only the overtone of
command implied by *donna,* but giving, too, some sense of the
conventional use of the word for the Beloved and its most neutral
significance as a formal title: Donna Pietra = Mistress Stone. It
is, however, an awkward word, and one which seems to me out of
tune with the other monorhymes; "lady" would harmonize much
better, making a partial rhyme with "shade," and this is, of
course, what Rossetti uses: "Of the Lady Pietra degli Scrovigni."
But "Lady" demands the capital again; without it, it has lost for
us any meaning more than "woman"—and with it, seeming a
shade nostalgic.

There is capital trouble enough in the problem of rendering
"Petra" as "stone" or "Stone." Unfortunately, it yields up no
common given name in English (why could the poet not have
had the good grace to pun on, say, Rose!); and though Stone is
not impossible as a family name, it seems improbable that a
reader will remain sufficiently aware of the play on words it suggests; yet that pun must be as evident as the one on "Will"

in Shakespeare's sonnets, or on "Rose" in Henry Green's *Back*.

No, "queen" is the best rendering, after all, the last title for a woman which suggests in our society the fiction of an immense social distance between the lover and the beloved on which this whole tradition depends. Moreover, the word has only one syllable, and this English meter demands. In Italian, of course, the monorhymes are all bisyllabic and each closing cadence feminine. Though it would be possible with some strain to maintain this pattern in English: "shadow," "verdure," "herbage," "mountains," etc., the eleven-syllable line closing on the offbeat is for us a pointless affectation, which clamors to become a ten-syllable one ending on the stress.

To maintain such a rhythm for five rhymes and not the sixth seems to me intolerable. But what other monosyllabic honorific for woman is there? "Dame" is ridiculous, and to use "lass," as does Grandgent (or "maid" or "girl"), blurs an important point. It is true, I think, that we should be aware of the beloved as really a girl, so absurdly young that the hopeless passion of an aging man seems all the more degrading; but there is a tension in such phrases as "*la giovane donna*" between the lady's actual youth and her status for the poet, best rendered by the paradox in "little queen."

Indeed, the whole poem must be conceived of as a series of ironic contrasts, some subtle, some stark almost to the point of melodrama; and nothing must conceal its nature as a nest of Chinese boxes, paradox within paradox down to the vanishing point. This sense no translation I know renders with real success, yet without this it, the poem, loses its *raison d'être*. Not only the logic but also the music of the sestina depends upon the establishing of this pattern of duality against a background of tripleness. It is as if the right hand played in double time against the triple time of the left. Over all, there is the balancing off of the three-line *congedo* against the preceding thirty-six verses; inside of this, a contrast of stanza one with stanza two, and of five with six. Stanzas three and four make quite separate units, each containing a sharp clash between opening and conclusion. But this, of course, is merely the beginning.

Stanzas one and two are linked by the adverb "*similemente*," which the earlier translators ignore, but which is the hinge of the wriest joke and the most delightfully ironic transition of the poem. I have rendered it "just so constantly" (literally it is "similarly") to make the point as clearly as possible. He and his beloved (the poet boasts) are equally faithful and unchanging; for quite as he remains the sole note of spring in winter, she remains the last vestige of winter in the spring. It is no more possible to make her love than to make him cease from loving. Yet there is a hint from the start that her kind of stubbornness will outlast his. The basic antimony of spring and winter suggests others: sunlight and shadow, white and green, grass and hills. The final pair introduces a further reach of irony; for if grass by virtue of its color stands for hope, it is also the symbol of impermanence; while the hills (associated with darkness, constriction and cold) are the type of what abides forever.

Though the winter is one of a set of contraries, it contains within itself a further contradiction described in terms of "*poco giorno*" and "*gran cerchio d'ombra.*" That this represents more than the simple-minded contrast of short days and long nights, already a commonplace by Dante's time, can be seen by comparing it with its Provençal counterparts: "Anigh short days and evenings long," "The longest night and the smallest day of all the year," etc. Only the Dantesque version evokes the cosmic image of the great globe itself beneath its inverted cone of dark, and the diminishing focus of daylight inside of which the tiny protagonist prepares to face an overwhelming destiny. From this vast background, the poem shrinks to the final foreground detail of the stone lost in grass. Simply to give up, as Rossetti does, this opening contrast of "small" and "great" is to risk losing the leitmotif of the poem. The sigh of "alas!" cannot be spared either; and to render the straightforward "*giunto*" as "clomb" rather than "come" is to submit to the sort of archaizing which takes the accidents of aging for the essence of poetic appeal.

That hopeless desire wear the color of hope when the grass has yielded it up before the cold is a further twist, compounded by the revelation that the fertility of that desire is based on its rooting not in rich soil but in "*dura petra,*" that strange stone as sentient as a woman. The second stanza, being the mirror image of the first, suggests no new images, presenting only the complements of those already established. The only real problem of translation is the phrase "*nova donna*," in which it is hard to know whether the adjective means "new" in the sense of "just discovered" or "unique" or whether it rather signifies "curious" or even just "young." This ambiguity is not resolved until the final stanza, where "*giovane donna*" establishes the last possibility beyond question. It would have been nice to find a similarly ambiguous word in English, but I discovered none. "Little" has, however, parallel possibilities of its own, and it is for that reason that I have chosen it over "youthful."

The third stanza stands by itself. For the first four lines, it is the least "stony" in technique of any of the verses; the lady with the leafy garland is a stock figure of Dante's imagination (Fioretta, too, is crowned in this way); and the expected references to the gold of her hair and to love's finding a resting place in her eyes are not redeemed from banality by Dante's stunt of substituting "curling gold" for "gold curls"—or by his periphrasis which speaks indirectly of love's traditional seat as the shade of the garland. To emphasize the conventional sweetness of this opening, I have tried to out-Rossetti Rossetti, building up for the shock of the concluding turn with a diction quite mannered and verging on the cliché.

Dante does not repeat the word "love" in launching his reversal, which turns the conventional personification of *Amor* into the warden of the prison of the hills. A simple relative pronoun suffices him; but I did not dare risk confusion. I am aware that "*calcina petra*" in the final line may be subject and object rather than a compound noun, in which case the translation ought to read "More stubbornly than mortar stone on stone"—but this image would rather disconcertingly make the lady "mortar," the poet "stone"; and besides I was reluctant to give up the satisfying ring of "calcareous stone."

In the fourth stanza, the ratio between conventional opening and ironical counterstatement is reversed. The first two lines draw upon stock again, with quite conventional references to the *vertù* of gems and the medical properties of herbs. The redeeming twist here arises from the suggestion, implicit in the fact that

a single word means both "jewel" and "rock," that the magic of
the lady, her essential power, is inseparable from the very stoni-
ness which baffles her lover. These lines are a real trap for the
translator; both "stone" and "grass" seem to me to demand qualifying adjectives to make them mean unequivocally "gem" and
"herb"; while the word *vertù* almost defies a rendering succinct
enough to stay inside the poem. Rossetti's "more bright than is
a precious stone" is an abject surrender.

The four-line reversal links a new pair of paradoxes: that the
lover in fear has fled from the "queen" he really desires to possess
through a nightmare landscape of rise and hollow; and that he
seeks to hide from the lady's light in that same nightmare world
whose humps and frondage cast no shade. The final two lines,
though intended merely to specify the horror of a queen whose
very radiance is terror, reflect back on the whimpering poet, who
has begun by complaining of the "*gran cerchio d'ombra*" but now
begs for the small shadow of wall or tuffet, later of the lady's
skirts. Having narrowly resisted the temptation to make "*cotal
donna*" "so cruel a queen," I feel free to express my disdain for
Rossetti's "so dangerous a lady." "This kind of queen" seems to
me finally just right in its bare suggestiveness, an example of
Dante's tactful reticence.

The fifth and sixth stanzas are linked like the first and second, but this time with a frank adversative conjunction, while
elements of the third and fourth stanzas enter into the beginning
of the passage, somewhat transmuted. The lady wreathed in
green changes slightly into another recurrent shape of Dante's
fantasy, the woman draped in green (one thinks of Beatrice in
the *Purgatory*, "*sotto verde manto*"); and the nightmare of flight
through a shadowless waste, which closes four, is converted into
a dream of the beloved herself on fire with love and sealed off
in a meadow surrounded by hills. Rossetti, misled by the verb
"*chesta*," which he apparently took to mean "wooed" instead of
"wished for," translates into fact what should be presented as an
unreal vision.

The elegant syntax of the conclusion of stanza five, more
Latin really than Italian, with the adjectives deliberately dis-
placed ("*chiuso*," which modifies "*prato*," huddles next to

"*donna*"; while "*innamorata*," which modifies the pronoun in the phrase "*l'ho chesta*," is shifted close to "prato") has baffled me. The effect of the original is to blur lady and meadow into each other as in a dream, until the queen almost becomes the grassy field in the hollow of the hills. The confusion of reference I have been able to retain; but the simultaneous delicate sorting out depends on the agreement of the endings beyond the power of English to simulate.

The impress of Latin verse extends into the sixth stanza, with its vaguely Vergilian figure at the opening ("sooner will the rivers climb the hills"); but the stanza soon swings violently in a new direction. The point of the "but" (or as Rossetti would have it "yet") on which the counterstatement hinges is lost in his rendering. In my fantasy, Dante is saying, I have imagined the *Donna Pietra* in love, but in fact I know her to be incapable of being kindled. The figure in "*s'infiammi*" I have carried back into the previous stanza, making "*innamorata*" not merely "in love" but "fired with love."

The subtlest development in this section seems to me to come in the new meaning of *verde* exposed in the second line: the adjective green applied to the wreath and the garment, this time is attached to the lady herself; but here the word *verde* signifies neither springtime nor hope, only youth in all its cruelty. For a moment she is imagined not as a rock, hard and lifeless, but as *legno* (I have translated "sprig" rather than simply "wood" to emphasize the elusive note of youthfulness), which is *molle*, soft but also damp, and *verde*, living but also uninflammable. Stone or sprig, she is not a "*bella donna*," "a fair and proper queen," but an unawakened child, still ignorant of that ultimate obligation of her sex, which Francesca remembers even in hell: "*Amor, ch'a nullo amato amar perdona.*"

And yet, the poet protests, the man whom she so ungraciously rejects is ready for any sacrifice, would consent even to wander about "*pascendo l'erba*" and for the rest of his days "*dormire in petra.*" There is, I suspect, a triple pun, wicked and complex, in that last phrase. If Dante did not desire it, the sestina did: the terms of the game he accepted demanded it, and I am delighted to preserve (or even introduce) it in my own version. The basic meaning of "*dormire in petra*" restated in the alternative figure "*gir pascendo l'erba*" is to live like a beast; yet one must, I think, resist the temptation to make this too explicit, as Rossetti does with "feed like beasts on grass." To sleep out in the open, on stony ground, is then the first significance of the phrase; but the poet does not say "ground." He says "stone" and "stone" is "*petra*," which is also the lady's name. It is a tart and hopeless jest, reinforced by the ambiguity of "*per veder do'suoi panni fanno ombra*"—consent to sleep in Petra, indeed!

But there is another level, even beyond the sexual one, a final convolution. In the double sestina, the poet foresees the time when "this gentle Stone shall see me prone within a little stone," and the concluding phrase of that poem "*coricare in petra*" fades into the "*dormire in petra*" of this one, to introduce the note of death that intrudes near the close of all the *rime petrose*. To sleep, to possess and to die—the three significances mingle in a bitter music.

The *congedo* is both unorthodox and mysterious; a gnarled but haunting passage, obscure in syntax, but possessing an odd beauty and power of implication beyond anything else in the poem. In these three lines, the symbolic exponent of the whole sestina is raised. Each of the other attested *rime pietrose* ends with the conventional address to the song: *Canzone, io porto ne la mente donna; Canzon, vattene dritto a quella donna*, etc.; Arnaut's classic sestina itself has a comparable close: *Arnutz tramet sa chansson d'ongla e d'oncle*. But here Dante has rejected the merely formal close in order to deepen and complicate his series of paradoxes with a final reversal—graceful enough, though anything but the conventional curtsy to spell *finis*.

About my own interpretation, I have more to say below; for now, I want only to make the point that I have accepted the established text, the editor's punctuation, etc., of all recent Italian editions. I therefore read the last phrase "*com'uom petra sott' erba*" as if "*uom*" were the subject, "*petra*" the object and the verb "*fa sparire*" understood: literally then "as one [makes] a stone [disappear] beneath the grass." Just a couple of years ago it was argued that the whole passage could be reinterpreted in a new and fascinating (though finally unconvincing) way. In this new reading, "*uom petra*" would be understood as the compound "*uom-petra*," and the whole passage would then read "as a stone man (or petrified man) [is buried] beneath grass." This would make a characteristically grim conclusion, blending death and despair as in the other *rime pietrose:* the man who loved a stone instead of a woman is himself turned to stone and buried beneath the sod. The hyphenated *uom-petra* strikes me, however, as a contrived monster; and the meaning as not worthy of the richness, the quiet melancholy that one feels in the *commiato.*

The end of stanza six has been a desperate declaration of the poet's fidelity to the unyielding beloved; no longer does he flee or moan, but offers himself in almost hopeless humility. The *congedo* moves naturally enough from this into a compliment to the "little queen," a piece of hyperbolic praise, carefully keyed so as to tone down toward gentle melancholy the bitterness that has come before. "Whenever the hills cast blackest shade," the final counterstatement begins, echoing not only the thematic noun, but this time also the verb of the preceding line: "*fanno ombra*" "*fanno . . . ombra.*" (This echo Rossetti sacrifices to pointless variation.) In the transition from stanza to stanza, however, the pleasant shade of the lady's skirts (with its suggestion of a *double-entendre*) has been transformed into the ultimate blackness "*più nera ombra*"; and the poet finds himself in the very Valley of Shadow.

The verb after *quandunque* ("whenever" not "howsoe'er") is the generalizing present, which we feel as a future until the repetition of the tense in the second verb, *la fa sparer*, shocks us into an awareness that "whenever" is now! Not only do the hills cast their blackest shadow now, but at this moment, too, the lady triumphs over their terror. "Yea, though I walk through the valley of shadow, my *donna* is with me." "No medicinal grass" can cure the wounds she inflicts; but she, who has more *vertù* than a jewel, can assuage suffering even as she bestows it, even perhaps raise again the one her cruelty has killed.

It is by virtue of her greenness that she has a power over the power of blackness, overwhelming it as hope triumphs over death and as the living grass covers insentient stone. The metaphor of "drown" is my own, not Dante's; but its evocation of a green tide and its connotations of disaster suit so well my reading of this passage that I have not been able to resist it. The ambiguity of *verde* here reaches a final rest; from the thesis of "*vestita in verde*" we have moved to the antithesis of "*molle e verde*," from awakening of hope to its bafflement; the *bel verde* of the *commiato* announces the synthesis: the birth of a greater and more metaphysical hope and the defeat of the *ombra* which has lain over the poem since the first line, "my little queen annuls it—"

But we are not yet through: the confrontation of *ombra* and *verde* suggests the parallel matching of *petra* and *erba;* and the simile introduces a new ambiguity which seems to tilt the resolution once more toward despair "as a stone is drowned in grass." Grass, as we have already noticed, is not simply the emblem of springtime, it is also the symbol of mortality; and when it is *petra* (Petra!) which disappears *sott'erba*—the notion of a new life covering lifeless rock threatens to blur into the image of a dead girl committed to earth. The balance of the final phrase is so delicate, a hope which is despair and a resurrection which is an entombment, that no further synthesis is required, no answering statement possible. The poem has exhausted its paradoxes at the same moment that it has rung the final changes on its rhymes.

AL POCO GIORNO . . .

> *Al poco giorno e al gran cerchio d'ombra*
> *son giunto, lasso, ed al bianchir de' colli,*
> *quando si perde lo color ne l'erba:*
> *e'l mio disio però non cangia il verde,*
> *sì è barbato ne la dura petra*
> *che parla e sente come fosse donna.*

> *Similemente questa nova donna*
> *si sta gelata come neve a l'ombra:*
> *ché non la move, se non come petra,*
> *il dolce tempo che rescalda i colli,*
> *e che li fa tornar di bianco in verde*
> *perché li copre di fioretti e d'erba.*

Quand'ella ha in testa una ghirlanda d'erba,
trae de la mente nostra ogn'altra donna:
perché si mischia il crespo giallo e'l verde
sí bel, ch'Amor lí viene a stare a l'ombra,
che m'ha serrato intra piccioli colli
piú forte assai che la calcina petra.

La sua bellezza ha più vertú che petra,
e'l colpo suo no può sanar per erba:
ch'io son fuggito per piani e per colli,
per potere scampar da cotal donna;
e dal suo lume non mi può far ombra
poggio né muro né fronda verde.

Io l'ho veduta già vestita a verde,
sí fatta ch'ella evrebbe messo in petra
l'amor ch' io porto pur a la sua ombra:
ond'io l'ho chesta in un bel prato d'erba,
innamorata com'anco fu donna,
e chiuso intorno d'altissimi colli.

Ma ben ritorneranno i fiumi a' colli
prima che questo legno molle e verde
s'infiammi, come suol far bella donna,
di me; che mi torrei dormire in petra
tutto il mio tempo e gir pascendo l'erba,
sol per veder do' suoi panni fanno ombra.

Quandunque i colli fanno piú nera ombra,
sotto un bel verde la giovane donna,
la fa sparer, com'uom petra sott'erba.

SESTINA: OF THE LADY PIETRA
DEGLI SCROVIGNI
(translated by D. G. Rossetti)

To the dim light and the large circle of shade
I have clomb, and to the whitening of the hills,

There where we see no color in the grass.
Natheless my longing loses not its green,
It has so taken root in the hard stone
Which talks and hears as though it were a lady.

Utterly frozen in this youthful lady,
Even as the snow that lies within the shade;
For she is no more moved than is the stone
By the sweet season which makes warm the hills
And alters them afresh from white to green,
Covering their sides again with flowers and grass.

When on her hair she sets a crown of grass
The thought has no more room for other lady;
Because she weaves the yellow with the green
So well that Love sits down there in the shade,—
Love who has shut me in among low hills
Faster than between walls of granite-stone.

She is more bright than is a precious stone;
The wound she gives may not be healed with grass:
I therefore have fled o'er plains and hills
For refuge from so dangerous a lady;
But from her sunshine nothing can give shade,—
Not any hills, nor wall, nor summer-green.

A while ago, I saw her dressed in green,—
So fair, she might have wakened in a stone
This love which I do feel even for her shade;
And therefore, as one woos a graceful lady,
I wooed her in a field that was all grass
Girdled about with very lofty hills.

Yet shall the streams turn back and climb the hills
Before Love's flame in this damp wood and green
Burn, as it burns within a youthful lady,
For my sake, who would sleep away in stone
My life, or feed like beasts upon the grass,
Only to see her garments cast a shade.

How dark soe'er the hills throw out their shade,
Under her summer-green the beautiful lady
Covers it, like a stone covered in grass.

TO SMALL DAYLIGHT: THE STONY SESTINA OF DANTE ALIGHIERI
(translated by L. A. Fiedler)

To small daylight and the great circle of shade,
I've come, alas, and to the blanching of the hills,
That season when the color leaves the grass
And only my desire keeps its green,
So rooted is it in the rigid stone
That speaks and harks as if it were a queen.

And just so constantly, my little queen
Lies frozen fast, a snowbank in the shade,
And is not stirred except as is the stone
By time's sweet turning that now warms the hills
And changes all their whiteness into green
With blossoms and a blanketing of grass.

When she is garlanded with plaited grass,
She lures our longing from each other queen;
So intertwined the curling gold and green,
Love loves to lounge there in its shade—
That Love which locks me here in little hills,
More stubborn even than calcareous stone.

Her beauty's magic mocks the precious stone;
Her blows are eased by no medicinal grass;
And I have fled through fens and over hills
To find my freedom from this kind of queen;
But from her light there is no sheltering shade,
Not wall or tuffet or the leafiest green.

Yet there was once I watched her dressed in green,
So winsome she might wake within a stone
That love which wracks me for her merest shade;
And then I dreamed her in a field of grass,
More fired with love than ever any queen,
And sealed there by an arc of alpine hills.

But sooner will the rivers climb the hills
Than for my sake this sprig, too moist and green,
Be kindled like a fair and proper queen,
For me, who would consent to sleep on stone
For all my days, and pasture me on grass,
So I might see where her skirts cast their shade.

Whatever time the hills cast blackest shade,
Beneath a lovely green, my little queen
Annuls it, as a stone is drowned in grass.

Shakespeare and the Paradox
of Illusion

There is a sense, annoying I think to the more tender-minded reader or beholder, in which a work of art is a history of itself, a record of the scruples and hesitation of its maker in the course of its making, sometimes even a defense or definition of the kind to which it belongs or the conventions which it respects. The artist in most times is driven to conceal, with a wariness that becomes habitual and unconscious, this face of his work from all but the canniest of his audience, for he comes early to realize the resentment which a betrayal of this inward concern is like to arouse. "Treachery!" the reader cries. "Unfair!" For to him the *maintenance* of the illusion is what counts, though to the artist the primary thing is the *justification* of the illusion. And so their relationship has been conventionally based upon a complementary blindness and deceit.

Within the last few generations it has become possible to admit openly the aspect of self-concern in a work of art, even to flaunt it in the tradition of *épater la bourgeoisie*. One thinks of the classic device of Gide's *Counterfeiters*, of the novel within the novel. Gide tells us brazenly of a novelist writing a book in which he exists writing precisely the book in which we have met him writing the book in which, etc., etc. It all opens up, or more accurately opens *inward*, toward the fake infinity of the girl on the cereal box holding a cereal box on which another girl (or perhaps the same one) holds a cereal box on which another girl holds a cereal box on which—and so on until the label blurs to a breakfast-table indeterminate.

Not only in the twentieth century, however, are such games played. Melville in *Pierre* contrives a quite similar relationship between the novel his hero is vainly trying to write and the novel in which he is trying to write it; and Cervantes in the Second Part of *Don Quixote* treats his First Part as a fact of the fictional world through which his paired protagonists move, a favorite book of every cultured lady and gentleman they meet. When in the early twentieth century or the mid-nineteenth or the closing years of the sixteenth such jugglery becomes a primary concern of the artist, we feel ourselves in the presence of the kind of art our age calls Mannerism—stripping that term of its original pejorative sense. Critics like Arnold Hauser have accustomed us to see in Shakespeare, as well as in Cervantes, the Mannerist at work; and it is, perhaps, this aspect of his inexhaustible talent with which we are most at home, preferring Shakespeare the Mannerist to Shakespeare the Child of Nature, Shakespeare the Melancholy Romantic, Shakespeare the Healthy Soul or Shakespeare the Businessman-Playwright.

Yet it will not do to confuse him with André Gide. The contriving of fictive infinities is the concern of both, but in Gide that concern has finally the air of an intellectual joke, a suitable fraud in a world in which we are all coiners, and the currency of the artist presumably as counterfeit as our other media of exchange: the book is not really by Uncle Edouard, but rather Uncle Edouard by the book, and the Gide who composes them both, it is inevitably suggested, was composed for just that purpose by a more ultimate Gide. Here is a general problem reduced to a special irony, stated in terms of a travesty on Romantic notions of authorship, and in the context of an age that is ready to think of the artist primarily as an illusionist, a perpetrator of hoaxes (consider Joyce's key image of Shem the Penman, the forger as artist, or Mann's gamut of symbols for the writer from Felix Krull the Confidence Man to the charlatan hypnotist of "Mario and the Magician").

Still the general problem persists; in any age a work of art is on one level about the problems of its own composition, the threat to the illusion it attempts to create; and just so far as it comments on those perils, it further endangers the basic illusion. The use in comedy from the Greeks to the Marx Brothers of the deliberate breaking of the illusion (the deprecatory aside: "That's what it says here!") tries to laugh the danger out of existence, to anticipate the audience's awareness of art's essential hokum or at least to shock them out of feeling superior in that awareness by a defensive self-exposure; but such a method is a desperate and degrading expedient— "Anything for a laugh!"—and is, of course, quite inadequate for serious art.

But there has long existed in drama another expedient, capable at once of confessing and exorcising art's central illusion ("Now you see it, now you don't!") and of objectifying the artist's need to make his creation a record of its creating. That expedient is the "play within a play," which, though used sometimes for partial or even trivial ends, can be said to have as its essential meaning the solution of the dilemma we have been considering. The "play within a play," like the Happy Ending or the Reversal, is an example of a technical or structural myth: a plot configuration or a technical device with an archetypal meaning quite independent of any individual's conscious exploitation of it.

It is an easy step from *The Counterfeiters* to *Hamlet*, for the "novel within a novel" of *The Counterfeiters* is a translation of the "play within a play" of *Hamlet* or, more precisely, a profanation, an honorific parody—that is to say, a critical analysis of the myth. The myth, by definition, cannot be conscious, and the moment we take pains to know it, it is degraded, profaned—the Joseph story in Genesis is mythic, in Thomas Mann an endless, middle-aged joke. In *Hamlet*, however, we have, rather than an analysis, the *realization* of the myth: its meaning is evident but unstated; all its ambiguities are in solution; its mystery is intact but at rest. Add to *The Counterfeiters* and *Hamlet* the *Spanish Tragedy* of Kyd (or Shakespeare's own *A Midsummer Night's Dream*) and we have a full triad: the myth imperfectly exploited, the myth realized, the myth analyzed.

Kyd and Shakespeare share certain assumptions about the role of the artist and the relation of art to the given world which separate them sharply from Gide: to them the type of the artist is the Man with the Mirror, not the Swindler; the process is not forgery but imitation. And even when the Mannerist holds up a mirror to a mirror, catching the endless interplay of reflection, he does not deny the final reality of "nature." "It's all done with mirrors," we say and echo ironically the Shakespearean "hold the mirror up to nature," with all the sad denigration of the mirror as metaphor that lies between. The Renaissance mind was convinced from one side of the "truth" of artistic representation in a context in which arithmetic, theology and rhetoric subscribed to a single criterion of truth; just as from the other it was convinced of the "falsity" of art in a context in which the meanings of "lie" and "fiction" had not yet been discriminated. This impossible contradiction, like a thousand others, the Renaissance mind ordinarily endured, with a lost art of accommodation that we must by turns envy and despise.

To Shakespeare, however, the contradiction was apparently a lifelong vexation, a conflict which he strove at first to conceal by all the grace of his art, but which ultimately he attempted to reconcile in a solution that abandoned the stratagems of technique for those of metaphysics. The Shakespearean corpus is a self-justification (one remembers the vaunt: *Non sanz droict!*), a justification of his art, of the art of the playwright as practiced in his time down to the last detail: the patching of plays, the use of the boy actor—eventually of all art, of the lie as truth. But that is a possible definition of myth, the lie as truth, and it is the extraordinary achievement of Shakespeare to have created the myth in defense of the illusion, to have revealed the universal symbolic relevance of those devices which persuade us to suspend disbelief.

Shakespeare seems to have felt the illusion of his art imperiled on four main fronts, and to have evolved, in response to those four threats, four essential myths that come to full flower in the last plays: the myth of the *Cosmic Drama*, the myth of the *Cosmic Dream*, the myth of the *Beardless Beloved* and the myth of *Qualitative Immortality*. I hope someday to treat all four of these topics in detail,* but here I shall concentrate on the first, touching the others only incidentally. I should like, though, before returning to a consideration of Hamlet and my center, to

---

* I no longer believe I shall really come to terms at great lengths with Shakespeare, but I leave the hope of 1948 in the text to remind myself of what seemed possible twelve years ago.

indicate briefly the four threats to illusion from which Shakespeare's mythical trajectories begin.

First, that the actors are merely actors; that is, they are today this, tomorrow that; and that there persists, behind the this or that they put on and doff, a recognizable self, inevitably felt as more real, the *real* self. There was in the Elizabethan theater at least the beginnings of a star system—of all systems the one which most emphasizes the actor as existing outside of his role. Further, the Shakespearean stage seems to have been at an uneasy point between frankly conventionalized presentation and realistic production, making for a certain basic shakiness of conviction.

Second, as a special and extraordinarily difficult case under the first, the actors of women's parts were not even women, but boys never quite sure of avoiding the gauche gesture or the cracked voice that would betray utterly the possibility of acceptance. "Boy my greatness i' th' posture of a whore," Cleopatra says, foreseeing her possible travesty on the stages of Rome in terms of the actuality of the performance in which she, the actor-she, moves.

Third, that the dead live. The corpses which fall to the stage, stabbed or poisoned or asp-bitten, will rise to acknowledge the audience's applause. Even before they are carried off, the closest of the "understanders" in the pit will have seen the eyelid's betraying flutter, the heaving of the chest.

Fourth, that the play ends. The action is framed with an arbitrary beginning and close, moves its three or four hours to an inevitable concluding couplet. Jack has his Joan, or the villain his quietus, and the stage is empty; but the felt mode of lived experience, of "real life," is continuity.

The third and fourth problems demand apparently contradictory solutions and indeed seem to get them; but if we are left at last with a contradiction, it is not the elementary one with which we begin. In the simplest apprehension of life, there seems to be a continuity, an immortality of the general, though the individual dies. The show, that is to say, goes on—and on and on. The world survives our particular endings; but in the uni-

verse of play acting, the individual survives his age, his world
—which is to say the actor survives the play. Four hours and
there's an end to Denmark, but Burbage is resurrected next night
in Illyria or Bohemia or Rome.

The author's immediate problem is to deceive his audience,
to leave us unshakably convinced that the stage dead are really
dead; and for the elementary reinforcement of the illusion Shakespeare is full of devices, from the expedient of *Romeo and Juliet,*
in which Juliet first *appears* to Romeo within the play to have
died (though we outside *know* she "really" lives), and then dies
actually for *us;* or by the simulated death of the Player King in
the inner play in *Hamlet,* a remove of "pretend" from which we
return to find the death of the actor who plays Claudius "true."

But this device is perilous; for, though the double order of
belief proposed by the play within the play on the first convolution inveigles us into belief, on second thought, or to the naturally
more complicated mind, it suggests that just as the Player King
has not really died, no more has *this* king, after all a Player too,
and leaves us the more emphatically undeceived. But this disenchantment, Shakespeare has apparently decided by the end of
his career, is precisely what he is after—nobody is dead at all,
not in any ultimate sense, for all death is appearance only. And
by the time we have got to the final plays, to Hermione or
Imogen, the hoax of stage-death seen through by the wary has
been translated into the symbolic statement that *all* death is a
hoax, a seeming. The presumed failure of illusion becomes the
revelation of a higher truth, and the last plays are, as Wilson
Knight has so convincingly argued, myths of immortality.

In an analogous way, the poet begins by resenting the arbitrary ending, the betrayal of the play's fictional time by the
inevitable close of the last act. In the young and "arty" *Love's
Labour's Lost,* there is an outright refusal even to pretend that
the play ends at all, but that particular stratagem only a bright
young man in a work aimed at a special audience can afford.
Things are just *beginning* when the play is through. But a mass
audience demands other devices, less frank, more conventional.
A closing marriage or a birth or coronation helps to create the

sense of an open ending, a conclusion without finality—and in *Hamlet*, as we have seen, the inner play is used to create a double continuity of intension and extension, a fake circular infinity. But in the *Tempest*, Shakespeare makes his typical reaffirmation of the breach of illusion, abandons any attempt at concealing the play's limits. In the speech "Our revels now are ended . . ." he explicates the meaning of the interrupted masque, the performance arbitrarily brought to a close, as a symbol of the world's transience, collective impermanence.

"The great globe itself . . . shall dissolve." The world *does* decay, and only the individual, in his moment of discovery or passion or tragic insight, is forever. In this sense, the apparent contradiction between our being immune to death ("Not a hair perished") and yet "such stuff as dreams are made on" is reconciled.

The problem of the ambiguity of sex and the stratagems demanded by the stubborn convention of the boy as girl in Elizabethan production deserve, and I hope someday to give them, a full-length examination. *Cymbeline* appears to me now to be the climactic play in the study of that problem and its mythic implications. It is probably sufficient to say here that Shakespeare begins in his customary fashion with the aim of defending the illusion of femininity against the inevitable shortcomings of the boy actor; but that, before he is through with those disguised boys who are really girls who in turn are actually boys, those master-mistresses who win the hearts of men and women alike, often both at once, he has established the myth of an androgynous Beloved, the focus of whose attraction is neither femininity nor masculinity but the delightful ambiguity of youth —the Beardless Beloved. And that myth enables him, without abandoning the Heroine altogether, to maintain his determining sexual attitude (clear in the Sonnets and elsewhere) which regards the blatant, the mature female (especially the mother) as a symbol of evil, blackness, lust, and so on. Connected with this syndrome, too, is the concept of the perfect Hero as the man without a female component, the child born not of a living mother but of death, that strange deliverer who breaks through the tragic circumstances of *Cymbeline* and *Macbeth* (paired plays that mark Shakespeare's escape from an obsession with unmitigated tragedy), the "man not born of woman."

There is a single tormented point of view dramatically working itself out from the blandly obscene puns of Sonnet XX ("the master-mistress of my passion . . . prick'd thee out for woman's pleasure . . .") through the intricate web of disguise and impersonation in *As You Like It* (in one scene of which, a boy actor—destined in the Epilogue to reveal his sex—plays a girl pretending to be a boy pretending to be a girl) to the soliloquy of Leonatus Posthumus in *Cymbeline,* so grossly anti-feminist that the milder Philistine scholars of the nineteenth century sought to persuade themselves that it was an interpolation. Even read in private, one of them notes, it seems "of doubtful propriety"; and, indeed, the savagery with which it imagines the sex act (". . . perchance he spoke not, but/Like a full-acorn'd boar, A German one,/Cried 'O!' and mounted . . .") and comments on female vice ("Is there no way for men to be but women/Must be half-workers? We are all bastards . . .") must have disconcerted those committed to a belief in Shakespeare's mental health. The poetic sensibility at work in this sequence seems less that of the genial, nature-loving optimist once postulated as the author of Shakespeare's plays than that of such a character as Antonio in *The Merchant of Venice* (with Hamlet and Prospero, a self-portrait which only the most obtuse scholar can fail to see), whose melancholy so oddly mitigates the gaiety of that play; and whose loss of his young friend the marriages at the play's end cannot quite make into a Happy Ending. Perhaps to avert such melancholy from himself, Shakespeare has chosen to portray the distinction of male and female as finally as meaningless as that of life and death, fiction and actuality. In the "play within the play," all such distinctions are dissolved; and it is to that archetypal device we must return in quest of further understanding.

In the "Pyramus and Thisbe" of *A Midsummer Night's Dream,* we have the "play within the play" used as a stunt to maintain a precarious illusion, to reinforce the reality of the larger production. Shakespeare trades upon the inevitable audience conviction that characters shown planning a play cannot themselves be characters in a larger play; the run-of-the-mill "under-stander" cannot get back past the second convolution; and the few who can, who are able to *see the lie,* fulfill the poet's other wish: to have someone know the deft machinery of the illusion he manipulates, appraise his skill. But the *Dream* with its loose structure makes no real attempt to integrate the inner play into the outer plot; rather it deliberately holds it off as mockery, as foil: bumbling tragedy versus graceful comedy—a courtly joke, all kept down among the peripheral vulgar characters, who seem to exist so often in Shakespeare, like Negroes in Hollywood films, largely to amuse the gentry.

Thomas Kyd in his *Spanish Tragedy* transfers the inner play from subplot to plot, from comedy to tragedy (or at least melo-drama), from dream to nightmare. Kyd's is a considerable achievement, and is the cue, either directly or via his lost *Ur-Hamlet,* to much in Sheakespeare's *Hamlet;* but he still muffs something essential to the integral, the mythic meaning of the inner play. The relationship of Kyd's double play is concentric; the play within and the play without dissolve into each other. Hieronimo and Bel-Imperia, disguised as the Bashaw and Per-seda, kill Lorenzo and Balthazar, in the roles of Erastus and Soly-man. The pivot of revenge upon which the whole structure turns, the climactic action of the whole fable, falls within the inner play, so that the outer play has no true ending but trails off into supere-rogatory and unconvincing horrors (Hieronimo biting off his own tongue, as if to confess what the author will not admit), merely to have something more to add, though there is nothing more to say. The characters are all involved, and no one remains outside to define the innerness of the play within—only the audi-ence and its proxies, the King and the Viceroy, who are, more accurately perhaps, rather its Dr. Watsons than its proxies; for they do not know, as the audience does, that the deaths they behold are "real," but take the murders as entertainment, illusory horror performed with exceeding conviction. That irony (the audience all the time *knowing!*) is for Kyd the sufficient meaning of the inner play, and beyond that, to be sure, the irony of the irony, the esoteric irony: the characters whose deaths had first seemed "fabulously counterfeit" and who were then revealed really to have died we know, outside the illusion, are not dead at all, but prepare to take our applause, bowing, as we move toward the exits.

This is a more complex device than that of the *Dream,* ending on a third convolution, but like the simpler comedy it offers the cream of its jest only at the expense of its over-all credibility. It remains a technical expedient, a dodge to protect and complicate the illusion. In Shakespeare's *Hamlet,* however, where the ironic climax has been detached from the inner play and isolated in the duel scene, in which the Prince and Laertes "play" at swords whose real threat is known to neither Hamlet nor the Queen mother, the "play within the play" is freed for its more essential, its pure mythic, function.

With an insistence that risks the obvious, Shakespeare hammers home the artificiality, the counterfeit of the inner play: we see the entry of the professional actors (that they are *professionals* to begin with is the first turn of the screw), and we are given, at some pains, a sense of their existence as persons outside their performance (the boy has grown; there is danger of his voice cracking); we are shown them being lectured on the art of gesture and delivery so that their technique cannot fail to show through their acting; we are permitted to hear an impromptu recitation set in a context of remembering lines; and lest, listening to that recitation, we have been betrayed into a suspension of disbelief, there is Hamlet's subsequent soliloquy to remind us that the player's passion and its occasion exist only in fancy: "What's Hecuba to him or he to Hecuba?"

The fictive nature of the inner play, its play-ness, is insisted upon almost desperately, suggesting at first that Shakespeare must have doubted the credibility of his main plot, strained between its sources and its meanings; or that some imperative need for an utimate verisimilitude moved him. What is at stake? Surely, the playwright must have sensed that such an extraordinary emphasis on the contrived nature of the play within threatened to defeat itself, increased proportionally the peril to the illusion and made more drastic the eventual shattering of belief, when the audience passed inevitably from the convolution of increased credence to that of disenchantment. But that may, after all, have been precisely Shakespeare's point.

For by a simple expedient the poet *forces* us toward the disruptive realization: just such a contrived fabric as this, is the whole tragedy in which it is set! The inner play and the outer play *are the same play.* To be sure we get that point (*Hamlet* is pre-eminently a work in which no chances are taken), the inner play is acted twice, first in the dumb show, in a striking departure from Elizabethan custom that either treated such pantomimes in terms of allegory or used them with a narrator to speed up the action; yet here the dumb show re-enacts literally the crime later to be played with speech: "Into the porches of mine ear . . ."

It has been a disturbing scene for actors and commentators ever since. Why, the question is asked over and over, does the King, later so rattled by precisely the same thing, not rise in fright at the pantomimic crime? To make his behavior credible, he is traditionally shown occupied in conversation with the Queen throughout the dumb show. This is what is conventionally called "the problem of the dumb show," but the ulterior, the real problem has, as far as I know, never been raised: Why does Shakespeare, in the first place, fall into this difficulty which can at best be solved only by a somewhat awkward piece of stage business? Surely, because he is convinced that at any risk he must clinch in the minds of the least subtle the *identity* of the two plays. In the pantomime there is no disturbing limitation of names (indeed, even in the inner play proper the characters do not name each other; only Hamlet, a chorus and proxy for the playwright, with a foot in each world, gives mockingly their Italianate names, their locale and pretended date): these are, quite simply, the King, the Queen, the Betrayer, the very ones who, as in a nightmare at once within and without, look on or haunt the scene.

It is necessary for the prosecution of the plot that the plays be similar, of course, and on the plot level Shakespeare has explained away an improbable degree of coincidence between the inner play and the actual events at Elsinore with Hamlet's added "dozen or sixteen lines"; but consider, in terms of the mythic convention we have been tracing, the import of this coincidence. Hamlet has, with those dozen or sixteen lines, imposed a meaning upon an old playlet (and we know that this is precisely the sort of tinkering that Shakespeare himself had done with the *Ur-Hamlet*) in which we have just reached the point at which, had Claudius not interrupted with his terror, his ironic cry of "Give me some light!" a Hamlet-character, some melancholy sniffer out of evil, would inevitably have had to come upon the scene to contrive another play to catch the conscience of Gonzago, and in that play another Hamlet, and so on.

In that sense the play narrows inward like *The Counterfeiters* toward a vortex of infinity; but it opens outward, too, unlike the modern work, in a widening circle toward an infinity of extension. Is not the very piece we are seeing, the inner play suggests, precisely that play Hamlet has arranged before us— and are we not then a stage audience, beheld as well as beholding, at a play within some greater play, actors all in a universal drama which inevitably defines all our plays as "plays within a play"? If Hamlet is Shakespeare—and who can really deny that Romantic insight?—Shakespeare in turn is Hamlet to some more ultimate Shakespeare, in whose reworking of a recalcitrant matter we as onlookers are, according to our guilt, Ophelia or Gertrude, Polonius or the usurping King, walking shadows, poor players.

"All the world's a stage." Reality dissolves around us to that fearful metaphor, ordinarily meaningless for us who have memorized it as children. It is Shakespeare's most obsessive figure, "the conceit of this inconstant stay," spoken not only through the ambiguous mouths of characters in his plays, but confessed in the personal voice of the Sonnets: "this huge stage presenteth nought but shows/Whereon the stars in secret influence comment." In *Hamlet* the figure is never reduced to a tag, but at the focus of the inner play the whole tragedy is epiphanized as that metaphor in infinite extension. That the playwright understand the world's illusion in terms of his own craft is understandable enough, for such a conceit at once familiarizes the cosmic mutability he feels and dignifies his own despised profession; the final Maker, too, it suggests, is concerned with just such shows as devour the poet's talent and lay up a modest fortune for his old age. The playwright's very life is mythic, the limitations of his art a clue to the meanings of life.

On one level certainly *Hamlet* is (or *can* be, once we have thought of it) an account of the writer's essential experience: the tragic vision, the relapse into doubt (what ghost is true?), the shaken faith in the adequacy of his medium ("Must like a whore unpack my heart with words") and the final restitution of belief in art as a symbolic act.

"The play's the thing," Hamlet cries in the anguished moment of recovering his faith in the efficacy of talk. For in the end, notice, he does not, for all his envy of the inarticulate soldier, cease verbally to unpack his heart, but learns to organize his words into the cunning form that gives them consequence in action. His only deliberately chosen act, his only real *success* in the course of the tragedy, is dramatic: the play within the play of passion and free will and fate—emended by some dozen or sixteen lines.

"Wherein I'll catch the conscience of the King." The phrase oddly suggests the Joycean conception of art's function: to re-create the conscience of the race; but in Shakespeare the accent is upon the sly disclosure, the revelatory trick. Art is a trap, the mousetrap, a miching mallecho that promises to amuse us with a lie—and shows in its unforeseen truth ourselves caught in the compulsive pattern of the fall. There is an apt mockery in the taunt: "Let the galled jade wince." Who is ungalled? Our consciences caught, we rise, our guilt confessed, to call out, "Give me some light!" and retire to plot our various and singular dooms.

This is a subtle and apt parable of art's genesis and role, its hesitations and its incredible victory snatched from defeat; but it is more. It is a *particular* instance, scrupulously defined; it is a singular account of itself. Perfectly circular (the two plays, we remember, are one), it comments on its own history, on the career and genesis of the very *Hamlet* at which we assist in all its particularity—the old play, the Oedipus horror, the playing style of the actors, the mystery of repetition—and thus redeems at the last minute its peculiar failure to its peculiar success.

Commentators have long though dimly felt the ambiguity

of success and failure in *Hamlet* and in its protagonist, and the special difficulty of disentangling the Prince's failure from the play's. No one who has read T. S. Eliot's acute, wrongheaded discussion can doubt that in some sense the play does not quite work out, that there is an unexorcisable incoherence at its heart—and yet, when the last lines are spoken, we are somehow *satisfied*, and convinced that our satisfaction is more ultimate than the sense of incoherence. And this is precisely how we feel about Hamlet the character: he has envied the soldier's readiness, the philosopher's dispassion, but his own actions have invariably been at the mercy of both passion and circumstance—and so, at last, ineffectual. He thrusts at a King, and an old fool dies. The denouement he does not achieve, but suffers; and he dies at the almost accidental consummation of his revenge, not really convincing us that he must.

Yet we do not feel as ironic the elegiac praise of Horatio and Fortinbras, who read the wreck of feeling and the wreck of enterprise as success. Hamlet does, in some sense, succeed, as only failure can succeed where success is bound either, like Claudius, to embrace evil or, like Fortinbras and Horatio, utterly to ignore it in simplicities of commitment or self-control. To this dubious victory the play's incomplete assimilation of its sources is a perfect objective correlative; the given plot defies the control of the poet's meaning and yet obliquely fulfills it, as the rottenness at Elsinore defies and yet fulfills in its own way the Prince's plan to set it right.

The refusal of life ever wholly to conform to the poet's plan is one of the inevitable meanings of art, and the intrinsic sadness of the artist before that failure is the sadness of *Hamlet*. That Shakespeare inherited a genre and a tradition which defined the artist as Patcher, Emender of the recalcitrant given, and that the disparities of *Hamlet* fix formally the hopelessness and glory of his task, conspire to make *Hamlet* a play upon itself and on all plays. Hamlet is sad because he cannot write the perfect *Hamlet*; but the record of his sadness becomes his triumph, our second-best and only play. The ultimate, the real *Ur-Hamlet*, is irrecoverable, unwritten, yet for a moment glimpsed and lost again at the dizzying focus of the play within the play within the play.

Further than *Hamlet*, Shakespeare could not go in terms of tragedy; its end term, revealed through the metaphor of the play within the play, is the myth of the Cosmic Drama. "All the world's a stage . . . the men and women merely players"; "struts and frets his hour upon the stage and then is heard no more." There is a double implication in this view: a strong determinism (the plot is given, and at best we can only amend it) and a conviction that the stage survives the player, that the universe persists and the individual perishes. In the life of the individual only his death—that is, his departing the stage, his becoming nothing—is "true." The myth of tragedy is a pagan myth, or in the current atheistic sense an "existential" one.

But the end term of Comedy, the concealed meaning of the Happy Ending, is the myth of the Cosmic Dream and of qualitative immortality, death as a dream and transformation. "These our actors . . . were all spirits." "Like this insubstantial pageant faded, leave not a rack behind." There is a contrasting twofold implication in this view: a strong emphasis upon free will and a conviction that the player survives the stage. There is no death, only the individual, the master of dreams, the magician dreaming for as long as forever is. The myth of comedy is a Christian myth.

Hamlet is an actor who desires to become a playwright trapped inside a tragedy, at last, a patcher of an old play, an emender of a pattern given like a fate. Prospero, the artist as magician, is not within a play at all, but the play, become his dream, is within him. Not necessity but wish controls the action, and the protagonist does not die to his situation, but wakes from it.

Prospero does not have, like Hamlet, to die with the plot he sets in motion; he must, though, be abandoned with its consummation. His is the failure of success that matches the success of Hamlet's failure. Only the disinherited, or as we say now the "alienated," controls the means of art; the magic of dreams is given in exile and loneliness, a weapon for casting out the usurper, for creating the brave new world in which love is a thing of innocence and law, and death is dead—in short, for redeeming the Fall. But the perfection of the dream is the dream's ending, and the Dreamer must let fall his cloak and wand, bid the powers of air depart, stand outside illusion forever and, naked as all men are essentially naked, learn to ask men's prayers as he has once compelled their applause.

> *. . . Now I want*
> *Spirits to enforce, art to enchant;*
> *And my ending is despair,*
> *Unless I be relieved by prayer . . .*

Walt Whitman: Portrait of the Artist as a Middle-Aged Hero

Originally the Introduction to *Whitman*
in The Laurel Poetry Series

The reader opening a volume of selections from *Leaves of Grass* should be aware first of all that, in intent, it is a single poem; though during the almost forty years which Whitman devoted to it, that poem grew from a modest book of about one hundred pages to a self-assured two-volume set of more than 450. The thin volume which appeared in 1855 (legend, truer than fact, says on the Fourth of July) included only thirteen untitled divisions; the authorized final edition of 1891-1892 contains 423 subpoems, not only named and often divided into helpfully numbered stanzas, but grouped under sixteen section headings, themselves duly labeled. Many of the present titles represent the end of a long search and several changes of heart: the verses now known as "Song of the Answerer," for instance, started as two separate poems of which the first was originally called "Poem of the Poet," then "Leaves of Grass, Number 3," then "List to My Morning's Romanza"; and the second "Poem of the Singers, and of the Words of Poems," then "Leaves of Grass, Number 6," finally "The Indications."

The changes of title, however, represent only the smallest part of the metamorphoses of this strange book, which could not leave off growing and shifting shape as long as its author lived. Not only were new subpoems added (often merely new tries at saying again what had been said already over and over), but old ones were shifted in position, even dropped; lines were cut or emended; the punctuation and ways of forming compounds altered; the very names for the days of the week and the months transformed. The prose introduction to the first edition was

translated into a poem; and in its finally modified form appears as
"By Blue Ontario's Shore"—not, however, before a short existence
under the more formidable name, "Poem of the Many in One."

The very portrait of the author which faced the frontispiece
of *Leaves of Grass* grew old along with him and his book,
changed in character with the mask or *persona* through which
Whitman chose to speak in succeeding editions of the work. In
the beginning he confronts us as "one of the roughs," shag-
bearded, open-collared, his hat cocked at an insolent angle; but
the very phrase "one of the roughs" is cut from "Song of Myself,"
and the beard grows not merely longer and whiter but more
gentle and patriarchal. The hat itself is doffed for the photog-
rapher, though the verse remains in which the poet boasts, "I
wear my hat as I please indoors or out. . . ." In the end Whitman chooses to address us in the role of "good, gray" prophet
rather than the cocky disturber of the peace whom an early
satirist described as "the dirtiest beast of the age," and who, as
late as 1865, lost a government job for having written a "pornographic" poem. The final form of the book reflects this final
revision of himself.

In the process of excision and addition, the nucleus from
which the whole *Leaves of Grass* developed, that bewildering
group of thirteen poems (only one of which, "Great Are the
Myths," was dropped completely) in which the poet found his
authentic voice, loses somehow its original jaunty and disreputable air. It is hard to read the last revision of *Leaves* with a
catch of the breath, a terrified and exhilarating sense that nothing
less than the whole poetic tradition is at stake. Yet Whitman, to
the few who read him in 1855, must have provided just such a
shock. Either the poem one picked up at the bookshop of a phrenologist would have to be judged as nonsense spiced with obscen-
ities—or all other poems would have to be reread, reassessed in
order to make provision for an unforeseen species of excellence.

Surely one goal of any new selection from Whitman ought to
be the redemption (from his later self as well as from those who
adulate and imitate him at his dullest) of that pristine poet, that
"dirtiest beast," whom, in a world grown ever more genteel, we
cannot afford to lose. A great poet who is also a great technical

pioneer is as offensive as any disturber of received ideas, as up-
setting as Copernicus or Darwin, Nietzsche or Marx or Freud.
And Whitman, if he is to be read as a living poet rather than
sanctified as a dead one, must come to seem again as offensive as
he really is.

Some selections in the past have been made with precisely
the opposite intent. Indeed, in England neither "Song of Myself"
nor "The Sleepers," the two most ambitious poems of the first
edition and the keys still to Whitman's total meaning, was reprinted until the nineteenth century was almost gone. They
were excluded, of course, because of the boldness of their erotic
imagery, and more especially for their odd habit of describing
spiritual crises in specific sexual terms. Though "Song of Myself"
has long since received proper recognition, "The Sleepers" has not
profited equally from the relaxation of old taboos. It is as effectively suppressed by its position in the final version of *Leaves of
Grass* as it ever was by any bowdlerizing editor. Pushed further
and further into the deadly center of the burgeoning poem, it
stands now at a place where few readers, starting boldly from
page one and resolved not to skip a line, will ever reach it.

Elementary honesty requires an editor to say that even if
Leaves of Grass has a satisfactory over-all form, few ordinary
readers survive to discover it. There is simply too much bulk,
too much of it too soggy even for the undiscriminating appetite
of the neophyte. Theoretically, Whitman's work may be a single,
unified poem; actually, it is sampled as if it were an anthology
of self-sufficient shorter pieces. The average reader is, unfortunately, most often his own unguided anthologist, and his selection
more the product of his attention-span than of critical choice.
The neglect of "The Sleepers" is only one instance of the damage
done by such unplanned, lay anthologizing, but it is typical.

"The Sleepers" is typical, too, in another respect: an exceptional, but not altogether unparalleled example of the way in
which Whitman's own cutting and revision could betray his
original vision. His emendations are by no means always inept,
nor are they invariably dictated by a desire to substitute for an
earlier version of himself more current ones. Sometimes a line
will be rewritten as the poet feels his way toward his essential

music. For instance, the line "Out of the rocked cradle" becomes after eleven years "Out of the cradle endlessly rocking"; and we find it hard to believe that this was not the metrical pattern from which the poem began.

Occasionally, however, changes result from a desire to cover up or tone down rather than genuine poetic concerns, as when in "Song of Myself" "I hear the trained soprano—she convulses me like the climax of my love-grip" becomes the much less crude and striking "I hear the train'd soprano (what work with hers is this?)." Only rarely are more extended passages of first excellence sacrificed out of fear of self-betrayal, but there are examples. Surely few poetic scenes in Whitman are more precisely imagined or richly phrased than:

> *The cloth laps a first sweet eating and drinking,*
> *Laps life-swelling yolks . . . . laps ear of rose-corn,*
> *   milky and just ripened:*
> *The white teeth stay, and the boss-tooth advances in*
> *   darkness,*
> *And liquor is spilled on lips and bosoms by touching*
> *   glasses, and the best liquor afterward.*

Yet these lines have been left out of the final version of "The Sleepers," along with the seven verses which precede them, in order presumably to conceal from the reader the poet's uneasy sexuality and the fact that loneliness and terror are as essential to him as gregariousness and euphoria. The advocate of nakedness as a way of confronting life did not choose finally to betray his nightmare-fear of being found naked.

> *O hotcheeked and blushing! O foolish hectic!*
> *O for pity's sake, no one must see me now! . . . my*
> *   clothes were stolen while I was abed,*
> *Now I am thrust forth, where shall I run?*

The reader will find here the uncut 1855 version of "The Sleepers" along with that confession of anguish and hopeless love suppressed by Whitman himself, "Hours Continuing Long,

Sore and Heavy-Hearted." Both are moving works of art which need no longer be expurgated or excluded in order to keep secrets long since out. "The Sleepers" is reprinted as originally spelled and punctuated, with the run-together compounds and the recurrent four dots which gave to the pages of the first edition of *Leaves of Grass* a peculiar air of stuttering urgency.

In the main, however, Whitman has managed to change the values of his earlier work not so much by revision or outright expurgation as by rearrangement of context. For this reason the order of the pieces in the present selection abandons the final order of *Leaves of Grass,* whose point is to make the varied product of forty years seem consistent with the poet's last version of himself. To an editor it seems desirable (especially in a selection from Whitman's poetry) not to resume briefly what the poet himself called the "form'd and launch'd work," but rather to give some sense of what that work was in the beginning and in "the subsequent adjusting interval."

Much is accomplished along these lines simply by sloughing off certain poems in which Whitman betrays his initial private vision to his later public role as Prophet or Unofficial Laureate of America. "O Captain! My Captain!" is not included, for instance, since that poem is not only banal but banal in a way utterly untrue to Whitman. It has persisted in school anthologies because it suits the bureaucratic bad taste which submits to Whitman's reputation but yearns for the trite and sentimental. The perpetuation of "O Captain! My Captain!" is the secret revenge of the bourgeoisie on the poet who most challenged it.

Also excluded from this selection are blatantly editorializing poems like "By Blue Ontario's Shore" and "To a Foil'd European Revolutionaire." The former, in its bardic Americanism, represents a frequent strain in the later Whitman, but it is by no means his most effective; and the reader can find latter-day examples of it aplenty in the sound tracks of government-sponsored documentaries and the folders of Chambers of Commerce. "To a Foil'd European Revolutionaire" is remarkable not only for one of Whitman's silliest lines ("Then courage European revolter, revoltress!"); but it has the distinction of having been distributed by Soviet troops to the American Expeditionary Forces in Siberia in 1919. As an American chauvinist or a Romantic internationalist, however, Whitman is unworthy of his own talent; of his several voices, that of the soapbox orator seems least congenial to current taste.

Even the Columbus poems ("Prayer of Columbus," "A Thought of Columbus," "Passage to India") are not entirely successful, though in the figure of Columbus, Whitman discovered a mask which could represent at once his vision of himself as the Spiritual Discoverer of America and the Neglected and Aging Great Man. "Passage to India" ("Ah Genoese thy dream! thy dream!") represents his major attempt to make poetry of the theme. Though much admired in some quarters, it remains a forced and turgid effort, lapsing into the sort of unrecitable, faked language into which Whitman falls when he is being self-consciously religious: "copest, frontest God, yieldest, the aim attain'd." (A handy rule of thumb says beware of Whitman when he uses the "thou" instead of the "you.") His larger religious statements, like his patriotic ones, are omitted here. The often-reprinted "Chanting the Square Deific" is excluded because the not-quite-believable adjective "deific" gives away the game; the verb "chanting" describes only too precisely the pulpit tone assumed by the poet when he addressed himself to such solemn subjects as "America" and "God."

It is the aim of this selection to focus on neither Whitman the booster nor Whitman the preacher—not even on Whitman the imagist—except as all these subserve another Whitman yet to be defined. His "imagist" aspect, however, deserves to be better known, and is represented by such purely visual little poems as "A Paumanok Picture" and "The Dalliance of the Eagles," to which Whitman applied not our contemporary word "images" but his own term "pictures." "O Walt Whitman, show us some pictures . . ." he wrote in an abandoned fragment, and went on to boast, "Yes, in a little house I keep suspended many pictures. . . ." But in another place, he compares unfavorably "what we call poems," which are "merely pictures," with "the real poems," which are humans in action. Surely his deepest aim was to transcend the image, to make a kind of poetry which was the equivalent of action, a very act of love.

In this he did not, could not quite succeed. Yet if one regards as the poet's most considerable achievements "Song of Myself," "The Sleepers" and "Out of the Cradle Endlessly Rocking" (with its pendant "As I Ebb'd with the Ocean of Life"), it becomes clear that his characteristic method is no more imagistic than it is rhetorical. His mode is reverie; his voice that of one talking to himself as he falls asleep in the haze of lazy noonday or at the onset of night. What binds Whitman's poems together is not the logic of persuasion or pictorial form, but what we have come to label a little misleadingly "stream of consciousness": the secret order of repressed wishes and fears that links impression to impression when the conscious mind abdicates or relaxes its control. Dreaming or reminiscing, the poet wavers between what he calls "vision" and "fit," an access of heightened awareness that at some moments elates, at other moments terrifies him. This alternation of joy and anxiety sets up poles around which his inner flux of ideas and associations take on objective forms.

But what are the forms in which Whitman's feelings are objectified? What are his subjects, his themes, symbols and myths? Unlike the writers of earlier times, Whitman does not find wating for him a body of legend and mythicized history already known to the whole community for which he writes. Of this he is quite aware. "Cross out please," he cries, making a virtue of necessity, "those immensely overpaid accounts,/ That matter of Troy and Achilles' wrath, and Aeneas', Odysseus' wandering. . . ." His essential mythology is not even provided by the American past; it is derived from his own personal experience, lived or dreamed, and his hero is, therefore, himself. He is, in this sense, the first truly modern poet with epic ambitions, the first author to portray himself as the mythic representative of his people and his time. His Odysseus is Walt Whitman; his Descent into the Underworld, the plunge into the darkness of his own mind. The irony of this, the absurdity of treating heroically such anti-heroic matter does not escape him. "Do you suppose yourself advancing on real ground toward a real heroic man?" he asks his reader, tipping his own hand with a wink. It is not out of simple vanity, nor without self-mockery, that Whitman attempts in *Leaves of Grass* his odd autobiographical Epic, his mythicized Portrait of the Artist as a Middle-aged Hero.

The key poems of Whitman's book were written from sometime just before 1855 to 1860; that is, from the moment the poet approached his thirty-fifth year to the moment he left behind his fortieth. They are, therefore, the expression of what the French call the *crise de quarante*, the crisis of entering middle age, of accepting once and for all what one unredeemably is. Whitman is a Romantic poet in many senses; but he is not, like most Romantics, a poet of adolescence, except as the nostalgia of adolescence in him survives and blends into the disenchantment of middle age. His production before his thirty-fifth year is trivial and conventional, his few poems, inept in form and melancholy in tone, concerned with death and the vanity of ambition. Most of his earliest writing is in prose, chiefly newspaper stories, but also a temperance novel and a handful of shorter fictions centering around fantasies of children beaten, abused and murdered. The almost pathological self-pity projected in such stories, the fear of authority and the desperate identification with the misunderstood child are a clue to all of Whitman's work; but it is not till his youth is over that he is able to make of such symptoms works of art.

The poetry written by Whitman after his fortieth year consists by and large of variations on the themes established between 1855 and 1860. The Civil War and especially the death of Lincoln provided him with what seem new subjects for verse. But even that remarkable threnody "When Lilacs Last in the Dooryard Bloom'd" in the main merely recapitulates the feelings and even the symbols of "Out of the Cradle." There is, indeed, a disturbing vagueness about the former poem, a sense that its occasion is only nominal, that it mourns someone or something only accidentally represented by Lincoln. The shorter war pieces are least successful when they are concerned with actual combat, most convincing when they deal with Whitman in his role of "The Wound-Dresser," male nurse and loving consoler of the dying—a role he had already imagined for himself in "Song of Myself."

> *To anyone dying, thither I speed and twist the knob*
> *of the door . . .*
> *Let the physician and the priest go home . . .*
> *I am he bringing help for the sick as they pant on*
> *their backs . . .*

It is as if, after his fortieth year, Whitman could not even live (much less write) anything he had not already set down in the work from which he was unable to disentangle his aging self.

At any rate the crisis of his own middle age remained always more real for Whitman *as a poet* than the great national crises of secession and war, and at the center of that personal crisis is a crushing sense of loneliness, of being unloved. In the years between 1855 and 1860, he apparently came to realize more and more clearly that not only would he never get married (he probably never experienced any deep heterosexual love), but that there would never be for him any stable, continuing relationship either with male or female. This terrible truth his heart had guessed (he tells us in "Out of the Cradle") even as a child; for him there would be no love not intimately blended with death, no satisfaction for all his yearning this side of the grave.

Only with the creatures of his fancy, with an imagined "you" (sometimes conceived as a lost lover; sometimes as the perfect "Camerado," God; sometimes as an indiscriminate Everyman; often as the reader; most often as a second self, "the real Me") could he enter into an orgasmic unity. His poems are at once a prayer for such a union and that imaginary orgasm itself. No poet engages the reader with so fervid and intimate a clasp; no writer describes the act of reading so erotically.

> *(Is it night? Are we here together alone?)*
> *It is I you hold and who holds you,*
> *I spring from the pages into your arms . . .*
> *Your breath falls around me like dew, your pulse lulls*
> *the tympans of my ears,*
> *I feel immerged from head to foot,*
> *Delicous, enough.*

"Song of Myself," though it stands at the center of Whitman's epic attempt and can be read as a heroic poem intended to define the ethos of a nation, is also a love poem: simultaneously a love song, a love affair (the poet's only successful one) and a love child (the only real offspring of his passion, for surely the five illegitimate children of whom he liked to boast were fantasies). But who is the poet's beloved, the Beatrice he could never leave off wooing, the Penelope to whom he could never return? As the hero of his poem is called "I," so the loved one is called "you"; and their vague pronominal romance is the thematic center of "Song of Myself." It is an odd subject for the Great American Poem: the celebration (half-heroic, half-ironic) of the mating between an "I" whose reality is constantly questioned and an even more elusive "you." The latter pronoun in Whitman's verse almost always is followed by the phrase "whoever you are." "You whoever you are"—this must be surely the most compulsively repeated four-word phrase in *Leaves of Grass*, for it embodies a riddle which torments the poet even more than that of the Self: the riddle of the Other.

Is there an Other to whom one can speak: a real beloved, a real audience, a real God? Unless such a "you" really exists, there is no point, no possibility of converting private "vision" into public "song." It is because Whitman's personal concern on this score coincides with a more general problem that he touches us so deeply. His loneliness becomes a symbol for the alienation of the modern artist and of modern man in a godless universe. He lived, after all, at a moment when some thinkers were declaring the death of God, and wrote at a time when poets grew increasingly unsure of whom they were addressing.

Unlike Homer and Dante, Whitman could not assume a certain class of reader, but had to create his own public even as he had to create his own themes. His pose of being a popular poet, the bard of the common man, fooled neither him nor the common man, and must not deceive the unwary reader. Like most modern poets, he addressed and continues to address a shrinking and uncertain audience.

That is why to write at all required of him an act of faith, faith that a real "you" existed somewhere; and that faith he desperately sustained. "Song of Myself" begins with the word "I" but ends with "you," a "you" believed in though never possessed.

I stop somewhere waiting for you.

It is, then, a poem of faith, its doubts incidental and repressed. "My foothold is tenon'd and mortis'd in granite," the poet insists. "I accept Reality and I dare not question it . . ." "The Lord will be there and wait till I come . . ." In other poems, however, this faith falters or is utterly lost. In "The Sleepers," for instance, the daylight has departed and with it all certainty. The poet begins "wandering and confused, lost to myself," and ends seeking through his dreams the embrace of a "you" who is not this time the Great Camerado, but the Great Mother: the darkness out of which his "I" has emerged and to which it must return.

I will duly pass the day O my mother and duly return
    to you.

Though "The Sleepers," like "Song of Myself," moves from a concern with "I" toward a commitment to "you," its tone is altogether different, melancholy and subdued. It provides a transition to the third of the great "I-you" poems, "As I Ebb'd with the Ocean of Life," which opens on the line which gives it its title and closes, "You up there walking or sitting,/ Whoever you are, we too lie in drifts at your feet." The final verses are thoroughly ambiguous, referring at once to God (whoever that may be) and "this phantom looking down," which is to say, the poet's "real Me," which he imagines eluding him, "untouch'd, untold, altogether unreach'd,/ Withdrawn far, mocking me with mock-congratulatory signs and bows,/ With peals of distant ironical laughter at every word I have written. . . ." There is no elation this time, no boasting, however hysterical; the poet begins "baffl'd, balk'd, bent to the very earth" and ends confessing, "I have not once had the least idea who or what I am."

But what happens to the love affair of "I" and "you" when the poet cannot even believe in his own "I," which blurs and dissolves as he contemplates the "Mystery of Being"? After his initial nausea before the ambiguity of his own existence ("Steep'd amid honey'd morphine, my windpipe throttled in fakes of death"), the poet of many masks and poses finds a kind of amusement in conceiving of all life as a cosmic hoax ("Have you no thought O dreamer that it may all be maya, illusion?"). Indeed, the play of illusion and reality, the teasing search for and the trifling with the "real Me," "the real real," "the real of the real," becomes a major theme of Whitman's poetry, a theme on which the last word is spoken in the poem Whitman himself chose to stand at the end of his book, "Good-Bye My Fancy."

> *May-be it is yourself now really ushering me to the*
> *true songs, (who knows?)*
> *May-be it is you the mortal knob really undoing, turn-*
> *ing . . .*

The poet of dogmatic assertion has come to rest on the tentative hope of "may-be"; and the meanings of "you" (you, lover, whom I fancy—you, poem, which my fancy has created) have grown even more complex.

The dissolution in doubt of the "I" and "you" does more for Whitman's poetry, however, than turn it in the direction of self-mockery or pseudo-Oriental references to maya. It permits the emergence of another pair of symbols or "myths," which he himself thought of as representing the deepest layers of his experience. In *Specimen Days,* Whitman writes:

Even as a boy, I had the fancy, the wish, to write a piece, perhaps, a poem about the sea-shore—that suggesting, dividing line, contact, junction, the solid marrying the liquid. . . . Hours, days, in my Long Island youth and early manhood I haunted the shores. . . . I remember well, I felt that I must one day write a book expressing this liquid, mystic theme. Afterward, I recollect, how it came to me that instead of any special lyrical or epical or literary attempt, the sea-shore should be an invisible *influence*, a pervading gauge and tally for me, in my composition. . . .

The sea and the shore: these are more than settings; they are the essential themes, the deep shadowy protagonists of the work which Whitman never quite wrote but of which all his writing is a projection. We are not surprised when in "As I Ebb'd with the Ocean of Life" the middle-aged poet, remembering the child he was, calls sea and shore his mother and his father.

> *Where the fierce old mother endlessly cries for her*
> *   castaways . . .*
> *I throw myself upon your breast my father,*
> *I cling to you so that you cannot unloose me . . .*

To no other scene is the poet bound with such filial ties. There are many landscapes in *Leaves of Grass,* evocations of mountain and plain, the South and the West—the whole breadth of America. But only the beaches of Long Island, that "Paumanok" where the poet played as a boy and mooned as a young man, live for his imagination. What the Hill of Howth and the River Liffey are to James Joyce or the Mississippi to Mark Twain, Coney Island and Rockaway, Hampton and Montauk are to Whitman. They define for him that small span of authentic experience which (though it covers only a few years, months, even days) means more to a writer than the whole stretch of nonsignificant life which frames it. Normally the vividly experienced moments on which the poet feeds throughout his career belong to childhood and adolescence, to the golden age before the natural scene has lost its primal magic. Walt Whitman is no exception. His "holy places" belong to the Long Island of his earliest years.

When he deserts such sanctuaries for other places, he becomes abstract, forced, false. When he cries, "I cross the Laramie plains, I note the rocks in grotesque shapes, the buttes . . . I see the Monument mountain and the Eagle's nest, I pass the Promon-

tory, I ascend the Nevadas . . . ," one does not believe him.
He has obviously worked it all up out of guidebook or gazetteer.
Only Brooklyn and New York exist in his work as compellingly
as Long Island; but this is because "Mannahatta" is for him an
island city, a city of ships, a city in the sea.

> *Choice aboriginal name, with marvellous beauty,*
>   *meaning,*
> *A rocky founded island—shores where ever gayly*
>   *dash the coming, going, hurrying sea waves.*

Whitman is an urban poet as surely as Baudelaire or T. S. Eliot,
but even more deeply a poet of beaches and harbors. His ocean
does not, like the watery desert of Melville's imagining, lave
only exotic shores; it is the sea seen from the bathing beach or
the wharf (an arm over some rough companion's shoulder), the
island dweller's sea. And so land is for him also the island
dweller's land, never removed from the sound of breaking waves
or the sight of the mastheads of ships.

Everything essential to Whitman is the gift of the ocean,
cast up even as he was cast up (mama's boy to the end) by the
"fierce old mother." Shipwreck and windrows are for him the
natural symbols of terror and grace. Even the obsessive image
of merging, of unity which works everywhere in *Leaves of Grass*
seems abstracted from memories of the mingling of water and
sand at the tide line. "The rim, the sediment that stands for all
the water and all the land of the globe." He may never have held
in a final embrace a human lover, but the sea, embracing him,
taught him to love, and he responded with love. "Dash me with
amorous wet, I can repay you." Not only in the crucial central
section of *Leaves of Grass* called "Sea-Drift," but throughout the
long poem, the sea intrudes in image and sound, the sea as Great
Mother presiding over dying and being born.

Even in the evocation of the inland funeral cortege of
Lincoln the ocean is improbably present: "The ocean shore and
the husky whispering wave whose voice I know . . ." Wherever
death is named or suggested, the off-stage noise of the sea is
heard. For it was the sea (we are told in "Out of the Cradle")

that first lisped to the poet the true name of his best-beloved, the final secret, the answer to all riddles, "the low and delicious word death . . ." The revelation comes like an ectasy, a caress ("laving me softly all over"). If Whitman is the singer of the death of love, he is also the singer of the love of death. Indeed, it is as the laureate of death (not of democracy or self-love or healing or sex) that we finally remember him, even as he himself remembered the moment of his poetic awakening as the moment of the sea's revelation: "death, and again death, death, death, death."

> My own songs awaked from that hour,
> And with them the key, the word up from the waves,
> The word of the sweetest song and all songs,
> The strong and delicious word which, creeping to my
>   feet,
> (Or like some old crone rocking the cradle, swathed
>   in sweet garments, bending aside,)
> The sea whisper'd me.

R.L.S. Revisited

Originally the Introduction to *The Master of Ballantrae* by Robert Louis Stevenson, Rinehart, 1954

"That angel was a devil . . ."

One hundred years after the birth of Stevenson, the question of his worth as a writer remains still very much at issue. Unless we are willing to surrender him completely to children or to indulge a sneaking fondness for him as unanalytically as if we were ourselves children, we must make a really critical assessment of his work. We must meet the question: Is a liking for *Treasure Island* a literary enthusiasm or a minor subliterary vice, like reading detective stories? The enthusiasm of the first generation of Stevensonians found a critical approach to what seemed to them all charm and magic impertinent; but today we are inclined to be suspicious of the easy triumphs of the R.L.S. style; and the genre of Romance to which Stevenson's reputation is tied has been relegated among us to the shelves of the circulating library. David Daiches has recently attempted to redeem Stevenson for our time by showing him progressing from the lesser form of the Romance to the Novel proper; but this approach concedes too much by assuming a derogatory evaluation of the Romance as such (to which I am not prepared to subscribe), and leads to a failure to understand the intent of the conclusion of *The Master of Ballantrae* and of the proposed ending to the *Weir of Hermiston*.

If we remember that Long John Silver appeared for years in the "Katzenjammer Kids," we will, I think, begin to see the possibilities of a quite different approach. Imagine Anna Karenina or Stephen Dedalus appropriated by the comic strips! It could be done only in vulgar burlesque; but the Sea-Cook can be kidnapped without impertinence. Like other Stevensonian characters (Jekyll and Hyde, for instance), he exists, as it were, in the public domain—along with Thor and Loki, Hansel and Gretel. The characters of Stevenson seem to have an objective existence, a being prior to and independent of any particular formal realization. They are, in short, not merely literary creations, but also embodiments of archetypal themes—and it is in the realm of myth, which sometimes overlaps but is not identical with literature, that we must look for clues to the meaning and unity of Stevenson's work.

Modern prose fiction has handled the myth in two quite different ways, one sophisticated, one naïve; the former, that of James Joyce, for instance, leads from the inward novel of character, through psychological naturalism, to symbolism and beyond to the conscious manipulation of the mythic; the latter begins with the outward Romance of incident, the boys' story or thriller, and moves through allegory, often elusive, to the naïve or unconscious evocation of myth. To the latter group belong such varied writers as Melville, Arthur Conan Doyle, Graham Greene—and Robert Louis Stevenson. They are possessed of a double ambiguity: on the one hand, they are likely to deny point-blank the symbolic intent which the critic can not help seeing in them; and on the other, they tend to define a wavering line between literature and subliterature—falling sometimes to the side of achieved formal statement and sometimes to that of a shoddy and cheaply popular evocation of archetypal themes.

Sophisticated exploiters of the mythic (Joyce, Mann) are inevitably limited in their appeal, and in their work the traditional "story" plotted in time tends to be replaced by the timeless movement of archetypes in the psyche. Such naïve exploiters of the mythic as Greene and Stevenson, on the contrary, preserve the "story" and its appeal intact; in them the picturesque never yields completely to the metaphysical—and they can always be read on one level as boys' books or circulating-library thrillers.

To understand and examine Stevenson as a writer of this

kind is at once to take him seriously and to preserve the integrity of his Romances qua Romances. More than that, such an understanding may lead to the more general appreciation of an honorable alternative to realism, somewhat out of fashion but by no means exhausted in its possibilities, a genre in which the serious contemporary fictionist may find a strategy for closing the distance between himself and the large audience of novel readers ordinarily immune to serious literature. It is well to realize, however, the difficulties inherent in such a strategy; and when we have come to see Stevenson's development as a writer of fiction, in terms of a struggle to exploit ever more deeply the universal meanings of his fables, with the least possible surrender of their structure and appeal as "howling good tales," we shall be able to understand, perhaps better than their author ever did, certain contradictions of tone and intent in the later books.

Over and over again since his reputation was first questioned, critics have asked: Is there in Stevenson's work a single motivating force, beyond the obvious desire to be charming, to please, to exact admiration—that seems to us now a little shallow and more than a little coquettish? Frank Swinnerton, who led the first reaction against the uncritical adulation of R.L.S. found in only one book, *Jekyll and Hyde*, a "unifying idea." But "idea" is a misleading word; a single felt myth gives coherence, individually and as a group, to several of Stevenson's long fictions—and it is the very myth explicitly stated in *Jekyll and Hyde*. The books besides the latter are *Treasure Island*, *Kidnapped*, *The Master of Ballantrae* and the *Weir of Hermiston*; the organizing mythic concept might be called the Beloved Scoundrel or the Devil as Angel, and the books make a series of variations of the theme of the beauty of evil—and conversely the unloveliness of good. The Beloved Scoundrel makes his debut as Long John Silver in *Treasure Island*, a tale first printed, it is worth noticing, in a boys' magazine, and written to explain circumstantially a treasure map drawn for a child's game that Stevenson had been playing with his young stepson.

There can be little doubt that one of Stevenson's motives in marrying was to become a child—and finding himself at the age of thirty at long last a child enabled him unexpectedly to become for the first time a real creative writer; that is, to sustain a successful long fiction. All of Stevenson's major loves had been older, once-married women—which is to say, mothers. There was his "Madonna," Mrs. Sitwell, who in the end married his friend Sidney Colvin, and to whom he used to sign his letters of passionate loneliness "Your Son"; there was the agreeably alien and mature Mme. Garischine, whom he assured "what I want is a mother"; and there was, at last, the woman he actually wed, Fanny Osbourne, some eleven years older than himself, the mother of three children.

His marriage to Mrs. Osbourne not only gave him a mother to replace his own, from whom he felt estranged and to whom he could not utterly commit himself without feelings of guilt toward his father, but provided him for the first time with a brother in the form of his twelve-year-old stepson, Lloyd. An only child and one isolated by illness, Stevenson had never been able to feel himself anything but a small adult (his parents observed him, noted down his most chance remarks with awful seriousness); against the boy Lloyd he was able to define himself as a boy. Together they *played* at many things; toy soldiers, printing (they founded the Davos Press to publish accounts of their mock warfare)—even writing. Before Lloyd had fully matured, he and Stevenson had begun their collaboration with *The Wrong Box*. Writing to R.L.S. seemed always a kind of childish sport; "to play at home with paper like a child," he once described his life's work, a glance over his shoulder at his disapproving forebears, good engineers and unequivocal adults. But there is in such a concept of art, not only the troubled touch of guilt, but the naïve surge of joy; and Stevenson's abandonment to childhood meant his first release as an artist—produced *Treasure Island*, *Kidnapped* and *A Child's Garden of Verses*.

Long John Silver is described through a boy's eye, the first of those fictional first-person-singulars who are a detached aspect of the author. It is Jim Hawkins who is the chief narrator of the tale, as it is Jim who saves the Sea-Cook from the gallows. For the boy, the scoundrel par excellence is the Pirate: an elemental ferocity belonging to the unfamiliar sea and uncharted islands hiding bloodstained gold. And yet there is an astonishing inno-

cence about it all—a world without sex and without business—
where the source of wealth is buried treasure, clean gold in sand,
for which only murder has been done, but which implies no grimy
sweat in offices, no manipulating of stock, none of the quiet
betrayals of capitalist competition. The very embodiment of this
world, vain, cruel, but astonishingly courageous and immune to
self-deprecation, able to compel respect, obedience—and even
love—is John Silver; and set against him for a foil is Captain
Smollett, in whom virtue is joined to a certain dourness, an immediate unattractiveness. Not only Jim, but Stevenson, too,
finds the Pirate more lovable than the good Captain. In one of
his *Fables* written afterwards, he sets before us Alexander Smollett and John Silver, debating with each other while their author
rests between Chapters XXXII and XXXIII; and Captain Smollett
is embarrassed by the Sea-Cook's boast that their common creator
loves him more, keeps him in the center of the scene, but keeps
the virtuous Captain "measling in the hold."

    Kidnapped, like *Treasure Island,* was written for a boys'
magazine, and in both all important relationships are between
males. In *Kidnapped,* however, the relation of the Boy and
the Scoundrel, treated as a flirtation in the earlier book, becomes
almost a full-fledged love affair, a pre-sexual romance; the
antagonists fall into lovers' quarrels and make up, swear to part
forever, and remain together. The Rogue this time is Alan Breck
Stewart, a rebel, a deserter, perhaps a murderer, certainly vain
beyond forgiveness and without a shred of Christian morality.
The narrator and the foil in this book (certainly, technically the
most economical—perhaps, in that respect, the best of Stevenson) are one: David Balfour is Jim Hawkins and Captain Smollett
fused into a single person. David must measure the Scoundrel
against himself, and the more unwillingly comes to love that of
which he must disapprove. Here good and evil are more subtly
defined, more ambiguous: pious Presbyterian and irreverent Catholic, solid defender of the status quo and fantastic dreamer of
the Restoration—in short, Highlander and Lowlander, Scotland
divided against itself. It is the Lowlander that Stevenson *was*
who looks longingly and disapprovingly at the alien dash, the
Highland fecklessness of Alan through the eyes of David (was

not Stevenson's own mother a Balfour?); but it is the Highlander he *dreamed* himself (all his life he tried vainly to prove his father's family were descended from the banned Clan Mac-Gregor) that looks back. The somber good man and the glittering rascal are both two and one; they war within Stevenson's single country and in his single soul.

In *Dr. Jekyll and Mr. Hyde,* which Stevenson himself called a *"fable"*—that is, a dream allegorized into a morality—the point is made explicit: "I saw that of the two natures that contended in the field of my consciousness, even if I could rightly be said to be either, it was only because I was radically both." It is the respectable and lonely Dr. Jekyll who gives life to the monstrous Mr. Hyde; and once good has given form to the ecstasy of evil, the good can only destroy what it has shaped by destroying itself. The death of evil requires the death of good. *Jekyll and Hyde* is a tragedy, one of the only two tragedies that Stevenson ever wrote; but its allegory is too schematic, too slightly realized in terms of fiction and character, and too obviously colored with easy terror to be completely convincing; while its explicit morality demands that evil be portrayed finally as an obvious monster.

In *The Master of Ballantrae,* Stevenson once more splits in two for dramatic purposes what is in life one: unlovely good and lovely evil, restoring to the latter the glitter and allure proper to his first vision. *The Master* is a splendid book, Stevenson's only truly embodied tragedy—and the wittiest of his works, in its device of placing the narration of the tragic action in the mouths of comic characters, a story told turn and turn about by the comic alter ego of the graceless good man and that of the winning scoundrel, the burlesque Scotsman and the burlesque Irishman, MacKellar and the Chevalier Burke—comic both of them, it is worth noticing, by virtue of their cowardice. To Stevenson, as to all small boys, cowardice is the laughable vice—as courage is the unimpeachable virtue. And yet for this book, the boys' scoundrel, one-legged Pirate or Kilted Highland Rebel will not do; there must be an adult villain, though he must live and die in terms of a "howling good tale." That villain is James Durrisdeer, the Master of Ballantrae.

He is, like John Silver or Alan Breck, absolutely brave and immediately lovable, though unscrupulous and without mercy, two-faced and treacherous, inordinately proud and selfish. But he is all these conventionally villainous things in an absolute sense; he is the very maturity, the quintessence of evil. He is for a time like Long John a Pirate, like Alan a Rebel (and like the later Frank Innes a Seducer), but these are for him mere shadowy forms of what he is ideally. Stevenson, as if to make sure we understand, brings the Master face to face first with the protagonist of *Kidnapped*, "Alan Black Stewart or some such name," and next with Teach himself, the infamous Blackbeard—surely a fit surrogate for Silver and all his crew—and shows each of these in turn shamefully outwitted by the Master. Alan's conduct in their encounter is described as "childish," and Teach, called first "a wicked child," meets his defeat at the Master's hand "like a wicked baby." Beside ultimate villainy, the Pirate and the Highland Rebel seem scarcely adult; theirs is the rascality of the nursery, laughable rather than terrible—and they serve at last only to define the Master's "deadly, causeless duplicity," that final malevolence which must be called "beautiful," the "nobility of hell."

In a letter in which he first discusses his plans for the book, Stevenson writes, "The Master is all I know of the devil," and later to Henry James, "The elder brother is an INCUBUS!" One of the happiest strokes of invention in *The Master* is the presentation of elemental good and evil as brothers: Esau and Jacob in their early contention, Cain and Abel in their bloody ending. It is an apt metaphor of their singleness and division.

Henry, the younger brother of the Master, James, is patient, loyal, kind though not generous, at first more than reasonably pious and humble. He has, however, the essential flaw of Stevenson's virtuous men: the flaw of Alexander Smollet, who was "not popular at home," perhaps even of R.L.S. himself appealing to his "Madonna" to assure him that he is not "such cold poison to everybody." Henry does not compel love, not his father's nor that of Alison, the woman who marries him believing that her real beloved, his malefic brother, is dead. He feels his lack of appeal as a kind of guilt, and when his wife is morally unfaithful to him (he is, like the hero of *Prince Otto,* in everything but physical fact a cuckold), he can reproach only himself.

Ephraim Mackellar, called "Squaretoes," the Steward of Durrisdeer and the loyal supporter of Henry, is everything that his Lord is—exaggerated toward the comic—and a pedant and a coward to boot. It is through his dry, finicky prose (with the exception of two interpolated narratives by the Chevalier Burke, the comic alter ego of James) that the story unfolds, and it is in his mind that the conflict of feeling—repulsion and attraction—toward the Master is played out.

There is no question of James Durrisdeer having some good qualities and some bad; it is his essential quality, his absolute evil, that is *at once* repellent and attractive. The Master *is* evil, that imagined ultimate evil which the student Stevenson naïvely sought in the taverns and brothels of Edinburgh, another Mackellar, his notebook in hand! It is the quality that, Stevenson found, women and unlettered people instinctively love—the dandiacal splendor of damnation that even a Mackellar must call at one point "beautiful!" The study of such double feeling is not common in the nineteenth century, which preferred melodrama to ambivalence; and it is the special merit of Stevenson to have dealt with a mode of feeling so out of the main stream of his time.

From the beginning of the book, the diabolical nature of the Master is suggested, at first obliquely and almost as if by inadvertence. "I think you are a devil of a son to me," the old father cries to James; it is merely a commonplace, a figure of speech, but later it becomes more explicit. Henry, veiledly telling his young son of his duel with the Master, speaks of "a man whom the devil tried to kill, and how near he came to kill the devil instead." They are the words of one already half-mad with grief and torment, but the eminently sane Mackellar is driven to concur in part: "But so much is true, that I have met the devil in these woods and have seen him foiled here." All leads up to the moment of recognition and unwilling praise, when Mackellar says of James: "He had all the gravity and something of the splendor of Satan in the 'Paradise Lost.' I could not help but see the man with admiration. . . ."

But if James is in any real sense the Devil, he must be immortal; his defeats and deaths can be only shows—and this, indeed, the younger brother comes to believe: "Nothing can kill that man. He is not mortal. He is bound upon my back to all eternity—to all God's eternity!" Actually—which is to say according to the account of Mackellar—at the point where Henry breaks forth into near hysteria at the news of yet another presumed death the Master has been falsely thought dead twice. "I have struck my sword throughout his vitals," he cried. "I have felt the hilt dirl on his breastbone, and the hot blood spirt in my very face, time and again, time and again! But he was never dead for that. . . . Why should I think he was dead now!" And truly, he is to rise once more. Which account is then *true?* Mackellar's dry literal report, or the younger brother's hallucinated sense of the moment of strife, the unreal death repeated again and again through all time—James and Henry, Esau and Jacob, Cain and Abel?

It is Stevenson's difficult task to juggle both truths: to contain in a single tale the eternally re-enacted myth and the human story, the historical event—and to do it in "Mackellarese"! Small wonder if he felt his problem almost impossible, and if, to some degree, he failed. I do not think he understood the precise nature of his difficulty ever (there is a price to pay for choosing to be a child), but he sensed its presence. "My novel is a tragedy . . . ," he wrote to Henry James. "Five parts of it are bound [sound?], human tragedy; the last one or two, I regret to say, not so soundly designed; I almost hesitate to write them; they are very picturesque, but they are fantastic; they shame, perhaps degrade, the beginning. I wish I knew; that was how the tale came to me however. . . . Then the devil and Saranac suggested this *dénouement,* and I joined the two ends in a day or two of feverish thought, and began to write. And now—I wonder if I have not gone too far with the fantastic? . . . the third supposed death and the manner of the third re-appearance is steep; steep, sir. It is even very steep, and I fear it shames the honest stuff so far. . . ."

The "honest stuff," the "sound, human tragedy" is the story of the hatred of two brothers and its genesis: the love of Alison for the Master; his supposed death at Culloden; her marriage to Henry, who has all the while loved her; and the Master's reappearance. It is an episode doubtless suggested in part by the actual experience of Stevenson's wife, whose first husband, presumed dead, had reappeared to his supposed widow. Indeed, Samual Osbourne seems to have been in his own right a scoundrel worthy of sitting for James Durrisdeer. This aspect of his novel Stevenson has handled with great psychological accuracy: the Master's reappearance causing the disconcerting transformation of what had been a touching loyalty to the dead into a living infidelity; the Master's two faces, graceful charm for Alison and his father, careless scorn for Henry and the Steward; the timid rage of Mackellar mounting toward the climactic moment at sea when he discovers he is not quite the coward—or the Christian—he has thought himself, and prays blasphemously in the midst of a storm for a shipwreck that will destroy him and the Master together.

But the "steep" denouement that joined itself to the soundly human story, one freezing night at Saranac, impelled the original material toward allegory, in the direction of the mythical. In that remote place, Stevenson had remembered a story told him by an uncle many years before: a tall tale of an Indian fakir who could, by swallowing his tongue, put himself into a state of suspended animation that would permit his being buried alive and later exhumed without any permanent ill effects. The last presumed death of the Master was to be such a deliberate East Indian sham, translated to the Province of Albany. To justify so "fanstastic" a conclusion in terms other than the merely picturesque, Stevenson would have had frankly to abandon ordinary standards of credibility, to make the Master *really* a devil, and to risk the absurdity of a myth of the deathlessness of evil. But that would have impugned the *human* tragedy he had already blocked out, and he dared be in the end only fantastic enough for a yarn; that is to say—far from too fantastic—not fantastic enough. Even in *Jekyll* Stevenson had felt bound to explain the transformation to Hyde in the "scientific" terms of a graduated glass and a compound of salts—and that story he considered an outright "Fable"—immune to the human limitations of the novel.

Stevenson will have the fabulous, but he will have it rationally explicable too. The Master must be provided with an Indian servant, must indeed have been in India himself; and there must even be an interpolated narrative to give us a glimpse of him there. The voice which frankly terms him supernatural, which asserts, "He's not of this world. . . . He was never canny!" must be that of a man nearly mad. If *The Master* seems to pull apart a little at the seams, it is this timidity on the part of its auhor that is the cause, rather than the fact, customarily insisted upon, that the book was begun in upstate New York and only completed after a lapse of inspiration in Honolulu. After all, the beginning and the end, whenever actually written, were *conceived* together. Perhaps the real trouble was that Stevenson, unlike his characters, did not really believe in Hell.

And yet the ending is effective all the same. The Master, who had seemed to die at Culloden, and had turned up again only to be apparently killed in a duel with his younger brother, is carried off by smugglers, healed, and returns once more to pursue his brother on two continents; but Henry, finally tormented out of humility and reason, turns on James, who, at last trapped by the cutthroats his younger brother has hired to kill him, "dies" and is buried in the midwinter American wilderness. Dug up by his Hindu servant under the eyes of his brother, the Master revives for a moment, just long enough to cause the death by heart failure of the onlooking Henry, and to ensure their burial under a single marker in that remote waste.

The point is the point of *Jekyll:* evil will not die until it has corrupted the good to its own image and brought it down by its side to a common grave. "He is bound upon my back to all eternity—to all God's eternity!" Henry had prophetically cried; and Mackellar, noting the universal meaning of his degeneration, its relevance to that struggle of us all—in which combating evil we come to resemble it—said, "I was overborne with a pity almost approaching the passionate, not for my master alone but for all the sons of man."

Toward the end of his life, Stevenson seems to have lost faith in the worth of *The Master*, though the book had received great critical acclaim, and he had begun with a sense of its being

"top chop," "a sure card!" One of his last recorded remarks about
the book is that lacking "all pleasureableness," it was "imperfect
in essence"—a strange judgment surely, for it is precisely a pleas-
urable story, a work of real wit: a tragedy seen through the eyes
of a comic character. Much more just seems to us the comment
of Henry James, written out of his first enthusiasm: "A pure
hard crystal, my boy, a work of ineffable and exquisite art." The
word "crystal" is peculiarly apt; it is a winter's tale throughout,
crystalline as frost, both in scene, from the wintry Scottish up-
lands to the icy, Indian-haunted Albanian forest; and in style,
the dry, cold elegance of "Old Squaretoes"—preserved in a
subzero piety in which nothing melts. The quality of the writing
alone—the sustained tour de force of "Mackellarese," that merciless parody of the old maid at the heart of all goodness and of
Stevenson himself, which makes style and theme astonishingly
one in this book—is the greatest triumph of Stevenson's art.

In the unfinished *Weir of Hermiston,* alone among his important novels, R.L.S. attempts to write in the third person, in
his own voice—and consequently, there is in that book, as there
is never in *The Master,* downright bad writing. Stevenson's
instinctive bent was for first-person narrative; and when in his
last book he attempts to speak from outside *about* his fiction, his
style betrays him to self-pity (we *know* Archie is really the
author, and the third-person singular affects us like a transparent
hoax), sentimentality and the sort of "fine" writing he had avoided
since *Prince Otto.*

The *Weir* is the first of Stevenson's books to deal at all
adequately with a woman and with sexual love (Alison in
The Master becomes quickly a background figure; and the earlier
efforts along these lines in *Catriona* and *Prince Otto* were failures,
sickly or wooden); but even here the most successfully realized
character is not the Ingenue, young Kirstie, but Old Kirstie, the
epitome of all Stevenson's foster mothers from his nurse, Cummy,
to his wife. The division of the desired sexual object into two,
the blonde and the dark, the young and the old, joined with a
single name: a relatively frank mother-projection and the more
conventional image of the young virgin is an intriguing example
of what the psychologists like to call "splitting"—but in the *Weir,*

despite this unconscious camouflage, sex is at last openly touched upon and a further meaning of Stevenson's sexually immature or impotent heroes is revealed. To possess the desired woman can be for Stevenson only to possess the Mother, to offend the Father and court death. He desires to *be* a father, for to inherit a son is harmlessly to emulate his own admired begettor, but himself to *beget* a son is to become his father's rival, to commit symbolic incest. I do not think it is an accident that R.L.S. had no children of his own, was in fact a foster father.

In his books, Stevenson's protagonists are often foster sons, orphans in search of a spiritual father: Jim looking to Long John, David leaning on Alan, Louden Dodd turning from Jim Pinkerton to Captain Nares. In one sense, all the Beloved Villains *are* Fathers, physically prepossessing, obviously strong, sexually vigorous—but by the same token they are bad sons, betrayers of their own fathers, possessors of the Mother—those who have, as in Stevenson's harrowing fable, *The House of Eld,* cast off the gyve that is loosed only by patricide. They are almost always shown as murderers, but in the earlier books and the books written in collaboration they themselves are spared by the pseudo-son who feebly contemplates their death (Herrick of Attwater, Jim of John Silver). The unloved virtuous are dutiful sons, sexless or impotent, because they had flinched before the killing of the Father, but they are racked by guilt, for the Beloved Villain is an externalization of what they have dreamed but not dared; and the Father, seeing deep, is offended none the less.

Parallel to the series of books I have been chiefly describing are the books written by Stevenson in collaboration with his stepson, especially *The Wrecker,* in which the father-son relationship is more openly treated, in the surprisingly contemporary terms of the relationship between the son as the insecure artist and the father as the assured bourgeois. The pursuit of the muse is felt as a device of Oedipus; and the making of fictions as a prolonged betrayal.

In the *Weir* the two themes at last coalesce, in what might have been, if Stevenson had lived to overcome the stylistic difficulties of its opening portion, the most complex and adult of his fables. Even in the fragment we have, read with the projected conclusion, we can assess Stevenson's achievement, his realization of a solution to the archetypal plight of sonship, placed between the alternatives of murder-incest and impotence-cowardice. Once R.L.S. had dared to confront face-to-face the sexual crisis underlying his fictions, that crisis ceased to be an ultimate explanation, became merely another symbolic level from which he could push on toward more ultimate and more metaphysical explications of the problem with which he had begun: the grace of evil and the unloveliness of good. In the *Weir*, the Lovable Rogue makes a final appearance, this time as the Seducer, Frank Innes, a school friend of, and foil to, the protagonist Archie Weir, the prototype of all those "good" Stevensonian characters who are somehow unworthy of love. The Master, who contains in himself all of Stevenson's lesser scoundrels, had already foreshadowed the Seducer, in intent upon his brother's wife, and in fact upon the village girl Jessie Broun, casually abandoned after a brief and brutal amour by the older brother, but provided for by the kindness of the younger. Young Kirstie in the *Weir* is something of Alison and something of Jessie, a Cressida at heart, neither untouchable nor yet a harlot.

In the book as originally planned, Young Kirstie, baffled by the principled coldness of Archie, who loves her but whom she cannot understand, was to be got with child by Frank Innes, who would then be killed by Archie, and Archie in turn would be condemned to die on the gallows by his own father, a hanging judge of terrible integrity. It is the ending of *Jekyll* and *The Master* all over again—good destroying itself in the very act of destroying evil—but Stevenson relented. In the projected ending reported by his amanuensis and much deplored by most of his critics, Archie was to have broken prison just before the day of his execution and to have escaped with Kirstie to America, making her his wife and taking as his own the child she was carrying, the by-blow of the Scoundrel he has killed.

It was to be a complete merging of good and evil, not as before in mutual destruction and the common grave, but in the possession of a single woman able to love—though in different senses—both; and in the seed which virile evil is able casually to sow, but which only impotent virtue can patiently foster. To cavil at this as an unmotivated "Happy Ending," and to wish that Stevenson had survived once more to change his mind, is to miss utterly the mythic meaning of the event: a final resolution of man's moral duality this side of the grave.

Three Jews

1. Peretz: The Secularization of the Absurd

Originally a review of *Prince of the
Ghetto* by Maurice Samuel

It is fifteen years now since I first read Peretz; and before
that for perhaps another ten years I had been aware of him dimly
as a name, an institution, a folk hero belonging to the darkness
of Europe, the double-darkness of the ghetto from which my
grandparents had fled to a sunlit America. It is an irony of communal memory that the bitterest critic of a way of life should be
identified in recollection with the world he attacks, and yet it is
a constant irony: an enlighened Aeschylus is confused with the
bloody world of Agamemnon; a liberal Hawthorne blurs into
the rigid Puritan commonwealth of Hester Prynne, an emancipated Peretz fades back into the ghetto from which in pain he
escaped. This irony Maurice Samuel chooses to perpetuate in
the title of his book, *Prince of the Ghetto*. Prince of the ghetto
indeed—that believer in statistics, popular science, socialism, that
"free" intellectual in a short coat who would not go home on
Seder night: enemy of the ghetto, scourge of the ghetto, destroyer
of the ghetto—Prince only in the sense that a revolutionist of '89
was Prince of the Bastille. And yet—

And yet there is possible another Peretz, a quite "real"
Peretz, though one the living author would, I suspect, have had
to deny: the *folk* Peretz—not, as Samuel misleadingly asserts, a
writer of folk stories, but himself a myth of the folk, re-created
by the Jewish people out of what was least conscious, most
instinctive in his work. It is characteristic of greatness in writing,
or of a certain kind of greatness at least, that it is amenable to

313

precisely such mythic appropriation. There is a type of writer who permits himself to be transmuted, reinvented in response to the shifting needs of his audience; and eternally transformed, he yet integrally survives. It is Shakespeare, of course, who most spectacularly exemplifies this infinite lack of resistance to adaptation. Peretz, on his level, is almost equally responsive.

There are many possible Peretzes to be extracted from his whole work: the socialist, the enemy of orthodoxy, the exponent of Jewish self-hatred, the Yiddish Hans Christian Andersen, the rhapsodist of Romantic Love; and for some reader each of these must be especially valid, especially useful. It is always a question of *use*—and for Samuel's fictive Prince there is a clear and urgent use: to act as a mediator between the American non-Yiddish-speaking Jew (particularly the intellectual) and what is valuable in his Yiddish past—that is to say, the East European, the ghetto past as opposed to the Hebrew past. It is true, for better or worse, that for such a Jew the ethos of his recent ancestors is most easily available as "literature," at a level where not belief but the suspension of disbelief is exacted.

To such a Jew, for example, Hasidism, in its native context of intolerance, dirt and shabby magic, is somewhat repugnant; even in Buber's modernist presentation (out of the Baal Shem Tov by Kierkegaard), it remains stubbornly alien. But in the ironic-sentimental tales of Peretz, Yiddish mysticism and ethics come to seem, by virtue of the familiar tone, usable. The American Jewish intellectual fumbling uncertainly backward toward the sacramental values of ghetto life cannot quite reach that vanished world; he cannot achieve the innocence, and will not tolerate the narrowness necessary for the full return. He reaches back, back—and falling short, finds Peretz within touch and comprehension; for Peretz had in revolt moved as great a distance from the Orthodox community as the contemporary intellectual has in nostalgia moved back toward it. The American Jewish intellectual of this generation from his side, and Peretz from his, bound between them a rich area of what might be called alienated Jewishness, in which flourish Kafka's K. and Joyce's Bloom, the most compulsive modern images of Citizen and Artist.

In this light, it is not strange, though Peretz could not have foreseen it, that his chance of survival as a writer, his opportunity to enter the mainstream of Western literature depend on his survival in the English language and in America, where alone the Jews in Exile substantially survive, a community capable of producing intellectuals peculiarly prepared to achieve the liaison with Europe which is indispensable to American spiritual life.

Peretz was never sure of his language or his audience; he experimented with Polish and Hebrew, turned to Yiddish as a *pis aller* and not without regrets. On the one hand, he was tempted outward toward Europe as an audience, and on the other, he felt drawn inward as a teller of tales to his own people; but he could contemplate neither possibility without irony at his own expense. In a piece called "Stories," Peretz satirizes his European orientation in a portrait of the Jewish writer spinning yarns to a stupid, anti-Semitic *shiksa* in hope of charming her into forgetting his ugly Jewish mug and giving him a kiss (surely, at some level he was ironically recalling *the* Kiss, the Kiss of the Shechina, the ultimate hope of the mystic Jew); and in one sketch he reports no less bitterly the attitude of an ordinary Polish Jew to his work: "What is the good of it? I don't mean to *you*. God forbid! A Jew must earn a living if he has to suck it out of a wall. But what do *they*, your readers, get out of it?"

In the end, Peretz seems to have spoken to the Europeanized Jew (a prospect rather than a fact), the cosmopolitan, rationalist, socialist Jew made in his own image; in lectures and by tracts, he tried himself to create his own ideal audience, though his total success would have meant the death of his work. After all, Yiddish is the ghetto language, and with the complete Europeanization of the Jew that Peretz dreamed, it would have disappeared as a living tongue, along with the caftan and the *sheitel*. Part of the tragic impact of Peretz' work arises from its being in intent an act of *suicide*, art's immolation of itself for the secularization of Jewish morality, and the Jew's subsumption into a common humanity.

Indeed, Yiddish is just about dead, though it died not in

the triumph of universalism that Peretz foresaw, but in mass extermination and the Zionist exodus from Europe. Jewry survives not on the continent Peretz loved and preached as the Jews' future, but in America and Israel, drawn toward the poles of assimilation and Zionist nationalism, both of which Peretz despised as profanations of Universalism and the Allegorical Return.

What Peretz can mean to those intent on becoming *Hebrews,* in face of the anti-European, anti-Yiddish tenor of life in Israel, I cannot say; but for those of us in America, his meaning is evident, his uses clear. We have become aware that we must achieve, if we are unwilling to become shadows of shadows, a double assimilation, back to a stable past as well as forward toward a speculative future, and in that act Peretz is a potential ally. To make available to us what Peretz carried from the house he helped fire (we must not forget that the death of the Yiddish community, as distinct from the deaths of individual Jews, was not only a murder, but a suicide), he must first be translated, then interpreted—which is to say, somewhat misinterpreted. This pious and necessary misrepresentation, re-creation if you will, is the function of Mr. Samuel's book; and Mr. Samuel, who has done a similar job for Sholom Aleichem, is peculiarly suited for the job, as one who did not inherit but had to learn by an act of choice and will the language of Peretz.

On the whole, he has skillfully disentangled the living Peretz from the ninetenth-century corpse of the same name: the optimistic believer in material progress, science and rationalism, the popularizing lecturer, the despiser of ritual. He has perhaps made him, out of nostalgia and a desire to simplify, too single, too gentle and beneficent. For a juster balance we might have been given more of the bitter, the dark Peretz: his commentary on the Jew's comical and soul-destroying pursuit of *parnosseh* (livelihood), his sketches of the degradation of woman in the Jewish community, his studies of the stultifying impact of hopeless poverty and the rule of the spiritually dead in Jewry. There is in Peretz a blackness that denies his avowed optimism, and an ambivalence toward his people that cannot be mitigated without sacrificing him as a writer.

My one major objection, however, is to Mr. Samuel's habit of referring to Peretz' artfully contrived fictions as "folk tales" or "Hasidic tales." Quite aside from the technical objection that the self-conscious writer for publication does not compose "folk" material, such loose terminology obscures the problem of Peretz' precise relationship to the folklore elements which he incorporated into his work. As a European writer, Peretz comes toward the end of a long tradition (which begins with Percy's *Reliques* and Ossian and includes the work of such men as Novalis and Hans Christian Andersen, Goethe and George MacDonald) of appropriating to high literature folk material, and of creating a pseudo-folk literature. It is a chapter in the long history of the writer's effort to domesticate to his task what was once called the *merveilleux* and is now fashionably called the Absurd.

The problem of the nineteenth-century Jewish writer in this regard was markedly different in two main respects from that of the Gentile manipulators of the fairy tale: first, the Jewish folk tale had not sunk in social prestige to something told by old women to children; the haggadic tradition had made it possible to keep the *maase* unseparated from the main body of Jewish belief and ritual; and the Hasidic movement had instituted the Tale as one of the centers of religious life. The Jewish folk story was in the lifetime of Peretz not an old wife's tale, a degraded myth, but Myth in full flower; and the writer's problem was to secularize rather than to redeem the Absurd. Second, for Jewish literature, whose development takes place in an incredibly short time, Enlightenment and Romanticism are telescoped, so that the ideological bias of Peretz is not the anti-rationalism of, say, Andersen, but a mixture of rationalism, sentimentalism and philosophical optimism that reminds the English reader, quite improbably, of Alexander Pope.

The myth becomes literature in Peretz, therefore, by a double process: by the sentimentalizing of the Absurd and the rationalizing of the Absurd. Let us take a single example, the story called "And Even Beyond," in which the "absurd" contention that the Rabbi of Nemirov spends the mornings of the Penitential Days in Heaven is challenged by a skeptical Litvak. In the end, the Litvak is content to grant the claim, after discovering that the Rabbi, disguised as a peasant, actually spends the holy mornings chopping wood for the old and the sick. For the Hasid's daring ambiguity of "Heaven," the Litvak and Peretz have substituted the rationalist (What else could Heaven mean to us moderns?), sentimental (to split kindling for a widow—what could be more Heavenly?) concept, "aiding the poor." What survives in the story, despite Peretz' conscious attempt to eliminate legend and magic, is the irreducible absurdity present as soon as the term "Heaven" is evoked, though the sentimentality endemic to Jewish emotional life nearly smothers it. Sometimes, as in "Silent Bontche," one of Peretz' best-known stories, a third and saving element enters: the joke, the Jewish Joke which secularizes the Absurd as the absurd; granted the pick of Heaven's abundance, the holy simpleton asks for "every morning a hot roll with butter, please!" But jokes are not frequent in Peretz, and he is ordinarily left to fend without the protection of wit against the shallow rationalization, the easy emotional response; so that most often, his reworkings of folk material are reductions, unintentional parodies of myth. More typical of Peretz' sensibility, though rare in its noncommittal tone, is such a study of Hasidic madness and devotion as "The Kiss of Moses"—in which, for once, Peretz succeeds in maintaining toward the Absurd a quizzical detachment, suspended between irony and sympathy, that makes *everything* seem possible: even the rightness of superstition and folly, even the Kiss of God.

II. Kafka and the Myth of the Jew

Originally a review of
Parables by Franz Kafka

A public word on Kafka is a piety, almost obligatory amongst us, to the *Zeitgeist*. At the focus of love and fashion, we assent to the unforeseen lucidity of the obsession, the stubborn integrity of the fragment, the irreducibility of meaning maintained like a martyrdom. "Yes, it is like this!" we cry. "Yes, *I* am like this!" —and the "it," the "I," object and subject, do not for once deny each other: that mediation, that peace is the function of Kafka's anguish.

It is not, after all, strange that behind the "this" with which most passionately we identify ourselves is—the Jew! "Spiritually," the Catholic Church itself has cried, looking, it is true, in a somewhat different direction, "we are all Semites." And more specifically, the artist, turning from the nineteenth-century sentimentality of the *poète maudit* but still concerned with his alienation, finds in the Jew, inseparable from the dignity of his ultimate exile, the noblest metaphor of the Outsider.

It is the essential Jewishness of Kafka that this slim collection, one volume in "a home library of great Jewish writings," attempts to establish. Most of these "parables" we have seen before; it is their occasion that differs. Extracted from novel, story, sketch or personal jotting, they place Kafka in the central parabolic tradition of Jewish teaching. From Esther and Jonah to the tales of the Hasidim, the haggadic method has survived in Jewry, the love of the story indistinguishable from the love of wisdom, the sense that what evades the precept flourishes in the tale. Kafka's comments on the Coming of the Messiah or the Tower of Babel might be the lost words of a *Zaddik*, at once a confession that some things are unsayable and that a Jew (why not?) can say them. This is one source of the humor, the essential Jewish humor, that not lightens but enriches despair (think again of Jonah!) and that plays over, an additional qualification, Kafka's reflections on possible versions of Abraham or the scene Before the Law.

Nor is Kafka's multivalence without ancestry; behind his devotion to the multiplicity of meaning lies the teaching that there are seventy true interpretations of each word of Scripture; and his obliquity evokes the Zohar's injunction that meaning should play lightly over the text, like the Spirit of the Lord hovering over the face of the waters.

But most central of all is Kafka's concept of the traditional: not the *strain* to recapture or redeem pastness, but the sense that all archtypical patterns of Fall, Expulsion or Redemption happen now and forever. The Passover celebration each year dramatically projects this for all Israel: "I was in Egypt. Thou broughtest *me* out," etc. These are Kafka's words: "The expulsion from Paradise is . . . eternal: consequently the expulsion from paradise is final . . . but the eternal nature of the occurrence . . . makes it possible . . . that we are continuously there whether we know it or not." Yet our suffering and our hope are in time and they are no less real.

What, then, of Kafka's cry that he could not feel anything in common with himself, much less with the Jews? The question, of course, answers itself; the lowliest member of Israel knows it for a "Jewish" remark. Is it not, after all, one of the things we may mean when we speak of the Exile?

To call Kafka a Jew is not, of course, to deny that he is a heretic. But Judaism is not in the habit of disowning its great heretics completely; rather, through them, it defines a negative orthodoxy. The monstrous Zevi continues to haunt the Jewish imagination, and in response to him modern rationalistic Judaism began. Who has not sensed possession in the way an old Jew says the name of Spinoza, or smiles to see the archheretic, Freud, who tried at last to take Moses from Israel, become the new Moses of a best-selling wing of the Reformed Synagogue? Jewish jokes betray the refusal of Israel to give up its heretics: "Let's throw out the *goy*," a Yiddish story reports Trotsky as having said, pointing to Lenin, at the first meeting of the Supreme Soviet, "and we'll have a *minyan*."

The grounds of Kafka's heterodoxy are clear: his distrust of the Promise, his incapacity to accept sex as sacramental (not till the end of his life did he fulfill the Cabalistic prerequisite for wisdom; for it is taught that only he who takes the lower Shekhina can receive the Higher, that a wife must be taken before the Presence come), but most essentially his refusal to leap to faith where reason eventuates in anguish. What of the Incommensurate is Imminent in natural experience he perceived, but its intolerable contradictions he demanded be explained in terms of his own reason. His work is a baffled theodicy, for he simply cannot conclude; lacking even the minimum wisdom of Job (who was, after all, merely a *goy*), he would not clap his hand over his mouth. It is just that he became *our* mythic Jew, humorous, heretic, fragmentary, incapable of being still.

III. Malamud: The Commonplace as Absurd

Originally a review of *The Natural*
by Bernard Malamud

The simplest of the pleasures of criticism is that of discovery. But after adolescence, when it is possible to come for the first time even on that which has been known forever, it is the most difficult to attain. The book written yesterday and just today entrusted to print falls into its foreknown place, seems a mere confirmation of certain expectations, further evidence of certain already charted trends. One is tempted to blame it all on the state of letters; but it is hard to believe really that literature fades so precisely with the fading of one's own capacity to be astonished. The new books of our youth cannot possibly have been that much newer; it was surely that we read them, re-created, reinvented them better.

To be sure, each book worth rereading, reread *is* new again, at least newer than we had dared expect. It is with those that we pick up the first time that we have the most trouble. They seldom seem as new as we foolishly continue to expect them to be, demand that they be, rage at them for not being. I suspect that the professional critic, that Don Giovanni of literature still dreaming himself the young lover of his first book, secretly hopes for so dazzling a progress in the art of his time that he will never become aware of his diminishing ability to respond.

This utopian hope disappointed, he is tempted to seek refuge in the expression of his disenchantment, which has the advantage over more positive responses of flourishing rather than declining with age. Since most books merit scorn rather than praise, this gives the critic a better batting average as an evaluator; and since the young, who are great consumers of criticism, aspire to disenchantment, a better box office. Besides, our world being what it is, a declaration of love in print lays the writer open to the suspicion of currying favor or submitting to fashion, while a vicious or snide attack is accepted as honest and independent by definition.

It is hard for us to love what we do not feel we have discovered, what we cannot convince ourselves is especially ours. And it is here that the critic finds himself the victim of a contradiction in his own divided soul. Half publicist, he is driven to share, to *sell* what he has come upon in loneliness; but half lover, he resents the sharing, feels himself the pimp of his beloved. Ideally, he would like—*I* would like (let me drop the mask of the third person or even the first plural; surely one of the legitimate subpleasures of criticism is that of talking about oneself) to have three or four secret books, exclusive loves.

They would have to have been published, of course, for everybody, but ignored or despised or simply misunderstood, left for me alone. As a matter of fact, I do have a handful of favorites which I share only with a few other eccentric appreciators: the *Dionysiaca* of Nonnus, *The Honorable Picnic* of Thomas Raucat, Henry Roth's *Call It Sleep*, *Edgar Huntley* of Charles Brockden Brown, etc. Even my poor *Master of Ballantrae* must be put in this class, I fear; for while a movie remotely related to Stevenson's book has lately done well at the box office, a new paper-backed edition (as I learned recently from the disconsolate editor I persuaded to do it) has found in the course of a year and in all the United States only thirty-seven readers! I am not, please notice, making a plea for any of these books; I suspect that certain accidents of my own experience have endeared them to me; yet I have, of course, mentioned the titles as a kind of bait for the curious.

I certainly do not wish for any of them that pseudo-success of being adopted by a smug, tight minority; the embattled orthodoxy of an enlightened literary splinter group is more disheartening than the relaxed, mindless conformism of "everybody." Nonetheless, I feel impelled to speak out on behalf of a book I have come upon recently; for it deserves to run the risk of all the popularities and pseudo-popularities upon which a work of art can be wrecked.

It is called *The Natural* * and is written by Bernard Malamud, whose short stories I have seen, and, I must confess, have never been attracted to, in *Commentary* and elsewhere. The book was first published by Harcourt, Brace in 1952 and is, I should guess, out of print. I cannot even remember reading a notice of it at the time; and I did not see it at all until a month or two ago when I came across it in a cheap paper edition by Dell. There is on the cover an enthusiastic plug by Alfred Kazin (I trust it was as enthusiastic as it is made to sound with the aid of three dots) and a complimentary phrase from the *New York Times;* but I have no sense of the book's having made an *impression.* I, at any rate, was completely unprepared for the pleasure it gave me.

There are two things I think it strategic to say about it to begin with. First, that I have not found so much simple joy, so much sense of zest and rewarding nuttiness and humor, in anything I've read for a long time; and second, that the book has the distinction of being immune to misrepresentation by any jacket the publisher chose to dress it in. It is, that is to say, in certain ways a vulgar and disreputable book, really about sex and baseball as the cover of the paper edition unsubtly suggests. One of the library journals made the point that this is an especially likely book for men who do not think of themselves as readers, meaning, I suppose, that it is disarmingly unliterary. This is an absurd contention in one sense, but quite right in another.

If "literary" implies an almost principled avoidance of invention (and I think we have just about reached this point), then this book is something else than "literature." Our younger writers, whether naturalists or Jamesian impressionists or conventional symbolists, have come to despise narrative ingenuity as something naïve or primitive, well lost for the sake of documentation or sensibility or allegory. Harried into choosing between the Dreiserian or Jamesian academies, many of our young novel-

* Since the appearance of this review, Mr. Malamud has come securely into his own; but *The Natural* (I am a little pleased to note) remains still unappreciated.

ists end up performing ritual acts of piety when they believe they are in fact achieving verisimilitude or expressing insights. Academy answers academy and permits each side to believe it has left outmoded convention and achieved "truth" or "form." Dullness has become so expected a part of seriousness in literature that we are likely to suspect the writer who does not proffer it among his credentials. But Mr. Malamud is neither naturalist nor impressionist, and he is not even dull; his fancy, confined neither to the limitations of the sensitive observer nor the narrow world of "real experience," manipulates the details of his fable in the interests of surprise and delight.

The epigraph of his book might well have been that melancholy popular phrase, "He could of been a hero!" It is about heroism that the story turns: the obligations of the heroic and its uses. For Roy Hobbs, the protagonist, the problem is the proper and pious use of his gift, that natural (or magical) talent which has its meaning only in its free exercise, the gratuitous, poetic act. For the fans, which is to say for *us*, the problem is our relationship to the hero and the question of whether he can survive our bribes and adulation, make the singular, representative act which alone can fulfill us, before we corrupt him into our own sterile image. For in truth, we need almost as desperately to hate and destroy the hero as to love and live by him; our self-hatred is projected as ferociously onto the representative figure as our reverence before our own possibilities. To say that in our world (the world of the Judge who pays for the defeat of the team he owns and the depraved dwarf in the stands ready to hoot down with his automobile horn defeated excellence) the hero fails is scarcely necessary.

Mr. Malamud finds in baseball the inevitable arena in which to play out our own version of this drama: part ritual and part commerce and part child's game, bounded by stupidity and corruption and sung only in the clichés of the sports writers, there yet survives in its midst a desecrated but indestructible dream of glory. The ball team of *The Natural* is real, its slumps, its fans, the absurd psychologist who comes to hypnotize the players, their charms and spells; and being real, it is comic. The details are the details of something which remains stubbornly a fact for all of its abstract meaning, not of a contrived device which functions only for the sake of that meaning.

Having said this, I dare confess at last that behind the literal fable, there is the presence of a legend, of the Grail Legend. Mr. Malamud reaches out with one hand to Ring Lardner and with the other to Jessie Weston. If this is outrageous, it is the sort of outrage I enjoy. Why none of the critics have noticed the influence of Miss Weston, whom Eliot has made almost a platitude of critical approach, I don't know; but they have not, though the hero, slain once with a silver bullet and miraculously resurrected, returns in a time of drought to a disease-ridden team called the Knights, presided over by a manager called Pop Fisher, etc., etc. I have thought it wise to save this modest revelation for the end of my comments, fearing to misrepresent the achievement of Mr. Malamud's book. The use of myth and symbol as a *machine* (an artificial and external device to lend the semblance of metaphysical depth to a half-imagined story) has become a convention and a bore.

The weariest sort of journals for aspiring hacks run these days articles headed, "Symbolism Can Save *Your* Story," and we should all be aware that we have had too many books (even ambitious and moving ones) in which the function of the myth is to save the book—to do the work of imagination, invention and coherence. But the point is, of course, quite the opposite; and we have had all too few books that have attempted to save the myth, to revivify an ancient insight without which we cannot fully live. Mr. Malamud has in *The Natural* found, not imposed, an archetype in the life we presently live; in his book the modern instance and the remembered myth are equally felt, equally realized and equally appropriate to our predicament. It is this which gives to his work special authority and special richness; for he has not felt obliged to choose between the richness of imagined detail and that of symbolic relevance. He is out of the trap! It is for this reason that I have been moved to ignore the small failures of technique and consistency in his book and to say quite simply, "Hurrah!" There is no real way to pay for the pleasure a work of art gives us; but one can at least record that pleasure and his gratitude.

Originally a review of *The Assistant*
by Bernard Malamud

In his second novel, Bernard Malamud has turned away from the rich playfulness, the free use of myth and magic which made of his first book, *The Natural,* so welcome a sport in the dim world of contemporary fiction. It is impossible, I think, to appreciate the kind of discipline and self-denial which motivates the muted style of *The Assistant* without a knowledge of the earlier work, and a consequent awareness that Malamud is doing what he does because he *chooses* to, not because he lacks the fancy to conceive anything else or the invention to accomplish it.

He is playing a dangerous game in *The Assistant* all the same; and in the earlier portion of the book, his resolve to treat gray lives grayly, to render dull conversations dully, threatens to succeed only too well. The material he deals with seems at first depressingly familiar: we have read before of the lives of poor Jews, proprietors of groceries and candy stores, just as we have encountered before Jewish writers, plagued by an ideal of imitative form and impelled, in the face of their material, to give us not the poetry of banal lives but their banality.

Long before we have reached the end of the book, however, we realize that, though muted, the poetry is never denied and that Malamud's theme remains here what it was in the more extravagant *The Natural:* the Absurd—here specifically the absurdity of existence in its most commonplace forms. It is odd how the subdued tone, the show of "realism" in Malamud take us in, as life itself takes us in, with its routine surfaces. We tend to accept on the level of mere realistic observation and reporting an account, say, of a young man wedged perilously in a dumbwaiter shaft watching the daughter of the man he has robbed but loves strip for a shower; or the description of the same young man crouched in guilt and fear and hunger in the basement of a store, feeding frantically and in secret on stolen bottles of milk.

A slight shift in emphasis, a slight heightening of tone—and we would be face to face with some quasi-surrealist image of the Underground Man, not unlike, perhaps, the hallucinatory opening of Ralph Ellison's *The Invisible Man*. But Malamud has chosen to create the least melodramatic of all possible versions of the Absurd: a vision of the commonplace as absurd. One is reminded by his ambition and achievement of Saul Bellow, especially in *The Victim*, and back, through Bellow, of Daniel Fuchs, author of *Homage to Blenholt*.

One is even tempted to say, on such grounds, that Malamud has with this book entered into the main Jewish-American tradition in the novel, taking up the frustrated experiements of writers like Fuchs or Nathanael West, ignored in the thirties in favor of "the proletarian novel," and overshadowed by the inflated reputations of Steinbeck and Dos Passos and Farrell. In a strange way, Malamud's novel *is* a belated novel of the thirties. It is not, I think, definitely located in time; but one imagines its events as happening in the dispirited years of the Depression. Only in that context does the struggle of the poor Jew, Morris Bober, to keep his store open achieve a proper sense of desperation, or the desire of his daughter Helen to go to college touch a full note of pathos.

But how different *The Assistant* is from any novel *written* in the thirties! The kind of politics which informed the "proletarian novel" is, of course, quite gone, as is the note of hysteria, the apocalyptic shrillness which characterizes all novels of the period, whatever their politics. Not even the humor of West or Fuchs is present, neither the half-mad belly laugh nor the self-deprecatory giggle by which such writers came to terms with terror and desolation. Indeed, Malamud's book is willfully, almost perversely humorless, even as it is apolitical. Helen Bober and her Jewish boy friends may talk the same stilted, hyperurban speech (indeed Malamud is masterful at reproducing it) as that of Arthur Kober's "Dear Bella" and her beaus; but here *it is no joke*.

Just as Malamud will not permit us the luxury of righteous indignation and political protest before the prospect of an honest man incapable of earning a living or a warmhearted girl cut off from the possibilities of love—so he will not let us snicker or guffaw at their plight either. He compels us to contemplate the absurdity of their situations—and that of Frank Alpine, the Gentile who alternately robs and aids them—with the pure response of *pity*. Beside this, politics and humor are revealed as rival opiates of the people: devices to prevent the confrontation of the full and terrible ridiculousness of human loneliness and desire, unsuccess and death. His is a book and a viewpoint essentially (questions of doctrine aside) *religious*.

The quite unpredictable, though distressingly up-to-date, absurdity of *The Assistant* belongs to the nature of its religiousness. We live in a time of an at least nominal revival of interest in religion, and the appearance of conversion stories surely surprises no one. *The Assistant,* however, is concerned with a conversion *to* Judaism—a theme by no means usual even at this moment of the ascendancy of Marjorie Morningstar. Marjorie, after all, is only confirmed in what Religious Emphasis Week speakers like to call "the faith of our fathers," and for her such subsidence means accommodation and "peace of mind." Malamud's Frank, on the other hand, is painfully impelled toward Judaism and accepts it as he accepts pain itself. After he has rescued Helen Bober from assault and more than half-raped her himself; after he has been cast out by Morris and has witnessed his quietly heroic death; after he has taken on himself the burden of the store which becomes in the novel scarcely distinguishable from the burden of life itself—Frank takes the final step. "One day in April," the book concludes in its characteristic low key, "Frank went to the hospital and had himself circumcized. . . . The pain enraged and inspired him. After Passover he became a Jew." As a happy ending, a springtime close for a story which begins in the chill of autumn, it is all quite ridiculous. Surely nothing is more conducive to titters and bad jokes than the notion of the circumcision of a grown man; and to *become* a Jew when it is hard enough to remain one—nothing could be more improbable.

At first glance, such a conclusion seems more sentimental than absurd; but it is saved from sentimentality by a further turn of the screw, a final note of the ridiculous. Frank becomes a Jew without knowing in any explicit way what a Jew is; and we are asked to accept his conversion knowing as little as he what he is converted to. What *is* the content of Jewishness as Malamud understands it? Easiest of all is to say what it is not: not an imaginary revived orthodoxy, not a literary man's neo-Hasidism out of Martin Buber by T. S. Eliot, not the rational "normative Judaism" of the Reformed. It is apparently nothing more than what an unlearned immigrant, who has not been in a synagogue in twenty years, but whom *everyone* would agree in calling a Jew, happens to live by.

Morris Bober is the book's exemplar of Judaism: a man who not only sells but eats pork, who knows scarcely anything of the Talmud, who can hardly answer when asked what a Jew is. Yet it is he, through the example of his life, who converts Frank Alpine, to whom being a Jew means practically taking on the responsibilities of Morris: his wife, his daughter, especially his accursed, ill-paying store. The nearest thing to an explicit definition of Morris' Jewishness is spoken by a rabbi called in after his death, a rabbi who has never known him and who improvises in broken English a eulogy on the basis of hearsay and the conventional lies one says in honor of the dead.

Yet in this speech, the novel reaches its climax of poetry and pity and truth. It must be read entire and in context for its full impact, though its sense can be resumed in a few excerpts:

> My dear friends, I never had the pleasure to meet this good grocery man that he now lays in his coffin. He lived in a neighborhood where I didn't come in. . . . He caught double pneumonia from shoveling snow in front of his place of business, so people could pass by on the sidewalk. . . . He was also a very hard worker, a man that never stopped working. . . . Fifteen, sixteen hours a day he was in the store, seven days a week, to make a living for his family. . . . This went on for twenty-two years in this store alone, day after day, except the few days when he was too sick. And for this reason that he worked so hard and bitter, in his house, on his table, was always something to eat. So, besides honest, he was a good provider. . . .
>
> When a Jew dies, who asks if he is a Jew, we don't ask.

Is this, then, what Jewishness has become for us, our world —not at its worst but at its human best—"to take care of the store"? One is reminded of the oldest of Jewish jokes, of the dying man who blindly asks for all his family one by one, and when he discovers all are present, cries out, "Then who's taking care of the store?" Is this, after all, a joke not on the dying man, as we have always thought, but on *ourselves* who laugh at it? Is that ridiculous deathbed cry the cry of a *lamedvavnik*, one of the hidden just for whose sake the world is preserved? To believe it would be absurd.

William Faulkner,
Highbrows' Lowbrow

Originally a review of *The Collected Stories of William Faulkner*

No one can write about Willam Faulkner without committing himself to the weary task of trying to disengage the author and his work from the misconceptions that surround them. It has taken me ten years of wary reading to distinguish the actual writer of *The Sound and the Fury* from a synthetic Faulkner, compounded of sub-Marxian stereotypes (Negro-hater, nostalgic and pessimistic proto-Fascist, etc.); and I am aware that there is yet another pseudo-Faulkner, a more elaborate and chaotic Erskine Caldwell, revealing a world of barnyard sex and violence through a fog of highbrow rhetoric. The grain of regrettable truth in both these views is lost in their misleading emphases; and equally confusing are the less hysterical academic partial glimpses which make Faulkner primarily a historian of Southern culture, or a canny technician whose evocations of terror are secondary to Jamesian experiments with "point of view." Faulkner, also distorting Faulkner, once told a class of young writers that he never considers form at all! I am moved by the publication of Faulkner's collected short stories to propose another partial view as a counterweight to the others.

There have been in the last weeks predictions from various quarters that Faulkner, now that *Intruder in the Dust* was chosen by the Book-of-the-Month Club, will shortly win a wider audience. But he has been, though the fact has been astonishingly overlooked, for nearly twenty years the most widely read American writer of whom any respectable critic has been tempted to use the word "great."

In Dixon Wecter's recent history of American life during the years of the Great Depression, the name of Faulkner is not even mentioned; yet in the years covered by Mr. Wecter's book, Faulkner published not only two of his greatest novels, but also some sixty stories, nearly twenty of them in the *Saturday Evening Post*, which is, I suppose, the magazine most likely to be picked up by the common man when he has seen all the movies in town. One must make certain qualifications, of course; neither *The Sound and the Fury* nor *Light in August* has had a wide sale; but as a short-story writer, Faulkner has sold consistently to the mass circulation magazines, apparently pleasing the widest of our reading publics.

It is a strange experience for those of us to whom Faulkner's name is associated with the critical journals in which his fiction almost never appears to find his stories, dressed up with the obvious pictures of the weekly family magazine, flanked not by a Kafka or Joyce, but by the dismal hacks whose names I cannot even now (though I have just looked) remember. Sometimes Faulkner writes for *Harper's*, but never for anything even as pretentious as *The New Yorker*. The only "little magazine" which has printed any of the present stories is *Sewanee Review*, in which first appeared the charming but rather slick "A Courtship."

If Faulkner's stories were the work of his left hand, their appearance in popular magazines would be of little consequence (a man has to live!), but Faulkner is essentially a short-story writer. He has no special talent for sustained narrative, though at least twice he has brought off a tour de force in long fiction. The forty-three stories in the present collection are by no means his total achievement. In it are included most of the stories from two earler collections now out of print, *These Thirteen* and *Dr. Martino;* but the seven stories of *Go Down Moses* are not included, nor those loosely worked together in *The Unvanquished,* nor the four magazine tales woven into the text of *The Hamlet,* nor the Gavin Stevens detective stories (*Saturday Evening Post* favorites) which were gathered together last year in a pseudo-long narrative called *Knight's Gambit.*

Faulkner as a storyteller is apparently short-breathed by nature, and his years of writing for the stringent space limits of the magazines have confirmed his tendency to write in gasps. What look like novels at first glimpse, *The Hamlet* or *The Unvanquished*, for instance, come apart into loosely linked short narratives; *Light in August* achieves substance by intertwining two separate stories and *Sanctuary*, slim enough in finished form, consists of various subplots out of the Sartoris-Snopes background, tacked onto the original money-making shocker. Only in *Absalom, Absalom!* and *The Sound and the Fury* has Faulkner worked out genuine full-length narratives by extension rather than patchwork; and even in these two books, he attains novelistic thickness not by inventing a long, complex fable, but by revealing in a series of strict "point of view" accounts of the same experience the amount of narrative material proper to a short story. It is this experiment with "point of view," a virtue made of a short-breathed necessity, that has concealed somewhat the essentially popular nature of Faulkner's work, and has suggested to his critics comparisons with Proust or Joyce or James, rather than Dickens, whom he so strikingly resembles. The inventor of Popeye and the creator of Quilp have a great deal in common besides an obsession with the grotesque, and especially they have a demonic richness of invention (typified by their equal skill at evoking names that are already myths before the characters are drawn) and a contempt for the platitudes of everyday experience.

Like Dickens, Faulkner is primarily, despite his intellectual *obiter dicta*, a sentimental writer; not a writer with the occasional vice of sentimentality, but one whose basic mode of experience is sentimental, in an age when the serious "alienated" writer emblazons anti-sentimentality on his coat of arms. In a writer whose very method is self-indulgence, that sentimentality becomes sometimes downright embarrassing, as in the stories of World War II in the present collection, "Tall Men," "Two Soldiers," etc., in which the soupiest clichés of self-sacrifice and endurance are shamelessly worked; he is not above the crassest "Happy Endings," stage-managing creakily the fulfillments that we had hoped for against all logic and probability. Even in so good a story as "Uncle Willy" the subtlety of tone and the ingenuity of development serve the conventional soft tale of the town lush opposed to the embattled forces of spinsterhood in a struggle for the old man's life and a boy's soul. Since Romanticism, the reservoir of the sentimental has been nostalgia, and in popular American literature this reservoir has been pre-eminently the nostalgia for boyhood and for our only home-grown Middle Ages, the antebellum South. The South conquered the popular imagination at the moment of its defeat, and the number of synthetic latter-day supporters of the Confederacy is exceeded among us only by the synthetic rooters for Notre Dame. When the bloody corncobs are brushed aside, we can see there is a large area of popular commitment which Faulkner shares with the author of *Gone with the Wind*.

Always in Faulkner there has been a counterimpulse to his basic sentimentality, a rage at the world for baffling his dream of nobility, a black violence bred of his nausea before what culture makes of man's primitive strength and loyalty; and in such a book as *Sanctuary*, or even *The Hamlet*, nausea, violence and rage drive out before them the last vestiges of sentiment, transform all into horror, grotesquerie and the mad humor which so oddly consorts with these when Faulkner is most himself. It is only when he leaves the world of the Snopeses and the Sartorises for the countryside that he reveals himself as a Rousseauist in an age when most serious writers learn to mock the Noble Savage even as they learn their letters.* Recently, in a general recantation of his early bitterness, Faulkner has been telling us that *all* men are if not good at least better than their circumstances would lead us to expect. But this he has always believed and asserted of small boys, peasants, Indians and Negroes. The American extension of Rousseauism through James Fenimore Cooper and Mark Twain leads directly to Willam Faulkner. The great unpopular novels of the twentieth century are urban in nature, but his writing has been largely nonurban, even anti-urban, like the most popular subliterature. Faulkner is surely the last serious writer in the United States to attempt the old-fashioned noble

---

* At the moment several recusant intellectuals are in the process of founding a magazine to be called *The Noble Savage*—but this represents for them a bold rejection of the past and a challenge to their former friends!

Redskin story ("The Courtship," "Lo!") and one of the last to do tales of horsemanship, hunting and fishing without even the exotic setting used by Hemingway to redeem such material from the level of *Field and Stream* or *True*. What other novelist of first rank can address so directly the average American male?

The subject matter par excellence of the modern novel, the alienation of the artist—and the hero par excellence, that artist wandering the city in a vain search for his citizen father—these are foreign to Faulkner. Only in one of his collected stories and in one early novel does he make an artist his protagonist; and this, too, is part of the good fortune with which he begins. To be sure, Quentin Compson, the central intelligence of much of his best earlier work, seems an artist in embryo; but he remains always a boy, taking his own life on his twenty-first birthday, refusing maturity. For the rest, Faulkner's "intellectual" mouth-pieces are (when they are not other boys, as in *Intruder in the Dust*) poor men's intellectuals: Ratliffe, the sewing-machine salesman, or Gavin Stevens, who can mingle unnoticed with the boys on the front porch—wearing the Phi Beta Kappa key which no one recognizes. They are symbols of the *nonalienation* of the right kind of artist; and they represent Faulkner's sentimentalized image of himself: not a writer but a peddler or a lawyer, accepted and admired by the people, for whom he reveals the truth of their plight, not as a prophet (intruding unbidden and unappreciated) but as a *detective*—called upon in moments of need and recognized always.

The detective story is the inevitable crown of Faulkner's work; in it (the stories in *Knight's Gambit*, for instance, and *Intruder in the Dust*) many strains of his writing find fulfillment, not least his commitment to the "switcheroo" and the surprise ending. Such devices are regarded in highbrow quarters these days as old-fashioned and factitious, but Faulkner has always shared with the mass public a sneaking fondness for them. "A Rose for Emily," in some ways the best of his short stories, is marred by the last-minute use of such machinery; and many of his other efforts, good and bad ("Hair," "A Courtship"), employ that disreputable device. In that subliterary form, the detective story, the "switcheroo" has not only survived the devaluation of the O. Henry formula, but has remained the whole point of the genre; and it is, therefore, inevitable that Faulkner turn more and more to that form, as, indeed, Dickens was doing at the end of his career.

The resemblance of Dickens and Faulkner has been concealed by the fact that the former was essentially a city writer while the latter is with equal faithfulness the laureate of the small town and the farm; but in each case the commitment represents the same kind of closeness to a popular audience; and like Dickens' London, Faulkner's Jefferson is inhabited by grotesques who have, oddly enough, in both cases been taken for "realistic" characters. Stereotypically, however, Dickens is thought of as a comedian, while Faulkner is read as terror-ridden and even "morbid." But Dickens has more recently come to be recognized as an obsessed manipulator of irrational images of evil, while Faulkner is seen to have been all along a humorist. There are various kinds of humor in Faulkner, the most obvious form being connected with the standard folk-tale type of the trickster tricked. Just as in Dickens, however, his humor scarcely ever remains pure; there is no clear line in his fiction between the horrible and the funny, both verging toward that disconcertingly ambiguous blending called these days "the Absurd."

The cast of most of Faulkner's comic stories is drawn from the Snopeses, the perpetrators of his most revolting horrors and the symbol in his work of all that is most nauseating and terrible about the rising bourgeoisie. One of the best stories in the present collection, "Barn Burning," is a tale of unrelieved evil told through the eyes of a boy watching his criminal father, the aboriginal Ab Snopes, founder of the whole shabby clan; and from the seed of that story is developed much of *The Hamlet* (which in turn spawns *The Mansion, The Town* and the movie, *The Long Hot Summer*), a tale that begins in terror and passes through the affair of the idiot and the cow to a climax of horse-trading and treasure-hunting, by turns atrocious and simply funny; and it is the offspring of the Snopeses who provide the comic relief in *Sanctuary*, turning up as two burlesque cornballs who mistake a brothel for a hotel. The art of the grotesque, however, whether Dickensian or Faulknerian, has always a popular appeal; for it transforms as it exaggerates, turning every man into his own Archetype, and thus making possible the playing out of moral conflicts as melodrama or farce.

There are, of course, obstacles between Faulkner and complete popular acceptance. His monstrously involved "point of view" is a lion in the path, but it poses a problem in only three or four of his more than twenty books, and is not troublesome at all in the short stories. Then, there is his prose style, whose sheer pretentious ineptitude often puts off all readers, popular or highbrow; but pseudo-poetry is rather an attraction really for the common reader with his dim sense of rhetoric as desirable. If it were only easier to skip in Faulkner! It is necessary in simple self-defense; but his connecting links are so often lost within the double parentheses of precisely the most unreadable passages that one skips only at the price of confusion.

In general, the subject matter of Faulkner is congenial to popular taste, but he suffers in two respects, by an omission and an emphasis. His concern with sex at its most lurid, his monotonously nymphomaniac women, his lovers of beasts, his rapists and dreamers of incest put off the ordinary reader, who tends to prefer his pornography pure. The average reader is no prude about sex; he merely insists that it be kept in its place—that is, in trash and not in literature—demanding a distinction much like that between the harlot and the honest woman he marries.

More important, I think, is Faulkner's avoidance of young love, his almost hysterical campaign against the myth of the pure young girl,* which joins him to most post-Flaubertian serious novelists but cuts him off from the providers of popular entertainment. The purest passionate relations in Faulkner are between men in love with the same woman, who is usually quite unworthy of either; the tenderest feeling he evokes (barring the almost sickly-sweet idyll of Ike and the cow) are between brother and sister, or a boy and an old man, whether a white hophead,

* In his latest fiction, Faulkner has been redeeming the bitches of his earlier work; and in *The Town,* he invented his first full-fledged ingénue—virginal, witty—and destined at the volume's end for a career in Greenwich Village.

an Indian hunter or a proud Negro. Even in *Knight's Gambit,*
the most syrupy of Faulkner's works, he cannot quite bring himself to redeem the ingénue for love, but saves the final clinch for
a middle-aged pair, to whom a nineteen-year-old boy says at the
curtain, "Bless you my children!"

But American literature, popular and serious, has a counter-
tradition to the boy-girl-marriage routine, a pair of juvenile, sub-
sexual myths of love, perhaps even more deeply rooted in our
land: unconsummated brother-sister incest (from the very first
American novel through Hawthorne, Poe and Melville to a recent
successful movie, *Miss Tatlock's Millons*), and the Platonic passion of white boy and colored man, the dream of a love stronger
than our strongest guilt (most splendidly expressed in *Huckleberry Finn*) that reaches a climax in *Go Down Moses* and *Intruder in the Dust.*

That Faulkner is an uneven writer everyone knows; but the
good and bad in his work cannot be equated with the popular
and highbrow elements. The two distinctions cut through his
achievement on different planes; he is neither a natural storyteller confusing his talent with forays into the "literary" nor a
great artist prostituting his talents for a living. His successes and
failures are alike rooted in each level; and, indeed, he is often
a "bad" writer both by purely slick standards and in light of
the higher criticism.

Why he is such a supereminently good "bad" writer, sur-
mounting excesses of maudlin feeling and absurd indulgences in
overripe rhetoric alike, is a mystery. We can only cite the
astonishing richness of invention and specification, the ability to
realize characters and tensions with a power to coerce our credence that has nothing to do with a resemblance to "real" life or
the technical standards we had fondly supposed would be demanded of any first-rate fiction in our time. It is only the just and
delightful final turn of the screw that so baffling a writer has
pleased over twenty-five years two audiences, each unaware of
the fact, much less the grounds, of the other's appreciation.

Three Notes on
Robert Penn Warren

1. Toward Time's Cold Womb

Originally a review of
World Enough and Time

The popularity of Robert Penn Warren's fiction is a paradox that he, as a connoisseur of paradoxes, must especially relish. In an essay on Katherine Anne Porter, then as now honored and "unpopular," Warren once reflected on the immitigable divorce between serious and "popularized" writing in our time; even so tough and accomplished a writer as Faulkner, he observed, could publish in *Collier's* only cruel parodies of his best work.* What, then, of the story Warren himself has recently had printed in *Cosmopolitan;* and what of his novel *All the King's Men,* which became a best seller, won the Pulitzer Prize and has been made into an Academy Award picture? For a work of real merit to win any of these doubtful distinctions is highly improbable; and the compounded improbability of its winning all three is staggering. Are these works of the left hand of an avant-garde editor, poet and critic?

We cannot answer that question affirmatively when we remember that a section of *All the King's Men* first appeared in *Partisan Review,* and that *Kenyon Review* printed a part of Warren's newest book, *World Enough and Time,* which is also a current Literary Guild selection! The vulgarity of the taste to which the Literary Guild successfully panders is one certainty of

* Yet "The Bear," which some critics consider Faulkner's best short story, appeared in the *Saturday Evening Post* in a version perhaps preferable to its final form.

339

our ambiguous world, while *Kenyon,* as the *Saturday Review of Literature* has been recently warning us, is a hotbed of "obscurantists" who carry literary discrimination to the point of un-Americanism. Warren is more than an occasional contributor to the little magazines; for years he has been an editor of one or another, and indeed he is a charter member of those "New Critics," who have touted poets like Eliot and Pound, prose writers like Joyce and Kafka, who are an offense to the readers of *The Robe, Dinner at Antoine's*—and the last two novels of Warren.

That a fictionist, only ten years after the publication of his first novel, should be honored by both our publics, ordinarily hopelessly at odds, is an extraordinary and astonishing case. We have so long been committed to believing that the popular and serious are antithetical, that not a few avant-garde critics, admirers of Warren's first novel, *Night Rider,* have conscientiously argued themselves into believing that *All the King's Men,* even if they had not noticed it until reading the account of its sales, represents a selling out, or at least a falling off. But if, as is the fact, *All the King's Men* is a subtle, complex, integrated work, astonishingly plotted and eminently successful in its language and imagery—even though a best seller—we must confess that there are strategies possible here and now which can mediate between mass audience and serious writer.

It is doubtless true that to the majority of its readers, who will classify it as "heavy but good" and rank it with the season's other "great" novels, *The Wall* and *The Way West,* many meanings of *World Enough and Time* will go unperceived and its formal excellences be quite overlooked, but their readings of it, though partial, will not be false. It is the nature of Warren's work that it is available on many levels, but that each level states, in terms appropriate to a certain degree of sensibility, the same meanings. For the ideal reader, an immensely complicated structure of meaning and motifs awaits experiencing, but there are lesser satisfactions all along the way.

Warren is not a novelist in separation from his other activities as teacher, critic and poet, and to grasp fully the extensions of his themes, to know his uses of language and developing narrative technique, one should know, at least in a generous sample, his whole versatile body of work: the essay on Hemingway, who with Faulkner is the master of Warren's prose, a study prefixed to the most recent edition of *Farewell to Arms;* the long essay on the *Ancient Mariner* which appeared in part in *Kenyon,* Summer 1946; his first book, a re-estimate of John Brown, a little obvious in its ironies but showing his eternal concern with history and motivation; of his shorter work, his first published fiction *Prime Leaf* and, perhaps, *Blackberry Winter;* his textbook, done with Cleanth Brooks, *Understanding Poetry,* which has destroyed the long tyranny of Tennyson and Longfellow for a generation of college students; and, especially, his poetry, unread and even unseen by those of his readers outside of a few large cities and college towns (as a start, *Eleven Poems on the Same Theme* and *The Ballad of Billie Potts*).

In light of the whole corpus, any single work within it is seen as at once more complex and more lucid. One should begin with *Billie Potts* and the *Eleven Poems,* for they state most clearly the first of his two compulsive themes: Original Sin.

In a score of fables, Warren has tried to re-create our sense of awakening into a web of guilt and responsibility we never made, and our dawning consciousness that we, knowing or unknowing, in every act extend and involve that web for lives of which we may never be aware.

Unable to bear the burden, most of us attempt to flee toward an imagined innocence, pursuing the Ideal, maintaining the illusion of Time. Time is beginnings only, the forever new, the mirage of innocence, the Dream; in terms of America, the Dream of an inexhaustible West. And "had we but World enough and Time," that illusion could be projected forever, kept aloft in an eternal juggling act. But we carry with us, beside the Dream, the Nightmare, "Nodding, its great head rattling like a gourd,/And locks like seaweed strung on stinking stone . . . ," the knowledge of our death, our limitation and the sign of our Fall. And at last, in despair at the failure of escape, we accept the brute world, turn back to nature, go home, hoping to exorcise our haunting by returning to the place of its origin; and at the point of no-Time our parents await us, not in welcome, but in the Oedipus horror, the son killing the father like Jack Burden, or slain by him like Little Billie Potts; the womb holds not peace but the death we did not suspect we wanted, the "mistake" plotted from our beginnings.

The pattern of flight and return, often capitulated in a single life, becomes in America the rhythm of our history, the Westward movement of the fathers, and the sons hunting the past for a vanished certainty. In a poem called "History," Warren sees his own concern, the rummaging in the past, the writing of historical novels, as a part of this archetypal pattern,

> *Though some,*
> *Of all most weary,*
> *Most defective of desire,*
> *Shall grope toward time's cold womb;*
> *In dim pools peer*
> *To see, of some grandsire*
> *The long and toothéd jawbone greening there. . . .*

The passage is typical not only in its self-deprecatory irony, but also in the imagery common to the novels and the verse. As the symbols of illusory Innocence are roads and rivers, the "strip" down which Sugar Boy drives Willie, and the streams penetrating virgin land, so Home is a quiet water, a dim pool or the deep underneath of a lake, even Jeremiah Beaumont's last dismal swamp.

In the realm of public life, the denial of the Fall is the politics of the Idealist who tries to impose on the Nightmare world the purity of the Dream. To ignore the real evil of the world, or to try by force to make it fit some abstract vision of good, leads to a terrible adoration of the self. Yet the problem confronts us always: how to accomplish justice in a world of iniquity, where not only the means available are corrupt, but the very knowledge and will of the self-imagined reformer corrupted from the start. To the moralist like Warren, the act can never be judged pragmatically by its fruits, but only by its motives, the state of the will that puts it in motion. And are such motives really knowable?

The ineluctable ambiguity of justice is the second central theme of Warren's work. To his very first published fiction, Warren prefixed the tag from Horace that mocks Spense 's Romantic dream of a Golden Age when Truth was simp e and apparent. "Nor is nature able to distinguish between iniquity and justice, as it separates the good from the bad, and what is to be sought from what is to be avoided." The illusion of a primal innocence makes living possible for those who cannot face up to the fact that experience is ambiguous, truth elusive, the only certainty that we are born to sin and death.

And yet (to use a favorite figure of Warren's) there is a jewel in the forehead of the toad Adversity—the jewel of hope: the stoical, tragic hope that acceptance triumphs over fate as in the cases of Cass Mastern or Jeremiah Beaumont; and beyond that, the Christian hope that death is only a new definition, that the dream of Innocence thus redefined may be a partially understood truth. It is simple people who grasp this hope with certainty in Warren, Ashby Wyndham of *At Heaven's Gate* or Munn Short in *World Enough and Time*. "Body dyin hit ain't nuthin. . . . But dyin what ain't body, hit is different. Hit begins and hit don't stop. Till Jesus come in my heart. Red rose don't brag in the dark, but hit shore smell sweet, and Jesus lays in my heart in the dark and is sweet-smellin." In the direct lyrical statement, the perception of grace is more qualified and ambiguous, "That hope: for there are testaments/That men, by prayer, have mastered grace. . . ."

There is no hope, though, short of the abandonment of the dream; and insofar as Romanticism is pledged to the mirage of a natural Innocence, Warren is anti-Romantic. If his latest book is called a "Romantic Novel" to the confusion of some critics, it is as an irony, a truth to be understood on the second convolution. His whole work is a critique of Romanticism, whether it be an explicit defense of John Donne and a deflation of Shelley, or "just a story." In the "impure" art of Warren, the Garden into which his lovers enter is the Garden of Shakespeare and not of Tennyson. What Romeo and Juliet momentarily forget within the wall, Mercutio remembers outside, and the Nurse mutters in the bedroom: the toad is as real as the rose, the chancre as true as the moon.

What makes the anti-sentimental, ironic Robert Penn Warren palatable to the mass audience, which instinctively prefers the easiest romanticisms, the lushest sentimentalities; and asserts that they detest "ideas" in fiction? Warren's appeal depends primarily upon his deep flair for narrative, an instinct not merely for "telling a good yarn," which is within the scope of the weariest hack, but of touching archetypal plot material that embodies, quite apart from any explicit statement, ultimate mythic meanings. The author who can exploit plot significance, concrete meaning beside abstract, has a *chance* at least of reaching the great public whose responses and perceptions, where they have not been already vulgarized, are still more *mythos* than *logos*. Such great modern fictionists as Mann and Joyce, even Proust, have surrendered the direct use of the fable—and can move relatively few, though those deeply. To the naturalist, the pragmatist, the nominalist, plot can only be a "machine" and must in honesty be abandoned; but to the believer in the reality of guilt and grace, the "fable" with its immemorial reversals and recognitions is the formal vestige of a way of believing and a celebration of belief. The hunger for plot among the people is a hunger for ritual satisfaction, and the writer who can feed their hunger without condescension may satisfy them and his own alienated self at the same time. Besides Warren, only Graham Greene and perhaps Faulkner among contemporaries have this talent.

In the world of Shakespeare or the Greek dramatists, playwrights were happliy *required* to draw on a body of archetypal material; in our world, it is only with great daring that they can attempt to kidnap for high art such popular, mythic forms as the "thriller" or the "historical romance." Warren has moved uncertainly, fumblingly in this direction. In *Night Rider* he touches his authentic material, but apparently without knowing it; in *At*

Heaven's Gate, the most incoherent of his books, he loses it almost completely; in *All the King's Men,* he exploits a modern instance of the myth of the tragic hero, vaguely adumbrated in the life of Huey Long (had not three or four popular novelists already compulsively approached it?). But before his current novel, he seems to have clearly realized his proper subject matter and approach only in *The Ballad of Billie Potts,* a poetic version of a story, told in a score of literatures as "true," and for all one can tell erupting again and again from the fable into "real life," the account of the son of murdering innkeepers, who returns home rich and unrecognizable and is murdered for his money by his mother and father before he confesses his identity.*

The story is told on two levels, the actual instance in a rich colloquial language tied to the time and place of nineteenth-century Kentucky, and in a more universal and abstract vocabulary by an ironic observer detached in time. This device of the double vision was not possible in *All the King's Men,* except partially in the Cass Mastern episode, for Jack Burden was at once too close to the events on which he comments and too individualized to be the ideal "trapped spectator," in whom the death of Willie accomplishes the catharsis that justifies its terror.

In *World Enough and Time,* as in *Billie Potts,* the "trapped spectator" is impersonal and contemporaneous with us, becomes in fact *us,* a reinvented Chorus looking back through time at the archetypal situation, invested in its Byronic dress: the lover Jeremiah Beauchamp, who slays the seducer of the "wronged" woman he marries, for inextricably tangled reasons, personal and political. This episode, an actual case already written about by many writers from Simms to Poe, is held to its historical context, the semi-frontier of Kentucky in the 1820s, in a series of pseudo-quotations, fixed in the period diction. Read simply, the case seems to us melodramatic and a little ridiculous; so that the ironic commentator, who is our deputy, is driven to reconstruct in the light of our current psychologies the hidden motives that might really have produced so fantastic an appearance.

* Interestingly enough, this story is retold twice by Albert Camus— once, by the way, in *The Stranger,* and once as the main plot of a play, *Le Malentendu* (*Cross-Purpose*).

But the quotation from *The Faerie Queene* which prefixes the novel indicates that this is merely one more avatar of an eternal myth: the Knight-Errant slaying the Dragon (who is also, Freud save us, the Father) to rescue an incarcerated and tormented Princess. And, in still another sense, it is the account of a Dostoevskian doubter of his own motives, the victim of a literary tradition (Byron possesses the imaginations of the protagonists like an evil spirit) imposing an archetypal pattern on the resistant facts of experience; forcing a neurotic "Princess" to command him to kill, forcing himself to believe the gentle and sensitive Colonel Fort a true Dragon. In the interplay of archetype and fact, and in the movement of the commentator back and forth between various fictional times and our own, the time which seems to the characters so real is revealed as the nothingness it truly is. Behind the dreamlike, compulsive repetitions of the mythic pattern, we glimpse eternity, the "unwinking eye." And we learn finally what the "historical novel" has all the time been trying to *mean* through its costumes and nostalgia. When that form has been rid of sentimentality, it can serve us as a mirror that destroys time and shows in the experience of the past what we cannot perceive in the flux of the present: the typical mechanisms of self-confusion and damnation, of illumination and hope.

If *World Enough and Time* has any major flaw, it is the insistence on remaining still a novel—the expected, popular form; for it constantly aspires to become a narrative poem, an epic. One feels that the finally successful work toward which Warren has been groping will finally accept what is for narrative in our time, alas, the *burden* of verse. Certainly, Warren's imagery and command of texture, his concern with music and pattern, his sensitivity to language, all demand the freer scope and tighter discipline of poetic form. Perhaps his talent and skill, which have redeemed the metaphysical novel for the mass audience, may accomplish as much for the serious verse narrative.

II. Seneca in the Meat-House

Originally a review of
Brother to Dragons

To read *Brother to Dragons* is to experience the uneasy sense of familiarity we have sometimes in a repeated dream, the impression that we have moved through the same climate before in other utterly forgotten nights. The fable is new: the brutal murder of a Negro by two brothers for a trivial reason and their agreement to shoot each other over their mother's grave; and the reaction to that event of the murderers' uncle, Thomas Jefferson. The event is historical, the reaction imagined; the crime in time, the reflection upon it in a limbo of memory where the participants in the action and the poet can converse together. It is the rhetoric which seems familiar, the pitch of terror, the resonance of the words that try to encompass it.

To one who has followed Warren from nightmare to nightmare, his new poem is a reminder that there is only a single bad dream from which he has always striven to awake to art, a suggestion that perhaps for all of us there is a single archetypal experience of terror, unsayable and, therefore, forever to be said. This is not quite the point that the critics continue to make about Warren's works, observing that he returns to the same themes of Justice and Guilt, to the same reflections on the ambiguity of History, to the same exploitation of the dissonance between the intent of an act in time and its infinitely echoing meaning, to the same symbolisms of West and East, Wilderness and City, to the same Faulkner-ridden milieu.

These are the excrescences of something deeper, and by themselves suggest only an accidental entrapment, an obsession harmful to art. The reader of Warren who sees just so far is tempted to suggest that it might be well for him to find other concerns, to move on. . . . But his major theme seems to me to be precisely the paucity of possible themes, the terrible singleness

of the truth under the multiplicity of our lies, the ineffable one-
ness of Nightmare, or, as he preferred to call it in an early poem,
Original Sin.

Everyone is aware of the diversity of techniques with which
Warren attempts to formulate his single vision (his "aghast"
vision, I am tempted to say; for the adjective out of Faulkner
inescapably offers itself), a profusion of means that ends finally
in an almost indifference to means. The same fable is worked
as a poem, a play in verse, a play in prose, a novel (as in *All the
King's Men*), as if to demonstrate that the inexpressibility is a
part of the essential meaning. The title of an early collection of
verse can be extended to the whole corpus of his writing simply
by changing the number, *Eleven Poems on the Same Theme*.

> *. . . There is no form to hold*
> *Reality and its insufferable intransigence.*

Brother to Dragons contains the relics of a ballad that was
its first formulation, and a confession of the inadequacy of that
form.

> *. . . I once intended*
> *To make a ballad of them long ago.*
> *And I remember how the thing began:*
> > *The two brothers sat by the sagging fire.*
> > *Lilburn and Isham sat by the fire,*
> > *For it was lonesome weather.*

The poem itself, its fable and rhetoric, lives cannibalistically
amidst the ruins of other fables and rhetorics; for to Warren not
even his successes succeed finally, but must be consumed in the
next attempt.

I have the feeling that this would be an incomprehensible
poem to anyone who had not read the earlier novels, the lyric
poems and *The Ballad of Billie Potts*; certainly, the tone, the
almost hysterical pitch would seem to an uninformed reader excessive, as would the melodramatic occasion itself. No one would
scream like this who is trying to tell us something for the first

time; the voice behind *Brother to Dragons* neither sings nor
narrates nor speaks (I am talking about the over-all voice into
which all the other admirably modulated voices blend) but
insists, *insists!* This is a bombastic poem in the technical sense
of the word: bombast as in Seneca or the Jacobean dramatists,
a straining of language and tone toward a scream which can no
longer be heard, the absolute cry of bafflement and pain. Such a
tone becomes in Warren, as in Seneca or Torneur or Thomas
Lovell Beddoes, ridiculous on occasion, ridiculous whenever we
lapse from total conviction. Even the simple act of urinating
beside the road is turned into a little melodrama:

> *. . . stopped just once to void the bladder,*
> *And in that stunning silence after the tire's song*
> *The July-fly screamed like a nerve gone wild,*
> *Screamed like a dentist's drill, and then a million*
> *Took up the job, and in that simultaneous outrage*
> *The sunlight screamed, while urine spattered the parched soil.*

It is a Senecan tragedy that Warren has composed, a play
that cannot be played, a poem that must be imagined as acted
in the high, ranting style, complete with ghosts and prophecies
and dire forebodings, shakings of the earth and raw skulls, sui-
cides and obscene murders and crimes too horrible to define.
The real climax of action is, in this sense, not the explicit act in
the meat-house, but the unutterable Thing performed by Lilburn on his wife.

> *There's just no name to lay to the worst things,*
> *And that's what makes them worse than anything,*
> *For if they had a name, then you could name it.*
> *At least to name it would be something then,*
> *If you could bear to name it . . .*
> >   *And it was an awful thing*
> *I didn't even know the name of, or heard tell—*
> *Or if I had heard tell, I'd plain forgot,*
> *It was so awful that folks could do so awful.*
> *But when he did it, even if I'd never heard,*

It came just like an awful remembering
Like it had happened long back, not now, not now . . .

Here, for the first time, his form has allowed Warren to use all the trappings proper to the shrillness of his need. *All the King's Men* suffered not only because its hysterical rhetoric had to be disguised as the tough-guy patter of Jack Burden, but because its historicity prevented the appearance on stage of gibbering ghosts and portents out of nature. Even the considerably superior *World Enough and Time* permitted itself only a literary, metaphorical dragon; and the excuse of its Romantic milieu did not quite justify the more than Byronic bombast.

In *Brother to Dragons*, Warren has found the form most nearly suiting his obsessive theme, and it is consequently his most convincing and moving work. The Nightmare appears almost nakedly as Nightmare, disrupted only by the appearance of Jefferson as its improbable dreamer. We are upset finally not only because of the too easy triumph of the poet over the dead apostle of perfectibility; but even more because the obvious irony of a Rousseauist confronted by the Fall is a little beside the authentic point of the poem; and chiefly because the stubborn historicity cannot be purged out of Jefferson, who remains the history-book image of a waking man interpolated into a dream.

The unredeemable public nature of the Jeffersonian imago (and this is true also of the Meriweather Lewis who makes a brief appearance) tends to reduce Lilburn Lewis and his little brother, Aunt Cat and the dismembered slave to participants in a backwoods horror story. If the figure on the chopping block is chopped forever, the fable and the bombast work; if it happened once (and the reference to the records, the givenness of the case are either a frivolous irony or a mistake) nothing could be less important. No, the truth of the event must be consonant with the unexplained booming Lewis and Clark heard in the mountains, with the dog that rooted up the telltale bone, with the earthquake that struck at the very moment of the crime. To accept the rhetoric we must accept the fable; to accept the fable we must accept the ghosts. The factual notes are a tic that has survived an attitude, the last stand of the Archivist, the character who becomes confused with the protagonist in almost all of Warren's books.

I suppose Warren felt the need to root the Nightmare into experience, to insist on its naturalistic surfaces; but for this end, much more tactful and effective are the touches that bind the fable to the relationship of the poet and his aged father, to the personal pain of some barely hinted personal tragedy and to the change of season (real and mythical at once) that open and close the poem.

We have come somehow to believe that bombast and melodrama are hopelessly corrupted, that these shrill, honorable means are in themselves despicable. But we need them to complete our sense of ourselves, to do justice to the absurdity of terror, its failure to be well-behaved. That Warren has handled them with skill and poignancy in a time of careful and genteel poets, that he has made for perhaps the first time in a hundred years a successful long poem of them (Faulkner has, of course, exploited them dazzlingly in the novel), must be said first of all. It is because no one else has been making this point that I have foregone for its sake comments on the philosophical implications of the poem (the notion of a natural Fall and a natural Virtue, and of the glory born of their confrontation), or the handling of character and narrative (which have been sufficiently applauded), in order to praise the skill and courage with which Warren has pursued a difficult, improbable, heartbreaking rhetoric.

III. Fiction as Opera

Originally a review of
Band of Angels

Robert Penn Warren occupies a unique and baffling position in the history of our recent literature. He belongs to an interim generation, a group easy to ignore, caught between Faulkner,

Hemingway and Fitzgerald on the one hand and those whom we call, with greater or less latitude, our "young writers" on the other. It is not so much a matter of the year in which he was born as of a myth of himself: immune to the disenchantment of World War I and to the lure of expatriation, he has also not been touched by Marxist notions of alienation or the dream of a high bohemia of elegance and taste. He represents a line of development which begins with Faulkner's vision of the South as the landscape proper to the terror of us all; but he is not what we ordinarily mean these days by a "Southern Writer," not one of those feminizing Faulknerians, who via Katherine Anne Porter and Eudora Welty have burgeoned into the full-blown epicene school.

Warren, however, manages to preserve the shrillness of Faulknerian tone, the provinciality of his diction and the sense of a rhetoric more controlled by passion than design. He is, indeed, the only serious contemporary writer I know able to achieve the typical Faulknerian corkscrew motion of action, that inward and downward circling toward a climax of horror, which makes of plot an outward symbol of our inward flight from and attraction toward the revelation of guilt. But the author who clings to plotting remains by that token closer to the semiliterate reader than any exponent of sensibility; and this is by no means the only "popular" aspect of Warren's art. He is different from Faulkner in this respect, but no less sympathetic to those lovers of a "good story" so often baffled by current literature; for he has relinquished the hunting yarn, the comic folk tale of sharp dealing and the detective story only to substitute for them the Historical Romance, the debased and apparently unredeemable Bosom Book. We should be aware, however, that Warren's turning to the Historical Romance is an accommodation neither mercenary nor naïve; he exploits it for sophisticated and strategic ends.

In one of his roles, the extremely versatile Warren has stood for a long time as a representative New Critic—which is to say, an embattled highbrow; and his name is associated with the new Metaphysicals who once gathered around the *Southern Review*, Ransom, Tate, etc. The nonacademic reader may not realize that with Cleanth Brooks, Warren is the author of a book of readings and commentary which has done more than any other single text to make the kind of poetry and critical approach associated with T. S. Eliot standard in the freshman classroom. It is significant, I think, that Warren's chief critical accomplishment be such a piece of mediation between avant-garde aesthetics and practical pedagogy. There is something in him that longs to close gaps.

Warren is more than a critic and pedagogue turned novelist; he is also a poet of subtlety and distinction, who has long hesitated between prose and verse as a favorite narrative form and has finally achieved a special brand of heightened language, intermediate between verse and mannered prose, which can be drawn upon indifferently for a poem like *Brother to Dragons* or a novel like *Band of Angels.*

I have been convinced for a long time that Warren was feeling his way toward a form which would be neither prose nor poetry, but I have never been able to find a metaphor to define it. Since reading *Band of Angels,* I have become aware that what he has been approaching for so long is something not very different from nineteenth-century Italian opera: a genre full of conventional absurdities, lapses of good taste, strained and hectic plots—all aimed at becoming myth and melody. Though I feel deeply the *necessity* of such a contrivance and respect the courage of Warren's attempt, I am not quite sure that either the novel or the long poem intended to be read as a novel can stand such a metamorphosis.

Given the vast distances of the opera house as it has evolved, the glare of lights and the stir of the audience, one can accept the bellowing, the gilt trimmings, even the vulgarities as finally satisfactory, part of a gross but coherent whole. In the intimate situation of reading a novel, however, there is not enough public rumor, not enough basic space to save the illusion. I see the grease paint; I am aware of the contrived effects; I cannot believe in the pasteboard sets. Or rather, by fits and starts I am carried away; and then my doubt returns. There is, at last, no sufficient poetry, perhaps no way of attaining it, to make an equivalent for the music into which all the oafishness and coarseness of effect of the opera flow and are redeemed.

Introducing Cesare Pavese

At the moment when Italy is becoming for us a country of the imagination, a contemporary cultural fact for the first time in perhaps fifty years, we have a special obligation to come to terms with the writer who moves her newest authors most deeply, who seems to them, indeed, to have defined their newness, their very function. Cesare Pavese is that writer, the best of recent Italian novelists, though so far less known and honored in our country than Moravia, Vittorini, Berto or Pratolini—in some quarters even ranked under a sentimental entertainer like Guareschi, the creator of the insufferable Don Camillo. We have been slowly graduating from the notion that under Mussolini the Italian novel died except as maintained in exile by Ignazio Silone, confessing that both the overestimation of the author of *Fontamara* and the blindness to his contemporaries which sustained it were primarily the products of political piety rather than critical insight. And we have begun reprinting such books as Moravia's *The Indifferent Ones* (rechristened *The Time of Indifference*), which in the thirties we ignored, as if recognition of the merits of an Italian novelist who had not fled his country would have betrayed the anti-Fascist cause.

But Pavese has been reached late in our current rediscovery of the Italian fiction of the last twenty years; indeed, he was translated last among contemporary writers of merit, so that the publication of *The Moon and The Bonfires*, his major novel,* has an almost inescapable sense of representing just "another Italian book" to be received with the enthusiasm or dismay proper to one's reaction to recent Italian novels in general. Though I feel bound to write chiefly about the single novel available to Americans who read no Italian, I feel an obligation to put it back

* Since the publication of this essay, *Among Women Only* and *The Devil in the Hills* have been released in paperback editions, but they have not succeeded in stimulating a general interest in or understanding of Pavese.

355

into the context of Pavese's whole work and his prototypical life, in order to rescue it from the misleading general context into which it has been cast by chance and the extra-artistic calculations of the publishers.

Read by itself, in translation and especially between the covers of the twenty-five-cent reprint (whose cover portrays not the world of the book but our latest legendary Italy, all *vino* and sex and red peppers), the story scarcely betrays the poetic and problematical qualities which made the publishers hesitate so long before committing the book to the market. The brief introduction by Paolo Milano is not enough, despite some just observations, to offset the effect of the translation itself, which seems not so much technically bad as *critically* wrong in the writer it finds and tries, without much grace, to English; just another young Italian exploiter of sex and violence and the sentimental myth of the Resistance.

Poetry, however, notoriously escapes translation, and insofar as Pavese is the most poetic of recent Italian fictionists, he is doomed somewhat to be misrepresented; but he has also a more viable quality of contemporaneity which should survive translation, and which distinguishes him sharply from all other recent Italian writers (with the possible exception of Vittorini), who either present shabby counterfeits of modernity or are solidly old-fashioned in ways no longer available to quite serious writers among us. Moravia is an instance of the latter; he has been grotesquely misrepresented for Americans by being introduced in such advanced periodicals as *Partisan Review;* though he is actually, for all his grim frankness, technically timid—a sort of Italian Somerset Maugham who, being Italian, must look rather more like de Maupassant than our own bourgeois traditionalists.

We are apt to be a little casual about contemporaneity—perhaps a little disenchanted with it, since it is the easiest of graces for our own writers (indeed, it sometimes seems for us not a virtue but a fate, even a curse); in Italy, however, the symbolic abstractness and the peculiar violence toward language which modernity implies demand an almost superhuman effort of the will—and result in a tension in the diction itself which disappears in translation. To be contemporary, in the field of the novel at least, is, as Pavese discovered quite early, to be American—a feat, comprehensibly enough, not as impressive (or as disturbing) to us as to the Italians. What seems at first ironical—namely, that Pavese, who is to the Italians their chief "Americanist," * should have been recognized so late by the Americans themselves—seems in light of the foregoing observations natural, perhaps inevitable.

To understand Pavese at all, we must learn to see in him as strangeness what strikes us as most familiar, his "Americanism." All his life, he pursued or retreated from a legendary America, a legendary American Novel, *the* American Novel. Pavese never made an actual journey to the United States; his older, pro-Fascist contemporary Emilio Cecchi had in a book of essays called *America Amara* (*Bitter America*) turned a real visit to this country into a fact of the imagination; and that mythical America, half-dreamed, half-discovered in our literature, proved sufficient to the young men of Pavese's generation, who judged quite differently but did not trouble to redream Cecchi's America.

Cecchi had found in our quite alien culture the threat of anarchy, the nightmare of modernity; younger anti-Fascist Italians like Pavese found in it a promise of freedom, cultural as well as political, a clue to a new kind of literary tradition, "a tradition of seeking tradition," to set against their own official culture, the legendary Mediterranean past which, under Fascist auspices, was being transformed from a museum to a prison. Insofar as Pavese's Americanism was a politics, it was doomed by its Utopian contempt for facts not to survive a contact with real Americans, the intrusion of our troops as liberators and occupiers of Italian soil; though for a while it provided the possibility of writing anti-Fascist polemics in the guise of literary criticism. But insofar as that Americanism was an aesthetics, a search for the secret of contemporaneity, it was a lifelong commitment that survived Pavese's conversion to Communism and his latter-day concern with myth.

The real unity which is discoverable in Pavese's work under its superficial shifts from realism to regionalism, from the political

---

* Recently there has been a misguided (and thoroughly unconvincing) attempt to prove Pavese not "American" at all, but *Italianissimo*. It is just another sign of his success, his becoming an established author.

to the archetypal, is his preoccupation with the meanings of America; as essayist, poet, novelist, translator and critic, his chief effort was directed toward defining, discovering an America for his country and his time. The assimilation of Melville to the Italian imagination, the long effort which has finally made a nine-teenth-century American writer a living force in contemporary Italian fiction, was not begun by Pavese, but realized itself chiefly in his astonishingly successful translation of *Moby Dick* and in his various essays on Melville; while his total body of critical work, gathered together posthumously, has established for the younger Italians a new canon of American literature. There are certain absurdities in the process by which the individual preferences and blindnesses of a single man (his misguided enthusiasm for Edgar Lee Masters and O. Henry, for example— as well as his juster estimates of Anderson, Gertrude Stein, Hemingway, etc.) have achieved the status of an orthodoxy; but there is something impressive, too, in the singlehanded achieve-ment. I do not mean, of course, that other Italian writers have not commented illuminatingly on American literature (Vittorini comes immediately to mind), or that there have not been a host, a very plague of imitators of the techniques and themes of our contemporary novel, but that, for better or worse, the taste which controls and the values which judge this widespread enterprise are essentially Pavese's.

At a certain point, Pavese even attempted to throw his weight against an Americanism that had been transformed from an aesthetic quest to a fad, a tic of Italian literature. Impelled partly by political reasons (he was then a Communist), but partly, too, by a sense of how parodies of Saroyan and Heming-way had become themselves a sterile tradition (there was for a while at least a prize offered every year by Hemingway for the best of these parodies—technically for the best novel by a younger writer), he declared that "the days are over in which we discovered America," and went on to insist on the multiplicity of available traditions, adding finally that he himself had found through translation and study of American authors chiefly how *not* to write—a purely negative definition of his situation as an Italian writer.

It is certainly true that various specific problems of the Italian writer remain outside the scope of the American example. The difficult relationship between the continually invented literary language of Italy and the dialects her writers naturally speak is a case in point; and Pavese, like all Italian novelists since Manzoni, like all Italian poets since Dante created the problem, had to learn to graft into the "pure" language of art his own local speech, the Piedmontese. Even when he found on occasion cues for dealing with concerns common to Italy and America, these required special adaptations for the Italian scene. In Sherword Anderson, for instance, who was a special favorite, he came on certain strategies for treating the relationship between province and center which seemed to him, too, a major theme; but Pavese had to rework that theme in terms of a country dominated by an almost completely Fascized Rome (to Pavese any Roman writer is *culturally* a "Fascist," regardless of his avowed politics) in which certain sterile rhetorical ideals had joined with the urban "neutralization of nature" to produce a literature equally elegant and empty of belief; while in the provinces ritual and magic still persisted inside the forms of peasant life.

And yet in rhythm and movement, and in a conviction, an understanding of art that underlie both, Pavese's art, profoundly Italian as it is, is rooted in our literature and could not have existed without it. It is necessary, however, to be quite clear about what Pavese discovered or felt he had discovered in our novels; for it is easy to misunderstand his art utterly on the basis of a failure to comprehend what "Americanism" meant to him. The Italians have a misleading way of equating it with what they call "neo-realism," a term applied indifferently to the moving pictures of De Sica and the work of the younger novelists; and Pavese himself has compounded this confusion by referring (playfully to be sure, and in order to avoid making public judgments of his fellow novelists) to De Sica as the greatest of contemporary Italian storytellers. Now, insofar as "neo-realism" implies an immediacy, a frankness, a brutal and anti-rhetorical disavowal of the traditionally "artistic" subject, it illuminates equally the method of *Paesà* and of *The Moon and the Bonfires*; but insofar as it suggests that Pavese, who preferred Herodotus and Plato as "poets" to Homer and Sophocles, was content to remain on the observational and particularizing level of "realism," it is utterly misleading.

Pavese's impulse as an artist was toward a dimension he liked to call "mythic," a dimension he found in Melville and not in Flaubert. It is primarily through the author of *Moby Dick* that Pavese approaches American literature, and it is through him that he finds in our books an identity of word and thing that goes beyond mere anti-rhetorical immediacy to a special sort of symbolism: not the aristocratic *symbolisme* of the French, whose watchword is absolute transcendence and whose hero is the Dandy (the Italians had had their fill of this through the "angelic" and the "ineffable" of their own hermeticists)—but a democratic faith that a "colloquy with the masses" might be opened on the level of myth, whose unity underlies the diversity of our acquired cultures.

Just as American literature had found a third way between the European poles of naturalism and *symbolisme*, so Pavese felt we had found an escape from the dilemma of classicizing traditionalism and romantic rebellion, between academicism and futurism. The American artist, Pavese believed, had discovered how to reject conformism without becoming "a rebel in short pants," how to be at once free and mature. The clue to this new kind of maturity Pavese found in the "intemperate autobiographism" of American books. "They are," he wrote, "memoirs for which the real is not a datum, but an inexhaustible discovery. And here precisely is the secret of their excellence; while for our European art, maturity means customarily a coming to terms with the traditional-collective, a recognition of the limits and norms of a pre-existent historical classicism, and hence individual mythologies have previously been able to realize themselves only by celebrating an infantile anarchy—for the Americans even the age of maturity, the kingdom of history and conformity, has presented itself as an irrational to be resolved into symbolic clarity, a wilderness to be reduced to cultivation."

In our classic books, Pavese found a method for making biography symbol, for transforming the most private impulses of the heart into myths of social utility; and for him the first of these myths was the image of America itself, a legend of a search for freedom, which Pavese used in order to transcend the limits of his own personality, to move his obsessions from the level of confession to that of communication. But there were other public legends to which he turned to redeem his private anguish, especially Communism and the myth of the Resistance, the Italians' fable of themselves as their own sole deliverers. To admit an outside liberation would have destroyed the underpinning of their self-respect, the belief that their heroism had finally been equal to their guilt, that what they had themselves wished and suffered, the whole burden of Fascism, they had been able to throw off. To maintain this self-righteous myth, the Italians have been forced to deny in their imaginations (as they have come to deny in their political pronouncements) the very presence of Americans on their soil, except as invaders; and for Pavese, who embraced the new legend, America had to be transformed into the image of a false paradise, finally exposed as the land of universal lovelessness, alienation and discontent.

Toward the end of his life, Pavese seems to have been approaching a break with Communism, but to what new legend he was preparing to turn we can only guess. Certainly, there seems in him everywhere a baffled religiosity, and some of his fellow contributors to the magazine *Cultura e Realtà* have since become Catholics; that he would in some sense have remained political is indubitable; for he was political out of the instinct of self-preservation. Politics was never to Pavese a convenient source for literary themes and symbols, nor was it a natural expression of temperament and conviction, but the sole method for converting his hunger for an absolute freedom from a wish for death into a drive toward social commitment. At the deepest level, indeed, political activity remained for Pavese always a second-best to death—and he was drawn finally and inevitably at the age of forty-two to make the gesture he felt to be the only true action, the gesture of suicide.

Long before that final surrender, he had begun the struggle to force himself into public life, into the actual fight against Fascism. Under Mussolini he suffered first a brief term in prison, then confinement; and at the moment of the Civil War he took to the hills outside of Turin, to avoid allegiance to the last Fascist regime, the so-called Republic of Salo. This earlier activity, plus his post-war public role as a Communist propagandist, convinced many of his readers (especially, one suspects, the half-readers) that he was essentially a political figure; so that there was dismay and revulsion in certain quarters when the posthumous publication of his journals revealed how *willed,* how nearly irrelevant his politics had been. In the whole of the *Mestiere di vivere* (*The Art of Living*), there is only a single sentence devoted to a political question; as if in Pavese's deepest conversation with himself, that whole area of public discourse were excluded as trivial.

One is left with the portrait of a man buffeted between vanity and fear, of one turning from bouts of self-pity to vain attempts at breaking out of an isolation that public fame and recognition could not mitigate nor political allegiance qualify. A reader feels spasms of disgust toward the spoiled child who could scarcely reach out toward his friends, yet vilified them in private for failing him, alternating with impulses of pity toward the irredeemable outsider, incapable of any of the final commitments of love. The records of the marriages of women he had desired, notes on their children, the terrifying cry: "The last indignity— a woman who smells of sperm that is not your own"—all testify to a final impotence, physical and spiritual. His truest passion was for death, and even with this most desired bride, he could achieve no consummation for twenty years. From the earliest pages, the diaries record his longing for suicide, the overture to the long flirtation, the approaches and withdrawals, the self-reproaches for cowardice and the desperate excuse that to kill oneself would be to lose the pleasure of looking forward to death.

But finally the last book is completed, the most naked version of his life (his American prototypes had taught him that there is no other book), and with the entry, "No more talk!" he is ready for the ultimate, the only real Act. But Pavese's suicide could end only his own talk; to that of others it served as a new impetus—until the imagined pure action of his death became almost lost in the speculation about it. Some tried to make political capital of it as a *de facto* disavowal of Communism; others through gossip and psychologizing sought a clue to his failure in his deepest self; while still others, by a double twist, read that discovered self as a condemnation of the corrupt society which had conditioned it. On all sides, Pavese's suicide was felt as typical, legendary, an event in the world of culture as much as in that of his own personal anguish; so that for the Italians, his death has come to have a weight like that of Hart Crane's for us, a meaning that penetrates back into his own work and functions as a symbol in the literature of an age.

It is difficult to distinguish the facts of his end from the overlay of fictive elaboration: the girls who followed his coffin weeping, hoping to be taken for old mistresses, the self-appointed insiders who will tell you his "real secret." To have been associated with Pavese means for the younger writers in Italy to have been *there*, to have shared the mana of the god. But the figures who seem really to have presided over his death are, justly enough, three Americans: a movie starlet, a great writer long dead, a more recent suicide. The death of F. O. Matthiessen seems to have shaken Pavese enough to help precipitate his long-suspended decision to die; for in Matthiessen he thought he had discovered something of himself in pure American form, his own vision of the literature of the United States, his own desperate commitment to a politics of the masses, the terrible definition of maturity toward which he had been groping along his own lines. It is in the essay on Matthiessen, called "American Maturity," that Pavese quotes for the first time the line that was to become his touchstone, as its comprehension and acceptance had been for Matthiessen the touchstone of tragic greatness in literature: "ripeness is all . . ."—the verse, Pavese reminds us, which Melville had underscored in his copy of *King Lear*.

Matthiessen and Melville, and between them the Shakespearian line: these give to Pavese's suicide the aspect of a boast, an assertion that he had broken for one instant at least out of the trap of adolescence, attaining what he calls in a final essay "a level of just maturation, of perfect and virile equilibrium for the love of which, as the father of us all has already said

> *man must endure*
> *his going hence e'en as his coming hither;*
> *ripeness is all. . . ."*

But there is a third American who stands beside the poet and critic, the Hollywood starlet C., the last of Pavese's hopeless loves, the final avatar of the dream of America with which he could never be done—the phantom he could not grasp. There is a kind of bathos in the conjunction of Melville and C., a descent, at least, from the tragic to the pathetic, but for the sake of the whole legend of Pavese, she is of equal importance; and the inept, touching poem to her called "Last Blues," written in Pavese's uncertain English (he would have said American), survives as his truest epitaph.

> *Twas only a flirt*
> *you sure did know—*
> *some one was hurt*
> *long time ago.*
>
> .   .   .
>
> *Some one has died*
> *long time ago—*
> *some one who tried*
> *but didn't know.*

It is with this mythicized Pavese that we must finally come to rest, lest we are betrayed into taking the figure of the diaries as his real self. The greatest of all errors would be to read the image he confided to his journal as a kind of giveaway; to suppose that the anguished, vanity-driven creature incapable of love was somehow more real than the public man who committed himself each day by an act of will to the almost impossible feat of living in the world of events and others. It is the special heroism of Pavese that despite his temperamental aversion to all things public, he not merely dreamed himself but, in however limited a way, *was* a political man. And yet to see that political man as his final transcendence, or even to find his identity in the dialectical interplay of his private and public roles, would be still a mistake. Pavese felt his life, as he understood his work, to be threefold: individual, communal, mythic—private anguish, public commitment and the death which gives to both their ultimate meanings. The rhythm of life, he seems to have been convinced, must be realized by the finality of suicide, as the rhythm of the poem is set by the finality of publication; and with his final gesture he turned himself quite deliberately into a person "sacred" in the anthropologist's sense: one who represents "once and for all" an experience forever unique no matter how often recounted or how widely shared.

One does not have to *impose* on Pavese these terms out of the no man's land between anthropology and literature; that marginal terrain he made his own. Especially toward the end of his life, the concern with myth became his central one, and he wrote a double series of essays on the subject, exploratory and apologetic. For he had not only to find in the modern anthropologists and in Giambattista Vico a theory of myth, but also to defend that theory against his Communist critics who felt in his preoccupation a concealed disloyalty, a desertion to hermeticism and mystification. Undaunted, Pavese proceeded from speculation on myth to a general theory of literature based on that speculation; and though inevitably his system is a rationalization and defense of his own instinctive ways of working, it possesses also a more general applicability. Certainly, it is revealing to watch how an Italian, conditioned by Vico, though committed on the one hand to American "realism" and on the other to Communist social theory, comes to terms with the problem confronted everywhere in contemporary literature at its best, in Mann, in Kafka, in Yeats and in Eliot.

Great literature, Pavese came to believe, moves us because what it reveals to us is felt as remembered as well as discovered, felt "for a second time"; yet the "first time" is known only by implication, in a sense never existed, except mythically, for it occurred before time began for us, in childhood when we do not know our experiences but are them. From this it follows that a work of literature, though it has to deal with parochial and local forms, things rendered as they are known "for the second time," does not finally depend for its force and conviction on "truth" of action, character or detail, but upon how much of the daemonic energy of the myth survives its rationalization. A work of art is successful insofar as it can recapture for us the "state of grace" which as children we live and as adults we know,

when before a stream, a hill, a holiday or birthday, we experience
(that is to say, remember-create) the inexhaustible reality of the
unique event, which is there forever, because it was there "for
the first time." The evocation of the sacred event (the ritual) and
the sacred place (the shrine), and the *knowing* of them (this is
what distinguishes art from religion) is the chief function of a
poem.

His sense of the obligation of the artist to myth leads Pavese
in one main line of his work to become more and more abstract,
to abandon ever more the fable in favor of the ritual, until in
Feria d'agosto (*Summer Holiday*), a series of stories, essays and
poems (the genre is indifferent) are worked into a musical
confrontation as three hypostasized themes: the Sea, the City
and the Vine; while in the *Dialogues with Leuko,* the book which
Pavese considered his most significant work and which is surely
his most beautiful, his most achieved effort, action has disappeared completely, and the characters have become "beautiful
names, charged with a destiny but not a psychological character,"
who confront each other two by two to discuss certain classic
myths in all their "problematic and anguished ambiguity."

As a matter of fact, Pavese himself insisted that all of his
books were essentially as little realistic as the *Dialogues,* that
in every one "the theme is the rhythm of what happens." But
this contention taken alone is misleading; for, certainly, the line
of books which reaches its climax in *The Moon and the Bonfires*
has a tension between the temporal and the ritual lacking in
the *Dialogues.* These novelistic books are by no means merely
their metaphysics; but are full of jokes, local excitement, incest,
murder, religion, politics, scenery, dialectics and poetry. It is
true enough that *finally* every village fair becomes the Fair, every
hill, the Hill—and even every life, Life, or as Pavese preferred
to say, Destiny; and that therefore every book, even the most
novelistic, is *at last* a dialogue between symbolic worlds, with
their appropriate rhythms and images: the Hill and the Sea, the
City and the Village, Virtue and Vice, the Child and the World,
the Moon and the Bonfires . . . But before the "finally," the "at
last," there is room enough for all the accidents of grace, for
the unpredictable collaboration of luck with art.

It is profitable in this light to compare Pavese's earliest work with his latest, to see what he did with certain characteristic themes before he really knew what they were trying to declare or had acquired the skill to control them. In *Paesi tuoi* (1941), all his compulsive situations, the very ones he will be manipulating still in his last novel *The Moon and the Bonfires* (1950), already exist but as mere obsessions and titillations, rendered in a tough, nervous style, self-consciously "American." The novel smacks of Erskine Caldwell in its gratuitous brutality, its pretended realism which is really an exoticism of the sordid. The story, seen through the eyes of a city-bred mechanic, deals with a peasant who ends by killing with a pitchfork the sister with whom he has been sleeping, when she tells him to use a dipper instead of drinking water directly out of a pail.

Implicit in the conception is a confrontation of City and Farm which is scarcely worked out, and the whole complicated fable of guilt and betrayal eventuates in detached images of violence which cry out to stand for something, but instead merely betray the writer's personal rage and frustration. The girl is obviously killed because her sexuality frightens Pavese, and must be at once penetrated and subdued, canceled out in blood; while the craftiness and brutality of peasant life (a whole society turning on the question of who will *fregare* whom, in all the senses of the word) is exploited only to reveal the author's sense of his own exclusion, his outsidedness. Under the hard-boiled surfaces, it is the book of a terrified adolescent who can believe in society only as his private nightmare.

But when in *The Moon and the Bonfires* Pavese returns for the last time to his familiar violated landscape, the same Piedmontese river and hill, to the compulsive themes of the beautiful girl slain in the full flush of her sexuality and the almost pointless violence of peasant life, the blood under the fig tree—the valence of the images has changed. To begin with, Pavese has reached the peak of his mature style (which must be taken on faith through the translation), the control of prose rhythms which makes his language at once absolutely lucid and completely incantatory, weaving into the texture of the sentences the sense of remembering rather than inventing, of returning to something impossibly remote yet knowing it for the first time.

But more than this, there is the feeling that Pavese is at last the master rather than the victim of his obsessions, that he has finally found a way to transform his realization of all that separates him from society and its typical experiences into a breakthrough to communication, a communion which must mean recognition and success. Pavese was, of course, never really read by large numbers of ordinary readers; he remained to the end a writer of the avant-garde, regarded by his nominal comrades with mingled pride and suspicion; but he seems at least to have felt that in his last books he had escaped the prison of himself and was opening that "colloquy with the masses" which could only be completed when the people as a whole had achieved a cultural emancipation to match his emotional one.

He had, at any rate, first politicized, then mythicized his themes: seeing the violence of the peasant now as a function of the *miseria* bred by the social system and upheld by the church; while the murdered enchantress became a symbol of the double agent, beauty as the whore of both sides in the struggle for social justice, and finally the accomplice of the Fascists. The death of all that is most desired becomes transformed into a brutal civic necessity, a crime which is also a deliverance, and toward which one must feel in unequal balance guilt and righteousness. But Pavese is not content to rest his case on social arguments, sensing that violence may merely call up counterviolence in an endless regress, and that crimes which depend upon a postulated future to justify them may remain merely crimes when that future fails or is fumbled. It is on magical grounds that he finally stands, equating the death and burning of the beautiful daughter of a disappearing ruling class with the bonfires lighted to ensure, not practically but ritually, the fertility of the earth.

For all the obliqueness of its reference, *The Moon and the Bonfires* is the most autobiographical of Pavese's fictions, almost cannibalistic in its effect; as if having been victimized by his life and having learned to control it, he wants now to consume it in a final fiction. The dedication of the book is "To C." and its epigraph the quotation that is Pavese's suicide note to the world: "Ripeness is all." The protagonist is called "the American," for he is returning, as the action begins, from a sojourn in America, as Pavese has returned to his own native earth from his imaginary expedition to the New World. There is irony in the plight of the returner, a bastard who does not know his parents, coming back to a home he has never had, to what is only a home by contrast with the lunar landscape of America, absolute home-lessness made desert and mountains.

The homecoming of "the American" is played out against two living persons and the memories of three dead girls—which is to say, against two exponents of the future he had never been able to imagine as a hired boy, and three golden ghosts repre-senting all in his past he had longed for and not possessed. En-dowed now with money and power, he returns to find the world he had longed to enter gone, and with it the girls, daughters of the well-to-do farmer for whom he had worked; destroyed by typhus, betrayal and the guns of the Partisans, the three splendid sisters still haunt the book, and when their fate is finally and completely known the novel must end.

The living survivors are Cinto and Nuto, the former a crip-pled and abused boy of perhaps twelve, the boy "the American" had once been and that somehow he becomes again in returning; the latter the man he might have become had he stayed home instead of pursuing his imagined America—or rather the man he can only love and envy, but *not* be, a Partisan, a Communist, who has chosen a life of public usefulness rather than private success. But even at the moment of "the American's" return, the world of Nuto's hope is threatening to disappear, the dreamed future following into darkness the desired past as the legend of the Resistance which sustains it begins to be vilified by priest and politician, and the corpses of Fascist soldiers gloriously murdered by the Partisans begin to seem merely corpses, the property of the priests. The old beauty has been destroyed but the new order does not appear; and the boy Cinto looks on still from under the vine with timeless terror and alienation and pain.

Only what eternally abides can be recaptured, and only this is truly new with the newness of the recurring seasons: the Hill, the River, the Grape Harvest, the Festivals with the young dancing until they fall in their places, the musicians playing their way home through the sleeping countryside, the magic bonfires lit on the hills for the sake of the crops. To this alone can the bastard return, to the archetypal earth: father and mother of the orphan, home of the homeless. If America is the land for which we can only set out, this is the anti-America, the land to which we can only come back.

But somehow the dead beauty of the past and the lost hope of the future survive, too, together and unforeseeably transformed into the eternal present of the myth. For the book ends as "the American" learns what has happened to the youngest, most desirable and most vicious of the three sisters he has sought: Santa, her name an obvious irony, yet somehow a portent. Caught in a flagrant betrayal by the Partisans, she was shot, soaked in gasoline and burned to ashes; but the place of her destruction remains as a scar on the hillside, the cold bed of yet one more ritual bonfire. Dreamed by a boy's nostalgia for what is gone, destroyed by a man's fury for what is to come, she persists as what endlessly *is*, in a world before charity or passion, before society or the person: the world of myth where "ripeness is all."

Part Two: The Generations

The use of myth theory to illuminate works of art has become standard in our time, though a few voices continue to cry scandal; and the reader has by now seen several examples of my own efforts in the field. I have, in addition, striven throughout my writing life to make clear how statements which are superficially concerned with large groups of people; such as the generations of the twenties, the thirties and so on, may more deeply (perhaps inevitably *have* to) be concerned with the speaker's hopes and fears for his own psychic economy, his attitudes toward his rational and impulsive selves. But this means that such statements, whatever their claims to credence, belong to the same realm as poetry and are to be believed or disbelieved, on one level at least, as poetry is to be believed or disbelieved.

Certain highly publicized and passionately followed trials have, however, seemed to me to offer even apter occasions for mythic commentary. I see them as symbolic events in which a whole society objectifies and acts out its inner conflicts, its most pressing archetypal terrors. And I have tried to show, therefore, in terms of specific problems of race and generation how the Leopold and Loeb case had—and continues to have—the same *mythic* resonance (no matter how lacking it may have been in political significance) as the cases of Hiss and the Rosenbergs, which I treated in *An End to Innocence*.

The Ant on the Grasshopper

Originally a review of *The Twenties*
by Frederick J. Hoffman

I am a little ashamed of the difficulty I have had in getting through this book. I tell myself that it is orderly, well-documented, immune to the more ridiculous prejudices about the period with which it deals; a combination of the most admirable attributes of old-fashioned scholarship and newfangled criticism. It scants neither political and social background nor close textual analysis; its acknowledgments range from Mike Gold to Ezra Pound, and it makes no concessions to Communist-baiting on the one hand or to the ill-humored exposure of anti-Semitism on the other. Its canon of admired works rests on a consensus of the liveliest critical minds as of the very latest report (Eliot, Pound, Tate quoted highly—Robert Frost and Edith Wharton falling fast); but it is not unreasonably up-to-the-minute, and tempers some of the harsher current assessments. It is, in short, good-tempered, well-informed, inclusive, balanced—and thoroughly unreadable.

There are faults one can find with the book even on its own terms. However one rates him finally, one cannot ignore Frost utterly in a comprehensive history of the twenties; nor fail to say a word about that redemption of Melville which was the period's most important and revolutionary revaluation of our past; nor treat Faulkner quite so cavalierly. Nor can one really discuss Stevens' "Sunday Morning" without mentioning the word "Christianity," or confront Pound's Brennbaum and Eliot's Bleistein without saying the word "Jew." Mr. Hoffman is the victim of his own genteel anti-polemicism, as well as of his literary prejudices. But the chief point is not that the book is sometimes not as objective as it pretends to be, but that too often it *is*.

373

I have, I admit, a low tolerance for detached chronicling and cool analysis, but I have tried plunging through the book doggedly in the order Mr. Hoffman has imposed on it; skipping about on the basis of selected references from the index; opening it at random. Always I am bored. It is, I suppose, partly my own unregenerate nature. I long for the raised voice, the howl of rage or love. When I cry in protest, "But you *can't* be sensible all the time—not about this silly, annoying period—not about writers who have helped make our minds and who may even be great!" the author answers me, unruffled in the midst of his evidence, "Oh, can't I though!" And, God bless him, he can.

Mr. Hoffman's is not, I fear, a particularly lively or original mind; but it cannot, I am sure, be as dull as it seems to me. On the other hand, my distress cannot be merely a matter of the incongruity of our tempers. No, I am convinced that he is, in large part, the victim of his subject—or more precisely, of a difficulty inherent in our connection with the twenties.

Certainly, our relationship to that time is a difficult and degrading one; and what is most difficult and degrading about it is our awareness of that fact. How hard it is to be the sober and hard-working children of grasshoppers—and to *know* it! To know that we were born middle-aged, older than our forebears knew how to become; and to feel at once our own indignity and theirs: the indignity of never having been quite young, and the equal and opposite one of being forever barred from growing decently old. We have our revenges, of course: nasty and superior essays puncturing the dated poses of the survivors of the twenties (*The New Yorker* on Hemingway or *Life* on Faulkner), bibliographies, Ph.D. theses, collections of critical essays. These are, after all, coals of fire heaped on our own heads. No matter how often we assure ourselves that the twenties overestimated the worth of their own achievement (and they did, they *did!*) and that we underestimate the value of our own, we must still face up to the fact that they had the nerve proper to their excesses and we have only the caution proper to ours.

In the eternal comedy of fathers and sons, we have been left only revolt against which to revolt, only nonconformism to which to refuse to conform. The only real blasphemy still possible to us is to write a history of blasphemies between the Great War and the Great Depression in which we prove those blasphemies merely manifestations of a deeper piety than ours—and this, I should be happy to believe, is the secret motive of Mr. Hoffman's book.

What irks our age and drives us to the more shameful excesses of "scholarship" ("After such experiences," Mr. Hoffman asks, "what forms of . . . defining . . . the human condition?" Answer: the glossary, the lexicon, the footnote!) is that we feel ourselves trapped among the clichés of anti-cliché that we have inherited from the great stereotype-mongers of the twenties. We should be ashamed to be as nakedly square as Fitzgerald, as unawarely sentimental as Hemingway or Faulkner, as prone to maudlin self-pity as Ezra Pound, as ignorant or as absurdly self-educated as any of these. Yet our irony, sensibility, objectivity and culture have not made us capable of seeing around the great literary platitudes of the twenties.

All the novels about World War II could never convince an intelligent observer from Betelgeuse that such an event had ever occurred; for they clearly represent the reaction of sensitive young men to a conflict they had read about during their high-school days; though, to be sure, they have tricked it out with exotic names from the back pages of an atlas, and have played out the trite events among coconut palms. Indeed, a veteran of the twenties like Faulkner can write in 1954 the same anti-war book he might have produced in 1924, as if nothing had happened since 1919—as, in the realm of the imagination, his and ours, it had *not*.

In the same way, no one has succeeded since the age of Sinclair Lewis and Sherwood Anderson in seeing an actual American small town or a living member of the Kiwanis club. The gross pathos of Anderson or the journalistic thinness of Lewis is beside the point; for all of us, the real facts of experience have been replaced by Winesburg, Ohio, and by Babbitt; myth or platitude, we have invented nothing to replace them. Perhaps the most distressing of the stereotypes that have persisted since the twenties is that of Sacco and Vanzetti—that is to say, the political morality-play constructed out of the handful of facts about the case anyone was able to know and remember past the passionate fiction of *Boston, Gods of the Lightning,* etc. It is notorious how such recent quite different affairs as the Hiss-Chambers case have been confused in the minds of many decent people with the legendary event which reached its climax in 1927. An age which by and large thought of itself as "realistic" has taught us the odd lesson that not the real but the mythic prompts our feelings and actions.

We have lived for thirty years in the world of someone else's dreams: a compulsive world in which Lieutenant Henry forever declares his private peace, Sherwood Anderson eternally walks out of his office, the Artist forever leaves the world of Puritanism and Respectability for the utopias of bohemia or expatriation. To be sure, we do not all relive the legendary pattern, or even believe it; but we have been unable to imagine our choices in any other image. It is strange and revealing how little residue or legend the Marxist thirties have left; how little their criticism of the twenties affected their image of themselves; how naked we are of all but knowledge and irony among the monuments of the period: those undraped figures in noble poses still declaring, "Be Free! Be Lost! Have Fun! Make It New!"

Under the enduring spell of the twenties, we cannot convince ourselves that the clichés against which we must fight for our imaginative autonomy are not patriotism, honor, God and country—but their mirror opposites which the twenties substituted for them. The world which the twenties invented in desperation and we inherit in smugness is a world in which we can no longer breathe. Their innocence and their assurance poison us; these are the bitter grapes that have set our teeth on edge.

And yet the twenties, which seem in one sense our Cities of the Plain, seem in another (or perhaps it is the same sense—for in all innocence they created for us the notion of Gomorrah as Utopia) our lost Eden. There are some, of course, among the dewier Beatniks, who have never heard of the expulsion from the Garden, and who are engaged in naming the platitudinous animals of an unfallen bohemia—as if Scott and Zelda had never turned East of Eden from the flaming sword. Mr. Hoffman, however, is well aware that he is neither acting nor writing a Holy story—merely performing exegesis upon it. Indeed, it is as the Talmudist on Eden that Mr. Hoffman seems most depressing (out of such joy, such wisdom!) and the lost paradise of the weary scholar is inevitably the world without Talmuds. But it is not the "freshness" of the period alone which intrigues us—or even its mythopoeic power; it is perhaps above all the *unity* of the times, real or legendary, that drives us to despair.

For if the men of the twenties were lost (as they never grew tired of asserting) they were lost together, lonely together: a single "we" of artists, intellectuals and emanicipated spirits exiled from the single "they" of Rotarians, Y.M.C.A. secretaries and generals. In the realm of technique, the single phrase "make it new" presided over an alliance ranging from Mencken to Eliot, Sandburg to Stevens, James Branch Cabell to Arturo Giovannitti. The fall to division was yet to come: Paleface against Redskin, Whitmanian against Jamesian, neo-Catholic against Marxist; and the rites for Sacco and Vanzetti were the last prelapsarian celebration, a prelude to the end of unity as well as innocence.

It is an awareness of all this which has impelled us recently on various levels to seek to come to terms with our lost Eden, to be done with it at last. But sentimental rescues of Fitzgerald or Wyndham Lewis, or gallant last stands for Ezra Pound, are beside the point—we cannot thrive on reconstructed truculence or repentance; these are the equivalents in the world of literature of popular evocations of booze and sex in the rumble seat. We must get past the barrier of the final stereotype: not only the myth of the Lost Generation but that of the Morning After, too—our last inheritance from the dying twenties, the image of Babylon Revisited.

Probably the only way to exploit the real comedy of the situation is to realize quite clearly that we are not dealing with an "actual" past, but with a tricky relationship between a literary image of the twenties and a present in part invented by that period, in part defining itself in opposition to it. Fiction seems the only device complicated enough to do justice to our plight;

and in *The Disenchanted,* for instance, Budd Schulberg seemed within striking distance of the real point; but he had finally too blunt and earnest a mind to distill from the relationship between his young Communoid protagonist and Halliday-Fitzgerald even the modest insights Henry Green achieved in the more frivolous fable of *Nothing.*

Insofar as it is a literary work, Mr. Hoffman's study belongs to this series of comedies, intentional and unintentional. When he is not being victimized by the notion that the "actual past" resides in newspaper files, he quite realizes the subtlety of the relationship he sets out to describe; and he is admirably on guard against certain standard oversimplifications. Indeed, he has a double formula to protect himself against error: on the one hand, "the saving grace of an irony" directed against both his own time and the time he is examining; and on the other hand, "scholarly forms of ordering the subject." His irony, which is Eliotic in inspiration, I find a little ineffectual; his scholarship quite deadly.

Of all the great cliché-mongers of the twenties ("objective correlative," "dissociation of sensibility"—the platitude on the loftiest plane), the one with whom the contemporary critic has the least trouble is T. S. Eliot, a grasshopper who lived so long and became the slyest and most charming of ants. Mr. Hoffman finds in Eliot's own playfully deprecatory relationship with himself an acceptable method for coming to terms with his subject; and, naturally enough, he has little trouble in submitting examples of Eliotic verse to Eliotic analysis. Each of the eight main sections of *The Twenties* ends with a text presumably exemplifying some key tendency of the age: Traditionalism, Experiment, Critiques of the Middle Class, etc. Four of the texts are poetic—and they are all, of course, safely inside the Eliot family circle: Pound, Eliot himself, Hart Crane and Allen Tate. Such textual demonstrations are, to put it as kindly as possible, redundant; and they seem joined to the sociological discussions that precede them more by a determination to have the cake one eats than by any demonstrable unity of meaning.

If the spirit of Prufrockian irony presides over the exemplary texts, the spirit of scholarly-journalistic documentation presides over the prefatory generalizations. I give, tempering justice with mercy, only one example of the latter:

> Choosing some eighty-five writers . . . I have consulted such books as Peter Neagoe's anthology, *Americans Abroad* (1932). . . . Of the number, 58 were from twenty to thirty years of age in 1920, 20 from thirty to forty, and 15 from fifteen to twenty. . . . They had been born in the East (29) and the Midwest (25) for the most part; 8 came from New England, 11 from the South, 2 from the Southwest, and 4 from the Northwest . . . only 5 had no college education at all; 15 of those who had gone to college had not finished, the remainder had at least a B.A. degree. . . . Harvard graduated 12, Yale 9, Princeton 4 and Columbia 7. . . .

This incredible attempt to substitute the methods of the box score for the insights of criticism is, I confess in all fairness, Mr. Hoffman at his worst; but it is a not untypical worst—and it reveals the conviction behind the veil of irony: that the truth is in the verifiable, the statistical "fact." It is difficult to see how a vulgarized positivism could be pushed to more ridiculous lengths; and yet only last week I was sent an offprint beside which Mr. Hoffman's statistics seem relevant and subtle. It was a "qualitative analysis" of Currier and Ives (in seventeen prints one finds fourteen chickens, three dogs, eleven Negroes, etc.), guaranteed by its author to introduce some of the certainty of social science into the shifty realm of writing about art. In this direction, no indignity is impossible.

One cannot, I am convinced, exploit such an approach and remain a critic in any traditional sense; and this Mr. Hoffman knows, for all his efforts to make the best of his two worlds. Confronted with D. H. Lawrence's *Studies in Classic American Literature,* he takes his anti-critical stand. To me, Lawrence's book is by all odds the most committed, wickedly apt appraisal of our past I know, the nearest thing I have ever encountered to what our classics must come to be in *us* if they are to remain alive. But here is Mr. Hoffman: "Lawrence came to American literature as a fresh, original, in many ways a naive reader, not especially concerned with—and not very well informed about—prevailing academic or scholarly forms of ordering the subject. . . . In almost every detail the insights are Laurentian and worth while for their revelation not of the American past but of the Laurentian present. . . ."

"Not of the American past . . ." One could never guess from these remarks that in Lawrence is to be found a defense of Melville written in the very teeth of the well-informed scholars of his time busy ordering their subjects, as well as what remains the only pertinent literary criticism of Cooper in print. Instead, there is the scholar's gentle snub and the scholar's failure to distinguish between the reconstructed and the resurrected past; with the final judgment saved, in the scholar's cautious way, for a representative quotation in a footnote. The quoted critic is H. I. Brook (and who the representative hell is he?) in the *New York Times* of September 16, 1923: ". . . you are driven to conclude that at bottom D. H. Lawrence is a bore, and, like most bores, complacently concerned with himself, bent buzzingly on his own pre-occupation." "After such knowledge" (as Mr. Hoffman himself concludes by asking in the apt enough role of Gerontion) "what forgiveness?"

The Search for the Thirties

Originally a review of *Part of Our Time* by Murray Kempton

I have found this an oddly moving book, though it is sentimental, philistine and a little ingenuous. As a matter of fact,
it has brought me as near as I hope I shall ever come to an
appreciation of those mild vices. For it is precisely his sentimentality, his ingenuousness and his philistinism which enable Mr.
Kempton to tell certain truths about the '30s—or, as he prefers
to say, "the myth of the thirties." Now "myth" is a tricky word
but Mr. Kempton makes it quite clear what he wants it to mean.
"Any myth," he tells us, "is the creation of the very few who
cannot bear reality." And the reality intolerable to the "very few"
Communists and fellow travelers turned informer, bureaucrat and
Hollywood hack with whom his book deals is "the reality that
man is alone on this earth." Mr. Kempton's victims and sufferers
turned from the realization of this truth to the "myth of community," which is for him not only false but viciously false, "the
malignant unreal." And those who subscribed to it can only be
classified as "a little group of the sick" still (in large part) trying
to convince themselves that once, for better or worse, they were
the voice and conscience of the nation.

I do not want to argue here the nature of "reality," but I
must insist that it is hard to see in what essential way the statement that "no man is an island" differs from the assertion that
"man is alone on this earth." Both are poetic generalizations
aimed at coming to terms with incoherent experience—and there
is no sense in which one qualifies as a "myth" more than the other.
In my book, *both* are entered as gospel. As for Mr. Kempton's
contention that all those drawn toward the declared ideals of
the Soviet Union in a time of depression and disenchantment

381

were no more than a handful of the sick, an "island of guilt in a sea of innocence"—this is obviously a polemical exaggeration, prompted by the desire to neutralize an opposite exaggeration of certain repentant radicals. I am sure that it is Mr. Kempton's kindly intent to call off the dogs of the investigating committees by proving that there was never any large-scale, meaningful internal Communist threat in our country; and it seems churlish to protest so benign a piece of apologetics. But I cannot help believing that there is more truth in the counterproposition, the cry of a young fellow I once overheard at the point where he was being refused a commission in the navy for the political sins of his adolescence. "Hell," he shouted, "in those days anyone with guts and brains was a Communist or fellow traveler."

How hard it is for those who did not *live* the mythic life of their own generation to realize that so far as imagination is concerned, they have never existed at all! It is not a matter of talent or intelligence or wit (the dullards Ethel and Julius Rosenberg are relevant and hence real, the brighter Harold and Bernard Rosenberg irrelevant and unreal); nor is it a question of belonging to the majority (more Baltimoreans, surely, were like Murray Kempton than Alger Hiss; but it is Hiss who counts); and it is all, therefore, intolerably unfair. No wonder the invisible men of each generation cry out in rage that there are no generations, that though a minority presumptuously calls itself "we," there is no we. How humiliating it would be now if one were, say, an earnest left-philistine like Harvey Swados or Herbert Gold to grant that the mythic "we" of the declining fifties was constituted by a no-talent novelist called Jack Kerouac and his friends.

But Mr. Kempton goes astray not only in his ignorance of what gives a decade its mythic identity; behind his temperate dismissal of the committed minority of the '30s (not evil, you understand, just sick) is the philistine conviction that our major problems have all been solved—were, indeed, being solved by the uncommitted while those incapable of facing reality were pursuing their myth. How hard it is to be just in these matters! Of course, it is a fact that men without a dream have improved Negro-white relations, taught labor and management to mitigate their conflicts, extended social security, etc., etc. But the real and remaining problem that vexed those sensitive and desperate enough to dream the dream of community Mr. Kempton does not trouble to mention: the drying up of creativity, the flight to conformity, the obsession with violence, the enervating fear of war and poverty, the alienation of men from each other, from their work and from the natural world itself. Has our revulsion from the '30s gone so far that we have to say things like this as if they were a revelation?

In America no large portion of the working class was ever impelled toward Communism; not economic but moral dissatisfaction drove a sizable portion of the intellectuals into the arms of the Communists. To call their real revulsion from real lacks in our life a flight from reality is utterly misleading. True, they were not especially good people, these marginal malcontents, not if measured by the goodness they dreamed of, since they were hopelessly children of the world they despised. They were, God knows, no worse than the "innocent" who never flirted with Communism—rather a little better in their discontent, their unwillingness to confuse, like Mr. Kempton, man's essential loneliness with his special lostness in an industrialized, dehumanized society.

Yet it is Mr. Kempton's temperamental inability to think of man as truly a political animal that gives his book its special value and appeal. To him the struggle over leadership in a union, the fight for a program in a party, is a matter not of issues but of personal antipathies and private passions. There is something ironically apt in an author who is capable of believing only in the lonely person writing about a period which found it hard to believe in the person at all. For the uninitiated reader, who never even sat in the largest mass meeting of the most thinly spread front organization, perhaps this is the only way of communicating some sense of the times: not in terms of insight and understanding, but of the *feel* of the thing.

But even the simplest soul must find it hard to convince himself finally that the Communist movement is simply the sum total of the pathologies of its members. In the midst of biographical detail and psychological surmise, one longs for the evident, the obvious historical or political fact, for the rich and complicated social context in which Mr. Kempton's heroes and villains lived their individual lives. There are two lacks which seem to me especially disabling.

The first is any specific understanding of the relationship of the American radical movement to Russia and the Communist International. I find in Mr. Kempton's book no awareness of the decisive fact that at the moment when Communist-oriented individuals were entering for the first time positions of influence in the American government and in the trade unions, all autonomy in national Communist parties had disappeared. Russia, itself hopelessly committed to autocracy, was making even the most trivial local decisions for all member countries. One of the things that gives the appearance of utter madness to American Communism is the fact that its tactics were a response not to American conditions but to European-Asiatic affairs as understood by parochial and ill-educated members of the Russian Politburo. The very decision of a Communist organizer in Akron, Ohio, to learn or not to learn to dance or play bridge was dictated by what a leading Bulgarian member of the Comintern had said at the Sixth Party Congress.

More than this, American comrades (and at their proper remove, sympathizers, fellow travelers, etc.) came to live in the half-invented world of the party press and to judge themselves by its editorials rather than by the reactions of their neighbors. If there is a legendary world that replaced the real world for the vanguard of the '30s, this is it, and not the quite proper notion of the indivisibility of mankind. What baffled American Communists was the fact that what was real abroad remained lunacy or a game here. If a slight difference in doctrine made or broke the Chinese Revolution, why did it not also matter cataclysmically on the campus of City College? Ben Gitlow, one of Mr. Kempton's favorite misunderstood examples, "shambling from one splinter group to another, still hoping to find the true light somewhere in their weak phosphorescence," differs from a tragic Trotsky or a triumphant Tito only by the accident of his living in the United States. But this immense joke on Gitlow and history and us, Mr. Kempton is not political enough to appreciate.

For similar reasons, he fails to understand that there is not even in his sense a single "myth" of the '30s, that inside the Communist mind there is no unified '30s at all, but rather two distinct and contradictory "myths": the surviving superrevolutionary dream of the Third Period; and, after 1935, the genteel dream of conformity proper to the Popular Front. This is a clue to all sorts of discrepancies which Mr. Kempton tries vainly to analyze in terms of personal limitation and cowardice: the sudden collapse of the "Proletarian Novel" in the middle of the decade, the replacement of the Edmund Wilsons by the Donald Ogden Stewarts as the intellectual mouthpieces of Communism, the contrast between the amazing spread and minimum effectiveness of the front organizations, the shifts in trade union policy, etc. Even the odd contrast of Hiss and Chambers, to which Mr. Kempton dedicates an interesting chapter, rests upon their embodying the two contrasting myths which arise ultimately from the maneuverings of the Russian Foreign Office.

The price which Mr. Kempton pays for preferring a personal to a contextual approach is great enough in political matters; but there at least it reveals from time to time the real way in which tics of character actuated men who saw themselves as the personifications of the march of history. In the field of literature, the same sort of narrowing down brings much slighter rewards—and Mr. Kempton's essay called "The Social Muse" is for me the least effective in the book. This seems an especial shame, because we have still no satisfactory study of the general literary scene in the '30s and of the "Proletarian Novel" in particular. In setting up his customary sentimental melodrama of a reality-loving hero battling a group of myth-ridden failures, Mr. Kempton has drafted James T. Farrell to play the Joe Curran of the literary world.

Now Farrell is beyond question a decent, dogged and admirable man, who has never betrayed his real if limited talent; but as a writer, he is far from being the most successful or interesting of the period. There is in him no new technical achievement, no breakthrough to a new way of seeing or rendering reality; but there was during those years one figure who, though he died before resolving all his problems of technique and feeling, did catch in three novels the bitterness, the mad humor, the tempo of the times. This is, of course, Nathanael West, whom Mr. Kempton does not mention.

And there was, in addition, one novel whose pathos and truth make it the most distinguished piece of fiction based on Jewish life in America. This is Henry Roth's *Call It Sleep*, a book Mr. Kempton misleadingly lumps together with *Studs Lonigan* as "unvarnished" and "without much grace"—an example of "plebeian naturalism." Actually, it is the adaption of Joycean techniques to a border region where two cultures meet—a constant shifting from the mind to the world, from symbol to fact, from poetic levels of language to the grossest talk of the street. The introductory chapter alone could stand as a short story capable of redeeming ten years of literature with its spare rendition of all the rage and hopelessness of a Castle Garden reunion of husband and wife. Henry Roth, who after this single novel lapsed into silence, has never had the recognition due him—and Mr. Kempton's cursory dismissal will not help.

The chief task confronting a historian of the literature of the '30s is to define the typical novel of the period, not simply to describe books that happened to be written in that decade. Indeed, some novels written then (Faulkner's *The Sound and the Fury* is an example) belong in tone and inspiration to the '20s; though *Sanctuary* by the same author belongs, perhaps alone among his works, to the era of the Great Depression. What is the difference? Some doctrinaire and artificial definition of the Proletarian Novel out of *The New Masses* will, of course, not do at all. It is not a matter of political allegiance, though the influence of Marxism at some remove is a requisite; books as different in commitment as Wyndham Lewis' *Revenge for Love*, Hemingway's *To Have and Have Not*, Fitzgerald's *The Last Tycoon*, reflect what is essential: a vision of the world so desperate that it breaks through the lyrical self-pity characteristic of the '20s to a kind of impersonal rage and nausea.

There is another sort of depression literature, too—the kind of sentimental, middlebrow melodrama practiced variously by such authors as Budd Schulberg and the John Steinbeck of *Grapes of Wrath*. But this is only accidentally and by virtue of subject matter implicated in the world of the '30s; change the setting a little, make the redeeming hero a priest rather than a Communist organizer and one can play it out with the same writers, director and cast in the mid-'50s, as *On the Waterfront* eloquently testifies. No, the real sensibility and passion of the Depression years for me find their literary expression in the penultimate scene of Nathanael West's least popular book, now long out of print, *A Cool Million: or The Dismantling of Lemuel Pitkin*. The protagonist (who is later to become the hero of an American Fascist movement) stands on the stage of a cheap theater between two comics, who belabor him with rolled-up newspapers until his wooden leg, his artificial arm, his false teeth and glass eye roll out onto the floor while the crowd howls in delight. Or there is Faulkner's impotent Popeye, spawn of alleys, slobbering over someone else's lust.

Here, in the poet's sense of the word, is the true "myth" of the '30s: the sense of sterility, the despair, the outrage before the senseless waste of the human turned crazy laughter and at last art; but for most people this is too strong, too "morbid," too *real* a vision to be endured. And so we do not have finally any shared myth of the age. The '30s do not yet exist in our common imagination—as do, for instance, the '20s, securely fixed in a single continuous legend from John Held, Jr., to Scott Fitzgerald.

This imaginative vacuum the newspaper accounts of confessions and accusations and invocations of the Fifth Amendment cannot fill; and it is into this vacuum that Mr. Kempton has nobly rushed. What he gives us is no more real poetry than it is real history; but it is a substitute for what the literature of the times has not given, perhaps cannot ever give to more than a few. It is the beginning of the search for an age; and it has encouraged me to rummage a little in the untidy attic of my own mind for what I was surer than I should have been that I had safely stowed away. For this at least I am grateful to Mr. Kempton.

The Un-Angry Young Men

America's Post-War Generation

"Be careful what you wish for in your youth," says an aphorism of Goethe's by which I have long been haunted, "for you will get it in your middle-age." It is a terrifying thought, but at forty I feel capable of amending it into one still more terrifying: "Be careful what you wish for in your youth," my new version runs, "for *the young* will get it in your middle age." Since what I wished for when I was young was maturity and an end to innocence—in short, middle age itself—I thought I was playing it safe; and, anyhow, I always added under my breath, like Augustine praying to be delivered from the lusts of the flesh: "Not yet, dear God, not *yet!*" First violence and despair, the flirtation with failure and the commitment to radical politics; then all the savor of slow disenchantment; and only at long last the acceptance of responsibility and accommodation—this was the pattern I imagined and approximately lived, the pattern of many of us to whom the Great Depression seemed perversely enough our Great Good Time; and the Spanish Civil War, to which most of us did not even go, *our* war.

Only the other day, someone now just past thirty recounted to me a childhood memory: his mother knocking her head against a refrigerator door, over and over, until his sullen and blustering older brother had promised he would not go to Spain after all. That older brother has become, only too aptly, a millionaire; but it was a long haul from the kitchen in Brooklyn to his present office in Toledo or South Bend or wherever. God knows the "not yet!" we prayed under our breath was answered. We have notoriously had the most prolonged youth on record: a youth wished on us by our predecessors of the 1920s, who could

389

conceive of no greater good, and from which we must recover as from a wasting disease. To the younger generation now defining itself, I am grateful for at least one thing—it has lifted from me the burden of being young, under which I had begun to feel myself aging without dignity, like some fading beauty obliged to pretend her wrinkles do not exist. No one will, I hope, ever again refer to my fortyish contemporaries (now busy deploring the *much* younger young) as "young novelists," "young critics," "young intellectuals." We may now proceed to become grandfathers in peace.

To be sure, none of us will ever be as old as most of those who are now around thirty, just as none of us were ever as young as, say, Scott Fitzgerald;* for the new young in America are mature with the maturity we dreamed. We ended their innocence before they knew they possessed it; and they passed directly from grade school to middle age with a copy of *Partisan Review* or *Kenyon Review* as a passport—their only youth our youth, which is to say, the mythical youth of the '30s.

My own high-school-age son, reliving for the third or fourth time the attitudes I first remember noticing in the freshman classes I taught just before World War II, complains sometimes that my generation has robbed his of the possibilities of revolt. He sees clearly enough that for him the revolutionary gesture would be an empty piece of mimicry, incongruous in a world which has found there is no apocalypse and that contemporary society threatens not exclusion and failure but acceptance and success. What he does not yet perceive is the even more crippling fact that, by anticipation, my generation has robbed his of new possibilities even of accommodation, of accommodation as a revolt against revolt. The single new slogan available to his generation is the pitiful plea: "Get off my back!" Yet it is they who should be on ours!

To me the most appalling aspect of the writing of the post-war generation in America, as of its life-style, is its familiarity.

---

* Or as young as some of those current Youth Leaders, like Kerouac or even Mailer, representing, as they push toward forty, the "program" of those approaching twenty. I wonder if they strike the actual young as comic or pathetic—or neither!

I will not conventionally deplore (though to deplore at all has become now the conventional form of our relationship) their sterility in art—their obsession with criticism. Each does what he can; and construing a poem by John Crowe Ransom, though it may not be as good as writing it, is considerably better than biting your fingernails. Frankly, I like criticism; and I find myself nodding with approval from time to time over an attractively written essay by a younger critic, perhaps some piece of high-handed abuse, only to wake with a start to the realization that my approval is *self*-approval; that the ideas and attitudes are much like my own or those of my contemporaries, unearned intellectual income.

The young who should be hard at work, fatuously but profitably attacking us, spend a good deal of their time discreetly amending, expanding, analyzing and dissecting—when they are not simply cribbing from us. They fatuously attack chiefly themselves—and I fall into their trap, adding my voice to that of the schoolteacher telling them that they no longer read, or to that of the camp director assuring them that they do not even make casual, summertime love with the vigor of the generations before them. How dull they are! Which is to say: How dull *we* are without our pasts; how banal our dissent from dissent without the living memory of a commitment to dissent.

The young are able to share our essential experiences only vicariously; neither the Great Depression, which begins our youth, nor World War II, which ends it, are to them more than classroom history. Yet our reaction to both they not only live again, but live *by*. How soon they grow comfortable (not rich, of course, but secure on a level that does not even have the baleful fascination of really cashing in) on echoes of echoes of the attitudes of the '30s or earlier.

The generation of the 1920s and the '30s existed for the imagination, as well as for the census taker, because they had their own myths of themselves, their own books, their own programs, their own journals. The young today do not even have a magazine. What, say, the *Hound and Horn* was for the '20s, what *Partisan Review* (even briefly *The New Masses*) for the '30s, is represented for the '50s by nothing at all—or worse. The most substantial and successful of recent literary quarterlies is the *Hudson Review*, a genteel, prematurely middle-aged version of the *Kenyon Review*, edited by younger men endowed with a solemnity before literature almost indistinguishable from *rigor mortis*, but sustained by contributions from older men not yet so close to death. The only "new" political journal is *Dissent*,* edited chiefly by aging radicals unwilling to leave the Garden of the '30s, and representing nostalgia at the point where it fades into academicism. The situation is superficially not unlike that in England, where two of the most recent journals, *Encounter* and *The London Magazine*, are presided over by two of the chief surviving representatives of the '30s, Stephen Spender and John Lehman. In England, however, where there is considerable evidence of liveliness among the young, this seems to be more a matter of the failure of finances than of spiritual resources.

The new generation in the United States has found no new journal, because it has found no new voice and no new themes. I do not mean that there are no younger writers who are interesting and no books worth reading; I do mean that by and large there is no coherent body of new fiction or poetry which indicates a direction or creates a strikingly new image of the new age. The Angry Young Men of Britain have managed, whatever their shortcomings, to project themselves and their dilemma in such figures as Kingsley Amis' Lucky Jim; for the nearest equivalent our new young must look to a middle-aged *New Yorker* regular, J. D. Salinger. A *Nation* symposium on the college student agrees that the one novel they feel is truly *theirs* is Salinger's *Catcher in the Rye;* and I myself have seen several imitations of that book in prep-school literary magazines, some quite frankly labeled, "Holden Caulfield in Baltimore," "Holden Caulfield in Philadelphia," etc. Yet whatever the merit of Salinger's novel as a work of art or of Holden as an archetypal figure, the disturbing fact is that he is the creation of a man past thirty-five; and that he was first created in a story in *Good Housekeeping*, which took

---

* There are, to be sure, certain Beat journals, chiefly unread, like *Big Table*—but occasionally as successful as the *Evergreen Review*, which balances the bad poetry of the young with certain good things by elderly European avant-gardists like Beckett or Ionesco, and is underwritten by the profits earned from the unexpurgated *Lady Chatterley*.

place before World War II. The same dark-haired, tall, lost, young man, broken loose from school and heading for a breakdown, traveled then through Europe as he traveled later through New York; he has only grown a little younger with the passage of fifteen or sixteen years, having been a college student at the moment of his birth and having become a secondary schoolboy in his reincarnation. He is not, in any case, a creation *of* the latest young—only, like so much else, a creation *for* them, an inheritance.

Having no new matter, the young need no new medium; the older quarterlies are open to them (and one can even earn academic credit toward promotion by publishing in former anti-academic journals like *Partisan Review*), as are the back pages of such weeklies as *The New Republic* and *The Nation; The New Yorker* itself is not unfriendly, and if one has the proper tone and themes, he is more than welcome in *Mademoiselle* and *Harper's Bazaar*. The latter, swollen with ads for ladies' lingerie and jewelery, pay extremely well, as do such recently founded, but not new, publications as *Playboy, Nugget,* etc. Such "men's magazines," which have become the favorite reading matter of male college students, particularly in private Eastern universities, are attempts to be what *Esquire* was in the early '30s, a happily commercial combination of semi-pornographic art and serious fiction. The colored photograph has reached a point of technical excellence which makes *Playboy's* nude "Playmate of the Month" more lush and convincing than all her predecessors; but no writers have been turned up so far to match *Esquire's* Hemingway and Faulkner, so that few readers are tempted to read much beyond the description of how the photographers persuaded the "Playmate" to pose. It is, of course, doubtful that most of *Playboy's* subscribers ever find out what the quality of its stories are; as the editors of *Harper's Bazaar* assume that their readers will seldom get past the ads, so the editors of the men's magazines assume that theirs will never get past the pin-ups. Printing stories amounts more to subsidizing writers than really publishing them.

It is all, as Trotsky once remarked of quite another problem, like hitting one's head against an open door. When a young poet does appear (as one has recently in California), who bucks current fashion enough to choose William Carlos Williams rather than Wallace Stevens as a master, and gets himself censored— at this point *Life* magazine moves in with cameras; and he becomes merely another feature, lost somewhere between a contest for girl baton-twirlers and a spread on intercontinental ballistic weapons.* Opportunities are distressingly plentiful everywhere —not only for publication and publicity, but for study and travel. Scholarships and fellowships abound; the great Foundations are eager to invest in the young, to send them to school or Europe or Asia or up and down America. Whatever the imagination can conceive, there is plenty of money to achieve; and when the imagination withers away before the limitless possibilities, money begins to usurp its function. Half of the academic young (and a higher and higher percentage of talented youth goes into academic life) are engaged in the kind of project that can be contrived only by a bureaucracy driven half-mad by money which increases faster than it is spent.

In a fantastic way, all the traditional strategies of the intellectual for evading the pressures of his world are transformed into subsidized programs. Expatriation (renamed, of course, the Prix de Rome or Year-after-Year Abroad) is financed with the same evenhanded munificence that sponsors a scholarly study of population pressures or right-left asymmetry in the atom. Only one goal becomes increasingly difficult—perhaps impossible: failure. Only one satisfaction is forbidden: violence.

From childhood on, the new young have been supervised by parents and teachers, influenced at one remove or another by Freud and the universal pacifism which attacked the American middle class after World War I and deeply troubled over whether their charges should be allowed to play with toy bazookas, read the horrors of Grimm or of the latest comic book.

---

* Ginsberg is a poet not without talent—and the maudlin point of view from which he speaks one that has proved, since this article appeared, of considerable mythic potency. I admire the Beats for their enemies; if they were young, they would constitute a youth movement; as it is, they provide only another model for the young, essentially that of the twenties—superficially brought up to date.

Some have been forbidden all these, some allowed only therapeutic doses; on the whole, however, American society seems to have decided to let children and adolescents indulge vicariously in massive bouts of aggressiveness and terror. On the screen, in popular literature, on television and radio, these are permitted —with the tacit understanding: *this is all!*

Foreign observers find it easy to see the mythology of violence on which our children are raised: the crash of fist into jaw, the crumpling of bullet-ridden bodies, the bright red gobbets of blood. What they often miss is the anxiety which hedges that mythology about, the sense in which what is fostered with one hand is forbidden with the other: the PTA meetings that discuss censorship; the testifying psychologists hinting darkly of evil to come; the popular guides for new mothers which advocate expurgating from the child's life all mention of disaster and death. This is the first of the contradictions which have conditioned our young.

Even more critical is the one which arises from the fact that the present generation is perhaps the first in the United States born into an era of social peace. Since our beginnings, violence has been the very pattern of American life: a continent violently appropriated, a national life created in revolution and defined in the midst of Indian warfare, the degrading brutality of slavery and the conflict between competing national groups. Even after the closing of the frontier, the Civil War and the end of mass immigration, violence persisted in America, not as the threat of war but as the shape of everyday life. World War I brought to our people for the first time the shocking vision (still at long distance) of violence as a threat imposed from outside on an entire nation. This left behind a further complicating factor: a heritage of compulsory pacifism for the young, and a pattern for the war novel based on that pacifism which in almost forty years no novelist has managed to recast.

The imagination of the '20s lived off that remembered feast of terror as well as a mythology of murder and nighttime pursuit bred by Prohibition. The '30s subsisted on the social violence always present in our life but exacerbated by the Great Depression: the death of Sacco and Vanzetti set the tone before the period had properly begun, and was succeeded by images of Pinkertons and smashed picket lines, Gastonia and Paterson and South Chicago; of Bonus Marchers and hostile troops; of the quieter terror of despair in the bread lines and among the unemployed selling apples. The Civil War in Spain was a first climax; and World War II, with its guilt-ridden atomic conclusion, the end of all. At this point, the imagination faltered before the bureaucratization of terror—not merely its immensity, but the dispersal of personal responsibility. Before Dachau, before Hiroshima, older perceptions of horror failed; and the older responses of sentimentality and righteous indignation (how hard it is to remember the furor over the Fascists' amateur bombing of Guernica) were revealed as impotent. Yet for the majority of Americans still, war remained something remote, something belonging "overseas"; and to many, though an occasion for suffering abroad, it proved an occasion for prosperity at home.

For our younger generations, World War II is a dim childhood recollection, reinforced by facts learned in the classroom from a teacher who seemed, perhaps, incomprehensibly and unforgivably "shook" by it all. The oldest of the newer young went off to that war in time for peace; the armed forces to them meant schools and post-war billets, chances for culture-mongering, sightseeing or black-marketeering, depending on their tastes. The Spanish War, of course, scarcely exists for them at all. I can remember as early as 1941 overhearing one college girl complaining to another (they were studying, no doubt, for an exam in "Spanish Civilization"): "Franco? Franco? I can never remember what *side* he was on!" Even the conflict in Korea, presumably *their* war, touched directly only a relative few; and the reactions even of those few were so set in the older G.I. pattern of cynicism and compulsory griping that they were able to leave no record of it for the imagination.

Since Korea, we have lived under the Eisenhower dispensation in a kind of social truce. The sort of labor violence that made the typical street scene of my childhood (the mass picket line, the striker clubbed, the scab kicked in the groin) is by and large out of sight and even of existence. In the South, to be sure, recent events have stirred up again riots and bombing; but even there events are strangely limited in their consequences. What looks like the beginnings of civil war ends with an irate citizen getting his hand cut by a bayonet; and meanwhile, concealed for a little beneath the upsurge of brutality, the long-term change proceeds: the lynching of Negroes reaches the point of vanishing completely and a Negro singer becomes a leading matinee idol of the whole nation. Outside of the South, certainly, the young must produce their own violence—with autos or knives or brickbats—if they are to have it at all.

The latest concern with the depredations of juvenile delinquents is sharpened, I think, because their outbreaks seem so isolated on a generally peaceful scene. I do not intend to say that violence has disappeared utterly from our lives; the daily newspaper is there to remind us it has not, but it has ebbed away. Never has the violence of the young seemed so nonfunctional, so *theoretical*, as it were—so sought after for its own sake. Most of the traditional motives for violence are gone: defending the frontier, making the world safe for democracy, teaching the Jew or Dago or Nigger his place, demonstrating against war and Fascism; the young have lost their faith in all the ancient excuses for violence; they have only a vestigial hunger for it for its own sake. It may have been in part self-deceit when my own generation hung Hitler in effigy, tore off its silk stockings and underpants to hurl into anti-Japanese bonfires—or rioted in the streets against the cops: crying all the while that these were blows for the cause of humanity. We felt at least the *need* to pretend, to invest our aggression in a sanctioned cause; and our actions were congruous with our world.

The young now, however, inhabit a world where their truer movies are not, like those of the '30s, black-and-white images of violent action, but gray ones of suffocating inaction. Compare, say, *I Was a Fugitive from a Chain Gang* with *Marty*, in the latter of which nothing much happens at all, and violence has shrunk to a dream dreamed over the latest adventures of Mike Hammer, best-selling Private Eye. The function which Mickey Spillane performs for the semiliterate, the books of Hemingway and Faulkner and Nathanael West perform for the more informed and subtle young. They provide, that is to say, images of violence, in which the intellectual new young can find satisfaction.

Incapable of actual politics, the intellectual young sometimes find it possible to commit themselves to politics-once-removed: to a kind of ghostly anti-Fascism, or the rewarmed dream of the New Deal as embodied by Adlai Stevenson. A few —progressively fewer and fewer, I suspect—of the very young and bright (the sort of boy or girl, say, who goes through the New York public-school system in an accelerated program and graduates from a special high school at fifteen) even manage to repeat the Communist experience, circulating official petitions against the Bomb and singing the pseudo-folk songs with which that Movement keeps alive its own sentimental version of the New Deal:

> *Was at Franklin Roosevelt's side*
> *Just a while afore he died,*
> *Said, "One world must come out of World*
> *   War II"—*
> *Yankee, Russian, White or Tan—*
> *Lord, a man is just a man. . . .*
> *We're all brothers and we're only*
> *Passing through!*

It is the ghostliest manifestation of all; but outside of such tiny groups, few of the young so utterly inhabit the past. Yet the sensibility of all who read has been conditioned by the literature of the '30s, bereft now of political meaning but based on violence and postulated on the expectation of failure. Their dreams are possessed by images that their society cannot fulfil. In a world rent by violence, and plagued by disaster, America remains strangely immune at home. Only the newspaper headlines grow shriller, though they cannot disturb Ike's round of golf and the sense of security which it represents for the people to whom that game is a necessary symbol.

It seems impossible for the young to identify themselves with some distant cause. The sides are no longer so neatly de-

fined, allegiances no longer so naïvely given. The daily newspaper falls from hands that clutch the latest reprinting of Orwell's
Homage to Catalonia, which provides, in a way, a ready-made
disillusionment applicable to any cause. The dream of violence
and the fact of security, the dream of failure and the fact of success—here is the center of our new comedy; but it is not yet written, for no one seems to stand at the proper vantage point.

The trouble is that there are at the moment no new social
groups out of which a truly new generation can emerge. The
'20s marked a climax in the breakthrough of provincial writers,
of the displacement of New York and Boston by the Midwest as
the source of imagery and thematic material in fiction and poetry;
such books as Fitzgerald's *The Great Gatsby* and Hemingway's
In Our Time conplete the process begun by *An American Tragedy* and *Main Street* and *Winesburg, Ohio.* The '30s saw the
interruption of urban Jews (the final blow in the smashing of the
Anglo-Saxon domination of American culture) and the establishment of their pattern of struggle and accommodation as essential
American themes. This pattern has remained, in diluted form,
sovereign to this day. First rebellion; then a pleasant university
job, teaching the young in turn to rebel (only vicariously, after
a while); these then move on to their own jobs teaching the still
younger how to . . . There is no end.

Just as the second-generation intellectuals in New York
were moving from dispossession to possession, wave after wave
of young Southerners were, as the '30s wore on, emerging from
their areas of deprivation. They clutched not Marx in one hand
and a "proletarian novel" in the other; but a volume of neo-
metaphysical poetry in one and of "close" criticism in the other
—only to disappear into the colleges to the North, still crying the
slogans of agrarianism to their students, who were, alas, only
interested in John Donne.

The first pity of the contemporary situation is that the relationship of the new young to the generations just before them is
that of pupil to teacher, their common ground the schoolroom.
No longer is the young writer, bored in college, able to set up
against the teacher who bores him the image of some lonely poet
slumped over his empty Pernod glass in a Parisian cafe. The

lonely poet *is* the teacher, and if he is momentarily in Paris (or Athens or Rome), he is there to give a series of lectures under the auspices of the State Department.* On the other hand, we who are teachers no longer have the privilege of seeing before us alien minds with destinies quite different from our own, chafing to be free as we would wish them to be free, but as we cannot, of course, *teach* them to be. Not only are the new young our students; they are our younger brothers, our nephews, the children of our best friends, following behind us and distinguishable from our shadows only when they, dutifully and perfunctorily, raise an occasional cry of protest against us.

How committed they are in advance to academic life or the salons of upper bohemia or suburban peace! Ever more young men arise out of a world gone prosperous to the core, and head for the places which we before them have already occupied, mapped and cleared for comfortable living.

In this respect, the situation of our new young is completely different from that of their opposite numbers in England. The young British writer has the inestimable advantage of representing a new class on its way into a controlling position in the culture of his country. He is able to define himself against the class he replaces: against the ideal of "Bloomsbury," which is to say, against a blend of homosexual sensibility, upper-class aloofness, liberal politics and avant-garde literary devices. When he is boorish rather than well-behaved, rudely angry rather than ironically amused, when he is philistine rather than arty—even when he merely writes badly, he can feel he is performing a service for literature, liberating it from the tyranny of a taste based on a world of wealth and leisure which has become quite unreal. His books are, indeed, about the comedy of his relationship to the writers of the '30s (who are not only a generation but

* Even the occasional student who breaks out of the pattern, leaves, let's say, Lionel Trilling not for Downing College but San Francisco's provincial bohemia, comes back to New York after he's made it to lecture before the latest students of Trilling—or testifies in a City College classroom to the virtues of the nonacademic life, Hip or Beat. The terms have been defined and written on the blackboard the night before!

a class away from him) and he finds it easy enough to reject them.

He is not in any case excoriating (merely in order to be as nasty in his own way as they were, and are, in theirs) predecessors who are scarcely different from himself. The British writer in Swansea or Reading is a long way from Oxford and Cambridge, and merely to report what life is like in such places is to have found a new and fertile subject matter. American writers are, however, at least two generations deep in their Swanseas and Readings—in Bloomington (Indiana) or Madison (Wisconsin) or Moscow (Idaho). The baby sitter moving, soiled diaper in hand, across a declassed and blighted landscape is no longer for us a sufficient muse; and our own tradition of strategic bad writing goes back as far as Melville.

Even the main subdivisions within our new generation are secondhand, reflections of the older ones between New Yorker and Southerner, urbanite and agrarian (theoretical now, since the two are likely to be teaching in the small Midwest town), sociologue and new critic, contributor to *Partisan Review* or *Kenyon Review*. Long since, our Augustan peace has blurred those once bitter distinctions. This is an age of interfaith tolerance, after all; and only an occasional challenge to a duel disturbs the truce that finds Philip Rahv and Allen Tate presiding over the same school for training young critics, who may, indeed, bypass the traditions of both masters and be translated directly into the back pages of *The New Yorker*.

It is, however, worth distinguishing still the major subgroups within the new generations. First, the New York academics, who represent the latest form of status-striving among descendants of East European immigrants. In the first generation, there was a simplehearted drive to found fortunes in woolens, ladies' underwear, junk—no matter; in the second, an impulse to enter the (still financially rewarding) respectability of the public professions of law and medicine; in the third, an urge to find a place in publishing and the universities, to become writers and intellectuals. In my own generation, there are notorious cases of men with no taste (much less any love) for literature becoming critics out of sheer bafflement. Never have so many natural operators and minor Machiavellians pushed so eagerly and with less reason into the academy. The old tragedy of the poet forced into manufacturing paper bags becomes the new comedy of the prototycoon lecturing on the imagery of Wallace Stevens.

The New York intellectual in academia is typically a product of Columbia (although he may have gone to some large, Midwest university to get away from home), a student of Lionel Trilling, who has received his finishing touches at the Kenyon School of Letters or one of the British universities (preferably Downing College at Cambridge) or the Harvard Graduate School. Nurtured on critical dialects and trained in "close reading" by the New Critics, he (a little ostentatiously) handles a body of learning appalling in scope. This learning is deep and real, though such writers do not carry it lightly; and they are never, therefore, guilty of gross lapses like those of the more sketchily informed younger British writers—like Kingsley Amis, for instance, who is able to refer quite blandly in an American publication to Faulkner's lack of humor.

In addition to contributing to a vast, communal, talmudic commentary on the literary canon defined in the '20s and '30s— Melville, Faulkner, Stevens, etc.—such intellectuals normally occupy themselves with problems of "Popular Culture" or the "Mass Arts." Indeed, there is a sense in which this is their special subject; though here, too, they are likely to follow the lead of such a writer of the '30s as Dwight Macdonald. Among writers of this breed, such a concern is in part an inverted snobbism, a resistance to culture-mongering, which leads them to prefer a standard Hollywood Western to an "art film," and boxing to ballet. It is also, however, a kind of vestigial anti-bourgeois politics: a protest against the vulgarization of life in a commercial society; and finally, it is a professional protest against a world which will sponsor and support them, but which will not look up from the latest copy of *Life* to read their works or those they admire.

Yet they are, after all, members of the first generations to have grown up under the full impact of triumphant mass culture;

and it is their interest in this subject which connects the New York intellectuals with their British contemporaries (who, however different in other respects, share a concern with jazz, say, and science fiction—a sense that these give direct evidence of their new situation), and even with their less literate confreres, right down to the current high-schooler. The first cultural snobbism of the very newest young tends to be based on taste in jazz. "Do you dig Bird?"—that is to say, "Do you like the music of Charlie Parker?"—is a question that separates those in the know from those who are "nowhere"; and beyond the "Bird" there are ever retreating horizons of modern or progressive jazz. "It's a way of life," I remember hearing a young drummer in Missoula, Montana, explain quite solemnly to a graduate student, who had asked him why, if he read books (he was an admirer of Norman Mailer), he also blew jazz. "A way of life." I suppose it is also a way of life to the high-school kids I used to watch this past summer in Washington Square Park in New York, their shirts unbuttoned to the waist and a pair of bongo drums between their knees.

Expectedly enough, the nearest thing to a spokesman for the very new young is (or rather was briefly over the past couple of years—in and around New York) Jean Shepard, a disc jockey with some training in psychology, who used to lecture his listeners on the perils of conformism when he was not spinning records or singing a commercial which began:

> *Nedicks, shmeedicks,*
> *Double deedix,*
> *Pipkins all agree . . .*

Under his guidance, highly disorganized meetings (he preferred to call them "mills") were held in some Eastern colleges, at which he spoke endlessly, while the audience clambered around the hall, making a racket and turning off and on the lights. He finally gathered together his "Night People," those who listened to his program after midnight, in a kind of public demonstration at which several hundred kids were supposed to fly four-inch kites to express their contempt for everything ("Go fly a kite!").

Quite appropriately, on the appointed day, the wind failed to blow, and the Night People trickled off sullenly.

The situation in American Popular Culture is, at the moment, a thoroughly absurd one. On its own level, it has never been in a duller or less promising condition. Movie houses close down or play to smaller and smaller audiences—more and more, just the young; though in my own town this year for the first time in history there was no appreciable jump in box office receipts when college began. Popular music is in so dismal a state that the disc jockeys, to fill their time, have to play a larger and larger proportion of revivals of old hit tunes; Broadway subsists on importations and revivals and especially the rewriting of its own dramatic repertoire as musical comedies. Everywhere Popular Culture begins to live parasitically on its own past (the role of old movies on TV is too well known to need more than a bare reference). On the other hand, everyone, and not least the highbrows, wants to *read* about popular culture. There have been two recent books anthologizing the mass of new writing on the subject, and one of them is at the moment being distributed as a bonus by a large book club. The study of popular culture threatens itself to become a branch of Popular Culture.

The interest of the urban academics in the "mass arts" is matched in intensity by that of the radicals-once-removed, who may, indeed, sit side by side with them (they are more distinct ideally than in action) in a New York University or Harvard classroom. Such belated or symbolic revolutionaries, the youngsters who insist on reliving step by step the political past of the '30s, may have become (if they are old enough) Trotskyites in 1945 or '46, and certainly now subscribe to *Dissent,* approving especially the articles blasting Lionel Trilling or David Riesman, who are portrayed as archdefenders of the status quo and to whom they are bound by spasms of filial rejection. They cannot, however, in role or function distinguish themselves from their colleagues who admire Riesman and Trilling and subscribe to *Encounter.* They, too, sit behind desks in the offices of Rinehart or Doubleday; they, too, teach at Columbia or Minnesota or Brandeis University; and the Ford Foundation is only too delighted to subsidize what their politics has largely become: the writing of histories of the radical past. Needless to say, their youth, too, comes at secondhand.

If on his left, the urban intellectual finds a *Dissenter*; on his right (this time, say, in R. P. Blackmur's class in The School of Letters or at a lecture in Cambridge by F. R. Leavis), he may find a writer for the *Hudson Review:* a limp, Hugh Kennerish admirer of Ezra Pound or Wyndham Lewis, dreaming that all their manly spite and vigor are his own; and writing careful exegeses of the *Cantos,* in which he conceals certain bitter political comments for the initiated. It is a figure like Yvor Winters that he is likely to emulate, finding in him a moral ferocity not incompatible with a Christian gentleman's version of taste. Such a young intellectual sometimes imagines a pure politics of the literary right, which would make clear to anyone with real sensibility how a love of the best in art and a dignified McCarthyism can go hand in hand. It is these right-wing purists who like to think of themselves as the new radicals, isolated and despised by liberals with hardening arteries and professorships; but they, too, are welcome among the "celebrities" on Mike Wallace's TV interview program; for they, too, are still fighting in terms of a concept of right and left antiquated enough to seem undisturbing in any parlor.

Beyond all these groups (and within them) are the homosexuals, the staunchest party of all. Indeed, one feels sometimes that homosexuality is the purest and truest protest of the latest generation, not a burden merely, an affliction to be borne, but a politics to be flaunted.* Certainly, there is a logic to their identification of their sensibility with that of the artist in a country like America, where an undue interest in the arts is likely to bring on a boy the stigma of being a "sissy." Unlike England, America has no long tradition of allowing the homosexual to tyrannize over literary taste, nor indeed a tradition of fiction asserting (behind the most perfunctory of disguises) homosexual responses to experience as the cultivated norm. The sort of thing

---

* Even in Beat circles, they are heard above the rest making inversion part of a platform that includes disorder, madness and anti-hygiene.

which would seem in Britain dull and routine, trapped in a world of platitudes as old as Oscar Wilde, strikes an American reader as comparatively fresh. The earliest work of Truman Capote—or more strikingly of Carson McCullers—as well as such a recent novel as James Baldwin's *Giovanni's Room*, seem in our context to be conquests of new areas of feeling, an opening up. On the stage and in the movies, a similar breakthrough occurs on the middlebrow level; the young men with bare chests (all looking like Marlon Brando) and the middle-aged slatterns who assault their purity (all looking like Anna Magnani) become standard not only on Broadway but in movie houses in the remotest mountain town; while such films as *Picnic* propose to the American woman the homosexual's ideal of the handsome young man as her own. Leopold and Loeb are suddenly exhumed from comparative obscurity to be made the center of two recent novels and one current play.

Implicit in the whole trend is a certain impatience with the customary taboos and restraints; and particularly in its highbrow manifestations the celebrations of homosexual sensibility imply a rejection of the ideal of marriage and the family and of men who are men (*i.e.*, Gary Cooper). It is, perhaps, more than that, too: the last possible protest against bourgeois security and the home in the suburbs in a world where adultery is old hat. But they come so fast, the new homosexuals, queen treading on queen: and we are so ready for them, so eager to prove our own emancipation by understanding and accepting. It is the same old trap, though more elegantly upholstered. For each group there is its fitting and proper mode of accommodation; this one usually finds publication in the pages of *Harper's Bazaar*, *Mademoiselle* and *Vogue*. Indeed, such publication is their passport into an upper bohemia, where good manners are appreciated and high style is savored, a world of chic, eager to read the latest effete exploitation of the Faulknerian scene and the Faulknerian themes of dissolution and infertility.

What is finally most distressing about this is not that the devices of the young are so dismal and unfruitful, but that they are not even theirs. If I draw as dark a picture as legitimate distortion can make of their plight, it is not to blame them but to blame us who have dreamed them—and have taught them the dream as they sat before us in class. I would not rob them of free will and the possibility of guilt—but *they* must blame themselves. It is depressing enough to look in the mirror the young hold up to nature and see a host of little Trillings and Riesmans; more horrible yet to think of an endless proliferation of James Burnhams and Arthur Millers; and the mind falters at the thought of catching sight of something one fears is intended to be oneself. Enough, dear friends, and students, enough!

Yet it does not matter really—for so long as the imagination lives, every plight is potentially the stuff of a vision that will transcend it by capturing it. It is not generations, thank God, that write books or come to understanding; it is men. The generations are what the books are about, what the understanding comes to terms with. At the moment, one has the sense of young writers at a loss for a subject; poets all technique and no theme; novelists desperately contriving factitious subjects because they need somehow to keep writing books. But the subject is there: the comedy of themselves in their passionate and absurd relationship to us. When a young writer arises who can treat this matter in all its fresh absurdity, we will be done with symposia on the Younger Generation, with self-recrimination and sullen defensiveness and abuse. And I (I fondly hope) will be leaning from a window to cheer him on and to shake down on his head the torn scraps of all surviving copies of this article.

Class War in British Literature

During the past four or five years, there has been the sense in England that something painful at least, perhaps critical, is occurring in the world of literature. Cries of rage are heard, mingled with shouts of triumph; insults meet counterinsults, and everyone seems astonished that it has all come to *matter* so much. Certainly, there has been nothing like it since the thirties, when Auden and Spender and the other wild boys came down from Oxford crying the names of Freud and Marx and Kierkegaard as battle slogans. But the excitement of the thirties was confined almost entirely to poetry, while the new changes affect the novel, prose drama and criticism as well; and, oddly enough, the survivors of the earlier literary breakthrough are among those who cry out most loudly against the newer writers.

For an American such recent developments have a special meaning. Over the last twenty-five years, there has been little in English literature which has deeply moved us by seeming itself to move out of impulses anything like our own. Dylan Thomas, to be sure, proved an import article successful beyond belief; but in general, British writing has threatened to become merely exotic—more foreign to us and less relevant than the fiction, say, of France or Italy.

Now, however, distant sounds of pain and elation begin to reach us; and even before we have read the verse or the novels which inspire them, we realize that at last new writers have arrived on the English scene capable of giving offense as only the truly new gives offense. The correspondence columns of *The Spectator, The New Statesman* and *The Observer* are kept full; and we learn that there are even public debates on the new movement, special discussions in the theater following the production of certain new plays.

The young have not only, it appears, managed to please

themselves (which is simple enough), but to displease the elder statesmen of their literature, critics pledged to a dishearteningly broad range of tolerance. Unlike most of our own younger writers, the British ones have succeeded in appearing shockingly impossible! Literary rebels of the thirties, retired from their rebellion or grown confirmed in it, have looked to the young for the kind of rebellion which they themselves once provided—and have found, of course, only a rebellion against their own.

Everyone in England is aware that, with the close of the last war and the election of a Socialist government, a cultural as well as a political era has closed; and some at least are equally aware that the death of certain literary magazines (*Criterion, Horizon*—even *Scrutiny*, which represented an almost official opposition to the official literary orthodoxy) has signaled the disappearance of a kind of literature and of the taste which sustained it. To the young, something else, much more disconcerting, has become clear, too: that the literary revolt of the thirties did not make any really basic changes in the values which have informed British art since before World War I.

Auden and Spender, Day Lewis and MacNeice had extended, even strained those values, but had not fundamentally broken through them; and the poets of the forties had disrupted them no more than had their predecessors. T. S. Eliot could welcome Stephen Spender as cordially as Spender could hail Dylan Thomas; and all of them, everyone from E. M. Forster to W. H. Auden, came to tea with Virginia Woolf, whose husband could remember lunching with the Empress Eugenie.

It is this which offends (rightly or wrongly scarcely matters) the newer English writers, who are resolved to break at last out of a world of taste which has been, it seems to them, too long confined to the circumference of a tea table. It is, of course, possible that certain of them will be lured into the orbit of the witty and charming self-perpetuating society that they began by attacking; but in general that society is doomed. Already there are young men willing to write the sort of frank review of a dull and repetitious volume of verse by Edith Sitwell that no one would have written earlier; because (though it was possible, indeed expected, to comment on that dullness and repetitiveness in private malicious gossip) one did not publicly attack a member of the official first family of the arts.

The new writers are, in short, not *gentlemen* like their forerunners; if born to that status, they flee from it guiltily; if lucky enough to be sons of factory workers or furniture dealers, they exult in their origins. The ideal of the gentleman they associate with what they call (like its other enemies before them) "Bloomsbury." What "Bloomsbury" was historically, even the question of whether in fact it existed at all, does not matter; it has become a *myth*, a handy label for a hated world. In the minds of the new writers, "Bloomsbury" means quite simply a society pledged before all else to an ideal of elegant style in conversation, art, life itself; a society in which the liberal and aristocratic are subtly blended; an international society bounded in England by Oxford and Cambridge on the one side and London on the other, but existing, too, in colonies at Cagne-sur-mer or on Capri or Ischia.

In "Bloomsbury," all that had seemed "new thought" at the end of the nineteenth century had been grafted onto the grace and wit of an upper bohemia invented in the days of Oscar Wilde. Its origins indicate its hospitality to the politer forms of homosexuality and Marxism, and perhaps suggest why it has also welcomed the new economics of Keynes or admired such conventions of avant-garde literature as stream of consciousness.

Members of this world (it is more loosely organized than the term "Bloomsbury" perhaps suggests) know at one and the same time that they must fight to defend a far from ignoble ideal of life; and that they are doomed—that the world of television and Public Health Service and the disappearance of servants is more congenial to their enemies than to them. Their resistance is already half a surrender; yet the newer writers feel this resistance as a "conspiracy" against youth and art. At least they choose to describe it so. Young writers tend everywhere to classify those who do not admire them in McCarthyite terms, finding it easier to believe in a behind-the-scenes plot than in a simple difference of taste; and identifying themselves so totally with the main development of literature that they cannot distinguish an attack on any one of them from an assault on the whole future of art.

From this side of the Atlantic, it is obvious that the struggle is not between "gangs," plotting and counterplotting, but between classes trapped in a common plight in a world of transition. Ultimately it is a conflict between two worlds: the class world of the past and the declassed world to come—from our point of view, between a world very different from ours and one which becomes ever more like it. The special irony of the situation lies, of course, in the fact that the defenders of the caste system of "Bloomsbury" are, in large part, declared proponents of the "classless society," and that *politically* they have always worked to undercut the order which maintains them.

It must be embarrassing for them now to discover themselves on the barricades in a literary class war, attacked by the kind of scholarship boy they themselves have sponsored. They had dreamed, I suppose, of the intellectuals in the New Order adopting their values and imitating their literary manners as individual lower-class writers had done for so many decades. The new writers are, however, no longer V. S. Pritchetts, eager to assimilate culturally to a level of society into which they have not been born. They are no more impressed by his example than they are by the fact that writers they regard as superseded still function; that Leonard Woolf, for instance, still attacks and rejoins, and, in a certain sense, *writes better than any of them.* The latter is one of their chief grievances against him. They no longer aspire to the canons of taste he and Pritchett variously represent. Clumsy and sullen and defensive as young outsiders always tend to be, they make of their clumsiness and sullenness and defensiveness their definition; they will neither be bullied into adapting or flattered into assimilating.

In the Welfare State, whether under Conservative or Labor rule, they find nothing to encourage the courtliness and grace once considered the hallmarks of literature as well as the adornments of conversation in a salon. For an older generation, the drabness of contemporary society is tempered by an awareness that it is they who have made it; for the young it is simply a world they did not make, someone else's utopia. They are its awkward and diffident offspring, to whom it is, despite its faults, merely *home*. When they challenge the codes and values which survive from an earlier state of affairs, they do not raise their voices with the vehemence of those who fought "Bloomsbury" in its palmier days. Unlike D. H. Lawrence or Wyndham Lewis or even F. R. Leavis, the young are not driven to shrillness and paranoia in the fight against what seems invulnerable. Chiefly, they *laugh*. They are angry enough at the deepest level, in earnest all the way through; yet their typical response is the horse laugh. For, in a way, they know what they do not like to confess: that they have already won a victory (a victory not entirely satisfactory) by being born at the right time, by being now rather thirtyish than somewhere near forty or fifty.

Rather typically, they have no journal of their own to celebrate this victory, no special publication to say precisely what it is that is being born out of the collapse of older values. It is not only that journals are these days too expensive for any except the middle-aged, well-heeled or at least well-known to sponsoring foundations; it is in the very nature of the new literary revolution that it should make itself known through the back door of journalism. There are, indeed, two new magazines in England, *The London Magazine* and *Encounter* (the latter, of course, only in part literary); but these are edited by survivors of the thirties, John Lehman and Stephen Spender, the latter a favorite whipping boy of the new writers.

To be sure, Lehman and Spender print the newer writers along with older ones and between editorials deploring their aims; for it is their code to be eclectic and tolerant. What is wanted, however, is precisely a partisan magazine, strident and narrow, to speak for what has come to be called the "Movement." Meanwhile, the only forum of the new young is the back pages of news magazines and papers, particularly *The Spectator*. Members of the Movement have consistently been book reviewers for that journal, and a leading article which appeared in its pages in the fall of 1954 comes close to being a manifesto for the group. Its poets have been published in a series of slim pamphlets, sold for ninepence and published under the title of Fantasy Poets by the Oxford Poetry Society. In addition, of course, there have been individual volumes of criticism, verse and fiction; and some of the latter have even become best sellers, one at least (Kingsley Amis' *Lucky Jim**) being translated into a movie.

Typically again, however, the real introduction of the Movement to a larger public came through one of the newer mass media which distinguish its special world. John Wain, novelist, poet, critic and teacher of literature, was entrusted in 1953 with a literary program called *First Reading* that was being broadcast over the Third Programme of the BBC. He used the occasion to present the ideas behind the Movement and to introduce over the air the work of several writers now counted among what their detractors call the Angry Young Men. A nasty review in *The New Statesman* by Hugh Massingham attacked Wain's "maggoty and bureaucratic" style, and unleashed a controversy which drew letters to the editor for weeks. Before the first furor died down, various major literary figures from Graham Greene to V. S. Pritchett had put themselves on record (chiefly against), and a kind of definition of the Movement began to take shape.

That many of the new writers are "bad" writers, inept, overserious, heavily magisterial, has been evident from the first. What became clear only in the event was that they were not just bad, but bad in a special way—a strategical and perhaps necessary one. Certainly, it was not only their ineptness which enraged their foes; it was their program of which that ineptness was improbably a part.

But what is that program? It is not easy to say; indeed, there has been a growing tendency recently to deny that any Movement exists at all. Deep within the British mind, there lurks a profound embarrassment at being caught out in so seemingly ideological a position; "Movements" are for the French! Yet it is undeniable that certain new writers are linked together in their own awareness and that of the larger reading public. There are the novelists John Wain (who wrote *Hurry on Down* and *Living in the Present*), Kingsley Amis (author of *Lucky Jim* and *That Uncertain Feeling*) and Iris Murdoch (who has three novels: *Under the Net, Flight from the Enchanter* and *The Sand Castle*).

---

* And now, of course, John Braine's *Room at the Top,* a quite bad book became a quite good movie!

Amis has come to seem in most ways an epitome of the group, his first protagonist Lucky Jim and his own person blending into a composite portrait of the Angry Young Joker at Work and Play.* Miss Murdoch, a teacher of philosophy at Oxford, seems often only loosely associated with the others; and her latest book rather turned away from their typical themes and tone in an (unsuccessful!) attempt to show she could compete with the older school of writers on their own home grounds.

John Wain is the spokesman for the group of which Amis is the embodiment. It is not only that Wain is more seriously polemical than Amis, but also that he sums up in himself almost all aspects of the Movement as well—a pattern typical to many of its members of turning indifferently from genre to genre. A poet like Amis himself, Donald Davie, Elizabeth Jennings and Philip Larkin, Wain is also a critic like Al Alvarez and Lawrence Lerner. Drama is the one field he has not yet tried; and here the new values have been represented chiefly by John Osborn, whose *Look Back in Anger* was successfully played in New York, after annoying critics and intriguing playgoers in London.

Wain is also (more accurately, has been until recently) a teacher of literature; and in this respect, too, he is not unusual. The movement is largely academic; at least its members are teachers in the lower ranks and in the remoter colleges. Here he and his colleagues are not unlike many of our contemporary American writers, though quite different from such earlier rebels against "Bloomsbury" as D. H. Lawrence. Imagine Lawrence settling down to a lifetime of lecturing on Metaphysical poetry at a university in, say, Leeds! Like their authors, the protagonists of the new novels are teachers, and their conflicts are fought out in terms of teaching jobs won or lost.

It would be wrong, however, to think of these writers as sitting securely behind the walls of a traditional British university. They cluster rather in the provincial universities (the "red-brick" schools founded during the nineteenth century in the grimmer industrial cities of England), whose faculties are drawn

---

* By now *Lucky Jim* has become so much a part of popular mythology, that the characters in more recent post-Angry books are shown reading it, comparing themselves to its protagonist.

more and more from sons of working-class and lower-middle-class parents, seeking security and worrying not about the quality of the port but about the availability of baby sitters. The new British writer finds himself in a college, that is to say, when the colleges are well on the way to becoming merely other centers for the status-hungry.

It is easier to say what the new writers are against than to define what they are for. In general they are against the alliance of high culture, fashion, Fabian socialism and homosexuality which has been described earlier; but this begins to seem more and more like being against the Holy Roman Empire, for "Bloomsbury," whatever life it may once have possessed, is now dying. The novels of the Movement are, in this sense, weapons in a class war which is already over. Yet the fight must still go on—if not against the fact, against certain illusions which survive it. What the new writers satirize is the tendency in themselves to pretend to the standards of an upper class which no longer has roots or function, the tendency in their more insecure colleagues to turn themselves into parodies of artists in a (lovely, after all!) world, which they have destroyed in the act of entering.

The poets of the thirties, who had seemed to challenge but had ended by adapting themselves to the values of "Bloomsbury," irk them especially. They are less appalled by the defection of Guy Burgess to Moscow than they are by the fact that Stephen Spender can sit at peace with E. M. Forster. They refer contemptuously to the "hygienic Marxist-Freudian" approach of Auden and his followers, and comment wryly on their desire to be "one with a vaguely conceived People." Charles Lumley, protagonist of John Wain's *Living in the Present*, doubtless speaks for his author as well as himself when he boasts that he had been "right to despise them [the intellectuals of the thirties] for their idiotic attempt to look through two telescopes at the same time: one fashioned of German psychology and pointed at themselves, the other of Russian economics and directed at the English working class."

Part of the problem arises because the Marxist intellectuals became the schoolmasters of the newer generations, generations to which, therefore, the obsessive social concerns of the earlier period took on the peculiar irreality of classroom "history." Donald Davie puts it succinctly in a poem which has infuriated certain survivors of the thirties:

> The Anschluss, Guernica—all the names
> At which those poets thrilled, or were afraid,
> For me mean schools and schoolmasters and games;
> And in the process someone is betrayed.

Not only the social concerns, but even more the religious impulses of their elders baffle and bore the new writers. When Kingsley Amis, invited to comment on Colin Wilson (one pretentious young man exaggeratedly praised by his elders, though quite out of tune with his contemporaries), asks who the hell is Kierkegaard, this is in part a pose; but it is also the reflection of a fundamental indifference to any religious thinkers and a furious contempt for the more fashionable ones. The atheist existentialists are scarcely more congenial to the new young than the believers; though Iris Murdoch has written a sympathetic book on Sartre, John Wain expresses a more typical response: "he was English enough to feel a savage contempt for modish philosophers who went about preaching a profitable brand of nihilism, blandly informing their fellow creatures that they were already in hell. . . ." The philistine tone, the half-information are both revelatory; but "*English* enough" is the critical phrase; for the younger writers have turned inward to domestic concerns and home-grown virtues, turning away from all internationalisms, whether of chic or Marxism.

The literary enthusiasms of their predecessors seem to the newer writers as alien as their other allegiances. John Donne, Gerard Manley Hopkins, the French symbolists, the "revolutionists of the word" associated with *transition*—these they reject as they reject the guarded irony of tone with which the poets of the thirties played their literary games. Davie's poem comments on this, too:

> They played the fool, not to appear as fools
> In time's long glass. A deprecating air

Disarmed, they thought, the jests of later schools;
Yet irony itself is doctrinaire . . .

For the thirties, the new writers have, I think, a certain residue of respect—at least the sense that there one finds foes worthy of engaging. The forties, on the other hand, apparently strike them as thoroughly despicable; and perhaps the strongest charge they have to make against the surviving upper-class Marxists is that they were taken in by later fads; that they cooperated in the "canonization of Dylan Thomas" and of the turgid Romanticism for which he stood. To many of the new young, Thomas has come to seem the apotheosis of the False Poet: operatic, sodden, all shapeless dithyrambics and professional Welshness. Though they are domestic, the new writers are not parochial; and local color offends them as much as internationalism.

A character shamelessly drawn from Thomas plays the role of "a dirty little sod" in Amis' *That Uncertain Feeling,* and a professional Scots bard, equally drunk and devoted to chasing women, makes a similar appearance in Wain's *Living in the Present.* The writers of the Movement like to claim they have their own anti-Thomas (R. S. Thomas, author of *Song of the Year's Turning*), an Anglican clergyman who believes that poetry should be read to oneself, heard with the inner ear.

What most disturbs them is finally not Dylan Thomas himself so much as his *cult;* for the latter seems to them to sum up all they hate in intellectual pretentiousness and faddism. They are driven by a rage against ladies' literary societies, chamber-music groups, recorder concerts, amateur dramatics, academic flummery—any kind of culture-mongering. At their worst, they list toward a true middlebrow (and English) sort of anti-intellectualism, not unlike that which motivated George Orwell, who is one of their models. It must be said frankly that philistinism is a part of their artistic program, a New Philistinism, to be sure, nurtured not on pious tracts but on science fiction and jazz records. In their hands, however, militant middlebrowism sometimes functions as a useful weapon in the fight against a quiet, upper-class reign of terror based on a frozen high style and a rigidified good taste.

The new writers are not above or beyond politics; yet they seem in an elusive way to be *past it*, having come to maturity after what the thirties had meant by politics had lost most of its sense and significance. They are generally pro-labor and opposed to anything that reminds them of Fascism; but they are post-Marxist as they are post-Freudian. In various political parties, they find fragments of what seems to them a true view of society; in none do they appear to find a sufficient embodiment of their own aspirations. They vote Labor not unlike certain American intellectuals, who, without great enthusiasm, support Adlai Stevenson. The authors who most move them range in politics from Willam Empson, whose sympathies with the Communists have led him to swallow the most flagrant tales of germ warfare in Korea, to George Orwell, whose vision of all that was worst in England and Russia blended into the anti-Utopia of *1984*.

If in politics they must be called post-Marxist, in religion they are *post*-post-Christian, pupils of teachers who themselves had lost all orthodox belief, unbelievers twice removed. The shadow of Wittgenstein falls over them and they tend to assume that metaphysics is meaningless. Yet they cannot avoid being shaped by the religious commitments of the class whom they represent in its final avatar; they are the last manifestation of English nonconformism, dissenters without God. Their most immediate ancestor is the Cambridge critic F. R. Leavis, harried veteran of a long war with "Bloomsbury"; and it is, in large part, his world-view that the new novelists adopt: areligious yet moralistic, nonpolitical yet aggressively class conscious, the faith of a British Last Puritan.

They are, indeed, secular Puritans, "distrustful of too much richness or too much fanaticism," and their protagonists, like all fictional projections of the Puritan mind, are typically on the run, a step or two ahead of fell temptation. The tempter is for them sometimes the homosexual (with alarming regularity, their characters brush off the clutching, pale hands of queers), sometimes intellectually pretentious upper-class women, offering sex as a bait in the trap of accommodation. Chiefly, however, it is some more abstract symbol of compromise which the hero flees: a raise, a promotion, a better job—finally, respectability itself. Typically enough, in our time of easy living, it is not failure and poverty against which the protagonist struggles but their opposites. In the book of the new young, nothing fails like success.

The hero of the new British novel is, then, the lonely individual narrowly evading respectability, or the harried, petty-bourgeois couple just escaping prosperity. Poverty and loneliness and exclusion are the touchstones of morality and merit—the Puritans' materialist measures of grace not refused but turned upside down. Rejection is offered as a way of life, though never *total* rejection which threatens to become religious or at least fanatic. The newer British fiction is plagued by knowing much better where to begin than where to end; its heroes flirt with self-destruction, suicide or utter declassing, but in the last chapters they tend to be bundled shamelessly into some sentimental compromise. Back goes the protagonist to the colliery in which his father worked, back to the old school or into the arms of a Good Woman.

One does not know exactly how to take these pre-emptory Happy Endings. Are they the outcome of utter confusion, or mere strategies to please the public, like the typical last scenes of movies? Certainly the new writers, though they woo failure in the name of their characters, are eager for success in their own right. They *want* to produce best sellers, and would consider it outmoded snobbishness to refuse to tickle the average reader in order to gain the approval of a sensitive few.

Yet plot is less important in revealing what the writers are after than are the attitudes of their protagonists: Jimmy Porter with his trumpet and sweet stall more important than the fable of *Look Back in Anger,* Lucky Jim and the "faces" with which he secretly mocks his fate more significant than what happens in the book called by his name. Whatever other characteristics the new hero possesses, whether he be a "card," a *schlemiel* or a self-torturer, he must possess two qualities: a fear of success and a talent for anger. As the fear is the substance of his politics, the anger is the substance of his self. These new heroes are irascible men above all, impossible husband and lovers, impotent bullies gifted with a rough eloquence whose source is their rage at their own predicament and the state of the world. Such irascibility is at least a relief from the self-pity which has been too long the keynote of the novel; and it leads outward into action rather than inward into elaborate analyses of motive and sensibility, toward the picaresque rather than into stream of consciousness.

There have been impassioned arguments recently over whether these fictional figures are true to their own time—representative of the young as they are. Such debates seem most often to end in absurd, though heated, queries about why in hell Osborne's Jimmy Porter didn't get a job with a band if he were really all that talented; and they are, of course, essentially pointless from the start. It is a little like asking whether Hemingway's Jake Barnes really existed; whether, after all, there *was*, in fact, a Lost Generation.

What we are beholding is the creation of a *myth* of a generation, the response of a certain kind of just-short-of-thirty anti-intellectual intellectual to life in contemporary England. What such a writer renders is the way in which he enjoys being, or is forced to be (the two get mixed up), aware of himself, his consciousness of the drama of his existence. That drama is not history, it is an inner or imaginative drama that is felt rather than lived. Whether or not the Angry Young Men existed before the books which embody them, they exist now—for us as well as for themselves. It is their spokesman who is sent off to the Youth Congress in Moscow to register the "British view" for the British press, at the very moment that his right to represent anything is being challenged. And this is a joke that the younger writers can especially relish.

Indeed, they are very good at jokes in general; for though they look back in anger, they report in humor. The interior drama to which they bear witness, as well as the outer drama which it obliquely reflects, they regard finally not as tragic or pitiful, but as *funny*. Theirs is not, of course, the delicate, protective irony of an Isherwood, much less the superior and polished mockery of a Waugh or a Huxley. Amis, for instance, who is the funniest of them all, can sound like P. G. Wodehouse when he recounts the flight of his hero, dressed in female Welsh costume and pursued simultaneously by an angry husband and a drunk and amorous workman.

Most often the new writers plunge from satire to brutal farce, as deliberately vulgar as Wain's description of Edgar Banks (in *Living in the Present*) doing an imitation of himself vomiting in a phone booth and of a cop attempting to arrest him for committing that nuisance. Amis is the master of the pratfall, the minor indignity which forever bars his characters from seeming more than fools. Here is one of his husbands trying to strike a convincing attitude before a jealous and reproachful wife:

> "No, we just met by chance. Honestly."
> "I bet she was glad to see you like that."
> "Like what?"
> "You've got a bogey on your nose. Improves your looks no end."
>
> I was near the mirror I used for shaving and which hung above the washbasin. I peeped in and saw the bogey. It was large and vermiform and clung to the wing of my right nostril. I removed it feeling a little downcast. Even the dignity of Charles I on the scaffold, I reasoned, would have been deflated by the executioner telling him what Jean had just told me. . . .

At its furthest metaphysical reach, this becomes the grotesque gallows humor of Iris Murdoch's *Flight from the Enchanter*, a symbol of the Absurd in the full existentialist sense of the word. The new writers do, indeed, feel their lives as absurd, but usually with a small "a" rather than a capital. They have no vision of their plight as cosmically horrible or ridiculous, even as they have no vision of themselves as authors of cosmically significant works. If they write loosely strung, picaresque novels, "funny books," it is because this seems modest, proper to their diffidence. A poem by Philip Larkin (in the opinion of many, the best poet of the group) puts it quite candidly—so candidly, in fact, that it quite enraged one reviewer in *Encounter,* who found so bland a refusal to be outrageous the ultimate outrage.

To the Daughter of a Friend

May you be ordinary,
Have, like other women,
An average of talents:
Not ugly, not good-looking,
Nothing uncustomary
To pull you off your balance,
That, unworkable itself,
Stops all the rest from working.
In fact, may you be dull—
If that is what a skilled,
Vigilant, flexible,
Unemphasized, enthralled
Catching of happiness is called.

Dedicated to such an ideal, it is no wonder that the poets of the Movement sound a good deal more like the English versifiers of the late eighteenth century than either William Empson or Wallace Stevens, whom they like to speak of as their favorites. For similar reasons, the novelists turn rather to the consistently flat prose of Orwell than to more elegant examples for their models. "Amis," V. S. Pritchett has written in uncomprehending annoyance, "writes with his boots." This is true, as it is true that Wain is imprecise and clumsy in his polemics (his more graceful opponents leave him thrashing helplessly in their web of wit) and quite unsubtle in his fiction. Even Iris Murdoch, the most artistically ambitious of the lot, often is confused and blurred to the point of chaos. But this is, of course, exactly the point!

For too long the British novelist has had to submit to an imperious ideal of good writing which began as a liberation and has ended as a tyranny. The impulse of the new novel is back toward the popular ineptness of the Victorians: back through the drawing-room finish, the upper-class grace and wit, which give so odd a uniformity to English fiction from Firbank to Waugh, E. M. Forster to Isherwood, and Aldous Huxley to Henry Green. Once more we can see that it is a class war which is being waged in British literature; that we are witnessing an attempt to redeem fiction and poetry in theme, diction and decor from the demands of one social group in the interests of another. With the weapons of crudity and righteous anger and moral bluntness, the new writers are trying to deliver literature from the circles which captured it early in this century, and to restore it—to whom?

To a group not yet, it must be confessed, clearly defined even to itself—to the New Men in a New Society which proposes to itself the ideal of classlessness, to the real or imaginary Common Readers who are (or anyhow *should* be) emerging from the "Americanization" of British culture. The conflict over the new literature is sometimes spoken of in the correspondence columns as a debate between metropolitans and provincials, Londoners and outsiders; and it is true that many of the new writers live, or have lived, in places like Reading or Swansea or Sheffield, where they teach in "redbrick" universities. But it is hard to be provincial in the older sense in a world of mass communications and mass culture, where the former provinces threaten, indeed, to become the center. More properly, the new writers must be regarded not as provincials but as an "intellectual proletariat" of the Welfare State—perhaps even better as a kind of degraded petty bourgeoisie of the spirit.

Trained in the great universities themselves, though often as scholarship boys and after preparation in county or municipal schools, the members of the Movement find themselves compelled to teach literature, though they would like chiefly to make it. They are not "dons" in any traditional British sense, gentlemen by definition, living in semi-monastic retirement from the vulgar. They are plunged, armpit deep, into a society of largely misguided cultural aspiration and feebly camouflaged illiteracy, where their third-year students may never have heard of Homer and cannot without great pain make sense of a passage from Shakespeare.

The manners and codes of what they call contemptuously "Oxbridge" are irrelevant to their worlds, unreal; and yet these still hedge their lives about—in the form at least of shoddy emulation. Though the newer writers despise old-line philological criticism, having been trained by such "New Critics" as F. R. Leavis, they are urged to publish "scholarly" articles if they would hold their jobs and win promotions. Similarly, though they distrust the relaxed literary gossip of London and the amateur appreciation that passes for criticism in such circles, they find their own work unfavorably compared to that appreciation.

Most wounding of all, perhaps, though artistically most stimulating, is their sense of their own situation: their vision of themselves as the first self-conscious New Men of a dingy New World—not deposed aristocrats in the republic of letters, but minor cultural employees of a bureaucracy. The sordidness of their lives especially obsesses them, the ugliness of their habitual surroundings, which emerges not only in the backgrounds against which the buffoonery of their books is played out, but in their personal complaints and apologies. In 1953, John Wain begins by speaking of the "ugly, industrial city" in which he finds himself, then cries out in answer to those who have called him a "don," "I sit not in a gracious, panelled room —but in a tiny, slum-clearance bungalow."

Similarly, Kingsley Amis is quoted on the jacket of *Lucky Jim*: "I write in a small room facing the blank wall of the house next door, between lectures in English literature at the University College of Swansea." From their unspectacularly difficult position, the new writers judge and portray their world in terms of a satire rooted in bitterness and self-mockery. That bitterness and self-mockery, as well as its seedy setting, we know in our country, too. It is to be found among graduate students and junior instructors in Bloomington or Evanston or Madison or Chapel Hill—our own Readings and Swanseas, where the young sit looking out of their windows at blank walls.

Their critics sometimes accuse the "kitchen sink" school of letters of indulging in sordidness for its own sake, of exploiting the disgusting out of some obscure love of filth. Yet it is no private nightmare but a real public world the new writers have made their theme—a world more real now than the lovelier world of the Sitwells and Russian ballet, the dying world in which art is a final grace of cultivated life and eccentricity its spice. The world of Amis and Wain is the declassed, uniform world of mass culture, where the country house and the common room of Oxbridge enter only via the detective stories of Dorothy Sayers: a world where graciousness has followed the last servant out the door—or is about to. It is a world best rendered by Kingsley Amis, who has made it impossible for anyone in England to pretend any longer that it does not exist:

> The baby, his upper lip hidden behind his lower one, was sitting on the pot, crying steadily; Eira was crouching naked with her face in Jean's lap . . . Jean, herself apparently wearing only a dressing gown, was vigorously towelling Eira's hair . . . Around them was a multitude of objects such as might, in a memory test, be shown to spectators for one minute and then withdrawn. Apart from clothes, adult and juvenile, male and female, ironed, newly washed and fit to be washed, there was a half-eaten browning apple, several broken biscuits, a plastic doll, the torso of a rubber doll, some children's books with pictures of clothed animals on the covers, a cup, a card of blue safety pins, an orange with one of my pencils stuck into it, a bottle of cod-liver oil, a pair of plastic knickers . . . some nappies in varying states, the defaced cover of my *Astounding Science Fiction,* and a lot of other things.
>
> "Well, hullo," Jean said.

This, we must grant, is a world we inhabit, too—not any of the exotic worlds of Evelyn Waugh or Nancy Mitford Jones, but the depressing One World, with which all of us must come to imaginative terms. It is the merciless delineation of this long-familiar (to us) terrain which is "new" to the British novel; and it is the acceptance of such a world and of the limitation of passion and ambition among those living in it—in short, the acceptance of the *declassing of experience*—which makes such literature new and disturbing in its own country. In Amis, Wain *et al.*, the "American novel" has arrived in England after its more touted triumphs in France and Italy.*

It has come not by deliberate invitation as in other parts of Western Europe, but inevitably as the result of certain changes in society, especially the shift in status of the intellectual in general and of the writer in particular. The embarrassment of the English reader at this unforeseen and unsolicited event explains a little the almost hysterical tone of his response to it. For us, the problem is considerably easier. No class allegiances or national pride stand in the way of our recognizing a literature that makes an attempt (whatever its crudity or occasional downright philistinism) to possess imaginatively the classless, grim world which has become our common home.

* But it will not *stay* in England! Understandably enough, the kind of writer I have been talking about, given a taste of life in the United States, wants to stay here. Poets, novelists, playwrights among the "Angries" keep escaping from the United Kingdom via lecture tours, fellowships, New York productions, etc. And, meanwhile, their inspiration runs down or is denied. Amis' books have got progressively worse; Iris Murdoch has renounced her own early work as "neurotic" and writes sentimental ladies' books dedicated to love; Osborne grows rich; only the new academics proliferate—and the myth threatens to outlive the literature composed in its name.

Leopold and Loeb: A Perspective in Time

In its first intention, a review of a
spate of books based on the Leopold
and Loeb trial

In an age which no longer believes in sin, crime becomes
the capital concern of the moral imagination. Questions of
innocence and guilt are thought of as being resolved in the
public arena of the courtroom rather than in the privacy of the
confessional or the heart. We are, despite our sense of religious
recommitment, such an age; and we seem never to tire of crime
novels and stage versions of court trials, of newspapers directly
translated from the police blotter and televised adventures of
cops. Generation after generation of us have grown up identifying ourselves, according to temperament and training, with the
criminal or detective, the prosecuting attorney or the defense;
indeed, none of us can enter a courtroom without the sense of
walking onto a stage where we have already played a part. The
criminal trial, the congressional hearing, the grand jury are
natural dramas before which a whole community, the nation
itself sometimes sits entranced; but more than that, they are
rituals—realer to us than communion or prayer, rituals whose
event decides for us the riddle that obsesses us: *Who done it?*
Who is guilty, who innocent?

It is never a wonder, then, that a novel based on a crime
become a best seller, be read with peculiar intensity by the
popular audience. The only question is why at a given moment
one crime seems to that audience the crime par excellence, an
epitome of the moment's own awareness of guilt. God knows the
newspapers provide us every few weeks with another Crime of

the Century; and there seems, on the face of it, small reason to ransack dead files for old causes. Yet we have recently seen within the span of a year the publication of two novels (one already a play and perhaps on its way to becoming a movie) based on the same criminal case, decided more than thirty years ago. It seems an anomaly—two grave robbers after the same corpse, but this is not all. The publishers have sensed the demand behind the double event and have rushed back into print a journalistic account which first appeared in 1925 (camouflaged as usual to seem new to the unwary newsstand customer) and the autobiography of one of the principles in the crime. But what has the Franks case, what have Leopold and Loeb to do with us in 1958?

The renascence of interest in their case is not a literary phenomenon so much as a reflection of a crisis in popular culture: the reappearance of a legend appropriate to our times. None of the works which embody it is, in the real sense, "literature." Even Meyer Levin's *Compulsion*, put together with skill and a certain passion, does not finally transcend the interest of the documents upon which it is based. It remains parasitic upon the earlier newspaper stories, the psychiatrists' published case reports, but especially upon our collective memories of the shocking crime: the naked boy's body thrust up a culvert, and the two adolescent "degenerates" (it was the term of those days), who killed him quite at random, tittering to each other at the trial.

Leopold and Loeb, or to give them their fictional names, Steiner and Straus (it is symptomatically difficult to remember the transparent pseudonyms) are not the inventions of Meyer Levin, as Raskolnikov is, for instance, the invention of Dostoevsky. Their case has not been re-created out of an unnoticed newspaper clipping or a trivial piece of gossip to embody the larger social vision of a writer, as in *Crime and Punishment, Madame Bovary* or *An American Tragedy*; their significance belongs not to art but to not-quite-current events. Since, therefore, the meanings of the crime of Leopold and Loeb are implicit in the act itself as that act is apprehended by the popular imagination, all Levin and James Yaffe can do is to explicate those meanings—

in effect, to solve the crime. Their books are consequently detective stories in the sense that Dostoevsky's or Dreiser's are not; indeed, they resemble more a book like Poe's *Mystery of Marie Roget,* not fiction but the fictionized version of a puzzling and much publicized act of violence.

Levin, like Poe, projects himself into the events of his case in the guise of an investigator: a poor young Jewish student called Sid Silver, a part-time newspaperman to whom are attributed several critical discoveries which lead to the exposure of the criminals. The real solution of the case for Levin, however, goes beyond finding out what hand held the chisel that cracked the skull of fourteen-year-old Bobby Franks; more important to him is discovering what impulse moved that hand. To the aid of the student-reporter-detective comes another Jewish student: the embryo psychoanalyst, played in *Compulsion* by Willie Weiss; but the psychic detective investigates crime for reasons exactly opposed to those of the ordinary cop. His aim is not to dispel the show of innocence and reveal the fact of guilt, but to dissipate the conviction of guilt and reveal the fact of innocence: to deprive us of the belief in the reality of crime as we have already been robbed of faith in the reality of sin.

To this issue, so vital in the Franks case, whose courtroom revelations were those not of private eyes but of psychiatrists, we shall return; for now it is enough to insist that Levin's novel (and by the same token Yaffe's) is, in its attempt to "solve" a given situation rather than to create one, a documentary rather than a poetic book: what is called by its author in a preface (unfailing appendage of the genre) a "historical novel." The paradoxical nature of this kind of fiction was aptly described by Manzoni, who himself made one of the major attempts at the form, and his description defines Levin's failure: The historical romance is, he writes, "a hybrid form in which fiction and history must be introduced, without the possibility either of balancing the elements or indicating in what proportion or relationship they are introduced; a hybrid form, in short, which there is no right way to create, since its assumptions are intrinsically contradictory."

Yaffe attempts to bypass the problem by stripping from

his protagonists all their historical differentia, by rescuing Leopold and Loeb from history rather than rendering them in history. His protagonists, called this time Barry Morris and Paul King, are no longer specifically Jewish, no longer overt homosexuals, no longer rich college boys in the Chicago of the twenties; they are, in intent, timeless figures of juvenile delinquency, in fact, ciphers thinly disguised as New York prep-school boys of the fifties. Yet we know all the time that they are *really* Leopold and Loeb, and are disconcerted by the documented facts which slip by Yaffe's censorship (Leopold's fantasies, for instance, or the scheme for collecting ransom), facts which detach themselves from his perfunctorily contrived context, and, improbable enough in their own right, seem now doubly improbable. Neither "history" nor fiction seems adequate to the legend; but no more is autobiography.

Nathan Leopold, writing from prison thirty-three years after his crime, in an attempt to set the record straight by substituting for what he calls "Mr. Levin's long-distance, do-it-yourself psychoanalysis" a truer portrait of himself, ends only with a handful of irrelevant clichés: "I felt a little dejected of course. But there was only one thing to do: pull in my belt another notch and try to face up to the future as courageously as possible. . . . There is always one consolation in touching rock bottom: you know that any change has to be for the better!" Reminiscence and remorse cannot create a Leopold adequate to our memory of his crime or our sense of what his suffering in prison must have been. His crime and trial he announces he will not even treat; but he cannot quite forbear an attempt to retouch the image of his still loved accomplice (whose death at the hands of a fellow convict, Leopold insists, was not occasioned by a homosexual pass in the showers) or even mitigating a little his own guilt. How earnestly he argues (and apparently now believes) that he never said, "It is easy to justify such a death, as easy as to justify an entomologist impaling a butterfly on a pin"—that he used the metaphor not to describe his own attitude to the murder but rather to upbraid certain reporters for their attitude toward him.

Far more than any fiction, Leopold's account serves to remind us of what is legendary in our reconstruction of his crime and, indeed, of the criminals who perpetrated it. It is, after all, neither disgraceful nor disconcerting that he assert for the sake of his own peace as well as for the edification of the parole board facts which do not accord with our reading of the documents; what is disturbing is that his style (which cannot lie) reveals a man of fifty-two impossible to connect with the nineteen-year-old boy tried in 1924 or, at least, with our image of that boy.

It is all very well for Leopold to assure us, in words as flat and banal as those of any other self-made man, that he has been a good prisoner, that he has never departed from the code of his fellow cons, that he is a good citizen ("O.K., let's face it: I was and am patriotic; I love my country") and once risked death by malaria to help a wartime medical experiment. He has every right, too, to remind us that he reads the *Yiskor* service on the anniversary of his parents' death—and to invoke in the next breath the spirit of Christmas; he can even insist we read his verse on the death of a pet bird:

> *And I think, too, he'd started to love me,*
> *(I'd taken his mother's place)*
> *For when on my hand I would lift him,*
> *He'd cuddle up to my face.*
>
> . . . .
>
> *And I found in my heart to wonder*
> *If this little mite of a bird*
> *Hadn't learned more of Christ's own teachings*
> *Than some men of whom I'd heard.*

But how are we to connect the balding ex-quiz kid, the author of such lines, who looks up at us from the jacket of his improbable success story (he is, as he writes, a trusty, with a TV set and a framed letter from Einstein hanging on his cell wall) with the well-groomed boy who acted out the "crime in a vacuum," the *acte gratuite* of which French intellectuals dreamed. The relation of the two Leopolds seems accidental and unconvincing: the one perfected correspondence courses for prisoners (under the aegis *Ratione autem liberamur,* by reason, however, we are freed), the other killed Bobby Franks. In Leopold's account the two are simultaneously linked and separated by an act of repentance; in us, they must be joined by an effort of imaginative faith, a suspension of disbelief.

It is the myth, however, which finally concerns us, not the man who has survived it; for the myth has a life of its own, though it lay dormant for over thirty years and has revived only at the moment that the man emerges from prison. Between its resurrection and his release there is surely some connection; both awaited a certain evolutionary development of the popular mind, the creation of a new middlebrow definition of innocence and guilt. One can understand Leopold's horror at confronting in *Compulsion* his legendary image; but he is surely wrong when he wails that the appearance of the novel means "the death of my hopes." Levin followed up his book with a published plea for Leopold's parole; but the book itself had already made clear that in the court of middle-class, middlebrow opinion, which had condemned Leopold before the judge passed sentence, that sentence had already been revoked. The old rigorous anger had long since died away.

It should be remembered that the rage which the revelation of the murder of Bobby Franks stirred in the newspaper-reading public of 1924 was, for the more enlightened at least, more the product of bafflement than of fear. The surliest lowbrows found in the case just another atrocity to justify their distrust of Jews, atheists, intellectuals and "perverts." Titillated to discover in the daily press the mention of sodomy, they yielded to an orgy of righteous pornography, refusing to the last to give up the comforting belief that the Franks boy had been buggered before (or even after!) being killed. It was only what they had always suspected went on in those plush South side mansions. Their attitude is summed up in the vulgar, almost hysterical plea of the State's Attorney, who reviled the accused as "these two perverts, these two murderers," "these poor, little sons of multi-millionaires," "these young, egotistical smart alecks"; and cried out that "they are entitled to as much mercy as mad dogs are entitled to."

The conscientious middlebrows, on the other hand, did not know what to do with a crime rooted in perversity rather than politics, in prosperity rather than poverty. Liberals by and large, they were committed to the sentimental thesis that murder and kidnapping were the crimes of the desperate poor. The rich they looked for not in the docket but on the side lines crying for the condemnation of victims driven to violence. In the beginning they were tempted by the same simple slogan that satisfied the lowbrows: "Kill them!" though they eschewed anti-Semitic and anti-intellectual arguments in favor of the pious demand that wealth not be allowed to buy off justice. Clarence Darrow should have spoken for *them*, as he had so often before, but was committed on principle to the defense; and this time the defense was on the side of the rich! In the end, their true spokesman turned out to be the Judge, who wept a little as Darrow summed up, and saved the accused from death; though he urged that they never be granted a parole, and remarked (perhaps to persuade himself that he had not really been moved to mercy) that "to the offenders . . . the prolonged suffering of years of confinement may well be the severest form of retribution and expiation." Life imprisonment, without the possibility of parole—this is the middlebrows' last word in 1924.

The real intellectuals, the highbrows, however, were simply not interested, for to them the case made no symbolic sense; it remained always just a courtroom trial and not a cause. The issues were too hopelessly confused: if the boys were rich and spoiled (on the other side, the side of the oppressor), they were also Jews and students (on "our" side, the side of the scorned), as well as young, neurotic, lost (on *no* side?). For the highbrow the case failed utterly to define a clear-cut "we" and "they," to distinguish "our" innocence from "their" guilt. Darrow, who was defending Leopold and Loeb, had, to be sure, defended Debs, and Debs represented to the intellectuals untainted innocence; but the middlebrows' insistent whispers about a "million dollar fee" made it easier to believe that Darrow was "selling out" than that he was carrying on the good old fight in a new guise. The notion of the Sell-out to Big Money was an even more firmly established cliché than the concept of crime as the product of private property.

Besides, Darrow for all his passionate dedication had begun

to seem more than a little old-fashioned: with his sentimental rhetoric and self-conscious folksiness, his poetic repertoire limited to A. E. Housman and the *Rubáiyát of Omar Khayyám*, his small-town Baptist-baiting, his war against free will and his crusade to end capital punishment. What had any of this to do with the sexual revolution at home, the artistic revolution in Paris or the Soviet Revolution in Russia, with any living movement of protest or dissent? Dating even faster than H. L. Mencken, Darrow had begun to look like yesterday's liberal, the provincial and slightly ridiculous spokesman for the not-quite-enlightened middlebrows.

If anyone in the case represented the intellectuals, it was Nathan Leopold, with his tortured Jewish face and his quotations from their own kind of literature. Yet in him, all their attitudes and commitments were parodied: the blatant atheism, the theory of the Superman ("the only mistake he . . . can do, is make a mistake, that anything that gives him pleasure is right"), but especially the absurd questions he had left sealed to be answered after death by his spirit, if it survived: "Is there complete omniscience?" "Is life on earth correct in judgment, or is there a higher judgment?" "What is happiness?" Leopold and Loeb were not so much intellectuals as the middlebrows' image of the intellectual: the young "genius," the "prodigy" who reads outlandish books and skips grades in school (were they not the yongest graduates in history of the Universities of Michigan and Chicago?). Leopold is especially true to type, from his owlish glasses and faintly condescending air, to his painstaking classification of birds, his study of the Oscan and Umbrian dialects, his dazzling scores on the intelligence tests—just then becoming for the earnest parent more important than report cards or diplomas. Twenty years later he would have been a quiz kid, thirty years later a winner (subject ornithology, of course) on the $64,000 Question; and watching mothers would have held him up to their sons as an example of how hard work in school pays off in America.

The Franks case was then, and remains now, the middlebrow American Tragedy; and it is fitting that Leopold's autobiography (composed after he "had all but mastered twenty-seven languages") be introduced by the best-selling authority on crime and dean of the paperback market, Erle Stanley Gardner. But what were the intellectuals of the twenties to do with these travesties of themselves improbably come to life and notoriety? Even to plead that they were mentally sick was dangerous at a moment when anyone arguing (as Leopold and Loeb seemed to argue) that bourgeois morality ought to be transcended was classified as a "nut."

Moreover, the New Psychology, called upon by the defense and debated with ignorant vehemence in the daily press, was only watered-down psychoanalysis, old stuff to the advanced— to whom it seemed useful chiefly as a weapon against the sexual mores of the middle classes. They were not yet prepared to go beyond the dated daring of Darrow and launch a general defense of the sexual deviant (Hemingway, who was to be their spokes- man, was at that moment in Paris, scorning queers even as he scorned Mencken); nor were they inspired by Darrow's con- tention that no one was responsible for anything, that crime was only disease. Their special interest lay in asserting that accepted morality was disease. But this sounded embarrassingly like the callow assertion of Leopold and Loeb.

Indeed, G. K. Chesterton was making precisely this point in one of the few lively, though, of course, wrongheaded, com- ments produced by a case remarkable for the dullness of the responses it stirred. His piece, written for *The Illustrated London News* and reprinted by that household cultural staple, *The Liter- ary Digest*, charged bluntly that the crime of "these young Yankee Jews," these "completely educated . . . Jewish intel- lectuals" was the product of an irreligious education and the "philosophy of experience." For him, Leopold and Loeb were, like "the boy and girl experimentalists" of avant-garde literature and bohemian life, pledged to the pursuit of "anything that will make a bored person happy."

If all experience is (as he insists the intellectuals assert) desirable per se, then murder is an experience no more to be shunned than adultery. Of all literate commentators on the case, only Chesterton seems to find it perfectly compatible with all his beliefs. There are implicit in it no contradictions for this black Catholic socialist; rather it provides him with an occasion for trotting out all his favorite whipping boys: modern youth, the

New Education, millionaires ("one of the exceedingly few attempts ever made in the modern world to punish a millionaire for anything"), Jews and especially Americans. The case had, indeed, in this last respect an appeal to all shades of British opinion from the intellectual left (*The New Statesman* sneered coolly at the "American institution of trial by newspaper" and "that world of American riches and indulgence") to the solid right (*The Saturday Review* lauded the accused for having managed to commit "as finished a murder as we . . . can expect even from America").

The simpler pleasures of post-World War I American-baiting were, however, denied to our own serious observers, whose quarrel with their country was based on quite different grounds. Even so critical and self-righteous a journal as *The Nation*, speaking for the minority of enlightened middlebrows who favored sentencing Leopold and Loeb to life imprisonment, preferred to concentrate on psychology and penal reform. In an editorial, taking its cue from the psychiatric defense, the editors assured their readers that "when we cease talking in terms of guilt and begin talking in terms of psychological cause and prevention, lawyers . . . may no longer be needed." This pious and optimistic prognosis they underlined some weeks later with the testimony of a practicing psychiatrist, who asked, "What do we know about human responsibility for human behavior?" and promptly answered himself, "I do not think the time far distant when all crime and bad behavior will be approached as human illness is now, where moral questions do not enter in."

Most middlebrow readers, however, even of *The Nation* were not yet ready to scrap their inherited notions of free will and guilt. The innocence they were eager to establish was not a universal innocence, but only that of the exploited and injured. The psychiatric issue, therefore, fell quickly from the lofty "philosophical" level on which it had been proposed by Darrow and *The Nation's* psychiatrist to that of a family squabble among American doctors. Though the presiding judge had specifically discounted the entire plea of pathological disability, and had mitigated the sentence of Leopold and Loeb on the basis of their youth alone, he had recognized the pertinency of such psychological testimony for future legislative reform, and this encouraged certain long-time critics of our courts and jails.

The case had been made a forum not only for the clash of oldsters and youngsters: "formal, orthodox psychology" versus "dynamic psychology"; it had served also to air the quarrel of psychiatric penologists in general with lawyers and the law. This long-term quarrel, given new impetus by a new instance, soon resumed its cool expert tone in the professional journals, much to the relief of the academic specialists, who had been embarrassed by the sensational aspects of the court case. Typically enough, Nathan Leopold, in the years when he was busy making good in jail, contributed statistical pieces of his own to the "scientific" literature on penology, collaborating in the process by which legends are reduced to footnotes.

Meanwhile, the intellectuals of the waning twenties had found other, more congenial courtroom legends. Even the Scopes trial, the occasion for Darrow's next spectacular performance, offered possibilities, however shopworn, for symbolic melodrama: once more the Bible-belters against the sophisticated, the fundamentalists versus the enlightened, this time refighting the Darwinian battle of 1859, seventy years late. It was two old men who faced each other in this last Menckenian circus, Bryan and Darrow, memorializing the end of an era, confronting their own deaths. In 1927, a new era was formally initiated; the thirties prematurely opened even before the Crash, as Sacco and Vanzetti brought together middlebrow and highbrow, liberal and Communist, alienated poet and suburban do-gooder in a single protest. Their trial and conviction provided the archetype for which the liberals had been waiting: the innocent victims, aliens, radicals, poor workingmen—and against them the prosperous Anglo-Saxon community genteelly howling for blood. The event combined all the pathos of innocence, abused and framed, with all the security implicit in an enemy clearly defined, battle lines cleanly drawn.

It was a case no one involved in the defense ever willingly forgot, more like a dream than an event in history; but the succeeding years, ever more ambiguous and unkind, refused to repeat it, though there were those who sought to recapture its pattern in a host of others: The Scottsboro Boys, the Trenton Six, even the Rosenbergs. In literature, highbrow and middle-brow, the events were almost ritually kept alive: in Upton Sinclair's *Boston*, in John Wexley's *Gods of the Lightning*, in *Winterset* and Howard Fast's belated *The Passion of Sacco and Vanzetti*, the scriptures of an Age of Innocence. Excerpts from Vanzetti's letters were printed as poems in a serious anthology of modern American verse; and at least one other work (*The Male Animal* on the stage, in the films, and lately on TV) created from the drama of a teacher persecuted for reading those excerpts to a class. For the age of Marxism and united fronts, this was the tragedy of the class struggle, *their* Case of the Century, in which the state was the criminal, the accused not guilty but framed.

What could be made at such a moment of the psychiatric record of the teen-age sons of millionaires, indeed, with any case in which the defendants were guilty as charged? When Richard Loeb was slashed to death with a razor in 1936, only a single major magazine in the United States considered the event worth an article. This time *The Nation* was silent, while *Time* exhumed all the discredited lowbrow canards (even the report that the Franks boy had been "violated"), excoriated the prison authorities who "pamper wealthy prisoners, place perverts in positions of authority." It reported, though with some skepticism, the popular fantasy that Loeb had not been killed at all, but spirited away alive by the omnipotent, rich Jews from whose ranks he came. In the end, the whole account seems anomalous, irrelevant, sandwiched between a feature story on John L. Lewis and the latest news on Stakhonovism in the Soviet Union.

The single literary treatment produced between the time of the case and the mid-fifties was Patrick Hamilton's play *The Rope*, a commercial thriller, which converted Leopold and Loeb into Oxford undergraduates, whose crime is uncovered by a poet and war hero embarrassingly reminiscent of Rupert Brooke. This play, performed in 1929, had to wait nearly twenty years for a movie version, in which Alfred Hitchcock moved the principals back to America (though only as far as New York) and converted the soldier-bard into a guilt-ridden schoolteacher, who attempts to make amends for having exposed his neurotic students to Nietzsche by exposing their crime. Beneath a rather perfunctory gesture at anti-intellectualism, Hitchcock is, like Hamilton before him, exploiting the case chiefly for the audience appeal of horror in an upper-class setting; and the film seemed not so much a revival of the case as a Technicolor tombstone on its grave. The crime that had shocked all middlebrow America appeared to have expired in the first film to be made without cutting, a vehicle for Jimmie Stewart.

Yet ten years after the release of Hitchcock's film, Leopold and Loeb had become once more a staple of mass culture on its middlebrow levels. Signaled not only by new novels, a play, an autobiography and the reprint of the McKernan book, but also by a series of articles in the *Saturday Evening Post,* an appeal for clemency by Meyer Levin in *Coronet* and a piece in *Life* itself, the revival has culminated in the freeing of Nathan Leopold— who had been consigned, presumably forever, to prison and oblivion. Already his plea for a decent obscurity, delivered at the prison gates, has been compared by a radio reporter to the prose of Vanzetti; and one foresees the revised anthologies, the next *Male Animal.*

It is as if the middlebrow mind has at last discovered the true meaning of the case it abandoned for Sacco and Vanzetti, its own true meaning in that case, and moves now to rewrite its past. Something it had denied in itself has been paroled along with the gray-faced murderer, puking on his ride toward the freedom he had awaited for thirty-three years. In an odd way, Leopold owes his freedom to the collapse of Marxism in America, to the middling liberal's rejection of economic determinism as a sufficient explanation of innocence and guilt. With the rejection of the clichés of social consciousness, the thirties are excised from the popular imagination; the preferred past of the prosperous and disenchanted fifties is the prosperous and disenchanted twenties—the two post-war decades reflecting each other as if the intervening decades did not exist. In this sense, Leopold and Loeb belong to a more general revival which brings back the early Hemingway to the films (not *For Whom the Bell Tolls* but *The Sun Also Rises*), the cloche and the dropped waistline to women's fashions, beards and bohemianism to the advanced young, archetypes of the flapper age to the current novel—and, at last, the posthumous conversion of *Lady Chatterley's Lover* into a best seller!

As Budd Schulberg redeemed Scott Fitzgerald for the middlebrow readers of fiction, so Levin rescues Leopold and Loeb. It is not, of course, in the heedless euphoria of their beginnings that we resurrect the heroes of Before-the-Crash, but in the pathos of their ends: Fitzgerald blind-drunk and mocked by Dartmouth undergraduates; Leopold, diabetic and pot-bellied, at the moment of his parole. The reader of my own generation and the one just before it, I suppose, responds most sensitively to the recalled twenties. This was our childhood, our youth, and we conceive it grown old along with us: the world of Big Bill Tilden and Al Capone, of Babe Ruth and Jack Dempsey—faces on the picture cards we played for or the newsreels we endured between the serial and the Western.

With the resurgence of the twenties, there has come a resurgence of Freudianism, too. Psychoanalysis as a method of treatment, a theory of the mind, has been a part of our culture uninterruptedly for nearly half a century; but as a *Weltanschauung*, a world-view, it has affected us in two major phases, quite different from each other. The first wave represents its capturing of the intellectuals' imaginations during the twenties, when it seemed to a restless avant-garde (never clearly aware of where D. H. Lawrence stopped and it began) a cue for sexual emancipation, deliverance from bourgeois taboos. The second wave reaches its climax just after World War II and is marked by the Freudianization of the middlebrow liberal. It is at this point that the ladies' magazines devote more and more space to superficial psychoanalytic articles on sex in marriage or sibling rivalry, PTAs sponsor sex-education films and enlightened parents learn to smile benignly at masturbation. It is an age in which the analyst becomes as standard an adjunct of modern living as the dentist.

To be sure, the Freudianism which triumphs in the suburbs and the housing developments is somewhat expurgated—stripped of its bleak stoicism, its tragic view of man and its more disturbing moral implications. At this point, Dr. Freud is confused with Dr. Kinsey and Dr. Spock, read as a good, gray guide to tolerance and understanding, a bourgeois prophet of the social adjustment which supplants the class struggle as an ideal image of society.

"The point is not to change the world but to *understand* it," runs the new anti-Marxist critique of the social philosophy of the thirties; and Freud seems somehow to sanction this revisionism. In the name of such a doctrine, at any rate, Levin brings to Freud the case to which Freud himself would not come (despite Colonel McCormick's offer of "$25,000 or anything he names" and a specially chartered yacht). What an orgy of understanding the psychiatric record of Leopold and Loeb makes possible; and what infinitely extended possibilities of higher and higher understanding are implicit in their plight. In an age which prefers explaining social forces in terms of psychological motivations to deriving such motivations from those forces, the case of the two young murderers seems to offer a clue to the nature of Fascism itself. "Had we not seen," Levin writes, "massive demonstrations in our time of entire populations so infected with some mad leader's delusions?" And again, "There in 1924, in the Chicago courtroom, far from the Munich where another Nietzschean began his march in 1924, the tocsin for the era was scarcely heard." It is more sentimental rhetoric, perhaps, than political theory, but it convinces certain minds.

Understanding, however, even for the middlebrow, must begin with the case itself, be rooted in a sympathy with the very lusts of the principals, and identification of id with id. Their confessions, that is to say, must be matched with our own; and in an only slightly camouflaged way, Levin's book is precisely such a confession, at home in an age of confessions. Half peep show and half confession, it titillates as it purges, a sure-fire hit. At its climax, Levin avows his own urge to commit a similar act of darkness, his own kinship to Leopold and Loeb; for he is a child of their generation, also a one-time "prodigy" and a Jew.

The Jewishness of the accused, once an embarrassment, ignored by every one except the most hostile, becomes now an added attraction, a further recommendation to the righteous; for it is in the understanding of "persecuted minorities" that the new middlebrows excel. Nurtured by *The Wall* and the fiction of Irwin Shaw, they no longer feel even a nostalgia for anti-Semitism but rejoice in purer philo-Semitic delights. The Jew has become on all levels from *Marjorie Morningstar* and *For Two Cents Plain* to *Augie March* and *Goodbye, Columbus* the symbol in which the American projects his own fate; but nowhere does he more successfully possess the imagination than on middlebrow levels. The culturally ambitious middlebrow is already an imaginary Jew—and the archetypal face of Leopold is the one they dream their own.

Compulsion profits by the new freedom this tolerance makes possible. Levin's identification with the accused (private in 1924, when, as he tells us in his autobiography, "I felt that I understood them, that I, particularly, being a young intellectual Jew, had a kinship with them . . .") belongs in 1957 to everyone —at least to the everyone to whom Levin qualifies as an "intellectual." At any rate, he feels free to insist that "Jewish self-hatred" is the essential clue to the crime, that there is "an inverted, subterranean way in which there was a meaning to their all being Jewish," to their victim's having been the child of a pawnbroker, to their attempts to destroy the mark of circumcision on their victim. The book becomes finally almost a regional novel of South Side Jewry, like Levin's earlier *The Old Bunch* a gallery of Jewish types: the Jewish culprits, their Jewish victim, the Jewish reporter-author-detective, the Jewish student of psychiatry. And over all hovers the spirit of the famous Jewish doctor and his "Jewish science," which provided a way to illuminate the connection of Jewishness and the crime.

The criminals are, however, apter occasions for tolerance than mere Jewishness could make them, for they are also homosexuals; and the despised fairy, though he offers a tougher test, excites the good will of the modern middlebrow quite as much as any other case of discrimination. What reader of Levin does not consider himself something of an expert in these matters, able to smile condescendingly at his presumably sophisticated young men and women who read each other Walt Whitman without "any suspicion in those days that he could be singing of another kind of love"? Has not Tennessee Williams made it clear to us all what it is to be queer and how we must meet revelations of sexual aberration with tolerance rather than contempt? And have not all playgoers learned how young Nathan and Dick might have been saved for heterosexuality and freedom had they met the kind lady of *Tea and Sympathy?* Have not all the enlightened finally read the Kinsey Report?

To love the Jew and understand the homosexual: these are basic criteria of decency in the middle of the twentieth century; and the Franks case is a test for us on both scores. But even this is not yet all! Leopold and Loeb were (before the tag had been invented) Juvenile Delinquents, too, precisely the sort of problem children who most concern the liberal philistine in our time. It is just such cases he reads about in the teen-age columns of his daily newspaper, discusses with his neighbors at the Child Study Group or listens to his children debate at the High School Forum. JDs, Rebels without a Cause, members in good standing (had they not stolen the electric cars of old ladies, cruised the drag in their fire-engine-red Stutz Bearcat?) of the first Beat Generation: how familiar they are—or at least seem, stripped of all particulars and adapted to current stereotypes. They were, Erle Stanley Gardner argues in his pious foreword to Leopold's book, "merely the first shocking symptom of a change which was destined to sweep across the country. Youth had broken away from the pattern of thinking which had been the ironclad rule."

But why, to begin with, the shrill concern with juvenile delinquency on which Gardner trades, the almost hysterical response to the problem on which the revival of interest in the Franks case feeds? To be sure, the JDs are our last rebels and last gangsters: public enemies shrunk to adolescent dimensions and YCL-ers without a banner rolled into one pimply skin; and they *do* flourish, growing (apparently) younger and younger, more and more frantically pointless in their violence. It is almost as if they realized that these days one must explode early or not at all; that the age of compulsory maturity has been moved back, and that they will be wheeling a baby carriage across campus before they know it. Yet the most intriguing problem lies not in the quantity of the provocation, but in the quality of the response. What is especially baffling is the willingness, even eagerness of parents to declare themselves guilty of the misdemeanors of their children—their almost neurotic insistence upon their responsibility and the innocence of the young.

An unforeseen consequence of the second Freudian wave, with its emphasis on the critical role of the parent in the psychic development of the child, is to have left the generation of the American middle classes whose children are now adolescent ridden with anxiety and guilt. Caught between succeeding schools of child-rearing that advocate contradictory theories of permissiveness or rigor, they are unable to cast all theory aside, but chase madly after the latest, reproach themselves for having followed the next-to-the-last. Their commitment to a science of family life only aggravates the normal concern of any parent confronting the inevitable imperfection of his children and reflecting on his own inevitable mistakes. Who, in this context, is not guilty as charged, whatever the charge? Who has not slipped up in toilet training, discipline, selection of books, supervision of TV? Who has not at some moment seemed to reject (most terrible of words to the analytically oriented) his child?

Under the impossible burden of wisdom and love demanded by the marriage of Freudianism, philistinism and Puritanism, a generation of middle-aged Americans have staggered and slipped; and they see now backward in the Leopold and Loeb case an exemplar not of juvenile viciousness or the curse of wealth but of the Failure of Parents. How far we have come from 1924, when the psychiatrists who examined Leopold (paid, of course, by his family and Loeb's) felt it expedient to declare: "There is nothing in the family training, either of omission or commission, which is responsible for his present condition." Told this nowadays, an enlightened parent, avid for blame, would demand his money back.

The Children who reveled in their own innocence have become parents who wallow in their own guilt. There is an overwhelming concert of opinion, from John Barlow Martin in the *Saturday Evening Post* ("We are all involved in this. Are we surprised that kids drive fast and drink? A generation ago we made a revolution. Well, the revolution is over now. These are its children.") to James Yaffe ("Their peace of mind, their freedom from fears, their chance to develop into happy men, all this depends on their parents. But the parents of these two boys have never fulfilled their responsibility . . . these boys have been neglected children. Their parents have never given them an ounce of real affection . . . or moral guidance"). How easily the old philistinism blends into the new; how seamlessly religiosity and psychologizing are joined.

A counterrevolution has been fought and won in the pages of the journals of popular culture, a coup accomplished, whose beneficiaries search now for an ideology and an American Tragedy to dramatize it. Their Sacco and Vanzetti they have found in Leopold and Loeb. What the highbrows learned in the case of Alger Hiss, their former middlebrow allies have been learning here: that there is no pure "We" engaged in a legendary battle with a corrupt "They," no melodramatic encounter of innocence and guilt. Either all are innocent or all guilty! Thirty-three years ago, Clarence Darrow opted for the first alternative: "There is no such thing as crime. . . . I do not believe that there is any sort of distinction between the moral condition in and out of jail. One is just as good as the other." His opposite numbers today choose the second.

For them, there is only an all-inclusive "We" involved in universal complicity: the accused guilty of the fact of crime; their parents guilty of the failure of love; the middlebrow spectator (who clamored once for the death sentence or imprisonment without hope of parole) guilty of the failure of sympathy and understanding. But just as there stood behind the accused their guilty parents, behind those parents stood *theirs*, guilty like them and like us, of having undercherished or overprotected their children (how can one ever be sure?). And behind them, there are *their* parents in turn—an infinite regression to some dim, original source of moral failure. Only the latest generation are pure victims, only those who have not yet begot children innocent. But our innocents are JDs.

What is left except forgiveness—a parole, perhaps, rather than a pardon, a conditional remission of guilt? Yesterday morning, Leopold left jail, a seedy figure in his prison-made blue suit, and was carsick four times on the first stage of his way to freedom. But who of those who had wished his death in 1924 and his release in 1958, who had been titillated by the newspaper accounts then or *Compulsion* now, could believe in the man behind the symbol, forgive anyone but himself?

Part Three: The Excluded

The term "minority groups" has never seemed to me a satisfactory one to describe those segments of humanity (women, for instance, or dark-skinned peoples, children or Jews), sometimes indeed constituting majorities, who represent for everyone else an ambivalently regarded Other—that is, an excluded and feared aspect of themselves. Men tend everywhere to divide themselves into opposed groups, only one of which has a symbolic value for the other. Women, that is to say, have a symbolic, even a mythic significance for men that men do not have for women; so with Jews for Gentiles, children or adolescents for adults, preliterate peoples for literate ones, etc., etc.

This has long seemed to me the profoundest and most troubling, as well as the least understood, kind of social inequality. In our time, Negro and Jew especially (the day of the feminist is over; the teen-age revolt only threatens to be born) long to be delivered from their mythical status, to be translated from dream to history. But the way to such a deliverance lies through understanding, an understanding to be sought in literature, where myth and dream are made flesh. Yet an anthropological approach to literature irks the "pure" critic, just as a literary approach to society irks the "pure" social scientists. All the better.

My essay "The Eye of Innocence" began as a speech before a regional meeting of Child Welfare Workers; and I have often imagined drafting analogous ones for delivery before meetings called to combat juvenile delinquency, eliminate segregation (or vice versa), censor comic books or pass leash laws for dogs.

Negro and Jew: Encounter in America

Originally a review essay based on
Notes of a Native Son
by James Baldwin

I have never read anything by James Baldwin which has not moved me. Both his novel, *Go Tell It on the Mountain,* and his recent collection of essays possess a passion and a lyricism quite unlooked for in another book about "the Negro." There is no securer or more soporific refuge from the realities of Negro-white conflict than most of the writing on the subject; and the greatest tribute one can pay to Baldwin is to state unequivocally that he does not contribute to that pious bedtime literature. Since I am impelled to take off from, and in certain respects to amend what he has to say about the relations of Negro and Jew to each other and to America, I feel his honesty as a challenge. To write with less involvement or risk of pain would be an offense.

I am moved to begin with Baldwin's title. Unlike the Negro, the Jew is apt to feel himself not a "native son" but a sojourner in America. I do not mean that he cannot by assimilation and adaptation become as American as anyone else, merely that he knows he can only achieve that end by accepting a role which he has played no part in creating. The Jew is, by and large, a late-comer in the United States; and when he begins to arrive in significant numbers toward the end of the nineteenth century, he and America are already set in their respective ways; theirs is a marriage of the middle-aged. The guilts and repressions, the boasts and regrets of America are already formulated when he debarks, waiting for him. Their genesis goes back to an experience he does not share; and he himself is determined by quite

451

other experiences—twice determined, in fact: by the dim pre-history of *Eretz Yisrael* and by the living memory of Exile.

Indeed, the Jew may already have been determined a third time, by the impact of the Enlightenment, perhaps even in the form of anarchism or socialism. Whatever the shape of his own life, the Jew comes to America with a history, the memory of a world he cannot afford to and does not want to deny. But the Negro arrives without a past, out of nowhere—that is to say, out of a world he is afraid to remember, perhaps could not even formulate to himself in the language he has been forced to learn. Before America, there is for him simply nothing; and America itself, white America, scarcely exists until he is present. Whatever the fate of the Jew in America, he knows he has not helped forge the conscience of the country. He may give a special flavor to New York or Hollywood, even to one or more of the arts in recent days; but he does not exist for the American imagination at those deep levels where awareness is determined. The encounter with the Jew is irrelevant to America's self-consciousness.

Nowhere in all of American literature is there a sentence bearing on the Jew with the terrible resonance of Benito Cereno's cry in Melville's story, "It is the Negro!" This is an exclamation of terror, to be sure; but it is also a statement of fact: the black man is the root of our guilt and fear and pain. Similarly, in Whitman's "Song of Myself," where the United States found in the mid-nineteenth century a lyric voice, the Negro is evoked in all his suffering: "I am the hounded slave, I wince at the bite of dogs, Hell and despair are upon me . . ." but there is no Jew. No more than he can forget he was a slave can the Negro forget that he was the occasion, whatever the cause, of a war which set white American against white American and created a bitterness we have not yet ceased to feel. It is the historical fact of the Civil War, not specifically alluded to in Baldwin's book, which gives special sanction to his grim vaunt: "The time has come to realize that the interracial drama acted out on the American Continent has not only created a new black man, it has created a new white man, too. . . . One of the things that distinguishes Americans from other people is that no other people has ever been so deeply involved in the lives of black men. . . ." Certainly, none has witnessed its white citizens killing each other over the question of their relation to the blacks. Yet at the time of the Civil War, the single Jewish member of my own family by marriage or blood who was in this country (and I suspect this is not untypical) was called on to mount guard on the roof of a Fifth Avenue shop during the draft riots in New York. Baldwin's boast is one no Jew could make; and "Thank God for that!" one is tempted to add, for the Negro, insofar as he considers himself responsible for that war and all it sums up that is dark and ambiguous in the American experience, must endure a sense of guilt of which we are free.

Indeed, superficially at least, the history of the Jew in America is singularly free of guilt on either hand. We represent, rather disconcertingly, the major instance in America of an ethnic minority redeemed rather than exploited or dispossessed. Other foreign groups, the Italians or Scandinavians, for instance, were also welcomed in the time of the great immigrations; but they did not arrive like the Jews, on a dead run, universally branded and harried. Only the Irish can be compared with us in the urgency of their flight. We fled to the Golden Door not merely from poverty and hunger, but impelled by an absolute rejection and the threat of extinction; and it is, therefore, no accident that the lines on the Statue of Liberty: "Give me your tired, your poor, your huddled masses yearning to breathe free . . ." were written by a Jew. They are sentimental enough, to be sure; but they could at least be inscribed by one of our people without the destructive irony that would have undercut them had they been written by a Negro.

The Jews have prospered in the United States, the single Western country never to have had a real ghetto, as they have nowhere else in the world. Even the niggling social snobbery, the occasional outbursts of violence against us can be understood, without extraordinary injustice to the facts, as hangovers from the European experience we have all fled, remnants of debased religion and ancient terror that we have not yet sloughed off. The American, who must wince when the Negro is mentioned, thinking of the slave ships; stutter when the Indian is brought up, remembering the theft of the land; and squirm when the Japanese are touched on, recalling the concentration camps of the last war—can cite the Jews with pride. We are (it is fashionable to forget this now, but salutary to recall) the boast of the United States, as the Negroes are its shame; and it is across the barrier of this discrepancy that our two peoples confront each other. The Negro boasts grimly that he has helped shape with terror the American spirit; we admit shamefacedly that we have profited by its generosity. It is no good showing our minor wounds, on the one hand; or insisting, on the other, upon the squalor and brutality of the Africa out of which the Negro was kidnapped; the guilt of Isaac toward Ishmael can not be so easily dispelled.

The problem, however, is more complicated than that; the relationship of Negro and Jew to America involves their relationship to Europe; for America, transmuted as it is, remains still somehow the Europe it thought to flee. But Europe is "the West" —that is to say, Christendom in decay. What, then, is the relationship of the Jew to the Christian world he invented and rejected; and how does it compare with the relation to that world of the Negroes—that is, of the last heathen to be converted by force? We are strangers both, outsiders in some senses forever, but we are outsiders with a difference.

America is for the Negro a way into the West, a gateway to Europe—and not only for the young colored writers and students and artists, like Baldwin himself, whom one sees sitting in the cafés of Paris and Rome, sustained by awards from our large Foundations. They are merely the vanguard, the symbolic representatives of their whole people. The Jew, conversely, is the gateway into Europe for America; for he has carried with him, almost against his will, his own history, two thousand years of which is European. The anti-American Frenchman or Italian condemning our culture and its representatives will brush aside the names of certain writers and thinkers offered in our defense, protesting, "But he's a *Jew*," meaning, of course, a European, not really an American. And there is a kind of miserable half-truth in the rejoinder.

Certainly, no young Jewish-American writer (*returning* to Europe, after all) can feel what Baldwin does confronting a group of ignorant Europeans in a remote Swiss village, "the most

illiterate among them is related in a way I am not to Dante,
Shakespeare, Michelangelo . . . the Cathedral of Chartres says
to them which it cannot say to me. . . ." Alien as the Jew may
feel himself, he is an alien with a culture ambiguously related
to that which informs all the mounments of European art. It is
not merely that people of our blood, whether converts to Christianity or skeptics or orthodox believers, have been inextricably
involved in the making of the European mind: Leone Ebreo,
Maimonides, Montaigne and Spinoza and Marx—perhaps even
St. John of the Cross and Christopher Columbus; but that we
have haunted the mind of Europe for two thousand years as the
black man has haunted that of America for two hundred. Standing before the cathedrals that make Baldwin feel a stranger, we
remember that here a spokesman of our people was dragooned
into debating the incarnation; there, every Sunday, the elders
of the ghetto were forced to listen to a sermon on the destruction
of the Temple. Walk down into the Forum, and there is the arch
of Titus; enter the palace of the Dukes of Urbino, and there is
Uccello's painting of the Jew burning the bleeding host; open
Shakespeare, and there is Shylock.

But even this, of course, is by no means all. The Jew is
bound to Europe not only by ties of guilt and mutual hatred, and
he lives in its imagination not only as the sinister usurer and
defiler of altars. The images of all it most aspires to and reveres
are also Jewish images: the David and Moses of Michelangelo,
the Virgin of Dante—the very figure of the Christian God are
collaborations of our mind and theirs. Before the Cathedral at
Chartres, the Jew can not help thinking, wryly, ironically or
bitterly: this is our gift to the barbarians. And this the barbarians cannot deny. The boast of that Church most deeply rooted in
the history of Europe is "Abraham is our father. Spiritually we
are Semites." The West may, in occasional spasms, try to cast
us out; but it cannot without spiritual self-castration deny its own
Jewishness. The Jew is the father of Europe (irksome as that
relationship may sometimes seem on both sides); the Negro only
an adopted child. If Christendom denies us, it diminishes itself;
but if we reject the West, we reject not our legend, only a historical interruption of it. We are what we always were—our-

selves. The Negro, on the other hand, cannot endure alienation from the West; for once he steps outside of it, he steps outside of culture—not into Africa, to which he cannot return, but into nothing. The cases of Liberia and modern Israel make the point vividly: a homeland urged on the American Negro and (by and large) rejected, versus one denied the Jew, but fought for and, against ridiculous odds, achieved. Similarly, the Negro is the prisoner of his face in a way the Jew is not. The freedom of the Jew is no mere matter of plastic surgery and nose-shortening; this would be a vanity as pointless as the Negro's skin bleaches and hair-straighteners. A generation or two in America, however, and the Jew is born with a new face. A blond and snub-nosed little boy looks out of the Barton's Pesach ad in the *New York Times,* crying, "Happy Passover, Grandma!" and it is hard to tell him from the pink Protestant image of "Dick" in the school primers. But no Negro dares imagine his child with such a face. This, too, lies between the Jew and Negro in America: the realization that for one (whether he finally choose it or not) there is always a way out, by emigration or assimilation; for the other there is no exit.

Both Negro and Jew exist for the Western world, as I have already suggested, not only in history but also in the timeless limbo of the psyche—that is, as archetypes, symbolic figures presumably representing the characters and fates of alien peoples, but actually projecting aspects of the white Christian mind itself. It is the confusion between these legendary projections (necessary to the psychological well-being of Europe and America) and actual living men called by the same labels which makes the elimination of race prejudice a problem beyond the scope of mere economic and social measures.

The differences between the archetypes of Negro and Jew are especially illuminating. They begin with the fact, which we have noticed earlier, that the myth of the Jew is a European inheritance, or, perhaps better, a persistence; while the myth of the Negro is a product of the American experience and of a crisis in the American mind. The image of the usurer and bad

father with a knife that lies behind Shylock existed long before
even the dream of America; indeed, it represents a distortion of
our own myths of Jacob and Abraham in alien and hostile minds.
The evil Jews of American writers like Fitzgerald, Pound or
Cummings are no more than refurbishings of the original symbolic figure out of the Middle Ages; for there is, in the world of
the imagination, no American Jew. The key Archetypes of the
Negro, however, are purely American: Aunt Jemima and Uncle
Tom, those insipid and infuriating but (as Mr. Baldwin justly
observes) inescapable images that, still in the best American
tradition, belong really to childhood. From Uncle Tom, in particular, there descend such important characters of our literature
as Mark Twain's Nigger Jim and Faulkner's Lucas Beauchamp,
who symbolically grant the white man forgiveness in the name
of their whole race, redeem him by enduring the worst he can
inflict.

It is intriguing that the chief literary archetypes of the Jew
are frankly villains and figures of terror, while the myth of the
Negro as it takes flesh in our classic novels is more often than
not the symbol of a reconciliation more hoped-for than real, a
love that transcends guilt. It is the noblest American sentimentality. By the same token, the counterimages of Jew and Negro
in the "enlightened" fiction of the most recent past differ equally
from each other but in reverse: the conciliator has been transformed into the murderer, the murderer into the conciliator; that
is, Uncle Tom has become Bigger Thomas, while the Jew's daughter who lured Hugh of Lincoln to his death has been transformed
into Marjorie Morningstar.

The Negro, however, whether thought of as killer or pious
slave, has always represented for the American imagination the
primitive and the instinctive, the life of impulse whether directed
toward good or ill. The Jew, on the other hand, stands symbolically for the uses and abuses of intelligence, for icy legalism
or equally cold vengefulness. They represent the polar opposition of law and lawlessness, the eternal father and the eternal
child, who is also, according to the Romantic poets, "father of
the man." In Freudian terminology, the one can be said to stand

for the superego, the other the id, though both are felt, like the peoples with whom they are identified, as *other* by the white, Gentile ego.

Toward id and superego alike, the American, with his double inheritance of Romanticism and Puritanism, has a divided attitude; and this ambivalence is transferred to the symbolic Negro and Jew. The black man is associated with the primitive and the forest, with the "natural," which Americans like to think of as their element. But the Devil was called in Massachusetts the "Black Man," too; and what we label nowadays the unconscious had earlier no other name than the "satanic." The heart is another symbol for the same "natural" for which the Negro comes to stand, but so are the genitals; and if the Negro comes into classic fiction as a source of pity and love, he lurks in the back of the popular mind always as the rapist—the projection of the white man's own "dark" sensuality which he can neither suppress nor justify.

No Christian, however, can without calling Jehovah the Devil (and even this was tried long ago and condemned as a heresy) think of the Jews as wholly satanic; recalcitrant or rejected, they are still God's people. The final Puritan equivalent of the id is Satan, but that of the superego is God: and this is why no good Protestant American can, whatever the presumable Gospel justification, hate the Jew (who stands forever on Sinai, the Tables in his hand), without a sneaking suspicion that he is also hating God.

Perhaps this explains, too, why a certain kind of Romantic anti-Puritanism, which aims at setting traditional morality on its head and prefers whim to law, ends with a violent and sentimental espousal of the dark-skinned peoples and a complementary hatred of the Jews. D. H. Lawrence is one example of this tendency; but its clearest exponent is, as one would expect, an American. For Sherwood Anderson, the Negro in his *Dark Laughter*, his visceral, impulsive joy in life, represents a positive pole, while the Jew, cerebral, talkative, melancholy, the enemy of his own sexuality, stands for all that is negative and reprehensible in modern life.

Yet despite the many spectacular differences between the history and status of Negroes and Jews, between the ways in which they have come to America and the ways in which the American imagination uses them—they are somehow bound together and condemned to a common fate, not less real for being so hard to define. "Prejudice against Negroes and Jews"—it is a phrase that comes naturally and inevitably; and for all its banality, it contains a truth. As far as economic and professional opportunities are concerned there is no comparison between the status of Negroes and Jews; but in a certain kind of social exclusion, in the *quality* of that exclusion rather than its degree (for it is much more severe in the case of the Negro), they are one. Similarly though not equally, both peoples are bound by restrictions that determine where they can live, what clubs and fraternities they can join, what hotels they can enter and finally (and this is the crux, though we are often driven to deny its importance for what seem good strategic reasons) *whom they can marry.*

There are no other white ethnic groups against whom such thoroughgoing exclusions are practiced; for there is no other group which is felt, viscerally not rationally, as so completely alien, so totally other. Though none of our state laws against miscegenation apply, as far as I am aware, to Jews, every Jew knows that the spoken and occasionally printed injunction "FOR WHITES ONLY" may exclude him. There is at work everywhere in the United States, the Protestant-North European tendency to think of all Mediterranean peoples as more black than white, Dagos and Gypsies, swarthy fiddlers and actors, not to be trusted with women; but only in respect to the Jews among those peoples is there the true primitive fear of the *contamination of blood*. Historically, the Jew has been rejected on two grounds, for his religion and for his "race"; but in America in recent years the decay of piety into interfaith good will has rendered the former more and more negligible. The last irrational grounds of our exclusion are not very different from those which surround the Negro with horror: we are taboo peoples, both of us. The secret of our fraternity lies in the barbarous depths of the white, Gentile heart; and it is that shared secret which makes us aware of how we resemble each other and are mutually different from the Irish, the Poles or the Yugoslavs, discriminated against only for comparatively *rational* reasons: because they have arrived here later than other groups and now displace them in jobs, etc.

To be so alike and so different; different in ourselves and alike only in the complicated fear we stir in the hearts of our neighbors, this is what exacerbates our relations with each other. Surely the Negro cannot relish (for all his sentimental desire to think of himself metaphorically as Israel, "Let my people go . . .") this improbable and unwanted yoking any more than the Jew; and yet even physically our people have been thrust together. It is in the big cities of the industrial North, in New York or Philadelphia or Chicago or Detroit, that the Negro and the Jew confront each other and that their inner relationship is translated into a spatial one. The "emancipated" Negro fleeing poverty and the South, and the "emancipated" Jew fleeing exclusion and Europe, become neighbors; and their proximity serves to remind both that neither is quite "emancipated" after all. In America, to be sure, the ultimate ghetto (there is no way of avoiding the word, which gives its name to Baldwin's chief essay on the subject I am treating, "The Harlem Ghetto") is reserved for Negroes. Jews inhabit at one remove or another the region between it and the neighborhoods which mean real belonging, except for the marginal Jewish merchant who finds himself inside the Negro quarter, forced to squeeze his colored customers for his precarious livelihood and to bear the immediate brunt of their hatred for all white men.

It doesn't matter how much newer and richer are the homes which the Jews attain in their flight toward the tonier suburbs and how shabby the dwellings they leave to the Negroes always behind them, five years away or twenty or thirty; and they can never lose the sense of being merely a buffer between the blacks and the "real" whites. Insofar as they are aware of their undeniable economic superiority to the Negroes, middle-class Jews are likely to despise them for lagging behind at the same time that they resent them for pressing so close. It is not an easy relationship.

Most Jews have, I think, little sense of how the Negroes regard them specifically as Jews. They are likely to assume to begin with that Negroes are incapable of making subtle distinctions between whites and whites; and they are, moreover, accustomed to look for anti-Semitism chiefly from people who are, or whom the Jews believe to be, socially more secure than themselves. And so they are easily taken in by the affable play-acting of the Negroes, from whom they believe they have no cause to expect hatred. Jews, more often than not, take it for granted that the Negroes are grateful to them for the historical accident of their never having been the masters of black slaves; and they are shocked at the sort of black anti-Semitism which Baldwin describes: "But just as society must have a scapegoat, so hatred must have a symbol. Georgia has the Negro. Harlem has the Jew."

But why should the Negro hate the Jew? As far as he is aware, the Jew does not hate the Negro—at least not as much as the Gentiles do! To be sure, most Jews are conscious that the Negro is their lightning rod, that he occupies a ghetto which might otherwise be theirs and bears the pogroms which might otherwise be directed at them. But no Jew has ordained these ghettos, and if the owner of a Negro tenement happens to be a Jew, after all, he must live! In any court of law, the Jew would be declared innocent of major complicity in the oppression of the Negro in America. What if he sometimes bamboozles or overcharges a colored customer, or refuses to sell his house to the first Negro to try to enter a neighborhood? He and his ancestors have never owned a slave or participated in a lynching or impregnated Negro women while worrying publicly about miscegenation. Almost alone among Americans, the Jew seems to have no reason to feel guilt toward the Negro; and this is, though Baldwin makes no point of it, a matter of great importance.

Yet it is not true that the Jew feels no guilt toward the Negro; he merely believes that he *should* feel none, and is baffled when he does. There is no reason, the Jew tells himself, why he should be expected to be more liberal than any other Americans in regard to such problems as fair employment codes and desegregation; and yet I am sure that most Jews are. On the record and at the polls, they are the Negroes' friends; and if the overwhelming majority of them would object to their daughters' marrying Negroes, they would object with hardly less violence to their marrying *goyim*. If we discriminate against Ham in this regard, we discriminate also against Japheth. Some Jews, to be sure, adopt the anti-Negro attitudes of their neighbors in an excess of assimilationist zeal, as a way of demonstrating by the all-American quality of their hatred that they, too, are "white." There is, however, also a particularly Jewish distrust of the black man, buried deep in our own tradition. Are we not told in the Torah itself that the offspring of Ham will be cursed: "A servant of servants shall he be unto his brethren."

There is no use quibbling about it; though he does not oppress the Negro, the Jew does hate him with a double though muted hatred: for being at once too like himself and too like the *goyim*—for resembling what the Jew most resents in his own situation and also what he most despises in the whole non-Jewish world. The Jew sees in the Negro a carefree and improvident life-style, that he has also observed and envied a little, all around him, but which he feels he could not afford (even if, improbably, he could approve) in his rejection and devotion to God. Yet though the Negro is also poor and rejected and pious, he is able to laugh overloud and drink overmuch, to take marriage lightly and money without seriousness, to buy spangles at the expense of food, to despise thrift and sobriety and to be so utterly a fool that one is *forced* into taking financial advantage of him. Real or legendary, this Negro the Jew finds or thinks he finds in his run-down, slovenly house; and he considers him no more admirable at worship than at play, jerking and howling and writhing on the floor in a final degradation of the alien Evangelical tradition.

Perhaps the Jew cannot be taken to task for despising improvidence and superstition. And yet he knows that somehow he has failed an obligation that he does not quite understand, failed his own history of persecution and oppression by not managing to—to do *what*? What he might have performed he can never really say, some bold revolutionary blow for emancipation, some superhuman act of love. So he cries out, if he is disturbed enough, against segregation to a group of his friends who are also against segregation, or he writes a letter to the papers, or makes a contribution to the NAACP. And, after all, what else can he do? What else can *I* do?

At least it is necessary to say "I" and pass on from safe generalizations about what the abstract "Jew" thinks about the abstract "Negro," generalizations from which it is possible to be secretly exempting oneself all the time. Even at the cost of some pain, it is necessary to say what "this Jew," what *I* feel on these matters in my own quite unstatistical flesh.

I can begin by saying, in the teeth of the usual defensive cliché, that none of my best friends is black. I have known many Negroes in my life and have talked to some, chiefly comrades in one radical party or another, far enough into the night to have some notion of the distrust we would have had to overcome, the masks we would have had to penetrate, to discover our real selves, much less become real friends. I cannot see how that gap could be closed without genuine passion; and my only passionate relation to a Negro I do not even remember, but take on trust from stories of my mother. When I was little more than a year old, I was taken care of by a black girl, whom I loved so deeply, caressing and kissing her black skin in a way which horrified my family, that she was fired. I assume that I was desolate for a little while; I do not really recall, and my mother never carried her account that far.

My only other connection with a Negro that involves any tenderness comes at a much later date. I was thirteen or fourteen, working at my first job in a shoe store, and more than a little scared at the cynicism and worldliness of the other "boys" (some of whom were as old as sixteen!), much less the salesmen and the hose girls. My only friend in the store, the only one who never mocked me, intentionally or unwittingly, was the colored porter. We would eat our lunches together in the basement out of paper bags, while all the others were off at cafeterias or lunch counters. He would speak to me gravely and without condescension about life—mostly sex, of course, which he thought the salesmen made too much of in their boastful anecdotes and I was overimpressed with in my callow innocence. After we finished eating, I would retouch the crude sketch of a gigantic, naked woman that someone had roughed out on one of the cellar walls, while he leaned back and criticized my efforts. Before we went upstairs to work again, he would help me push a pile of empty hose boxes in front of our private mural.

In retrospect, it seems to me that I found in this Negro porter, quite in accord with the best American traditions, my own Nigger Jim or Sam Fathers—but with what a difference! Urban Jew that I was, I had no nighttime Mississippi for the encounter, no disappearing virgin forest—only the half-lit cellar with the noise of the city traffic rumbling dimly above and the rustling of rats in the trashbin. It was not, however, a relationship with a person, but with a type.

Aside from these, my early encounters with Negroes were casual and public. There was, of course, the colored tenor who could sing *"Eli, Eli"* in Yiddish and was therefore in great demand at all Jewish events as a curiosity, a freak. What his fellow Negroes thought of him God only knows! I can remember the old women shaking their heads incredulously as he sang, and the kids afterwards arguing about whether one could really be both black and a Jew. Beyond this, there were the Negro customers in the shoe store and in my father's pharmacy. The shoe-store customers fell into two classes: ignorant working girls and old servants with broad, horny heels and monstrous bunions, who could be sold practically anything (even extra arch-supports for their rubbers!); and middle-class Negro women from the suburbs whom we hated for assuming, quite correctly, that we were trying to put something over on them. My father's customers I would see less frequently; his drugstore was in a distant and disreputable part of the city, with a Mission for repentant drunks on one side and a factory across the street. I would visit him occasionally, taking along a "hot meal" that had grown rather cold on the long streetcar ride, and watch him wait on the Negroes who made up a large part of his trade and whom he supplied with asafoetida to charm off the "misery," hair-straightener and large boxes of candy tied with even larger pink ribbons.

Last of all, there were the maids—which is to say, the kind of part-time help that would appear at my grandmother's house or ours when we were prosperous enough to afford it. I think it was a long time before it entered my head that a maid might not be a Negro, or a healthy young Negro woman not a maid. In conversations between my grandmother and my mother, the girl who helped us was always referred to simply as "the *schwarze*," which did not really mean "Negro," nor, God forbid, "nigger," but only "servant." After a while, we settled down to one *schwarze*, Hattie, who was an ardent disciple of Father Divine, and would dance abandonedly in one corner of the kitchen when the spirit moved her or preach at us in the name of peace. It pleased my mother, I know, to be called "Miz Lillie" in an unfamiliar style handed down from plantation days and reminiscent of movies about the South; and she would certainly roar with laughter when Hattie clowned and grimaced and played the darkie for all she was worth. When I was adolescent and very earnest on the Negro question, I would rush out of the house sometimes, equally furious with Hattie for her play-acting and my own family for lapping it up and laughing at the display with winks and condescension.

Things have changed a good deal since I was a kid; and when I return now to the city where I was born, there are not only colored cops on the corners, but in the stores, even the biggest ones, colored salesgirls as well as customers, black salesgirls who do not hesitate to be as insolent as the white ones. Indeed, when my grandmother was dying and I came back to see her for the last time, I found not only Hattie, quite old but spry enough to caper on seeing me as absurdly as she knew was expected, but also a Negro nurse. The nurse was a follower of Father Divine, too, but this was her only bond with Hattie; for she was not only a "professional woman," but a West Indian, very light-skinned, and spoke a painfully refined brand of British English. She insisted on having a papaya every day for lunch, presumably to keep her origins clear in the minds of everyone; but she was kind and patient all the same, though she slipped away, quietly but firmly, a few hours before my grandmother's death. "It's coming," she whispered to my mother in the kitchen. "I'm sorry, but it's against my principles to stay in a house of death."

Despite my lack of intimacy with Negroes, I have possessed from my earliest childhood very strong theoretical opinions on the question of their rights. The first book I ever bought for myself with my own money (I was eight) was *Uncle Tom's Cabin*, which I read over and over, weeping in secret, and making vows to myself that I would work always (imagining, of course, a heroic stand against the ignorant multitude) until the last vestiges of racial inequality were wiped out. Needless to say, no heroic exploits followed, though I have a vivid memory of myself at twelve, shouting and pounding the table until I grew red-faced in an argument with the rabbi of the chief Reform temple of our city. I can still remember his face, unspeakably moderate (either he looked like the late Senator Taft or I have remade his remembered face into that image), nodding at me disapprovingly, while my family, acutely embarrassed, tried to signal silence from behind his back. His apology for discrimination was certainly one of the spiritual scandals that drove me in despair from the bourgeois Jewish community. The poor Orthodox Jews did not, it seemed to me, even know there was a Negro problem: while the richer, Reformed ones had, for all their "liberalism," surrendered to Gentile conformism.

If the first impulse that took me as a young man into the radical movement was a desire to be delivered of the disabilities of being a Jew, the second was the counterdesire to be delivered of the guilt of the discriminations practiced by Jews in their efforts to free themselves from those disabilities. Only in the Marxist scheme for remaking society could I then see the possibility of winning my freedom rather than buying it at the expense of somebody else—particularly of the Negro. Besides, I thought that one could discover in the Movement a society in which already Negro and white were living together on the basis of true equality. Did not white girls and Negro boys dance together at their social evenings? Were they not even lovers without special recrimination or horror? I soon became uncomfortably aware, however, that the radical movement was plagued by the same inability as bourgeois society to treat the Negroes as more than instances of their color. Turning this inability upside down helped very little.

That the girls chose Negroes as boy friends *because* they were Negroes, or that the top leadership (who were, it happened, Jews once more) appointed Negro organizers not in spite of their color but because of it—and that they would, when their directives changed, hurry them out of sight—all this became distressingly clear. That one could not call a sonofabitch a sonofabitch if he happened to be black, that a comrade who was sullen, uncooperative and undependable was immune to blame because he was colored—this became unendurable. The fear of being labeled a "white chauvinist" is as disabling as that of being called a "nigger-lover"; and to be barred a priori from hating someone is as debasing as being forbidden a priori to love him.

It is not, finally, a question of the Marxian movement failing its own dream, the dream of an assimilated Jew not above calling a political opponent a "Jew-nigger." Such a failure could be an accident of history, reparable under changed circumstances. The fatal flaw of all such approaches is that they begin with self-congratulation: permitting us to set ourselves apart from the guilty others and to think of ourselves as immune to the indignity and hatred which are the very condition of the coexistence of white and black in America. Only with the recognition of our own implication can we start to be delivered: not to fight for Negro rights as if we were detached liberators from another planet, but to know that those rights must be granted to ease us of the burden of our own guilt.

Of all my own experiences, the one which seems to me now central to an understanding of my problem, a real clue to the nature of Negro-Jewish relations, is that of merely *walking to school.* For some six months, when I was in the ninth grade, I went to what was called "The Annex," an aging, standardly dismal primary-school building used to catch the overflow from one of our high schools. It stood in a neighborhood largely inhabited by Negroes, though there were still Jewish delicatessens and kosher poultry slaughterers among the "race record" shops; and one of the streets was lined throughout the day with pushcarts, among which Yiddish was the commonest language spoken. The sons of butchers and the few trapped Jewish property owners left in the area seemed to become almost as often as not gangsters (one especially successful one, I recall, ran a free soup kitchen all through the Depression); and a standard way of proving one's toughness was "nigger-smashing." This sport involved cruising a side street at a high rate of speed, catching a lonely Negro, beating the hell out of him and getting back into the car and away before his friends could gather to retaliate. I remember that one of the local figures associated, in kids' legend at least, with "nigger-smashing" was himself called "Niggy" because of his kinky hair and thick lips, features not so uncommon among Jews, after all.

I had to walk to school through those streets, and it was not long before I was repeating to my friends what was quickly whispered to me: that it was not safe for either a white boy or for a colored one to walk there alone. It was a strange enough feeling to pass even in packs through so black a neighborhood to one's totally white class; for though the grade school was predominantly Negro, there was not a single colored student in my ninth-grade room. Especially on the warm days in late spring, when everyone was out on his stoop or sidewalk, in shirt sleeves or undershirt, one had a sense of an immense, brooding hostility. The fattest and most placid-looking woman leaning out of her window or the knot of yelling kids who parted to let one pass could suddenly seem a threat. It was like entering the territory of a recently subdued enemy, still too weary and disorganized for resistance but not for hatred. And saying to oneself, "I am a friend of the Negro people. I am on your side," didn't help a bit. It would have been absurd to cry it aloud, though sometimes the temptation was great; for in such a context, it would seem as false to the mouth that spoke it as to the ear that heard.

The sense of entering an alien country was exaggerated during my first month in school by the barricades which blocked off the streets just past the last plush Jewish apartment house and on the verge of that real ghetto. A smallpox epidemic had spread through the crowded, filthy living quarters of the Negroes, and only those with business in the neighborhood were permitted to enter, though even they were snatched up and rudely vaccinated on the spot. After a while, the sense of poverty and dirt, the dark faces looking out of the windows and the fear of the most dread-

ful of diseases blended into one; and even a kid going to school
had the sense that he was entering not a place but a condition,
that he was confronting the sickness and terror of his own soul
made manifest.

Once toward the end of my endless term there, I was walking with my mother down the same street I followed daily to
school. We were after something special, who knows, hot pas-
trami, maybe, or onion rolls or a fresh-killed chicken; when
suddenly and quite casually she pointed to one of those drab,
alien houses from which I had shrunk day after day, saying, "I
was born there." It is the familiar pattern of the decay of urban
neighborhoods; when the Jews are ready to go and it no longer
pays to patch and paint, the Negroes are permitted to move in.
The street where I myself was born is now almost all Negro, as
is my high school; and the neighborhood where I lived until I
was married is now surrounded. But at that moment beside my
mother, I heard behind her familiar voice another which
prompted it: the voice of a mild, horrified, old Gentile lady over
her tea: "First the Jews, then the Negroes . . ." But this is also
the voice of T. S. Eliot, "And the jew squats on the window sill,
the owner . . ."

Emancipated and liberal, I could scarcely shake off my resentment and rage; for I saw the comedy and pathos of our
plight, how *we* looked to the *goyish* eye at the very moment we
were looking at the Negro: the first symptom of a disease, as
inexorable as age itself, which eventually reduces newly seeded
lawns and newly painted houses to baked gray mud and scabby
boards. I could feel the Jew's special rancor at the Negro for
permitting himself visibly to become (there is no question of the
justice of such a notion, only of its force) the image, the proof of
the alien squalor that the white, Gentile imagination finds also
in the Jew. "As he to me," the Jew thinks helplessly, "so *I* to
them!" And the "them" refers to the Gentiles already in the new,
restricted addition to which the Jew will eventually come, by
hard work and with much heartburning, only to find the Gentiles
gone and the Negro still at his heels.

For the Jew, the Negro is his shadow, his improbable caricature, whom he hates only at the price of hating himself; and he
learns quickly (unless he allows rage to blind him) that for this
reason his own human dignity depends not only theoretically but
in terrible actuality upon that of the Negro. No Jew can selflessly
dedicate himself to the fight for the equality of the Negro; when
he pretends that he is not also fighting for himself, he is pretending that he is indistinguishable from a *goy*.

The Eye of Innocence

Some notes on the role of the child in literature

1. The Invention of the Child

We move through a world of books in which the child is so accepted a feature of the landscape that we are aware of him chiefly when he is absent. There he is (or she—it scarcely matters), his eye to the keyhole, his ear to the crack in the door, peering, listening, observing in his innocence our lack of it. He is the touchstone, the judge of our world—and a reproach to it in his unfallen freshness of insight, his unexpended vigor, his incorruptible naïveté. Or he is the hero himself: Tom Sawyer or Huck Finn or Holden Caulfield, the Good American, the unrecognized saint, living in a hogshead or thrown out of fashionable bars: the cornerstone the builders rejected, Christ as a J.D.

So ubiquitous and symbolic a figure is, of course, no mere reproduction of a fact of existence; he is a cultural invention, a product of the imagination. But what have we invented him *for*, and out of what stuff have we contrived him? There is something both ambiguous and unprecedented about the Cult of the Child; indeed, the notion that a mere falling short of adulthood is a guarantee of insight and even innocence is a sophisticated view, a latter-day Pastoralism, which finds a Golden Age not in history but at the beginning of each lifetime. The invention of special clothing, special books, a special role in literature for children belongs to a late, a perhaps decadent phase of our culture.

In Greek art, to be sure, the icon of the downy-cheeked boy is caressed in a thousand tender works of sculpture. The undraped adolescent, bent to remove the thorn in his foot or lying

471

with his back to the beholder, becomes the Aphrodite of the pederast; but he is considered a love-object only, not a small prophet or a guide to a lost innocence. In the Judaeo-Christian tradition, such erotic trifling with the image of childhood stirs only hostility; "he who offends the least of my little ones" is promised a fate which would make it better that a millstone were round his neck and he cast into the sea.

There is, however, no pious counteridealization of the child to replace the rejected image of the Greeks. In the Old Testament, indeed, there seems a willful, to us almost perverse, resolve not to exploit the possibilities of the child, even in stories which demand for him a central role. Isaac, who, in our reimaginings of the fable of the Sacrifice, has an outward shape and a psychology, is in Genesis a cipher. The rabbis when they commented on the story said that he was thirty when he submitted to his father's knife. Thirty! The revolution in imagination which lies between the Biblical account and our response to it is implicit in our difficulty in conceiving a middle-aged Isaac or making the legend come to life around him.

In the New Testament, there are other forces at work; and in the Gospel according to Luke, the Nativity story opens up what strike us as irresistible opportunities for creating images of appealing babyhood, the pure infant symbolically situated between beasts and Wise Men. It is not, however, until the Renaissance that the Babe escapes from the text to its Mother's pearly breast, fulfills itself as a significant image: innocence as infancy, the infant as Innocence itself. Earlier, the Christian imagination does not know what to do with the paradox of the child as Saviour; one recalls the rigid Christ Child of Byzantine mosaics, his tiny hand raised in a gesture of command and blessing—not an infant at all, only a miniature Emperor of the Universe. Indeed, not until the Renaissance blossoms into the baroque does the Christ Child come fully into his own; it is then that the prototypes of sentimental religious art are established once and for all: playing on the appeal of motherhood and babyhood in a maudlin upsurge of self-deception which ends by making quite good Christians (and parents of actual children) incapable of granting the possibility of infant damnation.

The orthodox and patriarchal Trinity of Father, Son and Holy Ghost is at this point replaced by a popular matriarchal anti-Trinity of Virgin, Cuckold and Infant; a group derived, the experts tells us, from ancient portrayals of Venus, Vulcan and Cupid, the antique form of the fatherless family. The dimpled Babe of the baroque tableau is still quite different, however, from the modern notion of the child as spokesman for the unfallen ego, still a part of the theatrical-sentimental attempt of the Counter-Reformation to wash away Protestantism—that rigid reassertion of Fatherhood as an all-sufficient principle—in a flood compounded of mother's milk, the tears of the Magdalene and the blood of Jesus' circumcision.

Expectedly enough, so liquid and maternal a revolt, reducing the male to infant size, a helpless burden in the lap of his adoring mother, stirred little response in the paternalistic Protestant North, particularly in the Anglo-Saxon world. There child witches continued to be hanged; while infant damnation continued to seem probable to those remembering in a colder clime Augustine's observation that the innocence of childhood is more a matter of weakness of the limbs than of purity of the heart.

Even in the Catholic South, no fundamental change in the view of childhood was possible, despite the exploitation of its painterly appeal, so long as the orthodox theory of Original Sin was unchallenged. If one began by believing that an originally corrupted nature must be trained (cajoled and beaten) into the semblance of orderly virtue, he ended by being convinced that an adult had some chance of attaining goodness, the child little or none. Similarly, so long as maturity and virtue were identified, so long as goodness was considered the function of conscience rath r than impulse, no adult could consider postulating the child as a noral touchstone. The occasional use of abused and suffering children for the sake of pathos, in Dante, say, or in Shakespeare, was necessarily peripheral. Children were, symbolically speaking, beside the point. It was no more possible to conceive of a child as hero than of a peasant in the same role.

One of the major shifts in modern thinking involves moving the child from the periphery to the center of art—and, indeed, to the center of life. Child-worship may begin as one of those pieces of literary hypocrisy (like the courtly adulation of woman), a purely theoretical gesture of compensation by those who, in real life, neither spared the rod nor spoiled the child (and felt a little guilty about it somehow); but it ends in a child-centered society, where the parent not merely serves but emulates his immature offspring. This revolution is, of course, merely the by-product of a much larger one, of the shift from a belief in Original Sin to one in Original Innocence—or to put it more precisely, to a belief that the same original disposition once called "sin" was more properly labeled "innocence."

The time of that major revolution is the mid-eighteenth century and its prophet (however many statements to the contrary scholars extract from his utterly contradictory works) is Jean Jacques Rousseau, whose waking on the road to Vincennes, his waistcoat wet with tears, marks the moment of a New Revelation. It is told that on the day Christ was born, certain sailors off the coast of Illyria heard a wailing from the woods and a terrible voice crying, "The God Pan is dead!" If on the day of Rousseau's vision, no one heard the countercry, "The God Pan is reborn!" that is because no one any longer listened.

The West that had for more than seventeen hundred years deified its superego turned again to making the id its god. The scholars have many names for the New Revelation in its various stages and aspects: Pantheism, Deism, *Sturm und Drang*, Sentimentalism, Romanticism, etc. In the light of depth psychology, which is one of the products of the movement and can be considered its "theology," let us call it the Psychic Breakthrough, the Re-emergence of the Id. We who are its children and its heirs live in an age characterized by the consciousness of the unconscious and by a resolve to propitiate and honor that dark force, so long surrendered to the auspices of unlettered witches and shabby wizards.

The keynote of such an age is revolution and its not-so-secret motto: "Whatever is up shall be down! Whatever is down shall be up!" It is an age which says the Lord's Prayer backwards because its predecessors have said it forwards. It is a time which prefers the New World to the Old because that World is its own invention; America may have been discovered for the geographers in the fifteenth century but it is discovered for the imagination in the eighteenth! Similarly, it glorifies new art forms at the expense of traditional ones: autobiography and the lyric, especially the novel replacing the classical genres, epic and poetic tragedy, as the forms in which the most ambitious writers dream of creating the self-awareness of their era. Finally, the diabolic principle is elevated above the angelic. In a very few years, the archetypal villains of the European mind, Don Juan and Faust, are transformed into heroes; "to make a pact with the Devil" becomes the hallmark of a real man and true artist. Since Hell had become the official name of the forbidden world of impulse and unreason, it is hailed by the poets as their natural home.

The greatest possible compliment to writers of the past is to insist that they had been secretly on the Devil's side without knowing it: so Blake attempts to redeem Milton, and Melville tries to save Shakespeare. Antiquity, Greek and Hebrew, is ransacked for satanic heroes: Prometheus and Cain and the Wandering Jew. The Jew in general profits by the catastrophic upheaval, in some quarters not so much because he was thought to be blackened as because he is still thought to be black. Audiences that had guffawed at Shylock's discomfiture and cheered his comeuppance learn to weep for him. Life itself is not immune to the movement that begins in art; the Black Mass becomes a pastime of amateur Devil worshipers and Byron feels called on to howl diabolic imprecations over his marriage bed.

Everywhere men engaged in a double search: on the one hand, for terms to describe the psychic split they feel, terms that will escape the prejudicial Christian dichotomy, body and soul; and on the other hand, for models in the actual world, for living symbols to represent, more vitally than literary archetypes, the too-long-denied half of the sundered soul. "Head" and "heart" are the terms that suffice for generations, from Rousseau, say, to Melville, for the warring sides in the Romantic melodrama; and the glorification of the heart over the head, of impulse over intelligence, lays a theoretical foundation for the anti-intellectualism which has become nowadays the property of the dullest reactionary but which was once the battle cry of a truly advanced guard in a war against culture.

Images of impulse and natural virtue were found readily enough, where one would expect them, in the virgin forests of the newer worlds: in dark-skinned natives in general and Indians in particular. But there were noble savages closer to home; one did not have to go abroad for counterimages to set against the corrupt figure of the European courtier. The peasant could be glorified over the city dweller; the idiot or the buffoon over the philosopher; woman over man—and within the female sex, the whore over the bourgeoise. All such oppositions are dangerous, however; no matter how abstractly, how theoretically indulged, they threaten a disruption of the social values by which bourgeois society lives; and bourgeois society was, in fact, consolidating its greatest triumphs at the moment of the Psychic Breakthrough. The sons of the burghers, indeed, were precisely the dreamers and insatiable revolutionaries who were extending the Psychic Breakthrough; and though their fathers had approved, while they were down, the slogans of reversal, it was quite another matter when they were up.

Where the artist is most firmly committed to bourgeois values, especially where there is no surviving aristocratic tradition with which he can identify himself (in the Anglo-Saxon world, for instance), there is available to him one safely genteel symbol of protest and impulse: the Child. It is possible to insist that the child is Father of the man, that he comes "trailing clouds of glory" which are dissipated in a world of duty and work, without seeming seriously to threaten the middle-class ethos, without, indeed, revealing to oneself one's own revolutionary intent. Do not all decent people, after all, love children?

In England and in America this most maudlin of primitivisms triumphs everywhere. The relationship of the "angels of pigmy size" exploited by this school to observable children is slighter than that of, say, Cooper's noblest Indians to their historical counterparts; and yet, after a while, so plausible did such images seem, living children began to be asked to conform to them—as no Indian was ever asked to live up to his image; but then one could not confine children to reservations or kill them in popularly sanctioned expeditions. In time, children were re-created by hairdressers and tailors into facsimiles of their literary representations, and were addressed as if they were really such monsters of virtue, both in life (by visiting uncles and aunts) and in literature (largely written by those uncles and aunts).

Indians and peasants and village idiots were mercifully spared the ultimate humiliation of having to read descriptions of themselves that were in fact projections of nostalgia, in a time of oppressive taboos, for a life at once impulsive and virtuous; they did not come to measure themselves against such projections and failing them, berate themselves, as (presumably) did the children of Anglo-Saxondom. Nor did they, what is much worse, become living counterfeits of literary inventions, imitations of imitations. It must have been difficult enough for children of the most genteel, Anglo-Saxon homes to live up to images created, if not in conformity with their inner selves, at least with the superegos their parents were preparing for them. But imagine in America, the children of immigrants, little Italians and Jews, imagine even the young Negro who has learned to read—confronting the most pale-faced of all ego ideals: those dead-white blonde Good Good Girls or sandy-haired, snub-nosed Good Bad Boys, under whose cover our timid revolutionaries attacked the world of Puritan conscience in the name of the sentimentalists' "heart."

II. Good Good Girl and Good Bad Boy

The holiest Ikon of the Cult of the Child, of the Dream of Innocence in its pristine Anglo-Saxon form, is the Good Good Girl, the blonde asexual goddess of nursery or orphanage, re-incarnated from Little Nell to Mary Pickford. In this single figure are satisfied the middle-class desire to idealize woman-hood; the Protestant resolve to celebrate pre-marital chastity; the North European wish to glorify the fair and debase the black; as well as the sentimental need to deliver childhood from the odor of diapers and the implications of Original Sin. Only the girl child seems a sufficiently spotless savior to the imagination of the North, which rejected the austere orthodox Trinity and the gaudy baroque one, the Son of the Father and the Virgin's Babe. The Son and his Sacred Mother (corrupted by "Papist Mariolatry") are reserved for other uses.

The New Holy Family is centered not around the Divine Boy but the Good Good Girl, imagined not in the arms of the mother but in those of the father, and not at the moment of birth but at that of death. The basic image is what has been called the Protestant Pietà (foreshadowed by Shakespeare in the final scenes of *King Lear*): the white-clad daughter, dying or dead, in the arms of the Old Man, tearful papa or grandfather or woolly-haired slave. It is the unendurable Happy Ending, as the white slip of a thing too good for this world prepares to leave for the next, while we, abandoned, sob into our handkerchiefs. The Good Good Girl must die, not only so that we may weep (and tears are, for the sentimentalist, the way to salvation), but also because there is nothing else for her to do—no course of action which would not sully her. Allowed to grow up, she could only become (forbidden the nunnery by the Protestant ethos) wife, mother or widow, tinged no matter how slightly by the stain of sexuality, a sexuality suffered, perhaps, rather than sought, but one in any case *there*.

Though the essential theme of the novel is love, it has never been forbidden the spice of death; and at its beginnings, it presented both in terms of an adult world. In the earliest bourgeois fiction, the reader was permitted to assist at the last moments of the betrayed woman: the polluted female redeeming both her honor and (by providing an occasion for repentance) that of her seducer. In the later, more genteel stages of the novel, however, when the reader is no longer allowed to witness female sexual immorality even as a preparation for repentance, he must content himself with the spectacle of the immaculate child winning her father to God by her courage in the face of premature death: little Eva, for instance, melting the obdurate St. Clare from skepticism to faith. What an orgy of approved pathos such scenes provide in the hands of masters like Dickens or Louisa May Alcott or Harriet Beecher Stowe.

"Dear papa," said the child, with a last effort, throwing her arms about his neck. In a moment they dropped again; and, as St. Clare raised his head, he saw a spasm of mortal agony pass over the face,—she struggled for breath, and threw up her little hands.

"O, God, this is dreadful!" he said, turning away in agony, and wringing Tom's hand. . . . "O, Tom, my boy, it is killing me!" . . .

The child lay panting on her pillows, as one exhausted, —the large clear eyes rolled up and fixed. Ah, what said those eyes, that spoke so much of heaven? Earth was past, and earthly pain; but so solemn, so mysterious, was the triumphant brightness of that face, that it checked even the sobs of sorrow. . . .

The bed was draped in white; and there, beneath the drooping angel-figure, lay a little sleeping form,—sleeping never to waken!

We learn that not softhearted women only, but the most tough-minded of critics once wept uncontrolledly over these climactic scenes, that sometimes the authors themselves could barely finish writing them in the midst of their own tears, could scarcely reread them afterwards. "The child has been buried inside the church," Dickens writes a friend as he prepares to finish off Little Nell, "and the old man, who cannot be made to understand that she is dead, repairs to the grave and sits there all day long . . . I think an hour-glass running out would help the notion; perhaps her little things upon his knee . . . I am breaking my heart over this story, and cannot bear to finish it . . ." If there seems to us something grotesque in such a rigging of the scene, so naked a relish of the stiffening, white body between the whiter sheets; if we find an especially queasy voyeurism in the insistence on entering the boudoirs of immature girls, it is perhaps the fault of our imaginations that have since learned to believe in the pre-nubile enchanter, the self-consciously sexy "nymphets" of Nabokov's *Lolita*.

For our predecessors, life was somewhat simpler; they felt it quite respectable not only to intrude into the bedroom of the Pure Young Thing but even to participate in the kill. Edgar Allan Poe could scarcely provide a more refined titillation—and in his work the sanctions of Christian morality are surrendered. To be allowed (vicariously) to murder the deflowered Clarissas of the earlier novel is, perhaps, satisfactory enough, since the appeasement of guilt, the hatred of sin lies at its root; but to murder (just as vicariously) the pre-adolescent Virgin is to be granted the supreme privilege of assaulting innocence, appeasing the hatred of virtue, which must surely have stirred uneasily before such atrociously pure examples. And it is all without "sex," as sex was then quite narrowly defined—*cleanly* sadistic to the pre-Freudian mind, in an age during which no one suspected the shadow of the Marquis de Sade might fall upon the social reformer, and that half-mad lover of nymphets, Charles Dickens, became a household figure. All was permitted the writer capable of combining such evocations of death with lay sermons against slavery or Southern corruption, the brutality of the male world or the factory system.

It is notorious that Dickens exploited all his life a version of the class struggle quite different from that of Marx. Not the proletarian but the child was his innocent victim; and his readers, convinced with him that all of adult society was a conspiracy against childhood, could sigh, wipe away the furtive tear and return to their ordinary tasks indescribably satisfied. "We are all child murderers!" his admirers were able to tell themselves, quite unaware that the realization titillated as much as it horrified them. The effect is, indeed, not unlike that of the film *Nous sommes tous assassins*, which, in the guise of arousing a passionate rejection of capital punishment, satisfies our secret desire to witness it—to become more intimately guilty of its horrors in these days when public executions are forbidden.

In Dickens, the dwarfish, albino monsters of forbearance and piety are not only Little Nells; his symbols of offended innocence include boys, too: Tiny Tim or Paul Dombey, who first asked what the wild waves were saying, and learned at last that they whispered the death, *his* death, necessary to redeem his father from pride and wealth; even Oliver Twist, who does not ever quite die, little tease that he is, but is in and out of the sickbed, constantly flirting with the final consummation. In America, however, such figures are somehow not quite acceptable; for in this country, genteel primitivism, like all else, must learn to abide by the double standard.

Little Lord Fauntleroy is an import once much admired by Europeanizing females but always scorned by rugged nativists no matter how sentimental. The Good Good Girl is naturalized without a qualm, for she is Daisy Miller's younger sister, "America's Sweetheart," whether in bottle curls or bangs; but the Good Good Boy seems the juvenile reminder of a tradition of aristocratic culture we left behind. He is the "little gentleman," which is to say, the villain: an insufferable outsider who wears his Sunday clothes during the week and would rather walk shod than run barefoot. Sometimes the "little gentleman" is called the "mama's boy," but this is misleading in the extreme, since all American boys belong to mother. Tom Saywer, who sets the pattern, is fatherless by definition, born into a world presided over only by Aunt Polly; and he melts with shame at the thought of her believing him faithless to the maternal principle.

To betray the mother—to deny her like the young rogue in *The Prince and the Pauper*: this is for Mark Twain, who speaks here for all of America, the only unforgivable sin. What then is the difference between the Good Good Boy and the Good Bad Boy, between Sid Sawyer and Tom? The Good Good Boy does what his mother must pretend to the rest of the world (even to herself) that she wants him to do, obey, conform; the Good Bad Boy does what she *really* wants him to do: deceive, break her heart a little, so that she can forgive him, smother him in the embrace that seals him back into her world forever. No wonder we can never have done pillorying the Good Good Boy in our books; no wonder we insist that no matter how he enters our fiction, he must exit whimpering, whipped, exposed as an alien and an imposter, no Saviour at all, though he may be the minister's son. Even his death does not shock us; and he is therefore chosen to play the part of the victim in *The Bad Seed* (even as Leopold and Loeb once chose him in real life), just the sort of little monster we have all righteously longed to kill, though we have not, of course, yielded to the temptation.

The Good Bad Boy, on the other hand, we all understand and love—at least feel obliged to pretend to understand and love. For a long time he was merely the "bad boy" without further qualification—his goodness needing no adjective to declare it to those who *really* knew him, his proud title almost enough in itself to ensure a best seller: *Confessions of a Bad Boy, Peck's Bad Boy*, etc. The male reader not enterprising enough to have been actually "bad" as a child himself could persuade himself as he read that this was, indeed, the true shape of his childhood; and his wife beside him could nod comfortably, believing, too, that her husband had been just so untamed before she had imprisoned him in the gentle bonds of her love. "Oh, you bad thing!" cries Becky Thatcher to her small noble savage, Tom, and the epithet is revealed as the supreme term of endearment. It is the fate of Good Good Girls to love such boys precisely because they play hooky, lie, cuss, steal in a mild sort of way, act the part of Robin Hood—refuse in short to be "sissies." Where taboos forbid the expression of sexuality except once removed in the form of aggression, such delinquency is the declaration of maleness. Besides, the Good Good Girls know all the time (what, of course, they never tell) that their young lovers are rugged individualists in embryo, boy philistines in training.

In quite the same way, the modern Bad Good Girl (no longer permitted to flaunt her virtue, but expected to preserve it in some sense all the same) knows that the young radical or bohemian she loves is *playing* at being bad, will, like Tom Sawyer before him, end up as judge or bank president, senior editor at Random House—at the least as author of some latter-day *Confessions of a Bad Boy*: *Memoirs of a Revolutionist*, perhaps, or *The Naked God, An End to Innocence* or *On the Road.* Our American bad boys are, alas, examples of natural virtue, and must not be confused with the monstrous little villains of exemplary British books for children—or even with the Katzenjammerish projections of infantile sadism whom the Germans find so amusing and satisfactory.

Still less are they the horny adolescents of Mediterranean fiction, bedeviled by desire, and falling via sex to adulthood. No American boy hero is, in the classic tradition at least, devirginated into participation in the moral ambiguity of life. At best he is *terrified* into it; at worst he grows away from it into the safety of respectability. The Tom Sawyer archetype, the junior Robin Hood, can only grow into goodness, *i.e.*, success; for his "badness" is his boyhood and he cannot leave one behind without abandoning the other. His fantasies of revolt are oral not genital, his dreams of indulgences the stolen slab of bacon and the forbidden pipeful of tobacco. Grown older he will alternately diet and grow fat, honor his dream of rebellion on the Sunday picnic or over the built-in Jackson's Island in his back yard.

The Good Bad Boy is, of course, America's vision of itself, is authentic America, crude and unruly in his beginnings but endowed by his creator with an instinctive sense of what is right; sexually as pure as any milky maiden, he is a roughneck all the same, at once potent and submissive. That the image of a boy represent our consciousness of ourselves and our role is scarcely surprising. We are, to the eternal delight and scorn of Europeans, inhabitants of a society in which scarcely anyone is too grave or mature to toss a ball around on a warm afternoon. Where almost every male is still trying to sneak out on mother (whom he demands *make* him sneak his pleasures); where, as Geoffrey Gorer has made quite clear, mothers are also fathers—that is, embodiments of the sugerego—growing up is for the male not inheriting the superego position, but shifting it to a wife, *i.e.*, a mother of his own choice. No wonder our greatest book is about a boy and that boy "bad"!

The book is, of course, *Huckleberry Finn* (with its extension back into *Tom Sawyer*), an astonishingly complicated novel, containing not one image of the boy child as a symbol of the good life of impulse, but a series of interlocking ones: boys within boys.* Tom Sawyer exists as the projection of all that Sid Saw-

* Some of these notions were suggested to me by James Cox's essay, "The Sad Initiation of Huckleberry Finn."

yer, pious Good Good Boy, presumably yearns for and denies; but Huck Finn in turn stands for what Tom is not quite rebel enough to represent; and Nigger Jim (remade from boy to adult between the two books) embodies a world of instinct and primitive terror beyond what even the outcast paleface boy projects. In most ways, Huck is closer to Jim than to Tom—that is, closer to what the white world of gentility fears and excludes than to what it condescendingly indulges in the child. He can *play* with Tom at being an outlaw and runaway, counterfeit the anguish of the excluded, but he is playing on the square as Tom is not.

But the novel *Huckleberry Finn* exists on two levels: as the tragic book Mark Twain half-unwittingly had to write, and as the comic one he was content to have most readers believe he had written. Twain himself confuses the two books hopelessly at the end, when Huck, calling himself Tom, *becomes* Tom; when Tom himself appears and reveals his whole role as fiction, a lie; and the tragic moral problem of Jim's freedom is frittered away in a conventional Happy Ending celebrated in the midst of furious horseplay. It is to this Happy Ending that we owe our idyllic vision of Childhood on the Mississippi.

Partly because of Twain's uncertainty, partly because of its own inability to accept his tragic vision of childhood, America has kept alive in its collective memory a euphoric series of illustrations to the comic novel Twain did not really write. In our national imagination, two freckle-faced boys arm in arm, fishing poles over their shoulders, walk toward the river; or one alone floats peacefully on its waters, a runaway Negro by his side. They are on the lam, we know, from Aunt Polly and Aunt Sally and the Widow Douglas and Miss Wilson, from little golden-haired Becky Thatcher, too, whose name Twain forgot between books: from all the reduplicated female symbols of religion and "sivilization."

They live in a mythicized rural hinterland of America, in the ante-bellum small town, in America's childhood; and they pass through a landscape based not so much on memory and fact as on an urban nostalgia for the countryside and the village, the rich man's longing for the falsified place of his poverty. It is these kidnapped images which the popular imagination further debases step by step via Penrod and Sam or O. Henry's "Red Chief" to Henry Aldrich or the insufferable Archie of the teenage funny books. They become constantly more false in their naïveté, in their hostility to culture in general and schoolteachers in particular; and it scarcely matters whether they are kept in the traditional costume of overalls and bare feet or are permitted jeans and sweaters decorated with high-school letters. On the riverbank or in the Coke shop, afoot or in a stripped-down hotrod, they represent the American faith in the boy who will not go to school willingly, who will not learn anything except what his heart whispers to him, who is always ready to hang up the sign: *Gone fishin'*; but who charms away our distrust, turning on us the shy grin of innocence that can still elect a president of the United States.

Anyone can counterfeit Tom Sawyers these days; Henry Aldrich, for instance, was composed by a long series of radio writers who succeeded each other without ever disturbing the prefabricated myth they passed from hand to hand. Most of these writers were city-bred Jews, but the image they kept alive remained still the expression of an America quite different from their own: Henry like Tom is white and Protestant and sexless, the son of a father who was (or would like to believe so) Tom Sawyer before him and whose own father had been Tom, too. How they long, all three generations of them, for the summertime when they can escape once more to the parks and national forests, the guarded places which conserve along with trout streams and ponderosa pine the good old badness that is our original innocence. But it is not only Henry Aldrich I, II and III, who fishes the big two-hearted river; let Jake Barnes shake off the queers and the women and the Jews, let him once cut loose with "good old Bill" and he can forget even in Spain that the sun also rises, remember only that he, too, is still the barefoot boy with cheek of tan. For Americans there is no other childhood —for some, indeed, no other life. In the end, readers of our classic books and their commercial derivatives are driven to counterfeit similar boyhoods (even in Brooklyn they wriggle into jeans) or to grant that they were not, in the mythical sense, ever boys at all.

III. Boys Will Be Boys!

The one realm of childhood experience almost completely excluded from the sentimental world bounded by the Good Good Girl and the Good Bad Boy is sex. Yet surely boys and girls even before the Civil War giggled at the sight of each other's underpants, crept off into private corners for intimate examinations, even played "doctor"; nor was all of this unknown to their elders. Indeed, Freud once complained that, despite all the protests raised over his theories of infantile sexuality, it was his dull duty merely to make public facts known to every nursemaid. If childhood is innocent to the Anglo-Saxon world of the nineteenth century, it is innocent by definition, pure by virtue of its symbolic function, sexless because the novelist in flight from sex demanded it be so.

The turning from the adult hero to the child represents not only a search for projections of pure impulse, but also a rejection of the themes with which the bourgeois novel began, themes rooted in sexuality. Though the child is understood to represent the "heart" as opposed to the "head," feeling as opposed to reason; the order of feeling figured forth by the "heart" is clearly distinguished from mere lust, the crude genital passions. In the symbolic psychology invented in the eighteenth century, the "heart" does not correspond precisely to what we would call the "id," but only to its more benign aspects. The sexual and demonic components of impulse and unreason, at first unconfessed (concupiscence is postulated as a cold product of the "head"), are later allowed for by splitting the basic "heart" symbols into polar opposites: Woman become the Fair Virgin and the Dark Lady, the Indian becomes Mingo and Mohawk, Pawnee and Sioux—Good Indian and Bad Indian! In each case, the Dark Double represents the threat of sex as well as that of death; the Bad Indian is a rapist as inevitably as the Dark Lady is a sexual aggressor. The child, however, refuses to do such double service, stubbornly resists becoming an image of fear as well as one of hope.

The badness of the Good Bad Boy is, as we have seen, a necessary spice to his goodness; the worse he is, the more "boy" he is, which is to say, the better. It is a trap hard to break through. There are, on the other hand, real possibilities in the girl who refuses the full burden of her "good goodness." Yet though there are tentative fumblings at defining a pre-adolescent Dark Lady, none of them really works. Pearl, the demon child of Hawthorne's *The Scarlet Letter*, represents one attempt to shadow forth in the guise of childhood the more demonic aspects of nature; for she is, indeed, a "natural child," that is to say, a bastard—and Hawthorne is still Puritan enough to suggest that her real father is that father of all illegitimates, Satan. His witch child, however, does not finally seem a child at all, but only an allegory of the aftereffects of sin: like the Scarlet Letter itself a symbolic prop rather than a living character; yet, interestingly enough, she is one of the few childhood figures from the literature of the mid-nineteenth century based not on stereotypes and nostalgic memories but on a systematic observation of the author's own living child.

Mrs. Stowe's Topsy is the product of yet another attempt at portraying the Really Bad Girl, though her badness is finally no more than mischief; and she comes to represent not so much the darkness of evil as a decorative blackness necessary to set off the whiteness of little Eva. Topsy and Pearl alike are not permitted to languish in their moral exile forever but are redeemed to the light, saved: the small and sooty pagan by the death of her white counterimage, the untamed illegitimate by the self-sacrifice of her adulterous father. In the end, they are only minor anticipations of the latter-day Good Bad Girl, that favorite of a newer sentimentality, who seems the trollop in Chapter I but proves the mere victim of appearances before the conclusion. Pearl, indeed, is not only redeemed but endowed with wealth, transferred into the dazzling figure of the Young American girl as the Heiress of All the Ages.

In *Tom Sawyer*, Mark Twain, who is often at the point of tipping off the game he always ends by playing, nearly gives away the secret sexual life of the Good Good Girl, when Becky is almost caught looking at the dirty pictures in the teacher's anatomy book. Tom takes not only her beating but the blame; and so circumspect is Twain in describing her actual fall that few readers remember (after all, it is only a child's book) the primal keyhole act at which she is surprised. There is something close to cynicism, at least to willful self-deceit, in Tom's complicity; for it is as necessary to him that Becky retain her mythical Goodness as it is for her that he retain his equally legendary Badness. It is hard to know which revelation would seem more scandalous: that she is not as pure as she is postulated, or that he is not as wicked.

In the genteel era, the Good Good Girl is more and more protected from contamination by sex; not only is she portrayed as innocent in herself; after a while, she is not even permitted to stir lust in the most ignoble heart. In America in particular as the nineteenth century wears on, Seduction, which as accomplished fact or omnipresent threat had been the staple of female fiction for a hundred years, is banned; and the heroine is moved back in age across the dangerous border line of puberty. In works like *The Lamplighter* and *The Wide, Wide World*, the woman's best seller becomes the book about the Good Good Girl, who is no longer harried by the lustful libertine, but has to content herself (and her readers) with being exploited by cheating salesmen, scared by hydrophobic dogs and runaway horses, or threatened with death by pleurisy or brain fever.

Only Lewis Carroll (who wept when the young girls he loved put up their hair and let down their dresses) was able to rescue the pre-nubile heroine from pious insipidity. His Alice moves through a fantastic landscape where the symbols of sexuality seem mere magic or nonsense, and the threat of puberty is waked from as from a bad dream. But the main line of female fiction, after its retreat back behind pubescence, leads inevitably to Elsie Dinsmore! The Good Good Girl expires in the sanctimonious bathos of juvenile fictions presented by maiden aunts to their nieces in a desire to teach them that a woman must weep, without really revealing to them for what. Even boy's literature cannot entirely escape the stereotypes and taboos; and

Huckleberry Finn, despite all its apparent distance from *The Wide, Wide World,* is like *Alice in Wonderland* an evasion rather than a breakthrough, an acceptance however devious of the genteel decree that *all* literature must be fit for the eye of the sexless child.

It is not only that Twain deprives Huck of the prostitute sisters who helped define the lot of his real-life prototype; he cannot even (beneath the comic high jinks and realistic dialogue) avoid creating him in the image of the child-heroines of contemporary best sellers: an orphan adopted by widows and old maids, an outcast, harried by his own father, and misunderstood by the respectable community—and, of course, an irreproachable virgin. One of the reasons it is so hard to tell Huck Finn's age (Twain *says* he's fourteen!) is Twain's unwillingness to confess that, capable as he is of shifting for himself, he is also sexually mature. Huck is permitted, it is true, to move in the world of the raree show; but he is not allowed to respond to the sexuality of such spectacles with the same awareness that he brings to the world of lynchings and cruelty which is its twin. Twain's scruples work in almost precisely the opposite way from those of our own latter-day sentimentalists: he is squeamish about sex, utterly frank about violence.

Yet his unwillingness to grant that Huck is physically a man makes it hard to assess the impact on him of the alienation he endures. Genteel taboos do not prevent Twain from rendering the brutal predicament of the child (adolescent?) buffeted between his own imaginary fears and the real terrors of the society that rejects him. We find it disturbingly easy, however, to forget the isolation out of which Huck comes and to which he returns: the fate of all those excluded from the comfortable, empty world of Aunt Sally. So much is he the "poor, motherless" boy, the "child of nature" that we confuse him with the barefoot boy with cheek of tan—demote him to moral imbecility of early childhood. Twain takes advantage of this ambiguity to make us approve his anti-social, "satanic" behavior, before which we might at least have hesitated, were his hero, say, unequivocally portrayed as old enough to desire a woman. Though we recall that Huck (in his innocence and ignorance) stole Jim, perpetrated, that is to say, what in terms of his world's values was a crime and sin, we smile smugly. The child is right, we tell ourselves, childhood is always right, intelligence and experience always wrong. But we have forgotten (because Huck is "only a boy") that he has performed precisely the arrogant act of Raskolnikov or Oppenheimer or Leopold and Loeb, has appointed himself the lonely arbiter of morality.

Huck Finn is, then, in one sense the really Bad Boy, a projection of insolence and contempt for authority; but he is also the persecuted orphan (blurring into the figure of Oliver Twist), a nonresisting rebel, gentle and scared and (alas!) cute. He emerges out of the earlier stereotypes of Abused Innocence and fades back into their later versions, one more forerunner of the grubby little boy and his dog, but also one more ancestor of the Juvenile Delinquent, whose badges of innocence are the switch knife and the hot-wiring kit. Before our own Hucks, the young hoods of the mid-twentieth century, we are disabled still by literature: unable to tell fact from myth, the real child from the projection of our own moral plight. The guilt of the J.D. seems to us somehow only one more sign of his innocence, of *our* guiltiness in failing to protect and cultivate his original purity with enough love and security. The "child of a broken home" replaces the orphan among our current stereotypes, as "psychic rejection" replaces old-fashioned bullying and flogging. We are, however, still attempting to appease the same unappeasable anguish which once wailed with Dickens over poor Oliver in the hands of Fagin or with Twain over poor Huck trapped in Pap's cabin; though now the villain is no longer projected as the evil Jew or the fishbelly-white village drunk, but as the harried bourgeois father oozing baffled good will.

Just as it is difficult for us to discuss our guilt toward Negroes or Indians, say, without really talking about our uneasiness over what we have done with our instinctive life, what reservations and ghettos we have prepared for our darker impulses— so it is difficult for us (even more difficult perhaps) to consider the plight of our children as if they had independent existence and free will, and were not merely projections of our unconscious. We permit that unconscious (and the child) more sexual freedom now and are deeply troubled that this has made no difference, that each still blindly rebels. Perhaps, we sometimes think, we are paying a price for having restricted the child's range of aggression in return for his erotic freedom. The Good Bad Boy can get himself laid these days even in the fiction of Anglo-Saxondom, but he is no longer permitted to glory in beating up on the Jewish kid next door, or the minister's son or the over-dressed stranger from the big city. It is all a little like the joke in which the mother calls to her son, "Jakey! Jakey!" and he answers, "Here I am, Mama, behind the fence with Shirley." "And what are you doing, son?" she asks. "Screwing, Mama." "All right, all right. As long as you don't fight."

It is easy to exaggerate the difference a few generations have made in the basic concept of the Good Bad Boy. He is not to our moral imagination less innocent, merely permitted a new innocence, that of sex. Yet even though he is allowed now a certain amount of good clean sex (not as the basis of a relation-ship but as a kind of exhibition of prowess) and forbidden in return an equivalent amount of good clean violence, his standard repertory of permitted crimes remains pretty much the same. What are winked at still as permissible expressions of youthful exuberance are crimes against school and against property. The hood can mock his teacher and play hooky like Tom Sawyer before him, though in our days of prosperity and the indefinite extension of adolescence, he runs away (like the protagonists of J. D. Salinger or the speaker in Allen Ginsberg's poems) not from grade school, but from prep school or the university. Similarly he is allowed still to "hook" things, though not, in these more expansive times, such meager loot as candles and a side of bacon, but rather the neighbor's '58 swept-fin car. So much and so little have the spread of culture and wealth influenced our deeper mythical versions of our young selves.

Recently a group of writers in their late youth and early middle age have appeared, who not only project in literature the image of the Good Bad Boy but even act out in life this standard role, as if they had just invented it. They think they are emulating Huck Finn, though in reality their model is Tom Sawyer, and even at times (so dewy and starry-eyed is their naïve acceptance of all experience) they rather resemble Becky Thatcher! Such writers range all the way from a suburban, upper-middle-class wing represented by Salinger and his image Holden Caulfield to Allen Ginsberg and Jack Kerouac with their transparent, not-quite-fictional representations of themselves. Rural no longer in their memories or nostalgia, they yearn still for boyhood, and submit in their books to speaking through their masks, in a language which simulates that of the Good Bad Boy himself whether in his prep-school or pseudo-hipster form. Unlike Twain, who makes poetry of inarticulateness, his latter-day imitators produce only slick parodies of the silent generation pretending to talk—or are content with exclamatory noises: "And I said to myself, Wham, listen to that man. That's the West, here I am in the West . . . Whooee, I told my soul, and the cowboy came back and off we went to Grand Island."

Such writers have found on their own upper-middlebrow or bohemian-kitsch levels, a theme, a myth common at the moment to much of our society from its scarcely literate to its almost highbrow limits: the theme represented in the mass arts by such wide-screen projection of the New Good Bad Boy as Elvis Presley, Jimmie Dean, Marlon Brando. The corn-pone Romeo (with his dry orgasms below the semi-paralyzed face), the refugee from Broadway (half Tennessee Williams dream-boy, half stage-proletarian salvaged from the abandoned props of the Group Theatre), the homemade Hollywood legend in jeans and horn-rimmed glasses (taught to mumble with the best by the old master, Elia Kazan) are all Boys together, pinned side by side on the walls of fourteen-year-old girls and indistinguishable from their dreams. They in the big features and their simulacra on a thousand TV programs and in a hundred quickie films—SEE THE NAKED TRUTH ABOUT THE GET-LOST GENERATION!—act out stories of apparently causeless revolt (the cause is in the stereotype whose existence they fail to recognize) and accommodation, while the rock-and-roll fans roar approval. So the more literary exploiters of the theme, talking of "total rejection," actually rehearse the Tom Sawyer pattern once more, though this time for an audience that digs Miles Davis and worships the memory of the Bird.

In *Catcher in the Rye*, Holden comes to the dead end of

ineffectual revolt in a breakdown out of which he is impelled to fight his way by the Good Good Girls in the guise of the Pure Little Sister, from whose hands he passes directly into the hands of the psychiatrist. In *On the Road*, whose characters heal themselves as they go by play-therapy, the inevitable adjustment to society is only promised, not delivered; we must wait for the next installment to tell how the Square Hipster makes good by acting out his role (with jazz accompaniment) in a New York night club, or even, perhaps, how he has sold his *Confessions of a Bad Boy* to the movies. In the book itself, all the stigmata of Tom Sawyer are already present except the return to Aunt Polly; Paul Goodman has, without recalling the stereotype, identified them precisely: "One is stunned by how conventional and law-fearing these lonely middleclass fellows are. They dutifully get legal marriages and divorces. The hint of a gang-bang makes them impotent. They never masturbate or perform homosexual acts . . . To disobey a cop is 'all hell.' Their idea of crime is the petty shoplifting of ten-year-olds stealing cigarettes or of 'teen agers joyriding in other people's cars . . . Their behavior is a conformity *plus royaliste que le roi.*"

Typically enough in our time, such Boys are also *plus religieux que le pape*, insisting on their dedication to God, their assumption of the Christ role (unlike poor Huck, who chose to "go to hell") in a way that would have made the anti-clerical Twain wince. To be sure, it is Zen Buddhism rather than Unitarianism or neo-Orthodoxy which attracts the Square Hipster and *New Yorker* contributor alike, binding together as improbable coreligionists Salinger and Kerouac; indeed, if James Dean had not yet discovered this particular kick before he smashed up in a sports car, it is because he died just a little too soon. Past the bongo drums and fiddling around with sculpture it was waiting for him, the outsider's religion in a day when there is room inside for the outsider himself, provided he, too, goes "to the church of his choice."

The fact that one is tempted, even impelled to speak of, say, Jack Kerouac at thirty-five as a Boy, the fact that he writes as one of the Boys, is symptomatic of the degree to which the image of Good Bad Boyhood has impinged upon adult life itself, has be-

come a "career" like everything else in America. The age of
Kerouac's protagonists is just as ambiguous as that of Twain's,
though for quite the opposite reasons. Twain blurred adolescence
back into boyhood to avoid confronting the problem of sex; the
newer writers, accepting the confusion of childhood and youth,
blur both into manhood to avoid yielding up to maturity the
fine clean rapture of childish "making out." The fictional counterparts of the provincial Hipsters have crossed the border line of
genital maturity, but in all other respects they have not left
Jackson's Island. *Plus ça change, plus c'est la même chose,* we
sigh, capable only of banality in the face of such banality; and
the American translation is, "Boys will be boys!"

iv. From Redemption to Initiation

Though the treatment of the child in twentieth-century
fiction is often merely an up-to-date adaptation of sentimental
prototypes, this is by no means universally true. The influence
of depth psychology has not always stopped at the superficial
level; on occasion it has gone beyond providing useful tags for
the stage of infantile sexuality or making explicit insights already
implicit in earlier fiction. Most crucially, it has helped undercut
the moral optimism of sentimentalism by restoring a concept of
the child (and of the world of impulse he represents) more like
that of Augustine than that of Rousseau. Yet the child remains
for us, less sanguine about the "natural" though not less concerned
with it, still a fascinating literary theme; indeed, writers have
come to depend rather more than less on the child's eye, the
child's fresh vision as a true vision, a model of the artist's vision
itself.

The child is, however, considered an examplar not of the
innocence of the spirit but of the eye. Implicated in aggression
and sexuality, he projects nonetheless an unfallen way of perceiving the world; and his ambiguous unfallenness is used ironically to portray the implication of us all in the guilt he shares

but about which he has not yet learned to lie. The confrontation of adult corruption and childish perception remains a contemporary subject, though we no longer believe in the redemption of our guilt by the innocence of the child. His act of perception is portrayed as the beginning of his initiation into full-blown, self-conscious evil—the start of moral life. "Initiation" is the favorite word of an age which aspires not to "salvation" but to "maturity"; and the initiatory story has become popular almost to the point of triteness.

In its sentimental form, the fable of the encounter of the child and adult represents, it must be remembered, a bowdlerized version of the seduction theme. Just as in, say, *Pamela* and *Clarissa* the question is posed: will the Seducer seduce the Redeemer before the Redeemer redeems the Seducer, will the conflict end in the victory of the (good, female) Heart or the (evil, male) Head, in marriage or death; so in the more genteel, apparently asexual terms of Child-Adult fiction, the same question is posed: will Fagin win out or Oliver, Tiny Tim or Scrooge? Up to the very last moment, it is possible for Scrooge to find grace through Tiny Tim and Tiny Tim to be spared; or, as we have seen, redemption may be bought by the death of the Redeemer, Dombey ransomed by the sacrifice of Little Dombey; or the Redeemer may live and the Seducer die unredeemed as in the case of Oliver and Fagin. Beyond these comic and tragi-comic resolutions, neither Dickens nor his more genteel American followers were prepared to go; in no case, at any rate, is the child-redeemer won over to evil.

Even Melville in *Moby Dick* is unwilling to portray the corruption of a child; though every other crew member on the *Pequod* is committed temporarily to Ahab's diabolic quest, the cabin boy Pip is unseduced. True, he cannot, though he is endowed with *all* the symbolic attributes of natural virtue (he is a child and a Negro and mad to boot), redeem Ahab to the "humanities," and he dies with the rest; but he dies pure, the innocence of his vision only refined by his suffering. J. D. Salinger (the last reputable exploiter of the sentimental myths of childhood) pushes the redemption theme a step further into blackness; in "A Perfect Day for Banana Fish" he shows how Seymour Glass, a not entirely vicious adult, is awakened by the innocence of a child to enough awareness of the lost world he inhabits to kill himself! Yet we are asked apparently to accept the act of self-destruction as a kind of salvation.

The *ambiguity* of the attraction to childhood remains as unperceived in Salinger as in any nineteenth-century Anglo-Saxon Dickensian. In Dostoevsky, however, leading Russian disciple of Dickens, the lesson of the master had long since been translated out of sentimentality into horror. Only he was capable of understanding the secret to which Dickens obliquely alluded when he spoke of Quilp (the deformed, grotesque persecutor of Little Nell) as a self-portrait. True to his preceptor, Dostoevsky sees the world as a conspiracy against the child. His works are full of child-victims, typified by Ilusha in *The Brothers Karamazov*, infant martyrs whose death redeems those who crush them; while his childlike saviors go out to the children, Myshkin rescuing the little Swiss girl from her small persecutors and Alyosha becoming the hero of the pack of boys who cheer him at the novel's close. In the dream of Dmitri in *The Brothers Karamazov*, the vision of Russia as a wasteland is explained by the cry, "The child is weeping!" And Dostoevsky himself in his journal reminds himself over and over, "Do not torment the children, do not soil or corrupt them."

Yet Dostoevsky boasted at least once in public that he had raped a thirteen-year-old girl in the bath, and the image of the violated child appears again and again in his works. This is the crime which haunts Svidrigailov in *Crime and Punishment* and Stavrogin in *The Possessed;* according to surviving notes, it was originally to have been one of the sins of Dmitri, too; and it was certainly a fantasy that possessed the author all his life, an obsession he was driven to confess as fact and to rewrite continually as fiction. Child-lover and child-rapist: these are two sides of a single coin, the sentimental and demonic aspects of the Cult of the Child, which elsewhere in the nineteenth century is presented as if it possessed only a single, benign side.

Even in Russian and in Yiddish literature, so closely linked to it, the Dickensian image of the starved and brutalized child as it is passed on via Dostoevsky is once more expurgated, deprived of its erotic overtones, and (in writers like Chekov or Peretz) restored to sentimentalism. How finally melodramatic and cloying all those East European portraits of tortured apprentices and starving schoolboys appear; not so much because the children themselves are travestied as because their true enemy the Lover-Seducer is not candidly portrayed. The drunken, miserly, heartless master, the caricatured Exploiter (it is a theme easily adapted to Marxian uses) replaces Svidrigailov, the tormented lover of what he destroys.

Implicit in the fable of the love affair of Seducer and Redeemer is the barest hint that the child seeks out evil not only to transform it, but also out of a dim, unconfessed yearning for it. Eventually this underground perception will develop into the revelation of the moral coquetry of the child, a sense of how his flaunted innocence is an invitation to violation. In nineteenth-century literature, particularly in England and America, this ambiguous insight is somewhat naïvely projected as the Innocent Flirtation. In such fiction, the child in his simplicity finds himself attracted to adult evil rather than adult good; for the former seems to him to possess a spontaneity and grace more like his own than anything in the safe, dull world of grown-up virtue. There is a hint of such a flirtation with evil in Huck Finn's apparent choice of the Duke and Dauphin over the Widow Douglas; but he is more their prisoner than their accomplice, and in the end he feels for them not love but pity.

Clearer examples are to be found in the standard American story in which the Good Bad Boy enters into an alliance with Rip Van Winkle, the town idler or drunk (William Faulkner's "Uncle Willy" is a classic instance) against the world of conscience and womanhood. Rip Van Winkle himself is not, however, a clear-cut example of dowright villainy, but a figure as ambiguous as that of the Good Bad Boy; indeed, he is perhaps only the Good Bad Boy grown old without growing up. The Negro, portrayed as shiftless, vain, thievish and even sexually promiscuous, is an alternative lover or pseudo-father for the Good Bad Boy, particularly in popular fiction. The Negro, however, is not in such fiction taken any more seriously than Rip; he is a symbol not so much of one who has fallen from morality as one who has not yet begun the arduous climb toward it, and as such is merely another version of the Boy himself. "Little children and big Africans," writes William Lyon Phelps condescendingly in an introduction to Stephen Crane's *Whilomville Stories*, "make ideal companions, for the latter have the patience, inner sympathy, forebearance, and unfailing good humour necessary to such an association. Both Stephen Crane and Booth Tarkington have given us permanent drawings in black and white." Such stereotyped black-and-white portraiture sets a bad example which even serious later writers like Sherwood Anderson and Faulkner have not been able to escape. The flirtation of the child with evil becomes transformed into a genre picture of the nature-loving boy and the watermelon-stealing darky.

It is Robert Louis Stevenson who most clearly develops the theme in his books, which, like *The Lamplighter* or *Huckleberry Finn* or *Alice in Wonderland*, appeal to that odd late-nineteenth-century audience which made adult best sellers of children's literature. In *Treasure Island* and *David Balfour*, Stevenson adds to the tale of adventure the boyish romance: the passionately ambivalent relationships of Jim Hawkins and Long John Silver, David Balfour and Alan Breck Stewart. In the boy's flirtation with the pirate and the outlaw, Stevenson is clearly projecting his own ambivalence as a writer (whose function he describes somewhere as "playing with paper like a child") before the criminal and outcast, before what is taboo to his own lowland, Protestant conscience. In the end, however, both author and characters are Good Bad Boys, who return from playing at evil to working at good. The threatened inheritance or the contested (and innocently won) treasure in their possession, they return from fabulous highlands or legendary islands to the gray world of unattractive virtue.

The Seduction-Redemption theme is not easily surrendered. In various forms its victimized small saviors survive: as the Salinger girl heroines of *Catcher in the Rye* and "To Esme with Love and Squalor"; as the protagonist of *Poile de carote*, whose motion-picture success has ensured his survival beyond that of the novel in which he first appeared; as the poisoned, tormented children of the Reggie Fortune mystery stories; and most lately as the child mutants (telepaths, teleports, superhuman monsters of virtue as well as intelligence) who in a score of science-fiction tales struggle with the dull world their merely human parents have made. *Childhood's End,* the most successful of such fictions is called; and, indeed, its author, Arthur C. Clarke, has reached the end of a much exploited myth of childhood. It is tempting to read the conclusion of his book, in which the superchildren he has imagined desert this world utterly, as a symbolic prophecy that we are through with them as they are with us; but the social scientists caught in a cultural lag will take up what fiction has outlived, the Dr. Werthams of our society talking about the *Seduction of the Innocent* long after the Dickenses of our time have turned elsewhere for pathos.

Most serious writers in the twentieth century, however, have given up the notion of seduction as well as that of redemption; they are no more moved by the concept of corruption than they are by that of salvation, substituting for the more traditional fable of a fall to evil that of an initiation into good-and-evil. In a sense, this represents a transition from the worship of innocence to that of experience, from a concern with the latency period of the child to a concentration of the moment of adolescence. *Huckleberry Finn* is sometimes thought of as the prototype of this newer kind of fable; and one of the most perceptive recent interpretations of that novel is James Cox's "The Sad Initiation of Huckleberry Finn." But it is hard finally to believe in Huck's having been initiated into anything; if he is at all different at the end of the book from what he is at its start, it is only in possessing a few more nightmares; but in such treasures he was rich enough to begin with. Sympathy he does not learn; for he has as much when he sets out as when he returns, and always it alternates with an astonishing callousness. The original innocence of Huck is not his ignorance of evil (he is the son of his father, after all) but his immunity to experience, his resistance to responsibility; and these preclude the fortunate fall we call initiation.

An initiation is a fall through knowledge to maturity; behind it there persists the myth of the Garden of Eden, the assumption that to know good and evil is to be done with the joy of innocence and to take on the burdens of work and childbearing and death.

Yet typically, in Anglo-Saxon literature at least, the child is not
a participant in the fall, but a *witness*, only vicariously inducted
into the knowledge of sin. In the modern version of the Fall of
Man, there are four participants, not three: the man, the woman,
the serpent and the child (presumably watching everything
from behind the tree). It is Henry James who sets the pattern
once and for all in *What Maisie Knew*, in which the details of a
particularly complicated and sordid adulterous tangle are presented to us as refracted through the half-ignorance of a pre-
adolescent girl. The fictional working out of the Vicarious Initiation presupposes the invention of a technique (the famous
Jamesian point of view) which leaves no doubt in the reader's
mind about who is witnessing the events related; and so the
perfection of a formal device makes possible the development
of a new theme.

Once James has achieved the convention and the image,
once he has established the Child as Peeping Tom, it is adapted
everywhere, on every level of literature from highest to lowest.
Eye to the crack in the door, ear attuned from the bed where
he presumably sleeps, curious or at idle play, the innocent observer stumbles upon the murderer bent over the corpse, the
guilty lovers in each other's arms, the idolized jockey in a whorehouse, a slattern on his knee. Such children are the presiding
geniuses of modern fiction, reborn in a hundred guises: as Hemingway's Nick Adams overhearing the gossip about his Indian
girl; as the baffled boy of Sherwood Anderson's "I Want to Know
Why"; as the little Jew of Salinger's "Down at the Dinghy" hearing the cook call his father a "kike"; as the upper-class child
confronted with the vulgar sin of servants in Graham Greene's
"Basement Room," or Walter de la Mare's "The Perfect Craftsman." Even in drama, where point of view is hard to maintain,
in Inge's *The Dark at the Top of the Stairs*, for instance, writers
are driven to emulate the prototype, to render the experience
of evil in terms of *what the child sees*.

But *why* have our writers welcomed so indirect an evocation
of the child's passage from innocence to experience? In a way,
it seems the last genteel reticence; a refusal to portray the child
as an actual sinner, though it is no longer possible to postulate

his innocence as absolute. In the fiction of France and Italy, indeed, the initiation of the boy into manhood is portrayed in frankly sexual terms; he is *devirginated* into maturity by the kindly, aging whore, who is the high priestess of this *rite de passage* in the stories of writers like Colette or Alberto Moravia; and he may even, released from the burden of innocence (as in the recent movie *The Game of Love*) then induct the young girl into the world of experience he has entered. Sometimes, even in European fiction, the initiation is the sexual experience fumbled rather than fulfilled, the visit to the whorehouse which ends in impotence or even in flight at the very threshold, as in Flaubert's *A Sentimental Education.* This quasi-devirgination, the fall via sexual queasiness rather than sexual satisfaction, has become a cliché in stories both here and abroad; but the *typical* American convention, where the Vicarious Initiation is spurned, is quite different.

In the United States it is through murder rather than sex, death rather than love that the child enters the fallen world. He is not asked, to be sure, to kill a fellow human, only an animal, deer or bear, or even fish, some woodland totem, in slaying whom (sometimes he is even smeared with the blood of his victim) he enters into a communion of guilt with the natural world in which hitherto he has led the privileged existence of an outsider. Hemingway and Faulkner are, of course, the leading serious exploiters of this theme, and "The Bear" its classic expression; but in pulp fiction and outdoor books it is repeated over and over on the level of the stereotype. The boy with "buck fever," the kid trembling over the broken body of his first rabbit or the first bird brought down with a sling, is the equivalent in the world of violence to the queasy stripling over the whore's bed in the world of passion. But even as the sexually inexperienced boy is redeemed by the old tart, so the child unused to death is initiated by the old Negro or Indian, the dark-skinned primitive who mediates between him and the world of wild beasts and prepares him for this bloody First Communion.

Yet even this last device, so implicated in the cult of nature which everywhere influences American life, cannot replace completely the theme of the Vicarious Initiation; for that theme is *more* finally than an evasion. Indeed, the stories which it informs embody in various disguises one or another of the two major crises of pre-adolescent emotional life: the stumbling on the Primal Scene, mother and father in the sexual act (or less dramatically the inference of it from creaking springs and ambiguous cries); or the discovery of heterosexual "treachery" on the part of some crush, idolized in innocent homosexual yearning. *What Maisie Knew* is ultimately the same old scandal that brought her into being; and "The Fallen Idol" is inevitably the desexualized substitute father caught out in turn in the primal defection. "At the track the air don't taste as good . . ." Sherwood Anderson makes his disillusioned Peeping Tom declare. "It's because a man like Jerry Tilford . . . could see a horse like Sunstreak run, and kiss a woman like that the same day . . . it spoils looking at horses and smelling things and hearing niggers laugh and everything . . . What did he do it for? I want to know why!" But he does know why already and it is what Maisie knew before him; the knowledge that was to make us as gods and taught us only that we die.

v. The Profanation of the Child

The fate of the child after his vicarious initiation can be variously portrayed; the work of William Faulkner provides a paradigm of all the possibilities. In *Light in August*, Joe Christmas, at the age of five, his mouth full of stolen toothpaste, witnesses the love-making of an orphanage nurse and learns from her that he is a Negro; at fourteen, brutally kicks the naked black girl upon whom he might have lost his virginity; and at thirty-three, decapitates the aging woman who has made him her lover, thus assuring his own eventual lynching. Quentin Compson (the chief mask of the young Faulkner) watches as a child a drama of passion and death in "That Evening Sun Go Down," which he relives as an adolescent witness and participant in

The Sound and the Fury and *Absalom, Absalom!*; and dies by his own hand on the verge of manhood, having learned his own implication in the human tangle of incest and nostalgia, murder and miscegenation.

For the earlier Faulkner, the fall to sexual knowledge is a fall to inevitable corruption and death; but the later Faulkner, plagued perhaps by declining powers and certainly converted to more "positive" attitudes, has revised his views of these matters, as he has revised his tragic view of life in general. Quentin is re-created as the bowdlerized boy, Chuck Mallison, who was born in a *Saturday Evening Post* detective story and has been kept alive through *Intruder in the Dust* and *The Town*. Unlike Quentin, Chuck is finally undismayed by any revelation of evil in his society or family, finding no ambiguous echo in himself; he is obviously destined to grow up into another consciously noble, impotent windbag with a Phi Beta Kappa key like his uncle Gavin Stevens—a second J. Alfred Claghorn. He represents, that is to say, a sentimental-comic version of initiation, initiation viewed not as a catastrophic ordeal but as a rather painful induction into compromise and responsibility. He belongs to a time when Supreme Court decisions on integration have taken the headlines away from lynchings; and is blood brother to the youngsters celebrated in neo-realistic TV scripts about family life, written by liberals without a cause and projected by actors with a Method.

The more serious successors of Faulkner, the homosexual-gothic novelists who have, unexpectedly enough, inherited his symbolic Southern landscape and his concern with evil, have ignored his later versions of the plight of the child in favor of the earlier ones. Their pre-adolescent protagonists confront still the decaying plantation house, the miasma-laden swamp, the secret lives of the Negro. They serve as symbols of exclusion as well as innocence, though no longer (as in Faulkner's case) merely of the exclusion of the fallen aristocrat and the unsuccessful writer. Like the circus freaks, the deaf and dumb, the idiots also congenial to their authors, they project the invert's exclusion from the family, his sense of heterosexual passion as a threat and an offense; and this awareness is easily translated into the child's bafflement before weddings or honeymoons or copulation itself.

Such child-figures are ambiguous, epicene, caught at the indeterminate point where the charm of boy and girl are scarcely distinguishable. Truman Capote is a notable contributor to this gallery of ephebic forms; but it is Carson McCullers who has adapted it to the popular imagination, breaking out of the bounds of the novel (with the help of Julie Harris) to stage and screen; so that her boy-girls, with their jeans and chopped-off hair and noncommittal first names, have made familiar to us all the fantastic image of the Good Bad Boy as Teen-age Tomboy, Huck Finn as F. Jasmine Adams. It is turn and turn about, for Huck once played the girl as these now ape the boy; but if his exigencies were similar Mark Twain did not know it. Much has remained the same, the Negro, for instance, still providing comfort for these transvestite Hucks in their moments of misery; though Jim, too, has been transformed from male to female.

The *Harper's Bazaar* Faulknerians remain faithful at least to the tragic implications of the initiation story; certainly, they are not tempted by the sentimental fables so popular with their British opposite numbers and recently worked by Angus Wilson into his *Anglo-Saxon Attitudes*. In the latter kind of story, a disgustingly female, aging wife is portrayed as engaged in a struggle with a young boy-girl (or girl-boy, it scarcely matters) for the soul and dignity of a gentle scholar-huband. A somewhat more camouflaged, middlebrow homosexual theme is the *Tea and Sympathy* defense of the "sissy": the delicate and effete Good Good Boy, presented as more worthy of the favors of some motherly female than the grossly male bully to whom she happens to be married.

Once the child has been remade by homosexual sensibility into the image of an ambiguous object of desire, the lust for the child is revealed as a flight from woman, the family, maturity itself; and unless the writer sentimentalizes pederasty on some romantic, English public-school model, he finds himself confronting a theme as dark and terrible as Dostoevsky's evocation of the child-rapist. Hints of this theme are everywhere in fiction of the McCullers school, but nowhere does it seem to me to be treated with full awareness. Oddly enough, J. D. Salinger (elsewhere more grossly sentimental about children than any contemporary writer of similar stature) comes once to the very verge of expressing it in "A Perfect Day for Banana Fish," when Seymour Glass trifles erotically with the child Sybil, playing with her fingers, kissing her feet in an appalling demonstration which the author will not quite let us accept as pathological. Actually, he demands that we accept this ambiguous love-making as a moment of sanity before suicide, that we read the child as the embodiment of all that is clean and life-giving as opposed to the vulgar, destructive (*i.e.*, fully sexual) wife. To have made the little girl a little *boy* would have given the game away; but this Salinger refused to do, clinging like a good American to little Eva even on the verge of the tragic.

In two European novellas by Ronald Firbank and Thomas Mann, however, the final step had already been taken, long before the time of Salinger or McCullers or Capote. Indeed, it had been anticipated before Firbank and Mann by Ibsen in *The Masterbuilder;* but he had projected the elusive image of youth teasing the artist toward his own destruction as a half-mad girl already past puberty. The not-quite-mature boy, dimly aware of his own homosexual allure, seems finally an apter, certainly a more sinister embodiment of the Romantic drive toward self-immolation. At any rate, in *Death in Venice* and *The Eccentricities of Cardinal Pirelli,* Mann and Firbanks have created with great tenderness but even greater truth portraits of boy-coquettes; on the literal level, they are callow flirts, cruel without any deep sense of the real pleasures or the true threat of cruelty; on a symbolic level, images of death itself. The last mad pursuit in which the naked Cardinal chases Don Skylark around the empty Cathedral, the "cage of God," and the final vision of the great writer von Ashenbach, painted and hectic at his shameful end, indicate the same thing: that what they have all along desired, known all along that the child really figured forth, was self-destruction. What such poetic treatments have once established, no later version of the lust for childhood can quite ignore. Like all sophisticated yearnings for the primitive and inchoate, the nostalgia for innocence and the child is suicidal.

The dis-ease with Romantic primitivism that underlies the tragic statements of Mann and Firbank is at work, though less profoundly, elsewhere in our culture. Even at the level of popular literature, certain anti-stereotypes of the child begin to establish themselves. The boy and his dog may still creep off into a corner to mourn, the misunderstood kid find in the town drunk his truest friend, or the golden-haired young girl win the crusty old curmudgeon to virtue and affection; indeed, in the comic strips such obsolescent archetypes are embalmed, preserved apparently forever. Little Annie Rooney and Little Orphan Annie play out latter-day versions of the Good Good Girl as outcast and wanderer, while Dennis the Menace revives the image of Peck's Bad Boy. The Small Angel in the House and the Little Devil survive side by side; and one can even suggest, as Stephen Crane did before the turn of the century, that the golden-haired girl is a little devil herself—as long as it is clear that one is (finally) only kidding! Such an authority on witchcraft and diabolism as Shirley Jackson can call a book about children *Raising Demons* and sell chapters of it to the ladies' magazines as long as her readers continue to believe that when she speaks of kids raising hell she is using a jocular metaphor.

For a long time, however, quite serious writers have suggested that children may indeed be instruments of the diabolic rather than embodiments of innocence. In some liberal quarters any such suggestion, especially if associated with New England Calvinism, is considered as absurd as asserting that some government officials may have been Communists; and, indeed, Arthur Miller managed to make a play whose two layers of meaning depended on associating charges of witchcraft against children with "McCarthyism." But ever since Henry James' *Turn of the Screw*, subtler writers have presented as objects of horror children possessed, children through whom the satanic attempts to enter the adult world. After all, "satanic" is merely another word for the impulsive, unconscious life otherwise called "innocent."

How equivocal our attitudes toward that subrational life in

fact are is best portrayed by the popular reception of *Peter Pan*, a fictional diatribe against adulthood and paternal authority, disguised as a tract in favor of fairies. The most ordinary Broadway producer knows these days the poor papa in his doghouse and the evil Captain Hook ought to be played by the same actor; but the Oedipal slaying (the triumph of boy over man, the father figure fed to the *vagina dentata!*) with which the play reaches its climax is sufficiently disguised in sticky cuteness to make its reading a nursery ritual, and the trip to see it in the theater a Holy Pilgrimage of the bourgeois family! Barrie's protagonist is Pan in a real sense; and therefore not only a callous, amoral, vain boy, but a *devil*, against whom all windows must be shut. But Barrie, sentimentalist and popular entertainer, equivocates before he is through, making Pan only a Good Bad Little Devil, who must be sewed for and told stories—although he will not abide mothering contaminated with sex, and in the end lights out for his territory!

Barrie's story is finally a "fantasy" (capable of being transformed by Disney's vulgar touch into a mere dream) and even Henry James' tale a "ghost story," an entertainment to which one condescends a little. Realer monsters, child-demons implicated in the actual world we inhabit are to be found in Saki's story of the small boy rejoicing in the killing of his evil governess by a pet mongoose, and especially in Walter de la Mare's "The Perfect Craftsman." The boy-protagonist of the latter, stumbling on a murder, helps in icy calm the rattled killer arrange all the evidence so that it looks like a suicide—then runs in panic through the dark passageways of a house haunted by imagined terrors. Beyond this, there is the sixteen-year-old in Paul Bowles' limpidly nauseating "Pages from Cold Point" who seduces his own father, luring him, unwilling but weak, to the final monstrous embrace. This is, of course, horror pornography—last product of the endless gothic search for something ultimately odious enough to shock our ultimately jaded tastes.

Two larger-scale attempts at creating counterstereotypes of the child are Richard Hughes' *Innocent Voyage* and *The Lord of the Flies* by William Golding. In each, we are presented not with a single child, but a gallery of children ranging in age from just out of infancy to just short of full adolescence; in each (in Hughes' nostalgic evocation of the end of piracy, by a typhoon; in Golding's more recent book, by an atomic bombing) a group of children is removed from the constraints of normal adult society; and in each the innocent protagonists are shown as reinventing the evil of which the sentimentalists had considered them the passive victims. In the Golding book, indeed, they recapitulate, on the island on which they are cast, the whole terrible history of civilization; and are engaged at the moment of rescue in a war, which their rescuers take as a game. "I know," says a bewildered naval officer. "Jolly good show. Like the Coral Island." The reference is to a childhood book based on older romantic clichés of good clean boyish fun which Golding quite deliberately mocks, leaving us with a view of Ralph, his most sensitive child observer, "with filthy body, matted hair, and unwiped nose" weeping "for the end of innocence, the darkness of man's heart . . ."

The Hughes book is even more terrible in its impact, finally, for it portrays a society in which girls play a leading part (Golding's island community is all male); and its fourteen-year-old Margaret, who becomes the forecastle whore, as well as its younger Emily, who kills a bound man, stabbing him in a dozen places, are profanations of the Good Good Girl—not mere antistereotypes but blasphemies. Emily's crime is not only unsuspected; it does not even bring her to self-awareness. Unlike Golding's Ralph, she sinks back into innocence without regret or self-reproach, is lost in a crowd of schoolgirls: "Looking at that gentle, happy throng of clean innocent faces and soft graceful limbs, listening to the ceaseless, artless babble of chatter rising, perhaps God could have picked out from among them which was Emily: but I am sure that I could not."

Emily has not remained an isolated case. In Faulkner's *Absalom, Absalom!*, the young girl Judith is discovered, leaning over the edge of a loft and screaming with the blood-lust her brother does not share (he trembles, nauseated), while her father wrestles naked and bloody with one of his field Negroes. Faulkner is as interested in profaning the myth of the Good Woman as he is in debunking that of the Innocent Child—and the image of the Child Witch serves for him a double purpose. Judith, after her first scene, he cannot quite make come alive; but in *The Hamlet* he tries again, on a less gothic, more comic level with Eula Varner, more Girl Bitch than Child Witch this time, but equally terrifying. The scene in which the schoolmaster Labove, helpless with the desire that an eleven-year-old girl has stirred in him and will not satisfy, chases her mindless, quivering flesh round and round the classroom comes closer than anything in American literature to the horrific vision of *Cardinal Pirelli*. Eula finally knocks him down. "Stop pawing me,' she said. You old headless horseman Ichabod Crane.'" She is magnificent at that ridiculous point, a prematurely developed temptress, more myth than fact, fit symbol for all Faulkner's ambivalence toward the flesh; and nothing in his vapid later novel, *The Town*, can convince us that so monstrous a figure was all along only a Good Bad Woman in embryo.

Eula belongs not with her adult namesake whom an aging Faulkner tries to redeem, but with Hughes' Emily or the child-murderer of William March's *The Bad Seed*, reading *Elsie Dinsmore* and acting out for unsuspecting adults the role of winsome innocent she has learned from such literature. The avowed "serious" theme of March's book (the question of whether criminal traits can be inherited, and the decision of a mother to kill her own child) scarcely matter before the evocation of the sweet, young thing as diabolical killer. It is the latter theme which filled the theaters and movie houses with middlebrow, middle-class beholders eager to participate in the defilement of their own sacred images. That defilement is carried even further in Vladimir Nabokov's *Lolita*, whose subject is the seduction of a middle-aged man by a twelve-year-old girl.*

The subject involves multiple ironies; for it is the naïve child, the female, the American who corrupts the sophisticated adult, the male, the European. In a single work, Richardson, Dickens and Henry James are controverted, all customary symbols for

* And there is no end in sight. The villain of Lillian Smith's latest novel, *One Hour*, is a girl of eight; and the most delightfully fiendish of female children is the marplot and moving force of Raymond Queneau's recent mad book *Zazie dans le Metro*.

the encounter of innocence and experience stood on their heads Nowhere are the myths of sentimentality more amusing and convincingly parodied, and it is surely for this reason that the book was, for a time, banned. True enough, the child's manipulation of her would-be seducer's excitement is documented, as it must be, physiologically and step by step, but Bowles' story is by all odds "dirtier"; and it is undoubtedly as an irreligious book rather than a pornographic one that *Lolita* was forced under the counter. It is the final blasphemy against the Cult of the Child.

Like most anti-religious literature, *Lolita* is perhaps too dedicated to assaulting belief to speak the disinterested truth; and like a good deal of the anti-stereotypical literature of childhood, it is not innocent of sadism, relished by writer and reader alike. Yet our latter-day sadism seems refreshingly pure compared to the necrophilia of Victorian deathbed scenes or the secret relish of the nineteenth-century exposures of the evils of child labor. Most importantly, *Lolita* and the tradition to which it belongs represent a resolve to reassess the innocence of the child, to reveal it as a kind of moral idiocy, a dangerous freedom from the restraints of culture and custom, a threat to order. In the place of the sentimental dream of childhood, writers like Faulkner and Nabokov have been creating for us a nightmare in which the child is no longer raped, strangled or seduced, but is himself (better herself!) rapist, murderer and seducer.

Their books reflect a growing awareness on the part of us all that our society has tended (at least aspired) to become not the conspiracy against the child against which our ancestors raged—but a conspiracy in his favor, against the adult. Certainly, in a permissive, family-oriented, servantless America, whose conscience is forged by popularizations of Freud, a new tyranny has become possible. If in the comics the baby sitter cowers in terror before Junior and in Nabokov the grown man trembles in passion before the pre-pubescent coquette, the causes are the same. We begin to feel that we are the slaves of our anxiety about our children, guilt-ridden by our fear of rejecting them, not giving them enough security or love, robbing them of spontaneity or creativeness; and like slaves everywhere, we grow sullen and resentful.

But the appeasement of the child is only one form of the

appeasement of the id, a resolve to give the (former) Devil his due. The child remains still, what he has been since the beginnings of Romanticism, a surrogate for our unconscious, impulsive lives; and the pattern of the family (at least as we dream it) is *a* symbolic representation of the way in which we have chosen to resolve certain persistent conflicts of what used to be called the Heart and the Head. The work of recent writers for whom tales of childhood are inevitably tales of terror, in which the child poses a threat, represents a literature blasphemous and revolutionary. Such writers have come to believe that the self can be betrayed to impulse as well as to rigor; that an Age of Innocence can be a tyranny no less terrible than an Age of Reason; and that the Gods of such an age if not yet dead must be killed, however snub-nosed, freckled-faced or golden-haired they may be.

Part Four: The Theory

The two essays in this section embarrass me a little, for they are examples of the kind of theorizing which threatens to leave literature and its appropriate delights for the sake of amateur philosophizing. I reprint them with the warning that they are not really literary criticism, which is for me a form of literature, a sub-genre of the essay. I am not sure how far they are the products of mere bravado, attempts to show the established theorists that anyone (even I) can play this sort of game.

I do know that I was amused to discover that they had earned me a page and a half in a recent New-Critical history of criticism and that I had made it into the same index with Coleridge, Hegel, Schlegel, etc. I reprint them at the end of this book to indicate that at best they are rationalizations, defenses of a practice which deliberately eschewed methodology and which existed long before their formulation. Rereading them

513

now, I am pleased to discover in them what seem to me occasional literary insights, even flashes of wit.

My Introduction, though literary theory too, is of quite another kind; of it I have said nothing and say nothing here, since it is really—despite its position—my last word.

In the Beginning Was the Word

Logos or *Mythos?*

To learn what an age most deeply believes, it is enough to discover what the acolyte is asked to be able to recite before he understands; for our age and for the arts, what the graduate student declares to his fellow or to the professor he particularly trusts: *a poem is not its ideas; poetry is not idea; the history of ideas is not the history of poetry; a poem should not mean, but be!* Dangerous thoughts become dogma, dogma platitude; nothing fails like success. When the callowest doctoral candidate shuns the heresy of paraphrase, the orthodoxy of nonparaphrase becomes unbearable, and someone tacks up a declaration on the church doors; *a poem is its ideas; poetry is idea,* etc. Meanwhile, the survivors of the last orthodoxy begin to adjust their faces from sullenness to superciliousness, as if they had always been right, instead of being (disconcertingly!) right again.

But at the point where one age is not quite out and another not quite in, when neither side is sure whose turn it is to feel defensive, whose advanced, it is possible to ask a new question instead of advancing alternative answers to the old one. We must, I am sure, be done for a while with the queries: How do ideas get into poems, and what becomes of them thereafter? What is the status of the Great Chain of Being in Pope, of Grace and Free Will in Dante? It will not even do to modernize the old chestnuts by concerning ourselves with Viconian evolution in James Joyce or the Dark Night of the Soul in Gerard Manley Hopkins; for such questions imply that ideas are merely added to whatever is essential in a poem, as it used to be believed that metaphor was added.

Since I am convinced that what are commonly called "ideas"

515

represent in fallen form an essential aspect of poetry, I prefer to ask, "How do ideas ever get out of poems at all, and what is lost, what gained in the process?" I would not deny that some poets in more sophisticated societies find it desirable to refer to previously detached ideas, but even in such cases, the proper question is: how do ideas get *back* into poems?

I shall try, then, to describe how certain ideas (or, more precisely, perceptions later developed in terms of logic and evidence) exist or pre-exist in works of art; and I shall attempt, by the way, to indicate how these insights are reclaimed by the poet, who has merely to redeem from use to wonder what was in the first instance drafted from wonder to use. From remote antiquity, it has been a commonplace that poetry is the "mother tongue of the human race"; but of late (for quite honorable strategic reasons) we have banished commonplaces not only from poetry but even from the discussion of it. Nonetheless, the old insight continues to be bootlegged into the latest scientific descriptions, in the form of an assertion that science specifies the mythic perceptions of the poet. But there is a whole school of thought which assures us that the assertions of a poem are outside the realm of belief; and that, since the only true knowledge is that which can be believed or disbelieved (fantastic inversion!), the ideas of poetry are pseudo-ideas, therapeutically valuable, but epistemologically untrustworthy. Certainly, most of us, even when we repeat the ancient wisdom in our own jargon, do it with a sense of indulging in pious rhetoric in honor of a humane discipline which we would hesitate to disown, though we cannot say why. To deny poetry would be like striking our parents, and though as good relativists, we know there is nothing *absolutely* wrong with taking a whack at mama, still . . .

It is, however, no mere piety to the past which demands we acknowledge and remember the priority of the poetic inventor over the purveyor of prose; without such a realization, it is hard to talk sensibly about the most important literary problems. I have, for instance, heard at a score of literary meetings the protest that a certain interpretation of, let us say, Shakespeare based on Freud or Jung cannot possibly be relevant, because Shakespeare belonged, "let us remind our younger colleagues, to the

Elizabethan Period while Freud . . ." The assumption is, of course, that ideas even about man's nature are established outside of and prior to their poetic expression; and that therefore any reading of Shakespeare not verifiable in Renaissance Humor Theory or speculation on Melancholy can only illegitimately be applied to his text. I do not think that the men who raise such objections would be quite prepared to admit that the psychologists in the sixteenth or twentieth centuries are the true "inventors," but what else can be the meaning of the assertion that to understand Shakespeare we must understand the science contemporary with him?

Perhaps they are only trying to express thus obliquely their distaste for the ideas of Freud, but their avowed reasoning plays into the hands of the positivist theoreticians who would have us believe that we did not really learn to know ourselves until we moved into the laboratory and bought a microscope. Freud was much more modest, claiming only to translate out of Sophocles and Shakespeare what had always been there, to state, in ways more useful to him as a doctor, what the poet had seized in the act of simultaneous perception and expression that precedes reason.

To insist on the priority of poetry to science is, it need hardly be said, an uncertain way of claiming for it honor in a world where an important segment of the population (and an important part of all of us) is prepared to identify "before" with "outgrown." It is, perhaps, a sense of this fact which has convinced some that it is impolitic to insist on the priority of *mythos* to *logos*. Where theories of progress have penetrated even into the kingdom of culture, it is a little risky to boast of ancient lineage. Peacock's essay on the *Four Ages of Poetry* is familiar at least by reputation to everyone who reads English; and Hegel's similar though less witty contentions at the end of the *Aesthetics* have made familiar to most of Europe the argument that poetry belongs to the childhood of humanity, realizing imperfectly the wisdom later better embodied in philosophy or science. The theory of poetry as the baby talk of the human race has passed into the common store of our ideas; while the notion that we have outgrown or are about to outgrow poetic statement continues to obsess minds dominated by concepts of progress, rational or mystical; and against a host of misconceptions based upon this view of poetry begins the debate to which Matthew Arnold gave classical form in his lecture, *Science and Poetry*.

Wherever the past is distrusted, whether as Father or Mother, as immemorial authority or primitive impulse, poetry is hated or, more or less hypocritically, mourned. It is, therefore, incumbent on anyone who would revive the ancient veneration for poetry (it would be better, of course, if one could pretend poetry were invented only yesterday and is even more up-to-date than science) to demonstrate not merely that ideas emerge from poetic insights, but that they are degraded in the course of their development. It is impossible to begin, however, without stating the conflict correctly, and that is not as easy as it seems. We are tempted to speak of the opposition of poetry and science, but it is better to say with Plato "the ancient quarrel between poetry and philosophy," understanding philosophy in the older inclusive sense; and it is, perhaps, best of all to define the issue as the dispute of *logos* and *mythos* as to which was the primal Word.

Poetry, however, is the representative of *mythos* in a much less direct way than philosophy (or science, its heir) is of *logos*; philosophy invented *logos*, but *mythos* created poetry. Poetry is historically the mediator between *logos* and *mythos*, the attempt to find a rationale of the pre-rational (which is to say, form)— and if philosophy quarrels with poetry, it is not because it considers its own mode of perception superior to the mythic way, but because it considers that there is *no* mode except its own; that mediation is therefore a betrayal of the truth. There is a *hubris* of science for which science has no way of atoning; for it denies poetry which could alone become its conscience.

In the poetry of primitive societies, in which philosophy has not yet detached itself as a separate discipline, insights about experience and relationship are *mythos* because they are not yet *logos*; and even in the most sophisticated communities, *mythos* survives below the margin of consciousness, and must until that community dies; since all power, even that invested in rationalization, must come from below the reason. But in ages which fear the irrational and conventionally assume its exclusion, *mythos* must disguise itself as the very *logos* it must cease to be if it is to function poetically. At certain times, the reigning poets are quite sure that they are merely versifying ideas; and they become poets only insofar as they are deceived.

In a similar way, we experience the controlling perceptions of poetry as poetry only when we experience them as something closer to *mythos* than to *logos;* and this, too, is independent of what we think we are doing, or what we call the satisfaction we have found: wit or realism or the Sublime. Having said so much, I am obliged now in order to proceed to define *mythos,* that is, to define what is prior to definition. But there are strategies for defining even God . . . and at the worst, I will have made clear another way in which the job cannot be done.

I should like to propose a multiple definition of *mythos.* First of all, it is intuition in the Crocean sense, an immediate intuition of being, pure quality without the predicate of existence. Implicit in this first definition are the notions that *mythos* is neither logic nor thought, that it involves no question of belief (and is therefore knowledge as opposed to opinion); and that, being a category of value, it is incapable of being evaluated except in terms of whether it is itself. Another way of saying that poetry is intuition is to call it, as Croce does, *linguaggio,* that is, Language as opposed to languages, conceptual rather than verbal speech—in short, the Word which was in the beginning.

But it is never quite clear in Croce of what *mythos* is an intuition; its materials, he says when pressed, are *sentimenti* and *imagini,* feeling and images. I should like to suggest, and this is the second part of my definition, that the intuited in *mythos* are the Archetypes, those archaic and persisting clusters of image and emotion which at once define and attempt to solve what is most permanent in the human predicament. The Jungian term locates in the unconscious mind that source of the simple, enduring poetic subjects which Romanticism felt to exist but sought so vainly in peasants, children, lunatics, savages and other figures that psychology has revealed to us as typical projections of the unconscious itself. It further adds another dimension to intuition by suggesting that the Word lies not only beyond all external languages with which the community strives to unify itself, but also behind the symbolic idiom of dreams in which the rent personality attempts to come to terms with itself and its fate. The Jungian term makes clear finally the *function* of *mythos* as mediator between the community and the individual, the person and his fate, the given and achieved.

But Archetype is a term somehow too modern and abstract to encompass the total richness of *mythos;* and I am forced against my will to use a word hopelessly compromised by fashion; to call *mythos* by its poor, prostituted cognate, myth. It is a word I would willingly have surrendered, if I could have found another capable of suggesting the relationship of *mythos* to *the* Myths, those ancient Greek stories that are our Archetypes par excellence, preserving for us the assurance which belongs to ritual alone: that what is done below is done above, what is done here and now is done forever, what is repeated in time subsists unbroken in eternity.

There is something beyond symbolism in the sense that the ritual act or its story does not stand for but *is* the archetypal fact; and as this ambivalence of the durative-punctual persists in poetry, it has been recognized as the Concrete Universal. The latter term, however, smacks of the University Chair rather than the altar or sacrificial fillets, and denies, with its connotations of a process moving from the particular to the universal, the primitive vision capable of perceiving most particularly what is most general. The word myth should remind us that the concept of an individual is not a beginning but an end, the last triumph of the power of abstraction; and that Achilles or Don Quixote are types, though, indeed, types not of the Warrior or of Misguided Chivalry, but of Achilles and Don Quixote.

Moreover, the word myth contains still what the more philosophical term has never possessed, overtones of the Marvelous; and no definition of *mythos* can end on any other note. *Mythos* is finally the Marvelous, or, as we say nowadays, the Absurd. I prefer the older word, grown unfamiliar enough to have lost its banality, while the newer has attained the status of a cliché without having got old. Besides, I have long been haunted by the suggestion of Jacopo Mazzoni in his *Defense of Dante* that poetry is the credible marvelous. In his explication of the term,

Mazzoni seems to me to have gone astray, opposing to Rhetoric, defined as the Credible as Credible, Poetry, defined as the Credible as Marvelous. This, it seems to me, is the error of a Virgil-ridden age, which takes wonder for an adornment of the rational, an accident rather than an essence; and which moves inevitably toward the rococo, initiating a process that can only end with—Truman Capote!

I should like to recast the classification a little, defining poetry as the Marvelous as Credible, and inserting it into an extended series: The Marvelous as Marvelous is *mythos;* the Marvelous as Credible, Poetry; the Credible as Credible, philosophy and science; the Credible as Marvelous, the ersatz of Poetry which appears in ages oppressed by philosophy or science: rhetoric, journalism, *kitsch* . . .

With the criterion of the Marvelous, I should like to complete my definition, in order to establish in general what is lost in the conversion of *mythos* to *logos,* and what we hunger for desperately today. The parodies and counterfeits of wonder which are peddled successfully on all sides testify to our awareness of a lack we are not usually prepared to admit. Certainly, it is in the power of scientific discourse to specify archetypal intuitions of man's relation to his own existence, his death and the universe around him, so that they are more viable for healing and social control and even the encouragement of civic virtue; so that, in short, they *work.* What is lost, however, is the sense of reverence and astonishment (another degraded name for what I am trying to describe is the Sublime) which alone breeds *pietas* —not religion, for even science can be a religion; but that natural piety without which we can approach the given world only as an enemy or a bore. The "neutralization of nature," of which we are tempted sometimes to boast, has made us aliens in the universe. The world has not abandoned us, but we it; for only as we love it can we know it, and the scientific knowing is a knowledge without love, a rape of nature. The world has not denied us, but we it; for only what we fear can we acknowledge, and scientific experiment is an experience without fear, an enlightened tolerance of nature.

In the light of these general remarks, I should like to examine one complex of myth, poetry and science, one fall from intuition to idea. Several possibilities tempted me in prospect, but I have had to abandon them for one reason or another: the Amphytrion *mythos,* so variously developed in poetry but so difficult to disentangle in philosophical or scientific thought; the *mythos* of the Trinity and its translation into the assumptions of modern physical science as demonstrated by Collingwood in his *Metaphysics;* the legend of Prometheus from Aeschylus to Karl Marx; Pandora, Eve and theories of human behavior. An ironic instance would have been I. A. Richards's translation into psychological terms of a view of contemporary sensibility expressed archetypally in Eliot's *The Waste Land,* in the midst of a proof that literature contains no ideas.

But I have chosen finally to deal with the Oedipus story, and I must begin by apologizing for the banality of my choice, though it is almost inescapable. On the practical side, there is the consideration that the major part of the materials for such an analysis have been gathered together by Patrick Mullahy (in an otherwise disappointing book called *Oedipus: Myth and Complex*); and further, the Oedipus myth is *our* myth, unriddled by our age, to which it has seemed an essential clue to the human situation.

The *mythos* itself, that essence which I have defined elsewhere as the Archetype without Signature, is almost irrecoverable in this instance; for us, the story exists always through, if not actually in, the formal rendering of Sophocles. The closest we can come to what the legend might have been before *our* Oedipus is in Homer's description of the "wives or daughters of princes" gathered around the dark pool of blood in Hades. "Then I met Oedipus' mother, the lovely Epicaste. She in her ignorance committed the sin of marrying her son. For Oedipus killed his father and took his mother to wife." How near bald statement the final verse comes, but it *is* a verse and lives in the remembered context. Some *mythoi* exist for us without individual coloring, the fables of half-familiar literatures, the plots of Saturday matinee movies made compulsively over and over; but the mythic Oedipus we know ordinarily only as the word made flesh in the trilogy of Sophocles.

Sophocles imposes not merely a Signature and the rationale

of form; he has already begun the fall from *mythos* to *logos,* and the moment of the expulsion from the Garden is the loveliest moment of poetry. Through his choruses, and especially those last words before which we do not tremble as we tremble before the naked fable, for they ask of us only belief, he interprets the legend of Oedipus in terms of "wisdom." "We must call no one happy who is of mortal race, until he hath crossed life's border, free from pain. . . ." "Great words of prideful men are ever punished with great blows, and in old age, teach the chastened to be wise. . . ." The absurd reduced to the commonplace, "interpreted" even by the greatest of poets, is already the stuff of rhetoric, capable of instruction or delight or persuasion, but not of transport, which inheres only in what transcends reason, what the poet himself does not "understand." The great works of art are those too untidy to fit the most elastic of explanations, no precise "objective correlatives," but constructs inadequate to what they must stand for, full of loose ends, buffoonery and mystery: *Hamlet, The Rape of the Lock, Don Quixote, Huckleberry Finn,* the *Antigone.* What the reasonable do not dare utterly to disown, they attempt to edit into rationality, cutting out of *Cymbeline,* for instance, the great speech of sexual disgust, or out of the *Antigone* the inviolably absurd passage beginning: "Never had I been the mother of children, or if a husband had been moldering in death. . . ."

But in Sophocles' time, at least the *Oedipus* was still acted in the presence of the god and before an altar, so that its mystery was implicit in the mode of presentation. It is interesting to compare the fate of the fable in a period that we call neo-classical —that is, one in which a sense persists that the old subjects contain a certain power that must be evoked, but where the magic of the Archetypal is hopelessly confused with concepts of decorum and rules. The Heroic Tragedy of a Dryden, acted under artificial light and to amuse the City, is a baroque tragedy, one which alternates the cool observance of rules with a hysterical shrillness over the fact that those rules do not guarantee the presence of power.

In Dryden's version of *Oedipus the King,* the original legend has been analyzed by common sense into morality (pride goeth before a fall), sensationalism (incest as titillation) and the "marvelous" (understood as make-believe). But though the central myth has been secularized into "entertainment," into precisely what is not *mythos*, the Archetypal re-enters unnoticed, in a subplot which seems the merest sop to the audience, the "love interest" an age demanded without knowing why. What is irrelevant to the mythic meanings of the Oedipus legend is paradoxically enough the story of Oedipus, whereas the father-son-girl triangle descended from New Comedy performs the function of myth for a public that can yield only unwittingly to its spell. We live, of course, still in the age of the comic Oedipus Archetype, fallen utterly now to a formula; but some of us begin at last to understand just why this trivial formula has moved us so deeply and for so long. Each age since Sophocles has read or retold his story in a way that profanes the myth; but in each there has been an unsuspected avatar of the same Archetype, in which Oedipus, Jocasta and Laios have become Youth, Girl and Father; Lover, Lady and Husband; Poet, Sister and Father. I am chiefly concerned here, however, only with the classicizing parodies, the re-evocations of the Pericleian Oedipus.

Most recently our poets have learned to exploit the myth not in the interest of classicism, but in search of the mythic itself. We are students of legend, anthropologists rather than humanists; and our errors arise from too much knowledge of what the Archetypal is rather than too little. We have substituted irony for make-believe, but we have not quite recaptured wonder. When, for instance, the contemporary Italian poet, Cesare Pavese, treats the legend of Oedipus he approaches it not only obliquely (in the form of a dialogue between Tiresias and Oedipus before the archetypal events unfold) but also with an awareness of his obligations to the absurdity and multivalence of the legend. Both the ancient Greek writer and the modern Italian one play off our foreknowledge of the events against the ignorance of the protagonist; but in Sophocles what we foreknow is Oedipus' fate, in Pavese it is his myth. The older poet assumes in his audience the knowledge of a legend, the modern the knowledge of their own plight as revealed by science. The contemporary writer effects a rapprochement between the Oedipus of Sophocles and that of Freud, rationalizing the figure of poetry and remythifying that of reason. But to understand so modern an instance, we must first glance at the actual interpretations of our scientists.

The first science to emerge from the total mythic view is philosophy; and the first interpreter of Oedipus is the first philosopher to find in poetry not merely a rival but a subject for analysis. The attempt of Aristotle is a strange one, for he has attempted to rationalize the myth as pure form; that is, prior to analysis, he has abstracted from the dramatic poem only what is already rational. Everyone realizes that *Oedipus the King* is Aristotle's ideal play, but scarcely anyone is sufficiently aware that his ideal play is only *Oedipus* stripped of its particularity. The form toward which Aristotle finds tragedy to have been tending turns out to be the schema of Sophocles' play, primarily its plot (this is, of course, what *mythos* has come to mean to that most unmythical mind), restated without individuation or wonder: a man, neither impossibly noble or villainous, commits against someone to whom he has the closest ties of blood, etc., etc. This is rather like what Kenneth Burke considers as establishing the essential meaning of a myth (*cf.* his treatment of the Bellepherontic letter)—but this method of myth interpretation, by formal abstraction, has few other followers.

All other derivations of *logos* from *mythos* follow one of the two classic patterns of myth interpretation, euhemerization or allegorization, reading fable as encoded history or personified description of nature and man. I am not referring merely to what are avowedly attempts at analyzing myths, the more or less scientific interpretations of Max Mueller, for instance (to whom the struggle of Oedipus and his father is a mythicization of the alternation of day and night or of seasons), or of Frazer (who finds in the Oedipus story traces of a matriarchal system in which the male had to become by adoption the son-husband of the Queen through whom the royal line descended); but to any systematic science of man or nature. Scientific systems are constructed by testing and measurement and controlled statement, but their informing assumptions and motivating "hunches" are in the first instance *mythoi*. I suspect that there are simply no other sources. The heart may have reasons that the reason knows nothing of, but reason has no reasons that the heart does not foreknow. From the myths of ether or four-dimensional space, from metaphors of the four elements and chaos, attraction and repulsion and Love, the science of mechanics is eternally reborn; from a poem of fifth-century Athens, the science of our age, psychoanalysis, is derived.

I shall not presume to discuss the interpretations of Oedipus found in Freud himself; even their vulgarizations do not belie the major insights of Freud and they are in the public domain. For my purposes, it is sufficient to remark that in the founder of depth psychology, we find both euhemerization and allegorization as typical modes of analysis. A prime example of the former is Freud's still half-mythical pre-history of the Old Man and the Pack, with the totemic eating of the father; and the latter is best exemplified in his treatment of the biological triangle and its effects on maturation. It can be objected, of course, that Freud found evidences of our universal hatred of the father and love for the mother in the facts of existence rather than those of literature; but we know that in no other culture did anyone ever find them, and that in our own they have been hinted at over and over by the poets before Freud. I suppose it is even possible to argue that the Oedipus complex has been as much made as discovered; and certainly one still finds in Freud that mythopoeic power which the Romantics called Imagination, and which they liked to understand as continuous with the great creative power of God.

In Jung, who is also something of a Romantic poet in a white jacket, there is further allegorization, the revelation that what Freud took to be final facts were still only symbols of a deeper lurking reality. The sexual basis of the Oedipus story, Jung asserted, is only a figure of speech; the relations to father and mother of the legend represent relations to the *pater imago* and *mater imago,* dreamlike projections of man, spirit, law and the state on the one hand—woman, feeling, family and the clan on the other: Laios and Jocasta, Antigone and Creon. The desire for incest with the mother symbolizes the desire to remain a child, to be unborn. The murder of the father signifies the rejection of fatherhood, of adult responsibility.

Once the process of interpretation has begun there is no end; an interpretation is no more immune to further interpretation than the story with which it started. To the essentially euhemeristic Otto Rank, Freud's Oedipus is exactly like Sophocles', a datum, revealing as much about Freud's age as it does about the remote hero of the legend. In every era, we struggle to come to terms with the essentially insoluble conflict that arises out of society's demand (called Fate in the older versions) that we be fathers and sons rather than selves. The Oedipus story reflects three major attempts to solve this problem. In the Heroic Age, when society was still essentially collective, Heroes (the superiors in whom the community saw the reflection of its ideal self) were granted the privilege of incest—that is, of becoming their own sons, of being reborn. In the Poetic Age, at the moment of the rise of the patriarchal family, such personal, representative immortality was renounced for immortality in children; but still an occasional heroic figure yearned to be his own son, like the "Oedipus" of pre-history. In our time, in the age of psychology and the anti-patriarchal family, the Oedipus wish, which began as a denial of fatherhood, has become its own opposite, the desire to be one's own father rather than one's own son.

In the depth psychologists of the first generation, the scientific reduction of the myth is not carried so far that the poetic overtones of the archetype are threatened; conditioned by nineteenth-century German literature, the founding fathers perpetuate something of the archaic and multilayered in their interpretations, though they are of course interested in use, in healing and self-illumination. But precisely for this reason they have seemed to their successors insufficiently "scientific." To some, indeed, the whole of psychoanalysis has appeared too "insightful" to be trusted, hopelessly involved in a compromise between *logos* and *mythos*, and they have disowned Freudianism in toto. Others who do not utterly deny the value of the Freudian approach but find it insufficiently detached from the mythic have tried to "neutralize" the archetypal overtones of Freud's work. To such revisionists the chief problem has seemed the irredeemably poetic concept of the Oedipus complex, which was for Freud himself the center of his theories. Karen Horney will do for the entire "scientizing" wing, with her doctrine that fixations do not arise from biological causes but from describable conditions in the family. Optimism, as well as rationality, demands the casting overboard of a myth which contains a kind of despair at its heart. Freud's formulation is "dangerous," Miss Horney teaches, for it obscures rather than underlines the important lesson to be learned: the need for "a real interest and respect for the child, the necessity of real warmth, reliability and sincerity by the parents. . . ."

Here is the final reduction to common sense and practical platitude, the inevitable end of demythification; for *logos*, where it does not find a formula and retreat to the laboratory and the sine tables, can confront the world only with the opposite of the archetype, the stereotype. That wife and daughter and mother of a Prince who rose beside the black pool of blood in Hell needed only to have read Miss Horney to have avoided trouble; and Oedipus need never have bawled his inarticulate cry or plucked out the eyes that had beheld the place which gave him birth. Some, indeed, may be healed by these platitudes as they have been healed by everything else, the laying on of hands, the rubbing of the soles of feet, the taking of chalk pills; but society cannot live by them. In the beginning was *mythos,* and each new beginning must draw again from that inexhaustible source.

Archetype and Signature

The Relationship of Poet and Poem

I

A central dogma of much recent criticism asserts that biographical information is irrelevant to the understanding and evaluation of poems, and that conversely, poems cannot legitimately be used as material for biography. This double contention is part of a larger position which holds that history is history and art is art, and that to talk about one in terms of the other is to court disaster. Insofar as this position rests upon the immortal platitude that it is good to know what one is talking about, it is unexceptionable; insofar as it is a reaction based upon the procedures of pre-Freudian critics, it is hopelessly outdated; and insofar as it depends upon the extreme nominalist definition of a work of art, held by many "formalists" quite unawares, it is metaphysically reprehensible. It has the further inconvenience of being quite unusable in the practical sphere (all of its proponents, in proportion as they are sensitive critics, immediately betray it when speaking of specific works, and particularly of large bodies of work); and, as if that were not enough, it is in blatant contradiction with the assumptions of most serious practicing writers.

That the anti-biographical position was once "useful," whatever its truth, cannot be denied; it was even once, what is considerably rarer in the field of criticism, amusing; but for a long time now it has been threatening to turn into one of those annoying clichés of the intellectually middle-aged, proffered with all the air of a stimulating heresy. The position was born in dual protest against an excess of Romantic criticism and one of "scien-

529

tific scholarship." Romantic aesthetics appeared bent on dissolving the formally realized "objective" elements in works of art into "expression of personality"; while the "scholars," in revolt against Romantic subjectivity, seemed set on casting out all the more shifty questions of value and *gestalt* as "subjective," and concentrating on the kind of "facts" amenable to scientific verification. Needless to say, it was not the newer psychological sciences that the "scholars" had in mind, but such purer disciplines as physics and biology. It was at this point that it became fashionable to talk about literary study as "research," and graphs and tables began to appear in analyses of works of art.

Both the "scholarly" and the Romantic approaches struck the anti-biographists as "reductive"—attempts to prove that the work of art was *nothing but* the personality of the Genius behind it, or the sum total of its genetic factors. In answer to both heresies of attack, the anti-biographist offered what he came to call the "intrinsic" approach, which turned out, alas, to be another *nothing but* under its show of righteous indignation—namely, the contention that a poem was *nothing but* "words," and its analysis therefore properly *nothing but* a study of syntax and semantics. An attempt to illuminate a poem by reference to its author's life came therefore to be regarded with horror, unless it confined itself to an examination of his "idiosyncratic use of words"! This is not parody, but direct quotation.

By this time a generation of critics has grown up, of whom I am one, to whom the contention that biographical material is irrelevant to the essential "experience" of a poem was taught as the basic doctrine of all right-thinking readers. The word "experience" is important; it comes out of I. A. Richards at his most scientizing, and along with the "extrinsic-intrinsic" metaphor is a key to the anti-biographist point of view. It must be understood for what the word "experience" is being substituted: as an "experience," a poem is no longer regarded as an "imitation," in any of the received senses of the word; nor even as an "expression" in the Crocean sense; and above all not as a "communication." All three possible substitute terms imply a necessary interconnectedness between the art object and some *other* area of experience—or at least an essentially intended pointing outward or inward toward some independently existent *otherness*. This is distasteful to the anti-biographist, who shows the ordinary nominalist uneasiness at any suggestion that there are realities more comprehensive than particulars, to which words only refer.

An odd phenomenon is the support of a position to which nominalism is logically necessary, by many confirmed anti-scientizers and realists; they are betrayed into their ill-advised fellow-traveling, I think, by an excess of anti-Romanticism. It is no longer as fashionable as it once was to publicly anathematize Shelley and Swinburne, but the bias persists as a real force in current critical practice, and cuts off many, to whom the position would be temperamentally and metaphysically attractive, from Expressionism. What the modern sensibility finds particularly unsympathetic in some Romantic writing has been misleadingly called, I think, "the exploitation of personality"; it is rather a tendency toward the excessively "programmatic." Just as music and painting can be too "literary," so literature itself can be too "literary." In reaction against the programmatic, there are two possible paths: more deeply into and through the personalism of Romanticism to Expressionism; or outward and away toward the sort of "abstraction" achieved in cubist painting. As a matter of fact, there has been at work all along in our period an underground, and probably harmful, analogy between poetry and the plastic arts. A poem, the feeling has been, should be as "palpable and mute" not merely as an actual fruit, but as the fruit become pure color and texture of Picasso or Matisse. As pictures have become frankly paint, so should poems be frankly words. "A poem should not mean but be." There is the slogan of the movement!

It is a rather nice phrase in the limited context of MacLeish's little poem, but a dangerous full-blown aesthetic position. The notion that a work of art is, or should be, absolutely self-contained, a discrete set of mutually interrelated references, needs only to be stated clearly to seem the *reductio ad absurdum* which it is. Yet this belief in the poem as a closed system, "cut off" in ideal isolation, descends from the realm of theoretical criticism to practical criticism and classroom pedagogy (if not in practice, at least as an institutionalized hypocrisy) to become the leitmotif of the New Teacher: "Stay *inside* the poem!"

The narrative and dramatic poem, finally poetic drama itself, is assimilated to a formulation, even *apparently* applicable only to a lyric of the most absolute purity—and it becomes heretical to treat the work as anything but "words," to ask those questions which attest our conviction that the work of art is "real"; that in the poem, the whole is greater than the sum of its parts; that certain created actions and characters exist, in some sense, *outside* of their formalizations. How long was Hamlet in Wittemberg? How many children did Lady Macbeth have? In what sense does Prospero speak for Shakespeare? What developing sensibility can be inferred from the Shakespearian corpus and be called (what *else?*) Shakespeare? We cannot ask these questions in the dewy innocence with which they were first posed; we restate them on the second convolution, aware of all the arguments against them, and the more convinced that they are essential, and cannot be shelved any more than those questions about the ends and origins of existence which have also been recently declared "unreal."

Closely associated with the Richardsian experiential-semantic approach in the total, eclectic position of the anti-biographist, is the psychological notion of the poem as the "objective correlative" or a complex of "objective correlatives" of emotional responses to the given world. Mr. Eliot's term is as elusive as it is appealing; but I am concerned here (Mr. Eliseo Vivas has elsewhere criticized it as containing some "non-intrinsic" contradictions) only with the adjective "objective" in one of its possible implications. Whatever its origins, Mr. Eliot seems to be asserting, a poem succeeds, as a poem, insofar as it is detached from the subjectivity of its maker. The poem is achieved by a process of objectification, and can be legitimately examined and understood only as an "object." This formulation leaves a somewhat second-best use for the biographical approach, as a way of explaining the particular badness of certain kinds of bad poems, *e.g.*, Romantic verse and Shakespeare's *Hamlet*.

From this presumed insight follows the deprivation of the

poet's right to explain his own poem, or at least the challenging of his claim to speak with final authority about his own work. Once realized, the argument runs, the successful poem is detached; and the author no longer has any property rights in what now belongs to the tradition rather than to him. And if, benightedly, he protests against some critical analysis or interpretation which seems to him wrong on the basis of his special biographical knowledge, he reveals that either his poem is not truly "successful," or even worse, that he has never read "Tradition and the Individual Talent."

There are, in fact, two quite different contentions, one valid, one invalid, confused in most statements about the poet as commentator on his own work. First it is asserted (and with real truth) that a poem may contain more meanings than the maker is ever aware of; and second (this is false, of course) that nothing the poet can tell us about his own work is of any *decisive* importance, because the poet cannot help falling into the trap of talking about his "intentions." But the notion of "intention" implies the belief that there is a somehow existent something against which the achieved work of art can be measured; and although this has been for all recorded time the point of view of the practicing writer, every graduate student who has read Wimsatt and Beardsley's ponderous tract on the Intentional Fallacy knows that we are all now to believe that there is no poem except the poem of "words."

The fact that all recognized critics have consistently spoken of intention shows merely that in the unfortunate past the writer about literature has often (unfortunately!) spoken more like the poet than the scientific semanticist. This regrettable looseness of expression we can only hope will be amended in the future, now that we have been duly warned. It is difficult not to be tempted by analogy. Why, we want to ask, can we properly laugh at the visiting dignitary in the high hat when he slips on the steps to the platform, because of the disparity between the entrance he *intended* and the one he achieved; and still not speak of a bathetic disparity between what a poem obviously aims at and what it does? On what respectable grounds can it be maintained that a poem is all act and no potentiality?

It is difficult to understand the success of the anti-biographist tendency in more respectable critical circles and in the schools, in light of its own internal contradictions. The explanation lies, I suppose, in its comparative newness, and in the failure of its opponents to arrive at any *coherent* theory of the relationship between the life of the poet and his work; so long as biographers are content merely to place side by side undigested biographical data and uninspired paraphrases of poems—linking them together mechanically or pseudo-genetically: "Wordsworth lived in the country and therefore wrote Nature poetry," or even worse, so long as notes proving that Milton was born in one house rather than another continue to be printed in magazines devoted to the study of literature, people will be tempted into opposite though equal idiocies, which have at least not been for so long proved utterly bankrupt.

A recent phenomenon of some interest in this regard is the astonishing popularity of such texts as Thomas and Brown's classroom anthology called *Reading Poems*—the very title reveals the dogma behind the book; in a world of discrete, individual "experiences," of "close reading" (a cant phrase of the anti-biographist) as an ideal, one cannot even talk of so large an abstraction as poetry. It is only "poems" to which the student must be exposed, poems printed out of chronological order and without the names of the authors attached, lest the young reader be led astray by what (necessarily irrelevant) information he may have concerning the biography or social background of any of the poets. It is all something of a hoax, of course; the teacher realizes that the chances of any student knowing too much for his own good about such matters are slight indeed; and besides, there is an index in which the names are revealed, so that unless one is very virtuous, he can scarcely help looking up the anthologized pieces. In addition, the good teacher is himself aware to begin with of the contexts, social and biographical, of a large number of the pieces. Frankly, that is why they make sense to him; and even when he admonishes the young to "stay *inside*" the poems, he is bootlegging all kinds of rich relevancies which he possesses because he is capable of connecting.

I cannot help feeling that the chief problem of teaching

anything in our atomized period lies precisely in the fact that the ordinary student cannot or will not connect the few facts he knows, the slim insights he has previously attained, the chance extensions of sensibility into which he has been once or twice tempted, into a large enough context to make sense of the world he inhabits, or the works of art he encounters. It is because the old-line biographist fails to connect his facts with the works they presumably illuminate, and not because he does connect them, that he is a poor critic. And the doctrinaire anti-biographist, like the doctrinaire biographist before him, secure in pride and ignorance of the newer psychologies, makes worse the endemic disease of our era—the failure to connect. There is no "work itself," no independent formal entity which is its own sole context; the poem is the sum total of many contexts, all of which must be known to know it and evaluate it. "Only connect!" should be the motto of all critics and teachers—and the connective link between the poem on the page and most of its rewarding contexts is precisely—biography.

The poet's life is the focusing glass through which pass the determinants of the shape of his work: the tradition available to him, his understanding of "kinds," the impact of special experiences (travel, love, etc.). But the poet's life is more than a burning glass; with his work, it makes up his total meaning. I do not intend to say, of course, that some meanings of works of art, satisfactory and as far as they go sufficient, are not available in the single work itself (only a really *bad* work depends for all substantial meaning on a knowledge of the life-style of its author); but a whole body of work will contain larger meanings, and, where it is available, a sense of the life of the writer will raise that meaning to a still higher power. The latter two kinds of meaning fade into each other; for as soon as two works by a single author are considered side by side, one has begun to deal with biography—that is, with an interconnectedness fully explicable only in terms of a personality, inferred or discovered.

One of the essential functions of the poet is the assertion and creation of a personality, in a profounder sense than any non-artist can attain. We ask of the poet a definition of man, at once particular and abstract, stated and acted out. It is impossible to draw a line between the work the poet writes and the work he lives, between the life he lives and the life he writes. And the agile critic, therefore, must be prepared to move constantly back and forth between life and poem, not in a pointless circle, but in a meaningful spiraling toward the absolute point.

To pursue this matter further, we will have to abandon at this point the nominalist notion of the poem as "words" or "only words." We have the best of excuses, that such terminology gets in the way of truth. We will not, however, return to the older notions of the poem as a "document" or the embodiment of an "idea," for these older conceptions are equally inimical to the essential concept of the "marvelous"; and they have the further difficulty of raising political and moral criteria of "truth" as relevant to works of art. To redeem the sense of what words are all the time pointing *to* and what cannot be adequately explained by syntactical analysis or semantics, I shall speak of the poem as Archetype and Signature, suggesting that the key to analysis is *symbolics;* and I shall not forget that the poet's life is also capable of being analyzed in those terms. We have been rather ridiculously overemphasizing *medium* as a differentiating factor; I take it that we can now safely assume no one will confuse a life with a poem, and dwell on the elements common to the two, remembering that a pattern of social behavior can be quite as much a symbol as a word, chanted or spoken or printed. In deed as in word, the poet composes himself as maker and mask, in accordance with some contemporaneous *mythos* of the artist. And as we all know, in our day, it is even possible to be a writer without having written anything. When we talk therefore of the importance of the biography of the poet, we do not mean the importance of every trivial detail, but of all that goes into making his particular life-style, whether he concentrate on re-creating himself, like Shelley, in some obvious image of the Poet, or, like Wallace Stevens, in some witty anti-mask of the Poet. Who could contend that even the *faces* of Shelley and Stevens are not typical products of their quite different kinds of art!

The word "Archetype" is the more familiar of my terms; I use it instead of the word "myth," which I have employed in the past but which becomes increasingly ambiguous, to mean any of the immemorial patterns of response to the human situation in its most permanent aspects: death, love, the biological family, the relationship with the Unknown, etc., whether those patterns be considered to reside in the Jungian Collective Unconscious or the Platonic world of Ideas. The archetypal belongs to the infra- or meta-personal, to what Freudians call the id or the unconscious; that is, it belongs to the Community at its deepest, pre-conscious levels of acceptance.

I use "Signature" to mean the sum total of individuating factors in a work, the sign of the Persona or Personality through which an Archetype is rendered, and which itself tends to become a subject as well as a means of the poem. Literature, properly speaking, can be said to come into existence at the moment a Signature is imposed upon the Archetype. The purely archetypal, without signature elements, is the myth. Perhaps a pair of examples are in order (with thanks to Mr. C. S. Lewis). The story of Baldur the Beautiful and Shakespeare's *Tempest* deal with somewhat similar archetypal material of immersion and resurrection; but we recall *The Tempest* only in all its specificity: the diction, meter, patterns of imagery, the heard voice of Shakespeare (the Signature as Means); as well as the scarcely motivated speech on pre-marital chastity, the breaking of the fictional frame by the unconventional religious *plaudite* (the Signature as Subject). Without these elements, *The Tempest* is simply not *The Tempest;* but *Baldur* can be retold in any diction, any style, just so long as faith is kept with the bare plot—and it is itself, for it is pure myth. Other examples are provided by certain children's stories, retold and reillustrated without losing their essential identity, whether they be "folk" creations like *Cinderella* or art products "captured" by the folk imagination, like Southey's *Three Bears.*

In our own time, we have seen the arts (first music, then painting, last of all literature) attempting to become "pure," or "abstract"—that is to say, attempting to slough off all remnants of the archetypal in a drive toward becoming unadulterated Signature. It should be noticed that the *theory* of abstract art is completely misleading in this regard, speaking as it does about pure forms, and mathematics, and the disavowal of personality. The abstract painter, for instance, does not, as he sometimes claims, really "paint paint," but signs his name. So-called abstract art is the ultimate expression of personality; so that the spectator says of a contemporary painting, not what one would have said in the anonymous Middle Ages, "There's a *Tree of Jesse* or a *Crucifixion!*" or not even what is said of Renaissance art, "There's a Michelangelo *Last Judgment* or a Raphael *Madonna!*" but quite simply, "There's a Mondriaan or a Jackson Pollock!" Analogously, in literature we recognize a poem immediately as "a Marianne Moore" or "an Ezra Pound" long before we understand, if ever, any of its essential meanings.

The theory of "realism" or "naturalism" denies both the Archetype and the Signature, advocating, in its extreme forms, that art merely "describes nature or reality" in a neutral style, based on the case report of the scientist. Art which really achieves such aims becomes, of course, something less than "poetry" as I have used the term here, becoming an "imitation" in the lowest Platonic sense, "thrice removed from the truth." Fortunately, the great "realists" consistently betray their principles, creating Archetypes and symbols willy-nilly, though setting them in a Signature distinguished by what James called "solidity of specification." The chief value of "realism" as a theory is that it helps create in the more sophisticated writer a kind of blessed stupidity in regard to what he is really doing, so that the archetypal material can well up into his work uninhibited by his intent; and in a complementary way, it makes acceptance of that archetypal material possible for an audience which thinks of itself as "science-minded" and inimical to the demonic and mythic. It constantly startles and pleases me to come across references to such creators of grotesque Archetypes as Dostoevsky and Dickens and Faulkner as "realists."

A pair of caveats are necessary before we proceed. The distinction between Archetype and Signature, it should be noted, does not correspond to the ancient dichotomy of Content and Form. Such "forms" as the structures of Greek Tragedy (*cf.* Gilbert Murray), New Comedy and Pastoral Elegy are themselves *versunkene* Archetypes, capable of being rerealized in the great work of art. (Elsewhere I have called these "structural myths.")

Nor does the present distinction cut quite the same way as that between "impersonal" (or even "nonpersonal") and "personal." For the Signature, which is rooted in the ego and super-ego, belongs, as the twofold Freudian division implies, to the social collectivity as well as to the individual writer. The Signature is the joint product of "rules" and "conventions," of the expectations of a community and the idiosyncratic responses of the individual poet, who adds a personal idiom or voice to a received style. The difference between the communal element in the Signature and that in the Archetype is that the former is *conscious*—that is, associated with the superego rather than the id. The relevant, archetypal metaphor would make the personal element the Son, the conscious-communal the Father and the unconscious-communal the Mother (or the Sister, an image which occurs often as a symbolic euphemism for the Mother)—in the biological Trinity.

It is not irrelevant that the Romantic movement, which combined a deliberate return to the archetypal with a contempt for the conscious communal elements in the Signature, made one of the leitmotifs of the lives of its poets, as well as of their poems, the flight of the Sister from the threat of rape by the Father (Shelley's *Cenci*, for instance) and the complementary desperate love of Brother and Sister (anywhere from Chateaubriand and Wordsworth to Byron and Melville).

Even the most orthodox anti-biographist is prepared to grant the importance of biographical information in the *understanding* of certain ego elements in the Signature—this is what the intrinsicist calls the study of an author's "idiosyncratic use of words." But they deny vehemently the possibility of using biographical material for the purposes of *evaluation*. Let us consider some examples. For instance, the line in one of John Donne's poems, "A Hymne to God the Father," which runs, "When thou hast done, thou hast not done . . ." would be incomprehensible in such a collection without author's names as the Thomas and Brown *Reading Poems*. Without the minimum biographical datum of the name of the poet, the reader could not realize that a pun was involved, and he could not therefore even ask himself the evaluative question most important to the poem, namely, what is the value of the pun in a serious, even a religious, piece of verse? This is the simplest use of biography, referring us for only an instant outside of the poem, and letting us remain there once we have returned with the information. Other similar examples are plentiful in Shakespeare's sonnets: the references to his own first name, for instance, or the troublesome phrase "all *hewes* in his controlling."

A second example which looks much like the first to a superficial glance, but which opens up in quite a different way, would be the verse "they'are but *Mummy*, possest," from Donne's "Loves Alchymie." Let us consider whether we can sustain the contention that there is a pun on *Mummy*, whether deliberately planned or unconsciously fallen into. Can we read the line as having the two meanings: women, so fair in the desiring, turn out to be only dried-out corpses after the having; and women, once possessed, turn out to be substitutes for the Mother, who is the real end of our desiring? An analysis of the mere *word* does not take us very far; we discover that the *lallwort* "mummy" meaning "mother" is not recorded until 1830 in that precise spelling, but that there are attested uses of it in the form "mammy" (we remember, perhaps, that "mammy-apple" and "mummy-apple" are interchangeable forms meaning "papaya") well back into Donne's period, and that the related form "mome" goes back into Middle English. Inevitably, such evidence is inconclusive, establishing possibilities at best, and never really bearing on the question of probability, for which we must turn to his life itself, to Donne's actual relations with his mother; and beyond that to the science of such relationships.

When we have discovered that John Donne did, indeed, live in an especially intimate relationship with his mother throughout her long life (she actually outlived her son); and when we have set the possible pun in a context of other literary uses of a mythic situation in which the long-desired possessed turns at the moment of possession into a shriveled hag who is also a mother (Rider Haggard's *She*, Hilton's *Lost Horizon*, and, most explicitly, Flaubert's *L'Éducation Sentimentale*), we realize that our original contention is highly probable, for it is motivated by a traditional version of what the psychologists have taught us to call the Oedipus Archetype. It should be noticed in passing that the archetypal critic is delivered from the bondage of time, speaking of "confluences" rather than "influences," and finding the explication of a given work in things written later as well as earlier than the original piece. Following the lead opened up by "*Mummy, possest*," we can move still further toward an understanding of Donne, continuing to shuttle between life and work with our new clue, and examining, for instance, Donne's ambivalent relations to the greater Mother, the Roman Church, which his actual mother represented not only metaphorically but in her own allegiance and descent. This sort of analysis which at once unifies and opens up (one could do something equally provocative and rich, for instance, with the fact that in two of Melville's tales ships symbolic of innocence are called *The Jolly Bachelor* and *The Bachelor's Delight*) is condemned in some quarters as "failing to stay close to the actual meaning of the work itself"—as if the work were a tight little island instead of a focus opening on an inexhaustible totality.

The intrinsicist is completely unnerved by any reference to the role of the Archetype in literature, fearing such references as strategies to restore the criterion of the "marvelous" to respectable currency as a standard of literary excellence; for not only is the notion of the "marvelous" pre-scientific but it is annoyingly immune to "close analysis." Certainly, the contemplation of the Archetype pushes the critic beyond semantics, and beyond the kind of analysis that considers it has done all when it assures us (once again!) that the parts and whole of a poem cohere. The critic in pursuit of the Archetype finds himself involved in anthropology and depth psychology (not because these are New Gospels, but because they provide useful tools); and if he is not too embarrassed at finding himself in such company to look about him, he discovers that he has come upon a way of binding together our fractured world, of uniting literature and nonliterature *without the reduction of the poem*.

It is sometimes objected that though the archetypal critic can move convincingly between worlds ordinarily cut off from each other, he sacrifices for this privilege the ability to distinguish the essential qualities of literary works, and especially that of evaluating them. Far from being irrelevant to evaluation, the consideration of the archetypal content of works of art is essential to it! One of the earlier critics of Dante says someplace that poetry, as distinguished from rhetoric (which treats of the credible as credible), treats of the "marvelous" as credible. Much contemporary criticism has cut itself off from this insight—that is, from the realization of what poetry on its deepest levels *is*. It is just as ridiculous to attempt the evaluation of a work of art *purely* in formal terms (considering only the Signature as Means), as it would be to evaluate it *purely* in terms of the "marvelous," or the archetypal. The question, for instance, of whether *Mona Lisa* is just a bourgeoise or whether she "as Leda, was the mother of Helen of Troy, and, as St. Anne, was the mother of Mary" is just as vital to a final estimate of the picture's worth as any matter of control of the medium or handling of light and shadow.

The Romantics seem to have realized this, and to have reached, in their distinction between Fancy and Imagination, for rubrics to distinguish between the poetic method that touches the archetypal deeply and that which merely skirts it. Even the Arnoldian description of Pope as "a classic of our prose," right or wrong, was feeling toward a similar standard of discrimination. It is typical and ironic that Arnold in a moralizing age should have felt obliged to call the daemonic power of evoking the Archetype "High Seriousness." Certainly, the complete abandonment of any such criterion by the intrinsicist leaves him baffled before certain strong mythopoeic talents like Dickens or Stevenson; and it is the same lack in his system which prevents his understanding of the complementary relationship of the life and work of the poet.

II

The Archetype which makes literature itself possible in the first instance is the Archetype of the Poet. At the moment when myth is uncertainly becoming literature—that is, reaching tentatively toward a Signature—the poet is conceived of passively, as a mere vehicle. It is the Muse who is mythically bodied forth, the unconscious, collective source of the Archetypes, imagined as more than human, and, of course, female; it is she who mounts the Poet, as it were, in that position of feminine supremacy preferred in matriarchal societies. The Poet is still conceived more as Persona than Personality; the few characteristics with which he is endowed are borrowed from the prophet: he is a blind old man, impotent in his own right. That blindness (impotence as power, what Keats much later would call "negative capability") is the earliest version of the blessing-curse, without which the popular mind cannot conceive of the poet. His flaw is, in the early stages, at once the result and the pre-condition of his submitting himself to the dark powers of inspiration for the sake of the whole people.

But very soon the poet begins to assume a more individualized life-style, the lived Signature imposed on the Archetype, and we have no longer the featureless poet born in seven cities, his face a Mask through which a voice not his is heard, but Aeschylus, the Athenian citizen-poet; Sophocles, the spoiled darling of fate; or Euripides, the crowd-contemner in his Grotto. The mass mind, dimly resentful as the *Vates* becomes *Poeta,* the Seer a Maker, the Persona a Personality, composes a new Archetype, an image to punish the poet for detaching himself from the collective id—and the Poet, amused and baffled, accepts and elaborates the new image. The legend asserts that Euripides (the first completely self-conscious alienated artist?) dies torn to pieces by dogs or, even more to the point, by *women.* And behind the new, personalized application looms the more ancient *mythos* of the ritually dismembered Orpheus, ripped by the Maenads when he had withdrawn for lonely contemplation. The older myth suggests that a sacrifice is involved as well as a punishment—the casting-out and rending of the poet being reinterpreted as a death suffered for the group, by one who has dared make the first forays out of collectivity toward personality and has endured the consequent revenge of the group as devotees of the unconscious.

In light of this, it is no longer possible to think of the *poète maudit* as an unfortunate invention of the Romantics, or of the Alienated Artist as a by-product of mass communications. These are reinventions, as our archetypal history repeats itself before the breakdown of Christianity. Our newer names name only recent exacerbations of a situation as old as literature itself which in turn is coeval with the rise of personality. Only the conventional stigmata of the poet as Scape-Hero have changed with time: the Blind Man becomes the disreputable Player, the Atheist, the incestuous Lover, the Homosexual or (especially in America) the Drunkard; though, indeed, none of the older versions ever die, even the Homer-*typus* reasserting itself in Milton and James Joyce. Perhaps in recent times the poet has come to collaborate somewhat more enthusiastically in his own defamation and destruction, whether by drowning or tuberculosis or dissipation—or by a token suicide in the work (*cf.* Werther). And he helps ever more consciously to compose himself and his fellow poets—Byron, for instance, the poet par excellence of the mid-nineteenth century, being the joint product of Byron and Goethe—and, though most of us forget, Harriet Beecher Stowe! Some dramatic version of the poet seems necessary to every age, and the people do not care whether the poet creates himself in his life or work or both. One thinks right now of Fitzgerald, of course, *our* popular image of the artist.

The contemporary critic is likely to become very impatient with the lay indifference to the poetizing of life and the "biographizing" of poetry; for he proceeds on the false assumption that the poet's life is primarily "given" and only illegitimately "made," while his work is essentially "made" and scarcely "given" at all. This is the source of endless confusion.

In perhaps the greatest periods of world literature, the "given" element in poetry is made clear by the custom of supplying or, more precisely, of *imposing* on the poet certain traditional bodies of story. The poet in such periods can think of himself only as "working with" materials belonging to the whole community, emending by a dozen or sixteen lines the inherited plot. Greek myths, the fairy tales and *novelle* of the Elizabethans, the Christian body of legend available to Dante are examples of such material. (In our world a traditionally restricted body of story is found only in subart: the pulp Western, or the movie horse opera.) In such situations, Archetype and "story" are synonymous; one remembers that for Aristotle *mythos* was the word for "plot," and plot was, he insisted, the most important element in tragedy. That Aristotle makes his assertions on rationalistic grounds, with no apparent awareness of the importance of the Archetype as such, does not matter; it does not even matter whether the poet himself is aware of the implications of his material. As long as he works with such an inherited gift, he can provide the ritual satisfaction necessary to great art without self-consciousness.

A Shakespeare, a Dante or a Sophocles, coming at a moment when the Archetypes of a period are still understood as "given," and yet are not considered too "sacred" for rendering through the individual Signature, possesses immense initial advantages over the poet who comes earlier or later in the process. But the great poet is not simply the mechanical result of such an occasion; he must be able to rise to it, to be capable (like Shakespeare) at once of realizing utterly the archetypal implications of his material and of formally embodying it in a lucid and unmistakable Signature. But the balance is delicate and incapable of being long maintained. The brief history of Athenian tragedy provides the classic instance. After the successes of Sophocles come the attempts of Euripides; and in Euripides one begins to feel the encounter of Signature and Archetype as a *conflict*—the poet and the collectivity have begun to lose touch with each other and with their common pre-conscious sources of value and behavior. Euripides seems to feel his inherited material as a burden, tucking it away in prologue and epilogue, so that he can get on with his proper business—the imitation of particulars. The poem begins to come apart; the acute critic finds it, however "tragic," sloppy, technically inept; and the audience raises the familiar cry of "incomprehensible and blasphemous!" Even the poet himself begins to distrust his own impulses, and writes, as Euripides did in his *Bacchae,* a mythic criticism of his own sacrilege. The poetry of the struggle against the Archetype is especially moving and poignant, but to prefer it to the poetry of the moment of balance is to commit a gross lapse of taste.

After the Euripidean crisis, the Archetypes survive only in fallen form: as inherited and scarcely understood structures (the seeds of the genres which are structural Archetypes become structural platitudes); as type characters, less complex than the masks that indicate them; as "popular" stock plots. The "Happy Ending" arises as a kind of ersatz of the true reconciliation of society and individual in Sophoclean tragedy; and the audience which can no longer find essential reassurance in its poetry that the superego and the id can live at peace with each other content themselves with the demonstration that at least Jack has his Jill, despite the comic opposition of the Old Man. Still later, even the tension in Euripidean tragedy and New Comedy is lost, and the Signature comes to be disregarded completely; poetry becomes either completely "realistic," rendering the struggle between ego and superego in terms of the imitation of particulars; or it strives to be "pure" in the contemporary sense—that is, to make the Signature its sole subject as well as its means.

Can the Archetype be redeemed after such a fall? There are various possibilities (short of the emergence of a new, ordered myth system): the writer can, like Graham Greene or Robert Penn Warren, capture for serious purposes—that is, rerender through complex and subtle Signatures—debased "popular" Archetypes: the thriller, the detective story, the Western or science fiction; or the poet can ironically manipulate the shreds and patches of outlived mythologies, fragments shored against our ruins. Eliot, Joyce, Ezra Pound and Thomas Mann have all made attempts of the latter sort, writing finally not archetypal poetry but poetry *about* Archetypes, in which plot (anciently, *mythos* itself) founders under the burden of overt explication or disappears completely. Or the poet can, like Blake or Yeats or Hart Crane, invent a private myth system of his own. Neither of the last two expedients can reach the popular audience, which prefers its Archetypes rendered without self-consciousness of so intrusive a sort.

A final way back into the world of the Archetypes, available even in our atomized culture, is an extension of the way instinctively sought by the Romantics, down through the personality of the poet, past his particular foibles and eccentricities, to his unconscious core, where he becomes one with us all in the presence of our ancient Gods, the protagonists of fables we think we no longer believe. In fantasy and terror, we can return to our common source. It is a process to delight a Hegelian, the triple swing from a naïve communal to a personal to a sophisticated communal.

We must be aware of the differences between the thesis and the synthesis in our series. What cannot be re-created as Plot is reborn as Character—ultimately the character of the poet (what else is available to him?), whether directly or in projection. In the Mask of his life and the manifold masks of his work, the poet expresses for a whole society the ritual meaning of its inarticulate selves; the artist goes forth not to "re-create the conscience of his race," but to redeem its unconscious. We cannot get back into the primal Garden of the unfallen Archetypes, but we can yield ourselves to the dreams and images that mean paradise regained. For the critic, who cannot only yield but must also *understand*, there are available new methods of exploration. To understand the Archetypes of Athenian drama, he needs (above and beyond semantics) anthropology; to understand those of recent poetry, he needs (beyond "close analysis") depth analysis, as defined by Freud and, particularly, by Jung.

The biographical approach, tempered by such findings, is just now coming into its own. We are achieving new ways of connecting (or, more precisely, of understanding a connection which has always existed) the Poet and the poem, the lived and the made, the Signature and the Archetype. It is in the focus of the poetic personality that *Dichtung und Wahrheit* become one; and it is incumbent upon us, without surrendering our right to make useful distinctions, to seize the principle of that unity. "Only connect!"

INDEX

Index

558 INDEX